P9-DUX-259

14.80

UNDERSTANDING THE TALMUD

Selected with Introductions by

Alan Corré

KTAV PUBLISHING HOUSE, INC.
NEW YORK
1975

© COPYRIGHT 1975
KTAV PUBLISHING HOUSE, INC.

Library of Congress Cataloging in Publication Data
Main entry under title:

Understanding the Talmud.

Includes bibliographical references.
1. Rabbinical literature—History and criticism—Addresses, essays, lectures. 2. Talmud — Theology — Addresses, essays, lectures. I. Corré, Alan D.
BM496.5.U52   296.1'206'6   78-138459
ISBN 0-87068-140-0

MANUFACTURED IN THE UNITED STATES OF AMERICA

CONTENTS

Foreword IX

Introduction 1

The "Vineyard" at Jamnia—*Israel Abrahams* 3

The Mishna—*Abraham Cohen* 8

The Talmud—*Israel Abrahams* 17

Gemara and Midrash—*Abraham Cohen* 21

The Midrash and its Poetry—*Israel Abrahams* 27

The Palestinian Talmud—*Louis Ginzberg* 33

"Open Thou Mine Eyes"—*Wm. G. Braude* 55

Rabbinic Exegesis—*David S. Shapiro* 62

BACKGROUND—THE WORLD WITHIN 65

Historical Antecedents—*Abraham Cohen* 66

The Economic Condition of Judaea—*Adolph Büchler* 73

Secular and Religious Forces—*Solomon Zeitlin* 107

BACKGROUND—THE WORLD WITHOUT 119

The Talmud in History—*Israel Abrahams* 120

The Burning of the Talmud—*Allan Temko* 124

The Graeco-Roman View of Jews—*Norman Bentwich* 141

The Talmudic Doctrine of God—*R. Travers Herford* 149

The Idea of Torah in Judaism—*Geo. Foot Moore* 160

MOVEMENTS 177

The Pharisees—*Ralph Marcus* 178

Pharisees, Essenes and Gnostics—*Ralph Marcus* 193

A First-Century Jewish Sage—*Joshua Podro* 198

The Persistence of Rejected Customs—*Louis Finkelstein* 216

The "Sons of Light"—*T. H. Gaster* 221

The Cave Scrolls and the Jewish Sects—*H. L. Ginsberg* 237

More Light from Judean Caves—*H. L. Ginsberg* 246

LAW 259

Life and the Law—*Louis Finkelstein* 261

Rabbinic Methods of Interpretation—*David Daube* 275

The Halaka—*Solomon Zeitlin* 290

Capital Punishment—*Gerald J. Blidstein* 313

Possession in Jewish Law—*Boaz Cohen* 325

RELIGIOUS IDEAS 331

The Religious Ideas of Talmudic Judaism—*Julius Guttmann* ... 333

The Religion of the Jews at the Time of Jesus—*Louis Ginzberg* ... 347

Some Rabbinic Ideas on Prayer—*Israel Abrahams* 360

The Rabbinical Conception of Holiness—*Solomon Schechter* ... 373

Divine Retribution in Rabbinic Literature—*Solomon Schechter* ... 381

Honor in Rabbinic Law and Ethics—*Chaim W. Reines* 394

In Praise of the Talmud — *Jacob Neusner* 403

Glossary 421

A Note on the Language of the Talmud 425

Notes 427

ACKNOWLEDGMENTS

"The Vineyard at Jamnia" from *Chapters on Jewish Literature* by Israel Abrahams, pp. 19-31 (Philadelphia, 1899)

"The Mishna," from *Everyman's Talmud* by Abraham Cohen, pp. xxi-xxx. Copyright 1932 by E. P. Dutton & Co. Reprinted by permission.

"The Talmud," from *Chapters on Jewish Literature,* pp. 43-53.

"Gemara and Midrash," from *Everyman's Talmud* pp. xxxi-xxxvii. Copyright 1932 by E. P. Dutton & Co. Reprinted by permission.

"The Midrash and Its Poetry," from *Chapters on Jewish Literature,* pp. 55-67.

"The Palestinian Talmud" from *Commentary on the Jerusalem Talmud* by Louis Ginzberg, Introduction to volume 1. Copyright 1941. Reprinted by permission of the Jewish Theological Seminary of America.

"Open Thou Mine Eyes" by Wm. G. Braude from *CCAR* Journal, vol. II no. 1, pp. 44-49. Copyright 1963. Reprinted by permission.

"Rabbinic Exegesis" from review of I. Frankel, *Peshat in Talmudic* and *Rabbinic Exegesis* by David S. Shapiro in *Judaism,* vol. 6 pp. 286-288. Copyright 1957. Reprinted by permission.

"Historical Antecedents," from *Everyman's Talmud,* pp. xv-xxi. Copyright 1932 by E: P. Dutton & Co. Reprinted by permission.

"The Economic Condition of Judaea after the Destruction of the Second Temple," by Adolph Büchler (London, 1912) Jews College, London, publication no. 4.

"Secular and Religious Forces," from "Rashi and the Rabbinate" by Solomon Zeitlin in *Jewish Quarterly Review,* vol. 31 pp. 1-20. Copyright 1941. Reprinted by permission.

"The Talmud in History," by Israel Abrahams, from James Hastings ed. *The Encyclopaedia of Religion and Ethics,* vol. 12 pp. 185-186. Copyright 1922. Reprinted by permission of Charles Scribner's Sons.

"The Burning of the Talmud in Paris," by Allan Temko, from *Commentary* vol. 17, pp. 446-455. Copyright © 1954 by the American Jewish Committee. Reprinted by permission.

"The Graeco-Roman View of Jews and Judaism in the Second Century" by Norman Bentwich in *Jewish Quarterly Review,* vol. 23 pp. 337-348. Copyright 1933. Reprinted by permission.

"A Unitarian Minister's View of the Talmudic Doctrine of God," by R. Travers Herford in *Jewish Quarterly Review,* vol 2 (1890) pp. 454-464.

"The Idea of Torah in Judaism," by George Foot Moore in *Menorah Journal* vol. 8, pp. 1-14. Copyright 1922. Reprinted by permission of David L. Hurwood.

"The Pharisees in the Light of Modern Scholarship," by Ralph Marcus, in *Journal of Religion* vol. 32 pp. 153-163. Copyright 1952. Reprinted by permission.

"Pharisees, Essenes and Gnostics," by Ralph Marcus, in *Journal of Biblical Literature,* vol. 73, pp. 157-161. Copyright 1954. Reprinted by permission.

"A First-Century Jewish Sage" by Joshua Podro, from *Commentary,* vol. 26, pp. 31-41. Copyright © 1958 by the American Jewish Committee. Reprinted by permission.

"The Persistence of Rejected Customs in Palestine," by Louis Finkelstein in *Jewish Quarterly Review,* vol. 29, pp. 179-186. Copyright 1939. Reprinted by permission.

"The Sons of Light" by T. H. Gaster, from *Commentary,* vol. 22, pp. 227-236. Copyright © 1956 by the American Jewish Committee. Reprinted by permission.

"The Cave Scrolls and the Jewish Sects," by H. L. Ginsberg, from *Commentary,* vol. 16, pp. 77-81. Copyright © 1953 by the American Jewish Committee. Reprinted by permission.

"More Light from Judean Caves," by H. L. Ginsberg, from *Commentary,* vol. 20, pp. 468-474. Copyright © 1955 by the American Jewish Committee. Reprinted by permission.

"Life and the Law" by Louis Finkelstein, from *Menorah Journal* vol. 24, pp. 131-143. Copyright 1936. Reprinted by permission of Louis Finkelstein and David L. Hurwood.

"Rabbinic Methods of Interpretation and Hellenistic Rhetoric" by David Daube, from *Hebrew Union College Annual,* vol. 22, pp. 239-264. Copyright 1949. Reprinted by permission.

"The Halaka," by S. Zeitlin, from *Jewish Quarterly Review,* vol. 39, pp. 1-40. Copyright 1949. Reprinted by permission.

"Capital Punishment—the Classic Jewish Discussion" by Gerald J. Blidstein, from *Judaism,* vol. 14, pp. 159-168. Copyright 1965. Reprinted by permission.

"An Essay on Possession in Jewish Law" by Boaz Cohen, from the *Proceedings of the American Academy for Jewish Research* vol. 6 pp. 130-137. Copyright 1934. Reprinted by permission.

"The Religious Ideas of Talmudic Judaism" from *Philosophies of Judaism* by Julius Guttman, pp. 30-43. Copyright 1964 by Holt, Rinehart and Winston, Inc. Reprinted by permission.

"The Religion of the Jews at the time of Jesus," by Louis Ginzberg, from *Hebrew Union College Annual,* vol. 1, pp. 307-321. Copyright 1924. Reprinted by permission.

"Some Rabbinic Ideas on Prayer" by Israel Abrahams, from *Jewish Quarterly Review,* vol. 20 (1908) pp. 273-290.

"The Rabbinical Conception of Holiness" by Solomon Schechter, from *Jewish Quarterly Review,* vol. 10 (1898) pp. 1-12.

"Divine Retribution in Rabbinic Literature" by Solomon Schechter, from *Jewish Quarterly Review,* vol. 3 (1891) pp. 34-51.

"Honor in Rabbinic Law and Ethics" by Ch. Reines, from *Judaism,* vol. 8, pp. 59-67. Copyright 1959. Reprinted by permission.

"In Praise of the Talmud" by Jacob Neusner © 1973 by Jacob Neusner, *Tradition,* vol. 13, pp. 16-35, 1973.

The editor wishes to acknowledge the assistance of Jeanette Rozansky and David Lowe with the text; the constant support of the Wisconsin Society for Jewish Learning, and the unfailing encouragement of his wife, Nita.

FOREWORD

An attempt to understand the spirit and writings of the Talmudic period in which Judaism crystallized in its classic form is confronted with a number of difficulties. More than a millennium has passed since that time, but years alone are not the source of the trouble; the Australian aborigine may still today be at one with the spirit of his ancestors at a much greater remove in time. Our society is different, and its norms and values erect all kinds of subtle barriers to understanding any other kind of society. Yet if we are to have any basis for the assessment of the values of our society, we must learn to understand other societies, especially those with which we have a historic connection—and many feel a pressing need to reassess those values ("progress" for example) the bright image of which has seemed to grow increasingly tarnished in recent years.

Attitudes toward the Talmud in the past have been marked by great polarity. On the one hand there were those who held the Talmud to be essentially valueless though a few scattered gems might be found by the persistent seeker; and on the other there were those who took it as the guide for every facet of life.

In the nineteenth century both Jews and Christians began the critical study of Rabbinic writings in the spirit of inquiry which characterized the era. This sympathetic yet not all-accepting attitude led to a calmer appraisal of these writings and to much of the research included in this book.

Understanding the society which led to the Talmud and similar works does not involve accepting all that its authors believed, but it does involve a tolerance of certain features, strange indeed to us, which they took for granted—in the context of their times indeed they could hardly have done otherwise. Some of these features will be pointed out here.

First, the supernatural was assumed without question to exist and to be active in the world. Although the problems arising from a theistic view of the universe were recognized, and some solutions—occasionally naive solutions—were proposed, belief in the existence of God was as natural as belief in the existence of man. Miracles were still everyday occurrences and the spirit world of demons was accepted readily. We may, if we choose, discuss *why* they believed in such things, which we may take to be impossible, but the fact that they *did* is indisputable and we must accept this if we are to get in tune with them at all. Nor should this acceptance be too condescending. I believe implicitly in the existence of bacteria even though I have never seen any. Possibly you *have* peeped through a microscope and can reassure me—but then those people had plenty of reassurers too. Much of what a human being holds to be true is based on the authority of others, and while I am convinced that we come closer to the elusive truth about the universe than the ancients, the principle cause of their error—relying on "authorities" rather than empirical tests—is not absent in our society either. A human life is just not long enough to ascertain the truth of everything. In looking at a culture in which the supernatural is assumed, we should avoid being annoyed or distracted by its pervasive influence.

The next point concerns the attitude to knowledge. We look upon knowledge as a discovery process: "research", "breakthrough" and "theory" are the kind of terms that science thrusts upon us. Many people in ancient times (not Jews alone) viewed learning as something given, eternal and immutable, and man's educational task was to study this given corpus intensively and to get to know it intimately. Originality consisted in the manner of manipulation of this given corpus since there was no really new learning to be discovered. What can man need beyond what God has told him? The negative effect of this was to inhibit the growth of experimentation of a practical character which might lead to the kind of science and technology with which we are familiar. The positive effect was that—within one's own group—everyone knew what constituted "education", why we should acquire it and what privileges and benefits resulted from its acquisition. Thus among the Jews, the man who mastered the written Torah (i.e. the Pentateuch) and the oral Torah (i.e. the traditions embodied in the Talmud) was entitled to leadership and respect in this world and a goodly portion in the next. The ignorant man might envy or even hate the scholar, but he did not deny the validity of his pretensions. Whether such a clear yet static situation is preferable to our present confusion over the means, goals and proper effects of education is a matter for discussion.

This attitude to learning had other results. Since law was part of the "given" it could only change organically, by manipulation rather than by outright repeal. Thus, capital punishment could never be abolished in Jewish law because it was expressly enjoined in Scripture. But it could be, and was, so narrowly interpreted as to maintain it in theory only, while in effect abolishing it in practice. "Legal fiction" is a term which for us has emotional overtones, suggesting sneaky little men "getting round" the "real" meaning of the law. But the "legal fiction"—and we must try to divest it of its overtones—is a natural outgrowth of any entrenched system, and we can perhaps more profitably judge the system as a whole by its end products rather than the esthetic quality of its mechanics. Is it just? Is it impartial? Does it inhibit and amend anti-social behavior? Does it lead to widespread satisfaction with life? It is perhaps better to ask these questions than to cavil at oddities of method. As a matter of fact the federal-state system of the U. S. is permeated by "legal fictions". Thus federal law enforcement cannot apply in a strictly intrastate situation; but it is "assumed" that a kidnaped child has been carried across state lines after a rather short period so that the superior federal investigation facilities may be utilized. Here too it is probably better to consider whether kidnaping is effectively controlled by this means, rather than discuss the truth or defensibility of the "fiction". And the ruling that struck down the "separate but equal" doctrine of treatment of the races was an interpretative act which changed no law but vitally affected practice.

Finally, we need to exercise care in assuming the superiority of our own culture and looking down from a lofty peak on the cultures of other times and places. This injunction is perhaps needed less now when many of the younger people especially are becoming increasingly aware of the contrast between the world of air conditioners and moon shots on the one hand and Belsen and Biafra on the other. Let us consider just this. Horrible methods of execution were known in Talmudic times; a criminal might have fiery liquid poured down his throat or be thrown to his death from a great height. "Cruel and unusual punishments!" Yet in August 1825—not really so long ago—a rapist in South Carolina was sentenced to be chained to a stake, soaked in turpentine and burned alive. The executioner submitted a bill for $1.12½ for the turpentine. This was not a lynching; it was the act of a duly constituted American court. In first century Palestine the criminal was given a stupefying drug before execution; the South Carolina expense account gives no evidence of such a mercy. And, as already noted, capital punishment was virtually in disuse anyway. Again, the Biblical code allowed 40 lashes, truly a savage beating. Yet in enlightened nineteenth century England a Tommy Atkins took *150* lashes for an act of insubordination—and died three weeks later of a "kidney complaint." If western correctional practices have passed those of ancient Palestine it would seem to be a rather recent development.

The inference is not to be drawn that Talmudic society was superior to ours or ought to be recreated. Human societies are so complex that only aspects of them can be fruitfully compared. But if we want to improve our own society, or try to see it with some degree of detachment, the attempt to understand Talmudic literature, and through it Talmudic society, may well prove enlightening. We can surely marvel at the judge who disqualified himself because the plaintiff had helped him step off the ferry thereby impairing his impartiality; or at this defense of a once learned man suffering from senility: "The tablets and the fragments of the tablets were placed in the Ark!"

This last utterance (pure poetry in my view) illustrates incidentally the point made earlier about agreement on a corpus of learning and helps us to understand its effects. Everyone who was not a total ignoramus knew that Moses broke the original tablets of the Law in anger at the Israelites' apostasy in worshipping the Golden Calf. Everyone knew that he kept the fragments along with the new Tablets which he obtained. Since Moses was a great prophet, his action in so doing must have been right, proper and commendable. Hence when a striking and poetic comparison is made between an old man, shattered yet holy still, with the fragments of the Tablets, shattered yet holy still, it follows that a doddering, senile old man must be cherished for what he once was. We may find ourselves quite unable to accept the simple faith that watched Moses ascend to God and fetch down his inspired word. We may lack the soaking in words of Scripture that set the Talmudic neurons atingle as soon as the comparison reached their ears with its irrebuttable conclusion in their terms of reference. But we can appreciate the abiding human concern that manifests itself here, and this makes worthwhile the attempt to understand the vehicle, exotic for us perhaps, which they used.

On the pages which follow the student will find some of the best English language contributions to Talmudic study which have appeared over the last eighty years, representing the researches or meditations of fine intellects. The aim has been to aid in the understanding of a literature and a culture which produced it; both the unique products of a people which has itself been unique in its history, its suffering and its contribution to world culture.

INTRODUCTION

The articles in this section describe the monuments of Rabbinic literature, how they were composed and what their contents are. It is difficult for us to comprehend the notion of *oral literature*, for we live in an age in which, until less than a century ago, *writing* totally dominated the cultural scene. We still judge a man's education largely by how much he has read, how well he can express himself on paper and even by his mastery of such arbitrary conventions of writing as the quirks of English spelling. Our educational system lays enormous stress on the significance of written materials; the pencil that we place in the hands of the five-year-old is the passkey to his success in life. This was not always so, and there is evidence that the advent of ever more ingenious machines for recording the human voice may change the situation once again.

The human memory has an enormous capacity which we do not use. The English scholar Sir Williams Jones was able to write out complete Shakespeare plays from memory. The Arab bard Hammad once offered to recite a hundred long odes for each letter of the alphabet.[1] Among many peoples, especially those who developed no writing system, the transmission of oral materials was highly organized, and in some pre-literate societies death could be the penalty for a mistake in transmission.[2] Mnemonic devices such as sticks, knotted cords or catchwords were used to aid correct transmission.

It might even be said that many ancient peoples trusted more fully a skilled oral transmitter than they would a written copy which was so liable to error in transcribing; and in this they may well have been correct. A young child will often object strenuously if a parent makes an inadvertent change in reading him a well loved story. Thoroughly memorized materials do not "sound right" if altered; by contrast the copyist's hand and eye may tire quickly.

Among the Jews the *tanna* ("repeater") was charged with the memorization of oral traditions. (The word is also used to mean a scholar of the Mishnaic period, but this is a different thing.) He acted as a kind of walking library who could pull out of his copious memory whatever those using him wanted to know. Translations into Aramaic of the

1

written Hebrew scriptures were also originally oral. There was great opposition to any attempt to write down this oral literature, but it eventually
was done. Accordingly the kind of organization required in a book is absent. The logical thought sequence to which we are accustomed must give
way to an order which aids the memory.

The first five essays in this section deal with the constituent parts of
the Babylonian Talmud and the Midrash. Ginzberg's essay deals with the
much less widely studied Palestinian or Jerusalem Talmud. Braude points
up the difficulty of getting in tune with the Rabbinic mind and gives
useful samples of the methods of the Rabbis. Shapiro's review shows how
the Rabbis regarded and utilized the text of Scripture, an important topic
which will be further explained in the section on *Law*.

THE "VINEYARD" AT JAMNIA
Israel Abrahams

The story of Jewish literature after the destruction of the Temple at Jerusalem in the year 70 of the Christian era, centers round the city of Jamnia. Jamnia, or Jabneh, lay near the sea, beautifully situated on the slopes of a gentle hill in the lowlands, about twenty-eight miles from the capital. When Vespasian was advancing to the siege of Jerusalem, he occupied Jamnia, and thither the Jewish Synhedrion, or Great Council, transferred itself when Jerusalem fell. A college existed there already, but Jamnia then became the headquarters of Jewish learning, and retained that position till the year 135. At that date the learned circle moved further north, to Galilee and, besides the famous school at Lydda in Judea, others were founded in Tiberias, Usha, and Sepphoris.

The real founder of the College at Jamnia was Jochanan, the son of Zakkai, called "the father of wisdom." Like the Greek philosophers who taught their pupils in the gardens of the "Academy" at Athens, the Rabbis may have lectured to their students in a "Vineyard" at Jamnia. Possibly the term "Vineyard" was only a metaphor applied to the meeting-place of the Wise at Jamnia, but, at all events, the result of these pleasant intellectual gatherings was the Rabbinical literature. Jochanan himself was a typical Rabbi. For a great part of his life he followed a mercantile pursuit, and earned his bread by manual labor. His originality as a teacher lay in his perception that Judaism could survive the loss of its national centre. He felt that "charity and the love of men may replace the sacrifices." He would have preferred his brethren to submit to Rome, and his political foresight was justified when the war of independence closed in disaster. As Graetz has well said, like Jeremiah Jochanan wept over the desolation of Zion, but like Zerubbabel he created a new sanctuary. Jochanan's new sanctuary was the school.

In the "Vineyard" at Jamnia, the Jewish tradition was the subject of much animated inquiry. The religious, ethical, and practical literature of the past was sifted and treasured, and fresh additions were made. But not much was written, for until the close of the second century the new literature of the Jews was *oral*. The Bible was written down, and read from scrolls, but the Rabbinical literature was committed to memory piecemeal, and handed down from teacher to pupil. Notes were perhaps taken in writing, but even when the Oral Literature was collected and arranged as a book, it is believed by many authorities that the book so compiled remained for a considerable period an oral and not a written book.

This book was called the *Mishnah* (from the verb *shana,* "to repeat" or "to learn"). The Mishnah was not the work of one man or of one age. So long was it in growing, that its birth dates from long before the destruction of the Temple. But the men most closely associated with the compilation of the Mishnah were the Tannaim (from the root *tana,* which has the same meaning as *shana*). There were about one hundred and twenty of these Tannaim between the years 70 and 200 C. E., and they may be conveniently arranged in four generations. From each generation one typical representative will here be selected.

THE TANNAIM

First Generation, 70 to 100 C. E.
JOCHANAN, the son of Zakkai

Second Generation, 100 to 130 C. E.
AKIBA

Third Generation, 130 to 160 C. E.
MEIR

Fourth Generation, 160 to 200 C. E.
JUDAH THE PRINCE

The Tannaim were the possessors of what was perhaps the greatest principle that dominated a literature until the close of the eighteenth century. They maintained that *literature* and *life* were co-extensive. It was said of Jochanan, the son of Zakkai, that he never walked a single step without thinking of God. Learning the Torah, that is, the Law, the authorized Word of God, and its Prophetical and Rabbinical developments, was man's supreme duty. "If thou hast learned much Torah, ascribe not any merit to thyself, for therefore wast thou created." Man was created to learn; literature was the aim of life. We have already seen what kind of literature. Jochanan once said to his five favorite disciples: "Go forth and consider which is the good way to which a man should cleave." He received various answers, but he most approved of this response: "A good heart is the way." Literature is life if it be a heart-literature—this may be regarded as the final justification of the union effected in the Mishnah between learning and righteousness.

Akiba, who may be taken to represent the second generation of Tannaim, differed in character from Jochanan. Jochanan had been a member of the peace party in the years 66 to 70; Akiba was a patriot, and took a personal part in the later struggle against Rome, which was organized by the heroic Bar Cochba in the years 131 to 135. Akiba set his face against frivolity, and pronounced silence a fence about wisdom. But his disposition was resolute rather than severe. Of him the most romantic of love stories is told. He was a herdsman, and fell in love with his master's daughter, who endured poverty as his devoted wife, and was glorified in her husband's fame. But whatever contrast there may have been in the two characters, Akiba, like Jochanan, believed that a literature was worthless unless it expressed itself in the life of the scholar. He and his school held in low esteem the man who, though learned, led an evil life, but they took as their ideal the man whose moral excellence was more conspicuous than his learning. As R. Eleazar, the son of Azariah, said: "He whose knowledge is in excess of his good deeds is like a tree whose branches are many and its roots scanty; the wind comes, uproots, and overturns it. But he whose good deeds are more than his knowledge is like a tree with few branches but many roots, so that if all the winds in the world come and blow upon it, it remains firm in its place." Man, according to Akiba, is master of his own destiny; he needs God's grace to triumph over evil, yet the triumph depends on his own efforts: "Everything is seen, yet freedom of choice is given; the world is judged by grace, yet all is according to the work." The Torah, the literature of Israel, was to Akiba "a desirable instrument," a means to life.

Among the distinctions of Akiba's school must be named the first literal translation of the Bible into Greek. This work was done towards the close of the second century by Aquila, a proselyte, who was inspired by Akiba's teaching. Aquila's version was inferior to the Alexandrian Greek version, called the Septuagint, in graces of style, but was superior in accuracy. Aquila followed the Hebrew text word by word. This translator is identical with Onkelos, to whom in later centuries the Aramaic translation *(Targum Onkelos)* of the Pentateuch was ascribed. Aramaic versions of the Bible were made at a very early period, and the Targum Onkelos may contain ancient elements, but in its present form it is not earlier than the fifth century.

Meir, whom we take as representative of the third generation of Tannaim, was filled with the widest sympathies. In his conception of truth, everything that men can know belonged to the Torah. Not that the Torah superseded or absorbed all other knowledge, but that the Torah needed, for its right study, all the aids which science and secular information could supply. In this way Jewish literature was to some extent saved from the danger of becoming a merely religious exercise, and in later centuries, when the mass of Jews were disposed to despise and even discourage scientific and philosophical culture, a minority was always prepared to resist this tendency and, on the ground of the views of some of the Tannaim like Meir, claimed the right to study what we should now term secular sciences. The width of Meir's sympathies may be seen in his tolerant conduct towards his friend Elisha, the son of Abuya. When the latter forsook Judaism, Meir remained true to Elisha. He devoted himself to the effort to win back his old friend, and, though he failed, he never ceased to love him. Again, Meir was famed for his knowledge of fables, in antiquity a branch of the wisdom of all the Eastern world. Meir's large-mindedness was matched by his large-heartedness, and in his wife Beruriah he possessed a companion whose tender sympathies and fine toleration matched his own.

The fourth generation of Tannaim is overshadowed by the fame of Judah the Prince, *Rabbi,* as he was simply called. He lived from 150 to 210, and with his name is associated the compilation of the Mishnah. A man of genial manners, strong intellectual grasp, he was the exemplar also of princely hospitality and of friendship with others than Jews. His intercourse with one of the Antonines was typical of his wide culture. Life was not, in Rabbi Judah's view, compounded of smaller and larger incidents, but all the affairs of life were parts of the great divine scheme. "Reflect upon three things, and thou wilt not fall into the power of sin: Know what is above thee—a seeing eye and a hearing ear—and all thy deeds are written in a book."

The Mishnah, which deals with things great and small, with everything that concerns men, is the literary expression of this view of life. Its language is the new-Hebrew, a simple, nervous idiom suited to practical life, but lacking the power and poetry of the Biblical Hebrew. It is a more useful but less polished instrument than the older language. The subject-matter of the Mishnah includes both law and morality, the affairs of the body, of the soul, and of the mind. Business, religion, social duties, ritual, are all dealt with in one and the same code. The fault of this conception is that by associating things of unequal importance, both the mind and the conscience may become incapable of discriminating the great from the small, the external from the spiritual. Another ill consequence was that, as literature corresponded so closely with life, literature could not correct the faults of life, when life became cramped or stagnant. The modern spirit differs from the ancient chiefly in that literature has now become an independent force, which may freshen and stimulate life. But the older ideal was nevertheless a great one. That man's life is a unity; that his conduct is in all its parts within the sphere of ethics and religion; that his mind and conscience are not independent, but two sides of the same thing; and that therefore his religious, ethical, aesthetic, and intellectual literature is one and indivisible—this was a noble conception which, with all its weakness, had distinct points of superiority over the modern view.

The Mishnah is divided into six parts, or Orders (*Sedarim*); each Order into Tractates (*Massechtoth*); each Tractate into Chapters (*Perakim*); each Chapter into Paragraphs (each called a *Mishnah*). The six Orders are as follows:

ZERAIM ("Seeds"). Deals with the laws connected with Agriculture, and opens with a Tractate on Prayer ("Blessings").
MOED ("Festival"). On Festivals.
NASHIM ("Women"). On the laws relating to Marriage, etc.
NEZIKIN ("Damages"). On civil and criminal Law.
KODASHIM ("Holy Things"). On Sacrifices, etc.
TEHAROTH ("Purifications"). On personal and ritual Purity.

THE MISHNAH
Abraham Cohen

With the invention of new methods of interpretation the Torah became a science, and only men who were duly qualified to expound the text spoke with authority. They received the designation of Tannaïm (Teachers). It is the name given to the Rabbis during the period which closed with the codification of the law in the Mishnah. A pioneer who left a profound influence on their work was Hillel. He was a Babylonian by birth and, so tradition related, a descendant of David through his mother. He migrated to Judea and for about forty years was one of the acknowledged guides of his community.

Hillel exemplified the Pharisaic standpoint at its best. He recognized that life, with its ever-changing conditions, was incapable of compression within a fixed and immutable written code; and he perceived in the freedom of interpretation allowed by the Oral Law an invaluable instrument for making the Torah adaptable to varying circumstances.

A good illustration of his method is afforded by the enactment of Deut. XV, 1 ff.: 'At the end of every seven years thou shalt make a release. And this is the manner of the release: every creditor shall release that which he hath lent unto his neighbour.' That is to say, if a loan had not been repaid by the Sabbatical year, it could no longer be claimed. The Scriptural ordinance really deals with an act of charity performed by an Israelite towards a member of his nation in distress and not with a loan contracted in the ordinary course of business. The sociological background of the law is a nation of small-holders, each living on the produce of his allotment. When conditions altered and a large section of the population derived a livelihood from commerce, the Biblical regulation became a serious impediment. Men must have been afraid to give credit when they were precluded from claiming what was due to them after the incidence of the year of release, and the attendant hardship was undoubtedly very great.

From the Sadducean standpoint there was no redress. Such was the law and it must be obeyed. Hillel disagreed, and contended that a close study of the text would disclose a way out of the difficulty. Starting from

8

the hypothesis that the Torah did not include a superfluous word, he pointed to the phrase 'whatsoever is thine with thy brother thy hand shall release' (ibid. 3). At first sight this appears to be an unnecessary repetition of the statement in the preceding verse: 'He shall not exact it of his neighbour and brother.' That, however, could not be, since there is nothing redundant in the Torah. Therefore the words, 'whatsoever is thine *with thy brother*,' must have been added to exclude a certain contingency, viz. the case where 'whatsoever is thine' is not with the debtor. By such reasoning Hillel deduced that if the creditor handed to a Court of Law a signed document which made over the indebtedness to its members, it was within his right to claim the debt through the Court even after the expiration of the Sabbatical year.

We may, if we so choose, criticize the argument as casuistry; but it served a vital purpose, which was to make the Torah a practical guide of life of everlasting validity. The Torah could never grow antiquated so long as it was capable of reinterpretation to comply with new contingencies.

Hillel was the creator of a School of *Tannaïm*. His contemporary, Shammai, also founded a School; and during the first seven decades of the first century, the two teachers and their disciples dominated the thought which was current in Pharisaic circles. On the whole the Hillelites favoured a more lenient interpretation of the law, while the other School took the stricter view. The Talmud records over three hundred points of divergence between them, and in the end the teaching of Hillel prevailed. The establishment of a School demanded a systematic presentation of the subject-matter of study. It must be borne in mind that in the Orient, even today, memory is more highly developed than in the West. A mass of learning is acquired not from books but from the lips of teachers. Hillel would therefore find it necessary to examine the rules of exegesis which had come down from previous generations, and recommend to his disciples those which he considered logically valid. He adopted seven such principles of interpretation which became generally accepted, though others were added at a later stage. In his instruction he would also have to arrange the large volume of traditional lore for the convenience of the learners. His arrangement was preserved orally and may be regarded as the first edition of the Mishnah.

The next personality to claim attention is Jochanan b. Zakkai, the youngest and most distinguished of Hillel's disciples, characterized by the master shortly before his death as 'the father of wisdom and father of (future) generations (of scholars)' (p. Ned. 39b). He was the outstanding authority at the time of the destruction of the Temple by Titus. Fore-

seeing the defeat of the Jews in their struggle with Rome, he urged peace
because the preservation of Judaism meant more to him than national independence. When his advice was rejected, he planned measures to prevent the extermination of the community when the Temple and State
would come to an end. A story tells that, in order to leave the besieged
city whose gates were closely guarded by the Jewish zealots, he circulated
news of his illness and then of his death. With the connivance of trusted
adherents, he was carried out of Jerusalem in a coffin for burial; and only
the respect in which he was held saved him from a spear thrust through
his body by the guards who adopted this method of assuring themselves
that nobody passed through the gates alive. He thereupon made his way
to the Roman camp, gained admission to the presence of Vespasian and
petitioned him: 'Give me Jabneh and its Sages' (Git. 56b). The emperor
kept his word and Jabneh was spared. At the end of the war Jochanan
removed there, with the result that its School, previously of small importance, became the centre of Jewish life and thought. Jabneh replaced
the Holy City as the seat of the Sanhedrin and virtually became the new
capital. By his foresight, he preserved the Torah from probable annihilation in the national disaster, and thereby assured the survival of the defeated people.

Before the occurrence of the catastrophe, Jochanan had been the
foremost antagonist of the Sadducean attitude towards the Torah. On rational grounds he proved it to be inadequate; but events were to provide
an even more convincing demonstration of the weakness of the Sadducean
position and the strength of the Pharisaic. With the Sadducees Judaism
was a hidebound system, fixed for all time by the written code of the
Pentateuch; it was also inseparably bound up with the ritual of the
Temple. Consequently, when the Sanctuary ceased to exist, the Sadducees
very soon afterwards disappeared. The Pharisaic theory of the Oral
Torah received remarkable vindication in that time of crisis. It unques-
tionably kept the religion of the people alive by adapting it to the new
conditions which had arisen; and nobody more than Jochanan b. Zakkai
achieved that result. In his School at Jabneh he transmitted to his pupils
the learning he had received from his master, and they in turn became
the teachers of the next generation. He thus forged another link in the
chain of Jewish traditional lore.

Passing over one generation we come to the beginning of the second
century, when two names stand out prominently. The first is Ishmael b.
Elisha, a martyr in the Hadrianic persecution, who was the founder of a
School. He specialized in the scientific study of Jewish law, and elaborated the seven rules of Hillel into thirteen, which became the recognized

principles of interpretation. His main work was the endeavour to co-ordinate the large number of decisions by attaching them to the Biblical texts from which they were deduced. He composed a commentary on the legalistic passages of the last four Books of the Pentateuch; but only that on Exodus, commencing at chap. xii, has been preserved, although in a later redaction. It is known as *Mechilta* (Measure). His work on the other books formed the basis of similar commentaries which were compiled subsequently to the Mishnah, but may be conveniently mentioned here. They are the *Sifra* on Leviticus which was edited by Chiyya b. Abba, who flourished in the earlier part of the third century, and the *Sifré* on Numbers and Deuteronomy, which doubtless had a separate editor for each book although issued together. The commentary on Numbers seems to date from the same period as the *Sifra* and that on Deuteronomy belongs to a somewhat later time.

Both the *Sifra* and *Sifré* display traces of the influence of another eminent teacher, Akiba b. Joseph, who suffered martyrdom under the Romans in 132. He developed the science of *Midrash* to its extreme limits. Not a letter of the Scriptural text was held to be without significance, and he gave proof of extraordinary acumen in his interpretations. By the application of his exegetical method, a traditional practice no longer remained detached from the written code. By some means or other it was provided with an authoritative basis in the text.

In addition to his work as expositor and teacher, he also did much as a systematizer. It was said of him that he made the Torah into 'a series of rings' (ARN XVIII), by which is to be understood that he collated the multitude of legal dicta which had accumulated down to his time and reduced them to order. He may be described as the architect of the plan of the Mishnah which was brought into existence a century later. Without his pioneer labours the Talmud may never have been ultimately produced. His disciples continued along the lines marked out by him and became the dominating influence in Torah-study during the generations that followed. The most important of them was Meir, for the reason that he was responsible for the edition of a Mishnah which was accepted by Judah the Prince as the groundwork of his codification.

The Talmud remarks that 'when Akiba died Judah was born' (Kid. 72b). As a statement of chronology this is not quite correct, because the date of Judah's birth was 135. The intention was probably to link together these two pre-eminent figures in the history of Jewish literature. What Akiba started Judah completed. The former was, as stated, the architect and the other was the master-builder.

Judah was the son of a famous teacher, Simeon b. Gamaliel II, and so belonged to a wealthy and influential family. He was given a liberal education, which included Greek, and he enjoyed the friendship of Roman nobles. His learning and social status combined to give him a position of unquestioned authority among the Jews of Palestine, and for over fifty years until his death in 219 or the following year he occupied the office of *Nasi* (Prince, Patriarch), i.e. he was the officially recognized leader of his community.

The great achievement of his life was the compilation of the corpus of Jewish law, called the Mishnah. The name is derived from a root *shanah*, 'to repeat,' and indicates oral teaching, what is learnt by repetition. The noun is the opposite of *Mikra*, 'the text (of Scripture) for reading.' It therefore signifies the codification of the Oral Torah in contradistinction to the Written Torah of the Pentateuch. He succeeded in preparing a code which was adopted throughout the Schools of Palestine and Babylon, and it resulted in the disuse of all other collections of laws made by individual Rabbis for their own academies. He established the uniform textbook for future study and discussion.

The language in which it is composed is a vernacular form of Hebrew, distinguished from Biblical Hebrew by a less strict conformity to grammatical rules and the infiltration of Latin and Greek words. It is characterized by extreme terseness of expression and the absence of literary flourishes. The language admirably suits the subject-matter.

Since the Middle Ages the question has been debated whether Judah committed his Mishnah to writing or whether it remained for some time a verbal arrangement. Scholars are still in disagreement, but the weight of opinion is gradually accumulating in favour of the view that it was issued in the form of a written code. It is arranged in six sections called *Sedarim* (Orders); each Order consists of a number of *Massichtoth* (Tractates), the total being sixty-three; and each tractate is divided into chapters and subdivided into paragraphs. There are 523 chapters in all.

The following is a summary of the arrangement and contents of the Mishnah:

I. Order *Zeraim*, 'Seeds'

1. *Berachoth*, 'Benedictions'. Regulations dealing with the liturgy.

2. *Peah*, 'Corner'. Questions arising out of the law concerning 'the corners of the field'.

3. *Dammai*, 'Doubtful'. Treatment of corn, etc., purchased from a person suspected of not having given the tithe to the priest.

4. *Kilayim*, 'Mixtures'. On mixture of seeds, cross-breeding, etc., prohibited by Lev. xix, 19.

5. *Shebiit*, 'Seventh'. Law of the Sabbatical year.

6. *Terumoth*, 'Heave-offerings'. Law of the heave-offering.

7. *Maaseroth*, 'Tithes'. Law of the tithe of the Levite.

8. *Maaser Sheni*, 'Second Tithe'. Regulations based on Deut. xiv. 22ff.

9. *Challah*, 'Dough'. The portion of dough to be given to the priests according to Num. xv. 21.

10. *Orlah*, 'Uncircumcision'. Law of fruits of trees during the first four years of planting.

11. *Bikkurim*, 'First-fruits'. The first-fruits brought to the Temple.

II. Order *Moéd*, 'Season'

1. *Shabbath*, 'Sabbath'. Prohibited labour during the Sabbath.

2. *Erubin*, 'Amalgamations'. Treats of a technical point which arises out of a Sabbatical law, viz. the boundary which may not be overstepped on the Sabbath and how it may be extended.

3. *Pesachim*, 'Passovers'. Observance of the Passover Festival.

4. *Shekalim*, 'Shekels'. The annual tax to the Temple treasury.

5. *Yoma*, 'The Day'. The ritual of the Day of Atonement.

6. *Sukkah*, 'Booth'. Observance of the Feast of Tabernacles.

7. *Betzah*, 'Egg' also called *Yom Tob*, 'Festival'. On prohibited and permitted labour on a festival.

8. *Rosh Hashanah*, 'New Year'. Observance of the feast which marks the New Year.

9. *Taanith*, 'Fast'. On the public fasts.

10. *Megillah*, 'Scroll'. Concerning the public recital of the Book of Esther on the Feast of Purim.

11. *Moed Katan*, 'Minor Feast'. Concerning the intermediate days of Passover and Tabernacles.

12. *Chagigah*, 'Festival Offering'. On the sacrifices offered on the three Pilgrimage Festivals.

III. Order *Nashim*, 'Women'

1. *Yebamoth*, 'Levirate Marriage'. Deals with the law of marriage with a childless sister-in-law and forbidden degrees of relationship in connection with marriage.

2. *Kethuboth*, 'Marriage Documents'. Treats of the dowry and marriage-settlement.

3. *Nedarim*, 'Vows'. On the making and annulment of vows particularly with regard to women.

4. *Nazir*, 'Nazirite'. Concerning the vow of the Nazirite.

5. *Sotah*, 'Suspected Adultress'. Relating to the wife suspected of infidelity.

6. *Gittin*, 'Divorces'. Laws relating to the annulment of marriage.

7. *Kiddushin*, 'Sanctification'. On the marriage status.

IV. Order *Nezikin*, 'Torts'

1. *Baba Kamma*, 'The First Gate'. On damages to property and injury to the person.

2. *Baba Metzia*, 'The Middle Gate'. On found property, bailment, sales, and hiring.

3. *Baba Bathra*, 'The Last Gate'. On real estate and hereditary succession.

4. *Sanhedrin*, 'Courts'. Deals with courts of law and their procedure and capital crimes.

5. *Makkoth*, 'Stripes'. On the punishment of perjurers, cities of refuge and crimes punished by lashes.

6. *Shebuoth*, 'Oaths'. On the oaths made privately or administered in a court.

7. *Eduyyoth*, 'Testimonies'. A collection of testimonies of Rabbis concerning the decisions of earlier authorities.

8. *Abodah Zarah*, 'Idolatry'. On heathenish rites and worship.

9. *Pirke Aboth*, 'Chapters of the Fathers'. An ethical treatise collecting favourite maxims of the *Tannaim*. There is also an Appendix called 'the Chapter of R. Meir on the Acquisition of the Torah.'

10. *Horayoth*, 'Decisions'. On inadvertent sin through the misdirection of religious authorities.

V. Order *Kodashim*, 'Sanctities'

1. *Zebachim*, 'Sacrifices'. On the sacrificial system of the Temple.

2. *Menachoth*, 'Meal-offerings'. Deals with the meal and drink offerings.

3. *Chullin*, 'Profane Things'. On the slaughter of animals and the dietary laws.

4. *Bechoroth*, 'Firstborns'. Concerning the firstborn of man and animals.

5. *Arachin*, 'Estimations'. On the value-equivalent of persons and objects vowed to the Temple.

6. *Temurah*, 'Substitution'. Treats of the exchange of animals dedicated as a sacrifice.

7. *Kerithoth*, 'Excisions'. On the sins punishable by 'cutting off'.

8. *Meilah*, 'Trespass'. On the sacrilegious treatment of Temple property.

9. *Tamid*, 'Continual Offering'. Describes the daily ritual in the Temple.

10. *Middoth*, 'Dimensions'. On the architecture of the Temple.

11. *Kinnim*, 'Birds' Nests'. On the offerings of birds.

VI. Order *Teharoth*, 'Purities'

1. *Kelim*, 'Vessels'. Deals with the ritualistic defilement of utensils.

2. *Ohaloth*, 'Tents'. On the defilement caused by a corpse.

3. *Negaim*, 'Plagues'. Laws relating to leprosy.

4. *Parah*, 'Cow'. Regulations concerning the Red Heifer.

5. *Teharoth*, 'Purities'. A euphemism for the defilements which last until sunset.

6. *Mikwaoth*, 'Baths'. On the requirements of cisterns to be used for ritualistic purification.

7. *Niddah*, "Uncleanness of Menstruation'. Deals with the laws of *Leviticus* XII, XV, 11 ff.

8. *Machshirin*, 'Preparations'. On liquids as a conductor of defilement.

9. *Zabim*, 'Persons Suffering from a Running Issue'. Treats of uncleanness caused by physical issues.

10. *Tebul Yom*, 'Immersed during a Day'. On the status of a person who has undergone immersion but whose purification is not complete until sunset.

11. *Yadayim*, 'Hands'. On the defilement of the hands and their purification.

12. *Uktzin*, 'Stalks'. Treats of fruit-stalks as a conductor of defilement.

APOCRYPHAL TRACTATES OF POST-MISHNAIC DATE

Aboth d'Rabbi Nathan. An elaboration of *Pirké Aboth*.

Sopherim, 'Scribes'. Deals with the rules for the writing of scrolls of the Torah for use in the Synagogue and other liturgical matters.

Ebel Rabbathi, 'The Great Mourning.' more usually called euphemistically *Semachoth*, 'Joys'. Regulations concerning burial and mourning customs.

Kallah, 'Bride'. A short tractate in one chapter on Chastity.

Derech Eretz Rabbah, 'Large Treatise on Behaviour'. On prohibited marriages and ethical conduct.

Derech Eretz Zuta, 'Small Treatise on Behaviour'. Collection of rules of good conduct.

Perek Shalom, 'A Chapter on Peace'.

Gerim, 'Proselytes'. Rules concerning conversion to Judaism.

Kuthim, 'Samaritans'. On practices of Samaritans in relation to Jewish law.

Abadim, 'Slaves'. Concerning Hebrew slaves.

To these must be added four small tractates published, together with the last three enumerated above, by R. Kirchheim in 1851.

Sepher Torah, 'Scroll of the Law'; *Mezuzah,* 'Sign on the Door-post'; *Tephillin,* 'Phylacteries'; and *Tzitzith,* 'Fringes'.

There has come down to us another work, analogous to the Mishnah, called *Tosifta* (Supplement). It is also a collection of laws in systematic arrangement, in many respects running parallel to the Mishnah, but containing additional matter. The style is more diffuse than that employed by Judah, and it frequently adds the proof-texts which are normally omitted in the Mishnah. Its exact relationship to the official codification has not yet been determined, and many problems connected with its authorship still remain in doubt. The nucleus of the work is now usually attributed to two Rabbis of the third century. Rabbah and Oshaya, although in its present form it probably dates from the fifth century.

THE TALMUD

Israel Abrahams

The *Talmud*, or *Gemara* ("Doctrine," or "Completion"), was a natural development of the Mishnah. The Talmud contains, indeed, many elements as old as the Mishnah, some even older. But, considered as a whole, the Talmud is a commentary on the work of the Tannaim. It is written, not in Hebrew, as the Mishnah is, but in a popular Aramaic. There are two distinct works to which the title Talmud is applied; the one is the Jerusalem Talmud (completed about the year 370 C. E.), the other the Babylonian (completed a century later). At first, as we have seen, the Rabbinical schools were founded on Jewish soil. But Palestine did not continue to offer a friendly welcome. Under the more tolerant rulers of Babylonia or Persia, Jewish learning found a refuge from the harshness experienced under those of the Holy Land. The Babylonian Jewish schools in Nehardea, Sura, and Pumbeditha rapidly surpassed the Palestinian in reputation, and in the year 350 C. E., owing to natural decay, the Palestinian schools closed.

The Talmud is accordingly not one work, but two, the one the literary product of the Palestinian, the other, of the Babylonian *Amoraim*. The latter is the larger, the more studied, the better preserved, and to it attention will here be mainly confined. The Talmud is not a book, it is a literature. It contains a legal code, a system of ethics, a body of ritual customs, poetical passages, prayers, histories, facts of science and medicine, and fancies of folk-lore.

The Amoraim were what their name implies, "Expounders," or "Discoursers"; but their expositions were often original contributions to literature. Their work extends over the long interval between 200 and 500 C. E. The Amoraim naturally were men of various character and condition. Some were possessed of much material wealth, others were excessively poor. But few of them were professional men of letters. Like the Tannaim, the Amoraim were often artisans, field-laborers, or physicians, whose heart was certainly in literature, but whose hand was turned to the practical affairs of life. The men who stood highest socially, the Princes of the Captivity in Babylonia and the Patriarchs in Palestine, were not always those vested with the highest authority. Some of the

Amoraim, again, were merely receptive, the medium through which tradition was handed on; others were creative as well. To put the same fact in Rabbinical metaphor, some were Sinais of learning, others tore up mountains, and ground them together in keen and critical dialectics.

The oldest of the Amoraim, Chanina, the son of Chama, of Sepphoris (180-260), was such a firm mountain of ancient learning. On the other hand, Jochanan, the son of Napacha (199-279), of dazzling physical beauty, had a more original mind. His personal charms conveyed to him perhaps a sense of the artistic; to him the Greek language was a delight, "an ornament of women." Simon, the son of Lakish (200-275), hardy of muscle and of intellect, started life as a professional athlete. A later Rabbi, Zeira, was equally noted for his feeble, unprepossessing figure and his nimble, ingenious mind. Another contemporary of Jochanan, Joshua, the son of Levi, is the hero of many legends. He was so tender to the poor that he declared his conviction that the Messiah would arise among the beggars and cripples of Rome. Simlai, who was born in Palestine, and migrated to Nehardea in Babylonia, was more of a poet than a lawyer. His love was for the ethical and poetic elements of the Talmud, the *Hagadah*, as this aspect of the Rabbinical literature was called in contradistinction to the Halachah, or legal elements. Simlai entered into frequent discussions with the Christian Fathers on subjects of Biblical exegesis.

The centre of interest now changes to Babylonia. Here, in the year 219, Abba Areka, or Rab (175-247), founded the Sura academy, which continued to flourish for nearly eight centuries. He and his great contemporary Samuel (180-257) enjoy with Jochanan the honor of supplying the leading materials of which the Talmud consists. Samuel laid down a rule which, based on an utterance of the prophet Jeremiah, enabled Jews to live and serve in non-Jewish countries. "The law of the land is law," said Samuel. But he lived in the realms of the stars as well as in the streets of his city. Samuel was an astronomer, and he is reported to have boasted with truth, that "he was as familiar with the paths of the stars as with the streets of Nehardea." He arranged the Jewish Calendar, his work in this direction being perfected by Hillel II in the fourth century. Like Simlai, Rab and Samuel had heathen and Christian friends. Origen and Jerome read the Scriptures under the guidance of Jews. The heathen philosopher Porphyry wrote a commentary on the Book of Daniel. So, too, Abbahu, who lived in Palestine a little later on, frequented the society of cultivated Romans, and had his family taught Greek. Abbahu was a manufacturer of veils for women's wear, for, like many Amoraim, he scorned to make learning a means of living. Abbahu's modesty with regard to his own merits shows that a Rabbi was not necessarily arrogant in pride of knowledge! Once Abbahu's lecture was besieged by a great crowd, but the audience of his colleague Chiya was scanty. "Thy teaching," said Abbahu to Chiya, "is a rare jewel, of which only an expert can judge; mine is tinsel, which attracts every ignorant eye."

It was Rab, however, who was the real popularizer of Jewish learning. He arranged courses of lectures for the people as well as for scholars. Rab's successor as head of the Sura school, Huna (212-297), completed Rab's work in making Babylonia the chief centre of Jewish learning. Huna tilled his own fields for a living, and might often be met going home with his spade over his shoulder. It was men like this who built up the Jewish tradition. Huna's predecessor, however, had wider experience of life, for Rab had been a student in Palestine, and was in touch with the Jews of many parts. From Rab's time onwards, learning became the property of the whole people, and the Talmud, besides being the literature of the Jewish universities, may be called the book of the masses. It contains, not only the legal and ethical results of the investigations of the learned, but also the wisdom and superstition of the masses. The Talmud is not exactly a national literature, but it was a unique bond between the scattered Jews, an unparallelled spiritual and literary instrument for maintaining the identity of Judaism amid the many tribulations to which the Jews were subjected.

The Talmud owed much to many minds. Externally it was influenced by the nations with which the Jews came into contact. From the inside, the influences at work were equally various. Jochanan, Rab, and Samuel in the Third century prepared the material out of which the Talmud was finally built. The actual building was done by scholars in the fourth century. Rabba, the son of Nachmani (270-330), Abayi (280-338), and Rava (299-352) gave the finishing touches to the method of the Talmud. Rabba was a man of the people; he was a clear thinker, and loved to attract all comers by an apt anecdote. Rava had a superior sense of his own dignity, and rather neglected the needs of the ordinary man of his day. Abayi, was more of the type of the average Rabbi, acute, genial, self-denying. Under the impulse of men of the most various gifts of mind and heart, the Talmud was gradually constructed, but two names are prominently associated with its actual compilation. These were Ashi (352-427) and Rabina (died 499). Ashi combined massive learning with keen logical ingenuity. He needed both for the task to which he devoted half a century of his life. He possessed a vast memory, in which the accumulated tradition of six centuries was stored, and he was gifted with the mental orderliness which empowered him to deal with this bewildering mass of materials.

It is hardly possible that after the compilation of the Talmud it remained an oral book, though it must be remembered that memory played a much greater part in earlier centuries than it does now. At all events, Ashi, and after him Rabina, performed the great work of systematizing the Rabbinical literature at a turning-point in the world's history. The Mishnah had been begun at a moment when the Roman empire was at its greatest vigor and glory; the Talmud was completed at the time when the Roman empire was in its decay. That the Jews were saved from similar disintegration, was due very largely to the Talmud. The Talmud is thus one of the great books of the world. Despite its faults, its excessive casuistry, its lack of style and form, its stupendous mass of detailed laws and restrictions, it is nevertheless a great book in and for itself.

GEMARA AND MIDRASH

Abraham Cohen

The purpose which Judah had in view in editing the Mishnah was not to fix the law. That would have been contrary to the spirit which animated the Rabbis and militated against the fundamental principle of the Oral Torah. His object was to facilitate its study. For that reason he records the opposing views of different authorities, but where an accepted decision had been arrived at he indicates what it is. His codification stimulated further research rather than checked it.

The Mishnah provided the schools with a much needed text-book, and its use rapidly advanced Torah-study both in extent and depth. Every clause was carefully examined and discussed for the purpose of testing its validity, definition, and scope. The editor had by no means exhausted the whole of the available material in his compilation, and teachers had handed down by word of mouth or in writing many legal opinions which had not been incorporated in the Mishnah. Such an excluded dictum is called *Baraita,* 'that which is external.' A debate on a paragraph of the Mishnah often opens with the quotation of a *Baraita* which appears to take different side on the law in question, and much ingenuity is expended in the harmonization of the two opinions.

For several centuries to come, scholarship among the Jews consisted mainly, if not entirely, in the acquisition of knowledge of the Mishnah and the commentary which gradually accumulated around it. This commentary is designated *Gemara* (Completion), because it completes the Mishnah. Its exponents, in contrast to the pre-Mishnaic Rabbis or *Tannaim,* were named *Amoraim* (Speakers, Expounders). The principal Schools where this study was prosecuted were Caesarea, Sepphoris, Tiberias, and Usha in Palestine, and Nehardea, Sura and Pombeditha in Babylon.

The Palestinian and Babylonian Academies carried on their researches independently, although Rabbis passed to and fro between the countries and in this way created an interchange of views. In Palestine the most distinguished teacher was Jochanan b. Nappacha (199-279), the head of the Academy of Tiberias. He began the collection of the reports of the discussions which were taking place on the Mishnah in the Palestinian Schools. He cannot be accredited, as used to be supposed, with the composition of the Palestinian Talmud, since authorities belonging to three generations after his death are cited in it. He may well have laid the foundation of the work which others added to until towards the end of the fourth century it reached its final form. The Mishnah, with its commentary the Gemara, are together denoted the *Talmud* (Study), an abbreviation of Talmud Torah.

The Palestinian Talmud, accordingly, consists of the text of the Mishnah and the glosses upon it which emanated from the Academies of that country. Simultaneously the same process was at work in Babylon. The Jewish community there was more numerous and better circumstanced than their co-religionists in Palestine, and they produced or attracted men of superior intellectual powers. At any rate, the teaching in its Schools was deeper and more thorough, and this distinction is clearly evident in the compilation of the Gemara which was made there. R. Ashé (352-427) began the task of its composition, to which he devoted thirty years, leaving it unfinished at his death. Rabina brought it to a close in 499.

Neither Talmud consists of a complete Gemara, although there is evidence that it existed on certain tractates where it is no longer extant. In the Palestinian Talmud it covers thirty-nine tractates and in the Babylonian thirty-seven; but the Babylonian Gemara is seven to eight times the size of the other.

The first complete edition of both Talmuds, as we now have them, was issued by Daniel Bomberg in Venice, the Babylonian in 1520-3 and the Palestinian in 1523-4. His pagination has been followed in nearly all subsequent issues. He printed the Palestinian Talmud without any commentary, two columns on each side of the folio; but the Babylonian Talmud he printed with a portion of the Gemara in the centre of each side surrounded by the commentary of Solomon b. Isaac (better known as Rashi, 1040-1105), and notes of later glossators called Tosafists.

The language of the two Talmuds also varies and represents two different dialects of Aramaic. The Palestinian Gemara is composed in Western Aramaic and closely resembles the Biblical Aramaic of parts of Ezra and Daniel. The Babylonian Gemara is in Eastern Aramaic, which is more akin to Mandaitic.

From the sketch which has been given of the history of the Talmud, it at once becomes evident that it cannot be regarded, in the strict sense of the term, as a literary work. The ordinary canons of literature do not apply to it. Although, in so far as it follows the text of the Mishnah, it is founded on a system, if taken as a whole it presents the appearance of a disorderly mass of the most heterogeneous material. As a record of the proceedings of the Schools, it faithfully reflects all that was discussed within their walls. Teachers and pupils allowed themselves to digress from the point under examination and wander off at will into every conceivable kind of topic. They relieved the tedium of a keen debate on an abstruse legal theme by taking up a lighter subject. They poured forth for mutual edification the treasures stored in their memories relating to history, legend, folk-lore, medicine, astronomy, botany, zoology, and a host of other matters. Not only the sharp battle of wits but likewise the ordinary conversation which passed within the Academies—all are vividly portrayed in the Talmud.

Furthermore, Torah, as understood by the Rabbis, touched life at every point. It dealt with the whole existence of the human being. Religion, ethics, and physical life—even his superstitions—in fact, nothing that pertained to man fell outside its purview. Therefore, instructors and disciples could not restrict their discussions to questions of law. They were in the closest touch with the mass of the people, and what the ordinary man and woman were thinking and saying penetrated into the Schools and found a place on the Talmudic folios.

The miscellaneous material which constitutes the subject-matter of the Talmud is divisible into two main categories known as *Halachah* and *Haggadah*. The former term denotes 'walking,' and indicates the way of life to tread in conformity with the precepts of the Torah. It therefore comprises the Mishnah and that section of the Gemara which treats of law. The *Halachah* is the logical working out by many generations of devoted scholars of the theory devised by Ezra for the salvation of the people of Israel. It provided the community as a whole and its individual members with a distinctive code of action which fulfilled the purpose of keeping the Jewish consciousness alive. The *Halachah* moulded the existence of the Jew. It directed his steps so that he walked humbly with his God. It also created a breakwater, behind which he found security from the alien influences that tended to sweep him from his racial moorings. Its efficacy as a preservative force has been thoroughly tested and proved by centuries of experience down to the present day. The Halachah is the regime under which the Jew lived *qua* Jew in past generations and still lives; and it supplies the answer to the question why a minority has for such a length of time maintained its identity and not been absorbed in the surrounding majority.

Even if it were possible to isolate the Halachah from the other elements in the Talmud, it would still be a mistake to envisage it as a system of dry legalism devoid of all spiritual content, as its critics invariably allege. A modern student of Rabbinic literature has truly said: 'The Pharisees and the Rabbis were, before anything else, teachers; and what they set out to teach was practical religion, the doing of right actions for the service of God and man. They sought to strengthen the factors which make for unity and peace amongst men—the sense of justice, truth, probity, brotherly love, sympathy, mercy, forbearance, and the rest—in a word, to raise the moral standard amongst their people from age to age. They had this purpose mainly in view when they developed the *Halachah* and kept it from becoming a rigid system. They made it a means of ethical training by defining right conduct in terms of a progressive morality, a standard which was raised and not lowered in course of time'.

But it is impossible to separate the *Halachah* from the other main constituent, the *Haggadah,* without creating a distorted picture of Rabbinic teaching. The *Haggadah* was the concern of the same teachers who pondered over the technicalities of the *Halachah*. The two were imparted side by side in the same Schools to the same pupils, and together they form the interwoven strands from which the Talmud was constructed.

Haggadah (Narration), therefore, signifies the non-legal sections of Rabbinic literature, and is equally important as the other for a correct understanding of the world of thought which generations of teachers lovingly evolved. Striking though the contrast be between *Halachah* and *Haggadah,* they complement each other, spring from the same root, and aim at the same goal. If the *Halachah* pointed out the way of the godly life, so did the *Haggadah*. 'Is it your desire to know Him Who spake and the world came into being? Learn the Haggadah; for from it you will come to know the Holy One, blessed be He, and cleave to His ways' (Sifré Deut. 49; 85a). They both grew from the same soil. Exactly as the Rabbi strove to derive sanction for a legal decision from the text of the Torah, he likewise endeavoured to corroborate an ethical or moral lesson by a quotation from that source. 'As it is said,' or 'as it is written,' followed by a Scriptural reference, is the ordinary way of presenting a piece of *Haggadah*. One important point of difference must, however, be noted. Whereas the *Halachah* remained the law to be observed in practice until it was abrogated by a competent authority, *Haggadah* was always held to be nothing more than the personal opinion of the teacher. It possessed no binding force upon the community as a whole or any part of it.

A Jewish scholar has happily defined the relationship of these two elements in the following terms: '*Halachah* is law incarnate; *Haggadah* liberty regulated by law bearing the impress of morality. *Halachah* stands for the rigid authority of the law, for the absolute importance of theory— the law and theory which the *Haggadah* illustrates by public opinion and the dicta of common-sense morality. The *Halachah* embraces the statutes enjoined by oral tradition, which was the unwritten commentary of the ages on the Written Law, along with the discussions of the Academies of Palestine and Babylonia, resulting in the final formulating of the Halachic ordinances. The *Haggadah,* while also starting from the word of the Bible, only plays with it, explaining it by sagas and legends, by tales and poems, allegories, ethical reflections, and historical reminiscences. For it, the Bible was not only the supreme law, from whose behests there was no appeal, but also "a golden nail upon which" the *Haggadah* "hung its gorgeous tapestries," so that the Bible word was the introduction, refrain, text, and subject of the poetical glosses of the Talmud. It was the province of the *Halachah* to build, upon the foundation of Biblical law, a legal superstructure capable of resisting the ravages of time, and, unmindful of contemporaneous distress and hardship, to trace out, for future generations, the extreme logical consequences of the Law in its application. To the *Haggadah,* belonged the high, ethical mission of consoling, edifying, exhorting, and teaching a nation suffering the pangs and threatened with the spiritual stagnation, of exile; of proclaiming that the glories of the past prefigured a future of equal brilliancy, and that the very wretchedness of the present was part of the divine plan outlined in the Bible. If the simile is accurate that likens the *Halachah* to the ramparts about Israel's Sanctuary, which every Jew was ready to defend with his last drop of blood, then the *Haggadah* must seem flowery mazes, of exotic colours and bewildering fragrance, within the shelter of the Temple walls.'

We have seen that from the time of the Babylonian exile the practice grew of Jews gathering together for the purpose of hearing the Pentateuch read and expounded, and from this kind of assembly the Synagogue originated. Right through the Talmudic period, not to speak of later ages, the Synagogue was the school of the public as well as the place of prayer. The mass of the people who had no time or inclination or ability for Halachic dialectics had their need of religious learning catered for within its precincts. In particular, the Sabbath afternoons were spent in listening to discourses which were intended to satisfy the eager audience intellectually, spiritually, and morally. Homilies corrective of prevalent faults, addresses to instil hope and courage into a harassed community and preserve its will to live, lectures on the relation of God and His Universe or of man and his Maker, skilful elucidations of Scriptural texts which revealed them in a new light or opened up fresh avenues of thought —such was the fare provided in the Synagogues for the instruction and delectation of the people.

With such a comprehensive goal in view, it will be readily appreciated that the preacher would not be satisfied with imparting to his hearers merely the superficial interpretation of the Bible. More than the desire to understand and teach the meaning of a verse was the eagerness to see what the verse could be made to mean. Four methods of exegesis were employed, and they are indicated by the consonants of the word for 'garden, Paradise' (*Pardes*). They were, respectively: *Peshat* (simple), i.e. literal interpretation; *Remez* (allusion), i.e. allegorical explanation; *Derash* (exposition), i.e. homiletical commentary; and *Sod* (mystery), i.e. esoteric teaching. By these methods the teachers garnered rich stores of ideas which contributed to the material of the *Haggadah*.

It follows, therefore, that apart from the Schools, a fertile source of Haggadic teaching was found in the Synagogues. In course of time a desire was felt to have this material collected for private reading and study. This need created the branch of Rabbinic literature called *Midrashim*. The most important of them is the *Midrash Rabbah* (Great Midrash), which has the form of a kind of Haggadic Gemara on the Pentateuch and the five *Megilloth* or Scrolls—Song of Songs, Ruth, Lamentations, Ecclesiastes, and Esther—which were read during the Synagogue services in the course of a year. These were compiled at various dates between the fifth and twelfth centuries, but the material belongs in the main to the period of the Talmud. Other notable Haggadic works are the *Midrash Tanchuma* on the Pentateuch, which emanated from a Palestinian Rabbi named Tanchuma who lived in the latter part of the fourth century, but in its extant form is of much later date; the *Pesikta d'Rab Kahana* on the lessons read on festivals and special Sabbaths, which belongs to the sixth century; and a Midrash on the Psalms.

THE MIDRASH AND ITS POETRY
Israel Abrahams

In its earliest forms identical with the Halachah, or the practical and legal aspects of the Mishnah and the Talmud, the Midrash, in its fuller development, became an independent branch of Rabbinical literature. Like the Talmud, the Midrash is of a composite nature, and under the one name the accumulations of ages are included. Some of its contents are earlier than the completion of the Bible, others were collected and even created as recently as the tenth or the eleventh century of the current era.

Midrash ("Study", "Inquiry") was in the first instance an *Explanation of the Scriptures*. This explanation is often the clear, natural exposition of the text, and it enforces rules of conduct both ethical and ritual. The historical and moral traditions which clustered round the incidents and characters of the Bible soon received a more vivid setting. The poetical sense of the Rabbis expressed itself in a vast and beautiful array of legendary additions to the Bible, but the additions are always devised with a moral purpose, to give point to a preacher's homily or to inspire the imagination of the audience with nobler fancies. Besides being expository, the Midrash is, therefore, didactic and poetical, the moral being conveyed in the guise of a *narrative,* amplifying and developing the contents of Scripture. The Midrash gives the results of that deep searching of the Scriptures which became second nature with the Jews, and it also represents the changes and expansions of ethical and theological ideals as applied to a changing and growing life.

From another point of view, also, the Midrash is a poetical literature. Its function as a species of *popular homiletics* made it necessary to appeal to the emotions. In its warm and living application of abstract truths to daily ends, in its responsive and hopeful intensification of the nearness of God to Israel, in its idealization of the past and future of the Jews, it employed the poet's art in essence, though not in form. It will be seen later on that in another sense the Midrash is a poetical literature, using the lore of the folk, the parable, the proverb, the allegory, and the fable, and often using them in the language of poetry.

The oldest Midrash is the actual report of sermons and addresses of

27

the Tannaite age; the latest is a medieval compilation from all extant sources. The works to which the name Midrash is applied are the *Mechilta* (to Exodus); the *Sifra* (to Leviticus); the *Sifre* (to Numbers and Deuteronomy); the *Pesikta* (to various *Sections* of the Bible, whence its name); the *Tanchuma* (to the Pentateuch); the *Midrash Rabbah* (the "Great Midrash," to the Pentateuch and the Five Scrolls of Esther, Ruth, Lamentations, Ecclesiastes, and the Song of Songs); and the *Midrash Haggadol* (identical in name, and in contents similar to, but not identical with, the *Midrash Rabbah*); together with a large number of collected Midrashim, such as the *Yalkut,* and a host of smaller works, several of which are no longer extant.

Regarding the Midrash in its purely literary aspects, we find its style to be far more lucid than that of the Talmud, though portions of the Halachic Midrash are identical in character with the Talmud. The Midrash has many passages in which the simple graces of form match the beauty of idea. But for the most part the style is simple and prosaic, rather than ornate or poetical. It produces its effects by the most straightforward means, and strikes a modern reader as lacking distinction in form. The dead level of commonplace expression is, however, brightened by brilliant passages of frequent occurrence. Prayers, proverbs, parables, and fables, dot the pages of Talmud and Midrash alike. The ancient *proverbs* of the Jews were more than mere chips from the block of experience. They were poems, by reason of their use of metaphor, alliteration, assonance, and imagination. The Rabbinical proverbs show all these poetical qualities.

He who steals from a thief smells of theft.—Charity is the salt of Wealth.—Silence is a fence about Wisdom.—Many old camels carry the skins of their young.—Two dry sticks and one green burn together. —If the priest steals the god, on what can one take an oath?—All the dyers cannot bleach a raven's wing.—Into a well from which you have drunk, cast no stone.—Alas for the bread which the baker calls bad. —Slander is a Snake that stings in Syria, and slays in Rome.—The Dove escaped from the Eagle and found a Serpent in her nest.—Tell no secrets, for the Wall has ears.

These, like many more of the Rabbinical proverbs, are essentially poetical. Some, indeed, are either expanded metaphors or metaphors touched by genius into poetry. The alliterative proverbs and maxims of the Talmud and Midrash are less easily illustrated. Sometimes they enshrine a pun or a conceit, or depend for their aptness upon an assonance. In some of the Talmudic proverbs there is a spice of cynicism. But most of them show a genial attitude towards life.

The poetical proverb easily passes into the parable. Loved in Bible times, the parable became in after centuries the most popular form of didactic poetry among the Jews. The Bible has its parables, but the Midrash overflows with them. They are occasionally re-workings of older thoughts, but mostly they are original creations, invented for a special purpose, stories devised to drive home a moral, allegories administering in pleasant wrappings, unpalatable satires or admonitions. In all ages up to the present, Jewish moralists have relied on the parable as their most effective instrument. The poetry of the Jewish parables is characteristic also of the parables imitated from the Jewish, but the latter have a distinguishing feature peculiar to them. This is their humor, the witty or humorous parable being exclusively Jewish. The parable is less spontaneous than the proverb. It is a product of moral poetry rather than of folk wisdom. Yet the parable was so like the proverb that the moral of a parable often became a new proverb. The diction of the parable is naturally more ornate. By the beauty of its expression, its frequent application of rural incidents to the life familiar in the cities, the rhythm and flow of its periods, its fertile imagination, the parable should certainly be placed high in the world's poetry. But its was poetry with a *tendency,* the *mashal,* or proverb-parable, being what the Rabbis themselves termed it, "the clear small light by which lost jewels can be found."

The following is a parable of Hillel, which is here cited more to mention that noble, gentle Sage than as a specimen of this class of literature. Hillel belongs to a period earlier than that dealt with in this book, but his loving and pure spirit breathes through the pages of the Talmud and Midrash:

> Hillel, the gentle, the beloved sage,
> Expounded day by day the sacred page
> To his disciples in the house of learning;
> And day by day, when home at eve returning,
> They lingered, clust'ring round him, loth to part
> From him whose gentle rule won every heart.
> But evermore, when they were wont to plead
> For longer converse, forth he went with speed.
> Saying each day: "I go—the hour is late—
> To tend the guest who doth my coming wait,"
> Until at last they said: "The Rabbi jests,
> When telling us thus daily of his guests

That wait for him." The Rabbi paused awhile,
And then made answer: "Think you I beguile
You with an idle tale? Not so, forsooth!
I have a guest whom I must tend in truth.
Is not the soul of man indeed a guest
Who in this body deigns a while to rest,
And dwells with me all peacefully to-day:
To-morrow—may it not have fled away?"

Space must be found for one other parable, taken (like many other
poetical quotations in this volume) from Mrs. Lucas' translations:

Simeon ben Migdal, at the close of day,
Upon the shores of ocean chanced to stray,
And there a man of form and mien uncouth,
Dwarfed and misshapen, met he on the way.

"Hail, Rabbi," spoke the stranger passing by,
But Simeon thus, discourteous, made reply:
"Say, are there in thy city many more,
Like unto thee, an insult to the eye?"

"Nay, that I cannot tell," the wand'rer said,
"But if thou wouldst ply the scorner's trade,
Go first and ask the Master Potter why
He has a vessel so misshapen made?"

Then (so the legend tells) the Rabbi knew
That he had sinned, and prone himself he threw
Before the other's feet, and prayed of him
Pardon for the words that now his soul did rue.

But still the other answered as before:
"Go, in the Potter's ear thy plaint outpour,
For what am I! His hand has fashioned me,
And I in humble faith that hand adore."

Brethren, do we not too often too forget
Whose hand it is that many a time has set
A radiant soul in an unlovely form,
A fair white bird caged in a mouldering net?

Nay more, do not life's times and chances, sent
By the great Artificer with intent
That they should prove a blessing, oft appear
To us a burden that we sore lament?

Ah! soul, poor soul of man! what heavenly fire
Would thrill thy depths and love of God inspire,
Could'st thou but see the Master hand revealed,
Majestic move "earth's scheme of things entire."

It cannot be! Unseen he guideth us,
But yet our feeble hands, the luminous
Pure lamp of faith can light to glorify
The narrow path that he has traced for us.

Finally, there are the *Beast Fables* of the Talmud and the Midrash. Most of these were borrowed directly or indirectly from India. We are told in the Talmud that Rabbi Meir knew three hundred Fox Fables, and that with his death (about 290 C.E.) "fabulists ceased to be." Very few of Meir's fables are extant, so that it is impossible to gather whether or not they were original. There are only thirty fables in the Talmud and the Midrash, and of these several cannot be paralleled in other literatures. Some of the Talmudic fables are found also in the classical and earliest Indian collections; some in the later collections; some in the classics but not in the Indian lists; some in India, but not in the Latin and Greek authors. Among the latter is the well-known fable of the *Fox and the Fishes,* used so dramatically by Rabbi Akiba. The original Talmudic fables are, according to Mr. J. Jacobs, the following: *Chaff, Straw,* and *Wheat,* who dispute for which of them the seed has been sown: the winnowing fan soon decides; *The Caged Bird,* who is envied by his free fellow; *The Wolf and the two Hounds,* who have quarrelled; the wolf seizes one, the other goes to his rival's aid, fearing the same fate himself on the morrow, unless he helps the other dog today; *The Wolf at the Well,* the mouth of the well is covered with a net: "If I go down into the well," says the wolf, "I shall be caught. If I do not descend, I shall die of thirst"; *The Cock and the Bat,* who sit together waiting for the sunrise: "I wait for the dawn," said the cock, "for the light is my signal; but as for thee—the light is thy ruin"; and, finally, what Mr. Jacobs calls the grim beast-tale of the *Fox as Singer,* in which the beasts—invited by the lion to a feast, and covered by him with the skins of wild beasts—are led by the fox in a chorus: "What has happened to those above us, will happen to him above," implying that their host, too, will come to a violent death. In the context the fable is applied to Haman, whose fate, it is augured, will resemble that of the two officers whose guilt Mordecai detected.

Such fables are used in the Talmud to point religious or even political morals, very much as the parables were. The fable, however, took a lower flight than the parable, and its moral was based on expediency, rather than on the highest ethical ideals. The importance of the Talmudic fables is historical more than literary or religious. Hebrew fables supply one of the links connecting the popular literature of the East with that of the West. But they hardly belong in the true sense to Jewish literature. Parables, on the other hand, were an essential and characteristic branch of that literature.

THE PALESTINIAN TALMUD

Louis Ginzberg

I

No student of the post-biblical literature of the Jews can fail to be struck by the fact that it is predominantly interpretative and commentative. At first sight this seems to be rather strange, for Israel's classic literature, the Bible, with all its richness and variety of literary forms, contains not the slightest trace of the form most favored by the writers of later periods. The literature of a people, however, is but a mirror of the ideas which rule that people, and in post-Biblical times the idea of "the Book" was all-powerful among the Jews. Nehemiah records a covenant entered into under the guidance of Ezra: "To walk in God's law which was given by Moses, the servant of God, and to observe and do all the commandments of the Lord our God and His ordinances and His statutes." Whether we accept the traditional view of Ezra as "the restorer of the Torah" or follow the opinion of some modern Biblical scholars who picture him as the creator of a new movement, the significance of this *covenant* cannot be over-estimated. By this solemn act a "book"—the Pentateuch—became the written constitution of the new commonwealth, its code of laws, and its way of life. But the dead letter needs to be made living by interpretation. Hence the interpretative character of the post-Biblical writings.

Old Talmudic sources call the spiritual leaders of Israel in the centuries between Ezra (about 450) and the age of the Maccabeans (175) *Soferim,* which means "men of the Book," interpreters of sacred Scripture, and not, as it is usually translated, "scribes." The most momentous event in the century and a half after Ezra was the conquest of Palestine by the Greeks. Another century and a half had elapsed before the Maccabeans freed the Jews from the Macedonian tyrants. This victory was made possible by the work of the *Soferim,* who had succeeded in establishing a normative Judaism that was able to withstand the allure of Greek thought and the attraction of Hellenic life. These *Soferim* had not only safeguarded "The Book," but had, by their interpretations and comments, made it workable under the new conditions that arose in Palestine with the arrival of the Greeks.

The enormous mass of "interpretation" thus accumulated during the centuries of the *Soferim* was further augmented in the century of the Jewish free state under the Hasmoneans, and this for more than one reason. With the final victory of "the pious over the wicked" the pendulum swung in the opposite direction. The problem now was no longer how to adjust the new ideas of Hellas to the spiritual inheritance of Israel nor how to respond to the demands made by foreign ways of life; it was actually the reverse. The strong national feeling engendered by the victorious wars in defense of Jewish religion and Jewish morals led to ordinances and regulations aimed at the complete isolation of Israel from the surrounding world. At the same time, the development of commerce and trade under the Hasmonean rulers peremptorily called for the building up of a code of civil law. The few rules found in Scripture bearing on this branch of the law were not sufficient and could not be made so, not even by the most subtle reasoning or the cleverest interpretation.

The time was certainly ripe for legislation. Every student of the history of jurisprudence knows that great as are the possibilities of interpretation and commentation, an old code has limits beyond which it cannot be stretched. When the breaking-point is reached, legislation comes to the rescue, abrogating obsolete laws and adding new ones which conform to the demands of the age. But how dare one tamper with sacred Scripture, in which the Divine Will is revealed? The sages and scholars of that time—about the middle of the Hasmonean era— had the necessary temerity. They took a very important step towards formulating what might be called, *de facto* though not *de jure,* a new code—they created the *Mishnah.*

To estimate adequately the radical changes that the Mishnah intro- duced, it is best to compare the mishnaic method of study with the midrashic (exegetical) method of the *Soferim.* These earlier scholars knew only one subject of study—Scripture; their comments and inter- pretations were interwoven with the text interpreted and commented upon. The creators of the Mishnah detached the enormous bulk of unwieldy material from the Biblical passages and studied it independently. The new method was not only highly practical, since the numerous laws based on interpretations of Scriptural passages could now be studied in a concise and systematic way, but it also gave "the oral law" an independent existence. Hitherto the laws, practices, and customs that had no Scriptural basis could only be studied by being connected in one way or another with some text in Scripture. Yet many of these orally transmitted laws and customs were as old as the oldest found in Scripture and were no less revered by the people. In the mishnaic method of study, a difference between the written Torah and the oral Torah hardly exists. The origins of the Mishnah and the rise at the same time of a militant Sadduceeism which reacted against over-emphasis of the oral law certainly stand in some causal nexus, though it is hard to tell which is cause and which effect.

The final compilation of the Mishnah toward the end of the second century C. E. by the Patriarch R. Judah completed a work at which scholars had labored for about three hundred years. While the Mishnah was in process of formation, two great national catastrophes overtook the Jews—the fall of the Jewish state in 70 C.E. and the Hadrianic persecutions after the defeat of Bar Kochba in 133 C. E. These sorrowful events were not without influence upon the final form of the Mishnah. One is safe in saying that had it not been for the political disorders and persecutions, the Mishnah would have been completed long before the time of R. Judah, and would have been a much closer approximation to a code. For it has been well said that truth becomes more liable to change as the distance from its origin across the ages lengthens. In the centuries that elapsed from the beginnings of the Mishnah until its completion, differences of opinion multiplied so greatly that the original aim of offering the doctors of law a norm for their decisions could be only partially realized. Of the sum total of five hundred and twenty-three chapters of the Mishnah, there are only six which contain no controversies. Is further proof needed of the uncertainty of tradition at the time of R. Judah?

The prolonged delay in codification had a further important bearing on the character of the Mishnah. Almost one-fifth of *our* Mishnah consists of laws and rulings concerning matters that at the time of its completion no longer had any bearing on contemporary life—they were studied but not practiced. This was true not only of the sections of the Mishnah dealing with sacrifices and other Temple laws, all of which became obsolete with the destruction of the Sanctuary, but also of that part of the Mishnaic criminal code which dealt with capital punishment. It is well known that capital punishment had not been exercised by Jewish courts after Palestine became a Roman province. An interesting illustration of the difference between the practical and the merely theoretical parts of the Mishnah is the following statement found in it. "R. Tarfon and R. Akiba said: If we had been members of the Sanhedrin nobody would ever have been executed." To which a very pertinent remark was made by one of their disciples to the effect that they would have caused bloodshed in Israel; meaning that murder is prevented by fear of punishment, and that when fear disappears crime increases.

Of course, the severe criminal code of the Bible was interpreted in later times in accordance with the humaneness of Pharisaic Judaism, but it can be assumed that many Mishnaic modifications probably date from a period when the problem had only academic importance. Since an integral part of Jewish piety is the study of divine revelation in Scripture and of the interpretation of revelation apart from its direct bearing upon life, the more extensively parts of the divine revelation lost their application, the more lovingly they were studied.

To speak of the Mishnah as a code would, as we have seen, not be correct, but to consider it only as a text book of "the oral law" would be still less accurate. The main purpose of the work is to teach the authoritative norm. While differences of opinion are frequent in the Mishnah, they are always presented in a way that clearly indicates which is authoritative. The accepted view is either given anonymously or introduced by the formula: "But the sages say." The most distinguishing mark of a code is that a people accept it as the authoritative statement of its *corpus juris*. The Mishnah might therefore be described as a close approximation of a code. Its authority was never seriously challenged either during the lifetime of Rabbi Judah or in the succeeding generations. This authority was due not only to personal distinction and his high position as the Patriarch, political as well as religious head of the Jews, but also to the fact that the Mishnah was, in the words of the Talmud, produced "by Rabbi Judah and his court," i.e., the cooperative work of all the prominent scholars of that period. It was not the product of a legislature but it was the work of judicial legislation.

II

With the proclamation of the Pentateuch as a code the *Soferim*—the interpreters—had arisen, and with the acceptance of the Mishnah as the norm of the oral law came the *Amoraim*—the expounders. The activity of the former had led to the creation of the Mishnah; that of the latter gave us the Talmud, or to be accurate, the Talmuds, Palestinian and Babylonian. Since the Babylonian Talmud, by virtue of its greater influence upon Judaism and the Jews, is the more important of the two, and is therefore usually spoken of as *the* Talmud, it shall engage our attention first.

The history of the Jews in Babylonia for almost seven centuries from the time of Ezra and Nehemiah, about the middle of the fifth century B. C. E., to the rise of the academies for Jewish learning about the first quarter of the third century of the common era, is shrouded in deep darkness. A few clay tablets of the first century after Ezra containing the names of Jewish farmers and craftsmen as parties or witnesses to documents of the Gentile banking house of Murashu Brothers; a report by Josephus of an attempt by Jews in the district of Nehardea to achieve independence; and the names of four native Babylonians who came to prominence in Palestine because of their learning and scholarship—that is all we know about Babylonian Jewry for many centuries. No trace whatsoever is to be found of any cultural or literary activity among them. We have not the slightest reason for the assumption that either Hillel the Babylonian, one of the most illustrious names in the history of post-Biblical Judaism, or Nahum the Mede, who filled the position of city magistrate in Jerusalem in the last years of the Jewish State, received their training in their native country. The first signs of spiritual and cultural life among Babylonian Jews became visible about the middle of the second century, and one can assume that this new life was infused into the Jewry of Babylon by the arrival there of the Palestinian emigrants who fled Palestine because of the Hadrianic persecutions then raging in the Holy Land, especially in the south, the home of Jewish culture and learning. For the understanding of the relation between the two Talmuds, their striking likeness, and their almost equally striking diversity, the pre-Amoraic activity of Palestinian scholars in Babylonia is of great importance.

The two Talmuds have much in common, both in form and content. Both are huge commentaries on the Mishnah, and of course contain a good deal of common matter. In addition, the personal relationships between the scholars of the two countries was a very close one. Interchange of opinions and ideas between them was carried on without interruption through the so-called "Travellers," emissaries sent from the Babylonian academies to those of Palestine and vice versa. Yet the dissimilarities between the two "Commentaries" are enormous, and as their likeness extends to form and content alike so also do their dissimilarities. The non-Hebrew portions of the Palestinian Talmud are in Western Aramaic; those of the Babylonian Talmud in Eastern Aramaic. The first has a large number of Greek words; the other a goodly number of Persian. The Palestinian Talmud is more concise; its discussions are much less diffuse. More important, however, than the differences in form are those which reflect differences in traditions and in economic, political and cultural conditions that prevailed in the countries of their origin.

To understand adequately the relation between the two Talmuds, one must of course have a clear idea of the activity of the "Expounders" of the Mishnah, an activity that culminated in the creation of these two monumental compilations. Whether we consider the Mishnah a code or only an approach to a code, we must not lose sight of the pre-eminence of the written Torah which has never ceased to be the pivotal assumption of Judaism. The covenant of Sinai has remained the Magna Charta. For many—one might be inclined to say most—of the commandments in the Pentateuch, however, neither mode nor measure is laid down. This task was left to the recognized spiritual leaders of the people—called by different names at different periods: Soferim, Tannaim, or Amoraim; leaders, who sought to interpret and define the intention of the Divine will as expressed in revealed writings. Hence the "Expounders" did not limit their study of the Mishnah to interpretation and explanation. The tracing back of the contents of the Mishnah to its origin, Scripture, forms a principal, perhaps the essential, part of both Talmuds.

The main source for this branch of the Expounders' study was the collections of exegetical comments on the Pentateuch by the scholars of former generations, the Tannaim. These collections, some small, some large, were very numerous. None of them, however, attained the degree of authority achieved by the Mishnah of R. Judah. While the latter became the standard work of study in all academies, Palestinian as well as Babylonian, the study of the Midrashim, as these collections are called in talmudic sources, remained more or less a matter of individual choice. Some of them, and among them those that were brought to Babylonia by the Palestinian immigrants during the Hadrianic persecutions, became very popular in the Babylonian academies, others enjoyed no less popularity with the Palestinian scholars. The use of different sources for the elucidation of the Mishnah inevitably led to differences in interpretation of the laws contained in it.

The study of the Mishnah in the light of the Biblical exegesis of the Tannaim is in a sense an attempt at an historical approach, though chiefly dictated by dogmatic interest—to establish Biblical authority for many of the laws laid down in the Mishnah. Of much greater interest to us for the understanding of both Talmuds is another branch of amoraic study in connection with the Mishnah. R. Judah, for practical reasons, eliminated much material that had been available for inclusion in the Mishnah. Admiring disciples maintained that by sound reasoning any doubtful case of law might be inferred from the material included in the Mishnah by R. Judah. But it is nevertheless true that very important laws are not to be found there, and that furthermore, those which are included are often not given in their historical development. This omission was purposeful; much of the dicta of the Mishnah was presented anonymously in order that it might be given the weight and authority which individual opinions do not command. For a work designed to approximate a code this was, of course, the ideal manner of presentation, but to the student who is interested in the origin and development of law, the Mishnah does not offer what is desired. Several younger contemporaries of R. Judah tried to correct the omissions, not only collecting a huge mass of material which had been excluded from the Mishnah but often also giving us the historical development of many of its laws. These collections, like the Midrashim mentioned above, were very numerous and form a substantial part of both Talmuds. The study by the Amoraim of the *Barayyata,* as these collections are called in the Babylonian Talmud, i. e. of the "extraneous" teachings and dicta of the Tannaim not found in the Mishnah, not only enriched their knowledge but also gave them some degree of independence towards the Mishnah. An Amora would hardly dare to oppose the Mishnah without the support of an old authority found in a Baraita. The discrepancies between the Mishnah and the "extraneous" teachings also afforded subtle minds an opportunity to display their acumen in reconciling apparently conflicting views. It was true of both Midrashim and of much of "extraneous" teachings that their lack of universally acknowledged authority led to many differences between the two Talmuds. Some of the Baraitot were highly thought of in Palestine but given little attention in the Babylonian schools, and conversely, the Babylonian scholars had "extraneous" teachings that were almost unknown in Palestine.

Midrash and Baraita were the basic materials used in Palestine as well as in Babylonia upon which their respective Talmuds were built, but the fabrics, while very similar, were not identical; hence the difference in the final products.

Even the Mishnah, the nucleus of both Talmuds, was not identical in both countries. Its compiler labored at this work for a great part of his long life, hence, the Mishnah reached posterity in several versions. The one used in the Palestinian schools was not identical with that recognized by the Babylonian academies; and these primary textual divergences were bound to result in divergences of interpretation. Many others have their origin in secondary divergences of text. In oral transmission, explanations, amplifications, and suggested emendations are apt to creep in. Granted that the Mishnah was reduced to writing by its compiler—a very moot question still!—we know for certain that as late as the end of the Geonic period, about the beginning of the eleventh century, the *oral* law, comprising primarily Mishnah and Talmud, was still taught *orally*. Consequently the text "expounded" by the Palestinian scholars was not always the same as that employed by their Babylonian colleagues. As the two Talmuds are commentaries upon the Mishnah, they would of course differ in their comments wherever their texts differed.

III

"Search it (the Torah) and search it again," says an old sage, "for everything is in it." One sometimes finds what one seeks but scarcely ever that for which one does not look. Objective interpretation of laws and authoritative dicta is an ideal toward which honest interpreters strive—it can, however, never be achieved completely. It is conditioned by emotion as well as by intellect.

Ample evidence of this striving for an unobtainable ideal is found in both Talmuds. The Babylonian, however, was at a disadvantage inasmuch as the Mishnah, Midrash, and Baraita, the three pillars upon which both Talmuds rest, were constructed of Palestinian material. The time that elapsed between the completion of the Mishnah and the completion of the Palestinian Talmud, roughly about two centuries, did not witness any violent changes in the economic, political, or cultural conditions of Palestinian Jewry. Its adjustment to the set of laws and customs which gave us the Mishnah was comparatively easy. Quite different were the conditions in Babylonia. Not only had Babylonian Jewry to grapple with the problem of adapting itself to the Palestinian Mishnah, but while occupied with this difficult task it was subjected to a radical change of government which was to be of far-reaching consequences for Babylonian Jews. When the Sassanids came to power, Zoroastrianism became the ruling religion in Babylonia and its Jewry had to struggle not only for its economic existence but also for its religious life, which was threatened by a hostile and aggressive priesthood.

Whatever branch of talmudic law or doctrine we study, the observation is forced upon us that numerous differences between the two Talmuds reflect the differences between Palestinian and Babylonian life and thought. Here are a few concrete examples. Important in the economic and domestic life of the Jews were the taxes which were collected almost entirely from levies on the products of the soil, for the support of the Priests and Levites who were originally the sole ministers of religion. Though the Priests and Levites were gradually outnumbered by lay teachers and ministers, the Biblical laws concerning tithes and other priestly dues were not abolished but remained in force in Palestine throughout the talmudic period. In Babylonia, however, as the result of the fearful depression precipitated by the protracted wars between the Persians and Romans during the third century, this set of priestly laws was abrogated. R. Johanan, the famous leader of Palestinian Jewry at the middle of that century, informs us of the important change that took place in Babylonia during his lifetime with regard to the Levitical tithes and the priestly share in the crops. Less than a century later a Babylonian Amora states: "Now the people do not give to the priest the first wool shorn," and we may add, nor his other dues.

The same Babylonian Amora also mentions the prevailing opinion of his time, supported by authority of the Babylonian Tanna, Judah ben Batira. This held that "The words of the Torah do not become impure"; thus an important element of Levitical purity was abolished. In Palestine vigorous insistence was placed upon a ritual bath after pollution preparatory to prayer or study. Similarly, the Palestinian authorities insisted upon washing the hands before prayer, while the Babylonians made light of it and strongly censured the delay of prayer on account of lack of water.

The disappearance of the Levitical laws of purity in Babylonia and their retention in Palestine can in part be explained by differences in the relationship between Jew and Gentile in these two countries. Palestinian law was largely war legislation, for Judaism and Paganism were locked in combat for many centuries. In Babylonia this state of war never existed. Says a Palestinian author of the second century, "Israel in the diaspora worships idols in all innocence; whenever there be a wedding among the pagans of the town, the entire Jewry participate in the wedding feast, easing their conscience by bringing with them their food and drinks." Less than a century later, a Babylonian Amora remarks "The Gentiles in the diaspora—Babylonia—are not to be considered idolators in the real sense of the word." Hence follows the rather lenient attitude of the Babylonian Talmud towards the old Palestinian laws which had their origin in the desire to avoid any dealings with a pagan which might encourage him in his idolatrous practices. From the Babylonian Nahum of Media to his countryman, Samuel, this tendency is marked. The Mishnah teaches that three days before a heathen holiday, no merchandise may be sold to the pagan since he might use it for idolatrous practices. Samuel limited the ban to the day of the festival. Certain old Palestinian regulations which had their origin in the economic self-defense of the Jews against the attempt of the Greco-Roman world to push them out of Palestine were transferred to Babylonia, but there they were interpreted on a purely religious basis. For instance, selling cattle to a heathen who would use them in tilling the ground was prohibited in Palestine, obviously for economic reasons. In Babylonia this law was regarded as a measure to insure the Biblical commandment that the animal world should rest on the Sabbath.

No other parts of the two Talmuds differ as much as those dealing with civil law—for lack of any better term I use "civil." These are the sections contained in the first three treatises of the fourth order of the Mishnah and Talmud. Theoretically, Rabbinic Judaism does not recognize a distinction between religious and secular law. Whatever law is found in the Pentateuch is Divine revelation and has supreme authority; it is inflexible and can never be abrogated. In practice, however, Jewish civil law in post-Biblical times shows in its very earliest stages the greatest independence of Scripture and hence the greatest possibilities for development. Without detailed examination of the principle that guided Jewish jurists in building up this branch of the law, there is one observation to be made. The distinction between religious law and civil law is to be found in the fact that the former expresses the permanent relation between God and man, the latter the changeable relation between man and man. It is true that private property is sanctioned by Divine Will as revealed in Scripture, but the concept of property in Jewish civil law is decidedly social. The Roman praetor constituted his praetorian law *propter utilitatem publicam* and similarly the Jewish jurists taught "that the entire Torah was given for the purpose of establishing harmony in human society." If for the welfare of society it becomes necessary to disregard the interest of the individual, "the court" has the power and the duty to act accordingly.

The potentialities for the free development of court-made legislation were enormous, and in both Palestine and Babylonia this development was closely linked with the prevailing economic and political conditions.

Palestine retained its agricultural character throughout the talmudic period, while in Babylonia, commercial activity among the Jews expanded noticeably during the same period. Talmudic law in Palestine was therefore dictated by the interests of the farmer; whereas in Babylonia commerce was given due consideration. A few examples will illustrate the difference.

Children: Potestas patris, which in Biblical times must have been very strong, as shown in the law concerning the rebellious son, is not to be found in rabbinic law. The two exceptions are the father's right to the earnings of his minor daughter and that of giving her in marriage. The latter "right" was recognized but strongly objected to on ethical grounds and hence rarely exercised. The complete emancipation of the adult daughter from the jurisdiction of the father is taken for granted in Palestinian as well as Babylonian sources and was established centuries before the compilation of the Mishnah. With regard to males, Palestinian authorities recognized the right of the father to the earnings of his children, male and female, minor or adult, as long as they were supported by him, while the Babylonians denied the father's right to the earnings of his adult children even when they were supported by him. The small farmer in Palestine could not easily afford to pay for the labor supplied by his grown children who were still supported by him; the merchant in Babylonia did not find it too arduous to compensate them for their labor. Another difference is the right of the father to the compensation allotted to his minor daughter for bodily injury, a right which was recognized in Palestine but not in Babylonia. The conservative character of Palestinian law is herein indicated; the Biblical law was not easily over-ridden.

Slavery: The Bible speaks of Hebrew slaves—perhaps it would be more correct to say Hebrew serfs—and slaves "from among the children of strangers." Hebrew serfdom no longer existed during the second Commonwealth, surely not in the time following the destruction of the Temple. Babylonian Jewry, however, practiced Jewish serfdom *de facto* and *de jure,* in the case of Jews seized as slaves by the Persian government for the non-payment of taxes. The poor Jew who was seized as a slave by the government for not paying taxes surely preferred to serve his fellow-Jew rather than the pagan until such time as his debt was paid. The status was somewhat similar to white labor servitude in America until about the beginning of the 19th century.

With regard to the non-Hebrew slave, note the following difference. About the beginning of the second century, leading scholars, following the Roman example, prohibited the emancipation of slaves. In Palestine this law subsequently lost its validity, but not so in Babylonia. The social position of emancipated slaves was very precarious in Babylonia, where great emphasis was laid upon purity of race, while in Palestine where the bulk of the Jewish population consisted of small farmers, slavery must have been practiced on a very limited scale, so that freedmen were too few to constitute a social problem.

Trade: Julius Paulus, the famous Roman jurist, remarks that it is quite natural for men "to cheat one another alternately and therefore, there is no reason for law to interfere." His Jewish contemporary, the compiler of the Mishnah, has elaborate legislation against over-reaching, most of which antedates him by centuries. *Onaah* in Rabbinic sources though etymologically connected with the Biblical *lo tonu* (you shall not wrong one another) is really a piece of later legislation which transmuted an ethical conception into law. Over-reaching beyond a certain amount, according to Palestinian law, entitles the injured party to invalidate the transaction, or to sue for refund of the amount over-paid. In Babylonia, commercial conditions modified the old Palestinian law to the effect that only when the over-reaching exceeded one sixth could the transaction be invalidated by the injured party. Palestinian authorities, toward the end of the third century, developed the law of *laesio enormis,* i.e., over-reaching exceeding one half, in cases where the general law of over-reaching could not be applied. Babylonian schools gradually accepted it, but not without some modification.

Usury: The Biblical precept against usury and increase not only was turned into law by the Rabbis but was developed to an extreme which made dealings in futures almost impossible, and thus a curb was put on speculation, a clear case of legislation for the benefit of the farmer. In Babylonia the development of commerce forced the scholars to modify the rigor of Palestinian laws. For instance, the *Mashkanah* was allowed; that is, the creditor was permitted to enjoy the use of landed property during the time the debtor had the privilege of redemption. A similar case is *Tarsha,* a sale on time at a price higher than the seller would take if he sold for cash; the Palestinians prohibited it, the Babylonians permitted it. The Babylonian practice of *'iska,* partial partnership—the capitalist to bear some small risk for part of the money he invested in the debtor's business and to be compensated by a considerable share in the profits of the investment—has the support of certain Palestinian scholars of the Tannaitic period, but the accepted law in Palestine would consider such dealings illegal.

In one respect the Babylonian jurists seem to have applied the usury laws much more strictly than did their Palestinian colleagues. Mishnah and Palestinian Talmud disqualify any man who takes interest from testifying—greed of gain will make him commit perjury as it made him transgress the law prohibiting the taking of interest. The Babylonian Talmud goes a step further and disqualifies the borrower on interest from testifying. In the light of what has been said of the differences in the economic structure of the two countries, the stricter attitude of the Babylonians is easily explained. In Palestine the simple conditions of Biblical times continued, relatively unchanged, in talmudic times. The borrower, a small farmer or an artisan, asked for a loan on interest because of personal need, and while from a higher ethical point of view he too was considered a "violator of the law"—the Mishnah describes as such all persons involved in an usurious transaction including the witnesses and the scrivener who draws up the contract—yet his motive was surely not greed of gain, and hence he was not considered likely to commit perjury. In a commercial society, on the other hand, both lender and borrower on interest engage in a business transaction for the same purpose, i.e. for the sake of gain, the lender to obtain interest and the borrower to invest the loan in a profitable undertaking. There was no good reason for the law to distinguish between them; neither could be trusted to act in accordance with the commandments of Scripture, whenever "gain" of money was concerned. They would commit perjury for its sake just as they had disregarded the prohibition against taking or giving interest.

The remarks found in the Talmuds relating to a gift *causa mortis* clearly corroborates the statement that the civil law of Palestine in Talmudic times mirrors an exclusively agricultural society, while that of Babylonia reflects a life greatly modified by commerce. Both Talmuds accept the mishnaic law that if the sick man gives away his entire estate, the act is revocable in the event of his recovery, and takes effect only on his death; but it also states that it is not revocable if he sets aside for himself sufficient land to enable him to earn his living. In comment upon this ruling of the Mishnah, the following remark is made by the Palestinian Talmud: "If he reserved for himself movable property it is as if he would give away his entire estate; for land even of a small size enables a man to support himself, but precious stones and pearls do not enable him to support himself." In contrast to this view of the Palestinian Talmud it is explicitly stated in the Babylonian Talmud that the kind of property the sick man reserved for himself is immaterial; it might be either real estate or personal property, so long as it sufficed to support him. The most valuable kind of personal property, such as precious stones and pearls, were not considered sufficient means of support in Palestine, since in an agricultural society consisting chiefly of small farmers and artisans, they were difficult to dispose of: in Babylonia, they were articles of commerce.

Jewish civil law being what it was, neither isolated nor independent, and developing as it did in connection with and relative to other manifestations of the socio-economic life of the people, it could not remain untouched by foreign influence. Greeks and Romans ruled Palestine, Babylonians and Persians ruled Babylonia, and *a priori* we assume that the law of the ruler left its effect on those who were ruled. The problem of the influence of foreign law, however, is a very intricate and complicated one. It is still a moot question whether parallel developments of law cannot largely be explained by the theory that the same economic or cultural conditions produce the same institutions. The recent discovery of new sources of Hellenistic and Oriental laws in the papyri has, however, cleared up one important point. Contrary to earlier opinion, it was not Roman law which exerted the greatest influence, but rather the Greco-Egyptian *Volksrecht* of the eastern provinces of the Roman empire. On the other hand, it is quite possible that the undeniable affinity between Greco-Egyptian *Volksrecht* and the Jewish civil law finds its explanation in their common origin, the cuneiform laws.

In support of this view, one might refer to the fact that there is scarcely any difference between the two Talmuds with regard to the use of these foreign elements of law. The beginnings of the Talmuds by the disciples and other younger contemporaries of the compiler of the Mishnah almost coincide with the issue of the famous *Constitutio* of Caracalla (212 of the common era), which bestowed Roman citizenship on every subject in the wide Roman empire. One might expect to see the effect of this radical change in the Palestinian Talmud, but actually one finds that Roman law, which now became the only law recognized in the empire, left no mark on the Talmud. The bulk of the Greco-Egyptian elements of law is found in the Tannaitic sources, a fact which points to high antiquity as the time of their absorption into Jewish civil law. The strongly "isolationist" policy of Pharisaism was not conducive to the adoption of foreign elements of law and furthermore this exclusiveness increased rather than diminished with time.

In this connection it ought to be pointed out that the Babylonian Talmud does not furnish any tangible proof that its civil law had been more influenced by the Assyro-Babylonian law than was true of the Palestinian Talmud. Traces of that influence are found in the oldest strata of tannaitic tradition which, in all likelihood, date from the very earliest times, perhaps from the period of "the children of Israel that were come back out of the captivity." It should, however, be mentioned that some clauses of Jewish conveyances have only Babylonian parallels. It is true that these characteristic clauses are met with first in post-Talmudic sources but there can be no doubt that they had their origin in Talmudic times. As an illustration of the strong hold which the Babylonian style of official documents had upon the Jewish courts, one might quote a formula in the Babylonian Talmud for a bill of divorce which was drawn up by a scholar of the fourth century of the common era; in this formula the third person is used. From earliest times, as early as the Elphantine papyri which date from 520 B.C.E., Jewish deeds had been written in the first, not in the third person, as was true of the Babylonian deeds.

A theory favored by many is that one of the characteristic distinctions between the two Talmuds is that the Babylonian Talmud, in contrast to the Palestinian, was greatly influenced by Persian law. In view of the new light shed on this question by the recent discovery of a Sassanian *Book of Laws*—so far the only one of its kind known—this theory can hardly be maintained. Fragmentary and obscure as this Persian *Book of Laws* is, it contains enough material to enable us to form an opinion on the relation of Jewish civil law in Babylonia to the Persian law in use in that country. Here too the observation made above is valid: the foreign elements in Jewish law date back to pre-Talmudic, even to pre-Mishnaic times. The parallels in the Sassanian *Book of Laws* to Jewish civil law are chiefly related to those parts of the latter which are also found in Palestinian sources such as the Mishnah and the Palestinian Talmud. If those parallels mean anything, they prove that in very early times, when Palestine was still a Persian province, old Persian law was not without influence upon the Jews of that country.

There is only one legal institution which the Jews of Babylonia may accurately be said to have borrowed from the Persians and which is therefore found in the Babylonian but not in the Palestinian Talmud. At about the beginning of the fourth century, the leading jurist of Babylonian Jewry, R. Nahman, introduced the oath of exoneration—an oath taken by the defendant to refute a claim not supported by any evidence at all—which is surely of Persian origin.

This Babylonian innovation in legal procedure, though not of very great importance for the development of Jewish jurisprudence, throws an extremely interesting light upon the cultural life of Babylonian Jewry. In antiquity, an oath was in reality one of the numerous forms of the ordeal. No trace of this concept existed in Palestinian Jewry of Talmudic times, but it continued in Babylonia long after the Talmudic period. The Persian oath was essentially an "ordeal," hence the adoption of the Persian "oath of exoneration" by the Jewish courts in Babylonia is understandable.

48   THE PALESTINIAN TALMUD

In one respect, however, the attitude of the authors of the Babylonian Talmud toward Persian law was radically different from that taken by their Palestinian colleagues with regard to "foreign" law in the Holy Land. The opprobrium attached in old Christian writings to the "publicans" has its origin not in the dishonesty or wickedness of the tax-collector but in the fact that Palestinian Jewry never recognized Roman rule in the Holy Land as legitimate, and looked upon the publican as an accomplice of robbers, not the servant of a legitimate government. In Babylonia, on the other hand, immediately after the conquest of the country by the Sassanids, the rule was laid down: The law of the government (Persian) is law. According to the Palestinian Talmud, therefore, a "publican" is automatically disqualified from testifying, while according to the Babylonian Talmud he is disqualified only if he is found to have discharged his office dishonestly, favoring the rich to the detriment of the poor.

Both Talmuds are commentaries on the Mishnah, a book of laws, and hence chiefly legal. Yet almost one-third of the Babylonian and about one-sixth of the Palestinian Talmud consist of non-legal matter, of so-called *Haggadah,* a very comprehensive term which includes theology and religious philosophy, folklore and history, mathematics and astronomy, medicine and natural science, and many other subjects. Because of the encyclopedic character of these non-legal parts of the Talmuds, the task of determining their Palestinian and Babylonian characteristics is almost insurmountable, though nobody will deny that they do exist. We shall cite a few illustrations from theology, a field in which we should expect to find the fewest divergences between the two Talmuds.

The main topics of theology and morals were established long before the Talmudic period; Scripture spoke plainly of them and the traditional understanding of them was fixed in its essentials. Where this was not the fact, there was free diversity of opinion among the Palestinian as well as Babylonian scholars and sages. However, even the wise and the learned are often influenced by the cultural conditions under which they live.

The chief difference between the two Talmuds in the field of theology is to be found in the fact that the Palestinian authors of the Talmud excluded, almost entirely, the popular fancies about angels and demons, while in Babylonia angelology and demonology, under popular pressure influenced by Zoroastrianism, gained scholastic recognition and with it entrance into the Talmud. Contrast these two sayings: The first, in the Palestinian Talmud, reads: "Cry not to Michael or Gabriel but to Me says the Lord." The second, found in the Babylonian Talmud, recommends: "One should never pray in Aramaic because the angels do not attend to him." An intermediary rôle for the angels is obviously assumed in the latter statement. In the Palestinian Talmud, angels are rarely mentioned and, with the exception of the passage just quoted from it, wherein Michael and Gabriel are but Biblical reminiscences, angels remain nameless—they have no individuality. The Babylonian Talmud, on the other hand, not only makes frequent reference to angels and their doings but knows some of them by name and describes their specific activities. The Palestinian Talmud intentionally avoids the use of the word *shed,* demon, though it is found in the Bible, and instead employs—three times in all—the designation "they who do damage." In the Babylonian Talmud demons are found as often as angels, and though most of them are nameless some have proper names and are assigned spheres of activity. It is of special significance that according to the Babylonian Talmud demons propagate their species by the union of males with females; while in the Palestinian Talmud they are sexless—spiritual beings.

The student of religion is often baffled by the problem of how to distinguish between the religious beliefs of a people and their fantasies, between religion and folklore. There can be no doubt that a great part, if not all, of the angelological and demonological material found in the Babylonian Talmud is folkloristic and has very little to do with the theology of its authors. It is nevertheless of importance to note that the compilers of the Talmud saw no objection to including the popular fancies, while their Palestinian colleagues ignored this branch of folklore almost completely. A certain chastity characterizes the Palestinian Talmud which, even when it relates a folk-tale, avoids the exaggerated role ascribed to supernatural beings by popular fancy. For instance, a legend in the Palestinian Talmud tells of Solomon's being deposed for his sins by an angel who impersonated him and ascended his throne. In the Babylonian Talmud, it is lustful Ashmedai (=Asmodeus) who became the occupant of Solomon's throne as well as the master of his harem. There is good reason to believe that the figure of Ashmedai, a being who combined most of the weaknesses of man with some of the superhuman qualities of the angels, was well-known to Palestinian folklore. The compilers of the Palestinian Talmud, however, were reluctant to accept the creations of popular fancies at their face value, and while they admitted some of them—not too many—into their Talmud, they used some discretion. The same cannot be said of the compilers of the Babylonian Talmud.

A similar observation can be made in regard to the difference in the attitudes of the two Talmuds toward sorcery, magic, astrology, and other kinds of superstition. There is very little of all this in the Palestinian Talmud and that little is cautiously stated. Not without a touch of humor is the following story, given there at the end of a number of folk-tales the purpose of which is to show the superiority of the sages of Israel who out-maneuvered their adversaries at their own game of witchcraft. I quote verbatim. "Said R. Hinanah son of R. Hananah, 'I saw while walking in Gobta near Sepphoris a sectarian (an adherent of gnosticism that consists of pagan, Jewish, and Christian beliefs and practices) who took a skull and threw it high up, and a calf came down. When I narrated it to my father he remarked: If you ate of the calf then, of course, it was a real one, but if not, what you saw was only a delusion.' " The Babylonian Talmud contains two opposing views. The one holds that magic and sorcery are vain efforts, for "the Lord, He is God, there is none else beside Him." The other, however, finds in the Hebrew word for sorcery an indication that it sometimes achieves its purpose against the powers on high. The magic bowls discovered in Babylonia which date from the talmudic period prove the popularity of the second view. Folk-medicine in the Talmud as well as the numerous stories about the effects of magic and witchcraft, and the remedies against them which it contains, are further evidence of the hold that these popular beliefs had on Babylonian Jewry.

IV

With the recognition of the Mishnah in both Palestine and Babylonia as the "Book of Law" for student and judge alike, began the activity of its expounders. In less than two centuries this culminated in the Palestinian Talmud and a few generations later in the Babylonian. The problems connected with the compilations of the two Talmuds are numerous and very baffling, and they relate some to both of them, some to the one or the other. The Babylonian Talmud refers to R. Ashi (died 427) and Rabbina as the two last representatives of "Talmudic" activity. The statement is very obscure and open to many interpretations, but at least we have a direct statement in the Babylonian Talmud itself as to the time and person (persons?) who participated in its compilation. The Palestinian Talmud maintains complete silence about its history. No editor is mentioned, no time of compilation is indicated, no editorial principle is given which would enable us to tell the process of elimination and selection of the vast body of material available. And yet in some respects our knowledge about the compilation of the Palestinian Talmud is more adequate than that relating to the Babylonian.

The few well-established facts concerning the compilation of the Palestinian Talmud are as follows. About the middle of the fourth century, the oldest part of the Talmud was compiled at Caesarea (Straton), which was then as it had been for some time, the seat of the Roman government of Palestine. This part of the Talmud consists of explanations and interpretations of the Mishnaic sections on civil law, which are contained in the first three treatises of the fourth order. These three Talmudic treatises not only differ in age from the rest of the Palestinian Talmud, and of course still more so from the Babylonian one, but also differ in form, style, terminology, and many other things. Two characteristics of this "oldest Talmud," its brevity and its almost exclusively legal contents, are of special interest. Its brevity is such that many passages would have remained unintelligible but for the parallels to them in the other parts of the Palestinian Talmud. The most likely explanation for this rather strange phenomenon is that this "old" Talmud was intended not for students but for teachers. The judiciary in Palestine during and preceding the Talmudic period included many nobles, political leaders, and members of the *Boulē* of the town, who, since they were not learned in Jewish law, often applied non-Jewish law. Some among them, however, had their "rabbinical prompters," who aided them in their judicial functions by instructing them in the rudiments of Jewish civil law. Intended as a guide for the instruction of the unlearned judges, this Talmudic digest of civil law is therefore extremely brief; it was more in the nature of memoranda to guide the teacher than a textbook for students or a book of laws for judges. While the compiler of the guide, in striving for extreme brevity, wisely excluded from it all non-legal matter—the so-called Haggadah that forms a very important part of the other sections of the Palestinian Talmud—he did, however, for practical, pedagogic reasons include a few telling stories which emphasize the ethical aspect of the law. The section on labor law, for example, closes with an anecdote about the Rabbi-judge who made a colleague cancel his claim against his laborers for breaking several kegs of wine, and in addition made him pay their wages. As reason for this decision, contrary to strict law, he quoted the verse of Proverbs: That thou mayest walk in the way of good men and keep the paths of the righteous. The Jewry of Caesarea was in part Hellenistic; in some of the synagogues Greek was the language used for prayers. One is therefore safe in assuming that many of the Jewish judges knew a good deal more about equity in Roman law than about the rabbinic admonition to act within the line of justice, i.e., that justice must be controlled by moral and social principles which often over-ride the strictness of the law. The non-legal matter in the "Caesarean" Talmud, consisting almost exclusively of stories about wise and kind judges, has no other purpose than to emphasize the rabbinic concept of equity.

Shortly after the completion of the "oldest" Talmud, a great calamity overtook Palestinian Israel. Because of local outbreaks between the Jews and the army, its commander, Ursicinus, in the year 351 wreaked vengeance on the three cities of Tiberias, Sepphoris, and Lydda, the seats of the three most famous academies in the Holy Land. The death knell had tolled for Jewish learning in the home of its origin. Some of the Palestinian scholars did what their forefathers had done under similar conditions about two centuries earlier when they had emigrated to Babylonia during the Hadrianic persecutions. Those who remained could read the signs of the times. Christianity had now become—in the second half of the fourth century—the established state religion of the Roman empire. Though Judaism continued to be a licit religion, in accordance with the edict of toleration issued by Constantine the Great, vexatious regulations interfering with the economic and religious life of the Jews increased daily. For centuries the Jew had to fight for his existence in his own home, first against the Greeks and later against the Romans. But with the exception of short periods like that of the Maccabean revolt and the Hadrianic persecutions, it was not Judaism but the Jew who was attacked. Now a militant church arose which, backed by the power of the state, undertook a war against Jew and Judaism alike. The academies in which the spirit of Judaism had been kept alive were forced to close. If the Jew were to retain his cultural and spiritual individuality, something had to be found to take the place of the living word that had been silenced—the Palestinian Talmud was the result.

It was compiled toward the end of the fourth century in Tiberias, yet it was not the exclusive work of one school, as is shown by the frequent references in it to the scholars of the other famous academy, that of Sepphoris. Less frequently are the scholars of Lydda and Caeserea mentioned, but their views were by no means ignored. It is this product of the Tiberian school that is called the Palestinian Talmud, a designation which is quite correct so long as we do not use it to convey the idea of unity for the entire compilation. The Tiberian scholars incorporated in their work the "Caesarean" Talmud on the three treatises of the Mishnah containing civil law. They certainly were not unaware of its many shortcomings pointed out above, but conditions were such that they could not spend their time in revising or supplementing the work of their predecessors. The work of the Tiberian scholars bears witness to the serious situation in which they found themselves, a situation that called for the utmost speed. If one compares the Palestinian with the Babylonian Talmud, one is struck by the relatively careful editing of the latter in contrast to the hasty compilation of the former. The closing of the Palestinian academies and the emigration of many scholars to Babylonia prevented the Palestinian compilers from doing their work as they would have liked to have it done. The critical position of Jewish scholarship in Palestine is chiefly responsible for the shortcomings of the Palestinian Talmud.

The superiority of the Babylonian Talmud over the Palestinian, from the point of view of system and arrangement, cannot be doubted. It is, however, not quite correct to ascribe it to the fact that the Babylonian scholars improved on the method used by their predecessors in Palestine. There is no reason to doubt the tradition, well supported by internal evidence, which declares R. Ashi, for fifty-two years the head of the academy at Sura (375–427), to have been the compiler of the Babylonian Talmud. But if this is so, one must question the dependence of that Talmud on the Palestinian. R. Ashi is said to have spent fifty years on his gigantic work, a statement which is not at all unlikely when one considers the enormously difficult task that he faced. By the time the Palestinian Talmud was compiled about 400, the Babylonian Talmud must have been far advanced. It is also very doubtful whether R. Ashi's compilation differed essentially in order or system from that produced by his contemporaries in Palestine. One must not forget that the "editorial" shaping of R. Ashi's compilation extended over nearly a century, and that if we consider the finishing touches of the Saboraim (the Babylonian scholars of the sixth century), one might say that two centuries were spent by the Babylonians on the final redaction of their Talmud.

The obvious shortcomings of the Palestinian Talmud are three—repetition, lack of continuity, and contradictions—but all three are not entirely missing from the Babylonian Talmud. Both Talmuds, since they were products of gradual growth over a period of about two centuries, betray their origins by these defects, which are more pronounced in the Palestinian than in the Babylonian. The work of the compilers in Palestine as well as Babylonia might be said to have consisted in making a Talmud out of numerous Talmuds. Each generation of the "expounders," each school of a generation had its Talmud, i.e., its comments upon the Mishnah. When the several Talmuds were combined into one, certain inconsistencies were overlooked, and the Palestinian Talmud because of the necessity for haste shows less editorial efficiency. One must not, however, measure by our standards of system and arrangement. The repetitions in the Palestinian Talmud are not due to lack of system but to the conviction that for practical reasons it is preferable to repeat things whenever cognate matter is dealt with. Much of the lack of continuity is only apparent: The order of the Palestinian Mishnah was not always the same as that of the Babylonian one, and some passages of the Palestinian Talmud seem to be disconnected only because they comment on a text of the Mishnah that differed in sequence from the Babylonian Mishnah. It is further to be noted that the text of the Palestinian Talmud was often badly transmitted, so that what seems to be faulty editing is sometimes actually faulty copying.

'OPEN THOU MINE EYES'

William G. Braude

For many years I worked on a translation of the *Midrash on Psalms*. The work was an obsession with me, its manifold problems—problems in text, in interpretation, in rendition—haunting me day and night. I felt I had to go on with the work, and could no more give it up than give up food or drink. In the manner of a man possessed I was certain that the *Midrash on Psalms* once published would sweep the English speaking world.

In my enthusiasm I was anxious to give visitors to our home a foretaste of the delights in store for them, so I used to read or recite for them passages from my manuscript. Most visitors were polite, responding with what I deemed adequate expletives of approval. But one visitor, a forthright gentleman, took to calling my work "The Rabbi's Mishmash." This epithet I smiled off in a superior kind of way. The poor fellow, I as much as said, does not recognize Beluga caviar when it is served to him.

Well, the years passed. The book—a two volume work—was finally published. It did not sweep the country. Not even members of my own family were swept off their feet. Though respectful, some of them remain either dubious about the work or bewildered by it. An officer of Brown University was quoted as saying of me that I looked particularly puzzled one day because I was trying to read my own book unsuccessfully.

So the description of Midrash as Mishmash would appear to be not altogether inapropos. Why should this be so? Why should Midrash strike people as Mishmash? Surely the minds of the teachers whose sayings are recorded in Midrashic works were clear, their speech simple and precise, their love of God and of His word great. Why then should their sayings often appear puzzling or trivial or both? Because these teachers and thinkers believed in the use of few words. If a thing could be said clearly in twenty words, cryptically in five words, they were apt to say it at times in only three words. And the listener or the reader was expected to mull over the statement, examine carefully the wording, the meaning, the intent of the passage or passages in Scripture upon which the cryptic comment was based. When that is done, as by means of examples I shall demonstrate, Midrash is no Mishmash. On the contrary, the meaning of every Midrashic statement becomes both luminous and clear.

Before citing specific Midrashim I ought to define the term Midrash and also set forth the premises and presuppositions upon which Midrashic interpretation of Scripture are based.

The term *Midrash* is derived from the root *drsh* (דרש) "to seek out" the meaning of a text. The Midrashic method of interpreting Scripture is in contrast to *pashut* or *peshat* (פשט) which means "spread out," "plain" or "obvious" meaning of a text.

That which is sought is סודה של תורה , the secret or undisclosed meaning of Torah; sought, too, are חדרי תורה the secret chambers of the Torah,[1] or the mysteries of Torah.

This quest into the underlying, the off-beat, so to speak, meaning of Scripture is an ancient concern and passion among Jews. Although we are speaking of men who lived and wrought in the first five centuries of the Christian Era, the process of interpretation and reinterpretation of Scripture is an ongoing one to this day among devout Jews. The way of Midrash, which is an unending quest into the inner meaning of Scripture, is described by a teacher who flourished in the Second Century: "Turn the Torah, and turn it over again, for everything is in it, and contemplate it and wax grey and old over it and stir not from it, for thou canst have no better rule than this."[2]

The basic rule or principle for men of Midrash, indeed for Judaism, is "that truth has to be discovered in and through the Bible . . . Every sentence in this Book not only tells something, it also means something . . . This is the word of God, and God speaks nothing that is aimless."[3] The Bible is not merely literature. It is not intended merely to please, merely to tell and retell old tales.

For the men who minted Midrashim the Bible has one overreaching purpose—instruction and guidance. For them each word, each letter, the missing and the superfluous letter alike, is intended to instruct. The extra word, the missing detail in a narrative or the apparently unnecessary addition of a detail—all have their special meaning which it is the business of the devout to dig out and to set forth.

Moreover, one meaning so dug out and set forth does not exhaust the pay gravel of the text whose riches in the realm of spirit are unfathomable.

To change the figure of speech, in every text in Scripture the range of meaning reverberates endlessly. "The Lord gave a word, great was the company of those that published it" (Ps. 68:12). That is to say, the overtones of meaning stored within a single word uttered by God echo and reecho to the end of time. "As when a man strikes an anvil and causes the sparks to fly off in all directions," says one teacher of Midrash, even so, "great is the company of those that publish it."[4] That is to say, infinite is the number of agencies and powers which promulgate and give currency to a single word of God.

To quote another teacher, "As the Holy One, blessed be He, lets a word out of His mouth it divides itself into many radiances,"[5] each radiance giving its special light and strength to the eyes that remain open, to the heart and mind which earnestly seek wisdom and guidance.

To the men of Midrash each text, each word in Scripture, not only describes reality but reflects it, indeed embodies it. If the full meaning of a text could ever be recovered the thing itself which the text describes would stand forth in full view.

Let me give a few examples of Midrashim to illustrate what men of Midrash did with material which to us might not appear promising and to illustrate, too, some of the methods these men followed and the goals they reached for.

Anyone who knows the Bible at all is familiar with the "begats." Generally a series of "begats" begins, as I suppose begats should, with the prefatory formula "These are the generations"—"the generations of the heaven and of the earth" (Gen. 2:4), "the generations of Noah (Gen. 6:9), "the generations of Shem" (Gen. 11:10), "the generations of Ishmael, Abraham's son" (Gen. 25:12), "the generations of Esau" (Gen. 36:1), "the generations of Jacob" (Gen. 37:2), "the generations of Aaron and Moses" (Num. 3:1), "the generations of Perez" (Ruth 4:18). I have not mentioned all such instances but for the benefit of those who are statistically minded the phrase, "These are the generations," occurs thirteen times in the Bible.

Nothing very startling in this datum for people concerned only with the plain meaning of a text, but for those who turn the text, "turn it over again and contemplate it and wax old and grey over it" even such statistical data are both meaningful and exciting. One such man, ever alert for the secret, the undisclosed meaning of Torah, noticed an inconsistency in the spelling of the Hebrew term for "generations." In all instances but two, the term תולדות "generations" is spelled defectively. That is, it is spelled תולדת , as though it were "gen'rations" without the second "e." In one instance, in the genealogy of Ishmael, the progenitor of the Arabs, it is spelled תלדת with both vowels missing, as though the word were spelled "g'n'rations."

Now in the genealogy of Ishmael and Esau, of two men who were not all they should have been, one might expect defective spelling, tell-tale evidence of defects in character. But in the genealogy of Aaron and Moses also, the term "generations" is spelled defectively. Only in two instances is it spelled in full—once at the beginning of time when in splendor and perfection the heaven and the earth were brought into being, and once again when the genealogy of Perez is given. Perez, the son of Judah and Tamar, was conceived under parlous and startling circumstances; and Perez in both Jewish and Christian tradition is regarded as the progenitor of the Messiah.

Now what is this Midrashic comment trying to tell us? This: that at the beginning of time, before man sinned, he was perfect; that at the end of time, with the coming of the Messiah, man will again attain perfection. In the meantime, expect no perfection in yourself and expect it not in your fellow man, and with all your crooked heart, if you please, love your crooked neighbor.

In the original Hebrew this meditation on the nature of man is stated briefly, even cryptically. In translation it goes something like this:

"These are the generations of the heaven and of the earth when they were created." Wherever the term "generations" occurs in Scripture it is spelled defectively except in two instances: "These are the generations of Perez (Ruth 4:18) and this one."[6]

At first blush this Midrashic statement appears as dry as a bookkeeping entry. Only careful examination of all instances where the term "generations" occurs reveals the intent of the Midrash to comment on the nature of man.

Let us now consider another Midrash, one based on a verse in Genesis which tells of the making of woman. The verse reads: "So the Lord God made Adam fall into a deep sleep and, while he slept, took away one of his ribs and s-ealed its place with flesh" (Gen. 2:21). In close study of this verse R. Hinena, a Palestinian teacher who lived in the 4th Century, observes that the letter samech, the sibilant in the word ויסגר which introduces the phrase "sealed its place with flesh," does not occur prior to the making of woman, for when woman was created Satan was created alongside of her.[7] Satan thus makes his first appearance with the rise of woman out of Adam's rib. The passions and drives, the frenzy and madness, the sultry winds of desire—all these are hinted at in the apparently dry comment that the sibilant "s" which stands for Satan makes its first appearance in Scripture as God shaped woman out of Adam's rib.

May I add, however, that in Midrashic teaching, sex is not considered to be solely satanic, a power which "merely mars, corrupts, and makes a massacre of men."[8] On the contrary, sex is spoken of as the mysterious drive which, through marriage, through the hallowed union of man and wife, makes the very existence of civilization possible. Here is the pertinent rabbinic comment on sex: As God made the heaven and the earth, He saw the light that it was good—the grass and the fruit of the trees that they were good; the sea monsters and the winged fowl were good. But only after God created man, male and female, does Scripture say, resorting to a superlative, "Behold, it was very good" (Gen. 1:31). Thereto a Midrashic teacher notes: The words *very good* referring to satanic drives in a man's heart, assert in effect that the supreme zest in life is linked to the mystery of sex.

But how can satanic drive, the passions of sex be termed very good? a more staid teacher asks. To which the first replies: "Because Scripture teaches that were it not for the satanic drive within us a man would not take a wife, nor beget children with her, and so the world could not endure,"[9] and God's work of creation would be undone. Hence the rise of male and female are proclaimed "Very good."

I have shown how men of Midrash made use of a missing vowel to set forth a theory concerning the nature of man; and how they used the first occurrence of a sibilant as a springboard for observations on the mystery of sex. I shall now show how they used the ambiguity of a Hebrew particle to drive home a subtle point in ethical behavior.

There is the statement in Genesis, "Whoso sheddeth a man's blood, by man shall his blood be shed" (Gen. 9:6), an injunction prescribing capital punishment. In the Book of Exodus there is a similar statement: "He that smiteth a man so that he die, shall surely be put to death" (Exod. 21:12).

Now we have said earlier that in the opinion of the rabbis, the Bible is the word of God and God speaks nothing that is aimless or repetitious. Why then is the injunction prescribing capital punishment stated twice? There must be a reason. Since God speaks nothing that is aimless, one of these texts may be assumed to be saying something not evident to him who reads on the run. Now the statement in Exodus, "He that smiteth a man so that he die shall surely be put to death," is clear, precise and contains no words which appear superfluous. On the other hand, the statement in Genesis, "Whoso sheddeth a man's blood by man shall his blood be shed," seems to have an unnecessary phrase—the phrase "by man." Scripture could say, "Whoso sheddeth a man's blood, his blood shall be shed." Moreover the Hebrew particle ב which is rendered "by" is ambiguous since it could be taken to mean "within." Let us re-read the verse in the new rendition: "He who sheds a man's blood within a man, his blood deserves to be shed." Under what circumstances can we be said to shed a man's blood within him? When we humiliate him in public, causing his face to turn white, to make the blood run out of him.

You remember the statement in Matthew, "Whosoever shall say to his brother *raca* (worthless, contemptible) shall be in danger of the council (punishable, that is, by the local court), and whosoever shall say 'thou fool' shall be in danger of the hell of fire." (Matt. 5:22.) This statement in Matthew may well be a Midrash on the verse, "Whoso sheddeth a man's blood within a man his blood deserves to be shed." For in rabbinic lore this text is construed as meaning that he who calls his fellow man *raca,* thus putting him to shame in public, has no share in the world-to-come,[10] shall in the words of Matthew, be in danger of the hell of fire.

You can see then how the precept, "Let thy friend's honor be as dear to thee as thine own,"[11] expressed in the Beatitudes in another form is essentially a Midrash taking off from a verse which appears to be repetitious and from a particle which, because of its ambiguous sense, may be rendered "within." The ambiguity of the particle thus provides the Scriptural fulcrum driving home the lesson that he who humiliates his fellow man, shedding his blood within him, deserves to have his own blood shed and is in danger of the hell of fire. This, I suppose, is the ancients' way of saying he is in danger of losing his very soul.

The opening verses in Genesis say that "God created the heaven and the earth," that He said, "Let there be light, and there was light," and that He divided the light from the darkness. They end with, "And there was evening, and there was morning, one day." The next section ends by saying, "And there was evening, and there was morning, a second day." And the next, "And there was evening and there was morning, a third day." Nothing very startling or suggestive, one would suppose, in this listing of the days of creation. But the men of Midrash discerned here a variation which puzzled them. The phrase "one day" (יום אחד) is a cardinal number; "a second day" (יום שני) "a third day" (יום שלישי) and so on, are ordinals. Why does the text switch from cardinals to ordinals? What is the text trying to tell us by means of the switch? Remember that a text in Scripture not only describes reality, but reflects it and embodies it. What then does Scripture seek to convey to us by the use of the phrase "one day"—not a "first day" which would be consistent with the way the other days of creation are spoken of but "one day?" Now "one day" יום אחד rendered literally means "day one" or "day of the One"—the One, the Unique One of the universe who, inhabiting the heaven and the earth illumined by the light which He summoned into being, was still a lonely One longing as He did for the companionship of a world inhabited by men, and yearning to dwell in the midst of men within sanctuaries which only men are capable of erecting.

Thus the phrase "day one" or "day of the One" is construed as God's confession of His need of man and, by implication, a promise of man's capacity to remain alive even in the face of cumuli of plutonium.

Let me summarize: Midrash is a quest into the overtones and undertones of Scripture. Those engaged in this devout quest look for meaning in every detail in Scripture, even if the detail seems trivial and insignificant—details such as variations in the spelling of the word "generations," the first appearance of a particular sibilant, the ambiguity of a particle, or the change from a cardinal to an ordinal number in listing the days of Creation.

Mulling over such details led men of Midrash to meditate on great themes: The imperfection in spelling the word "generations," even when the generations were those of Moses and Aaron, suggested the theme of man's universal proneness to evil. The sibilant making its first appearance in Scripture at the creation of woman suggested Satan's leering yet necessary presence at the play of sex. The ambiguity of a particle suggested the theme that man, who is capable of killing by the blow of a hand or the whiplash of a word, must refrain from both kinds of murder lest he, in turn, perish in both body and soul. And, finally, man, prone to sin, consorting with Satan, often on the verge of raising a murderous hand or a deadly epithet, is still a creature made in God's own image, for whose ennobling God prays and for whose companionship on earth God in heaven ever yearns.

The quest of Midrash which for Jews has been a vivid and exciting way of interpreting Scripture may be summed up in the petition of the Psalmist: "Open Thou mine eyes that I may behold wondrous things out of thy Torah" (Ps. 119:18).

RABBINIC EXEGESIS
David S. Shapiro

Dr. Israel Frankel has undertaken, in his doctoral thesis, the task of demonstrating the competence of the rabbinic sages in handling the plain exegesis (*peshat*) of the Holy Scriptures. Contrary to opinions prevalent among superficial students of Talmudic and Midrashic literature, the Rabbis were fully aware of the distinction between the true, literal meaning of the Biblical texts and the fanciful interpretations they often employed for mnemotechnical purposes or in order to clarify a moral lesson. Dr. Frankel makes it evident that the basic rules of Hebrew grammar and the characteristic forms of nouns and verbs were known to the Rabbis and were skillfully treated by them. Although Hebrew lexicography had not yet been developed as a formal science, the knowledge of its principles and details on the part of the ancient masters clearly emerges from the manner in which they dealt with the sacred writings.

All these facts would be rather obvious, were it not for the critical judgments of those who had maintained, over the ages, that the Talmudists had no sense of language, that their understanding of the Bible was fallacious, that they perverted and corrupted its meaning, and by transmitting their corrupt interpretations had impaired the understanding of the simple meaning of the Scriptures. The fact that the Rabbis used Hebrew as a spoken language and composed prayers in this language, which have never been surpassed in the beauty and perfection of their expression,[1] should give the lie to such superficial, untested notions. Prejudices, however, are hard in dying. Dr. Frankel deserves the gratitude of all students of the Talmud and the Midrash for making it clear, once and for all, that the judgments of the detractors of this literature are based on defective knowledge, and, in no way, reflect the actual mastery of the language and its forms by the sages of old.

Nevertheless, it appears to this writer that Dr. Frankel has not gone far enough in his evaluation of rabbinic exegesis. While one need not follow the conclusions of Mecklenburg and Malbim blindly, these great commentators have succeeded in demonstrating that the

Midrashic method is not the product of arbitrary whimsicality or capriciousness. It is grounded on a system of laws and principles. In this connection, mention should also be made of the works of Prof. David Hoffman (*Leviticus* and *Deuteronomium*), Rabbi Samson Raphael Hirsch (Commentary to the Torah), and David Golomb (*Hatorah ve' Hatalmud,* Berlin-Seini 1925-1932).[2]

It has been the experience of this writer, as a result of courses he has taught in Talmud and Midrash, that oftentimes those very passages and interpretations in these works, which seem to defy understanding and might serve as examples of inadequate or distorted exegesis, are the very ones which, upon closer scrutiny yield a richer understanding of the methods employed by the sages. To cite some examples: we read in the *Midrash Rabbah* to Genesis 16:2 as follows:

"And Sarai said unto Abram, 'Behold now the Lord hath restrained me from bearing; I pray thee, go in unto my maid; it may be that I may obtain children by her.' And Abram hearkened to the voice of Sarai."

On this Rabbi Jose comments: "He (Abram) hearkened to the voice of the Holy Spirit in her (Sarai), as it is written.[3] And now therefore hearken unto the voice of the words of the Lord". Rabbi Jose's statement seems, on the surface, to be mere fantasy. What proof does he offer that Abram listened to Sarai because he believed her to be inspired by the Holy Spirit? What evidence is there from the passage in I Samuel? Upon examination of the text, we learn that the Hebrew expression for *hearkened to the voice* in both of these texts is *shamoa lekol*. There are, of course, different ways of saying the same thing: *shamoa bekol, shamoa el kol* and *shamoa lekol*. An examination of the various usages of these expressions[4] reveals that *shamoa lekol* is generally used when one yields to the authority of another out of deference to his superior position or ability.[5] The two exceptions are in Gen. 16.2 and 3.17. In order to explain the discrepancy, Rabbi Jose maintains that Abram deferred to Sarai because the Holy Spirit spoke through her. Likewise in Gen. 3.17, where the same expression is used, the Midrash, in order to obviate the difficulty, interprets the phrase to mean that Eve frightened her husband into obedience by shouting at him, as in Jer. 18.19[6]

Another example might be cited from *Berachoth* 10a. In I Samuel 2.2, in Hannah's prayer, we read: "There is no Rock like our God." What is the meaning of this phrase: There is no Rock (*Tzur*) like our God? It means: There is no Artist (*Tzayar*) like our God." This interpretation is beautiful but, on the face of it, seems groundless.

What would compel anyone to give so strange an interpretation to a word whose meaning is so obvious? However, it seems that the Sages felt that, in a prayer of thanksgiving for the birth of a child, the expression *Rock,* which is ordinarily used to define God as a refuge from disaster, is out of place. For this reason, they reinterpreted the Hebrew *Tzur* as an ancient form of the late Hebrew *Tzayar.*[7]

In the Halakhah, likewise, one occasionally comes across interpretations of legal passages in the Pentateuch, or hypothetical suggestions of phraseology, which seem incomprehensible.[8] The Tosafists were already perplexed by the assumptions, on the part of the Talmudists, of the possibilities of grammatical constructions which have no parallels. However, it seems that the Talmudists discerned strange and unusual forms in certain texts, such as where the infinite absolute is used with *niphal* and *piel* forms in a manner different from other passages. Thus, contrast *himatze timatze* in Ex. 22.3 (both words in *niphal* form) and *heachol yeachel* in Lev. 7.18, 19.7, (both in *niphal*) with *ganob yiganeb* in Ex. 22.11 (one word in *qal,* the other in *niphal*) etc. Also contrast *rapo yerape* in Ex. 22.19 (instead of *rape*) with *shalem yeshalem*. The fact that even such minute nuances did not escape the attention of the Sages bears eloquent testimony to the profundity of their penetration of the intricacies of Hebrew grammar. One is lead to the inescapable conclusion that the Talmud and the Midrasn constitute nothing less than a depth-analysis of both the language and contents of Scriptures.[10]

BACKGROUND — THE WORLD WITHIN

The geographical area known as Palestine has had a varied, productive and often bloody history. The history of the area has been deeply influenced by its geography; it is a rather small but fertile area lodged between two larger fertile areas which cluster around the Tigris-Euphrates to the east and the Nile to the south-west. Although separated from both by a desert buffer, its position between two other, often physically stronger, centers of culture has ensured a constant progression of invading armies, travelling merchants and cultural influences. Present tensions in the area are to be attributed not only to contemporary events but to deep-seated characteristics of geography and patterns of human movement. The Talmudic period witnessed the most traumatic incident in Jewish history—the destruction of the second Temple and the dispersal of the Jews from their homeland.

Very unusual circumstances conspired to ensure the survival of the Jews despite the apparent destruction of their national polity. The written and oral literature to which they clung tenaciously and the way of life which it exemplified kept them separate even in exile; moreover it posited their national existence in their homeland as the norm from which they were made to depart as a punishment for sin. They always looked back to the time of independence and forwards to its restoration. Cohen's article gives us a sketch of the historical background which is supplemented by Zeitlin's discussion of political undercurrents. Büchler gives us an understanding of the economic and social conditions.

HISTORICAL ANTECEDENTS
Abraham Cohen

In the year 586 B.C. the Kingdom of Judea, which then represented all that was left of the people of Israel in Canaan, underwent a devastating experience. The Temple was laid in ruins, its ritual brought to an end, the best part of the nation led as captives to Babylon, and 'the captain of the guard left of the poorest of the land to be vinedressers and husbandmen' (2 Kings xxv. 12). There was bitter justification for the despairing cry: 'How doth the city sit solitary, that was full of people! How is she become as a widow! She that was great among the nations and princess among the provinces, how is she become tributary!' (Lament. i. I).

The crisis, from the national standpoint, was intensified by the circumstance that a century and a half earlier, in 722, the Northern Kingdom, comprising the ten tribes, had been overrun by the army of Assyria and the inhabitants driven into exile where they had, for the most part, become absorbed. If the disaster to Judea met with a like ending, the entire nation would be obliterated and the name of Israel blotted out of existence.

This grave thought must have given the leaders of the Jews in Babylon the deepest concern and induced them to concentrate on the problem of survival. How could the fate of extinction be averted? Recognizing that the distinctiveness of the Israelite people had always rested on its religion, which had centred around the Temple, they were forced to ask themselves by what means that distinctiveness could be maintained now that the Sanctuary had fallen and the people, resident in a foreign land, were exposed to powerful alien influences.

The Biblical sources, which deal with that period, do not provide detailed information, but certain references help to an understanding of the course of events. The outstanding personality in the captive community was the prophet Ezekiel, and he took the lead in the quest for the solution of the problem upon which, humanly speaking, the preservation of Israel depended. In his prophecies he tells of three occasions when 'the elders of Judah' assembled at his house, and we may fairly

66

surmise that at these gatherings the question which was uppermost in
their minds was discussed.

The solution which they evolved may be summarized in a single
word, Torah. This Hebrew word, incorrectly translated 'law,' means
'teaching, direction.' For the exiles it denoted the body of doctrine,
written and oral, which had come down from past ages. Without
entering upon the vexed question of the origin and date of the Pentateuch, we may assume that the Jews in Babylon had in their possession the Mosaic revelation in one form or another. They also had
some of the prophetical writings and Psalms. These relics of their
former national life constituted the only rock upon which the exiled
Jews could stand securely in a gentile environment until the time
God restored them to their homeland. These Scriptures must consequently be forced upon their attention and impressed upon their hearts;
then they would remember that though in Babylon they were not of
Babylon, and the sacred obligation rested upon them to remain a
people apart.

There is a general agreement among scholars that the institution of the Synagogue originated in the time and place of captivity.
Its Hebrew designation, *Beth Hakenéseth* (House of Assembly), accurately indicates its initial purpose. It was the rallying centre of a
homeless nation, and at the gatherings the Scriptures were read and
expounded. In course of time prayers were included and so the Synagogue developed into a place of worship. The effect of these assemblies
was the awakening of interest in the study of the Hebrew writings. The
desire for knowledge among the masses necessarily created a demand
for men who were equipped with the learning to qualify them to act as
teachers. These instructors are known as *Sopherim* (scribes), not in
the sense of writers, but 'men of letters.' Some of them are no doubt
referred to in the list of men who are described as 'teachers' in Ezra viii.
16, and as men who 'caused the people to understand the Torah' in
Nehem. viii. 7.

Foremost among this class of teachers was Ezra, who is characterized as 'a ready scribe in the Torah of Moses' (Ezra vii. 6), i. e. an
expert *Sopher*. He it was who worked out the solution of his predecessors to its practical conclusions. The Talmud, with justification,
compares the work he did for his people with what had been accomplished by Moses. As the great lawgiver created a nation out of the
released slaves by bringing them the Torah, so did Ezra renew the
vitality of a moribund community, both in Babylon and Judea, by

restoring the Torah as its guide of living. In admiration of his achievement the Rabbis declared: 'Ezra was worthy that the Torah should be given to Israel by his hand, were it not that Moses had forestalled him' (Sanh. 21b), and "When the Torah had been forgotten by Israel, Ezra came up from Babylon and re-established it' (Suk. 20a).

The policy of Ezra has been elsewhere described by the present writer in these terms: 'Zangwill once said, "History, which is largely a record of the melting of minorities in majorities, records no instance of the survival of a group not segregated in space or not protected by a burning faith as by a frontier of fire." This lesson of history had evidently been discerned by Ezra. He understood that the Jews could not be utterly segregated in space. Not only were there branches of the national tree in Egypt, Babylon, and Persia to be taken into consideration; but contact between the Jews in Judea and their neighbours could not be avoided. If, then, the Jewish nation was to be preserved, it must be ringed round "by a burning faith as by a frontier of fire"—a most apposite metaphor, since the Bible itself speaks of "a fiery law." The Jew must have a religion which would not only continually distinguish him from the heathen, but would likewise be a constant reminder to him that he was a member of the Jewish race and faith. The Jew was to be demarcated from his neighbours not merely by a creed, but by a mode of living. His manner of worship would be different; his home would be different; even in the common acts of daily life there would be distinguishing features which would constantly recall his Jewishness. His life, in every detail, was to be controlled by Torah—by the written enactments of the Mosaic code and their development in the corporate life of the people, as the altered conditions demanded change.'

Unless this viewpoint is thoroughly grasped, there can be no possibility of understanding the mentality of the Rabbis, the trend of their activities and their method of Bible-exegesis. It is the seed out of which the Talmud grew. We have it mentioned very distinctly in the account of Ezra's work: 'He had set his heart to seek the Torah of the Lord, and to do it, and to teach in Israel statutes and judgments' (Ezra vii. 10). The Hebrew verb used in this sentence for 'to seek,' *darash,* is of the utmost importance for our theme. Its true sense is 'to deduce, interpret' the ideas which profound study of the text could elucidate. This process of deduction is called *Midrash* and is the system of interpretation employed throughout the Rabbinic literature. By its aid a Scriptural passage yielded far more than could be discerned on the surface. The sacred words became an inexhaustible mine which, when quarried, produced rich treasures of religious and ethical teaching.

Starting from the axiom that the divine will is revealed in the Torah, Ezra taught that the daily existence of the Jew must be regulated in every phase by its precepts; and since the Torah has to be the *complete* guide of living, it must be made capable of yielding helpful guidance for every circumstance of human life. A prerequisite to the achievement of this aim was knowledge of the Torah. Before they could be expected to perform the commandments, the people had to be educated in them. He therefore introduced into Judea the public reading of the Pentateuch in order to make the masses familiar with its contents. 'They read in the book, in the Torah of God, with an interpretation; and they gave the sense, so that they understood the reading' (Nehem. viii. 8).

According to Jewish tradition, Ezra founded the *Keneseth Hagedolah* (the Great Assembly), a synod of teachers who received the corpus of doctrine which had been preserved to their day, adapted and developed it to suit the new conditions of their age, and then transmitted it to the pioneers of the Talmudic Rabbis. The chain of authority is thus described: 'Moses received the Torah on Sinai, and handed it down to Joshua; Joshua to the Elders; the Elders to the Prophets: and the Prophets handed it down to the men of the Great Assembly' (*Aboth* I.1).

The existence of such a synod has been questioned by modern scholars. While it must be admitted that the two and a half centuries which followed the career of Ezra are wrapped in obscurity and practically no historical data are available, yet there seems no sound reason to doubt that an official body of teachers must have functioned during that period. A far-seeing reformer like Ezra could not have failed to realize that his work would inevitably fall to pieces soon after his death unless he was succeeded by men who, imbued with his own zeal, would continue his policy. To create an authoritative council to which his people could turn for instruction appears the most obvious course for him to have adopted.

Furthermore, when the veil of ignorance lifts, we find ourselves in the early part of the second century B. C. witnessing a heroic struggle on the part of a small band of Jews to resist an attempt to destroy their religion. The Hasmoneans pitted themselves against the armies of Syria because Antiochus Epiphanes dared to order them to violate the precepts of Judaism, 'to the end they might forget the Torah and change all the ordinances' (I Macc. i. 49). Mattathias, on raising the standard of revolt, proclaimed: 'Whoever is zealous of the Torah, and maintaineth the covenant, let him follow me' (ibid. ii. 27); and before his death he exhorted his sons: 'Be valiant and show yourselves men in the behalf of the Torah' (ibid. 64).

Hence we see beyond all doubt that early in the second century the Torah had become firmly rooted among at least a section of the Jews. How can the deathless attachment to it which distinguished the Hasmoneans be explained if there had been no channel through which the knowledge of Torah passed to them from the fifth century when Ezra lived? The known facts of history postulate a body of teachers such as that which is named 'the Great Assembly.' If that be so, the probability is that its members would be drawn mainly, if not entirely, from the *Sopherim,* since they were the best qualified to discharge the duties which would fall to it.

Three leading maxims are attributed to this Assembly: 'Be deliberate in judgment, raise up many disciples, and make a fence around the Torah' (*Aboth* I. 1). These represent the three principles which motivated their activities. Judgment was to be deliberate in the sense that questions, which had to be determined by the rule of Torah, must be minutely studied and the closest investigation made as to the decision it suggested. That was one reason for the exact scrutiny of the Scriptural text which distinguished the Rabbis of the Talmud. A superficial reading could only result in a hasty judgment. An exhaustive inquiry was essential if the judgment was to be deliberate. The raising of many disciples had obviously to be the unceasing concern of the teachers if knowledge of the Torah was to be handed down to future generations. This ideal of spreading scholarship, and the consequent deference which was paid to the instructor and student of the Torah, provided a powerful urge towards the kind of learning which culminated in the compilation of the Talmud. To 'make a fence around the Torah' was a corollary of the desire to live by its precepts. If a person kept too close to its letter, he might inadvertently be led to transgress it. As a cultivated field had to be hedged round to prevent even innocent trespass, so the sacred domain of the Torah must be enclosed by additional precautionary measures for the purpose of avoiding unintentional encroachment. Accordingly, the purpose which actuated the members of the Great Assembly created the type of study to which the teachers of later generations conformed. Theirs was the sowing which ultimately produced the extensive harvest of the Talmud.

An important piece of historical information is contained in the statement: 'Simon the Just was one of the last survivors of the Great Assembly' (*Aboth* I. 2). Unfortunately its value is minimized by the uncertainty as to which man of that name is meant. Josephus mentions a High Priest, 'Simon who was called the Just, both because of his piety towards God and his kind disposition to those of his own nation' (*Antiq.* XII. ii. 5). He died about the year 270 B. C. Another High Priest, Simon, the grandson of the former, is also referred to by the historian (ibid. xii. iv. 10), and he died about 199. In favour of identifying the grandfather with the last survivor of the Great Assembly is the fact that he is actually called by Josephus 'the Just'; but against it is the circumstance that if the Assembly came to an end about 270 a chronological difficulty is created. The Tractate *Aboth* informs us that Antigonos of Socho was the disciple of Simon the Just and José b. Joezer, and José b. Jochanan received the Torah from them' (I. 4). These scholars died about the year 160, which seems to give too long a period of time if the sense of the passage is that they were disciples of Simon and Antigonos. To fill in the gap it has been suggested that 'from them' means from a succession of teachers whose names have not been recorded.

However this may be, the Great Assembly ceased to exist either towards the middle of the third century or at its end. It was followed by another organization, known as a Sanhedrin, which took charge of the affairs of the community in Judea. In a letter from Antiochus III to Ptolemy, preserved by Josephus, it is called a 'senate' (*Antiq.* XII. iii. 3). Jewish tradition relates that there were five *Zugoth*, or 'pairs' of Rabbis in succession, ending with Hillel and Shammai (died about A.D. 10), one of whom was *Nasi* or 'Prince,' i. e. President, and the other *Ab Beth Din* or 'Father of the Court of Law,' i.e. Vice-President (*Chag.* II. 2).

Modern historical study has come to a different conclusion. The Sanhedrin was a composite body of priests and laymen, presided over by the High Priest. In the deliberations which took place at its sessions a cleavage soon occured, resulting in the formation of two distinct parties. The priests favoured a policy of compromise with Hellenistic thought, even at the expense of complete loyalty to the Torah. Ranged against them were the laymen who were the direct heirs of Erza and the *Sopherim*, and they took a firm stand in demanding whole-hearted adherence to the rule of Torah. Their leaders were the Rabbis known as the *Zugoth*.

The rift between the two parties was closed during the Maccabean struggle, but manifested itself in a more pronounced form when John Hyrcanus (135-105 B. C.). came to the throne. It gradually widened until two sects appeared, called Sadducees and Pharisees. Among the differences which divided them was one of the utmost importance in the development of Judaism. Josephus refers to it in these terms: 'The Pharisees have delivered to the people a great many observances by succession from their fathers which are not written in the law of Moses; and for that reason it is that the Sadducees reject them, and say that we are to esteem those observances to be obligatory which are in the written word, but are not to observe what are derived from the tradition of our fore-fathers; and concerning these things it is that great disputes and differences have arisen among them' (*Antiq.* XII. x. 6).

This controversy over the validity of the Oral Torah stimulated its defenders to a fresh study of the Scriptural text. They set out to demonstrate that the Oral Torah was an integral part of the Written Torah, that they were warp and woof of the one fabric; and they further developed methods of exegesis previously employed by which the traditions rejected by the Sadducees could be shown to be contained in the wording of the Pentateuch. Exposition of Torah now entered upon a new phase and led directly to the creation of the Talmud.

THE ECONOMIC CONDITION OF JUDAEA
AFTER THE DESTRUCTION OF
THE SECOND TEMPLE

Adolph Buchler

I. THE PLACES AND THE POPULATION OF JUDAEA
PRESERVED AFTER THE YEAR
70.

Josephus, the contemporary historian of the Jewish war of the years 66-70, devoted a work of seven books to the events of that short period, and it should not be difficult to describe the condition in which the war left Judaea. Josephus seems rather anxious to register the rapid achievements of Vespasian, Titus, and their generals and officers, the Roman victories and the slaughter of thousands of Jews; an enumeration of all the places conquered or destroyed by the Romans could then reasonably be expected. Actually, however, the information from Josephus is rather fragmentary, though he describes the downfall of Jerusalem and reports the destruction of some parts of the trans-Jordanic country to Jericho in the western district, and in Judaea of the region from Antipatris southwards to beth-Gubrin.

1. From his fullness of material in these accounts the inference seems justified that whenever in a report of a campaign no destruction is mentioned, the towns and villages were spared by the Romans, probably in consequence of the early surrender of the defending Jews. This can be tested in his account of the way in which the Romans dealt with places on the main road from Caesarea, the residence of the governor and the starting-point of all military expeditions against Judaea, to Jerusalem, the centre of the Jewish rebellion. Owing to this geographical position Antipatris, Lydda, Emmaus, and beth-Horon had to suffer the first blows of the Roman revenge, and Josephus described fully its details. At the beginning of the revolution in the autumn of the year 66, Cestius Gallus on his march from Caesarea against Jerusalem left Antipatris without inflicting any harm (*Wars*, II, 19.1), but owing to the hostile, military preparations of some Jews in a tower near Antipatris he burnt many villages. In Lydda, a Jewish town (Philo, *Legatio* 28) he found no man, for all had gone up to Jerusalem for the feast of Taber-

nacles, but he killed fifty persons and burnt the town. A part of his army marched against Joppé and slaughtered all its inhabitants, 8,400 men, women, and children, plundered the town and burnt it (II, 18, 10).[1] Early in the spring of the year 68 Vespasian marched from Caesarea to Antipatris, where he spent two days to settle the affairs of the town (IV, 8, 1). On the third day he marched on and destroyed by fire and arms all the places round about. Having subdued the whole district of Thamma, he marched on Lydda and Jamnia that very soon fell into his hands, and now received as inhabitants a suitable number of such Jews as had deserted from the rebels to the Romans. Thence he went to Emmaus, where he seized the defiles which led to Jerusalem; then he passed through the district of Bethleptephai, laying it and the neighbouring district waste by fire. These statements of Josephus show that Lydda and Jamnia had been in Roman possession from 66 or 67 and were populated with loyal Jews, and that Emmaus was not destroyed.

Again, Josephus reports (IV, 9, 1) that Vespasian built a fortified camp in Adida, where he placed Romans and soldiers of his allies. He sent Lucius Annius with a squadron of horsemen and a great number of footmen against Gerasa. The town was taken at the first attack, all young men who had not escaped in time, numbering a thousand, were killed, their families were taken captive, and all property was plundered by the soldiers. After burning the town they turned against the neighbouring villages, where all fled, the weak were destroyed, and the abandoned places burnt. In this way the whole mountainous district and the whole plain were invaded by war. Gerasa cannot mean the Hellenistic city east of the Jordan, for it would not have been hostile to the Romans, but to the Jews. The term Oreiné and the immediate reference to the position of Jerusalem suggest that this Gerasa was in the mountains north or north-west of Jerusalem,[2] and we see the destruction of many places, but at the same time the escape of their inhabitants. In Sivan of the year 69 Vespasian marched from Caesarea to subdue all the districts of Judaea not yet conquered (IV, 9, 9). He went to the mountainous country, seized upon the district of Gofna and Akrabatene, then upon the smaller towns of Bethel and Ephraim, where he placed troops. Not one word suggests that these or other places in the district were destroyed, while the necessity of garrisons indicates the strategical importance of the towns, and also the presence of a Jewish population not quite to be trusted. Cerealis, the legate of the Fifth Legion stationed in Emmaus (IV, 8, 1), had to subdue Upper Idumaea, the southern part of Judaea. He burnt Kafethra and besieged Kafarabis. the inhabitants of which soon surrendered and were accepted (IV, 9, 9); this means the

place was spared. East of the Jordan, Gadara, the important and fortified city and inhabited by many wealthy men, asked for and in time
obtained a Roman garrison from Vespasian (IV, 7, 3). One of his officers, Placidus, continued in the spring of the year 68 the conquest of
Peraia, killing thousands of Jews (IV, 7, 4), among the first, the rebels
of Gadara that had fled to Bethennabris and had found there support;
then other villages with their inhabitants were destroyed. Abila, Julias,
and Besimoth, and all the villages down to the Dead Sea were conquered
(IV, 7, 5–6) and Jewish deserters placed there. Thus the whole district
from Peraia down to Machairus had either voluntarily joined the Romans or was conquered by force. During the winter of the year 68 Vespasian put garrisons in the conquered villages and townlets and made
many of the destroyed places habitable (IV, 8, 1).

2. Incidentally, Josephus mentioned that Vespasian and one of his
generals had settled Jews who had deserted to the Romans in Jamnia
and Lydda and in some places near the mouth of the Jordan, but he says
nothing about the original towns and villages of those Jews. They were
no Galileans; for those who had surrendered in the course of the Galilean war, as far as can be gathered from Josephus, remained in their
respective places, and no transplantation is reported. After the conquest
of Galilee in the year 67 only a few Galileans left their country to join
the defenders of Jerusalem. Only John of Gischala and his warriors of
the same town with their families left the place immediately before its
fall, and made for Jerusalem (IV, 2, 4). But 6,000 of the men were
overtaken by the Romans and killed (2,5) and 3,000 women and
children were forced to return. From Judaea great multitudes under
their respective leaders flocked into Jerusalem (3,3), zealots and sicarii
(3,4), but their numbers are nowhere stated. 20,000 Idumaeans came
to Jerusalem (4,2), but most of them soon left and returned home
(6,1). As the siege of the capital in the year 70 began on the day of the
Passover sacrifice (V, 13, 7, VI, 9, 3), to which naturally many thousands of pilgrims had arrived from all parts of the country, the number
of the besieged was very great. Among them were many from beyond
the Euphrates and other foreign lands (*Dio Cassius*, 66. 4). 1,100,000
men perished during the siege, 97,000 were taken captive (VI, 9, 3);
of these only 40,000 were preserved (8,2), all citizens of Jerusalem
(8,2), the rest were sold for slaves, some sent into the mines in Egypt
(9, 2), others distributed among the provinces for the circuses.

Considering the state of Judaea, the only questions are which section of the citizens of Jerusalem was preserved, and where did the
40,000 settle after having been allowed to go where they liked (V, 8, 2;

10, 1)? In the course of his account of the siege, Josephus several times refers to individuals who deserted to the Romans from Jerusalem and it is not evident whether they were included in the 40,000 ultimately preserved or not. He mentions one of the four sons of the high priest Matthias (V, 13, 1), the high priests Joseph and Jesus, and three sons of the high priest Ismael, four sons of a Matthias, and many other nobles who succeeded in escaping from the besieged capital to the Romans (VI, 2, 2). Many of the eminent citizens ran away to Titus (V, 13, 7) and told him the number of the poor who had died. Titus allowed these to retire to Gofna; there, he said, they should stay till his hands would be free from the war, when he would restore to them their property. Among the numerous deserters was the priest Jesus, son of Thebuthi (VI, 8, 3), who surrendered many costly vessels of the Temple, as well as the curtains and the robe of the high priest. The treasurer of the Temple also fell into the hands of the Romans and was exceptionally pardoned in exchange for valuable stuff, priestly garments, and costly spices. Already, after Cestius's defeat in the year 66, many of the nobles had left Jerusalem as if it were a sinking ship; for instance, the two brothers Costobarus and Saul, along with Phillip, son of Jakimos, who had been a general of Agrippa's troops (II, 20, 1). After the entry of the Romans into Jerusalem, Titus liberated all those Jews who had been thrown into prison by zealots (VI, 9.1); they also most probably belonged to the wealthy section of the population.[3] It may be assumed as almost certain that the members of both groups, of the priestly and of the lay nobility of Jerusalem, at the conclusion of the war received their landed property, and assisted the poor country of Judaea in recovering from its terrible downfall. Where they settled is nowhere indicated by Josephus; he lived in Rome and seemed to evince no interest in the state of his native country after the destruction. It is possible that, though owning land in Judaea, some of the nobles settled outside Judaea, as Josephus, who, in exchange for his fields near Jerusalem, received from Titus others in the plain, and was rewarded by Vespasian by additional property in Judaea (*Vita*, 76).

3. Though no historical work in the ordinary sense, the Talmudic literature in its incidental references to conditions of life and to property contains valuable information about Judaea during the sixty-five years from the destruction of the second Temple to the war of bar-Kochba. The Halakhah deals with all details of religious life that were placed before the rabbis of that period or were discussed in the schools; but here only facts and incidents reported within those discussions will be ad-

duced. Two high priests are referred to by R. Ishmael as testifying respectively to two different ways in which they had performed the same sacrificial act on the Day of Atonement.[4] A vice high priest, or the head of all the priests on duty, סגן הכהנים, was Haninah who had officiated in the Temple[5] and survived its destruction.[6] R. Ishmael, a priest (*Hull*, 49a), was the son of a high priest[7] who had worn the robe and the golden plate.[8] Simeon the Chaste told R. Eliezer that he once entered the space behind the altar with unwashed hands and feet (*Tos. Kelim*, I, 1, 6): he was a priest. R. Sadok, the priest (*Bekhor.*, 36a) who had once quieted the people assembled in the Temple excited by the murder of a priest,[9] was, with his son Eleazar, saved by R. Johanan b. Zakkai from among the captives (*Threni r.*, I, 5, *Gittin*, 56a), and both were later friends of R. Gamaliel II in Jamnia. R. Sadok gave, with R. Joshua, evidence about some customs in Jerusalem (*'Eduj.*, VII, 1-4), and his son reported many interesting facts and customs which he had observed there before the year 70. Another priest, Zechariah b. ha-Kassab, reports (*Kethub.*, II, 9) how he escaped with his wife from Jerusalem when the enemy entered the town; and we are informed of the arrangements which, on account of that, he made for his wife with whom, as a priest he could no longer live (*Kethub*, 27 b; *Tos.* III.2). Later on he gave evidence with Josê the priest, a disciple of R. Johanan b. Zakkai, about a point of law. R. Tarfon had once, as a young priest, stood on the platform in the Temple, from which the priests, among whom was his uncle, blessed the people. (*Kiddush.*, 71a), and he watched the blowing of trumpets by priests on the occasion when King Agrippa read from the Torah before the people assembled on the Temple mount (*Tos. Sotah*, VII, 16; *Sifrê Num.*, 75). After the year 70 he settled in Lydda and taught there.[10] Of high officials of the Temple, none is mentioned as surviving its destruction (see below); but R. Ishmael once met one of the grandsons of the Abtinas family who had for some time prepared the incense. R. Ishmael b. Luga told R. Akiba that he had once gathered plants with one of the grandsons, and R. Johanan b. Nuri told R. Akiba that he once met an old man, with a scroll on the preparation of spices in his hand, who belonged to the family of Abtinas.[11] The age of the last mentioned man shows that he had lived for some time before the destruction of the Temple which he survived. As the Talmud refers only incidentally to individual priests, it may be confidently assumed that many more escaped from Jerusalem and other places in Judaea. The institution of R. Johanan b. Zakkai, that also after the destruction of the Temple, priests should, barefooted, bless the people in the synagogue (*Rosh haShan.*, 31b), clearly shows the presence of priests in Jamnia. This is also evident from his other decree quoted by R. Gamaliel ('*Eduj.* VIII, 3) that no court should be constituted to deal with the question of whether a certain widow may become the wife of a priest, as priests refuse to accept the permission.[12]

Of Levites little is known. R. Joshua b. Hananjah had belonged to the singers in the Temple and had once wanted to assist Johanan b. Gudgeda in closing the gates of the Temple ('*Arakh.*, 11b). He had at the same time been a disciple of R. Johanan b. Zakkai whom he helped R. Eliezer to carry from the besieged capital and with whom he escaped into the Roman camp (*ARN*, IV, 12a, 2, VI, 10a). After the destruction of Jerusalem, he belonged for many years to the school of Jamnia, first under R. Johanan and later under R. Gamaliel II, and reported several interesting details of religious practice in Jerusalem. The other Levite, Johanan b. Gudgeda, had belonged to the gate-keepers of the Temple (*Tos. Shekal.*, II, 14; '*Arakh.*, 11b); he had in Jerusalem deaf-mute children who were entrusted with watching the levitical purification of vessels (*jer. Terum.*, I, 40b, 24; *Tos.*, I, 1). He survived the destruction of Jerusalem and gave evidence before the authorities in Jamnia about a point of law.[13]

4. Of the scholars who survived the destruction of Jerusalem R. Johanan b. Zakkai is to be mentioned first. He was probably a priest,[14] and had not only been the vice-president of the Synedrion beside Simeon b. Gamaliel as president, but had also fought the Sadducees in both their teachings and their practices (*Jadai.*, IV, 6, *Tos. Parah*, III, 8). After the destruction of Jerusalem he opened a school and constituted a beth-din in Jamnia by which he created the means for the continuity and the preservation of Judaism without the Temple. As important members of this beth-din, the sons of Bethera are mentioned in *Rosh ha-Shan.*, 29b. Though they seem to represent a whole party in the opposition, their name shows the stock to have consisted of a family that had survived the Temple, as a Joshua b. Bethera gave evidence about the marriage of a eunuch in Jerusalem.[15] Nahum the Mede was, according to R. Nathan (*Tos. B. bath.*, IX, 1, *Kethub.*, 105a), a judge in Jerusalem; he directed Nazirites who had come from Babylonia to Jerusalem to fulfil their vow, but found the Temple destroyed, as to their duties (*Nazir.* V, 4); and a few statements of his show him to have been a teacher in Judaea after the year 70. R. Dosa b. Harkinas, a member of the school in Jamnia, was old and blind when the discussions between the schools of the Shammaiites and Hillelites were being settled in Jamnia; he must, therefore, have been born long before the destruction of

Jerusalem. He remembered how Joshua b. Hananjah—born at the latest in the year 50—had been carried in his cradle by his mother to a school in order to accustom his ears early to the Torah (jer. Jebam., I, 3a, 72, b. 16a), and he was a contemporary of R. Johanan b. Zakkai and of R. Haninah, the vice high priest (Kethub., XIII, 1, Neg., I,4). Hizkijahאבי עקש,not otherwise known, gave evidence before R. Gamaliel II in the name of Gamaliel I (Bekhor., 38a, Sifra, 53d), so that he must have been born about the year 40. R. Gamaliel II himself, the son of Simeon b. Gamaliel the opponent of Josephus during the revolution (Vita, 38) and president of the Synedrion, was saved from the punishing hands of the Romans by R. Johanan b. Zakkai (Gitt., 56b) whom he later succeeded in the presidency of the beth-din in Jamnia. He remembered how his father counteracted, as to a law of the Sabbath, the interfering presence of a Sadducee living with him in the same lane ('Erub., VI, 2), and how he left the prescribed corner on fruit-trees (Pe'ah, II, 4) and what kind of bread was not baked in his father's house on a holy day (Besah, II, 6). From all this it is evident that he was at least a man of 20 at the death of his father. His co-president in Jamnia, R. Eleazar b. 'Azarjah, was a priest and probably quite young in the year 70, as R. Dosa b. Harkinas, though knowing his father, did not know him (Jebam., 16a); R. Akiba speaks of him as descended of great men and in the tenth generation from Ezra (jer. Berakh., IV, 7d, 10b., 27b). Also 'Elisha b. 'Abuja must have escaped young from Jerusalem where his father was a wealthy man; R. Joshua and R. Eliezer, the disciples of R. Johanan b. Zakkai, attended his circumcision in Jerusalem (jer. Hagigah, II, 77b, 38). Many years after the destruction he attended R. Akiba's school, and during and after the Hadrianic religious persecutions he lived in Tiberias, where he died about the year 140.[16] A R. Jehudah b. Gadish, not otherwise known, testified before R. Eliezer that his father's household bought fishbrine in Jerusalem for the equivalent of the second tithe.[17]

Incidentally, women who survived the catastrophe of the year 70 are also mentioned in the Talmud. R. Eleazar b. Sadok saw Martha, the daughter of Boethos and the wife of the high priest Joshua b. Gamala, tied by her hair to the tail of a horse and dragged from Jerusalem to Lydda.[18] R. Johanan b. Zakkai saw the daughter of Nakdimon b. Gorjon, one of the wealthiest men in Jerusalem, in Ma'on in abject poverty.[19] There are references to R. Tarfon's mother (jer. Kiddush., IV. 61b, 18, b. 31b) and his sister whose children he taught (Zebah., 62b) and also to R. Ishmael's mother (Niddah, 48b, Tos., VI, 8), R. Eliezer's mother (jer. Jebam., III, 13c. 60) and his wife, the sister of R. Gamaliel (*B. mes.*, 59 b). Naturally many thousands of men and women, nowhere specifically referred to were saved and remained in Judaea. There was no occasion for mentioning them, though general references are not wanting. It is also worth stating that some of the so-called Nathins survived the destruction of Jerusalem, for in the times of R. Eleazar b. 'Azarjah it was proposed to recognize them as proper Israelites.[20]

5. By tracing some places in Judaea in which, after the destruction of Jerusalem, Jews lived in greater or smaller numbers, a clearer and more complete view of actual conditions in the country can be obtained. Of Jerusalem, strange to say, very little is known from the Talmudic literature. It is true, some scholars state that soon after the catastrophe some Jewish and Christian families returned to Jerusalem, preferring to live in poor houses among the ruins of the holy city to cities in Judaea,[21] but no Jewish source is adduced, nor is such known to me. Only Eusebius (*Hist. eccl.*, IV. 5ff., V, 12) reports that the Christians, who during the siege of Jerusalem had fled to Pella, soon returned. And Epiphanius, just as reliable a historian as Eusebius, relates (*De mensuris*, §14) that, when visiting Jerusalem (130–1), Hadrian found the city and the Temple destroyed and only a few houses inhabited and a small church.[22] R. Simeon b. Eleazar of the second half of the second century reports (*Semah.*, X) that R. Gamaliel II had a hired grave in Jamnia for the temporary burial of members of his family whence they were later taken to Jerusalem. Whether other noble familes continued in the same way burying their dead in their family graves in Jerusalem is not reported, but it is not improbable. The ruins of the Temple were visited by scholars, as R. Gamaliel II, R. Eleazar b. 'Azarjah, R. Joshua, and R. Akiba (*Makk.*, 24b), who were grieved to see a fox coming out of the ruins of the Holy of Holies. R. Josê also entered one of the ruins of Jerusalem to pray (*Berakh.*, 3a); and 'Elisha b. 'Abuja told R. Meir that once, on a Day of Atonement that fell on the Sabbath, he rode by the Holy of Holies and heard a heavenly voice inviting him to repentance (*jer. Hag.*, II, 77b. 59, *Kohel. r.*, 7, 8). As he was then a sinner, it occurred about the years 120-135.

There is even some, though late, evidence that scholars and other Jews visited Jerusalem on the festivals. R. Shela of Kefar-Thamartha, between 280–300, states (*Cant. r.*, 8, 9, 3): though the Temple is destroyed, the Israelites have not stopped their pilgrimages three times a year. In *Threni, r.*, 1, 17, a number of differences between the present and the old pilgrimage are stated; and R. Berekhjah of the fourth century points out that both the going up and the return are very quiet; according to R. Levi of about the year 300 both are done secretly. In a

Baraitha, *Nedar.*, 23a, a man prohibited his wife by a vow to go on pilgrimage; when she still went up, the husband asked R. Josê's advice. It is true the destination is not stated, but it is hardly to be doubted that Jerusalem and not Jamnia is meant.[23] R. Eleazer b. Shammu'a, in the middle of the second century, took to his house a shipwrecked Roman when the Jews went on pilgrimage to Jerusalem (*Kohel. r.*, 11,1).R. Haninah, R. Jonathan, and R. Joshua b. Levi, about the year 250, on their way to Jerusalem bought some produce and wanted to redeem it outside Jerusalem, but an old man reminded them: your fathers did not proceed in that way, but declared such produce free property and redeemed it (*jer. Ma'as. sh.*, III, 54b, 20). Though the report is far from being clear, it is evident that the law concerning the second tithe in its relation to Jerusalem was still observed. Accordingly R. Eliezer b. Hyrkanos, about the year 100, declared the fruit of the fourth year of his vineyard free property and expected the poor who would take possession of it, to take it to Jerusalem (*Rosh haShan.*, 31b). And R. Akiba changed for R. Gamaliel and R. Joshua the money of redemption of their second tithe[24] to spend it in Jerusalem.[25] R. Jonathan was another time on his way to Jerusalem to pray there,[26] and fifty years before, about the year 200, R. Ishmael b. R. Josê went up to Jerusalem to pray (*Genes. r.*, 81, 3; *jer. 'AZ*, V, 44d, 41). In spite of the statements of the church fathers that the Jews were not allowed to visit Jerusalem, except on the 9th of 'Ab, they seem to have gone up regularly on various occasions, so that R. Johanan, between 250 and 279, was able to say that the city was open to everybody: whoever likes at present to go up, goes up, but in the future only invited people will go up to Jerusalem (*B. bathra*, 75b, top). R. Johanan b. Marja in the name of R. Pinhas says (*jer. Pesah.*, VII, 35b, 39): we see the scholars take off their shoes under the doorstep of the Temple mount;[27] and in *Threni r.*, 1, 17, Vespasian places guards 18 miles from Poma'im, who inquired of the pilgrims whom they recognized as their lord. All these reports agree in referring to a free pilgrimage to Jerusalem.

6. Lydda and Jamnia, we have seen, were populated in the year 68 by Vespasian with a suitable number of loyal Jews (*Wars*, IV, 8, 1). They were in no way interfered with by the Romans or the national Jews during the revolution of the years 69 and 70. Whether those Jews went up to Jerusalem to celebrate the Passover in April 70 and were there surprised by the Roman siege, is not reported; but as they had previously surrendered to the Romans, and Jerusalem was in the hands of the revolutionists, a pilgrimage of those Jews is not probable. Besides, as the Roman army began the siege of Jerusalem on the 14th of Nissan,

after one of the legions, the fifth, had marched from Caesarea by Emmaus to Jerusalem, it must have passed through or near Lydda at the
latest on the 12th of Nissan, and thus prevented the possible pilgrimage
of any inhabitants of Lydda or Jamnia which were at a day's distance
from Jerusalem. In any case, both these towns had organized Jewish
communities, and we can easily understand why R. Johanan b. Zakkai
asked Titus's or Vespasian's permission to settle just in Jamnia; and
even the statement that he asked for the scholars of Jamnia (*Gitt.*, 56b)
could be literally true, as there may have been scholars among the
settlers. Jamnia became the seat of the great school and the beth-din of
R. Johanan, which is often described as a meeting in the vineyard of
Jamnia.[28] Lydda had several schools, in one of which the teachers met
to decide questions, and before this meeting R. Tarfon placed a practical case (*Beṣah*, III, 5); [29] five members constitued the body.[30] R. Eliezer, who is pointed out as the authority in Lydda (*Synh.*, 32b), had a
school of his own, called the great[31]; it looked like a racecourse, and
there sitting on a stone R. Eliezer taught (*Cant. r.*, 1, 3, 1,). There were
also several synagogues in Lydda, some of which were built by the
ancestors of R. Ḥama b. Ḥaninah (*jer. Shekal.*, V, 49b, 33); one was of
the טרסיים.[32] A school for children is mentioned in the time of R. Akiba
in *Semaḥ.*, II, 4). Beside Alexa a man of importance and generally esteemed (*Tos. Ḥag.* II, 13), and the family of a Menaḥem (*Synh.*, 33a)
whose property will have to be referred to later, the family of Nithzah
is mentioned, with whom R. Tarfon and his disciples stayed on a Sabbath,[33] and the family of 'Aris in whose upper chamber the question
heavy with consequences was decided by a meeting of teachers, whether
in religious persecutions a Jew has to sacrifice his life for any religious
commandment (*Kiddush.*, 40 b. *Sifrê Deut.*, 41). A man Gornos, whose
little son committed suicide because the father threatened to punish
him (*Semaḥ.*, II, 4), is in the first century interesting for his name. The
same applies to a doctor Theodos, who in the presence of R. Akiba and
other teachers, examined human bones in the synagogue of Tarsijim
mentioned above (*Nazir*, 52a, and parallels). In the bakers' hall (in the
market of Lydda) R. Eliezer was found by R. Josê b. Darmaskith.[34] The
vendors of Lydda rejoiced when R. Tarfon fixed the amount of over-
reaching, permitting a buyer to return the article, at one-eighth of the
value; but when he added that the buyer may retract the whole day
of the transaction, they reverted to the accepted rule of the earlier rabbis, for they sold dear.[35] Strange to say, very few details are mentioned
of the life of the Jews in Jamnia, though sometimes 72 members of the
school were present in the town at the same time (*Zebaḥ.*, I, 3) and even

85 (*Tos. Kelim*, 3 II, 4). Only the family of a ben-Zaza is mentioned, for whose mother R. Gamaliel held a great public mourning (*Rosh haShan.*, 25a), and the bath of a certain Diskos used for levitically purifying vessels, which was once the subject of a discussion between R. Tarfon and R. Akiba.[36]

7. Around Lydda and Jamnia as centres several smaller places had Jewish inhabitants. When a certain Alexa died in Lydda, the men of the villages came to bewail him, but R. Tarfon prohibited the public mourning owing to the holy day.[37] In one of those villages, east of Lydda, Kefar-Tabi, R. Eliezer of Lydda had a vineyard;[38] another was Kefar-Luddim (*Gitt.*, I, 1) west of Lydda, already outside Palestine, although quite close to Lydda (*Gitt.*, 4a). R. Akiba had his school in benê-Berak,[39] a very fertile district near Joppé, R. Joshua b. Hananjah taught in Peki'in between Lydda and Jamnia,[40] R. Ishmael in Kefar-'Aziz,[41] his teacher Nehunjah b. Hakanah is once called a man of Emmaus[42] where R. Joshua visited him. This town had a cattle-market in which R. Gamaliel of Jamnia, accompanied by R. Joshua and R. Akiba, bought cattle for the wedding-feast of his son,[43] it was Amwâs in the Shefelah at the entrance into the mountains and reached from Jamnia by the valley of Surar.[44] Owing to its strategical importance it probably had a Roman garrison. R. Eleazar b. 'Arakh, the favourite disciple of R. Johanan b. Zakkai, after his master's death settled in Emmaus, a pleasant place with good water.[45] R. Akiba's teacher Nahum was of Gimzô near Lydda (*Shebu.*, 26a), R. Eliezer's son Hyrkanos lived in Kefar-'Etam,[46] near Bethlehem, one of R. Johanan b. Zakkai's disciples was R. Eleazar of Modeim, a disciple of R. Jehudah b. Baba was Simeon התימני , probably of Thimnah.[47]

In Ma'on in the south of Judaea, several hours' distance from Hebron, R. Johanan b. Zakkai saw a Jewish girl picking up grains of barley from the dung of horses (*Mekhil.* on Ex. 19, 1, 61 a); the presence of this teacher with disciples in Ma'on suggests with great probability that Jews lived in the place. Bethlehem seems to have retained its population after the revolution, as is suggested by the well-known legend about the birth of the Messiah (*jer. Berakh.*, II, 5 a; *Threni r.*, 1, 16, 51): an Arab told a Jew, who was working in the field with his cows, that the lowing of his cow announced that Jerusalem had been destroyed, and the lowing of the other cow that the Messiah had been born in birath-'Arabah of beth-Lehem in Judaea. The Jew left his work and, in order to find the future Messiah, went about selling flannels for children from village to village, from town to town, till he arrived at the village of birath-'Arabah where he found the child. This story assumes that whole districts of Judaea were not destroyed. Reland (*Palaestina*, 647) refers to Anastasius's Biographies of the Roman bishops, where it is reported that St. Euaristus of the times of Domitian and Nerva was the son of a Jew in Bethlehem; later when Hadrian defeated the Jews, he prohibited them to live in the district of Jerusalem and in Bethlehem; this—he says—followed from Tertullian, *Contra Judaeos*, 224, who remarked that in his time no Jew was left in Bethlehem, for none must live in its boundaries.[48] In the *Apocalypse of Baruch*, 47, 1, Baruch goes from the destroyed capital to Hebron to hear there the revelation of God; as the author wrote shortly after the destruction of Jerusalem, he seems to have known that Hebron was still a Jewish town. In Rimmon lived a Jew of means and several priests;[49] the position of the place is not defined, but as R. Jehudah and R. Simeon b. Gamaliel, both scholars of the school of Jamnia, report the incidents, and Rimmon in Judaea is otherwise mentioned,[50] it is probable that this was meant. At the Dead Sea So'ar was visited by several Levites (p. 78, note 13). Whether the oasis of 'En-gedi, with its balsam plantations administered by representatives of the Roman emperor themselves,[51] had any Jewish inhabitants left, is nowhere reported. But, as only the sicarii had during the revolution driven out the inhabitants (*Wars*, IV, 7, 2) and only the children and women, about 700 were killed, it is very probable that the men returned after the war to 'En-gedi. Eusebius (*Onom., s.v.*) indeed says that the place was in his time a very large Jewish town.

In Jericho R. Gamaliel with other rabbis stayed on some occasion (*Tos. Berakh.*, IV, 15, b. 37 a) which suggests a Jewish community there. As it was not destroyed by the Romans in the revolution and only a part of its population perished by the sword, while the greater part escaped into the mountains opposite Jerusalem (*Wars*, IV, 8, 2), many may have afterwards returned, or Jewish deserters loyal to the Romans may have been settled there under the protection of the garrison and the fortified camp (IV, 9, 1). Interesting evidence proves that Hadid and 'Onô in the north-west of Judaea had Jewish inhabitants after the year 70. R. Joshua and R. Jakim of Hadid[52] gave evidence (before the authorities in Jamnia) about a point of religious law. Hananjah of 'Onô obtained a ruling from R. Akiba when the latter was kept by the Romans in prison, and brought it before rabbis, among whom was R. Josê.[53] Further north, beyond benê-Berak, Kefar-Saba, which may be identical with Antipatris, had Jewish inhabitants. For R. Meir reports (*Tos. Niddah*, VIII, 5): a dead human body was suspected of having been buried under a certain sycamore in Kefer-Saba, but nothing was found.[54] A similar case is reported from beth-Horon, south-east of

Modeim, by R. Joshua, viz. that it was suspected that dead bodies were in a rock.[55] Gofna, a town north of Jerusalem, was conquered and spared by Vespasian (*Wars,* IV, 9, 9; VI, 2, 2), and Titus sent there the nobles who had deserted to him from Jerusalem, to stay there till the war would be over (VI, 2, 2, 3). Whether in addition to the original inhabitants of the town, mostly priests (*Berakh.,* 44a; *jer. Ta'an.,* IV, 69a, 57), any of the nobles of Jerusalem settled there, is not known.

Another place of interest is Adasa, of which R. Jehudah in a Baraitha (*'Erub.,* 60 a) reports: There was a village in Judaea called Hadashah where there were 50 inhabitants, men, women, and children, and being an annex itself, the rabbis measured by it annexes of towns (*'Erub.,* V, 6). It seems hard to doubt that R. Jehudah, as in his many other reports, referred to Judaea of his own times before the bar-Kochba war. Now Adasa is known from 1 Macc. vii. 40, 45, and was, according to Josephus (*Antiq.,* XI, 10, 5), 30 stadia from beth-Horon, probably identical with Adasa near Gofna.[56] But as R. Jehudah says that Hadashah was in Judaea and *jer. 'Erub.,* V, 22d, 54, quotes to it Joshua xv. 37, it must have been the one nearer Jerusalem, and was the small suburb of an unnamed Jewish town before the year 135. In *'Eduj.,* VI, 2, 3, R. Joshua gave evidence with R. Nehunjah b. 'Elinathan of Kefar-haBabli, obviously in Jamnia as is also evident from R. Nehunjah's discussions with R. Eliezer. His native place occurs again in *'Abôth,* IV, 20, as that of R. Josê b. Jehudah, who is identified with José or 'Isi the Babylonian.[57] In a *Baraitha Pesah.,* 113b, he is further identified with Josê of Husal; and as there is a place Husal of the Babylonians in Benjamin mentioned in *Kethub.,* 111a; *Megil.,* 5b, the matter seems quite clear.[58] There was then a village Husal in the territory of Benjamin, a Babylonian colony, about the year 150, which, however, must have existed earlier. In addition to these places where Jewish inhabitants can only be inferred, there are a few in connection with which Jews are expressly mentioned, but their geographical position can only be suggested. R. Jehudah reports[59] that about the levitical purity of some pots in Kefer-Signa a dispute arose between R. Gamaliel and other scholars; and R. Eliezer reports that a fire broke out on the threshing-floor of the same place and a doubt arose about the separation of priestly dues.[60] It was then a Jewish place that had survived the destruction of Jerusalem. R. Josê reports that from Kefar-'Iddim a case concerning more than 60 troughs was brought before R. Gamaliel to define their levitical quality (*Tos. Kelim,* 2, XI, 2). As R. Gamaliel measured the vessels they, had been all brought to Jamnia, the place cannot have been very far from that town; its inhabitants were either priests or trough-makers.[61]

8. A characteristic instance of a town that survived unimpaired the catastrophe of the year 70 is Betthar, the last fortress of bar-Kochba. R. José says in a Baraitha: Betthar continued for 52 years after the destruction of the Temple and then it perished, because it had lighted lamps (of joy) at the destruction.[62] And R. Simeon b. Gamaliel reports: There were in Bethar 500 schools for children, and the smallest of them had not less than 500 children.[63] It had bouleutai (*jer. Ta'an.*, IV, 69a, 26), and a beth-din as Jamnia (*Synh.*, 17b), and was consequently a town of importance. Add to this the full report of Dio Cassius, LXIX, 14, that the Roman general, Julius Severus, sent by Hadrian to Judaea against the Jewish rebels under bar-Kochba, razed fifty of their best fortresses and 985 of their most important villages, and that 580,000 men were killed in the sorties and battles, and the number of those who perished by famine, disease, and fire, could not be defined, so that almost the whole of Judaea became a desert, as it had been predicted before the war. Even granted that Dio grossly exaggerated the feat of the Roman general, it will have to be admitted that Judaea was fairly populated, as many thousands of those who had been driven from their towns and villages by the approach of the Roman armies in the years 66–70, after the restoration of peace gradually returned to their homes or settled in other places of Judaea that had been depopulated. Just as Betthar, there must have been several towns of greater or less importance. For in the report about R. Akiba's execution in the Hadrianic persecutions it is stated in rather obscure terms: within twelve months after this בוליאות in Judaea ceased. These were cities of importance of which there were at some time at least 24.[64] But apart from this, the material collected above about the existing cities and villages inhabited by Jews, conclusively proves that Judaea was still fairly populated after the year 70.

II. ECONOMIC CONDITIONS AND LANDED PROPERTY.

1. From Josephus we have derived the information that in the course of the long war in Judaea between the years 66 and 70, several towns and villages surrendered to the Romans and that the Jewish inhabitants probably retained their property and all their possessions. In some other places loyal Jews were settled, and they must have either received from the Romans or leased fields from Vespasian and Titus.

To many of the nobles who had deserted from Jerusalem into the Roman camp, Titus promised to restore their property after the war. Though the redemption of the promise is nowhere reported, Josephus's case in an instance of it, for his fields near Jerusalem were restored to him, and when they were required for the Roman garrison, Titus gave Josephus other property in the Plain (*Vita,* 76). On the other hand we are told (*Wars,* VII, 6, 6) that Vespasian declared the land of Judaea his private property and disposed of some parts, for instance, by giving to 8,000 veterans fields in Emmaus, near Jerusalem, and by rewarding Josephus. The rest had accordingly to be leased from the emperor, even by the former owners. Before order was restored in this matter, terrible conditions seem to have prevailed in some places of Judaea, as the following incident suggests. One of the wealthiest men of Jerusalem before its destruction,[65] Nakdimon b. Gorjon, most probably perished during the siege of the capital. After the catastrophe his daughter is found by R. Johanan b. Zakkai and his disciples starving and picking grains of barley from horses' dung,[66] and, when questioned by the rabbi, explained that the money of her father and her father-in-law was all gone.[67] Such cases of utter impoverishment may have been numerous, while such as continued on their property may also have been many. For Eusebius, in his short account of the bar-Kochba war (*Hist. Eccl.,* IV, 6), says: Tineius Rufus, the governor of Judaea, availing himself of the madness of the rebelling Jews under bar-Kochba, went out against them, killed indiscriminately thousands of men, women, and children, and, according to the law of war, brought the fields of the Jews into his possession.[68]

2. As to details reflecting actual conditions, Josephus offers none, and it is again the Talmud only that contains some very instructive information. Unfortunately this material is merely incidental and only in very few instances descriptive; in most cases it refers to the time between 80 and 135 in giving illustrative incidents and relating to the observance of the field corner for the poor, the sabbatical year of rest, the priestly dues, and mortgages. When once R. Joshua visited R. Johanan b. Zakkai in berûr-Hajil, the people of the villages brought them figs (see p. 83, n. 40); the farmers were Jews and lived in several villages. When R. Eliezer was put in the ban by the school in Jamnia, the world was smitten, one third on the olives, one third on wheat, and one third on barley (*Bar. B. Mes.,* 59 b). Evidently Jewish landowners suffered either in the close neighborhood of Jamnia or in Lydda, where R. Eliezer lived. R. Akiba remarks (*Tos. Pe'ah,* II, 21) that as to the

field corner to be left to the poor landowners (בעלי בתים) are liberal.[69] R. Josê relates (Kil'aj., VII, 5) how a man was reported to R. Akiba for sowing seeds in his vineyard in the sabbatical year; and R. Akiba himself once saw a man prune his vine in the sabbatical year (jer. Shebi., IV, 35 a, 36). The proselyte Akylas, who is found in the company of R. Gamaliel II, R. Eliezer, and R. Joshua,[70] acquired property in Judaea to export, from Judaea in Pontus, some produce of the Sabbatical year, is quoted as a mistake.[71] In benê-Berak, one sold his father's property and died; his relatives protested that he was a minor, and asked R. Akiba to examine his body, but the rabbi refused to have the grave opened (B. bath., 154 a; Semah., IV, 12). A security once signed a bill after the witnesses; when the debt was claimed from him, R. Ishmael ruled that only his movables were liable (B. bath., X, 8). Joshua, R. Akiba's son, married the daughter of a wealthy landowner and agreed with his wife that she should maintain him and allow him to study; when years of drought came, the husband and the wife divided between them her property (Tos. Kethub., IV, 7; jer., V, 29 d, 25). The son of R. Jehudah the baker gave by deed all his property to his wife who was his cousin; when creditors of the household claimed the property, the rabbis declared the wife's marriage settlement void owing to the gift from the husband, and the property liable for the debt, so that she lost all (B. bath., 132 a). R. Joshua once walked across a field by a trodden path; a Jewish girl reproached him for this, and when he pointed as an excuse to the path, she said: Robbers like you trod it ('Erub., 53 b). Once, walking in the road, R. Gamaliel and R. Joshua, owing to the unevenness of the road, walked beside it in the fields. When they noticed R. Pappos b. Jehudah approaching and walking deep in the mud of the road, R. Gamaliel found fault with this self-exhibition; but R. Joshua explained to him who the man was and how blameless his character.[72] The fields to which Jewish law was applied were Jewish property.[73]

The law concerning priestly dues and tithes was observed in spite of changed conditions of property, and as there were many priests in Judaea, among them several scholars, incidents reported about them will throw light on property. R. Tarfon, a priest who survived the destruction of Jerusalem, is termed a very wealthy men (Nedar., 62 a); he owned land and slaves. Once the unusually red face of his disciple, R. Jehudah, attracted his attention. He accounted for it as follows: Thy slaves last night brought us from the field beets, and we ate of those without salt; had we taken salt, our faces would look even more red (Nedar., 49 b).

R. Tarfon once gave R. Akiba 600 silver centenarii to buy a field, on the income of which they would live; but R. Akiba distributed the money among poor scholars.[74] R. Tarfon received priestly due, Terumah; once an old man met him and asked him why people should speak of him in disparaging terms for his accepting such dues all the year round from anybody, as otherwise all his actions were upright (*Tos. Hag.*, III, 36). R. Tarfon referred to a rule received by him from R. Johanan b. Zakkai on which he had based his acceptance of such dues; but he declared, he would henceforth act more strictly. As we learn of his especially solemn dealing with his priestly dues in the days of R. Gamaliel II,[75] it is most probable that also the incident just quoted occurred in Lydda or Jamnia, and not before the year 70 in Jerusalem. In a year of drought he betrothed himself to several women to enable them to eat of his priestly dues.[76] These reports presuppose several Jewish landowners in Lydda who gave from their produce the prescribed dues[77] to R. Tarfon. Probably one of them was R. Simeon Shezuri, whose untithed produce became once accidentally mixed with a tithed one, and when he asked R. Tarfon what he should do, he advised him to buy produce in the market and to separate from that the required tithe.[77a] R. Simeon had, accordingly, fields of his own; the market was supplied by non-Jews, as the context proves, and the Talmud expressly states. Another priest and scholar was R. Eleazar b. 'Azarjah, a very wealthy man (*Kiddush.*, 49 b), mentioned along with the fabulously rich Eleazar b. Harsom; he who dreams of him, may hope to become rich (*Berakh.*, 57 b). Since he died, the crown of scholars departed, for wealth is their crown (*Sotah*, IX, 15; *jer.* and *b.* end). He gave to R. Josê the Galilean the amount of his wife's marriage settlement to enable him to divorce his wicked wife (*Genes. r.*, 17, 3). No reference is found to R. Eleazar's fields; but as in Rabh's report (*Sabb*, 54 b) the tithe of his herds was 12,000 calves every year, even taking the figure as grossly exaggerated, it presupposes in R. Eleazar's possession either his own land or leased pasture lands of great extent.[78] He dealt in wine and oil all his life (*Tos. 'Abod. z.*, IV, I; *B. bath.*, 91 a); whether it was his own produce or bought from others, is not indicated. As a priest he used to receive the tithe of the produce of a certain garden till R. Akiba stopped it[79]; the owner was a Jew who kept the law about priestly and levitical dues.[80]

3. Several other scholars who had lived before the year 70 in Jerusalem, and now lived with the priests discussed in Judaea, were possessed of landed property. R. Dosa b. Harkinas (p. 78) was once visited by R. Joshua b. Hananjah, R. Eliezer b. 'Azarjah, and R. Akiba

(*Jebam.*, 16 a), and he offered them gilded chairs, and his house had several entrances; but of what his wealth otherwise consisted, is not reported, most probably of fields. R. Eliezer was before the year 70 assisting his father, a wealthy farmer in the country, in his work in the fields[81]; when, already a married man, he became a disciple of R. Johanan b. Zakkai in Jerusalem, and during the siege of Jerusalem he followed his master to Jamnia. He lived in Lydda in a house built in Greek style,[82] consisting of at least a room, an upper room, and a dining-room. He had a slave whom he freed when in the synagogue only nine of the requisite ten Israelites were present (*Gitt.*, 38 b). He had also a female slave (*Berakh;* 16 b; *Semah.*, I, 10), a vineyard (*Tos. Ma'as. sh.*, V, 16; *Rosh haShan.*, 31 b), fields planted with flax, olive-trees, and date-palms, (*Synh.*, 101 a).[83] R. Eliezer's wife, Imma Shalom, sent as a bribe a golden candlestick to a philosopher who boasted incorruptibility, and brought a fictitious civil case concerning her inheritance before him (*Sabb.*, 116 a, b). Her brother, R. Gamaliel II, the president of the beth-din in Jamnia after R. Johanan b. Zakkai, was a wealthy man. The style of living in his house was that of a rich man: his rooms were furnished with sofas for dinner (*Tos. Jom tob*, II, 13); guests dined with him on holy days, among whom were R. Ṣadok and his son Eleazar (*Beṣah*, 22 b, 23 a, and parallels); after dinner smelling spices were burnt, for holy days the scent was prepared beforehand and kept in boxes (*Tos. Jom tob*, II, 14; *jer. Beṣah*, II, 61 c, 57, 59, *b.* 22 b); special kinds of food were prepared in his house, some with Greek names (*Tos.*, II, 16, *jer.*, II, 61 d, 18. *b.*,22 b). As he gave tithes (*Ma'as. sheni*, V, 9), he had landed property[84], he had for his fields several farmers (אריסים *B. mes.*, V, 8) to whom he advanced wheat to be returned in kind and to be reckoned at the lowest price. He engaged laborers to work his fields whom he fed with produce bought from a Jew and not certainly tithed.[85] R. Akiba was a wealthy man, as he himself said to the crowd attending his son's funeral (*Semah.*, VIII) and there are various legends accounting for his great wealth.[86] To satisfy both opinions in the controversy of the schools, he gave two tithes of citrons which he collected, evidently in his own garden (*Tos. Shebi.*, IV, 21; *Rosh haShan.*, 14 a). A colleague of R. Akiba in the school, R. Jesheb'ab distributed all his property among the poor, and R. Gamaliel sent him the message that the rabbis approved of giving away only a fifth of one's possessions.[87] Where he lived and the kind of his property is not defined; but in *Nazir*, 65 a, a Baraitha says: Once R. Jesheb'ab examined a field for human bodies and found two which had been noticed before, and one that had not been noticed, and on this proposed to declare the field a place of tombs, but R. Akiba told him; All your work is useless, for only three known or discovered bodies constitute sufficient evidence. He lived, as other evidence shows, in Jamnia or Lydda, and probably owned land; as he can only have examined Jewish property, we learn of such in Judaea.[88] A friend of R. Eleazar b. 'Azarjah was Boethos b. Zonen in Lydda; in his house we find R. Gamaliel and his colleagues in the night of a Passover discussing laws of the feast (*Tos. Pesaḥ.*, X, 12), and as R. Jehudah reports (*Tos. Pesaḥ.*, I, 31; *jer.*, II, 29 c, 1; *b.* 37 a), he asked in Jamnia of R. Gamaliel and the rabbis a question about unleavened cakes for the same feast. At the advice of R. Eleazar b. 'Azarjah, he had eight books of the prophets bound together (*B. bathra,* 13 b, bottom). Once he brought in a ship dried figs on which heathen wine from a broken barrel came (*'Ab. zar.,* V, 2); the rabbis permitted the figs. He lent money to Jews and took their fields for pledges on the condition that, in case the debt would not be paid on the appointed day, the field should be sold to him; to avoid even an appearance of interest, he consulted R. Eleazar b. 'Azarjah as to the procedure (B. *mes.,* V. 3; *b.* 63a; *Tos.,* IV, 2, *jer.,* V, 10b, 13).[89] This precaution shows that his debtors were Jews, and we learn of another instance of property in Jewish hands.[90]

A few decisions of rabbis as judges in civil and other suits also prove that Jews in Judaea owned not merely landed property, but had also other means. A man who had promised his wife in her marriage settlement 400 zuzs in case of divorce, vowed that he would not live with her. At the complaint of his wife, R. Akiba upheld her claim to the full amount. When the man explained that his father had left to him and his brother altogether only 800 denars, so that he was unable to pay the amount, R. Akiba replied: Even if you should have to sell your hair, you must pay the marriage settlement (*Nedar.,* IX, 5). A man who offended a woman by uncovering her head in the street was fined 400 zuzs by R. Akiba when he, later on, proved that the woman herself, when seeing a jug of smelling oil poured out in front of her house, had uncovered her head in the street, R. Akiba adhered to his decision (B. *kam.,* VIII, 6). In the first case the money seems to have passed after the year 70 from the father to the son, and must have been saved in spite of the Roman conquest. In the second case, the amount of the fine shows the standard of wealth and of private honour. R. Gamaliel fined a man ten gold pieces for covering in anticipation, the blood of a fowl slaughtered by another man and thus depriving him of the merit of a religious act

(*Ḥull.*, 87 a).[91] There were in Judaea wealthy people, as we read that R. Akiba, who lived in Lydda and later in benê-Berak, showed honour to such (*'Erub.*, 86 a). They owned land, produce, cattle, and money; and it is noteworthy that the property could be sold or passed on as a gift or inheritance, showing the right of free disposition and fullest ownership. Josephus's statement that Vespasian declared the land of the province his private property that was to be leased (*Wars*, VII, 6, 6; Schürer, *Geschichte*, I, 640), must have referred to the towns and villages conquered by force, but not to those that had surrendered and were not deprived of their property; or the Romans sold the conquered land to any Jew for a nominal price, holding the new owner responsible for the taxes, as it mattered to them nothing who possessed the land, if only the taxes were paid. For this purpose it was the law that no property could change hands without registration at the competent Roman office, as several passages in the Talmud and Midrash clearly state.[92]

4. There were, naturally, also poor people in Judaea, in the first instance many orphans whose parents had either fallen in the War or were taken captive and sold. For in the upper chamber of R. Tarfon it was resolved, after a discussion between the assembled rabbis, that Psalm cvi. 3b, Blessed is he who practices charity at all times, enjoined the duty to bring up an orphan in one's house.[93] There were other poor who had inherited no property from their fathers, as R. Joshua b. Ḥananjah, who earned a living by making charcoal (*Berakh.*, 28 a) or needles (*jer.*, IV, 7d, 20)[94] and who once reproached the head of the school, R. Gamaliel, that he knew nothing of the troubles of scholars in earning a living[95]; his house was small, but had a gate in which once four scholars sat and studied (*Tos. Berakh.*, IV, 18). Especially in the first years after the War the struggle must have been very hard, as is evident from a statement of R. Ḥaninah, the vice high priest (*ARN*, XX, 36 a): he who takes the torah to heart, is relieved of many fears, the first of them being the fear of hunger. This is explained in full to mean: when one craves for a piece of barley-bread or a drop of vinegar or drink, or would like to put on a shirt of wool or linen, he does not possess it, everything is lacking; we are without a lamp, a knife, and a table.[96] R. Ishmael on one occasion said (*Nedar.*, IX, 10): Jewish girls are handsome, but poverty disfigures them. The Roman governor asked R. Akiba why God did not maintain the poor in Israel if He loved them (*B. bathra*, 10 a); he evidently based his question on actual conditions in Judaea.[97] It is related in a Baraitha[98] that the burial of a dead relative was, owing to the expense, a greater trouble to the family than his death, so that some left

the dead and fled, till R. Gamaliel expressed the wish to be buried in plain linen, when everybody followed his example. Though some scholars ascribe this to R. Gamaliel I, between the years 30 and 50, the name without the distinctive adjective 'the old' and the poverty are in favour of R.Gamaliel II.Poor students belonged to the school of Jamnia (*Sifrê Deut.*, 16; *Horaj.*, 10a, b) who were supported by wealthy scholars such as R. Tarfon (p. 88) and Neḥunjah b. Hakanah (*Megil.*, 28a), and sometimes invited to dinner by their masters (*Derekh' 'ereṣ*, VII). Some support was obtained by collections, great scholars not minding the journey for such a purpose to distant towns (*jer. Horaj.*, III, 48a, 44), and wealthy Jews contributed liberally. Characteristic is the statement of Naḥum of Gimzô that his old age was due to his never having accepted presents (*Meg.*, 28a).

5. It may be safely assumed that the landowning Jews in Judaea worked their fields as strenuously as before the War, as their taxes had increased owing to the revolution and living was under direct Roman rule not easier. Incidentally, we hear of very early work in the field.[99] Whether the wars left the Jew in possession of sufficient working animals, cows, and asses, is not evident from the scanty records. R. Eleazar b. 'Azarjah had very numerous herds, and he probably was no exception. Besides there are in connexion with priestly dues a few references to cows and sheep. The rabbis permitted 'Ela in Jamnia to charge four asses for his examination of a firstborn sheep or goat, and six for a calf, no difference whether it was found to be with or without blemish (*Bekhor.*, IV, 5). R. Ṣadok the priest had a firstborn animal (*Bekhor.*, 36a; *Berakh.*, 27b); R. Gamaliel had one, the lower jaw of which was larger than the upper, and this anomaly was declared a blemish (*Bekhor.*, VI, 9). About the nature of another blemish in the house of Menaḥem, R. Akiba and R. Joḥanan b. Nuri differed (VI, 6; *b.* 40a *Tos.*, IV, 8). A Baraitha in *Synh.*, 33a, reports another case in the same house: R. Tarfon declared a cow without matrix unsuitable for food and gave it to the dogs; when the matter was brought before the teachers in Jamnia, Theodos, the doctor, said that no cow or sow left Alexandria without its matrix being first removed to prevent it from bearing (IV, 4). A cow expired on a holy day, and R. Tarfon brought the question before the school whether the removal of the carcass was permitted, and of priestly due that was defiled (*Beṣah*, III, 5). R. Gamaliel had cattle, for his son Simeon said (*Tos. Sabb.*, XV, 26 *b.* 128b): We used to stimulate the maternal instinct of a clean animal on a holy day. R. Simeon of Timnah slaughtered on a holy day a calf, to appease a troop of soldiers (*Tos.*

Beṣah, II, 6; *b.* 21a). Abba Saul relates (*Tos Ṣabb.,* IX, 21; *Jebam.,* 114a): We used to suck milk from a clean animal on a holy day. It is noteworthy that the wealthy R. Gamaliel had only just as many cows as the working of his fields required; for when the wedding feast of his son was to be prepared, he had to buy some cattle in the market of Emmaus (*Ḥull.,* 91 b, and parallels).[100]

It must not be forgotten that R. Eliezer was asked by his disciples whether sheep or goats may be reared, and that he gave an evasive answer (*Tos. Jebam.,* III, 4), while R. Gamaliel replied to the same question of his disciples in the affirmative.[101] Perhaps the Shammaiite R. Eliezer would not abolish even a temporary prohibition in spite of changed conditions, while R. Gamaliel the Hillelite had no hesitation in doing so. It cannot be accidental that no flocks were mentioned of any rabbi or landowner discussed above; and it is most instructive that in the exhaustive enumeration of goods and possessions in the house of a wealthy farmer in Judaea in the Baraitha in *Sabb.* 127b, herds, but not flocks, are included, fully in accordance with R. Eliezer who is meant there (p. 90, note 83). Professor Krauss[102] tried by every possible argu-. ment to dispute the fact implied by the questions addressed to R. Eliezer and R. Gamaliel and to show that the prohibition against rearing sheep and goats was mere theory; but arguments cannot remove clear reports of facts. Though we may be able to point to instances of sheep reared,[103] we have to consider that R. Gamaliel had permitted it and 'Ela, the examiner of blemishes of firstborn sheep or goats, acted as such in Jamnia. There may have been farmers in Judaea who, even before R. Gamaliel's permission, reared flocks; but that is no proof against the prohibition and its general observance, as we find only herdsmen referred to incidentally with R. Tarfon ('*Erub.,* 45a), but no shepherds.[104] The fact that the prohibition of rearing flocks is put together with that of cutting down fruit-bearing trees, suggests some inner connexion between the two, in so far as the protection of newly planted trees, necessitated by the devastation of the country by the Romans, implied the prohibition of rearing especially goats.[105]

6. The success of the most careful farming depended to a very great extent on rain in proper time. R. Simeon b. Gamaliel, in the name of R. Joshua, said (*Sotah,* IX, 12): Since the day of the destruction of the Temple there has been no day without a curse, and dew has not come down for blessing, and the taste of the produce has been taken away. R. Joshua had known the years immediately preceding the destruction of Jerusalem, and though the bitterness of the fruit may largely have been

due to the bitter mood of the Jews, he must have noticed some change in the produce.[106] R. Eleazar b. Parta, who lived before the year 135, said in a Baraitha (*Ta'an.*, 19b): Since the day of the destruction of the Temple, rains have become scanty in the world; there are years when rains are abundant, others when they are too little, in some they come in time, in others out of season. Samuel the Young, a member of the school in Jamnia, instituted public fasts on two occasions, obviously for rain to come (*Ta'an.*, 25b); in Lydda the authorities, owing to a drought, ordered a fast on the feast of Hanukkah , but R. Eliezer and R. Joshua refused to recognize it.[107] R. Eliezer and R. Akiba instituted public fasts and rain came down (*Ta'an.*, 25b; *jer.*, III, 66c, 76); when once a fast was held in Lydda and rain came down before noon, R. Tarfon allowed the people to go and to eat and to drink and to have a holiday (*Ta'an.*, III, 9). In a year of drought, R. Tarfon betrothed to himself several women to enable them to eat of his priestly due (*Tos. Kethub.*, V, 1; *jer. Jebam.*, IV, 6b, 59); and in such a year Joshua, the son of R. Akiba, made special arrangements with his rich wife (*Tos. Kethub.*, IV, 7; *jer.*, V, 29d, 25).[108] Drought often entailed for many starvation and death; when once R. Eliezer prayed at a public fast meeting for rain, and in spite of several fasts his prayer was not fulfilled, he said to the congregation: Have you prepared graves for yourselves (*Ta'an.*, 25b)? The land was fertile, especially so in the western districts of Judaea. R. Jehudah, by birth a Galilean, who attended the schools in Lydda, Jamnia and benê-Berak, says (*B. bath.*, 122a): A se'ah of land in Judaea is worth five se'ahs in Galilee. And his colleague, R. Josê of Sepphoris, says in a Baraitha (*Kethub.*, 112a): A se'ah of field in Judaea yielded five se'ahs, one of fine flour, one of sifted fine flour, one of bran, one of coarse bran, and one of cibarium.[109] R. Jacob b. Dosithai tells (*Kethub.*, IIIb, bottom) how he once, early in the morning, walked from Lydda to 'Onô to his ankles in honey of figs.[110] The produce of the fields in ordinary years seems to have been sufficient for maintaining the population in spite of the heavy taxes in kind to be considered below.[111] As there were many without land, they had to buy provisions in the market; and we learn that R. Eleazar b. 'Azarjah dealt in wine and oil for many years (*B. bath.*, 91, a; *Tos. 'Ab. zar.*, IV, 1). Of export, we hear only in a discussion between R. Jehudah b. Bethera and another teacher. Boethos b. Zonen brought from outside, by ship, dried figs (*'Ab. zar.*, V, 2), perhaps in a year of drought.

7. A passing reference to the food of the Jews in the period considered may be of some interest. R. Eleazar b. 'Azarjah, in a sentence pre-

served in two forms, prescribes food according to one's means (*Tos. 'Arakh.*, IV, 27): He who owns 10 manahs, may eat every day vegetables boiled in a pot; if he has 20 manahs, he may eat the same vegetables first boiled and then stewed; if he has 50 manahs, he may buy every Friday a pound of meat; if he has 100 manahs, he may have a pound of meat every day. In the parallel (*Hull.*, 84 a) it reads differently: He who has 1 manah, may buy for his pot one pound of vegetables, with 10 manahs a pound of fish for his pot, with 50 manahs a pound of meat, if he has 100 manahs, let a pot (of meat) be put up on the fire for him every day. The difference is not due merely to varying traditions, but, it seems, to different parts of Palestine, which cannot be investigated here. The pupils of R. Tarfon ate of his beets, raw ones, with or without salt (*Nedar.*, 49b), but sometimes also meat with eggs; for R. Jehudah reports (Nedar., VI, 6) that when they—in the *Baraitha Nedar.*, 52 b, he—once vowed not to eat meat, R. Tarfon prohibited them—or him—to eat even eggs boiled with meat. What caused this vow would be interesting, but is not suggested. As was shown above (p. 94), R. Gamaliel had to go to the market in Emmaus to buy cattle for the wedding feast of his son (*Hull.*, 91 b), as eating meat was an essential expression of joy; and R. Josê reports (*Bekhor.*, 40a; *Tos.*, IV, 8) that in the house of a certain Menahem a cow was slaughtered, but no special occasion is mentioned. In R. Gamaliel's house, various dishes with Greek names are incidentally referred to (*Tos. Besah*, II, 16; *jer.* II, 61d, 18) with which pepper was used; but even on a festival a bucketful of lentils was in his house one of the dishes (*Besah* 14b; *Tos.*, I,22), and fish is also mentioned once as brought to R. Gamaliel (*Besah*, III, 2). Akylas the proselyte had a man-cook who once brought a levitical question before the school of R. Gamaliel (*Tos. Kelim*, 3, II, 4), as Akylas kept his food in high levitical purity (*Tos. Hag.*, III, 3). R. Joshua, when on a journey in lodgings, lived on beans (*'Erub.*, 53b), other teachers on vegetables. Wine, as far as incidental remarks allow judgment, was almost as rare as meat. At the wedding feast of his son, R. Akiba offered wine freely to his guests (*Tos. Sabb.*, VII, 9; *b.* 67b; *jer. Berakh.*, VI, 10d, 58), as it was done at every festivity (משתה , *Kiddush.*, 32b, *Sifrê* Deut., 38). In the houses of wealthy people wine may have been more usual (*Berakh.*, VIII, 1 ff., and *jer.*, VI, 10c, 76ff. concerning סעודה), so that R. Gamaliel and his companion drank wine on the way from Akko to Ekdippa (*Erub.*, 64 b, and parallels). Bread was made of wheat; barley as everyday food of a wife was, according to R. Josê, permitted only by R. Ishmael, who lived near Idumaea (*Kethub.*, V, 8); on the festivals, as on Passover, more luxurious cakes were baked, as

R. Akiba made on the Passover for R. Eliezer and R. Joshua a dough with oil and honey (*Pesah.,* 36a). As Joshua, R. Akiba's disciple, was a grit-miller (*'Erub.,* 21b), grits must have been common food.

All the food mentioned was in most cases derived from one's own field and required no outlay of money. Those who were compelled to buy provisions, had first to earn some money. R. Gamaliel engaged Jews as labourers (p. 90), and in addition to their food must have paid them some wages. Of trade, hardly any clear evidence is found, though there must have been grocers and bakers. R. Eleazar b. 'Azarjah dealt in wine and oil (*B. bathra,* 91a; *Tos. 'Ab. zar.,* IV, 1); R. Jehudah was a baker, and bakers' shops are mentioned in *Tos. 'Ahil.,* XVIII, 18; *Jadaj.,* 11, 16, and Joshua a grit-miller (*Erub.,* 21b). Lydda had vendors who sold their goods dear (*B. mes.,* IV, 3), and a synagogue of weavers or metal-workers (*Nazir,* 52a, and parallels). R. Joshi'a gave up his studies and took up business, for which his colleague R. Matthia blamed him (*ARN,* I, 1a), and R. Akiba seems to have been connected with shipping (*Nedar.,* 50a, b). A R. Johanan was sandal-maker (*Sifrê Deut.,* 80; *Midrasch Tannaim,* 58), a Jehudah a perfumer (*Hull.,* 55b, and parallel); Simeon a cotton-dealer (?); R. Ishmael a Torah-writer (*Sotah,* 20a); and Eleazar a writer (*Hull.,* 55b); and in connexion with the deposition of R. Gamaliel, a fuller is mentioned (*jer. Berakh.,* IV, 7d, 23).[112]

8. As almost natural after the terrible catastrophe, the mood of the Jews of Judaea was depressed. Not only immediately after the destruction of the Temple and of the country, when some men, on account of the sanctuary, resolved not to eat meat and not to drink wine, and R. Joshua had to dissuade them (*B. bath.,* 60b; *Tos. Sotah,* XV, 11)[113]; and when the author of the *Apocalypse of Baruch* voiced the despair of some religious leaders and of a section of the population. But also later, when a recognized authority gave expression to the feelings of the people by prescribing for joyful occasions some signs of mourning, the same mood still prevailed; for *Mishnah Sotah,* IX, 14, reports: In the war of Vespasian a decree was issued concerning wreaths of bridegrooms and the drum (*b.* 49b; *jer.,* IX, 24c, 4);[114] and *Tos. Sotah,* XV, 7, says: Since the Synedrion ceased, song ceased in the house of feasting. It is true, we find that the book of Canticles was sung as an ordinary song at feasts, and R. Akiba denounced such songs in the strongest terms[115], but the section of the population that feasted in this way did not seem to share the general feeling in this as in other respects. Other constant and spontaneous reminders of the loss of Jerusalem were suggested by a rabbi, probably R. Joshua: One may whitewash his house and leave merely a

spot not whitewashed in memory of Jerusalem; one may prepare every-thing for a dinner and leave one thing out in memory of Jerusalem; a woman may adorn herself and leave off one ornament in memory of Jerusalem.[116] The strict observance of the 9th of 'Ab, the day of the des-truction of Jerusalem,[117] the mourning for the Temple (*Threni* r., I, 2; IV *Ezra* 9, 38 ff.), the inclusion of a special prayer for the restoration of the holy city in the eighteen benedictions,[118] all show the mood of the people and the endeavor of the rabbis to strengthen the hope of the Jews for the restoration of Jerusalem and the Temple.

9. In conclusion, a few words must be said about the life and the position of women in Judaea between the years 70 and 135. The very strange discussion as to whether one is legally bound to maintain his small children suggests terrible poverty. R. Eliezer declared it a good deed to feed one's little sons and daughters (*Kethub.,* 50a), while R. Eleazar b. 'Azarjah formulated the law in the gathering of the rabbis in Jamnia that little daughters had no claim to maintenance (*Kethub.,* IV, 6).When a man refused to marry his niece,who was ugly, R. Ishmael said that all Jewish girls were bright, but poverty made them ugly (*Nedar.,* IX, 10). All men married, Simeon b. 'Azzai was an exception con-demned by himself and R. Eliezer.[119] As a rule girls married after attain-ing puberty (*Pesaḥ.,* 112 a, b) and later; but we find also a child married to a man, as in the case of R. Ishmael's son (*jer. Jebam.,* XIII, 13 c, 19; *Nidd.,* 52a), and another that came before R. Jehudah b. Baba (*Tos. Je-bam.,* XIII, 5). R. Eliezer married his niece, who was an orphan and lived in his house, when she attained puberty (*ARN,* XVI, 32a; in *jer. Jebam.,* XIII, 13c, 60, before that time). To marry one's niece was commended and practised, and among others 'Abba had R. Gamaliel's, his brother's daughter, for a wife (*Jebam.,* 15a), and he was the only instance reported of having had two wives.[120]

When R. Tarfon's wife died, he asked her sister, at the cemetery, to take charge of his children[121] and betrothed her. Once, when he saw a bridal procession pass by his school, he interrupted his teaching, brought the bride to his house and asked his mother and his wife to bathe, anoint, and adorn the bride, and then he danced before her and took her to her husband (*ARN,* XLI, 67a). R. Ishmael persuaded a man to marry his niece who was poor and whom Ishmael's mother adorned for her wed-ding (*Nedar.,* IX, 10). Those girls had hardly any dowry, but there was the rich wife of R. Akiba's son who was maintained by his wife and stud-ied (*Tos. Kethub.,* IV, 7, and parallel), and R. Eliezer's wife, the sister of R. Gamaliel. In a year of drought R. Tarfon betrothed to himself several women to enable them to eat of his priestly due (*Tos. Kethub.*, V, 1; *jer. Jebam.*, IV, 6b, 59). The husband had to write to his wife a marriage settlement promising her at least 200 zuzs in case of divorce or his death, and that document protected her against whims of her husband (*Nedar.*, IX, 5) and made it impossible for a poor man to get rid of a tyrannical wife (*Genes. r.*, 17, 3). The son of R. Jehudah the baker, who had married his cousin, gave all property to her; but when his creditors claimed their money, she had to pay the debts and even her marriage settlement was lost (*B. bath.*, 132a).[122] A married woman had to have her head covered in the street, and it was a serious offense to uncover it; R. Akiba fined a man heavily for it (*B. kam.*, VIII, 6). In moonlit evenings women met and while spinning, discussed the latest events in the families of the place (Gitt. 89a); if they talk ugly things about a married woman, R. Akiba says, she must be divorced. And R. Joshua says (*Sotah*, VI, 1) that if a married woman was alone with another man and women spinning in the moonlight talk about it, she must be divorced (see *Sotah*, 6b, bottom); R. Johanan b. Nuri objected most strongly to such evidence. Otherwise we find the wives and mothers of teachers in conversation with other rabbis, as Imma Shalom, the wife of R. Eliezer (*Nedar.*, 20b) and the mother of R. Ishmael and of R. Tarfon.[123] Women came to the schools with all kinds of religious questions,[124] and R. Ishmael and R. Eliezer asked their mother and wife respectively to examine girls as to their signs of puberty (*Tos. Nidd.*, VI, 8). R. Eliezer was once asked by a learned woman about a contradiction in the Bible, and his answer was: A woman's wisdom is in the distaff; in the parallel he replied: Words of the Torah should be burnt and not given to women.[125] He consistently prohibited teaching a girl Torah (*Sotah*, II, 4). R. Joshua's opinion was not favorable to women:[127] A woman is more satisfied with a kabh of food if intercourse is with it than with nine kabhs of food and rare intercourse: a woman separating from intercourse is one of the destroyers of the world.[127] Whenever Pappos b. Jehudah left his house, he locked his wife in that she should not speak to anybody; but this is stated to have been an exception and wrong.[128] In the home the wife had to attend to the house and to its requirements, she had to look after her children (*jer. Jebam.*, IV, 6b, 37), and, when free, she spun (*Kethub.*, V, 5); and we learn that she sold wool to dealers (*B. kam.*, X, 9; *b.* 119a). Of children we hear little, only of the deaths of several young men, the son of R. Johanan b. Zakkai, when already a scholar (*ARN*, XIV, 29b), of R. Ishmael's several sons (*Moëd k.*, 28b), and of R. Akiba's son (*Semah.*, VIII;

Moëd k.. 21b).[129] On the eve of Passover children were entertained with sweets by R. Tarfon or R. Akiba (*jer. Pesaḥ.,* X, 37b, 75; *b.* 109a). An anonymous Baraitha in *Jebam.,* 62b, allows an insight into the principles practised by the teachers in their homes: To him who loves his wife as himself, and who honours her more than himself and guides his sons and his daughters in the straight way and who makes them marry immediately after puberty, applies Job v. 24.

III. THE POLITICAL CONDITIONS IN JUDAEA AND THE ROMANS.

1. Though a great part of Judaea was saved in the catastrophe of the year 70, it did not escape an evil attending great wars; outlaws and robbers increased in number and enhanced the difficulties of maintainance and of recovery. Their place of activity was not only Galilee, where a son of R. Ḥaninah b. Teradjon of Sikhnin joined robbers and was ultimately killed by them as traitor (*Semaḥ.,* XII, *Threni r.,* 3, 16), but Judaea suffered even more from them, because there war followed war. When staying in Babylonia, in the lifetime of R. Gamaliel, on matters of intercalation, R. Akiba met in Neharde'a Nehemia of beth-Deli; they discussed the question of finding witnesses to testify to a man's death, and Nehemia referred R. Akiba to the fact that Judaea was infested with raiding bands (*Jebam.,* XVI, 7). In the neighborhood of Lydda R. Tarfon was once in danger of his life when, according to Shammaiite rule, he lay down in the road to read a prayer (*Berakh.,* I, 3). A man told R. Tarfon how he and a companion were on the way pursued by a raiding band; his friend broke a branch from an olive-tree to use it as a weapon and thereby invited the raiders to return, and was taken ill and died.[130] R. Jehudah relates[131] how a robber before his execution in Mazaga (Caesarea) in Cappadocia confessed to the murder of Simeon b. Kohen on entering Lydda; on this evidence Simeon's wife was allowed to remarry. The informant's person shows that the case was discussed in Lydda or in Jamnia; as R. Akiba once stayed in Mazaga,[132] perhaps he brought the confession to Judaea before the schools. R. Joshua prescribed a short prayer to be said in a place of danger (*Berakh.,* IV, 4) though he prayed therein for help for the remnant of the nation בכל פרשת העבור, the parallel (*Berakh.,* 29b; *Tos.,* III, 7) defines the danger as a troop of wild beasts and of robbers.[133] Some seem to have been Jews, as those who met R. Akiba's disciples on their way to Ekdippa (*'Ab. zar.,* 25b). It is true, most of these instances of robbery and robbers in the Roman province of Judaea could belong to one special period of unrest, the war of Quietus in the year 116, when some revolutionary movement and persecutions on the part of the Romans again disturbed the country.[134]

2. The Roman military power in the newly subdued province must have, since the year 70, been distributed all over the country (see *Wars,* VII, 6, 1), and we should expect, could, if it wanted, have reached robbers near the important town of Lydda without difficulty. Though there is no evidence for the places of garrisons, numerous or small, Lydda was certainly one of them.[135] R. Johanan b. Zakkai had conversations with a Roman official called in *jer. Synh.,* I, 19c, 16, Antoninus hegemon; I, 19d, 3, Antigonos hegemon; I, 19b, 18, Angatos hegemon; *Num. r.,* 4, 9, Hongatos; *Bekhor.,* 5a, Kontrakos the ruler;[136] in *Sifrê Deut.,* 351, Agnito shegemon, who asked R. Gamaliel a question. Hegemon does not necessarily denote the governor of Judaea; he may have been the commander of the garrison in Jamnia, and this all the more as none of the few governors known suits the name, nor any Greek or Roman name has so far been found to cover the form preserved in the Hebrew sources.[137] Jamnia was to the Roman administration of special importance on account of its imperial stores of produce. For in *Tos. Damm.,* I, 13, we read: R. Josê says: The rule mentioned applies to private stores only, but in the stores of the emperors we go as to the origin of the corn by the majority of it. R. Jehudah says: This applies to stores of Jews and non-Jews, but in stores of Jews and Samaritans we go by the majority of the produce. The rabbis then said to R. Josê: As you have told us concerning the stores of Jamnia before the war that the corn there was not certainly tithed, and most of the people who delivered there corn were Samaritans, we see that in the stores in Palestine into which corn is brought from abroad, as the stores of Regeb, all goes by the measure of the corn. R. Joshua b. Kaposai said that from the rules concerning the stores in Jamnia he derived a halachic lesson. Into those stores the taxes were delivered prescribed to be in kind, as *Tos. Damm.,* VI, 3, 4, clearly states: He who rents a field from a Samaritan, gives him the rent in kind after separating the tithes, then he weighs into the stores, he weighs to the centurion and then gives it to him. A Jew must not say to a non-Jew or a Samaritan or some one not trustworthy in tithing: Take 200 zuzs and weigh for me into the stores; but he should tell him: Free me from the stores.[138] The stores in Jamnia continued for a long time and existed still about the year 200. When once on the road, Rabbi and R. Josê b. R. Jehudah saw a non-Jew coming towards them; when he asked them who they were, what their occupation was, and where they were going, they replied: We are Jews and business men, and are going to buy wheat from the stores of Jamnia.[139] Here, then, produce could be bought by anybody. It need hardly be pointed out that such stores were supervised by officers, as the centurion mentioned and other officials, and guarded by soldiers; the Kontarikos who discussed a question with R. Johanan

b. Zakkai could have been a centurion of the stores.[140] Ben-Dama told
his uncle R. Ishmael that in a dream both his jaws fell off, and R. Ishmael interpreted it to mean: Two Roman soldiers devised evil against
you, but died (Berakh., 56b). Neither the place, nor the soldiers, nor the
kind of device are defined, and it may be, that in order to confiscate
his property, they wanted to accuse him of some invented crime,[141] as
happened to the nephews of R. Johanan b. Zakkai in B. bathra, 10a.[142]
Jerusalem was a Roman camp, with the greater part of the Tenth Legion
and all its usual following stationed there, and similarly other important
places must have had garrisons.

3. The administrative military centres seem to have had Roman
courts of justice. For R. Tarfon[143] says in Gitt., 88b: Wherever you find
agoras of non-Jews, even if their judgments are the same as of the Jews,
you must not apply to them. Also R. Eleazar b. 'Azarjah in Mekhiltha
on 21, 1, takes a stand against applying to these courts, and R. Akiba
refers to deeds made at non-Jewish offices (Gitt., 11a, Tos., 1, 4).[144] R.
Johanan b. Zakkai refers to human judges who can be appeased by gifts
(Berakh., 28 b). This seems to point to his experience with Roman
judges in Judaea.[145] To such, as R. Tarfon's strong warning shows, Jews
were inclined to apply, probably because the Roman officials suggested
it to them and such courts were everywhere near at hand.[146] Not merely
the wealthy Jews felt attracted by them, but also the poor who seem to
have received support from the Romans. For in an interpretation of
Prov. xiv. 34: The lovingkindness of the nations is sin, asked by R. Johanan b. Zakkai of his disciples, R. Eliezer says: All kindness done by non-
Jews is sin to them, for they do such only to boast. R. Joshua said: They
do such only to prolong their rule. The latter explanation clearly shows
that the Romans were referred to, whom also the interpretation of R.
Eleazar of Modeim fits, that they practise charity only to abuse us.[147]
Both rabbis presuppose that the Romans support Jews by alms.[148] In
this way and by persuasion the representatives of the Roman government and other non-Jews tried to win over the Jews of Judaea. For R.
Akiba, in a dialogue between Israel and the nations, makes the latter
say: Why do you die for your God, and are killed for Him? You are
bright and valiant; come and mix with us.[149]

The emperor owned property in Judaea; not only 800 veterans received land in Emmaus near Jerusalem (Wars, VII, 6, 6), but also other
property must have been in Roman hands. Apart from the agadic, but
certainly not groundless reference to Hadrian's vineyard of 18 by 18
miles (jer. Ta'an., IV, 69a, 18) which was manured by the blood of the
slain of Betthar, a very instructive address of R. Johanan b. Zakkai

(*Mekhil.*, 19, 1, p. 61b) refers to imperial vineyards. He said to some
Jews, as representing the whole nation: You would not pay the tax of
one beka' per head to God, now you pay 15 shekels to the government of
your enemies; you would not repair the roads and the markets for the
pilgrims, now you repair את הבורגסין ואת הבורגמין for those who go up
to the vineyards of emperors.[150] As R. Joḥanan spoke to all the Palestinian Jews, there must have been in Judaea several such vineyards. Schil-
ler[151] states that soldiers stationed in a Roman province were in peace
engaged in draining work and in planting vineyards, the latter especially
to facilitate the necessary supply of wine for the soldiers. In connexion
with such imperial plantations the Jews in Judaea had probably to do
compulsory work of various kinds; as R. Joḥanan's contrast of past and
present shows, in the first instance they had to keep up the roads. There
is express evidence that the balsam plantations of 'En-gedi were imperial
property and were farmed by the fiscus,[152] and the balsam was sold by
the fiscus.[153] The same applied to Jericho, as Pliny in his note on the bal-
sam-bush says (XII, 25, 112): Servit nunc haec ac tributa pendit cum
sua gente; presupposing that both balsam gardens had the same political
position, as in fact he says (113): Seritque nunc eum fiscus.[154]

4. The Roman taxes weighed heavily upon all the Jews. For even
those to whom, as to Josephus, their property was returned by Titus and
Vespasian, had to pay taxes, and Josephus himself reports (*Vita*, 76)
that the emperor Domitian freed him from the taxes of his property in
Palestine, which was the greatest distinction for any one.[155] The tax to be
paid in addition to the poll-tax varied in various provinces,[156] a fifth or
a seventh of the produce, in kind or in money, according to the value of
the field. What tax R. Joḥanan b. Zakkai meant by 15 shekels, the passage quoted does not suggest. Nor does the list of Jewish taxes in a papyrus from Arsinoë of the fifth year of Vespasian[157] constitute a parallel
to it. Though the Jews are there distinguished from the bulk of the native
population, and already children pay the Jewish tax by head and year, 8
drachmae and 2 oboloi, and in addition to it 1 drachma ἀπαρχῆς, and
again poll-tax, altogether about 40 drachmae, yet no relation of those
taxes is visible to the Judaean didrachma.[158] The fixed amount mentioned by R. Joḥanan shows that the tax was not varying according to
the produce of a field, but a fixed contribution, perhaps a minimum paid
on leasing one's own field from the Roman governor .The tax in kind to
be paid into the Roman corn stores to the centurion (p.101),was probably the income-tax or the annona. The forced labour mentioned by R.
Joḥanan at בורגמין seems to have concerned fields, for the nearest word,
of which it is evidently a corruption, בורגנין is found in connexion with

fields, though only in statements after the year 135.[159] In addition to those, a tax of food, bread, drink, and clothes was demanded, called cellaria,[160] which, according to R. Haninah's, the vice high priest's description (p. 92), was felt very heavily owing to the great poverty after the War. R. Gamaliel gives further information about Roman impositions (*ARN,* XXVIII, 43a): By four things the government consumes (property), by customs, baths, theatres, and annonae.[161] But very little is known about duties in Judaea in our period, except the Baraitha in *B. kam.,* 113a: One must not put on garments of mixed stuffs, not even over ten other garments, in order to defraud duty; R. Akiba, opposing the view, says: One must not defraud duty; R. Simeon, in R. Akiba's name, says: one may defraud duty.[162] But even this is doubtful; none of the other passages about custom, *Semah.,* 11, 9; *Nedar.,* III, 4; *Tos.,* II, 2, can with probability be referred to Judaea before the year 135. About Roman public baths, nothing is preserved in Jewish sources, though it is probable that for the Roman garrisons and officials such were built; R. Eleazar b. 'Arakh settled in Emmaus on account of its good water and its baths (p. 83 ff.). Even less is known about theatres in Judaea, as the only reference in R. Nehuniah b. Hakanah's sentence in *ier. Berakh.,* IV, 7d, 39, is not to be found in the parallel Baraitha in *Berakh.,* 28b (p. 88, note 69). And it is not probable that the Romans built in Judaea theatres, as no halachic or agadic reference deals with such. Nor is there any trace of any form of idols and idolatry which the rabbis would have certainly discussed for the guidance of the school and the people.[163] Jerusalem and Emmaus, important military stations, must naturally have had some Roman temple, just as the maritime cities inhabited by non-Jews.[164] Akko had a bath of Aphrodité (*Ab. z.,* III, 4), and Caesarea heathen sacrifices (*Hull.,* 39b; *Tos.,* II, 13). R. Akiba says (*Synh.,* 65b) that as a heathen obtains by fasting the spirit of his god, how much more should a Jew by fasting obtain the spirit of God; but our sins prevent it. And when Zonen asks R. Akiba his opinion about healings by sleeping in a heathen temple,[165] the master gives an explanation of such cures; in both cases he presupposes the existence of heathen worship in his neighbourhood. Either in Jamnia, where Roman officials resided, or more probably in Caesarea or Askalon, the seats of various heathen worships, R. Akiba and Zonen could have observed those rites. Askalon had a market which the rabbis used to frequent (*Tos. 'Ahil.,* XVIII, 18), and was a city which R. Gamaliel visited with Akylas (*Tos. Mikw.,* VI, 3),[166] and where R. Joshua was on a political mission (*Sabb.,* 127 b; 2 *ARN,* XIX, 21a), and where Asklepios was worshipped (Schürer, II, 24).

5. A few words have to be added about the presence of non-Jews in Judaea. The land having been declared the private property of Vespasian, and a million of its inhabitants having fallen or been sold in the War, it would seem the most natural thing that non-Jews, Romans, and non-Jewish Palestinians, flocked in great numbers into the country and leased property. But no information to that effect has come down, except a reference to property in the possession of a matrona who gave Hyrkanos, R. Eliezer's son, yearly 300 kors, tithe from her produce.[167] She was probably the wife or widow of a wealthy Roman or Syrian in the neighbourhood of Lydda, as we find a matrona in Askalon (*Sabb.*, 127b, above). R. Johanan b. Zakkai was asked by a non-Jew the difference between Jewish and non-Jewish festivals (*Deut. r.*, 7, 7); and as he enumerates Kalendae, Saturnalia, and Kratesis, he is a Roman official, provided the enumeration is no imitation of R. Meir's in *'Abodah z.*, I, 2. There was a non-Jewish laundry to which R. Gamaliel of Jamnia gave his linen to wash, as reported by R. Eleazar b. R. Sadok.[168] R. Johanan b. Nuri refers to a religious question raised in Jamnia about a hen, and his colleagues remind him that several non-Jews in Jamnia prepared hens for food (*Nidd.*, 50b). An incestuous heathen woman came to R. Eliezer and R. Joshua to be admitted into Judaism (*Kohel. r.*, 1, 8). A wealthy woman, Veluria, who owned slaves, became a proselyte;[169] she lived in Jamnia or Lydda, where she asked R. Gamaliel about a contradiction in the Bible (*Rosh haShan.*, 17b, bottom). R. Josê, the priest, former disciple of R. Johanan b. Zakkai, who was with R. Gamaliel when that question was asked, was so strict in his observance of the Sabbath that, to avoid a profanation of it, he did not allow any letter of his to be found in the hands of a non-Jew (*Sabb.*, 19a). Where they lived is not indicated. A non-Jew brought fish to R. Gamaliel on a Jewish holy day which he would not accept (*Beṣah*, III, 2). But all these references prove nothing as to an influx of non-Jews into Judaea after the War. The long preparations of the Jews for the great rising under bar-Kochba unnoticed by non-Jews, confirm the impression that beside the few and scattered officials of the Roman government very few non-Jews lived among the Jewish population in Judaea.

6. The main results of these lengthy investigations into the economic conditions of Judaea from the destruction of Jerusalem by Titus in the year 70 to the bar-Kochba war in the year 133 are the following. In the long war from 66 to 70 the Romans destroyed, besides Jerusalem, many towns, forts, and villages, and depopulated many other places.

But as the resistance of the country had not been sufficiently organized by the leaders of the revolution, many important places surrendered to the Romans and were spared. From Josephus and the Talmudic literature the names of several of those can be traced. Though a million Jews perished in Jerusalem, over forty thousand of its citizens went over to the Romans during the siege, and having been spared constituted, with the Jews spared in the country, the population of Judaea after the catastrophe. Among them were many priests of high standing, and nobles and wealthy land-owners, some with their wives and children, who, as a reward for their surrender, received their former property from Titus and Vespasian. Others bought or leased land, often their own, from the emperor who had declared the whole of Judaea his private property, so that a considerable portion of the country was farmed in the usual way. Among the survivors were several wealthy rabbis who, their property having been restored, were landowners and supported their own schools. The laws concerning the priestly dues and the sabbatical year were mostly observed, and the poor without land and money were supported, especially in years of drought. The representatives of the Roman administration in Judaea interfered little with the Jews; only the various taxes were heavy and retarded the recovery of the country and its population. Still, it progressed so rapidly that in two generations a hundred thousand Jews could again rise in several hundred places of Judaea against the Roman rule. The best-known towns were Lydda and Jamnia; they had received from Vespasian new inhabitants from other Judaean places which had surrendered to the Romans. Jamnia had Roman corn stores for receiving taxes delivered in kind, and it was the seat of the highest religious body, the beth-din. Lydda had many wealthy inhabitants, among them scholars at the head of schools for adults. Both towns are often referred to in the Talmud, and the material preserved affords some insight into the life of Jewish places. Around them were several Jewish towns and villages of greater and smaller importance. The discussion of many details of private and public life, of men and women, of property and farming, of schools and scholars, of goods and trade, of towns and villages, and of Roman rule and violence, affords additional information about the conditions in Judaea and the life of all sections of its population from the year 70 to 135.

THE STRUGGLE BETWEEN SECULAR AND RELIGIOUS FORCES FOR LEADERSHIP

S. Zeitlin

I
THE SECOND COMMONWEALTH

When King Cyrus of Persia issued his decree in the year 538 B. C. E. permitting the Jews to return to their homeland, thousands of Jews left Babylonia to return to Judea.

Two leaders directed the life of the early period of the new settlement: Zerubbabel, the grandson of Jehoiachin, the King of Judea; and Joshua, the grandson of Seraiah, the High Priest who was killed by the Babylonians at the time of the destruction of the Temple.[1]

The Jews were divided into two factions. Those who desired to organize the new community under the leadership of a civil authority wanted Zerubbabel for their leader, as he was a scion of the royal family, a descendant of King David. Those who were of the opinion that the new community should be organized on a religious basis maintained that Joshua, who came of a priestly family, should assume leadership. The group which supported Joshua triumphed; Zerubbabel disappeared as a political factor from Judea, and Joshua became not only the High Priest in the rebuilt Temple but the sole leader in the new community.[2]

One of the chief reasons for the victory of the religious party was the feeling that if the new Jewish community should be established under Zerubbabel, of the Davidic family, the Persian government would suspect the Jews of planning to set up an independent political state and would lay obstacles in the way of the development of the new community.[3]

It is also possible that many Jews were of the opinion that the calamities following the destruction of the Temple were due entirely to the policies of their kings; therefore they did not want any descendant of this royal family as leader.[4] Thus the new Jewish community, after the return from Babylonia, was established under the authority of the priests. In the year 458 B. C. E. the king, Artaxerxes, granted permission to Ezra, a descendant of Zadok, the first High Priest in the Temple built by Solomon, to assume the authority over the Jews there. The King

vested in Ezra the power to appoint judges, who were to instruct the
people and give them the right to punish by death, by confiscation of
goods or by imprisonment those who did not follow the laws of God
and of the King.[5] This authority was conferred by the subsequent kings
of Persia upon the High Priests. Thus, the new Jewish settlement was
established as a theocracy, since the jurisdiction was vested wholly in
the High Priests, who were the sole authorities over the Jewish people.

The first reaction against the sole authority of the High Priests came
after the successful revolt of the Hasmoneans against the Syrians. The
Hasmoneans revolted not only against the Syrians but also against the
High Priest Menelaus, who obtained the high priesthood from the Syrian
king, Antiochus.[6] By the success of the Hasmoneans over the Syrians a
Jewish state was established. Simon, the son of Mattathias the priest,
the brother of Judas Maccabeus, was elected High Priest and Ethnarch.
By the election of Simon to high priesthood and to the leadership of the
people, a radical step was taken in Jewish life. The high priesthood had
been hereditary and confined to the family of Zadok for many centuries,
throughout the period of the First Temple and into the period of the
Second Temple, up to the time of the Hasmonean revolt. Simon, however, was not of the family of Zadok, and thus the high priesthood and
the leadership of the Jews were given by the Great Synagogue to someone outside of the hereditary line. The high priesthood was given to
Simon until a "true Prophet should appear in Israel."[7]

The successful Hasmonean war, which brought political independence to the Jews, wrought a profound effect upon the entire life of
the Jews, both in its social and religious phases, since the victory over
the Syrians was largely due to the support of the masses who constituted
the rank and file of the Hasmonean forces. It was through this aid that
the Hasmoneans won their victory over the Syrians and established an
independent state. Therefore the masses could not be ignored in the
management of the new state.[8]

A graphic picture of Jewish life of the pre-Hasmonean period is
given by Ben Sira. He tells us that during his time the masses—artisans,
farmers, laborers—without whom a city could not exist, nevertheless
were excluded from the assemblies. "On the seat of the judges they do
not sit, and law and judgment they understand not."[9] He also tells us
that instruction in Jewish law was confined to the priests.[10] The reason
for this was that the Jewish state had been a theocracy. Entire authority
over the Jews in religious and political matters had been vested in the
Pontiff, the High Priest, who had sole power to appoint judges and in-

structors to regulate Jewish life. The High Priests of the pre-Hasmonean period were Sadducees. The common people had not participated in affairs of state. Now, after the establishment of a Commonwealth under the Hasmoneans, the rights of the rulers were curtailed.[11] Although the kings of the Hasmonean dynasty, by virtue of being a priestly family, were High Priests, they did not, however, guide the religious life of the people. A Sanhedrin was instituted in place of the aristocratic Gerousia.[12] While it is true that during the early period of the Sanhedrin the leaders were still priests,[13] in later days the leadership of the Sanhedrin was taken over by non-priests, Israelites.[14] Thus, for the first time, in the period of the Second Temple, the priests were stripped of religious authority, which was taken over by scholars who were not necessarily of priestly families.

By the successful revolt of Herod, when the last king of the Hasmoneans was killed, the government of Judea, with the assistance of the Romans, was usurped by him. Herod was not of priestly family and consequently could not assume the function of High Priest. Therefore a member of the priestly family was appointed High Priest. Thus, the three authorities which in the time of the Restoration were vested in one person—the High Priest—were now divided among the King, the High Priest and the Sanhedrin. So, in the Herodean period the political power over the Jewish State was held by the King; the authority over the Temple was in the hands of the High Priest (although he was appointed by the King; nevertheless, while he was in office the High Priest was the sole authority in the Temple); but the religious life of the Jews was controlled by the Sanhedrin. The Herodean family had power only over Judea, but not over the millions of Jews who lived in the Diaspora and particularly not over the Jews of Babylonia, which did not belong to the Roman Empire. The authority of the High Priest did not extend beyond the limits of the Temple. The Sanhedrin, however, had religious authority not only over Judea but over the entire Jewry all over the world.[15]

At the time of the Procurators, Judea lost its independence and became a province of Rome. The High Priest was either appointed by the Procurator or had to obtain his good will in order to become High Priest. The religious life of the Jews continued to be in the hands of the Sanhedrin. The office of *Nasi*—president of this body—now became hereditary in the family of Hillel. The family according to tradition descended from the royal family of David.[16] This tradition in later days became established as an historical fact.

The High Priest, by virtue of being the head of the Temple, which was the center of the entire Jewish life, exercised great influence over the people. He represented them before the Roman government. He was responsible for maintaining the peace of Judea. Hence he was actually the leader of the Jewish people.[17]

There always had been dissension between the scholars and the High Priests. The High Priests usually were not liked by the scholars and many High Priests were often despised by the common people.[18]

During the revolt of the year 65 C. E., after the early successes won by the Jews against the Romans, the High Priest Ananus was the head of the provisional government after the defeat of the Roman General, Cestius. Second in the leadership of the provisional government was Simon, a son of Gamaliel,[19] the president of the Sanhedrin. Thus the last government which the Jews established was headed by both the priesthood and the Sanhedrin.

II
AFTER THE DESTRUCTION OF THE TEMPLE

PALESTINE

After the destruction of the Second Temple in the year 70 C. E., the Jews were not only deprived of their independence as a state, but lost their Temple. With the burning of the Temple the position of the High Priest was gone. The only remaining authority in the religious life of the Jews was the Sanhedrin. This body remained the sole representative of the Jews of Judea before the Roman authorities. The president of the Sanhedrin, as well as its members, had to travel to Rome either to plead for the Jewish cause or for other political reasons.[20]

It is interesting to note that the first Sanhedrin which was established at Jabneh, after the destruction of the Second Temple, had a priest as its president,[21] Rabban Johanan ben Zakkai. Various reasons are suggested as to why Rabban Gamaliel, the son of Simon, who was the *Nasi* of the last Sanhedrin before the destruction of the Temple, was not elected *Nasi*. Some believe that Gamaliel was too young at the time to be given such an important office. This view is based on a passage in the Talmud wherein it is stated that among the favors asked by Rabban Johanan ben Zakkai of the Emperor Vespasian was one that he should not harm Gamaliel.[22] This episode must be classed as legendary.[23] In all probability the reason why Gamaliel was not elected was that he was *persona non grata* to the Roman authorities because his father had participated in the provisional government which was established during the beginning of the revolt against Rome. However, I believe that the election of Rabban Johanan ben Zakkai was influenced by the fact that he was a priest. Many of the old ruling authorities desired that the head of this body should be not only a scholar but also a priest, since the Sanhedrin, which was the only institution left after the destruction of the Temple, controlled the religious life of the Jews and represented them before the Roman government.[24] After the death of Rabban Johanan ben Zakkai, however, Rabban Gamaliel, who claimed descendancy from the family of David, was elected *Nasi*.

From time to time there were conflicts between the members of the Sanhedrin and Gamaliel as to who had greater authority—he, as *Nasi*, or the members of this body. Gamaliel had once been removed from the presidency. According to the Talmud the reason for his removal was because of difference of opinion on the Halakah—the members of the Sanhedrin thought he was arrogating too much power to himself in deciding the law.[25] A new president was elected, Eleazar the son of Azariah, who was of priestly family.

Was it only a coincidence that the new president, Eleazar, was of priestly family, or was it that the group which had always wanted the head of the Sanhedrin to be a priest had gained power enough to elect a priest as president? The Talmud merely says that they appointed as *Nasi* Eleazar the son of Azariah, a descendant of Ezra,[26] the priest who at the time of the Restoration was the head of the Jewish community.

After the destruction of the Temple, the priesthood as a potential power was not yet destroyed, since the Jews of Judea had hope for a new revolt against the Romans and looked forward to the rebuilding of the Temple.[27] The immediate cause for the removal of Gamaliel may have been due to differences of opinion between him and his colleagues. However, for the appointment of Eleazar we must look deeper. It seems that the priesthood was still struggling for leadership. The influence of the priesthood as a religious and political factor in Jewish history disappeared only after the collapse of the revolt of Bar Kokba, when the Jews gave up hope for the immediate rebuilding of the Temple.

After a short period of time, however, Rabban Gamaliel was reinstated as *Nasi* and Eleazar ben Azariah was appointed *Ab Bet Din*.[28] Gamaliel in his epistles to the Jews of the Diaspora addressed himself both in his own name and in the name of his colleagues.[29] This would indicate that he was not the sole authority. According to the Talmud, the phrase "in the name of his colleagues" was used by Gamaliel after his re-instatement.[30] Another source tells us that on one occasion when Gamaliel was delayed in his return from visiting with the Governor of Syria, the members of the Sanhedrin, finding it necessary to inter-calate another month into the year, did so on the condition that Rabban Gamaliel concur in their action.[31] From this we may conclude that the entire authority was vested in the *Nasi*. However, this event may have occurred before Gamaliel was removed from his office as *Nasi*.

The *Nasi* had the title of Rabban or master. The members of the Sanhedrin were called *zekenim* and each one had the title of Rabbi, my master. This latter title was given only to those scholars who had authorizations from the Sanhedrin. Those who did not receive the authorization, although they may have been great scholars, were not called Rabbi, but were addressed by their proper names.[32] They could not participate in the session of the Sanhedrin when the question of the intercalation of the year was under discussion.[32a]

In the year 140 C. E., after the Jews had recovered from the catastrophe which had befallen them in the Hadrianic period, the Sanhedrin assembled again in the city of Usha. The *Nasi* of the San-hedrin was Simon the son of Gamaliel. He, like his father, had difficulties with his colleagues.[33] It seems, however, that his differences were rather personal. In his time the power of the *Nasi* became more extensive. In his epistles to the Jews of the Diaspora he does not use the phrase, as his father did, "in my name and in the name of my colleagues," but solely "in my name."[34] This shows that his authority was formally established.

After the death of Simon his son Judah became *Nasi*. Judah was the first to be called by the name *Nasi,* because he was recognized by the Roman authorities as the Patriarch of the Jews. Therefore he bore the title *Nasi,* patriarch, president. His predecessors had been president only of the Sanhedrin and had been appointed by his col-leagues, the members of the Sanhedrin. In some cases prior to Judah the members had the power to remove the *Nasi,* as in the case of Gamaliel II, his grandfather, whereas Judah had his authority from the government, and his colleagues could not remove him, while he, on the other hand, had the sole authority to appoint members to the Sanhedrin.[35] His descendants continued to have sole power to appoint scholars to the Sanhedrin.[35a]

Beginning with Judah, the Patriarch, who became known in talmudic literature by the name Rabbi, the term *Semikah*—ordination—disappears from usage in the Palestinian Talmud. We find the term מנוי "appointment" instead of סמיכה "authorization." This is due to the fact that up to the time of Judah the members of the Sanhedrin had authorized their disciples to decide the law.[36] However, beginning with the time of Judah only the Patriarch had the authority to do so and he appointed judges.[37] Therefore the term מנוי replaces the term *Semikah*, authorization. The Patriarchs appointed judges for the Jews not only of Palestine but for Jews throughout the Roman Empire.[38] These appointments were made for a limited time, as in the case of Hiyya, the son of Abba, to whom the Patriarch gave authorization until his return to Palestine.[39]

It was charged that some judges were appointed not because of their great scholarship but because they paid the Patriarch for their office.[40] The Patriarch sometimes gave to his disciples permission to decide the law connected with ritual. This was called רשות.[41] The judges who were appointed by the Patriarch could in turn delegate their power to any one they thought fit. The Patriarch or the men who were delegated by him had the power to nominate and install the secular leaders in the Jewish community as well. These were known as *Parnasim*.[42] Usually scholars were chosen for this office.[43]

As already stated, the Patriarchs were representatives of the Jewish people before the Roman authorities. In the epistle of Emperor Julian the Apostate, Hillel II is called "Patriarch," which indicates that the *Nasi* was considered in the eyes of the emperor as the head of the Jewish community.[44] In many cases the Patriarchs, representing the Jews before the Roman authorities, suffered greatly from the whims of the Roman emperors.[45]

The office of Patriarch, as we know, was hereditary. It continued from the time of Hillel (approximately in the year 30 B. C. E.) until Gamaliel (circa 429 C. E.), and was abolished by the Emperor Theodosius.[46]

The authority of the Patriarchs to decide the law and delegate their powers to others was derived from two sources. One was based on the talmudic passage interpreting the phrase of Jacob's blessings to Judah, where we read, "The sceptre shall not depart from Judah, Nor the ruler's staff from between his feet." According to the Talmud this referred to the patriarchs descended from Hillel, who was of the Davidic family.[47] The second source was based on the tractate Abot, which traces the chain of tradition from Moses to Rabbi Judah, the

Patriarch, and his son. The Mishna Abot reads as follows: "Moses received the Law from God and transmitted it to Joshua who gave it to the Elders, who in turn transmitted it to the prophets. They gave the Law to the men of the Great Synagogue, who handed it to Simon the Pious, who transmitted it to Antigonus. From him it was received by Jose ben Joezer and Jose ben Johanan, who transmitted it to Joshua ben Perahya and Nittai of Arbella; they in turn transmitted it to Judah ben Tabbai and Simon ben Shetah. They turned over the tradition to Shemaya and Abtalyon, who conveyed it to Shammai and Hillel." From then on it remained in the hands of the dynasty of Hillel, up to the time of Rabbi Judah, the Patriarch, and his son. This passage shows that the authority vested in the Patriarch came from Moses.

Thus, the authority of the Patriarchs of Palestine over the Jews was claimed by them as descendants of the Davidic family, to whom God had promised leadership over the Jews forever and forever, while the spiritual authority was claimed by them because the tradition came to them from Moses, who received it from God on Mount Sinai.

III

BABYLONIA

When Cyrus, King of Persia, issued his decree permitting the Jews to return to their homeland, not all of the Jews left Babylonia. The great majority remained in their adopted country. The Jews of Palestine and the Jews of Babylonia were, however, politically united under the Persian flag. When the Persian Empire was conquered by Alexander, the Jews continued to live under one flag. After the death of Alexander, when his empire was divided into different parts and Palestine was conquered by the Ptolemies, and Babylonia was under the Seleucidae, for the first time the Jews of Babylonia were separated from the Jews of Palestine. The Jews were in separate kingdoms hostile to each other.[48]

In the war between Ptolemy III and Seleucus, the High Priest Onias II, who was at that time the head of the Jewish community, allied himself with the Syrian King Seleucus, for he was anxious that the Jews of Palestine and Babylonia should be united in one kingdom, under the flag of the Seleucidae. For Onias knew that if Palestine should be united with Egypt under the flag of the Ptolemies the Temple would lose considerable income, since the Jews of Babylonia would find it difficult to continue their pilgrimage to Jerusalem and to send their gifts and sacrifices to the Temple. He therefore sided with the Syrian king.[49]

After the victory of the Maccabeans over the Syrians, the Jews gained their independence and again established their own state, and thus were once more politically separated from the Babylonian Jews. During the time of the Roman domination of Palestine the Jews lived again in two different empires of opposing interests. They remained so almost up to the time of the Arabian conquest of Palestine.

We do not know who were the Jewish leaders in Babylonia in the Persian period. Tradition tells us that even in the time of the Persian period, and up to the Islamic period, the Jews had leaders of their own who were called Exilarchs, *Resh Galuta.* The ancestry of the Exilarch was traced to the House of David.[50] Even if we should accept this as authentic, the spiritual leadership was not in the hands of the Exilarch. In the Persian period most likely the High Priest interpreted the law for the Jews. In the Hellenistic period the Sanhedrin in Jerusalem did this.[51] We may also surmise that during the Second Commonwealth there were schools of instruction in Babylonia and many Jews went to Jerusalem to advance their studies in the law. It is known that Hillel, one of the outstanding scholars in the Second Commonwealth and the founder of the dynasty of the Patriarchs, was a Babylonian.[52] After the destruction of the Temple the Sanhedrin continued to interpret the law and to regulate the spiritual life of the Jews in Babylonia. This is indicated by the Epistles of Gamaliel and Simon to the Jews of Babylonia, in which they proclaim the intercalation of an additional month thus changing the order of the holidays.[53]

At the time of the revolt of Bar Kokba the Jews of Babylonia, who were very numerous and were in better political and economic circumstances, attempted to sever themselves from Palestinian authority; however they did not succeed.[54] The Jews of Babylonia continued to travel to Palestine to study, particularly during the time of Rabbi Judah, the Patriarch, when many young men came to his academy. Some remained there permanently, as for example Rabbi Hiyya; while others, like Abba, who became known in rabbinic literature by the name Rab, returned to Babylonia after acquiring the necessary knowledge and authorization. And so Samuel, who hailed from Babylonia, also went to Palestine. Abba received partial authorization from Rabbi (Judah), while his cousin Rabba received full authorization and Samuel, on the other hand, received no authorization.[55]

When Rab returned to Babylonia he established a higher academy of learning in the city of Sura. At this time there was an Exilarch in whose hands was concentrated the power of the entire Jewry of the country. This Exilarch supervised the social as well as the spiritual life. The judges who wished to make certain that their decisions would not be reversed in error, on objection raised by a litigant to the decision of the court, were compelled to accept authorization from the Exilarch.[56] This shows that the Exilarch had control over the appointment of judges. One of the well-known judges of the time of Exilarch Huna was Karna.[57] The Exilarch also appointed inspectors of markets to supervise weights and measures.[58]

In the course of time, however, the heads of the academies of Sura and Pumbedita gained more power and they contested the authority of the Exilarch. On one occasion Rabba, the son of Rab Huna, defied the Exilarch by saying, "I do not have my authorization from you, but from my father who received his from Rab, while Rab obtained it from Hiyya and Hiyya from Rabbi (Judah)."[59] In this way Rabba sought to trace his authority to Rabbi (Judah) who was a descendant of the Davidic family and whose tradition went back to Moses. By invoking this tradition the scholars of Babylonia declared their superiority to the authority of the Exilarch, and hoped to prove that to them rightfully belonged the leadership of the Jews. In the fourth century C. E. the power of the scholars of Babylonia was supreme over the Exilarch, who was dependent on Rab Ashi, the head of the academy of Sura.[60] Even in the early days before Ashi, when the Exilarchs governed the Jews, they never had any influence in choosing the head of the academies. We know that in many cases the members of the academies consulted Palestinian scholars in choosing the heads and it seems that they never even sought the advice of the Exilarch as to who should lead the academies.[61]

The heads of the academies in Babylonia were always chosen from among their members, while in Palestine they were appointed by the *Nasi,* the Patriarch. In Babylonia the scholars ordained their disciples; in Palestine, however, the ordination came from the *Nasi* and was by way of appointment. As the Palestinian Talmud says, "There (in Babylonia) they called מְנוּיֵיה appointment, סְמִיכוּתָא authorization."[62]

Thus, as we have shown, in Palestine after the destruction of the Temple the entire authority of the Jewish community was vested in the hands of a single person, the *Nasi,* Patriarch, thereby avoiding conflict between the secular and religious authority. In Babylonia, however, these two persons were separate, i. e., the Exilarchs and the scholars (the heads of the academies), thus creating friction as to their supremacy. In this later period of Amoraim the scholars succeeded in wresting authority from the Exilarchs by maintaining that they were the actual successors to Rabbi (Judah the Patriarch), who held civil authority by virtue of his descent from David and religious authority by the unbroken chain of tradition which descended from Moses.[63] The amoraic period ended at the close of the fifth century. This sudden termination may be explained by the social and political condition of the country. Babylonia came under the government

which was afflicted with the communistic doctrines of Mazdak. The
academies were closed and the Jews were persecuted.

BACKGROUND — THE WORLD WITHOUT

This section aims to give an insight into the relationships of the Talmudic world with the world outside it and also the reactions of the outside world to the Talmud and what it represented up to the present day. Abrahams' essay gives a conspectus of gentile reactions to the Talmud through the ages; this is treated in more detail for a specific instance in Temko's essay. There is much food for thought on the history of man's interpersonal relationships in these episodes. Bentwich discusses relationships between Jews and the outside world within the Talmudic period. Herford and Moore are the two men who have done most to encourage a more moderate view towards Rabbinic literature on the part of Christians. Without departing from their own standpoint they tried to correct the antagonistic viewpoint which was supported by the bad press received by the Pharisees in the New Testament. Their book-length studies in their fields of interest will repay close study.[1] At the present time we see a more serene and tolerant attitude towards the Rabbinic writings even on the part of those who for dogmatic reasons must reject them. Thus Hugo Odeberg in his *Pharisaism and Christianity* (Saint Louis, 1964) while speaking from a Christian viewpoint which rejects the notion that man is capable by himself of doing God's will, gives a sympathetic account of Pharisaism, although differing from it totally. This scholarly spadework has been the basis of the ecumenism which has lately begun to manifest itself in Christian-Jewish relations.

THE TALMUD IN HISTORY
Israel Abrahams

The century which saw the completion of the Talmud also witnessed the beginning of interference with the normal circulation of the Rabbinical literature. In the year 553 the Emperor Justinian was called upon to arbitrate on a difference which arose between two sections of Jewry in the Byzantine realm. Whereas some were desirous of publicly reading the Scriptures both in Greek and in Hebrew, others wished to use the Hebrew only. Justinian[1] ordered the praefect Areobindus to promulgate the imperial decision in favour of the use of Greek (the Synagogue might use Aquila if it preferred it to the Septuagint), or of other vernacular tongues such as Latin in the Italian provinces. The emperor, moreover, forbade any attempt on the part of the heads of the schools or elders to prevent the use of the vernacular by devices or excommunication. Most significant of all was Justinian's interdiction of the practice of giving the Haggadic exposition ($\delta\epsilon\upsilon\tau\epsilon\rho\omega\sigma\iota\varsigma$) after the reading of the Scripture. The opening words of the rescript explain Justinian's intention. The Jews, he suggested, should read their Scriptures with an eye to the hidden meaning and see in them a prophetic announcement of Christianity. Hence the emperor would naturally desire to curb the popularity of the Rabbinic exegesis, which of course would confirm the Jews in their refusal to admit Christological interpretations. Thus Justinian, who introduced drastic legislative enactments against the Jews, was also among the first to attempt interference with the free use and spread of their literature.[2]

We must here confine our attention to that phase of interference which concerns the Talmud. It was not till the 13th cent. that the attack assumed practical shape. Paris, in the year 1244, was the scene of the first public burning of copies of the Talmud. Before that date

120

the Rabbinic doctrines had been assailed in the *de Insolentia Judaeorum* of Agobard; but from the Paris incident onwards these assaults became far more frequent and dangerous. Nicholas Donin of La Rochelle had, while a Jew, been excommunicated by the Rabbi Yehiel of Paris because of his denial of the validity of the Rabbinic tradition. This occurred in 1225; he subsequently joined the Franciscans, and in 1239 he formally laid an accusation against the Talmud before Pope Gregory IX., who addressed bulls to many lands (including England) ordering the seizure of copies of the Talmud pending a public inquiry. In France the matter was seriously taken up. Charges of blasphemy, immorality, particularism, and absurdity were formulated; a public dispute between Donin and four Rabbis was ordered. The humours and futilities of such debates have been satirized in Heine's poem 'Disputation.' But the consequences were deplorable. The Talmud was condemned; many copies of it were burnt; and popular outbreaks against the Jews resulted.

Within a few years similar scenes were enacted in Barcelona. Here again the attack originated with a Jewish convert to Christianity, Pablo Christiani. He instigated a public debate between himself and Nahmanides in 1263, as to the attributes and coming of the Messiah, and the Rabbi was sentenced to exile because his defence of Judaism was pronounced blasphemous. In 1264 Christiani induced Pope Clement IV. to appoint a Commission of censors, who expunged all those passages which appeared derogatory to Christianity. In particular, as time went on, Talmudic references to ancient paganism were misinterpreted as being attacks on the Church. This charge was brought forward by yet another erstwhile Jew, Geronimo de Santa Fé, who engineered a public dispute in Tortosa in 1410, and, like Christiani, submitted to the verdict of the crowd the most intricate problems of Biblical exegesis in relation to Messianic belief. The practical outcome again was not a settlement as to the significance of Is. 53, but the confiscation of copies of the Talmud.

Of much greater interest was the controversy which waged round the Talmud at the beginning of the 16th century. Owing to the part taken by Reuchlin in this incident, the Talmud became the battleground between the old and the new, between the obscurantists and the humanists. Again the protagonist in the attack on the Talmud was one who had left the Synagogue for the Church. It must not, however, be thought that the proverbial zeal of converts has invariably assumed this guise. In the recent assaults made on the Talmud by representatives of modern anti-Semitism, powerful among the defenders of the fair fame of the Rabbinic system were such famous Judaeo-Christian scholars as Daniel Chwolsohn and Paulus Cassel. The opponent of Reuchlin was of a different type. We know very little as to the antecedents of Johann Pfefferkorn, of whom Erasmus said that from a bad Jew he became an execrable Christian ('ex scelerato Judaeo sceleratissimus Christianus'), for no reliance can be placed on the insinuations made by satirists that in his earlier days Pfefferkorn had added to the respectable calling of a butcher the disreputable career of a burglar. All that we know is that Pfefferkorn was animated by a strong animosity towards his former co-religionists, that his fanaticism far exceeded his learning, and that he found support for his campaign among the Dominicans of Cologne. Though the Jews had been excluded from that city in 1426 and only regained rights of free domicile there with the coming of the French in 1798, Cologne remained during the 15th and 16th centuries the headquarters of the campaign against Jewish books.

It would be unprofitable to repeat the details of the oft-told tale of Pfefferkorn's pamphlets and Reuchlin's rejoinders; of the seizure of Hebrew books in Frankfort-on-the-Main in 1509, their restoration, and the long-drawn-out struggle that ensued in Rome. Nor is it of any importance to us now whether or not Pfefferkorn wrote the works that bear his name. The whole incident would have been forgotten but for certain facts. In the first place, this battle of the books gave rise to a famous satire, the *Epistolae Obscurorum Virorum,* the first part of which appeared at Tübingen towards the end of 1514. The effect of this rather savage satire was instantaneous and permanent. As an exposure of obscurantism it remains one of the most masterly efforts ever put forward on behalf of humanism. The struggle between Reuchlin and Pfefferkorn became, in short, elevated to a higher plane. Reuchlin, once for all, struck the true note when he protested against the destruction of a literature because elements of it were distasteful to certain of its critics. 'If the Talmud contains errors,' he said, 'let us render them innocuous by studying to sift the chaff from the grain. Do not burn the Talmud, but read it.' It is to Reuchlin that we owe the foundation of Hebrew chairs in the universities; the first Hebrew text printed in Germany was the edition of seven Psalms used by Reuchlin in 1512. The study of Hebrew in Christian Europe commenced with him, was taken up by his immediate successors, and has never since been relinquished.[3] Reuchlin's devotion to Rabbinism began with his interest in the Kabbala. But Hebrew was the passion of his life. And there is no doubt that to him we owe that interest in the Talmud which soon led to the publication of a complete printed edition of all its tomes. There were, as we shall see, printed editions of parts of the Talmud available in 1510, when he wrote that 'he would like to pay the price for a copy of the Talmud twice over but he had not yet been able to obtain one.'[4] He was referring to MS copies. Within about a decade of the year in which Reuchlin wrote this lament it was easy to procure the Bomberg edition printed in Venice. It was fortunate for scholarship that Daniel Bomberg began to print the Talmud in 1520, before the censorship intruded its hand. Yet the censorship has this value. In 1550 the Talmud was placed on the Index. But the Tridentine Synod in 1564 provided that the Talmud might be circulated, if the passages obnoxious to Christianity were deleted. This was done, and between 1579 and 1581 there was completed the censored Basel edition which formed the model for many subsequent editions. In this form, claims the Basel editor, the Talmud may be read by Christians not only without reproach but even with profit ('etiam cum fructu a nostris legi potest'). The Inquisitor Marco Marino went through the Venice edition of 1546-50, censored it, and affixed his name to the expurgated version page by page. The expurgated passages have often been edited and commented on separately. Attacks on the Talmud, nevertheless, continued. As late as 1757 copies of the Talmud were publicly burned in Poland as a result of the Kamenetz-Podolsk disputation. Literary onslaughts have naturally continued, and modern anti-Semitism has displayed much energy in seeking in the pages of the Talmud grounds for attacks on the Jews. Those pages contain enough and to spare of superstition, narrowness, folly, and intolerance. But the faults are superficial, the merits fundamental; and it is because of the latter that the Talmud retains its permanent worth.

THE BURNING OF THE TALMUD IN PARIS

Allan Temko

To the Middle Age no subject of conversation was more fascinating than the Lord. Wherever men gathered—in the castle hall, the wine shop, the market place—they would forget all else, and talk vividly of God. If they disagreed, they argued; and since the times were violent, disagreements sometimes ended in blows and sword thrusts. Religion was a lively matter. Amateur theologians were as numerous as amateur politicians today, and took their ideas at least as seriously. For the world, in the 12th and 13th centuries, was a giant cathedral. The supernatural entered every part of human life, every day of the year, and from the ribald comedy of the *Fête des Fous* to the intense drama of Easter, served every human emotion. Daily activity was suffused by the moods of Heaven to an extent that we now find quite impossible to grasp. All we can do is stand in the portal of a medieval church, while the stone population of Paradise mounts overhead, and try to imagine that these Prophets and Martyrs, these celestial Queens and Kings, were once as real as any earthly creature, and indeed did sometimes walk upon the earth and speak.

And so men debated about the Lord wherever paths met. The Church, for very good reasons, did not find this enthusiasm altogether commendable. Public discussion has a tendency to break down dogma, and while the Gothic moment was an age of extreme faith, it was not an age of strict orthodoxy. The whole of Languedoc—almost one-fourth of France—lay in the passionate error of Catharism. The Rhône Valley, Champagne, and Flanders swarmed with itinerant preachers whose wild outcries compelled no less a figure than Saint Bernard to answer them in the name of the Church Universal. In the Schools of Paris, soon to become a University, independent thinkers like Abélard battered down conventional thought in *disputationes* that shook Christendom.

In this atmosphere of sharp theological disagreement, of popular error and heresy, the Jew had a special place. He was the most dangerous deviant of all. As Christianity rose to its most triumphant instant, hurling armies against the East, and conquering the sky with cathedrals, the Jew stubbornly refused to capitulate. This took courage. The Church had begun to abandon its age-old policy of gentle persuasion, and was now resorting to severe political pressure against him. Moreover, the Crusades had loosed anti-Semitic lynch mobs throughout Western Europe. When men adore their Lord as fervently as did the medieval Christians, they are inclined to make him absolute.

To the Christian intellectual of the Middle Age, the Jew needed only a firm push toward the light, and his conversion would be assured. This conviction was not as far-fetched as it might seem. Today, when differences between faiths receive more attention than their similarities, we occasionally forget that Christianity and Judaism share an enormous common ground. During the Middle Age, the one regarded itself as the child of the other, a natural growth that had sprung from Jewish monotheism like Jesse's Tree. The relationship was dramatized in thousands of works of art, but nowhere does it emerge more brilliantly than in the great transept rose windows of Notre-Dame of Paris. Through the northern rose flows the austere blue light of the Old Law; through the southern pours the sun-filled reds of the New. The two streams of color blend at the exact center of the cathedral, in the most mystical alliance that Western civilization has devised.

Coaxing, this wonderful light—and yet the Jew did not surrender to it. In his tiny synagogues he prepared his replies to Paris, Chartres, and Rheims; and when he ventured on the talkative streets, walking the tightrope of medieval tolerance, he would courageously answer Christian challengers. He argued as Jews have since Abraham (according to the Midrash) debated theology with Nimrod. In the face of continual proselytism, he responded with a proselytism of his own.

In general, these religious discussions were friendly. They occurred far too often to be otherwise. We know, too, that they had their share of good humor. Once a monk asked Joseph Kara why synagogues did not have bells. "Go to a fish market," replied the Jew, "and you will see that the high-quality stalls are silent. Only the sellers of herring shout their merchandise."

Jewish wit and learning grew famous, and the debates soon became a form of entertainment, as diverting as the songs of minstrels, before aristocratic audiences. Sometimes keenly intelligent women, like the Lady of Vitry, in Champagne, took part. But if the nobility found clever argument amusing, the Church did not. By the end of the 12th century France was hot with heresy, and Jewish criticism, for all its charm, was becoming too effective. About the year 1200 the Bishop of Paris threatened with excommunication anyone but qualified clerks who entered into theological argument. A Church writer, Peter of Blois, declared with some heat in his *Contra Perfidiam Judaeorum* (and *perfidiam* should here be translated simply as "disbelief") that it is "absurd to discuss the Trinity at street intersections." Finally, in a Bull of 1233, Gregory IX condemned all public controversy.

The Pope's edict was not obeyed. The debates went on, as passionately as before. Men could not keep silent. The Jews continued to give a good account of themselves, and provoked Saint Louis's celebrated remark to Joinville: "I tell you that no one, unless he be a very learned clerk, should dispute with them; that the layman, when he hears the Christian Law mis-said, should not defend it, unless it be with his sword, with which he should pierce the mis-sayer in the midriff, as far as the sword will enter."

If the foremost Christian spokesmen were trained in the young University of Paris, their leading adversaries were educated on the opposite bank of the Seine in the Talmudic School of the Paris Synagogue. There, with modest resources, the Jews had set up a center of learning that was renowned throughout the West. Its students, like the scholars in the Christian schools on the Left Bank, came from as far away as England and Italy. Occasionally even, Christian philologists would cross the river to receive special instruction from the rabbis in Hebrew.

Exactly where on the Right Bank the Talmudic School was located in the 13th century is a matter of doubt. It was situated in a newly acquired building, for the Jews had lost all of their ancient holdings in Paris when they were sent into a sixteen-year exile in 1182. The Crown had then seized not only their homes and lands, but also their seat of religious and intellectual life: the temple on the Ile-de-la-Cité, which was transformed into a church. After their return in 1198, the Jews did not come back to the Island and the Left Bank, where they had lived since Merovingian and even

Roman times, but settled in the expanding commercial quarter near the Halles. There they consecrated a new synagogue, which almost certainly housed the School. One might note that they have never left the vicinity of these great markets, except under periodic compulsion. They live by choice in the neighborhood today, in the twisting streets behind the Rue de Rivoli, as merchants and artisans and scholars.

With the exiled community had returned its leader and champion, Rabbi Judah ben Isaac—Judah Sir Leon[1] of Paris, one of the most accomplished Jews of the Middle Age. Sir Leon may have been a descendant of the superb teacher Rashi of Troyes (1040-1105), the father of Jewish medieval Scholasticism; at any rate, he carried on Rashi's cultivated principles of Tosafist education. A corps of brilliant rabbis developed under Sir Leon's supervision. Like their master, they had a perfect familiarity with the Talmud and the Old Testament, were widely read in other religious and philosophical literature, had a precocious knowledge of science, and above all loved theology for its own sake. They were also gifted poets, convincing preachers, and skilled controversialists. The most famous of Sir Leon's pupils were Moses of Coucy, Sir Morel of Falaise, and Yechiel of Paris, all three of whom would later defend their beloved Talmud at the risk of their lives, and see it condemned and publicly burned in Paris.

When Sir Leon died in 1224 at the age of fifty-eight, young Yechiel succeeded him as Chief Rabbi of Paris and head of the School. Young, and alive! Yechiel's name was translated literally into French as Sir Vives—or *Vivo,* as he is called in Latin documents. He was also called Yechiel the Holy, Yechiel the Pious, and when he in turn grew venerable, Yechiel the Elder. At the time he took charge of the School, however, he could scarcely have been more than twenty-five. He was born at Meaux, near Paris, sometime after the return of the Jews to France in 1198.

Under Yechiel the School flourished as it had under Sir Leon. More than three hundred students listened to his lectures; and when he was called upon to defend Jewish doctrine in open debates as official spokesman for his community, all Paris thronged to hear. He won admiration from Jews and Gentiles alike when he refuted charges that Jews are compelled by ritualistic demand to use Christian blood. Another time he successfully denied the allegation that Jews cannot, consistently, with their belief, bear witness in courts of law.

But Yechiel's oratory alone did not move the imaginative 13th century. It was his reputation as a Cabalist that gripped medieval Paris. A story circulated that he possessed a magical lamp which, after being lit Friday evening, burned an entire week without oil. Saint Louis was intrigued by the rumor, and according to one version of the episode, asked Yechiel if it were true. The Rabbi's reply was vague (it would have been fatal to confess to sorcery), and the King decided to surprise him in person late on Wednesday night, to see if the lamp were still burning.

An apocryphal bit of comedy resulted which is worth telling one more time—it has been repeated for ages in European ghettos.

In those days, says the legend, beggars and ruffians often chose the dead of night to beat on Jewish doors and disturb the sleeping households. Yechiel, of course, was never in bed at that hour, but wide awake in his study, poring over Cabalistic symbols. In order not to be interrupted, he had a sort of projecting peg or nail on his desk, which he pressed downward whenever he heard a knock As far as the peg entered the wood, the intruder sank into the earth outside.

When the King knocked, Yechiel pressed the peg immediately, and Louis sank to his waist. The King, a tall man, managed to reach up and strike the door again. Yechiel pushed the peg a second time. The device hopped backward beneath his finger! With a terrified cry he rushed to the door and prostrated himself before his monarch.

He found that Louis had been as frightened as himself. The King and his barons, as they felt the earth swallow them, had in one voice cried out: "Save us!"

Yechiel led them into his home, placed them near the fire, and entertained them with cakes and jam—the authentic medieval touch that is as impossible to duplicate as the pure blue glass at Chartres.

Louis then asked the Rabbi if he was really a sorcerer and if it was true that he possessed the marvelous lamp. Yechiel lifted his eyes toward the omnipotent 13th-century Heaven, and answered: "Let the Lord be pleased, I am not a sorcerer! But I *am* versed in physics, and know several properties of Nature."

Then he showed the King his lamp, which was burning brightly, and revealed that it was neither a miracle nor a work of enchantment, but that he had filled it with another combustible material rather than oil. This part of the tale rings true. Phosphorous had recently been brought to Paris from the East, and was a tremendous source of local excitement at the time. With reservations certain other details of the story may also be accepted, such as the proud Jewish claim that Louis afterwards made Yechiel a trusted counselor at Court. It is altogether possible that in the first years of Louis's reign, Yechiel was received at the palace on a friendly, if not official basis. Only one fact is sure: in the year 1254 the King for some reason categorically prohibited the practice of magic to the Jews of his realm.

By night, in his study, Yechiel may have enjoyed tranquility; as head of the School by day he led the stormiest of intellectual careers. Jewish theologians could disagree as violently among themselves as the Christian doctors, and Saint Bernard and Peter Abélard contended with no more bitterness than Yechiel and one of his students, Donin of La Rochelle. Donin, who in spite of his name seems to have spent most of his life in Paris, expressed sharp disapproval of the oral tradition of Talmudic teaching—the very foundation of Jewish Scholasticism. This was heresy. Yechiel of course denounced it as such, and for a full year after he assumed direction of the School, his conflict with Donin raged within its walls. Finally, when Donin's criticisms became irreconcilable with orthodoxy, Yechiel excommunicated him in the presence of the entire Congregation, with the usual humiliating ceremonies, in 1225.

The severity of this sentence cannot be overemphasized. The medieval man bereft of his Lord, Jew or Christian, was driven— quite literally—out of his community. After his scourging in the temple, he wandered as an outcast: shunned, feared, hated; denied any solace of religion, including burial in sacred ground. No man would dine with him, or receive him in his house, or—if the excommunication were observed to the letter—associate with him in any way, unless it be to urge him to repent. For ten years Donin endured this impossible existence. His only sympathizers seem to have been certain members of the clergy who saw his potential value as a *provocateur*. With their encouragement. Donin dramatically announced his conversion to Christianity in 1236. He was baptized under the name of Nicholas, and joined the Franciscan order.

There have been few more despicable renegades. Donin's first Christian action was to circulate through France during the summer of 1236, haranguing troops that were forming for the Sixth Crusade. The volunteers were in an ugly mood, and needed little pretext to renew the pogroms that had accompanied every Crusade for more than a century. Donin gave them their opportunity. He traveled through Anjou, Poitou, and Aquitaine, preaching to mobs in his friar's habit, and the atrocities followed. Homes and synagogues were burned. Torahs were torn to pieces. Then came a demand for mass conversion. Some five hundred Jews submitted and were baptized. Three thousand others perished, some in indescribable pain. The Crusaders had hit upon the idea of trampling men, women, and children with their war horses.

In desperation the Jews appealed to the Pope, and Gregory ordered Saint Louis and the prelates of France to protect them from further outrages. But as was usual in the Middle Age, the lynching mood had almost spent itself before the responsible officials acted. Through a wide band of central France, Jewish communities lay decimated. Donin, however, had not yet had his full revenge. Two years after the massacres, in 1238, he went to Rome and formally presented the Pope with thirty-five accusations against the Talmud and recommended its destruction as a mass of blasphemies. He added that the Talmud alone kept the Jews in error, that the rabbis valued it more highly than the Bible, and that without it the Jews would have been converted long in the past.

This last point in itself was enough to convince Gregory that an investigation, at least, was necessary. Nevertheless, the Pope was taken totally by surprise. In countless previous attacks on the Jews the Talmud had never before been called into question. Until Donin's denunciation they had been considered only as defenders of the Old Testament, not as blasphemers of the New. What then, after centuries of Christian indifference to the Talmud, had given Donin's charges their special effectiveness?

At the center of the situation lay the classic source of bigotry: ignorance. Not one Gentile in ten thousand had the faintest idea of the contents of the Talmud; not one in a million had an understanding of its ambiguities. An unprincipled apostate like Donin could easily take passages from context, and twist their meanings. But beyond ignorance of the Talmud, Christians had a distorted conception of the Jews themselves. Rabble-rousers everywhere, like Foulque de Neuilly, the organizer of the Fourth Crusade, had created a popular image of a monster. The Jew was vilified ingeniously. He was charged with ritual murder, with subterranean orgies of blood-drinking, with desecration of sacred objects that the clergy had left in his pawn. He was simultaneously reproached for poverty and for the practice of usury, both of which Christians had forced upon him. He was accused of being ugly, of being small in stature. Politically, feudalism adopted a notable decision of Saint Thomas Aquinas, and declared him a serf. Above all, the miracle plays that were staged before the cathedrals depicted him as a magician and agent of Satan.

To some extent, although it should not be exaggerated, the secrecies of Tosafism made these slanders more credible to the uninformed. This was the age of the Cabalists, strange creatures in peaked hats who were shrouded in mystery even to their own congregations. It is easy to see how the primitive science, like Yechiel's experiment with phosphorous, could instil fear and hate as well as wonder.

Underlying all these emotional sources of Christian resentment was a hard new code of Church law. The Lateran Council of 1215 had gone further than the oppressive Council of 1179, and formulated a complete pariah status for the Jew. It initiated the marked costume and other crude indignities which were to torment the Jew until the French Revolution. It also established the Inquisition, and the Talmud became one of its first victims.

If the investigation of the Talmud held no lesson for the 13th century, it might for the 20th. The methods of inquisitors have seldom been more striking. Pope Gregory considered Donin's accusations for a full year, and then decided that they were serious enough to invoke the entire judicial apparatus of Church and State. For this he would need the help of the secular arm, particularly the "strong right arm" of the Church's "eldest son," King Louis of France. But more than France alone, Gregory hoped for a joint civil and ecclesiastic action throughout the Occident. In an encyclical dated June 9, 1239, he requested the sovereigns of seven western kingdoms—France, England, Aragon, Navarre, Castille, Leon, and Portugal—to act in concert with their prelates, and simultaneously seize every copy of the Talmud in their realms. The date fixed for the coup was the first Saturday in Lent the following year—nine months off.

Strange, this delay. More strange, Gregory did not circulate the encyclical by papal courier. Instead he ordered Donin personally to deliver the text to the Bishop of Paris, William of Auvergne, who—at a time that seemed propitious—would send out the necessary letters to the various kings and bishops concerned. Hence the entire maneuver, as William of Auvergne's biographer has pointed out, was directed not from Rome, but from the Episcopal Palace of Paris.

The Pope's plan was more lucid than it seems at first. In William of Auvergne—the Bishop who was rushing Notre-Dame to completion—he had a hard-headed prelate from the tough southern hills near Aurillac, whose people are still among the most orthodox Catholics in France. William could be counted upon to conduct the investigation energetically; if it ended in fiasco, he would absorb any embarrassment rather than the Pope, who was publicly committed to protect Jewish freedom of religion. The Bishop was also in an excellent position to influence King Louis, whose palace stood a few hundred yards from the cathedral, at the opposite end of the Ile-de-la-Cité. Many historians have tried to prove that Saint Louis was not the "priest-ridden mystic" whom other scholars have described. In this case we can say only that he alone among the seven monarchs obeyed the Pope's instructions; all the other kings refused.

The Jewish Sabbath was a favorite medieval moment for a raid. On Saturday morning, March 3, 1240, while the congregations were praying in their synagogues, the officers of Church and Crown struck "a great blow." Every copy of the Talmud that could be found in France was seized and transported to Paris, where the book was to be judged for blasphemy before the Royal Court.

Whether or not Saint Louis was dominated by priests, we have it on the impeccable authority of Joinville that he was tyrannized by his mother, Blanche of Castille. This remarkable woman, whose courage and imagination had saved the throne for her young son when his barons rebelled, was a Spanish beauty who had been trained in the sophisticated courts of the south. Like her son, she possessed the ecstatic temperament in strong degree. Her artistic taste was faultless, and the northern rose of Chartres, which she endowed, is perhaps its most splendid example. She also gave license to poets and troubadors, and yielded utterly to that curious medieval emotion known as "courtly love." She adored chivalry and its tournaments of jousting. And now she conceived the trials of the Talmud as a tournament of eloquence in which champions would match dialectical lances for the delight of her courtiers. She named herself chief judge. For reasons never explained, Saint Louis did not attend the debate, and his devout and gifted mother took complete charge of the proceedings.

By June 1240, three months after the mass seizure of the Talmud, the Colloquy was ready to begin. In the great hall of the palace, before a brilliant assemblage of clergy and nobles, Queen Blanche took her place on the dais. A team of clerks and monks, led by Donin, entered as prosecutors, attired for pageantry. Then came the four representatives of French Jewry. According to a contemporary account, their bearing was "royal"; and, indeed, they could not have looked much different from the stately, bearded patriarchs whose images were carved about this time for the western façade of Notre-Dame.

Of the four rabbis, Yechiel was perhaps the most famous, but each had a great reputation in his own right. There was Moses of Coucy, an Italian-born intellectual and author who spoke not only French but Spanish and Arabic fluently; in 1235 and 1236 he had made a speaking tour through southern France and Spain, upbraiding congregations which had neglected the Law, and delivering sermons of such power that he became known as *ha-darshan*—the Preacher. Judah ben David of Melun, who was head of the School at that thriving city a few miles above Paris on the Seine, was a Tosafist scholar of the same stature as Yechiel and Moses. The fourth spokesman seems to have been Sir Morel of Falaise, whose Hebrew name was Samuel ben Solomon, but it is equally possible that he was Samuel ben Solomon of Château Thierry.

The pageant now took its first step toward tragedy. A burst of excitement swept over the spectators as the evidence was brought in. It was gorgeous. The illuminated parchments, with their bold Hebrew characters, were the treasure of the synagogues of France. Since few of the audience had seen the Talmud before, Nicholas Donin stepped forward and described the book briefly.

That day Yechiel alone remained in court, selected expressly by Donin. The three other rabbis were isolated, so that they could not consult with one another.

When Yechiel saw that Donin had been entrusted with the prosecution, he disdainfully asked what points of Jewish doctrine the apostate wished to question. Donin's reply was unexpected. Although the thirty-five accusations he had made before the Pope were supposedly the basis of the inquiry, he now declared that the discussion would be limited to the Talmud's treatment of Jesus. He added that he would prove the divinity of Jesus Christ in spite of the heresies of the Talmud, which he said had been composed some four hundred years previously.

"Fifteen hundred years!" thundered Yechiel who, like every pious medieval Jew, was certain that the Lord had dictated the book's oldest portions to Moses. And the Rabbi turned to Queen Blanche with this appeal: "Lady, I beg of you, do not oblige me to reply. The Talmud is a holy book of venerable antiquity in which no one until the present has been able to discover a fault. Jerome, one of your Saints, was familiar with all of our Law; if he had found the least blemish in it, he scarcely would have allowed it to remain. No prelate, no apostate even, has ever reproached us our belief. Your Doctors, and you have had many more learned than Nicholas these last fifteen hundred years, have never attacked the Talmud. They have recognized it as fitting that we should have a commentary on the Scriptures. . . ."

Yechiel then faced the entire court with defiance: "Know further that we are prepared to die for the Talmud. . . . our bodies are in your power, but not our souls."

One of the King's officers broke in: "Yechiel, who thinks of harming the Jews?"

Yechiel, recalling the recent Crusader slaughters, and aware of a rising pogrom sentiment in Paris, must have smiled bitterly: "Surely it isn't you who will protect us from the enraged people."

With the meticulous courtesy that she displayed throughout the hearing, Queen Blanche reassured the Rabbi. She declared that she would defend the Jews and their possessions, and would punish as a capital crime any violence against them.

Reassured that the forms of justice were to be observed, Yechiel requested an immediate appeal to the Holy See. This was a frequent and honorable legal technique in the Middle Age, since the papal tribunal—the Supreme Court of medieval Europe—often reversed the decisions of prejudiced or incompetent lower courts. Ordinarily the request would have been granted. This day it was shouted down by the clerks who told Yechiel to answer Donin, if he could.

The Rabbi had to submit. He protested angrily, however, when Donin demanded that he swear an oath before testifying. "Never in my life have I sworn upon the name of the Lord," he told Queen Blanche, "and I shall not begin today. If, after giving oath, I said merely one word which displeased Donin, he would cite me for perjury."

This time the clerks gave way, and Yechiel was not forced to swear, although Jews on occasion did take oath voluntarily during the Middle Age, with the right hand resting upon a Torah.

At last the two champions came to grips. To the delighted astonishment of the assembly, Donin began with a *tour de force*. He demonstrated, texts in hand, that the Talmud was filled with absurdities. It condemns to death, he pointed out, the man who sacrifices *part* of his progeny to Moloch, but provides no penalty for him who sacrifices *all* of it. This stroke put the clergymen in wild laughter.

Yechiel replied coldly. "One day," he told them, "you shall laugh no longer at these words. You wish to intimidate me, but ought you not at least hear me before vilifying our Law?" Then he explained that a total sacrifice was a sin so monstrous that it passed human punishment, and deserved only the wrath of God.

After this exchange, the discussion centered on the various passages in which the name Jesus appears in the Talmud, some twenty in all. Many of these references are without question uncomplimentary or openly insulting. They speak of an illegitimate son of a harlot, who was condemned as a false prophet, and later executed like a common criminal. Donin claimed that they applied to Jesus of Nazareth and his mother the Virgin Mary. The audience was shocked and horrified, and their indignation was skillfully exploited by Donin. As he translated each of the alleged blasphemies from Hebrew into the official court language, Latin, he added in French, the popular tongue which could later be quoted to illiterate mobs: "See how this people insults your God. How do you allow them to live in your midst?"

At this unhappy moment, when the Jewish cause must have appeared lost to everyone except the solitary Rabbi, Yechiel defended the 'Talmud proudly, and with success. He asserted that none of these insults concerned Jesus Christ, but other personages of the same name who had no connection with the Christian Savior. In particular he mentioned Jesus Gereda, the bastard son of Sotada, a soldier, and of Panthera, a whore. This Jesus, the Rabbi maintained, was a villain who fully merited the cruel punishment he received for false prophecy. Yechiel here had an irrefutable point, and he made it convincingly. Although the Talmud is not altogether definite on the method or exact place of execution, it makes it clear that Jesus ben

Sotada was not crucified, but either hanged or stoned and that his condemnation and death took place not at Jerusalem, but in or near Lydda.

This confident denial made a deep impression. It was further supported by Yechiel's counter-charge that Donin had known all of these facts, but had sedulously distorted them for motives of revenge.

The debate continued bitterly, until at last Donin and the clerks resorted to invective. At this point, according to a contemporary Jewish account of the episode, Queen Blanche brought them up sharply. "Why do you spoil your good odor?" she asked. "The Jew, out of respect for you, has succeeded in proving that his ancestors did not insult your God, and yet you persist in trying to make him confess to blasphemies. Aren't you shamed by such maneuvers?"

Yechiel was dismissed, and Judah ben David of Melun, who had been held incommunicado while Yechiel's testimony was given, was now called before the court. Donin went over the same ground, and saw his accusations exploded utterly. Judah's refutation was identical with Yechiel's, although the two Rabbis could not have possibly planned this specific defense together. The details coincided perfectly, and for the moment the Talmud was saved.

At the suggestion of the clerks, however, it was decided that the Royal Court was not the best qualified to judge theological quarrels, and that the dispute should be transferred to a Church tribunal. This would be a very different court of law indeed. Saint Louis personally appointed the new judges: the Archbishop of Sens, the Bishops of Paris and Senlis, the Chancellor of the University of Paris, and a preaching friar named Geoffroy de Blèves. They were joined by an Inquisitor, Henry of Cologne, and a new hearing was held in Paris shortly after the first.

Any reconstruction of these events is necessarily vague. Neither their dates, nor even the order in which they occurred, have been fixed beyond doubt. It would seem that the encounter between Yechiel and Donin began in June 24 or 25, 1240, and continued for three days while the Jewish community fasted and prayed for deliverance of the Talmud. Judah ben David of Melun apparently testified on the third day. As far as is known, the two other rabbis were not summoned to appear at all. The Church Court, with the same spokesmen participating before a new set of judges, would have convened sometime later during the summer of 1240.

Arsène Darmesteter, in a careful study, disputed these dates. He thought that the early meeting before Queen Blanche lasted a single day, June 12, and that the Church Court met June 25-27.

In any event, two trials were held, and we may be sure that the second was more severe than the first. Only one of the Church judges was impartial in the modern sense. The Archbishop of Sens, Gauthier Cornut, who on previous occasions had displayed sympathy for the Jews, was scrupulously fair. This earned him the slander that he had been purchased: the one explanation the Middle Age could offer when a high personage refused to be biased. The other prelates on the panel were openly hostile, especially Bishop William of Paris and the Chancellor of the University, Eudes of Châteauroux. The Jews feared and hated Eudes, with reason. It was he who had earlier challenged Yechiel on the use of Christian blood in secret Jewish rites. Eudes had lost then; this time he would win. He will stand forever as one of the most notorious anti-Semites the Middle Age produced.

During the second hearing, too, Donin had the assistance of Henry of Cologne, the Inquisitor. Between them they were able to make certain that the Talmud would not escape again.

It was now, before the Church tribunal, that Donin's thirty-five accusations were finally considered at length. In Isidore Loeb's masterly analysis of the arguments, the charges fall into five large classifications:

1. The exaggerated importance the Talmud had taken among the Jews; that it was more highly regarded than the Bible.

2. Blasphemies against Jesus Christ.

3. Blasphemies against God the Father and against morality.

4. Blasphemies against Christians. The Talmud allegedly prescribes that the "best of the *goyim*" should be put to death.

5. Errors, Stupidities, Absurdities contained in the Talmud.

None of these charges, Loeb demonstrated, can be sustained. That the Talmud had received an exceptional importance is a question of pure theology into which no court of law should enter. The charge of blasphemy against Jesus we have already seen proven false. The charge of blasphemy against God and morality is equally groundless: the Talmud is a deeply religious work of piety. Any arguments that may be brought against it in this connection—and Yechiel pointed this out—may also be brought against the Bible. As for the "Errors, Stupidities, and Absurdities," the charm and humor of the Talmud completely escaped its medieval judges. They were infuriated, for example, by the happy anecdote of an argument among rabbis which grew so heated that God intervened. Without hesitation one of the rabbis silenced the Lord with a brilliant *mot,* and God remarked—with one of the loveliest smiles that Jewish literature has given him: "My children have vanquished me!"

Only one of the five main charges, then, remains to be considered: the blasphemies against Christians. Here a problem of semantics arises. Donin claimed that the word *goyim* applies exclusively to Christians; the Jews retorted that it is not synonymous with Christians, but with pagans and Gentiles—in short, all non-Jews, Christians included. This distinction, in view of the abbreviated quotations Donin presented as evidence, had great significance. The Talmud is an enormous compilation which belongs to many epochs. It is punctuated repeatedly by outcries in the midst of suffering and disaster. The extravagant language of pain has a narrow meaning. It should never be lifted from context and given a wider sense than intended. This Donin did, crudely. Loeb cites the passionate curse uttered by Simon ben Yohai: "Kill the best of the *goyim!*" Simon did not intend his words to be taken literally. He had simply observed the Romans of the times of Hadrian, witnessed their cruel persecutions, and cried out specifically against them.

Were these ancient maledictions, the court demanded, still employed against 13th-century Christians? The question was not altogether fair, but Yechiel answered eloquently: "It is written that the poor of the *goyim* must be fed like the poor of Israel . . . that their sick must be tended like the Jewish sick, that their dead must be buried like the Jewish dead."

The judges did not reach an immediate decision. Instead, they deliberated in private for some time after the hearings. During these closed sessions, the disputed texts were read at least in part. Two clerks who had learned Hebrew in Yechiel's School aided the justices in this task, and presumably Donin helped too.

Finally the Talmud was condemned as a "tissue of lies," and sentenced, like Maimonides' *Guide* nearly a decade earlier in Montpellier, to be destroyed by fire.

The decision had been delayed because it was not unanimous. Gauthier Cornut, the aged Archbishop of Sens, made a strong dissent. He was the highest-ranking churchman present, and as primate of the Ile de France his word carried weight. The Bishop of Paris was his suffragan (Notre-Dame would not become a metropolitan church with an archbishop of its own until four centuries later). The Chancellor of the University of Paris was at a different level of the hierarchy altogether. Only the Inquisitor Henry of Cologne had a status approaching Gauthier's, and it was ambiguous locally in France.

For two years, from 1240 to 1242, the Archbishop prevented any violent action against the Talmud. The parchments remained under lock and key, while the Jews struggled frantically to save them. In spite of his obvious responsibility in the matter, Pope Gregory refused to assume it, and did not review the case. Nor did Saint Louis interfere. Then, in 1242, Gauthier died, the last great protector of medieval Jewry; and Bishop William and Chancellor Eudes were free to prepare their auto-da-fé.

In June 1242—the date has been contested, it may have been as late as 1244—wagon after wagon left the convents of the Preaching Friars, where the Talmud had been impounded, and were driven through Paris with a precious cargo. Manuscripts which would embellish any library in the world today were being carried to destruction. An immense throng had gathered, drawn by the novelty of the spectacle, for books had never before been publicly burned in Paris. The Jews remained hidden, in deepest mourning, terrified to venture on the streets. Slowly the tumbrils made their way through the multitude to the Place de la Grève, approximately where the Hôtel de Ville stands now. There the parchments were piled high, as the carts went back and forth to the convents for two days, until twenty-four heavy loads had been deposited. Then torches were brought, and the fire did its work.

The Jewish sense of loss was enormous. The blow to Talmudic learning was irreparable. The only outlet for Jewish anger and sorrow, as it has been so often, was literature. Elegies and bitter polemics were composed to commemorate the catastrophe. Both Jews and Christians also prepared their own versions of the trial, in Hebrew and in Latin. A copy of each manuscript is conserved at the Bibliothèque Nationale, and it is very much worth asking the special authorization required to examine them.

The Hebrew account of the trial begins with a sweeping, black Miltonic rhythm: "O dreadful and terrible day, filled with calamity! Anger and cruelty are spread upon the earth . . . and the clouds of horror and destruction have filled the sky. The sun and the moon are darkened, the heavens shattered, the stars driven away. Enormous lions roar. The giants of the past are called to life. The Universe mourns."

Yet this was not the nadir. The destruction of the Talmud was the beginning of a whole chain of disasters. A new law increased Jewish misery every two or three years until, in 1269, Saint Louis introduced the *rouella,* "the little wheel," which the Jew would wear for five hundred years as a mark of humiliation. The Jews of Paris, once so prosperous, found themselves in such poverty that money had to be borrowed from other communities to support the School. Yechiel lived to see his son Joseph unjustly imprisoned; and after his release was secured, the two of them traveled into exile, first to Greece, and then Palestine, where the great Doctor died a broken man of eighty, and was buried in a village near Acre. Thus, while Western Europe was moving toward what we are pleased to call the Renaissance, the Jew was being dragged into a Dark Age. He would have little but tragedy until the French Revolution.

The France that was responsible for these barbarities was passing its medieval prime. Jewish Scholasticism was violently put to death; Christian Scholasticism would gradually consume itself in subtleties. The Gothic, too, was losing scale and vigor. Before the 13th century would end, architecture would dissolve in a thousand forms of cleverness and show.

The smoke of the burning Talmud, however, rose in 1242 against a Gothic in full possession of its grand manner: the western façade of Notre-Dame of Paris. This tremendous sculpted wall—the most famous of postcard images—dates from 1200 to 1250, the classic instant of triumph. Flanking the central door stand two Queens, rivals across the centuries. The radiant figure on the left is the Church Victorious, crowned and imperial, and holding a chalice which is nothing less than the Holy Grail. The Queen on the right is posed in defeat, her staff broken in several places, her eyes covered by a coiling serpent, her signs of royalty removed or shattered. A reversed Tablet of the Law, falling from her hand, shows that she is the Synagogue. The statues at Paris are modern, the work of the 19th-century restorer. But at Strasbourg are two Queens in all their original beauty. The Church is magnificent. The Synagogue is amazing. We may stand before them for many hours, trying to decide which is the more lovely; and the decision will be purely a subjective matter of taste, as it should be; but as we look at the bandaged eyes of the captive Queen, and study the exquisite proportions of her broken staff, we shall not fail to realize the utter grace and majesty of her defeat.

THE GRAECO-ROMAN VIEW OF JEWS AND JUDAISM IN THE SECOND CENTURY

Norman Bentwich

The second century of the civil era saw the supreme crisis of the Jewish people and of Judaism. In the previous century the national center had been destroyed, and the national and religious existence were threatened. It was a fundamental principle of Roman policy to war down the proud, *debellare superbos,* as their great poet expressed it; and the "obstinate superstition" of the Jews, and the challenge of the small people to the might of the great empire seemed to call for the sternest and most thorough repression. The struggle against the Roman rule in the national rebellion of 66-70 C.E. was mainly confined to Palestine; but the audacity of the Jews of Palestine, as the Romans conceived it, reacted upon the Jews of the Diaspora in the succeeding era. There were violent outbreaks in countries where the Jewish population was considerable; and a determined attempt was made to exterminate the one national people who remained within the melting-pot of the Empire. In Palestine the Jews were continually bursting into desperate revolt for a half-century after the destruction of the Temple by Titus. And we may be sure that they were driven to these desperate outbreaks in and out of Palestine by an oppression of all that was dearest to them which could not be borne. During the so-called golden age of the Antonine Emperors, when Gibbon would have us believe that the world was happier and better governed than at any other period, the Jews were undergoing this prolonged agony. Rising followed rising not only in Palestine but over the whole of the East, and took on the form of wars of extermination.

Yet Judaism and the Jewish people survived, and not only survived but carried on an active and successful mission. They won for their faith the privilege of a *Licita Religio,* a privileged creed, and they spread their tenets in all parts of the Graeco-Roman world and outside it. The words which Seneca, the Roman statesman and philosopher, had used of them a few years before the struggle began:—"The customs of this most wicked race have prevailed so far as to be received in all countries. The conquered have imposed their laws on the victors." (*Usque eo sceleratissimae gentis consuetudo valet ut per omnes jam terras recepta sit;*

141

victi victoribus leges dederunt).[1]—These words still most aptly described the position of the Jewish people after that life and death struggle. It is interesting to bring together from the Greek and Roman writers of the second century and the succeeding epoch the notices of the Jewish people and of Judaism, and to reconstruct a picture of this obstinate race and obstinate creed, as it appeared to the writers of a perplexed pagan society.

It must be remembered, indeed, that the historians of that age are frequently, in fact usually, not witnesses of truth, but wrote consciously as rhetoricians and propagandists, and flatterers of their royal masters. The writers of history had lost a sense of exactness and of objective statement such as the historians of the golden age of Hellenism had affected. Now truth did not seem sufficiently impressive, and it must be embellished with exaggeration and distortion. To meet the "demand for brighter history," each writer tried to outdo the others in the luridness of his narrative and the forcefulness of his language. And the distortions of the pagan historians cannot be checked in this epoch by the writings of any Jewish chronicle. There is not even a Josephus of the second century. The only witness who can be brought to rebut the pagan is the Christian, and the Christian chroniclers of these times, who were not contemporary with the events, had their "tendency" to advance. They were, however, less induced or less tempted, to invent, and they had more understanding of what Judaism meant and stood for. But the chief and most valuable check on the aberrations of the historians is to be found in the incidental remarks and the asides about Judaism and the Jews which occur in the writings of the literary and philosophical masters of the decadent society. It has been said that "truth will out even in an affidavit"; and so too it may be claimed that truth about Judaism is to be found in the remarks of those who had nothing further from their minds than the giving of a testimonial to a creed which they did not understand and which they despised or even hated.

Let us consider first the passages in the historians about the wars of the Jews in this second century when there were the successive outbreaks against Rome in the days of Trajan, Hadrian and Antoninus Pius, that is from about 100 C.E. to 140 C.E. There is one contemporary historian who took part himself in the campaign against the Jews of Egypt when they rose in the reign of Trajan. He is Appian, a native of Alexandria, who wrote a series of books on the earlier Roman history upon an ethnographical plan, dealing with the Roman relations with the different peoples, Carthaginians, Parthians, etc. But his references to the Jewish wars are brief. In describing the tomb of Pompey who was assassinated in

Egypt, he says: "The burial place was destroyed by the Jews in the exigencies of war during my time, when Trajan was exterminating the Jewish race" (*Civil Wars* 2, 90). And in dealing with the Syrians he says that "the Jews were destroyed by Pompey, Vespasian and Hadrian in our time. And on account of their rebellions the poll tax imposed on them was heavier than that imposed on the surrounding peoples."[2]

A fuller and more lurid account is given in the history of Dio Cassius who wrote a century later, after there had been time for the stories to grow. His date is 160-230 C.E.; and he was a most industrious writer who compiled a history of Rome in 80 books from the legendary beginnings of Rome to his own age. A large part has survived only in epitome; and the account of the Jewish risings is in that part. He was of the impressionistic school, and loved the sensational picture. Thus of the rising in the time of Trajan against the Greeks in Cyprus, Egypt and Cyrene, he tells us that "the Jews were destroying both Greeks and Romans. They ate the flesh of their victims, made belts for themselves out of their entrails, and anointed themselves with their blood. . .. In all, 220,000 men perished in Cyrene, and 240,000 in Cyprus and for this reason no Jew may set foot in Cyprus."[3]

Of the struggle in Palestine against Hadrian he gives us similar striking details. "Hadrian founded a city in place of that which had been razed, naming it Aelia Capitolina; and on the site of the temple he raised a new temple to Jupiter. This brought on a war of no slight importance and of lengthy duration: for the Jews deemed it intolerable that foreigners should be settled in their city and foreign rites planted there. At first they conducted a guerrilla warfare and the Romans took no account of them. Then the Jews everywhere showed vigor, giving evidence of hostility to the Romans partly by secret and partly by overt acts. Many outside peoples were joining them, and the whole earth, so to say, was stirred over the matter. Hadrian then had to send his best generals against them. First of them was Julius Severus who was despatched from Britain. Severus did not dare to attack his opponents in the open, in view of their number and their desperateness. But by forming small groups and by depriving them of food he was able slowly but surely to crush, exhaust, and exterminate them. Few in fact survived. Fifty of their most important posts and 985 villages were razed to the ground; 580,000 men were slain in raids and battles; and the number who perished by famine, disease, and fire is impossible to find out. Nearly the whole of Judea was made desolate, a result of which the people had forewarning. For the tomb of Solomon which they revere fell to pieces of itself and collapsed."[4]

There is a more interesting reference to the beliefs of the Jewish people in the earlier part of the work of Dio. He is recounting the campaign of Pompey, and describing the capture of Jerusalem on the Sabbath day when the Jews would not fight. And he has a little aside on the name Jews which was "applied not only to the inhabitants of Judea but also to the rest of mankind, though of alien race, who have affected their customs. The class exists even among Romans; and though often repressed, it has increased to a great extent and has won its way to a right of freedom for its observances. They are distinguished from the rest of mankind in almost every detail of life, and especially by the fact that they do not honor the usual gods and show extreme reverence for a particular deity. They have dedicated to him the day of Saturn on which, among other peculiar observances, they undertake no serious occupation."[5]

Here we see the typical pagan's assumed or real surprise at the Jewish exclusiveness and his monotheism, and also the tribute to the effectiveness of the mission of a conquered nation. As regards the account of the Jewish rising, we can find some basis of comparison in the history of Eusebius the Church historian, Bishop of Caesarea, who wrote, indeed, two centuries after the events, but must have had access to Jewish and Gentile contemporary records. He, no doubt, was anxious to show that the Jews were suffering untold woes while the teachings of the Christians were spreading, and he therefore does not understate the calamity which befell them. But he has no word of the sensational outrages. Of the rising against the Greeks in the days of Trajan he says: "In the 18th year the rebellion broke out which destroyed a great multitude of them. For in Alexandria and the rest of Egypt, and especially in Cyrene, they were seized by some terrible spirit of rebellion; they rushed into sedition against their Greek fellows, and started a great war. In the first engagement they overcame the Greeks who fled to Alexandria and killed the Jews of that city. The Jews of Cyrene continued to plunder the country and ravage the districts, till the emperor sent against them Marcus Turbo who killed many thousands. The emperor, suspecting that the Jews in Mesopotamia would join, ordered Quietus to clear them out of that province; and he murdered a great number, and for his service was made governor of Judea" (*Hist. Eccl.* 4, 2).

Of the rising in Palestine under Bar-Kochba the same writer says: "Hadrian commanded that by decree the whole nation should be prevented from entering even the district around Jerusalem, so that not even from a distance could they see their ancestral home. When the ancient inhabitants had completely perished, it was colonized by foreigners and Romans with the name of Aelia in honor of the Emperor, Aelius Hadrian" (Ib. 4, 6).

We have one other but very inadequate authority about the origin of this last revolt of the Jewish people. In the time of the later empire a collection of the lives of the emperors was made and is known as "Historia Augusta." In the life of Hadrian there are two references to the war. "At the outset of the reign the emperor had to deal with risings of the various nations which had been conquered by Trajan. Palestine showed the spirit of rebellion, and the revolt was put down by Turbo." Then later: "the Jews began another war because they were forbidden to practice circumcision."[6] By the time these lines were written, the Jews were no longer the object of general hate; and it is notable that the reference to their struggles is cursory and unembroidered.

If we turn now to the other references in the Graeco-Roman literature to the Jews and to Judaism, it is interesting to trace three stages of good-humored contempt, bitter hatred, and enforced respect which are marked in the writings composed before, during, and after the dire struggle respectively. A typical writer of the first stage is Petronius who flourished in the second half of the first century and wrote satires and poems, and a famous study of Roman decadent manners, *The Banquet*. In that last book there is one Jewish character, a servant, who is a skilled imitator of animals. The one reproach against him, says his master, is that he is a Jew. And in one of the poems he writes of the Jew who may "worship his pig-god and denounce in the ears of high heaven; but unless he is circumcised he shall go forth from the holy city cast forth from the people and transgress the Sabbath by breaking the law of fasting."[7] This would seem to be a confused idea of the distinction between the "proselytes of righteousness" and the "proselytes of the gate." The pagan poet suggests that those who do not adopt the whole of the Jewish law are no better than the Gentiles in the eyes of the true Jews. Another writer of satires of the same epoch, Persius, gives the Jewish convert as the typical example of superstitious reverence. "But when the day of Herod comes, and the lamps on the grimy sills garlanded with violets disgorge their unctuous smoke clouds, when the tail of a tunny fish fills its red dish, and the white jar bursts with wine, you move your lips in silent dread and turn pale at the Sabbath of the circumcised."[8] Here, as with Petronius, there is no attempt to represent correctly the Jewish religion; or rather, there is a confusion, probably deliberate, of its beliefs and ceremonies. Similarly, the greatest of the Roman satirists of the Silver Age, Juvenal, writes: "Those whose lot it is to have a father that reveres the Sabbath worship nothing but the clouds and sky, and think that the flesh of swine from which their father abstained is closely related to that of man."[9] But if Judaism is misunderstood, it is recognized as the type of religion which is winning the common people.

With these statements of the Latin satirists it is interesting to compare the observation of a famous Greek writer of the same age. Plutarch is perhaps the most popular author who has come down to us from the period; and his testimony is the more striking in that he lived far away from the metropolis of Rome, in his Greek village of Chaeronea; and his opinions are those of the ordinary man of culture without any political prepossession. One of his *Moral Essays* deals with the topic of Superstition; and he gives as an example of unreasoning inhibitions the Jews who, "because it was the Sabbath, sat in their places immovable while the enemy were planting ladders against the wall, and did not get up, fast-bound in the toils of superstition as in a great net."[10] He is apparently using a commonplace from the contemporary historians about the capture of Jerusalem by the Roman Pompey who was said to have taken the holy city on the Sabbath when the Jews refused to fight. The current idea of the cultured pagan about Judaism was that it was a most profound superstition.

It was probably on account of this idea that Vespasian and Titus did not receive the title of Judaicus after their triumph over the Jewish people.[11] The name would be ambiguous. It might suggest that the conquerors had been infected with the superstition of the conquered.

Of the more hostile view which was taken during the struggle we have an example in the life of a curious figure of the social history of the Silver Age, the wonder-working Apollonius of Tyana. That worthy whose doings and sayings were recorded as a kind of gospel was for a time exalted as a rival of the founder of Christianity. He was at the height of his fame during the wars of the Jews against Titus; and Vespasian visited him at Alexandria during the campaign to obtain the omens for his bid for the imperial purple. Apollonius, it is said, refused to come to Palestine "a country which the inhabitants polluted by what they did and what they suffered."[12] The counsel of another sophist of Alexandria which is recorded in the same work is remarkable for its account of Jewish exclusiveness. One Euphrates advised that Vespasian should use his army against Nero and not against the Jews: "For the Jews have long been in revolt not only against Rome but against humanity; and a race that has made its own life apart and irreconcilable, that cannot share with the rest of mankind in the pleasures of the table nor join in sacrifices or in prayer, are separated from ourselves by a greater gulf than divides us from Susa or India. And what sense or reason was there in chastising them for revolting from us, when we had better never have annexed them."[13] Perhaps the sophist was a disguised Judaizer who sought in this way to divert the might of Rome from the destruction of the Jewish center. We find a similar expression of contempt in the writings of the master of oratory in the age of the Flavian Caesars. Quintilian (fl. 35-100 C.E.) gives as an example of the topic of denunciation that the vices of the children bring hatred on the parents: "And the founders of cities are detested for concentrating a race which is a curse to others, as e.g., the founder of the Jewish superstition."[14] Doubtless his royal patrons would expect any reference to the nation which they had conquered after a great struggle to be in this strain.

Half a century later the tone of the Graeco-Roman writers about Judaism is different. One of the teachers of the Emperor Marcus Aurelius was the orator Fronto, of whom a number of letters have survived. In one of these letters addressed to his royal pupil he writes: "I stick fast in Rome, bound with golden fetters, looking forward to September 1st, as the superstitious to a star at the sight of which they break their fast . . ." The reference is here to the Jews breaking their fast on the Day of Atonement when the star of evening is visible. And two things are notable; the writer knows something of Jewish ceremonial, and he treats the Jew as the ready illustration of religious zeal, as to-day a writer might treat the Christian Scientists.

Still more remarkable is the reference to the Jews in another guide of the Emperor and the friend of Hadrian, the Stoic philosopher Epictetus, who flourished at the end of the first and beginning of the second century. He belongs indeed to an earlier generation, but he was high-minded enough to be free from the utterance of prejudice or invective, which was usual concerning the Jews in his day. His *Discourses* have achieved lasting fame, and are taken as the finest expression of the creed of unemotional self-reliance. Dealing with the theme of sincerity, he writes: "Do you not see in what sense men are called Jews, Syrians, etc.? For example, when we see a man halting between two opinions, we are in the habit of saying, 'He is not a Jew: he is only acting a part.' But when he adopts the attitude of mind of a man who has been baptized and made his choice, then he is both a Jew in fact and is also called one. So we are counterfeit Baptists, ostensibly Jews but in reality something else, and not in sympathy with our own reason, and far from applying the principles we profess, yet priding ourselves on them as being men who know them."[15]

The meaning of the passage is not altogether clear, so far as it applies to Stoics themselves. But what is clear is that the Jews are the type immediately chosen of a missionary people who are making converts in great numbers, some being genuine and some half-believers. And this comes from a leader of a philosophical school who must have regretted that mission. It has been suggested that the Jews in the passage are a mistake for Christians; and the reference to Baptists gives some color to this idea. But in another part of his work Epictetus refers to the Christians as the Galileans,[16] which makes it clear that he distinguished them from the Jews. And while it is likely that he confused their tenets about baptism with the Jewish observances, the testimony to the Jewish mission is not affected by this fact. That the distinction between Jew and Christian was recognized in the Roman world from this time is indicated by the letters of Pliny (fl. 100 C.E.) who wrote to the Emperor Trajan about the treatment to be given to the followers of the heresy in the province of Pontus of which he was governor. He proposed to his master that he should execute those who were denounced and persevered in the superstition after being warned: For whatever the nature of the creed might be, I could at least feel no doubt that contumacy and obstinacy deserved chastisement."[17]

It was not till the beginning of the third century that the spirit of religious tolerance was firmly established; and then a distinction was still made between the tenets of Judaism which were *privileged,* and the tenets of Christian teaching which were *allowed.* In the lives of the emperors already mentioned, it is recorded of the noble Severus Alexander (208-235 C.E.) that "he respected the privileges of the Jews, and permitted the Christians to exist unmolested." And it is further recorded of him that he kept in his chamber, by the side of the pagan images, statues of holy men, including Abraham and Christ. He would quote too the golden rule, and had it written up in his palace and public buildings. He heard it from a Jew or a Christian, says the chronicler.[18]

By that time the Jewish religion was in no danger from the pagan rulers. It had not only won security for itself, but it was openly recognized as one of the great religious forces by the leading writers and thinkers of the Greek and Roman world. The new danger, then unseen, was to arise when its own offspring was to prevail in that empire which had sought in vain to crush the parent stem.

A UNITARIAN MINISTER'S VIEW OF THE TALMUDIC DOCTRINE OF GOD

R. Travers Herford

The zeal of orthodox Christianity, as professed by so-called Christian nations, has shown itself, from time to time, even down to the present day, in fierce hatred and persecution of the Jews. False, not merely to the teaching of Jesus, but to the natural instincts of humanity, the Church has looked upon the scattered and defenceless people of Israel as its lawful prey, and has dealt with them as enemies of God and man. Many a page of European history is stained deep with the records of cruelty towards the Jews, and no Christian can reflect without shame on the deeds which have been committed in the name of Christianity. As a natural consequence of the attitude of Christian orthodoxy towards the Jewish people, their literature has been reviled and derided, scoffed at as foolish or condemned as impious and profane, a tissue of blasphemy mingled with indecency. Where there was no pretence of fairness or impartial study, it is not surprising that Christian opinion of Jewish literature should be hopelessly in error. The means for an adequate investigation of that literature was not at hand, for the knowledge of Rabbinical Hebrew was confined to a few, most of whom used it merely to produce garbled evidence against Jewish writers; while on the other hand, there was naturally no inducement for Jews to translate their works into more familiar languages, and present them to unsympathetic readers. Even at the present day, though much has been written to elucidate the Rabbinical literature, and aid in the study of it those who are not Jews, yet there still remains a good deal of prejudice which seems to many writers to demand an apology for dealing with that literature. Nothing can be more one-sided or partial than some of the published selections from the Talmud; those of Hershon, e.g., are written with a strong Christian bias, and the same is true, to a large

extent, of Etheridge's *Introduction to Hebrew Literature.* There seems
still to be wanting an unprejudiced courtesy towards the Rabbinical
writings; and especially in regard to the Talmud there is needed a more
serious attempt to judge it fairly, and without at every step comparing
its teachings with other doctrines that may be preferred. Whether the
theology of the Talmud is adapted to the religious wants of the present
day is a question which must be left to those who have inherited the
Talmud; but considering the patient and devoted labour which was
expended through centuries in compiling it, there ought to be no question of its claim to careful and sympathetic study, with the sole aim of
understanding what its authors intended, and without regard to later
views on the same objects of thought.

The following pages are offered as a humble contribution towards a
fairer appreciation of the Talmud, and in particular towards the understanding of one feature in it which has been singled out for especial
attack, viz., its teaching about God. Charges of blasphemy and profanity have been freely brought against the Talmud for the strongly
anthropomorphic character of many of its statements about the Almighty, and it will be time well spent to inquire if a more satisfactory
explanation cannot be found than in mere abuse.

Explanations of a far higher order have been given and will be referred to below; but as these are contained in learned works not accessible
to all, and moreover do not appear to the present writer entirely satisfactory, it may perhaps be permitted to him to venture into a field already trodden.

What, in the first place, are the facts to be explained, and wherein
lies the riddle which must be solved? Briefly, the case stands thus, that
in the Talmud two conceptions of God are found, to all appearance
diametrically opposed to each other; one of them in which God is
refined to an almost colourless abstraction, the other giving a human-
ized representation of God, which puts into the shade the extremest
anthropomorphisms of the Old Testament. Of these two the latter is far
the more prominent, as could hardly fail to be the case, seeing that the
points of contact between humanity and the humanised God are far
more numerous than those between humanity and God conceived as
infinite and absolute. But both conceptions are present, and it becomes
a question what is the relation between the two.

The facts of the case are well given by Weber (*Alt-Synagogale
Theologie,* chap. xi., p. 144, *seqq.*). He illustrates the first conception
of God (the characteristics of which he defines as "den abstracten

Monotheismus, und den abstracten Transcendentismus") chiefly by the names or titles which are used to denote the Supreme Being. Thus, of very frequent occurrence is the title, רבונו של עולם "Lord of the World"; and with this may be compared the phrase, הקב״ה מתגאה על כולן ועל כל העולם " (*Chag.* 13b), "The Holy One, blessed be he, is exalted over them all, and over all the world." Again, it is said (*B. Bathr.*, 25a), שכינה בכל מקום "The Divine Presence is in every place." It.is significant that the name יהוה is not used, though various passages in the Talmud refer to its use on certain occasions, and others strongly forbid all mention of it. The obvious meaning of this reluctance to use what had been the personal name of the God of Israel is, that such a personal name was not in harmony with the idea of one Supreme God. Probably its occasional use was due to the desire to give additional solemnity to religious rites, by introducing the ancient sacred name, although the name had really lost its significance. (The name, under the form Jehovah, is still frequently used in Christian services, where so far as we can see, its only recommendation is that it has a majestic sound.) In place of the ancient name, God was spoken of or addressed as אדני, אל, אלהים , הקדוש ברוך הוא , or המקום, השם , besides the more descriptive epithets mentioned above.

This conception of God as high exalted above the world, far removed from contact with it, is the natural development of the Old Testament doctrine, culminating in the writings of the Second Isaiah. The Prophet of the Exile teaches the highest and most abstract monotheism to be found in the Bible, and clearly points the way for the still further abstraction which characterises the Talmudic idea of God. Weber (l.c., p. 147) maintains that this further abstraction was brought about by opposition to the trinitarian idea of God in Christianity, and no doubt this may have contributed to produce the result which appears in the Talmud. But apart from this there seems sufficient evidence in the Old Testament to account for the Talmudic idea.

The opposite conception of God, that which is anthropomorphic to the highest degree, also has its roots in the Old Testament. The wide gulf which seems to exist in the Talmud between the two conceptions of God may be discerned as a slight rift in the Old Testament, when the writings of Ezekiel are compared with those of the Second Isaiah. For Ezekiel is really the founder of the legal form of the Jewish religion, in spite of the fact that codes of laws existed before his time. Both he and the Second Isaiah attempted to interpret the religious significance of the Exile and its bearing upon the future career of Israel.

And while the one founded upon it his grand doctrine of the sole sovereignty of God, the other developed from it the doctrine that laws and regulations were needed to take the place of the free prophetic spirit which had been tried and found wanting. Though Ezekiel's scheme of legislation was never adopted (it was even proposed to exclude his book from the canon because it contradicted the Pentateuch),[1] yet undoubtedly it led the way to the legislation of Ezra, and thence to the Oral Law, the Tradition of the Elders, and thus finally to the Talmud. The anthropomorphic conception of God is the direct outcome of the legal and traditional form which Judaism assumed in consequence of the teaching of Ezekiel and his successors in the same direction.

To illustrate this side of the Talmudic doctrine of God is easy, for material is as abundant as on the other side it was scanty. It is not needful to search very long in the Talmud before meeting with statements about God which are, to say the least, startling. Perhaps the best general illustration will be the famous story of Rabbah bar Nahmani and his translation to heaven (B. Metz. 86a). After relating how this Rabbi fled from the pursuit of a king's officer, and took refuge in a marsh, where he sat down on the trunk of a palm-tree and began to read, the narrator goes on, "Now, there was a dispute in the assembly of heaven whether, if the bright spot comes before the white hair, the person is unclean, and if the white hair comes before the bright spot, he is clean. The Holy One, blessed be he, says he is clean; but all the assembly of heaven say he is unclean. Then they say, 'Who shall decide?' 'Rabbah bar Nahmani shall decide' (for R. b. N. had said, 'I am alone (i.e., an unequalled authority) in regard to "plagues"; I am alone in regard to "tents" (i.e., cases of uncleanness caused by the presence of a corpse).' They sent the messenger after him. The angel of death could not manage to approach him, because his mouth never ceased reading, until a breeze blew and rustled among the reeds. He thought it was a troop of horse, and said, 'May I die rather than be delivered up to the government.' While he spoke he died. He said, 'Clean, clean.' There came a voice (*Bath-Qol*), and said, 'Happy art thou: Rabbah bar Nahmani, because thy body is clean and thy soul is departed in purity.' A scroll fell down from heaven into Pumbaditha: 'Rabbah bar Nahmani was required in the heavenly assembly.' " The story goes on to say how his colleagues mourned for him seven days at the express command of heaven. The genius of anthropomorphic description could hardly attempt a more daring flight than that contained in the above story. But, though that is perhaps the most extreme case, there are many others which fall not far short of it in humanising (or, as Weber says, "Judaizing") the conception of God. Thus we are told (A. Zar., 3b), "Rab Jehudah says that Rab says, 'There are twelve hours in the day. During the first three the Holy One, blessed be he, sits and studies Torah; during the second (three) he sits and judges the whole world, all of it; when he sees that the whole of it is worthy of destruction, he rises from his throne of justice and sits upon his throne of mercy; during the third (three) he sits and feeds the world from the horns of the unicorns (ראמים) to the eggs of the gnats; during the fourth (three) he sits and plays with Leviathan, as it is written, "that Leviathan whom thou formedst to play with" (Ps. civ. 26).'" Further, it is said that God wears a Tallith (R. ha Sh. 17b)—a fact which, says R. Jochanan, could not be believed unless it were written, but which he obtains by interpreting ויעבור ה' על פניו ויקרא (Exod. xxxiv. 6) to mean "The Lord passed (the Tallith) over his face and read." It is only a slight step further that God should pray, and that the words of his prayer, or rather meditation, should be recorded (Berach. 7a).

Besides such anthropomorphisms as those contained in the above stories, there are many others of a more generally human and less specifically Jewish character. God is said to laugh, to weep, to roar, to be angry. He can even hate (Nid. 16b). And on the strength of a forced interpretation of texts, it is said that he plaited the hair of Eve (Ber. 61a), and by the help of the ministering angels shaved Sennacherib (Sanh. 95b). To these, other examples might be added, but our object is not to collect all the anthropomorphisms of the Talmud, but rather to attempt an explanation of their existence there. Sufficient instances have been given to illustrate the two dissimilar conceptions of God presented in the Talmudic literature. We have given them in what appears to us the order of the origin, viz., first the refined and abstract conception, then the Judaized form, and lastly the more generally human representation. We believe there were good reasons why the Judaized conception should arise; and this having arisen, a precedent was thereby set for extending the "humanity" of God into details not specially Jewish.

In attempting to account for the phenomena, of which the facts are now before the reader, we shall notice two explanations which have been offered. The first is that of Hirschfeld, and is contained in his work *Die Haggadische Exegese,* p. 100, onwards. We translate a few sentences which contain his views upon the subject. "Definitely pronounced *dicta* from the doctrines of philosophers, as well as from the belief of the common life of the people, had penetrated the (Pharisaic) circle of ideas, and were freely welcomed as soon as they found adequate foundation in the Bible, or as soon as they proved acceptable and appeared to be indicated in Scripture. Thus we find even gross, heathen, popular belief about the gods transferred to the God who is revealed to man in Scripture, because they were disseminated by authority." Then follow various instances of anthropomorphisms, such as those already mentioned; after which the author proceeds (p. 102): "All these views, which were taken over into Judaism from the coarse, sensuous heathenism, and to which graphic Oriental speech could offer at most analogies, arose from the lack of scientific culture, and from the dependence on authority in regard to belief which characterized the distant provinces at that time. Political and social conditions, the dreary pressure of circumstances, put a natural restraint upon higher thoughts, and forced the mind down to sensuous conceptions. The mind could not so far raise itself as to look above and beyond the prejudices of the people, and it emancipated popular forms of belief by canonizing the religious ideas of the masses." Finally (p. 106), at the end of the section on Pharisaism, he concludes, "In all sorts of ways the most various ideas were drawn into the circle of belief, which was thereby modified; but, nevertheless, the kernel remained unaltered, and while it drew to itself foreign notions, prevailed over their oppositeness and assimilated them."

Intercourse with Gentiles, political and social adversity and consequent depression of spirits, these are the causes to which Hirschfeld ascribes the anthropomorphic features of the Talmudic doctrine of God. But is this explanation probable? Is it likely that foreign philosophies should have affected Rabbinical thought, at a time too when the lines of demarcation between Jew and Gentile were being more and more strictly drawn? Surely, one great object of the Talmud was to define the true Israelite, to distinguish his religious, moral and social position, from that of all Gentiles and unbelievers. And if this be so, it is hard to understand how Gentile doctrines and superstitions could find an easy entrance into the circle of Pharisaic thought. This difficulty still remains, even if we admit that it was not the primary concern of the Talmud to lay down a doctrine of God, but rather to sketch the "whole duty of man." For still the fundamental idea of the Talmud was a religious one, and the intermingling of Gentile elements in its theology could hardly be a matter of indifference to its authors. It is true there is in the Talmud a most miscellaneous variety of subjects; the manners and customs of many nations are incidentally mentioned, and furnish abundant proof of intercourse between Jews and Gentiles. But it does not follow that this intercourse led to adoption by the Jews of Gentile belief and doctrines. The Talmud is a creation, not a mere compilation; its authors were not concerned to pick-and-choose what they approved in the religions of neighbouring peoples; they were concerned to develop a principle of their own, and did develop it with marvellous patience and ingenuity, needing no help from the Gentile world.

Besides the adoption of Gentile notions, Hirschfeld alleges as a second cause of the anthropomorphic representation of God in the Talmud, the social and political conditions of the times during which the Mishnah and Gemara grew up. The Jews suffered persecution at the hands of the Romans, at all events during a part of this period, and though they made heroic struggles to retain their political existence during the reigns of Vespasian and Hadrian, they were finally overcome, and the fall of Bethar was the death-blow of the Jewish State. From that time onward the children of Israel have been a scattered and homeless people, and if political calamity has any effect on the mental tone of a people, if it "puts a natural limit on aspiration, and forces the mind down to merely sensuous and material religious thoughts," as Hirschfeld maintains, then certainly we should expect to find abundant traces of this mental degradation in the Talmud. But it seems to us that the case is very different from what Hirschfeld describes. Persecution usually has the effect, not of deadening enthusiasm and lowering the tone of religious and moral thought, but of stimulating and inspiring it. In the early days, before the Romans had finally conquered, religious zeal flamed out strong and bright under the stress of persecution and two men who did more than almost all else for the future of Jewish religion were Jochanan ben Zaccai in the war with Titus, and Aqiba in the death-struggle under Bar-Cocheba. To say of these men, and especially of Aqiba, that they were men of low and degraded religious natures is simply to libel them. We might, with more reason, expect to find traces of this mental degradation in the long centuries after the war of Hadrian, during which the Jews never recovered their political status, and when "hope deferred" only too often "made their heart sick." But even then, the unflinching determination with which the great leaders and "masters in Israel" clung to their religion, and worked out its principles into ever minuter details, shows

plainly how unspeakably precious it was to them, and, as we think,
forbids us to assert that they sunk to coarse and materialistic religious
ideas. Doubtless their religion assumed a very peculiar form; but where
there was so much vitality in it, as there certainly was at least in the
case of the great Rabbis of the Talmud, it is hard to believe that a
religion which grew and made way against such difficulties should be
merely a degraded and materialistic belief. We are, therefore, unable
to accept Hirschfeld's explanation as an adequate solution of the problem contained in the Talmudic doctrine of God.

Weber, in his book already referred to, *System der Alt-Synagogalen
Palästinischen Theologie,* offers a different explanation and one which
seems to be much more satisfactory. He says (p. 153), "The decisive-
ness with which Legalism (der Nomismus) had asserted the Law to be
the absolute revelation of God, both beyond and in time, had this result,
that the idea of God was subsequently determined by the principle of
Nomocracy, and God was conceived as the God of the Torah; the
idea of God was thereby Judaized—a reaction against Transcendental-
ism, which did not lead any nearer to the goal of truth." The statements
made about God thus conceived of, are not, as he says (p. 146), mere
absurdities, still less blasphemies, as they were formerly designated. They
are the necessary consequences of the nomistic conception of revelation. "How else," he asks, "could the former purely abstract idea of
God be filled with life? Of necessity the Torah must appear as the
reflex of the inner life of God, Heaven must take the form of a realm
of Torah, and God must be Judaized. The older conception is certainly incompatible with this, and thus the result of Legalism upon the
Jewish idea of God is a harsh dualism." This explanation appears to
meet the case far more completely than that of Hirschfeld; but yet
we cannot feel quite satisfied with it. It certainly does account for the
anthropomorphic conception of God in the Talmud in a far more probable and reasonable manner than by the suggestion of accretions from
Gentile thought, or the depressing effects of hardship and suffering. We
admit with Weber the logical necessity according to which the Legal
conception of religion developed the belief in God as the God of the
Torah. But we think that his interpretation of this belief does not quite
do justice to the religious position of those who held it. It is true that
Weber protests against the notion that the anthropomorphic statements
in the Talmud are absurdities, or actual blasphemies; but yet he seems
to treat them as expressions of a much lower idea of God than the
older one, and maintains that there is a harsh dualism in Talmudic

Theology. A dualism there certainly is, if no more than the verbal expression be considered, but it may be doubted whether it extends deeper.
Is it not rather that such statements as those about God studying the
Torah have no meaning apart from the belief in him as the infinite and
eternal God? That the one doctrine, not merely logically followed from
the other, but was always held in connection with it, in the minds of
the Talmudic theologians? The anthropomorphisms seem to me to be
rather a species of cypher or symbolic language, liable indeed to be
misused and misunderstood, but employed by those who were masters
of it solely to denote great truths of their religion. This applies to those
expressions which connect God with the Torah; those which have no
such reference we take to be simply extensions of the anthropomorphic
principle into regions where it has properly no meaning.

Granted that the Torah, both written and oral, was looked upon as
the sole and perfect revelation of God, then there is no absurdity in
saying that God concerns himself with or studies it. If he studies it,
his angels may do so too, hence the Beth-hammidrash of heaven. And
if the sum total of divine knowledge and wisdom have been revealed in
the Torah, which is committed to his people on earth, then the assertion that a mortal should decide in the controversies of heaven loses
most of its apparent impiety. It is, of course, almost, if not quite,
impossible for us of modern days to think ourselves back into the mental position of the authors of the Talmud, but yet it seems possible that
such peculiar modes of representing the nature and the action of God
should go hand in hand with real reverence and piety towards him. To
take one of these startling statements and expound it as allegory, when
to all appearance it is intended literally, may seem unwarrantable and
unsupported by any evidence in the passage itself. We admit this, and
give as our chief ground for the view we take, the fact, that, judged by
its results, the religion which inspired the Talmud was a strong and
living faith; and such a faith we hold to stand in no need of either
accretions from without, according to Hirschfeld, or forced interpretations intended to give life and colour to an abstract idea, as Weber
maintains, and in such a faith there seems to be little room for a
"harsh dualism." Of course this applies to the religion of the Talmud,
as shown in the most distinguished of the men who made it. Amongst
the host of Rabbis whose words are enshrined in its pages are men of
very different gift, very different mental range. Many no doubt there
were who did not feel the religious importance of the task they were
engaged in, who were merely pedants of schools. And by these, very

probably, the statements about God were understood in a degraded and literal sense. But when it is borne in mind how the Talmud is the result of centuries of patient work, how the study of Torah was the absorbing task of men like Hillel, Jochanan ben Zaccai, Aqiba, Meir, Rab, Abahu, and many others, all of them men of great ability, then it is plain that religion, no matter how strange to modern ideas be the form in which they held it, was a real power in the souls of those who made the Talmud. The form, doubtless, was that of tradition and Legalism, but religion had not lost connection with its living springs in the soul, and thus it could renew itself and enter upon fresh developments, according to the changing needs of the time. The rise of Christianity, instead of being fatal to Judaism, gave it new life; all the latent energy of the old religion was roused to combat the opposition of the new; and even when the loss of the Temple, and later still, the political extinction of the nation, added crushing weight to the blows which had already fallen, still Israel stood firm, and clung to what God had given her to defend. Her sons lived for the Torah, and when that was no longer possible, they died for it. Faithfully each generation of teachers and scholars spent their strength, in face of danger and in spite of scorn, upon the task appointed for them; and to say that the power which inspired them was nothing more than a tradition from ancient days seems to me to fall far short of what truth and justice alike demand. Without this foundation of strong and living religion, the Talmud is inexplicable, for without it there is nothing to show why the best strength of Israel's greatest minds during nearly a thousand years, more or less, should be devoted to such solemn trifling as the Talmud, superficially considered, appears to be. Assuming, then, that the religion which lay at the foundation of the Talmud was strong and real, we maintain that the anthropomorphisms which logically result from the legal principle, are to be understood and interpreted, not literally, but in the light of the more spiritual conception of God, with which they are apparently at variance. Such, we believe, to have been the interpretation of those who framed these peculiar and startling statements of doctrine.

The above explanation applies, as had been said, only to those expressions which directly or indirectly associate God with the Torah. We should account for the others, which are not specially Jewish in form, by saying that the precedent having once been set, of using anthropomorphic language in speaking of God, such language came to be used in cases where it was really unmeaning. It could only be on the strength of such a precedent that such interpretations of texts could be adopted as those which say that God plays with the Leviathan, that he wears a Tallith, etc. (In the case of the first of these, it is probable that the Talmudic interpretation of Ps. civ. 26 is in accordance with the Psalmist's meaning; but, considering the lapse of time between the Psalmist and his Rabbinical interpreter, the adoption by the latter of the anthropomorphic explanation certainly calls for notice.) In expressions of this kind a hidden religious meaning is not to be sought for, at least it is hard to see what edifying truth is concealed in the statement that the Almighty and his angels shaved Sennacherib. But, nevertheless, it would be unjust to found upon these and similar expressions a charge of profanity against the authors of the Talmud; for amidst and beneath all its display of mingled wit and wisdom, fanciful imagination and close reasoning, there is a deep undercurrent of grave and solemn earnestness of resolute purpose, and of unassailable loyalty to religion. And although many isolated details of the Talmud may awaken surprise or aversion, yet it is only fair to consider them and judge them in connection with the entire mighty fabric to which they belong. It is our conviction that as the heroes of Israel, in Talmudic times, did well for their countrymen, so also they cherished a high and inspiring belief in God.

THE IDEA OF TORAH IN JUDAISM

George Foot Moore

The word and idea most characteristic of Judaism in all its history is "Torah," and when your committee did me the honor to invite me to deliver the Leopold Zunz Lecture, casting about me for a subject fitting the occasion and the purpose of the foundation, I could think of none more appropriate than just this central and, so to speak,constitutive idea.

I have used the Hebrew "Torah," not out of any predilection for foreign phrase but because I have no English for it. It is a common observation that terms in different languages do not cover one another in extension. There is, for example, no one English word that corresponds to the French *droit*, as we should find it used in a treatise on law. The case is much worse with Torah. For Judaism is implicit in that word. It means what it means because it belongs to a group, or system, of religious concepts which as such are peculiar to Judaism; it arouses feelings that come out of the peculiar history and religious experience of the Jewish people. The words by which we may try to represent it in another language—whether it be the Greek *nomos*, the Latin *lex*, the German *Gesetz*, or the English "law"—are not equivalent because they lack these implications and bring with them other and quite different associations. Even for the external aspect of Torah, *nomos, lex, Gesetz,* "law" are inadequate: they convey the idea of normative authority derived from the custom of the community, the edict of a ruler, or the statute of a legislative body; none of them suggest the divine origin and authority which is inseparable from Torah. Moreover, the word Torah itself does not mean "law," in the juristic sense, but something more like "instruction, direction"; nor is the Torah exclusively or even predominantly legal. The instructions or responses of the priests are Torah; the message of the prophets is Torah; the counsel of the wise is Torah; a Psalmist introduces his review of the great deeds

160

of God, "Give ear, my people, to my Torah"; in the Pentateuch, Genesis is as truly Torah as Leviticus, the story of the Exodus and the wandering, the exhortations of Moses in Deuteronomy, as truly as the strictly legislative parts of the books.

Still less do these various terms for "law" express the content of Torah, which may be concisely defined as revealed religion, with the further weighty implications, first, that the whole Torah is a revelation of religion; second, that all religion is explicitly or implicitly contained in the revelation; and finally, that revealed religion embraces the whole life of the individual and the nation; there is no partition between secular and religious; righteousness and holiness are the principles of civil and social life as well as of that which we set off as specifically religious, of morals as well as of piety, of ceremonial purity as well as moral integrity.

Scripture was a written deposit of Torah the authenticity of which was guaranteed by the fact that the writers had the holy spirit of prophecy. The fact was universally assumed, but there was no theory of the mode of inspiration; the Platonic conception which Philo adopted has no parallel in rabbinical sources.

The Rabbinical Attitude Toward the Scriptures

Where a religion possesses Scriptures to which divine authority is attributed, it sooner or later becomes necessary to determine what these Scriptures are, or to put it in the way in which the necessity actually arises, to exclude the writings to which this character is erroneously attributed. This process is commonly called the formation of a canon (list) of Sacred Scripture. This stage was reached in Judaism in the generation before the destruction of the Temple. By that time the custom had long prevailed of reading lessons in the synagogues from the Pentateuch and the Prophets, and their right, thus protected by liturgical use, was undisputed. Serious difference of opinion seems to have existed only concerning Ecclesiastes and the Song of Solomon, upon which about the turn of the century an authoritative decision was pronounced favorable to both. In the next generation a similar decision was reached to the effect that the book of Sirach was not Sacred Scripture, nor did this quality attach to the Gospel and other writings of the heretics (*minim*).

The Scriptures were conceived not only to be as a whole a revelation from God, but to be such in every single word and phrase, and to be everywhere pregnant with religious meaning; for religion, by precept or example, is the sole content of revelation. This led, as it has done wherever similar opinions have been entertained, to a fractional method of interpretation which found regulation, instruction, and edification in words and phrases isolated from their context and combined by analogy with similar words and phrases in wholly different contexts, and to subtle deductions from peculiarities of expression. To a student indoctrinated in modern philological methods, the exegesis of the rabbis and the hermeneutic principles formulated from their practice and as a regulative for it often seem ingeniously perverse; but we must do them the justice to remember that not only their premises but their end was entirely different from ours. We propose to ourselves to find out what the author meant, and what those whom he addressed understood from what he said; and to this end we not only interpret his words in their relation to the whole context and tenor of the writing in which they stand, but endeavor to reconstruct the historical context—the time, place, circumstance, and occasion of the utterance, its position in the religious development, and whatever else is necessary to put ourselves, so far as possible, in the situation of contemporaries. The aim of the rabbis, on the contrary, was to find out what God, the sole author of revelation, meant by these particular words, not in a particular moment and for particular persons, but for all men and all time. What they actually did was, speaking broadly, to interpret everything in the Scriptures in the sense of their own highest religious conceptions, derived from the Scriptures or developed beyond them in the progress of the intervening centuries. Thus they not only deduced piles of *halakhot* from every tittle of the Torah, like Akiba, with a subtlety that was quite beyond Moses' comprehension and almost made him faint, but found everywhere the enlightening truths and edifying lessons which they put into the text to take out again. But that has always been the method of religious exegesis as distinguished from historical.

The Written and the Unwritten Torah

The Scripture was for them a revelation of God, complete, and wholly consistent in all its parts and in every utterance. That it contains an imperfect record of the historical development of a religion, or in theological phrase, the record of a progressive revelation for the education of the human race—such modern ideas, if they could have understood them at all, would have seemed a plain denial that the Torah is from Heaven.

Torah was not coterminous with Scripture. Only the smaller part of God's revelation had ever been written down; the unwritten Torah handed on from generation to generation by tradition was much more voluminous. That the written Torah was from the beginning and all through accompanied by a living tradition is unquestionable. A large part of what we call the legislation in the Pentateuch could never have been carried out in practice, or even understood, apart from domestic and social tradition, the ritual tradition of the priests, and the juristic tradition of the elders and the judges. Indeed the lapidary conciseness of the formulation in the written law itself presumes such a concomitant. We are not here concerned with the history either of the written or the unwritten Torah as modern scholars endeavor to construct it, but only with the consistent doctrine of Judaism about them, in which the historical idea of development in our sense has no place. This did not, of course, prevent the recognition of certain epochs in the history of the Torah, such as the work of Ezra and the Men of the Great Synagogue, or the decisions and regulations of the Soferim, but what they did was conceived to be the restoration of Torah that had fallen into desuetude and oblivion, or the bringing to light what was implicitly contained in it.

The Chain of Tradition

From this point of view the unwritten Torah handed down by tradition was revealed no less than the written Torah—it would not otherwise be Torah; and inasmuch as the universal belief at the beginning of the Christian era, and doubtless long before, was that the whole religion of Israel, in idea and act, with all its distinctive institutions and observances, was revealed to Moses at Sinai, it necessarily followed that this revelation included the unwritten as well as the written Torah, down to its last refinements, and even to the last question an acute pupil might ask his teacher.

The written Torah in Scripture had by a singular divine providence been transmitted without the minutest change, even in the spelling since its origin. A similar guarantee of the authenticity of the unwritten Torah was necessary, and this was found in the chain of tradition: it had been transmitted from Moses, through Joshua and the Elders and an unbroken succession of prophets, down to the days of the Great Synagogue among whose members were several prophets, and thereafter through the "Pairs" to Hillel and Shammai, from whom it passed into the carefully guarded tradition of the schools. The genuineness of tradition as a whole and in particulars could only be assured if in every generation it had been in the custody of trustworthy men, especially qualified for the task. Similarly in Christian theory, the bishops were the keepers and transmitters of the Apostolic tradition.

Authority in Jewish Tradition: Scholastic—Not Ecclesiastical

The principal task of the schools in the first and second centuries of the Christian era falls under two heads: Midrash, the study of the Scripture by which the harmony of the written and the unwritten law, and of the one with the other, was established—and Halakhah, the precise formulation of obligations and prohibitions, practical regulations for observance in all spheres of life, and many cautionary ordinances designed to keep man at a safe distance from the unwitting infraction of a law. The Midrash was not in theory and intention a derivation of the unwritten law from the written or a discovery of authority for the unwritten law in Scripture; and whatever increment the unwritten law received from this source was, in the apprehension of those who made it, only a bringing to light of the unity of revelation.

The unity of the Torah in its two branches was always assumed. The authority of all parts of it was the same; for the divine revelation was one, complete and final, from which nothing could be subtracted, and to which nothing was to be added—nothing had been kept back in heaven. In theory and intention purely conservative, the work of the schools in the interpretation of Scripture and the formulation of tradition was in fact the way of progress; through it the unchangeable Torah was adapted to changing conditions.

As in other religions which recognize tradition as a concurrent authority with Scripture—in Christianity and Mohammedanism, for example—not only is a guarantee of the authenticity of tradition necessary, but an authoritative definition, exposition, and application of tradition. But in comparison with Christianity, it is a significant difference that in Judaism and in Mohammedanism this authority is not ecclesiastical but scholastic; it was the learned who were the voice of tradition, and this, it may not be superfluous to observe, in the sphere of the Halakhah only. Dogmas, in the proper sense of the word, are only the fundamental articles of Judaism, the unity of God and the revelation of religion in the Torah, to which was now added the resurrection of the dead. The Haggadic tradition, however highly esteemed, is not binding.

The Identification of Religion With Education

Since God has made a revelation of his character, of his will for man's conduct in all the relations of life, and of his purpose for the nation and the world, the study of this revelation in its twofold form is the first of obligations, the worthiest of occupations. When pursued for its own sake, such study is a religious exercise and a means of grace. The man whose "delight is in the Torah of the Lord, and in His Torah, doth he meditate day and night," is the ideal not merely of the scholar but of the religious man. Study, as well as prayer, is 'abodah, like the service of the altar. Familiar is the eulogy attributed to R. Meir in an appendix to Aboth: "He who studies the Torah for its own sake not only attains many good things, but deserves the whole world. He is called friend (of God), beloved, lover of God, lover of mankind; he delights God and men. It clothes him with humility and reverence, qualifies him to become righteous, pious, honest, and trustworthy. It keeps him far from sin and draws him near to virtue. Others have from him the benefit of good counsel, wisdom, understanding, and power, as it is said, 'Counsel is mine and sound wisdom; I am understanding, power is mine' (Prov. 8. 14). It gives him royalty and dominion and discernment in judgment; to him the mysteries of Torah are revealed; and he is made like a welling fountain and like a river that never fails. He is modest and self-controlled, and forgiving of insult. It magnifies and exalts him above all the creatures."

It would be easy to accumulate examples to show that the zeal of learning in the rabbis is a religious enthusiasm, and that the true end of learning is character. This conception of individual and collective study as a form of divine service has persisted in Judaism through all ages, and has made not only the learned by profession but men of humble callings in life assiduous students of the Talmud as the pursuit of the highest branch of religious learning and the most meritorious of good works.

The religion God had revealed was a religion for every man and for the whole of life, and the condition of the religious life, inward and outward, was knowledge of this revelation, that is of the Torah. This led to an effort, unexampled in antiquity, to educate the whole people in religion upon the basis of its sacred Scriptures. Elsewhere the religious tradition was preserved by a priesthood which made no attempt to instruct others in it and sometimes jealously kept it from the knowledge of the laity. This was true not only of the art and mystery of the cultus, but in even higher degree of the meaning of the cultus and of the esoteric theologies and philosophies which were evolved by priestly speculation. The profounder truths of religion were—in the view of those who possessed them—not only beyond the capacity of the multitude, but were mysteries that would be profaned by vulgar access. Egypt and India in different ways may be taken as illustrations of this attitude. In Judaism, on the contrary, the ideal was a people completely instructed not only in the observances of individual and household religion, and in the form and meaning of the rites of public worship, but in the highest conceptions of the character of God, His righteous will, and His beneficent purpose, to the end that all classes of the community might do intelligently and from the right motive what God required of them, and that every individual might share in those blessings which come from the occupation of mind and heart with religion. The instrumentalities created for this end eventually constituted what we should call a complete system of education, from the elementary stage to the most advanced professional training of the doctor of theology.

A Complete System of Religious Education for All

For the Jews in the dispersion, who had lost their knowledge of the ancient tongue, the Scriptures were translated into Greek; the lessons in the synagogues were read in this translation, and the expository homily or other discourse was delivered in the same language. We are so familiar with translations of the Scriptures as well as of other books into all manner of languages that it takes some effort to realize how radical this step was. The Greek translation of the Pentateuch is the oldest piece of translation on a large scale of which we have any knowledge; and even if the age had been more given to translation of secular books than it was, the translation of sacred books has always encountered strenuous opposition not only from the jealousy of the learned but on religious grounds: the words of sacred Scripture in the original are the very words of revelation, and this quality cannot be communicated to the words of another language, no matter how faithful the version may be. That this way of thinking and feeling was shared by the Jews is evident not so much from the occasional depreciation or condemnation of the Septuagint in utterances of Palestinian rabbis, as in the Alexandrian legends which endeavor to confer upon the translation the authenticity of the original by means of a divine supervision over the translation or the miraculous unanimity of the translators. But if the religious instruction of the masses in Greek-speaking countries was not to be abandoned altogether, it must be given in a language they understood; before this imperative neccessity all scruples had to give way.

In Palestine, and doubtless in Syria and Babylonia, the lessons were, in conformity with long established custom, read in Hebrew, and interpreted piecemeal in the Aramaic vernacular of the land; and in the same language the exposition followed.

The synagogue is a unique institution in ancient religion. Its services had no resemblance to the public worship in the temples; there were no offerings, no priesthood, no pompous ritual. Still less were they like the salvationist sects of the time, the mysteries, with their initiations and the impenetrable secrecy which enveloped their doctrines and their doings. To the Greeks the synagogue with its open doors, its venerable books, the discourses of its teachers on theology and ethics, seemed to be a school of some peculiar philosophy. A school it was in Jewish apprehension also—a school of revealed religion, which was itself for Hellenistic Jews like Philo the true philosophy.

Elementary schools for boys were early established, some supported by the community, some private enterprises. It was from the Hebrew Bible that the pupils learned to read. The lessons in the synagogue were read by members of the congregation, and the regulations for this part of the service which we have from the latter part of the second century assume that ordinarily there would be several present competent to participate in it—an indirect testimony to the existence and efficiency of the Bible schools. Many, doubtless, did not progress beyond this stage; but others continued their studies until they had acquired a more extensive knowledge of the Bible, for which the Bet ha-Midrash, where the better educated part of the community gathered, especially on Sabbath afternoons, afforded additional opportunity. Those who aspired to what we should call the academic career frequented the rabbinical schools, in which they learned Halakhah and Midrash, and at a more advanced stage Talmud (in the older sense of that word). These studies demanded unusual accuracy of memory and an acute intelligence, and many fell out by the way; only the elect few carried their learning to the point where they were recognized as qualified masters of the law and received the *venia docendi et decernendi*. A Midrash on Eccl. 7.28 ("I have found one man of a thousand") tells us: "Such is the usual way of the world; a thousand enter the Bible school, a hundred pass from it to the study of Mishna, ten of them go on to Talmud study, and only one of them arrives at the doctor's degree." Through the higher education was ensured a succession of qualified teachers in every stage; edifying homilists for the synagogues, and in the scholars and their academies a decisive authority for the definition and application of the norms of the Halakhah.

That this system of education as we know it in sources dated from the second century of the Christian era was in reality much older, whatever changes in form may have taken place in the meantime, is to be seen very clearly in Ben Sira, whose reputation as a coiner of aphorisms for the conduct of life sometimes makes us forget that he was an eminent member of the class of *soferim*, professional scholars.

The Universal Aspect of the Torah as Divine Wisdom

The Torah had, however, yet another aspect. For Judaism, while in history and in actuality a national religion, the religion of one of the smaller peoples of the earth, was in idea and in destiny universal. As there is but one true God, one revelation of His character and will, so in the future all mankind shall acknowledge the sovereignty of God, the *malkut shammaim,* embrace the true religion, and live in accordance with its precepts.

The revelation of religion, the Torah, is universal. A significant expression of this idea is the identification of Torah with Wisdom. It is the peculiar wisdom of Israel. Moses says of the statutes and ordinances which by God's command he delivered to the people: "Observe therefore and do them, for this is your wisdom and your understanding in the sight of the peoples, that when they hear all these statutes shall say, surely this great nation is a wise and understanding people" (Deut. 4.6). But it is this because Torah is divine wisdom, or to put it in the way the rabbis conceived it, the Wisdom that speaks in the eighth chapter of Proverbs is the Torah. The identification is a commonplace in the rabbinical literature, and many passages of Scripture referring to wisdom are interpreted in this sense; it appears in Sifré as a universally accepted truth. We can, however, trace it much farther back. In Sirach 24, 23 ff., after a eulogy of wisdom pronounced by itself as in Prov. 8, the passage concludes: "All this (that is, all the great things that he has said of wisdom) is the Book of the Covenant of the Most High God, the Law which He commanded Moses, an inheritance of the congregation of Jacob."

In Proverbs, Wisdom was present at the creation of the world, not as a passive onlooker, but as a participant in the making and in the joy of the Maker. She was at God's side as a skilled artificer, or artist. Identifying Wisdom with Torah, and taking the word *amon* in the sense of instrument, Akiba speaks of the Torah as the instrument with which the world was created. According to others it was the plan, or pattern, after which the world was made. Or again, the world was created for the sake of the Torah. It is permissible to modernize the last words: The world was created for religion; a stage on which, under the guidance of revelation, the right relation between God and men might be realized.

The identification of Torah with divine wisdom and its connection with creation made it premundane: "The Lord made me as the beginning of his way, the first of his works of old." For the Torah was *created,* however long ago; Judaism has no parallel to the eternal Koran of Moslem dogma, rival of the eternity of God. And since God foresaw that men would sin by transgression or neglect, He at once created repentance as the remedy. Without that provision He would never have created the world and frail man in it.

The Torah which was before the world is unchangeable for all time. In the World to Come, indeed, certain prescriptions for the law will have no application because the conditions they suppose cannot occur; but there is no abrogation and no supplement, only perfect fulfillment. And since perfect fulfillment supposes perfect understanding, God Himself will be the teacher there. The wisdom God has searched out and given to Israel is "the book of the commandments of God and the Law that exists to eternity" (Bar. 4.1). "Until heaven and earth pass away not the smallest letter (a *yod*), not an apex on a letter (one koṣ in the Tagin), shall pass away from the Law till it all be done" (Matt. 5.18); "It is easier for heaven and earth to pass away than for one apex of the Law to fall" (Luke 16.47).

The Torah Intended for All Nations

The Torah was in nature and intention for all men. How then

did it come that it was the exclusive possession of the Jews? The God of all mankind could not have been so partial in His revelation. The fundamentals of the Torah, it was taught, had been given to Adam; with one addition (*eber min ha-hai*) they had been renewed to Noah for all branches of his posterity. At Sinai, in the desert that was no man's land or every man's land, the Law had been offered to all nations in their several languages or in the four international languages, and been refused by them because it condemned their favorite sins; Israel alone accepted it. "All that the Lord hath spoken will we do and obey," was the response of the people at the foot of Sinai when Moses delivered to them the revelation of God's will he had received (Exod. 24.7; cf. 3). There for the first time the sovereignty of God, which hitherto had been acknowledged only by individuals, was confessed by a whole people. The Kingdom of Heaven in its national form was founded.

Of greater religious significance than the offering of the Torah in the remote past to the forefathers of all the Gentiles is the emphatic teaching that the Torah, by virtue of its origin and natuie, is for every man. R. Meir found this in Lev. 18.5; "My statutes and my ordinances, which if *a man* do, he shall live by them." It is not said, "priests, Levites, lay Israelites," but "*a man*," therefore even a Gentile; nay, such a Gentile who labors in the Torah (or, does the Torah) is in that respect on an equality with the high priest. Other texts are quoted in the same sense; for example, 2 Sam. 7. 19, "This is the Torah of mankind, Lord God"; Isa. 26.2, "Open the gates that a righteous Gentile (*goi saddik*) preserving fidelity, may enter in thereby" (cf. Psalm 118.20).

The Jews were the only people in antiquity who divided religions into true and false, affirming that Judaism was the only true religion and that it was destined to prevail over all the rest and become universal. Their pretensions and the manner in which they asserted them, especially their mordant satire on polytheism and idolatry, were resented by people of other races and religions, and contributed not a little to the general prejudice against the Jews that was so widespread in the Hellenistic and Roman world. If, as Philo complains, Judaism was alone excepted from the universal religious toleration of the times, it is fair to the heathen to say that Jewish intolerance toward other religions gave great provocation. Early Christianity, it may be added, inherited the attitude, and suffered the same consequences.

Judaism as a Proselyting Religion

But if some of the methods employed to turn the heathen from the error of their ways had a prejudicial effect, on the other hand the faith of Judaism in its truth and universal destiny made of it the first proselyting religion in the Mediterranean world. The universality of the true religion, in the age when "the Lord shall be one and His name one," and "the Lord shall be king over all the earth," was not, indeed, expected to come by human instrumentality or through historical evolution, but in a great revolution wrought by God himself, a catastrophic intervention such as the prophets had so often foretold. Meanwhile, however, the Jews had a twofold task in preparation for that great event; first, to make the reign of God a reality for themselves individually and as a people; and, second, to make known to the Gentiles the true God and his righteous will and convert them to the true religion. This conception of the prophetic mission of Israel among the nations had been set forth by the prophet in Isaiah 42 and 49: Israel is to be a light to the nations, that God's salvation may reach to the end of the earth; and not only reflection but the logic of the situation led to the same result.

In the two or three centuries on either side of the Christian era Judaism made great numbers of converts throughout the wide dispersion. Various Oriental religions in that age were offering the secret and the assurance of a blessed immortality through initiation into their mysteries, and drew into their mystic societies many seekers of salvation. Judaism on the contrary, as we have seen, appeared to ancient observers to be not a mystery but a philosophy. It had a high doctrine about God which was publicly taught in its synagogue-schools, a rule of life, and venerable scriptures in which both the doctrine and the rule were contained; and it sought to make converts by rational persuasion. In this aspect Judaism is sometimes called a missionary religion; but if the phrase is used it must be understood that it was a missionary religion without an organization for propaganda and without professional missionaries. The open doors of the synagogue, a noteworthy apologetic literature, and the individual efforts of Jews in their various social spheres to win over their neighbors, were the only instrumentalities in the conversion of the Gentiles.

Polytheism and idolatry were the salient characteristics of the religions in the midst of which the Jews in the dispersion lived. More intelligent Gentiles, instructed by the prevailing philosophies, regarded both as popular errors, but made no effort to combat them, and were not hindered by their personal convictions from taking part in the rites and festivals of their cities or of the state. Judaism alone was uncompromising. The worship of gods that were no gods was not merely an intellectual error but the sin of sins against the true God, the sin from which all others sprang. Its monotheism was not a philosophical theory of the unity of deity in the abstract, but a theological doctrine of the nature and character of God drawn from His revelation of Himself. There was nothing He was so intolerant of as the acknowledgement of other gods and the worship of vain idols: "I am the Lord, that is my name; and my glory will I not give to another, neither my praise to graven images" (Isa. 42.8).

To convert men from polytheism and idolatry was therefore the prime effort of Judaism among the Gentiles, and it might well seem that the renunciation of these from religious conviction was in principle the abandonment of heathenism and acceptance of Judaism. Even from Palestinian teachers come such utterances as, "Whoever professes heathen religion is as one who rejects the whole Torah, and whoever rejects heathen religion is as one who professes the whole Torah" (Sifré, Deut. 54, end; *ibid*. Num. 111, f. 31b. end).

The One Treasure That Could Not Be Destroyed

Next to this the emphasis was laid upon morality, which in Judaism—one of its singularities—was an integral part of religion, and especially on the avoidance of those vices which the Scriptures persistently associate with heathenism—*'abodah zarah* and *'arayot*.[1] If to this was added observance of the Sabbath and of certain of the rules about forbidden food, and attendance in the synagogue, a man might well be regarded as a convert to Judaism, even though he had not formally been admitted a member of the Jewish people by circumcision and baptism nor assumed as a proselyte the obligations, hereditary for born Jews, of the whole written and unwritten Torah. The number of such "religious persons" was large, and through them the leaven of Judaism was more and more penetrating the mass of Gentile society. Thus the Kingdom of Heaven was growing in the world and preparing for its consummation.

This rapid expansion was arrested by the climactic disasters that befell the Jews in the three-quarters of a century from Nero to Hadrian. But when everything else seemed to be lost, Judaism clung the more tenaciously to the one treasure that could not be taken from it, the Torah. The Temple might be destroyed and with it the whole sacrificial worship abolished, but in the study of the Torah and in good works it had the realities of which the ritual institutes of atonement were but symbols. Hadrian might suppress the schools and put the great teachers to death; the mere possession of a roll of the Law might invite the same fate; but persecution for its sake only made the Torah, sanctified by the blood of the martyrs, more inestimably precious. The disciples of the martyrs perpetuated and ordered the tradition of their teaching; and if one had to name the age in which the study of the Torah was pursued with the greatest zeal and the most epoch-making results, he would, I suppose, take the two or three generations between the catastrophe of the Bar Kokhba war and the death of the Patriarch Judah. It was the supreme proof of faith in the Torah God had given to his people and in God's purpose in it. Nor has Judaism ever lost this faith in itself and in the universal nature and destiny of the true religion whose prophet and martyr Israel has been through the centuries.

The Adaptation of Judaism to Changing Conditions

Today the situation of Judaism is again somewhat similar to that which it occupied in the Hellenistic world or in the Moslem world of the Middle Ages. In the lands of the modern Diaspora, and above all in America, it has, like contemporary Christianity, Catholic and Protestant, the conflict within itself of modernism and reaction. At bottom it is the question whether the finality of a religion lies in the tenacity with which it conserves forms that it has inherited from the past, or in its capacity for indefinite progress wherein its very fidelity to its constitutive ideas enables it to adapt itself to the present and to shape the future. The great epochs in the history of Judaism have been those in which it conceived its nature and mission in the latter way. It was so, as we have seen, in the Hellenistic age, when, in the midst of polytheism and idolatry and the vices of heathen society, it presented its Torah essentially as pure monotheism and a high morality, with the authority not only of revelation but of universal human reason and conscience. Philo interpreted Judaism in the light of the religious philosophies of his time, and expounded its theology and ethics to educated men as the highest and best philosophy.

The work of the Tannaim, which appears to be the deliberate

antithesis of this Hellenizing tendency, was itself a no less far-reaching adaptation of Judaism to the conditions which ensued upon the destruction of Jerusalem with the cessation of the Temple worship and the calamities that befell the nation under Trajan and Hadrian. The preceding period had been characterized by an adaptation to expansion, with the ideal of universality; now threatened with dissolution in the surrounding world, rabbinical Judaism became by force of circumstances an adaptation to self-preservation, and made of the unwritten Torah, with all its distinctive institutions and observances, not only a wall of defense without, but the organic bond of unity within. The survival of Judaism through all the vicissitudes of its subsequent history is proof of the thoroughness of this adaptation.

In the Middle Ages, again, from the tenth century to the thirteenth, the Jews, especially in Moslem lands, took an eager part in the intellectual life of the times. Scholars and thinkers equipped with all the scientific and philosophical learning of the time set themselves not only to prove the truth of the religion as revealed in its Torah but its eminent rationality. This movement, of which Maimonides is the conspicuous exponent, was again an adaptation to a new intellectual environment in the progress of the times.

Finally, when, in the eighteenth and nineteenth centuries, the Jews of central and western Europe emerged from their intellectual isolation, the same capacity for adaptation manifested itself not only in the assimilation of contemporary philosophy, as in Mendelssohn, but in the field of critical and historical investigation, of which Leopold Zunz, whose name we honor tonight, was one of the shining lights. Through these studies the way was made to a new apprehension of the ancient Torah. It had been accepted as a unitary revelation, which shared in its way the timelessness of its author; it had been interpreted in the sense and spirit of Hellenistic, or Greco-Arabic, or modern philosophies; it was now to be understood as an historical growth. This way of apprehending it led to a discrimination not only in the Talmud but in the Torah itself between forms and ideas that belonged to outgrown stages of the development and what is of permanent validity and worth, and so to the conception of a progressive development of the latter elements in the future.

But, however apprehended and interpreted, Torah remains the characteristic word and idea of Judaism. The much debated question, race or religion? is a false alternative. The Jews are a race constituted by its religion—a case of which there is more than one other example. Those who fell away from the religion were in the end eliminated from the people; while multitudes of converts of the most diverse ethnic origins have been absorbed in the race and assimilated to it by the religion. External pressure would not have held the Jews together through these centuries without the internal cohesion of religion—a living and progressive religion; and apart from religion no temporary exaltation of national feeling can in the end perpetuate the unity and peculiarity of the race.

MOVEMENTS

The exile which followed the destruction of the Temple brought with it a much greater degree of religious unity. Prior to this time various sects had flourished within Judaism—Sadducees, Pharisees, Essenes—known in some cases only through the literature of their opponents, which is surely not the best way to get to know them and what they stood for. The famous Dead Sea Scrolls have shed further light—and created new discussions—on the sects of the period since these writings represent a background clearly different from that of the "normative Judaism" of the rabbis. The first two essays here explain Pharisaism, the ancestor of all branches of modern Judaism, and its relationship to its rivals. Podro paints a picture of an important Pharisaic sage, who exercised great influence on the development of liberal Pharisaism and exemplifies the spirit which moved the men who were the bearers of Israel's law. Finkelstein shows how these movements were reflected in day to day practices. Gaster and Ginsberg describe the beliefs and practices of the men who wrote the "Dead Sea Scrolls" which remained buried in obscurity until the day when an Arab shepherd boy stumbled upon them in a long deserted cave.

THE PHARISEES IN THE LIGHT OF MODERN SCHOLARSHIP

Ralph Marcus

I

The name "Pharisee" is synonymous with "hypocrite." This association goes back many hundreds of years to the study of the Gospels and of the commentaries on the Gospels written by men who possessed great philological learning in many fields but not in the field of early rabbinic Judaism. It is one of the great achievements of modern theological scholarship, both Christian and Jewish, to have established the Pharisees as a group worthy of the respect and admiration of all religious men who have enough imagination to understand the methods and results of historical reconstruction.

The English plural form "Pharisees" comes to us indirectly from the Greek New Testament *Pharisaioi,* which in turn is based on the Aramaic *Perishayya,* corresponding to Hebrew *Perushim.* The Hebrew and Aramaic words mean "Separatists," being passive participles of roots meaning "to separate." This much is almost certain. What is not so certain is the origin of the name. Some scholars believe that the Pharisees adopted this name to signify their separatism from less pious Jews. This interpretation is thought to be supported by passages in rabbinic literature in which the *Perushim* are contrasted with the *'am ha-'areṣ* or the ignorant and religiously negligent masses and are equated with the *qedoshim,* "saints" (compare the Greek name *hagioi,* "saints," applied to themselves by the early Christians).

Other scholars think that the Pharisees stressed their separatism from their opponents, the Sadducees, especially in the reign of John Hyrcanus (who reigned ·in the last third of the second century B.C.), and were reproached as Separatists, somewhat as, centuries later, the Moslem pietists who broke with Ali were called Kharijites or "seceders."

A third, slightly different explanation of the name is that the

Pharisees assumed or were given the name of Separatists when they broke with John Hyrcanus over his nationalistic policies.

Finally, a number of scholars hold that the name of Separatists refers primarily to the distinction between pious Jews, on the one hand, and Gentiles or Hellenizing Jews, on the other. Those who hold this opinion cite such passages as Ezra 6:21, in which the priests and returning exiles are said to be "separated" (Hebrew *nibdalim*) from the unclean "peoples of the land." Compare I Macc. 1:2, in which the Hellenizing Jews deplore their "separation" from the Gentiles. In this passage the implication is that separatism from the Gentiles was advocated by pious Jews.

A similar kind of separatism is thought by some to be indicated in some ancient pagan Greek sources which refer to the clannishness of the Jews both in Palestine and in the Diaspora.

In the present state of our knowledge we cannot determine the precise kind of separatism signified by the name *Perushim*. At different times it may have included several of the meanings listed above. Whatever the origin and connotation of the name, it is at least certain that the Pharisees of the first century had no hesitation in applying the name "Separatists" to themselves.

II

Although the ancient sources represent the Pharisees as a distinct party or group (the name "sect" is simply a conventional rendering of Josephus' Greek term *hairesis*, which meant "school of thought"), it is now generally recognized that Pharisaic Judaism is synonymous with normative Palestinian Judaism of the early rabbinic period (which, of course, was preserved very fully throughout the Middle Ages). Many scholars also recognize that the Pharisees carried out the spirit of prophetic teaching.

Certain changes, to be sure, had to be made in the laws ascribed to Moses and the prophets in order to meet the needs of the more advanced post-Exilic community. In order to understand the nature of Pharisaism, therefore, one must bear in mind the social and religious history of the Palestinian community during the period of Persian rule (from about 530 to 330 B.C.).

Judaea as a province of the Persian Empire (and also under Ptolemaic rule in the third century B.C.) enjoyed a great amount of cultural autonomy. But in contrast to the pre-Exilic kingdom of Judah, in which the king and his official prophets and the state priests of the Zadokite line and the nobles of Jerusalem guided domestic and foreign policy, the post-Exilic community was a theocracy (Josephus' term) or, perhaps more accurately, a nomocracy, that is, a state governed by the Mosaic Law.

While the hope for a restoration of the Davidic dynasty was never completely given up, it gradually became more of messianic expectation than a political program. The new state was governed internally by a constitution, namely, the Law of Moses, which probably existed in writing in its present form from at least the time of Ezra (*ca.* 400 B.C.).

Aside from the governors appointed by the Persian king, the chief officers of the Jewish nation were the high priests and their priestly associates in the temple at Jerusalem and the nobles or princes (as they are called in Ezra 9:1 and Neh. 5:7) allied to them by marriage or political interest. These privileged classes were descended from the Babylonian captives who had returned to Judaea during the sixth and fifth centuries. The priests among them, claiming descent from the Zadokite line of the pre-Exilic Jerusalem priesthood, assumed religious and cultural primacy in the state. They regarded themselves as the only authorized interpreters of the Torah or Mosaic Law. Like their descendants, the Sadducees, they jealously guarded the written text of Scripture because any free interpretation of the Torah might undermine their vested rights as stated in the priestly legislation of the five books of Moses.

We should not, however, suppose that the conservative priesthood entirely ignored the prophetic teachings contained in the Bible, especially those of the Book of Deuteronomy, which seems to represent a compromise between the prophetic and priestly teachings of the pre-Exilic period. "That Ezra's law book turned Judaism into an arid ritualism and legalism is refuted by the whole literature of the following time."[1]

We may also suppose that the lay classes and the Levites, who now enjoyed less prestige and smaller revenues than in the pre-Exilic period, were dissatisfied with priestly domination. Just when this dissatisfaction became general and active it is difficult to say. Since Ezra, who was both a priest and a scribe (perhaps in his case meaning secretary for Jewish affairs in the Persian government), was regarded by the rabbis of the talmudic period as a second Moses and as the founder of Pharisaism, it is probable that the conflict of interests between the Jerusalem priesthood and the middle and lower classes had not assumed in his time the clearly marked form which it had in the days of the Pharisees and Sadducees.

It is also reasonable to suppose that in the differences of opinion in social and religious questions between the conservative Zadokite priests and the mass of observant Jews, the latter were supported by the lay scholars and jurists whom the later rabbis called scribes (*Sopherim*). Parenthetically it should be noted that the name "scribes" (Greek *grammateis*) applied to Pharisaic jurists in the Gospels is something of an anachronism, since the Jews of the first century no longer called their jurists by this name.

Rabbinic tradition ascribed to Ezra and the *Sopherim* various practices that furthered the interests of the lay classes, such as the reading of the Targum (Aramaic translation of Scripture) and synagogue services. "The Synagogue with its divine service took a place beside the Temple, the seat of the sacrifices."[2] Whether these lay scribes formed part of a legislative and judicial body during the Persian period we do not know. Rabbinic tradition speaks of the "men of the great assembly" (*anshê hakkeneseth haggedolah*) as if they were members of an official body like the Sanhedrin of the Hellenistic-Roman period, and it is quite possible that there was such a body to advise the high priest and that lay scribes were members of it. Unfortunately, the rabbinic sources about the "men of the great assembly" are too vague to be used with much confidence, although recently Professor Louis Finkelstein has given a plausible reconstruction of their history.[3]

We do know, however, that by the beginning of the second century B.C. there was a professional class of scribes, whose theological and social teachings not only were in line with prophetic doctrine but were also essentially the same as those held later by the Pharisees. This information comes to us from the Book of Sirach or Ecclesiasticus (esp. chaps. 38 and 39). Because of Sirach's admiration for the high priest Simeon and his omission of the name of Ezra from the list of national heroes in chapters 44-50, some scholars have concluded that the author was a Sadducee, but it is unlikely that distinct parties of Sadducees and Pharisees existed in his time. Moreover, his teaching is thoroughly Pharisaic.

Sirach's contemporary, the high priest Simeon the Just, is mentioned in the Mishnah (*Abot* i.2) as one of the "remnants of the men of the great assembly," who were followed by the *Zugoth* or "Pairs" of religious-legal authorities of the second and first centuries B.C. In the half-century or so that intervened between the high priesthood of

Simeon the Just and the emergence of the Pharisaic and Sadducean parties occurred the religious-political crisis that led to the Maccabean revolt against the Seleucid king Antiochus IV Epiphanes and the Hellenized priests and nobles of Jerusalem.

The history of this revolt need not be related here, but it is important to note that among the pious Jews who supported the Maccabees (as the Hasmonaeans are popularly called) in their armed resistance to the Seleucid king and his Jewish sympathizers were the *Asidaioi,* i.e., the *Hasidim* or Pietists. In I Macc. 2:42 they are described as "the strong in power from Israel, every one who volunteered for the Law," which undoubtedly means that they were spiritually strong. In I Macc. 7:12-13 they are associated with the scribes in an attempt to make peace with the high priest Alcimus and the Seleucid general Bacchides.

It is generally recognized that these *Hasidim* were the immediate predecessors of the Pharisees (and, it may be added, of the Essenes, who now, in the light of the recently discovered Dead Sea scrolls, appear to have been a subgroup of Pharisees, who were almost completely withdrawn from the Jewish community). At any rate the *Hasidim,* like the later Pharisees, were more interested in obtaining religious freedom than in seizing political power.

III

The two bodies of ancient writings that furnish the most detailed information about the doctrines and practices of the Pharisees that set them apart from other Jewish groups are the works of Josephus and the rabbinic literature of the Tannaite period, that is, the first two centuries of the Christian Era. There are also allusions to Pharisaic beliefs in the Apocrypha and Pseudepigrapha, but they are usually too vague to be used as accurate sources.

The explicit statements of Josephus and the rabbis should, however, be used with caution. Josephus wrote primarily for Gentiles and with an apologetic motive, and, in so doing, he presented the Pharisees and Sadducees as if they were philosophical schools (*haireseis*) like the Stoics and Epicureans. He therefore stresses their religious and poltical beliefs and neglects their differences in civil and ritual law. In his more extended pasages on the "sects," moreover, he is probably not so much giving his personal views as those of one of his gentile authorities, Nicolas of Damascus, who was an adviser of Herod the Great and an Aristotelian philosopher.

In contrast to Josephus, the rabbis were less interested in reporting the social and religious views of the two parties than in giving details of their disputes about matters of civil and ritual law. Moreover, these reports have come down to us in the writings of scholars who were themselves disciples of earlier Pharisaic leaders and lived at a time when the Sadducees no longer existed as a party of equal power with the Pharisees.

The information given by Josephus may be summarized as follows. The Pharisees, who had enjoyed the confidence of the Hasmonaean ruler John Hyrcanus early in his reign, were angrily repudiated by him when they objected to his retention of the high priestly office. His successors, with the exception of Queen Salome Alexandra, were even more violently hostile to the Pharisees. During the reigns of King Alexander Jannaeus and Aristobulus II many Pharisees were killed in open warfare.

As for the social and religious attitudes of the Pharisees, Josephus makes the following observations. In contrast to the Sadducees, who enjoyed the support of the wealthy few, the Pharisees had the masses of Jews on their side and were therefore able to force the Sadducees to follow their rulings. While the Sadducees accepted only the written law as binding, the Pharisees also made use of oral tradition. Whereas the Sadducees denied the intervention of Providence in human affairs, the Pharisees held that Providence ruled the universe; at the same time they recognized man's freedom of moral choice, resulting from his co-operation with God's will. The Pharisees believed in the survival of the soul after death and in the resurrection of the righteous and in the eternal punishment of the souls of the wicked. These eschatological beliefs the Sadducees denied.

Turning now to the evidence of rabbinic literature, we find what at first sight seem to be only trivial differences of opinion in matters of ritual or civil law. But thanks to the researches of modern scholars from Geiger to Ginzberg (whose contributions will be noted below), it is now clear that these seemingly casuistic interpretations of biblical texts are to a large extent rationalizations of significant divergences of social, economic, and religious attitudes. A few examples may suffice to support this view.

One of the controversies between the Pharisees and Sadducees

concerns the susceptibility of metal and glass vessels to ritual uncleanness, which would make them unfit for household use. To
understand the underlying motivations of the two groups, we must
bear in mind that biblical law mentions only vessels of wood, stone,
and pottery in connection with the law of ritual contamination,
since these were the materials in common use among the Israelites
of the early biblical period. We must also take note of the fact that
during the Hellenistic period wealthy Jews began to import vessels
of metal and glass. With these facts in mind we can understand more
fully why the Pharisees, who represented the masses, insisted that
the more expensive vessels should be subject to the same laws of
ritual contamination as vessels made of cheaper materials. The
Pharisaic extension of biblical law not only revoked the special
privilege of the wealthy but also served to provide the masses with
a sort of protective tariff, since local artisans who sold vessels of
wood, stone, and pottery must have suffered from the competition of
foreign manufacturers of the vessels of metal and glass which wealthy
Jews imported in their "conspicuous consumption."

A more puzzling controversy centers about the interpretation of
the biblical verses (Lev. 16:12-13) which prescribe the manner in
which the high priest is to cause a cloud of incense to rise when he
enters the Holy of Holies on the Day of Atonement (the only day
of the year on which he was permitted to enter this most sacred
place, which was separated from the larger chamber of the Temple
by a veil). The passage reads:

He shall take a pan full of coals of fire from the altar before
the Lord and a handful of finely ground fragrant incense and bring
them within the veil and shall put the incense on the fire before the
Lord, and a cloud of incense shall cover the Mercy-seat which is
on the Testimony (the ark), that he may not die.

The Pharisees interpreted this to mean that the high priest was
to cause the cloud of incense to rise only after entering the Holy
of Holies ("within the veil"). The Sadducees argued that he was
to cause the cloud of incense to rise before entering the Holy of
Holies ("before the Lord").

There have been several attempts made to discover the real
reasons for what on the surface seems merely a difference of opinion
about the literal meaning of the biblical text. Some of these modern
theories are extremely ingenious but not altogether convincing. With
some diffidence the present writer would like to suggest that the

concealed issue was the prestige of the high priest, a prestige which the hierarchical Sadducees constantly sought to enhance and the anti-hierarchical Pharisees to lessen. If we assume that the larger chamber of the Temple was visible to the priests and lay Israelites gathered in the Temple court on the Day of Atonement (which gave the high priest an opportunity to play the most important part in what was the most dramatic and spectacular ceremony in the Temple ritual), we can understand why the Pharisees tried to deprive the high priest of some of his glory by forcing him to send up the cloud of incense behind the veil in the Holy of Holies, where the spectators could not see him.

The preceding example has been cited precisely because the real motivation of the controversy is obscure; it may serve to explain why certain eminent Christian scholars have failed to understand the nonritual aspects of the rabbinic sources. Lest the reader remain skeptical that such assumed motivations really existed, a more obvious example of the social-economic background of a ritual controversy may be cited as the last of these illustrative instances.

Every morning and evening the priests of the Temple sacrificed a lamb as a burnt offering, called *Tamid*. The Sadducees held that the money used to purchase these sacrificial animals might be contributed voluntarily by individuals. The Pharisees insisted that the money must be taken from the public fund raised by levying a yearly half-shekel tax upon Jews throughout the world. Although the rabbinic account of this controversy makes it appear that their difference of opinion was based on the use of singular and plural pronouns in the biblical text (Num. 28:2-4), it is obvious that the democratic Pharisees, who were concerned to give laymen as large a share as possible in the Temple cult, were unwilling to let the conservative and wealthy Sadducees claim credit for privately financing what was originally and essentially a public sacrifice.

If we study the other halakic (ritual and civil) controversies between the Pharisees and Sadducees with the same contextual method, we see that the rabbinic sources agree on the whole with the differently oriented testimony of Josephus (or his source) in showing that the Pharisees were the party of what may be called progressive, democratic, and liberal Jews (with due allowance, of course, for the differences between ancient and modern social and political attitudes), while the Sadducees were members of a specially privileged and therefore conservative class.

IV

Scientific discussion of the Pharisees as a party may be said to have begun with the works of Abraham Geiger, one of the founders of liberal Judaism. In the latest formulation of his views in lectures delivered between 1872 and 1874 to German audiences, Geiger stressed the aristocratic nature of the priesthood and its control of the Judaean senate and the "Great Assembly," as well as its attempt to make the Temple in Jerusalem the great religious center of the country. According to Geiger, the Pharisees were the champions of freedom, who protested against the privileges of the hierarchic Sadducees. They therefore sought to give the liturgy of the synagogue equal importance with the sacrificial system of the Temple. Some of Geiger's critics have claimed that he conceived of the struggle between Pharisees and Sadducees as similar to that between the liberal and orthodox Jews in the Germany of his own generation. There is some truth in this claim, but the same kind of subjectivity and transference may be found in the views of his critics.

Writing about the same time as Geiger, the French scholar Derenbourg argued that the Pharisees or Separatists "substituted for the sanctity of the priesthood, which their birth denied them, a greater severity in morals and conduct." While some controversies between the parties remained in the realm of theory, others reflected the special economic interests of the two groups, such as that over the defraying of the cost of the daily *Tamid* sacrifices. Derenbourg believed that Josephus exaggerated the Sadducees' reliance upon worldly power into a denial of Providence, and their indifference to the afterlife into an absolute denial of it.

A wholly different estimate of the Pharisees was made by the eminent German Protestant scholar, Julius Wellhausen. He minimized the importance of the rabbinic sources and relied heavily upon the Gospel narratives (see below), as was to be expected from a theologian who regarded the Judaism of the scribes as a deterioration of prophetic religion. Believing, in his ignorance of rabbinic methods, that the scribes were chiefly concerned with regulating the minutiae of law, Wellhausen bluntly stated that "the strength of the prophets is the weakness of the Scribes and vice versa." Having in the back of his mind the supposed characteristics of his German Jewish contemporaries, he stressed the "excessive intellectualism" of the Pharisees and "the ethical and religious materialism" of their followers. He therefore contemptuously rejected Geiger's theory that the Pharisees were liberal and democratic. In spite of his prejudice, Wellhausen performed a useful service in calling attention to the distortions (of which he failed to recognize the largely subconscious nature) in the rabbinic accounts of the earlier history of Judaism.

Heinrich Graetz, author of the celebrated *History of the Jews,* (5th German ed., 1888) spoke of the essential difference between the Pharisees and the Sadducees as being a religious versus a political attitude. He rightly argued that the epithet "hypocrites" applied to the Pharisees could hardly have been justified in view of the respect and admiration which they received from the Jewish masses of their time. Some of the controversies between the two parties, Graetz believed, arose from their conflicting views on social and political questions, while others were due to the literalism of the Sadducees' interpretation of Scripture. But Graetz did not attempt to analyze the reasons for the literalness of the Sadducees.

More sympathetic toward the Pharisees than Wellhausen but more critical than Geiger was Emil Schuerer, author of the most widely used Protestant work on the history and religion of the Jews of Palestine in the time of Jesus. According to Schuerer, the Pharisees were "genuinely Jewish" in regarding political problems from a religious point of view, although they were obliged to take political action when the Hasmonaean rulers attempted to encroach upon the Law. While the Pharisees reflected the views of the Jewish masses, they were a small group, an *ecclesiola in ecclesia,* and were popularly regarded as representing the ideal type of Jew. Schuerer expresses skepticism of Geiger's attempt to find a general principle in the halakic controversies between the Pharisees and Sadducees as they are reported in the rabbinic sources.

An anti-Pharisaic attitude, almost as strong as that of Wellhausen though differently motivated, was shown by the Jewish scholar, Moritz Friedlaender, who preferred assimilationist Judaism to what he called "neo-Pharisaic" Judaism in his own day. According to Friedlaender, the Pharisees interrupted the natural development of prophetic religion by making it narrowly particularistic, whereas the spirit of prophetic universalism continued to exist only in the teachers of Wisdom and the intellectual leaders of the Hellenistic Jewish Diaspora.

Another Jewish scholar who disagreed with Geiger's appraisal of the Pharisees and Sadducees was Rudolf Leszynsky. He argued that Josephus' statements about the Sadducees' denial of resurrection and Providence (which he takes to mean a denial of the validity of prophecy) have misled modern scholars into considering the Sadducees as primarily a group of worldly politicians. Since they believed in an Aaronite rather than a Davidic Messiah, they naturally supported the Hasmonaean priest-kings. "That later the rich Sadducees, who had become powerful, developed in part into worldly people is a secondary result that has nothing to do with the essential nature of the party."

The eminent German historian of antiquity, Eduard Meyer, in discussing the Jewish parties in the second volume of his work on the origins of Christianity, expressed partial agreement with Leszynsky and rejected the view that the Sadducees were indifferent to religion. He makes an interesting comparison of the opposition between Sadducean conservatism and Pharisaic liberalism with that "between the frozen Lutheran orthodoxy of the seventeenth and eighteenth centuries and Pietism or between the English High Church and Methodism or between the Roman Church and the Franciscans." Meyer recognized that the Sadducees found their chief supporters among the priestly and lay aristocrats and that the Pharisees in opposing the worldly policies of the Hasmonaeans had popular support. But, he argued, only a marginal group of Pharisaic extremists came into armed conflict with rulers like Alexander Jannaeus. Most of the Pharisees, however, were opposed to any king and wanted a theocratic state.

In his authoritative work on Judaism in the first two Christian centuries George Foot Moore dealt only briefly with the differences between the Pharisees and Sadducees. While pointing out that in the ancient Jewish sources only the religious aspects of their controversies were presented, Moore admitted that the growing tendency to emphasize the social rather than the purely dogmatic differences between the leading sects "gives a good explanation of the fact that the Sadducees were almost exclusively of the upper classes."

Perhaps the most important contributions to the study of this problem since the time of Geiger have been made by Louis Ginzberg (whom, by the way, Moore in writing his *Judaism* frequently consulted as one of the "living repositories" of rabbinic learning). According to Ginzberg, there was a basic difference in outlook between the Apocalyptic and the "legalistic" (i.e., civic-minded) Pharisees. The latter, moreover, were divided into a conservative and a progressive wing from the beginning of the Pharisaic party, *ca.* 170 B.C. (We must bear in mind that the conservative Pharisees were more liberal than the Sadducees.) Both wings were represented in each of the *Zugoth* or "pairs" of religious leaders in the last two pre-Christian centuries. In the time of the first three *Zugoth* the conservative wing was more influential, while in the time of Shemaiah and Abtalion, and still more in the time of Shammai and Hillel (contemporaries of Herod the Great), the progressive wing was dominant. After this period the interpretation of Scripture became more theoretical and controversies increased until ca. A.D. 90, when the Council of Jabneh made the more liberal Hillelite interpretations binding upon all Pharisaic teachers.

In discussing the religious attitude of the Pharisees, Ginzberg stresses the fact that the Pharisaic idea of the Kingdom of Heaven was "neither eschatological nor political but the rule of God in the heart of the individual." The Pharisees "were strongly nationalistic but their nationalism was of a spiritual kind." Angelology and demonology played an unimportant part in Pharisaic Judaism, since the Pharisees sought help directly from God, and they regarded the "yoke of the Law" as a joyful burden. "The Sadducee taught the immobility of the Torah; the Pharisee maintained its immutability, which is not stereotyped oneness but the impossibility of deviating from its own course."

Like many contemporary scholars, Ginzberg holds that it is as little justifiable to characterize Pharisaic Judaism as legalistic as it is to identify Christianity with antinomianism, since the rabbis denounced legalism as severely as the Church Fathers denounced antinomianism.

Another notable defense of the thesis that the Pharisees were a group of progressive Jews who rebelled against the conservatism of the Sadducees was made by the late Jacob Lauterbach in a series of lectures delivered in 1928. In trying to explain the somewhat paradoxical fact that the progressive Pharisees championed the traditional Oral Law while the conservative Sadducees rejected it, Lauterbach plausibly argued that "the written Torah actually favors the priestly authorities, no matter how liberally you interpret it. But if the traditions of the fathers had preserved laws given by God to Moses and handed down to the teachers by word of mouth, the authority of these lay preachers would be established as equal with that of the priests. The Pharisees would therefore not limit God's revelation and teachings to the written Torah alone." Lauterbach suggests that the Pharisees were unaware of their radical departure from older views, such as those held by the Sadducees, and that they sincerely believed that in their interpretations of Scripture they were following the traditions of the fathers.

Less convincing is Lauterbach's theory that the Sadducees attributed such overwhelming importance to the written Torah because their fathers, in the time of Nehemiah, had taken a solemn oath to obey it. Surely their conservatism can better be explained by the fact, freely admitted by Lauterbach himself, that the written Torah heavily favored the priestly hierarchy.

An estimate of the Pharisees similar to those of Ginzberg, Lauterbach, and other Jewish scholars is made by the British Protestant theologian, R. Travers Herford, who in several influential books has insisted that the Pharisees continued to teach the beliefs of the Prophets but deepened them by laying stress on the nearness of God and the personal relation to Him of the individual soul.

During the past two decades considerable interest has been aroused by the theory of Louis Finkelstein, proposed as "a working hypothesis," that the Pharisees were originally an urban, and the Sadducees a country, group but that gradually the Pharisees, through their peculiar eschatological teachings and their democratic ideas, won to themselves the mass of Judean followers, so that by the time of Josephus there were left to the Sadducees only the wealthiest families of the nation.

Although Finkelstein in a two-volume work on the Pharisees has thrown much light upon the continuity of tradition in the period of the Second Commonwealth, his central thesis has not been generally accepted. He has not clearly established the rural antecedents of the Sadducees, nor has he shown that the social differences between urban and rural populations which exist today also existed in ancient Palestine and can be used to explain the controversies between the two groups which are cited in rabbinic literature. Furthermore, he has ignored the peculiar problem of ancient "agricultural cities," as they are called by Rostovtzeff in his *Social and Economic History of the Hellenistic World*. In his general characterization of the Pharisees, however, Finkelstein agrees with those scholars who hold that Pharisaism was a continuation of prophetic Judaism and was essentially liberal and democratic.

From this brief survey of modern scholarship in the field of early postbiblical Judaism it will be seen why an increasingly large number of Christian scholars working on the origins of their own faith have come to recognize the validity of the views held by Geiger and his successors and are prepared to vindicate the Pharisees of the age-old charge that they were narrow legalists and hypocrites.

V

We must now return to the initial statements of this paper and consider the attitude of modern Christian scholars toward the anti-Pharisaic statements attributed to Jesus in the Gospels. There is not space here for a detailed analysis of the specific passages, about a dozen in number, in which Jesus is reported to have criticized the Pharisees for being overscrupulous about the observance of the ritual laws or for showing too little regard for the needs of the poor and sick. It should, however, be noted that only in one or two instances, such as the lawfulness of divorce or man's right to forgive sin, does Jesus clearly challenge the Pharisaic interpretation of Scripture. In other cases, he merely goes further in the extension of privilege, and in some cases he even repeats a Pharisaic formula such as the statement that the Sabbath was made for man, not man for the Sabbath.

In explaining the unfavorable estimate of the Pharisees attributed to Jesus in the Gospels, many Christian scholars, including Harvie Branscomb, Frederick Grant, R. Travers Herford, George Foot Moore, and Donald Riddle—to name but a few—have suggested that Jesus was not attacking the Pharisees as a whole, since his own religious and ethical beliefs were almost wholly in agreement with theirs, but was attacking those Pharisees who took advantage of their position of authority to exploit or oppress the masses.

Another important point raised by modern liberal Christian scholars is that the authors of the Gospels were more hostile to the Pharisees than was Jesus himself. As Riddle puts it:

The piety of the Pharisees and the Jewishness of Jesus are found to be friendly rather than antipathetic. It is possible to witness Jesus living his life within the environment of first-century Judaism and in fact depending upon his background for much of his greatness. It is possible, with equal confidence, to witness the extension of Christianity as the cult of Jesus' followers into non-Jewish localities, and to see in it non-Jewish situations developing un-Jewish habits and customs. Indeed, it is possible to witness the shading over of their attitudes from un-Jewish to anti-Jewish positions.[4]

Writing in another connection, Henry J. Cadbury reminds us that "in spite of all their objectivity, the Jesus of the Gospels is not and was not meant to be merely a figure of history." This is merely another way of saying that the Evangelists were not scientific historians but were men possessed by a mission to present to the non-Christian, chiefly the pagan, world the argument that Jesus was the savior of mankind, whose divine nature had gone unrecognized by all but a handful of Jewish leaders, although he had won great numbers of simple Jews to his messianic faith.

Because of their own bias against the Pharisees the authors of the Gospels have not made it clear that many of Jesus' sayings and his use of parables to convey religious and moral teaching are not only Jewish but even Pharisaic in both content and form. This has been demonstrated by two Protestant scholars, Strack and Billerbeck, in their four-volume collection of rabbinic parallels to the New Testament.

That some of Jesus' charges of hypocrisy made against some Pharisees were justified is not only inherently probable but is confirmed by the existence of similar charges made by the rabbis themselves.

Where there was a clear difference between the views of Jesus and those of the Pharisees, it may reasonably be explained by the assumption that the institutional responsibilities of the Pharisaic jurists made it impossible for them to adopt the radical attitude toward traditional law that was possible for a non-professional teacher of unlearned believers such as Jesus.

Unpleasant as it is for modern Jews to carry on the long and wearying struggle to exculpate the Pharisees from the charges of hypocrisy and uncharitableness made against them by the Evangelists, it is the more consoling to realize how much modern Christian scholarship has done to correct the popular belief that there was an irreconcilable difference between Jesus and the Pharisees.

PHARISEES, ESSENES AND GNOSTICS
Ralph Marcus

About a hundred years ago Abraham Geiger inaugurated the modern phase of the discussion of the essential nature of Pharisaism, and his revision of views long current among Christian theologians may be said to have been accepted by the majority of modern scholars. The Pharisees as a whole are no longer generally considered narrow legalists but are recognized to have been the more liberal and democratic middle-class party of Palestinian Jews in the Hellenistic-Roman period, which consistently opposed the social and economic conservatism of the wealthy and hierarchial Sadducees of the higher priesthood and lay aristocracy.[1]

But two other influential groups among the Jews of that period have proved more difficult to understand and to relate to the other social-religious groups. These more enigmatic groups are the Essenes and the Gnostics. One reason for our greater uncertainty concerning the nature and origin of these two groups, as compared with the fairly well understood Pharisees and Sadducees, is that in their case we do not have diverse sources that can be checked against one another, for example, Philo, Josephus, and Rabbinic literature. The Essenes are not explicitly mentioned or clearly described in Rabbinic literature (unless we accept the doubtful theory that the Greek form *Essaioi* represents Hebrew *Hasha'im,* and Greek *Essēnoi* represents Hebrew *Senu'im;* it is far more likely that both Greek words represent the Aramaic plurals of the words *hasa,* "pious," corresponding to Hebrew *hasid,* and the word *hasid* has a great variety of meanings in early Rabbinic literature). As for the Gnostics, it is not certain, though probable, that they are to be identified with the *Minim* of early Rabbinic literature, but even if they are, we are told very little about the beliefs and practices of the *Minim.*

The discovery of the Hebrew scrolls in the caves of Khirbet Qumran on the western shore of the Dead Sea has, of course, brought new material of great importance for the study of these problems, but in the light of the texts so far published one may justifiably wonder whether the new material does not present as many new problems as solutions of old ones. It appears, however, that on the whole our knowledge has increased more than our ignorance. In this brief paper I shall attempt merely to outline in very broad fashion the picture of Palestinian Judaism that seems to emerge from a preliminary study of the Qumran scrolls and from a comparison of their contents with those of certain Hellenistic-Jewish writings, the apocryphal-pseudepigraphic literature and early Rabbinic literature.

First of all the Qumran scrolls clearly come from the same group that produced the Damascus Covenant. When this fragmentary document from the Cairo Genizah was published by Schechter in 1910 a few scholars suggested that the covenanters were Essenes, because they detected a resemblance between their institutional regulations and those ascribed to the Essenes by Josephus. This view was not generally or even widely accepted, perhaps because of the authority of R. H. Charles who ruled out Essene affinities on the ground that the Damascus covenanters performed animal sacrifice while the Essenes disapproved of this rite. His opinion, however, was based upon a misunderstanding of the two ancient sources which deal with the problem. Philo (*Quod Omnis Probus 75*) merely says that the Essenes enjoyed a reputation for piety "because they have shown themselves especially devout in the service of God, not by offering sacrifices of animals but by resolving to sanctify their minds," and Josephus (*Ant.* XVIII.19) says that though the Essenes sent offerings (anathemata) to the temple, they practiced a peculiar form of sacrifice and were therefore excluded from the temple precinct (*eirgomenoi* is always passive, never middle voice in Josephus).[2] Thus the Damascus covenanters might well have been identified with the Essenes or at least closely related to them. But Charles gave good reasons for recognizing them as close to the apocalyptic Pharisees. And in 1922 the great Talmudist, Louis Ginzberg, whose recent death is a heavy blow to Biblical as well as Rabbinic studies, in his unfinished work *Eine unbekannte jüdische Sekte* showed in great detail that the Damascus covenanters agreed in almost all points of Halakah with the Pharisees.

Is it possible, then, that the Damascus covenanters closely resembled both the Essenes and the apocalyptic Pharisees? The answer is yes; it is possible and even probable if we further assume that the

Essenes and the apocalyptic Pharisees were closely related. Such an assumption is in keeping with the fact that the Damascus covenant with its asceticism, allegorizing, pessimism and determinism resembles such apocalyptic works as Enoch, Jubilees, the Testaments and the like, which a good many scholars have held to be of Essene origin because of these features.

Apparently then in the second and first centuries B.C. there were Pharisees who exhibited certain tendencies that distinguished them, though it did not alienate them, from the Pharisaic authorities whose beliefs are preserved in the Mishnah and other Tannaite writings. Now we know that these early Rabbinic writings deliberately avoided apocalyptic speculation. Indeed, as the same Louis Ginzberg stated in a symposium on eschatology of the Society of Biblical Literature, held in 1921:

"It would therefore not be true to the ascertainable facts to maintain that for the leading Rabbis in the first and second generations after the destruction of the temple the Messianic hopes were not as actual and real as they were for the generation living at the time of the great catastrophe or shortly before it. . . . The great rabbis clearly perceived that the apocalyptic view which lacked touch with the vital problems of man really endangered the moral elements in the Jewish religion . . . yet very likely the vagaries and phantasmagoria of the apocalypses about creation . . . were primarily responsible for the disappearance of this kind of literature from among the Jews . . . the demonology and angelology of the apocalypses not rarely discussed by them in connection with the story of creation were again of a nature that could not but repulse (repel) those who were not blind to the danger lurking in the attempt to train popular fancy to a system of theology."[3]

To this statement of Ginzberg I would venture to add that in particular the Pharisee authorities were alarmed by the dualistic tendencies of apocalyptic, which they thought might lead to a belief in the *shtey reshuyoth* or "two powers," namely of good and evil. This theological tendency is one of the few ascribed to the *Minim* in early Rabbinic literature. For various reasons, into which I have not time to enter now, it has become clearer in recent years that while the term *Minim* in the Rabbinic and patristic literature of the third century and afterward may refer to Jewish Christians, in Tannaitic writings it chiefly designates Jewish Gnostics.[4] I may remark in passing that some scholars, e.g., R. Travers Herford,[5] who insist on taking *Minim* as referring to Jewish Christians, are in error partly because they take the doctrine of "two powers" to refer to the dual nature of Jesus Christ rather than to the two cosmic principles of good and evil.

From the brief outline given above, it appears that in place of Josephus' scheme of four Jewish social-religious groups, Sadducees, Pharisees, Essenes, and Galilaeans or Zealots, we may draw up a scheme that is more fluid and shows more gradual transitions from one group to the other. In the present state of our knowledge such a scheme as the following might be helpful.

- I. Extreme right — Sadducees
- II. Center — Pharisees
  - A. Right wing — Shammaites
  - B. Middle — Hillellites
  - C. Left wing — Apocalyptic Pharisees
  - D. Unclassified — 'Am Ha-areṣ
- III. Left of Center
  - A. Essenes
  - B. Gnostics
- IV. Extreme Left — Zealots

It should be noted, of course, that the terms "left" and "right" here refer not to theological but to social-economic orientation.

It may well be doubted whether modern analogies to ancient social groups are very instructive or helpful, but on the small chance that they may be, I should like to suggest that very roughly and *mutatis mutandis* (*quantum mutatis ab illis*), the following correspondences might be set up.

Sadducees	— Republicans
Shammaite Pharisees	— Conservative Democrats
Hillellite Pharisees	— New Deal Democrats
Apocalyptic Pharisees	— Radical Democrats and Progressives
Essenes	— Socialists
Gnostics	— "Lunatic fringe" (in Theodore Roosevelt's sense)
Zealots	— Communists

The above tentative scheme is based on the literature known before the Qumran scrolls but partly reinterpreted in the light of the scrolls. These new documents have converted earlier surmises into quasi-certainties. For example, the close resemblance of the Qumran covenanters' organization, as described in the Manual of Discipline, to that of the Essenes, as described by Philo and Josephus, as well as the location of the covenanters' headquarters north of En Gedi shows that they and the closely related Damascus covenanters were some sort of Essenes. The close parallels in the Damascus Covenant and the Qumran scrolls to Enoch, Jubilees, the Testaments, etc., show that the covenanters were also closely related to the apocalyptic Pharisees. Thus the Essenes were closely related to the apocalyptic Pharisees. Moreover, the Gnostic (I use the term in the restricted sense of Jewish Gnostic) elements in the Manual of Discipline, Hymns of Thanksgiving, and the Wars of the Sons of Light and the Sons of Darkness show that the Essene-like apocalyptic-Pharisaic covenanters were also closely related to the Jewish Gnostics.[6]

The Qumran scrolls also help to settle a long-standing controversy as to whether Essenism was essentially Jewish and a late form of early Israelite anti-urban, ascetic primitivism or whether it was essentially a syncretistic form of Judaism, deeply influenced by foreign doctrines whether Iranian or Syrian or Pythagorean or a combination of these. The answer seems to be that in most respects the Essenes accepted Pharisaic teaching, but from non-Jewish sources, chiefly Iranian,[7] had absorbed more deeply than the Shammaite and Hillellite Pharisees certain Gnostic beliefs, which are presented both in the apocalyptic writings of the Hellenistic-Roman period and in the Qumran scrolls.

In conclusion, I should venture to characterize the Essenes and the Qumran-Damascus covenanters as gnosticizing Pharisees, further specifying that they were probably more gnostic than most apocalyptic Pharisees but less gnostic than those Jews regarded by the Tannaite authorities as heretics and referred to by them as *Minim*.

A FIRST-CENTURY JEWISH SAGE

Joshua Podro

"Since Rabbi Joshua died, good counsel has ceased in Israel" (Sotah 49b). This was a contemporary opinion of the value of Rabbi Joshua ben Hananiah's leadership and the effect of his death on the Jewish people.

Born during Pontius Pilate's procuratorship, he lived under thirteen emperors, some crazier than others, but almost all of them gods in their own eyes: Tiberius, Caligula, Claudius, Nero, Galba, Otho, Vittellius, Vespasian, Titus, Domitian, Narva, Trajan, and Hadrian. A competent Greek scholar, he knew not only his own people but their enemies. He may well have realized how vulnerable the Roman Empire was to concerted attack, for not only the Jews but the Parthians and the German barbarians were watching for an opportune time to strike. Yet Joshua struggled with the people against the temptation to revolt. He belonged to a school founded by Hillel, which taught that the public good must be considered in terms of the misery or happiness of individuals. The Hillelite motto, "Seek peace and pursue it" (Psalm 24:14), amounted in the present context to the preaching of non-resistance, and Joshua declared himself for peace when the provocation to take up arms was almost irresistible. He gained the title of "good counselor" and, indeed, no one so truly translated into everyday action Hillel's humanitarian principles. He was an enemy of foolish piety, of hypocrisy, of visionary fanatics who tried to negate the values of this world by harping on the next. He opposed the imposition of additional ceremonial and legal burdens because the people might find them hard to bear. He did not, however, attempt to make life easier for himself.

While already famous as the outstanding religious authority of his generation he continued to work in an atmosphere of smoke and soot, earning a meager living as a smith. He was at the same time an eloquent defender of the Jewish faith before the outside world. If he lived frugally, it was because he would not "use the Torah as a coronet" or as a "spade with which to dig" (Aboth I. 13; IV.7).

Rabbi Joshua was the representative of a universalist Judaism which combined the prophetic with the Rabbinical outlook, and without inner contradiction. He believed in Judaism as a universal religion in which room could be found for all humanity. The doctrine of racial purity did not impress him. His attitude toward the admission of proselytes to Judaism was a revolutionary one. He argued that the circumcision was not necessary, only baptism (Yebamoth 46a). Whether he made this statement mainly to take some of the sting from Paulinist propaganda is a matter for speculation, but he certainly made the most liberal concessions to all foreigners who wished to meet under the "wings of the Shechinah."

Joshua converted the Emperor Hadrian's nephew, Aquilas. Whereas Eliezer the Shammaite distrusted prospective proselytes and became impatient at their questions, Joshua showed the patience of his master Hillel when confronted with those who came to scoff but stayed to learn. Aquilas did not come to scoff, but he might have been lost to Judaism but for Joshua's sympathy and friendship (Koheleth Rabbah VII.8).

Like Yohanan ben Zakkai, his master, whom he carried in a coffin, disguised as dead, through the Roman lines around Jerusalem, Joshua was prepared to be misunderstood and called a traitor in his efforts to avoid suffering. He realized that the Jews had to live with other nations, and he set himself to reduce bitterness and international discord.

Though one of the greatest figures of post-prophetic Judaism and, under Trajan and Hadrian (until the outbreak of the Bar Kokeba war), factually the leader of all Israel, Joshua is little known to non-Jewish historians. Not a single adequate biography of him exists. The references to him—as an authority, an opponent, or a witness—in both Talmuds, Sifre, Sifra, Mekilta, and other Midrashim occur in connection with subjects with which he was in many cases only incidentally concerned. Most of these references are only indirectly biographical, and cite opinions rather than events, yet we catch an occasional glimpse of his personal life from them. I have here tried to fit his life's story together from the scattered fragments. This has involved a reconsideration of the chapter in Jewish history with which his name is associated.

Joshua was born, probably in Jerusalem, about the year 35 C.E. He was a Levite, and he himself records that he sang in the Temple choir (Arakin 11b). Since a Levite could not have taken part in the Temple service before the age of thirty, he must have reached that age by 67 C.E.

Nothing is known of his father, but it may be assumed that he served in the Temple in one of the many trades and professions open to Levites, who worked as masons, potters, carpenters, doorkeepers, singers, money-changers, butchers, musicians, and so on. It is said that Joshua's mother used to bring him in his cot to the Beth Ha-Midrash so that his childish ears should become habituated to the sound of the Torah. Though perhaps figuratively intended, this is not a posthumous legend but a story told by a man older than Joshua himself, his colleague, Dosa ben Horkinas (Jer. Yebamoth I.6).

Joshua's childhood must have been spent in an atmosphere of continuous complaints against the High Priestly families, to whom the Temple service was now a mere formality. Their way of life resembled that of any aristocracy anywhere; scarcely involved with the life of the people, they were allied politically and economically with the Roman invaders. Joshua may well have been sent to a Pharisaic school at a very early age; certainly his later education was given him by men who had openly declared war against the "rulers of the Temple." The war was fought mainly in the lecture hall. The Pharisees taught the people not to depend on their priests for theological or even ecclesiastical service. In the first century the Pharisees spoke with authority on all vital matters of doctrine and Scriptural interpretation, while the priests' domain was limited to such matters as animal sacrifice, the diagnosis of leprosy, and the collection of tithes.

The thirty-odd years of Herod's rule—when most political activity was driven underground—had given the Pharisees an opportunity to work among the people, teaching them to read, to pray, and even to study. By the time Herod died the Pharisees had won a powerful hold over great numbers of Jews, and by the time of Joshua's birth, forty years later, education was almost wholly in their hands. Despite their economic and social disadvantages, the active left wing of the Pharisees, namely the Hillelites, were not only more numerous but more influential than the Shammaite right wing, who came from a richer part of the community. A spontaneity of approach, an unconcern with the dignities of rank, and, above all, a love of peace for the people's sake are implied in the Hillelite view.

Rabbi Joshua inherited this tradition from Rabbi Yohanan ben Zakkai, who often quoted the words of the prophet: "Not by arms, not by power, but by My spirit" (Zechariah IV.6). Rabbi Yohanan was Hillel's youngest disciple, but the fact that the Pharisees offered him their leadership at the death of Hillel's grandson, Gamaliel, suggests that he was also the worthiest.

The rigid discipline which later controlled the relations of master and disciples seems to have been unknown in his day: Yohanan treated disciples as friends and equals, praising them without stint when he saw the orchard in which he had labored beginning to bear fruit. He greatly encouraged the art of debate. Skillful debating was a necessity at this period: the Pharisees must "know how to answer the Epicurean" (Aboth II.14). Disruptive forces threatened not only from outside, but from within; many parties and sects claimed to possess the whole truth, and each treated the others as impostors. The smaller the sect, the larger its claim, the more vociferous its argument, the more insolent its attitude toward the rest of Jewry. A skillful debater himself, Yohanan trained his disciples to become defenders of the faith in accordance with the teachings of Hillel. Here Joshua emerged as his most capable pupil. Endowed with a dry scholarly humor, conversant with several languages, he was later to debate with Agnostics, Christians, Epicureans, Gentile philosophers, and potentates, including even the Emperor Hadrian. But it is in Joshua's formulation of attitudes to the problems of living, drawn from his interpretation of Judaism, that his true importance lies.

When new religious doctrines were aired before him, he showed none of the petulance that would have been expected from his contemporary, Rabbi Eliezer, but always said simply: "This must be an innovation of the scribes, and I have no comment to make" (Kelim III.7). Rejecting the "other-worldly" movement of those days, he looked upon life in this world as an important field of action, not without joy, and belonging to the "children of men." Pain and suffering were real, and he made it his task to reduce them wherever possible. He was, as I have said, against the imposition of new duties or restrictions upon the Jews: "Do not put on the people more obligations than they are capable of bearing" (Baba Bathra 60b).

Unlike his predecessors, he felt that there was a pressing need to prevent from hardening into law what had been originally only theoretical speculation or optional practice. Previously, the need had been to adapt the written law to changed social conditions by oral commentary; now this commentary had led to excessive control and needed a less rigid restatement. Thus in matters of Halachah, Rabbi Joshua was the leader of the "lenient" as opposed to the "strict" teachers. His opinion on the Rabbinic laws relating to vows, for example, was that ". . . the laws on Sabbath, Feasts, and Desecration of Holy Things have little Scriptural authority: many Halachahs are like mountains hanging on hairs with nothing on which to support themselves" (Tos. Hagigah I.9).

Extremism, both during and after the war against the Romans, was the curse of the nation. On one hand stood the remnants of a defeated and embittered Jewish army; on the other, numerous mutually hostile sects, each making extravagant claims. Among these was the sect called "Christian" in Antioch, whose members began to claim that they were the real Chosen People and all others worthless leavings, and who vied in piety with the Essenes and the other apocalyptic groups engaged in continuous prayer and in other "otherworldly" practices. But Rabbi Joshua reminded the people that they had work to do—"Six days *shalt* thou labor"—and had no right to abandon their normal occupations. Though not wishing to belittle the importance of Scriptural study, he suggested that "if one studies two Halachahs in the morning and two in the evening, it is counted as if one had fulfilled the whole of the Torah" (Mekilta Beshallah).

He commented icily on those who indulged in excessive fasting and mourning:

> Our Rabbis taught: "When the Temple was destroyed for the second time, ascetics who would not eat meat or drink wine increased in Israel: Rabbi Joshua approached them, saying: 'My sons, why do you neither eat meat nor drink wine?' They replied, 'How could we eat meat when it was once sacrificed on the Altar which has now ceased to be?' He replied 'In that case let me refrain also from bread because the meal offerings have ceased.' They replied 'Yes, we could live by eating fruit.' Joshua said: 'No, we should not eat fruit because the offering of first fruits has also ceased'" (Baba Bathra 60b).

When the people of Ludd declared a fast on a day of Chanukah, possibly to commemorate some local calamity, Joshua told them: "And now you should fast again, to win forgiveness for having fasted on a holiday!" (Tos. Taanith II.5.)

He tried to inculcate a practical and clear-headed attitude at a time when the apocalyptic visionaries had made converts in the most unexpected quarters. He poured cold water on the widespread belief that the present troubles were the "Pangs of the Messiah" and that the end of the world was imminent. He said:

> I received a tradition from Rabbi Yohanan ben Zakkai who received it from his teacher (Hillel), and his teacher from his teacher, as a Halachah given to Moses on Sinai, that Elijah will not come to declare unclean or clean, or remove afar or to bring near, but only

to remove afar those families that were brought near by violence and to bring near those that were removed afar by violence (Eduyoth VIII.7)

He meant that the return of Elijah, foretold by Malachi as a preliminary to the coming of the Messiah, would have as its sole object the return to Israel of those Jews who had been carried away from it, and of the removal of the non-Jews who had been settled in Israel in their place. Joshua's interpretation is directed, apparently, not only against the Pauline Christians, who claimed that Jesus as the Messiah hailed by "Elijah"—John the Baptist—had annulled the Mosaic distinction between clean and unclean, but also against the Essenes and all others who expected Elijah to recognize their exceptional holiness and give them preferential treatment in the world to come, after destroying the rest of the people. In effect, Joshua was warning his fellow Jews not to indulge in exaggerated hopes of new heavens and new earths, but to be content with the expectation that the Messiah would reunite Israel and inaugurate an era of peace.

In the name of common sense he also opposed arguments based on an appeal to miracles. In a memorable discussion with Rabbi Eliezer, Joshua uttered what was in those days a very daring opinion: that human beings should take no notice of heavenly voices (*Bath Kol*). The discussion concerned ritual, in which Joshua as a rule showed much less interest than did the conservative-minded Eliezer. The latter's position was rejected by an overwhelming majority of the scholars, whereupon he appealed—or so a picturesque legend has it—to magic. Eliezer said:

"If the Halachah be according to my view, let this carob tree prove it!"Whereupon the carob tree was rapt a hundred cubits out of its place or, as some say, four hundred cubits. They (scholars) replied: "One does not bring proof from a carob tree." He said again: "If the Halachah be according to my view, let the stream of water prove it!" Whereupon the stream flowed backwards. "One does not bring proof from a stream of water," they replied. Again he said: "If the Halachah be according to my view, let the walls of this schoolhouse prove it!" Whereupon the walls made as if to fall. Then Joshua turned and rebuked the walls, saying: "When scholars are engaged in a dispute over Halachah, what business is it of yours to interfere?" So the walls did not fall—in honor of Rabbi Joshua; yet they also did not resume their upright position—in honor of Rabbi Eliezer.

The argument did not, however, end there. Rabbi Eliezer invoked the heavenly voices to bear witness that his opinion was the correct one.

"If the Halachah be according to my view, let it be proved from Heaven!" Whereupon a heavenly voice cried out: "Why argue with Rabbi Eliezer, considering that in all such matters that have to do with Halachah his view is the correct one!" Then arose Rabbi Joshua and exclaimed: *"It is not in heaven—but very nigh unto thee in thy mouth and in thy heart to do it"* (Deut. 30:12 and 14). (The Talmud continues:) What did R. Joshua mean by this? Rabbi Jeremiah answered: "(He meant that) the Torah had already been given (once) at Mount Sinai, and we should pay no attention to a heavenly voice, because Thou, O Lord, hast long since written in the Torah: *After the majority must one follow* (Ex. 23:2)."

Joshua recognized that never had there been such need in Israel for common sense and moderation as after the crushing defeat by Rome. A steady untroubled routine of living was required if the wounds were to heal, and he opposed the extremists in both camps: the revolutionaries who advocated continuation of the war by guerrilla methods, and the Rabbis who wanted every waking hour to be devoted to study, without considering how the scholar was to earn a livelihood for himself and his family.

Mutual mistrust and even hatred clouded the relations between the scholars and the common people. Joshua was one of the few Pharisees who showed real tolerance and understanding in this matter. The term *am ha'aretz* (man of the land) was not limited to the farmers, for the alleys and side streets of Jerusalem were thronged with people who were called *am ha'aretz*; it implied either ignorance or a careless rejection of the Torah as interpreted by the Pharisees. Yet the Talmud contains a "favorite saying" dating from this time that is described as "a pearl in the mouth of the Rabbis of Yavneh":

> I am His creature and my fellow (the *am ha'aretz*, according to the Rashi) is His creature. My work is in the town; his work is in the country. I rise early for my work and he rises early for his work. Just as he cannot excel in doing my work, so I cannot excel in doing his work. Say, if you will, that I do much (study) and he does little? (The answer is), as we have learnt, that one may do much and one may do little; but what matter so long as each directs his heart to Heaven (Berakoth 17a).

This saying is attributed to the "Rabbis of Yavneh," yet it is known that most Rabbis distrusted the *am ha' aretz*. Alone among the

Tannaim at Yavneh, Joshua respected labor, being himself a worker in a physically exacting trade, and he may have been the sole author of this saying; in any case it is known that he tried to bridge the gap between the learned and the people.

Joshua grouped the over-pious with the evil-hearted and hypocritical as enemies of mankind, and said: "Foolish saints, cunning scoundrels, women ascetics, and the plague of the Pharisees are destroying the world" (Sotah III.4). The Gemara explains what Rabbi Joshua meant by a foolish saint: "If a woman is drowning in the river such a man would say: 'It is improper for me to look upon her (which I would have to do if I rescued her).' " Rabbi Huna defines a cunning scoundrel as "one who is lenient with himself and strict with others." By the "plague of the Pharisees," Rabbi Joshua meant those who pretended to imitate the true Pharisees, but were impostors and hypocrites. This passage has been misunderstood by Christian theologians who tried to find in it confirmation for the charge of hypocrisy leveled against the Pharisees in the New Testament.

Joshua held, further, that a holiday must not be devoted entirely to God: half should be devoted to God and half to merrymaking. In this spirit he ridiculed the fasters, the wailers, and the over-pious.

There was one respect in which Joshua's objectivity failed him, at any rate in general theory, though perhaps not in practice: I mean in his attitude to women.

His own domestic life was a sad one. He married a priest's daughter who contracted, probably soon after the marriage, a sickness from which she never recovered. He seems never to have married again nor to have had children. He made one cryptic remark about his married life: "Aaron was not pleased that I should cleave to his seed, and that he should possess such a son-in-law as me" (Pesahim 49a). This may mean that the marriage was opposed by the bride's parents, who may have been wealthy and influential Jerusalemites; or that it proved a failure since there were no children and the marriage was short-lived. He cannot have implied that fate was unkind to him, since this would have been to question God's purpose. But this personal experience may well have contributed to his negative outlook on woman's character in general—or perhaps it was this general outlook which made his marriage difficult. He would not accept a woman's word when she claimed that she had been raped unless she could produce some proof of her disinterestedness (Ketuboth I.6). He maintained that if a married woman were seen in the street with a man unknown to her husband, her protestations that he was an honorable man, or even a priest, were to be rejected unless she could produce witnesses to attest to the innocence of the meeting. He once said: "A woman has more pleasure in one *cab* (measure) with lechery, than in nine *cabs* with modesty" (Sotah III.4). Women's defects, he held, were a physical inheritance from Eve. To the question "Why is it harder to pacify a woman than a man?" he answered: "Men were created from dust; pour a drop of water on dust and it softens at once. But Eve was created from bone; though you pour on bone any amount of water, it will not soften" (Bereshith Rabbah XVII.14).

Nevertheless, he advised men to marry: those particularly who had already been married in their youth should take another wife, even if widowed in old age (Yebamoth 62b). He did not, however, follow his own advice—perhaps his lack of physical attractiveness was the obstacle (Taanith 7a). When Rabbi Yohanan ben Zakkai had asked his favorite disciples to answer the question: "What is the best thing to which you could cling?" Joshua's reply was "a good companion"—one with whom to share one's learning, confidences, and possessions, and to be bound to in reciprocal loyalty—rather than that good wife whom Solomon had rated above rubies (Aboth II.2).

Joshua's outbursts against women are quite out of keeping with the gentleness he otherwise displayed. Yet even his misogyny did not obscure his vision when dealing with particular cases. It is related that a Gentile woman came before Eliezer and asked to be converted. He inquired into her past. She replied: "My youngest son comes from my eldest son." Eliezer dismissed her, so she went to Joshua and confessed her past to him. He accepted her for conversion. His disciples said to him: "R. Eliezer drove her away, yet you brought her near!" Joshua replied: "As soon as she made up her mind to accept the Law she ceased to live in her (former) world: as it is written: *None that go unto her return, if they do return* (to their former ways), *neither do they attain unto the path of life* (Prov. 2:10)." He meant that the past was dead to anyone, even a woman, who sincerely wished to reform.

Two relationships, with Akiba and with Gamaliel, reveal much of Joshua's personal character, and show also his status in Jewry and his political vulnerability.

The Talmud records that Akiba studied under Eliezer before becoming Joshua's disciple. But Eliezer took so little notice of him as not even to be aware of his existence, until one day Akiba, now with Joshua, surprised Eliezer by his outspokenness. The discussion was one between Eliezer and Joshua on the proper sacrificial procedure when a Passover fell on a Sabbath, and Akiba intervened in support of Joshua. Though Eliezer would allow his friend Joshua to contradict him, he was not prepared to let Akiba, whom he all but accused of trying to uproot the written law, to do so. Joshua's comments on this occasion are not recorded, but on another he twitted Eliezer with having failed to recognize the brilliant scholar who had sat at his feet for years and was now his most formidable opponent. He quoted the Scriptural sentence: "These are the people you despised, now go out and fight against them!"

Joshua ordained Akiba as a Rabbi and even dared instruct him in the mystic secrets known as the "works of the Chariot," which were reserved for men of superlative wisdom and holiness. He watched Akiba closely, allowed himself to be defeated by him in argument, and apparently felt pride in his pupil's extraordinary grasp of the Torah.

His relations with Gamaliel, who was in his early twenties when elected president of the Beth Din, of which Joshua, then aged forty-five, was vice-president, is highly revealing with regard to the character of the national leadership of that age. The name Beth Din was given to the Sanhedrin as it reconstituted itself at Yavneh, after the siege of Jerusalem and the destruction of the Temple: it continued to legislate as the Jerusalem Sanhedrin had done and gradually obtained the recognition of Jewry as a whole. The Patriarchy was the presidency of this body, which was occupied by descendants of the House of Hillel, with two exceptions, Yohanan ben Zakkai and Eleazar ben Azariah.

Gamaliel stressed, and even overstressed, the need for unity. Since the Jews seemed incapable of achieving unity of their own accord, he was determined to impose it upon them by every means at his disposal. That he was less experienced than his colleagues, some of whom were twice as old as himself, may have induced a certain nervous arrogance in him, and his autocratic tendencies and his tactless treatment of his colleagues, particularly Joshua, are frankly admitted in the Talmud, where no attempt is made to cover up or justify any of his unjust acts. We should remember, however, the unhappy condition of the people whom Gamaliel was called upon to guide. No effective orders or prohibitions could be issued in Palestine by any Jewish authority. The Beth Din wished to become a national center of authority, but was divided against itself. The struggle was not only between those who accepted the unwritten law of the Pharisees and those who rejected it, but also between the Hillelites and Shammaites, who threatened to divide the Torah into two Torahs, and therefore the people into two peoples.

Joshua, too, sought unity in Israel, but did not believe that Gamaliel's iron discipline would achieve it.

Gamaliel, as a wealthy aristocrat, must have felt uncomfortable in Joshua's authoritative presence, perhaps feeling the latter's independence of mind to be rooted in a plebeian attitude of opposition. Clashes between the two would probably have occurred often but for Joshua's forbearance. None of the three momentous incidents that, as recorded in the Talmud, culminated in the dethronement of the Patriarch, and led to far-reaching reforms and changes at Yavneh, were of Joshua's seeking: furthermore, in all three he was the loser.

The first incident concerned a debate about the "fixing of the new moon." This most important prerogative belonged to the Sanhedrin, who presumably had delegated their authority to the Patriarch. The fixing of holidays depended on the first sighting of the new moon, and the matter was of particular importance in the months Tishri and Nisan, when the most important feasts occur. Once, on the eve of Tishri, two witnesses came before Gamaliel and testified that they had seen the new moon. Gamaliel accepted their testimony, but a very old and influential councilor, Dosa Ben Horkinas, did not. According to his calculations, the moon could not yet be visible and he declared that the witnesses had perjured themselves. Joshua, an astronomer himself, agreed with him, as did Akiba, but Gamaliel would not give way. As vice-president of the Beth Din, Joshua was himself qualified to fix the calendar (Eduyoth VII.7), but Gamaliel decided to make an example of him for having dared to challenge his decision. Joshua was ordered to appear in court in working clothes, with stick and wallet, on the day which, according to his own calculations, would be Yom Kippur.

Gamaliel sent this order to Joshua by Akiba. Joshua was so distressed at receiving it that he cried, "Rather would I lie on a sick bed for a year than bear this!" Akiba consoled him but advised submission. Joshua went to Dosa, but he too said that Gamaliel, as president of the Sanhedrin, must be obeyed. So on the day which he regarded as Yom Kippur Joshua dressed himself as ordered, took his stick in hand, threw a wallet over his shoulder, and presented himself to Gamaliel. As he entered Gamaliel stood up, kissed him, and said: "Welcome my master and my disciple! You are my master in wisdom, and my disciple for obeying my summons. Happy the generation when the great listen to the small!" Though this should have mollified those who resented the outrage to Joshua's conscience, the incident left a painful impression and Joshua's admirers in the Sanhedrin were determined to forestall any further attempt to undermine his dignity.

The second incident was that of the "blemished first-born animal." Joshua had opposed a number of Halachahs approved by Gamaliel, and though he refrained from public opposition once the vote had been taken, he nevertheless stated his views to his colleagues in private. This, Gamaliel seems to have regarded as a breach of discipline. Many Jews were at this time not only still paying their tithes to the priests, but even handing over to them those of their first-born animals which before the destruction of the Temple would have been sacrificed on its altar. What was to be done with a sheep or goat that could no longer be dispatched with the correct ritual? The Halachah agreed upon was that it should be allowed to graze with the priest's flock, but the priest might not claim and use it for his own purposes unless he discerned a blemish which made it unfit for sacrifice. But could a priest be trusted in a case like this? Might he not himself inflict a blemish on the animal and thus acquire it without delay, instead of allowing it to graze for many years at his own expense? Joshua held that if the priest were a Pharisee his honor should not be questioned He was overruled, the court deciding that every priest, whether a Pharisee or not, whose animal had suffered a blemish must rest under suspicion until he could prove that it was of natural origin.

Rabbi Zadok, who was a priest, privately confided to Joshua that one of the first-born animals grazing in his field had cut its lip while grazing. "Am I under suspicion?" he asked. Since Zadok was a fellow Pharisee and reputedly a man of honor, Joshua replied: "I cannot suspect you." But when the question was referred to Gamaliel, the latter said that so far as this Halachah was concerned there was no difference between Zadok and an *am ha'aretz*.

The more closely the case is studied, the more probable does it appear that Rabbi Zadok was acting provocatively. If the Halachah had already been decided by a majority vote, why did he privately ask Joshua for his opinion? Even if he had really wanted Joshua's opinion, why did he then reveal it? When the next public session of the court opened, Gamaliel asked: "Does anyone here challenge the truth of the accepted Halachah of the blemished first-born beast?" Joshua had no alternative but to admit that it was unchallengeable. It never occurred to him that his private assurance to Zadok, "I cannot suspect you," would come before the tribunal. But Gamaliel called on Zadok to testify that Joshua had expressed a view contrary to the Halachah. Not satisfied with this humiliation, he called upon Joshua to remain standing in his place until the end of the session. The temper of the assembly had now reached the boiling point. A third incident brought the opposition to Gamaliel to a head.

It was under Gamaliel that the *Sh'moneh Esreh* (the Eighteen Benedictions) were at last edited, and their repetition three times a day was made obligatory. Joshua, thinking how few of the uneducated would be able to learn this complicated prayer by heart or spend so long a time in prayer, composed a shortened version of the Eighteen Benedictions, which is recorded in the Talmud by Mar Samuel. This provoked no incident, but Joshua's equally definite views on the evening prayer of *Ma'arib* led to his third clash with Gamaliel. It seems to have been started, perhaps innocently, by a third party. The *Ma'arib* had just been made obligatory by Gamaliel and accepted by the Beth Din, despite the opposition of Joshua, who believed that it was optional. Soon after the decision had been taken a young scholar named Shimeon ben Yohai privately asked Joshua whether the prayer was optional and was answered in the affirmative. The matter came to Gamaliel's ears, and he regarded it as an affront to his authority. He said to Shimeon: "Wait and see what happens when the *Baale Tresin* (the armored ones) arrive in the Beth Ha-Midrash," and then arranged for someone to ask, as soon as the session opened: "Is the evening prayer obligatory or optional?" Gamaliel himself answered at once that it was obligatory. He then turned to the assembly and asked: "Does anyone dispute the ruling?" Joshua, realizing that the challenge was directed against himself, replied, "No."

This clearly contradicted his private opinion. (The only plausible explanation for his disowning his private opinion is that he did not wish to injure the interests of national unity.) Gamaliel showed his dissatisfaction with this brief "No" by pressing him: "Are you not reported to me as having said that the prayer should be optional? Stand up, Joshua, and let a certain man testify against you!" Rabbi Joshua stood up and said: "If I were alive and the witness were dead, the living could contradict the dead. But since both of us are alive, how can the living contradict the living?"

Gamiliel did not give Joshua leave to sit down again, but left him standing while he proceeded to expound a passage in the Torah unconnected with the prayer. In the end, both achieved the contrary of what they wanted: Gamaliel, instead of enhancing his authority, lost it, and Joshua, who had submitted to humiliation in the hope of unity, provoked disunity. For when the assembly saw Joshua standing before them like a punished schoolboy, while Gamaliel was proceeding with his normal exposition, ". . . all the people began to shout '. . . how long will you continue to insult him?' " (Berakoth 27b). Reminding Gamaliel of other occasions on which his lordly ways had caused resentment in the House, they cried: "Who has ever avoided being the victim of your ill will?" (Jer. Taanith VI.1). That same day they deposed Gamaliel from his presidency.

Not a voice was raised in his defense. He left his exalted chair and took his place, without a word, among the ordinary members. Realizing that he had overstepped the mark, he behaved with serene nobility; instead of sulking, he took an active part in subsequent debates and did not try to oppose the new, "revolutionary" conditions in the Beth Din, which lasted until he made his peace with Joshua.

It was difficult to find a successor to Gamaliel. Though Joshua was older and more learned, he was never proposed—probably because he was the cause of the upheaval, and no one wished to humiliate Gamaliel as he had tried to humiliate Joshua. Besides, Joshua was poor, and the Talmud, with strong historical backing, explains why a rich man was required as president; nor did he even come of a distinguished family. The next most worthy candidate would have been Rabbi Akiba, but he, too, was poor and had even less claim to distinguished ancestry than Joshua, having been an *am-ha'aretz* in his younger days and descended from a proselyte. Nonetheless, Akiba expressed keen disappointment at being passed over in favor of a man younger even than Gamaliel, namely Eleazar ben Azariah, who is described in one source as having been eighteen years old at the time, and in another as having been no more than sixteen. He cannot have already been a member of the Beth Din, because with his appointment its membership reached the unusual number of 72, instead of 71. Akiba grumbled: "It is not that he (Eleazar) possesses more knowledge than I, but that he has a more illustrious family: happy are those for whom their ancestors create privileges, happy are those who have a peg to hang themselves upon!" (Jer. Berakoth IV.1).

On the day of Gamaliel's deposition all restrictions were annulled that barred from the Beth Din scholars who did not comply with the standards he had set. When its doors next opened, several hundred scholars crowded in. The Talmud hints tactfully that they had hitherto been excluded in error as not being, as Gamaliel believed, "worthy disciples." At the same time Joshua's motion to abolish the exclusion of Ammon and Moab was passed.

Gamaliel must have realized that he had underestimated Joshua's influence among the people; feeling, no doubt, in the wrong, he decided to ask his pardon. On his arrival at Joshua's home, he was astonished to find it a miserable, soot-blackened hovel. He faltered: "From the walls of your house it would seem that you are a smith." Joshua replied: "It is a pity that you have taken so long to find that out. Woe to the generation whom you have led, men ignorant of the straits in which scholars live, and with what difficulty they make ends meet." Gamaliel said: I am humbled, forgive me." When Joshua did not reply, Gamaliel said: "Forgive me for my father's sake," whereupon Joshua accepted his apology.

When their reconciliation became known, a movement was started for Gamaliel's reinstatement as president. Akiba, however, led an energetic opposition; he had the doors of the Academy locked to prevent Gamaliel's followers from entering and "causing confusion among the Rabbis." Joshua, however, said: "Let him who is accustomed to wearing the robe (of office) wear it." Akiba protested to him: "Did we act for any other reason than to defend your honor?" But Joshua induced him to change his attitude, and Gamaliel was restored to the presidency.

Yet, despite his apparent victory, it was Joshua who came out the most discomfited. Gamaliel was restored, but the only way to remove young Eleazar ben Azariah without doing him deep offense was by appointing him vice-president of the Sanhedrin in place of Joshua. Perhaps it was then, and not earlier, that the latter moved to Peki'in, a small town between Yavneh and Lydda.

Joshua was around eighty at the accession of Hadrian, the thirteenth Roman emperor to whom Judea had been subject during Joshua's lifetime. Trajan had won the reputation of a bloody and vindictive ruler; Hadrian began as a man of peace and surrendered almost without a fight what was left of Trajan's conquests: Armenia, Mesopotamia, Assyria, and Parthia. He became the famous traveler, the brilliant conversationalist, the polymath, the philosopher king concerned for the welfare of his subjects. He bestowed freedom wherever he would ultimately have been forced to do so anyhow—Trajan had bequeathed him so many uneasy conquests that hardly a corner of the Empire remained placid.

Roman finances were in a confused, if not desperate, state. The Parthian war and the Jewish insurrection against Trajan had devastated rich districts at the expense of the Roman treasury, which was largely supported by provincial taxation; the need for pacification impressed itself on Hadrian, and he was willing to make large concessions to that end. Joshua led the negotiations with him. He hoped for the immediate granting of two urgent requests: the dismissal of Lucius Quietus, then Legate of Judea, and permission to rebuild the

Temple. Hadrian complied with the first by having Quietus, whom he regarded as a possible rival, executed. The Jews, ignorant in all likelihood of his real reason, concluded that Hadrian had removed their arch-persecutor to gratify them, and considerable relief was expressed.

It was not difficult for Joshua, as a well-known pacifist, to gain Hadrian's confidence and persuade him to grant his second plea, which after all demanded no political innovation. There is every reason to believe that it was Joshua who obtained the earlier promise from Trajan of permission to rebuild the Temple, the retraction of which had caused the latest Jewish rebellion. That this second promise was taken seriously is shown by the feverish activity reported from all Jewish communities. The story (by a Christian 'Father, Epiphanius) that Hadrian appointed Aquilas as the new governor of Jerusalem would mean, if true, another conciliatory gesture on the emperor's part.

As in the time of Ezra, the rebuilding of the Temple was opposed by Israel's neighbors, and also, it must be supposed by the Pauline Christians. The Midrash gives the following account, which appears to have telescoped two incidents but may nevertheless signalize Joshua's position after the rescinding of the second promise (Bereshith Rabbah LXIV.7):

> In the days of Rabbi Joshua ben Hananiah the wicked Kingdom ordered that the Holy House should be rebuilt. Thereupon Pappus and Lullianus established exchange stations (tables) from Acco to Antioch so as to provide the *olim* (Jews from foreign countries) with their needs in silver, gold, and the like. Then came the Kutheans (Samaritans) and said: "Let it be known to the Emperor that when the city is rebuilt and its walls are established they will not pay toll, tribute, or custom." The Emperor then said: "What are we to do? I have already given the order (promise)." "Tell them," they counseled, "to build the Temple on another site, or to increase or decrease its size by five ells; then they will withdraw by themselves." The people were thickly assembled in the Valley of Beth Rimmon and when the letters written in this sense arrived they broke out into weeping and wished to revolt. Then said (those in charge): "Let the sages come and pacify the people. Let Joshua ben Hananiah arise, for he is wise in the Law." Whereupon came Rabbi Joshua ben Hananiah and said: "A lion destroyed his prey, but a bone caught in his throat: he offered a reward to anyone who would remove the bone. A long-beaked Egyptian crane thereupon

came and removed it. When the crane asked for the promised reward, the lion said that it was enough reward that she could boast
of having put her head into a lion's mouth and suffered no harm.
So let it be enough for us to boast that we faced this people and
escaped in peace."

Joshua had lived through wars and rumors of wars, witnessed the
gradual impoverishment of the land, seen how after every struggle the
common people had become more brutalized, forlorn, and embittered
than before. The Zealots still believed that war would restore their
political power and allow them to rebuilt the Temple for themselves.
Joshua was convinced that no human effort could restore national
sovereignty, but only God—and His hand could not be forced. He
spoke with authority to this effect. His colleagues do not appear to
have contradicted him, and at the Valley of Beth Rimmon he succeeded in averting an open revolt—which may have been due in part,
it is true, to a lack of arms among the Jews.

So far from regretting his broken promise, Hadrian decided subsequently, it seems, that the Jewish religion, which recognized solely
its own God as master and king, and had spread far beyond the bounds
of Palestine, constituted a threat to the Empire. The record of the un-
yielding Jewish attitude to Rome ever since Pompey may well have
convinced him that the only way to overcome it was to destroy the
Jewish religion. There seems no other explanation for his ban on
Jewish rites, especially circumcision, which, like his plan for erecting
a pagan temple in Jerusalem, probably preceded Bar Kokeba's revolt.
Hadrian's severity toward the Jews may have been aggravated, moreover, by wounded pride: wherever else he traveled he was received
and worshiped like a god; these people alone would not offer him
sacrifices.

In 130 C.E. Hadrian broke his journey down the Syrian coast
from Antioch to Egypt to visit Jerusalem. Sixty years had passed since
the city had been sacked by Titus, yet he saw the Jews still clinging to the
ruins of what had once been the symbol of their nationhood. He decided to abolish the Jewish religion by wiping out every sign of
Jerusalem's former splendor and replacing the Temple with an edifice
dedicated to Capitoline Jupiter and to his own divine glory. This was
taken by the Zealots as a direct challenge and they prepared to resist.
Aware of the hopelessness of any armed struggle against the Romans,
Joshua exhorted the people to submit. But he now stood alone. Akiba,
hitherto a staunch member of the peace party, had at last been won
over by the Zealots. Joshua was over ninety when he made his last

attempt to dissuade Hadrian, then in residence at Alexandria, from his plan to make Jerusalem a heathen city. He went alone to Egypt; even the once faithful Akiba considered his attempt futile and stayed at home.

An echo of Hadrian's arguments at his last audience with Joshua may be recognized in a passage in the Midrash. He is reported as telling Joshua: "How great is the sheep that stands up amongst seventy wolves" (Esther Rabbah X.11). This was doubtless said ironically: Hadrian was pointing out the futility of the Jews' attempt to be different from the rest of the world. "Seventy wolves" means the seventy other nations of the world that are mentioned in Genesis, which Hadrian could not have been familiar with, but there is no reason to believe that he did not make the equivalent remark in Greek. The Midrash gives Joshua's reply: "Great (rather) is the shepherd who rescues his sheep and crushes the wolves; as it is written, *No weapon that is forged against thee shall succeed* (Isa. 54:17)."

Joshua's efforts to make Hadrian show consideration for the feelings of an outraged community were nonetheless doomed to failure. He died soon afterwards. The death of the *Tsaddik* (Just One) is, in Jewish tradition, a signal for the advent of calamities. In this case they lasted for eighteen hundred years.

At Joshua's deathbed the wise men cried: "How shall we now defend ourselves against the unbelievers?" (Tos. Sotah 15.3). Joshua's answer was dry: he quoted Jeremiah 49:7 thus: "If good counsel has gone from the Children (of God), so has also the wisdom of the others failed." In other words, the Jews were not wise enough to refrain from violence; but neither were the Romans clever enough to destroy their religion. He may also have been thinking of the Christians. Perhaps he did believe that Pauline Christianity, now spreading far and wide, lacked the strength to overcome Judaism, even though spiritual life in Palestine had greatly decayed since the days of Hillel.

The Jews rose almost immediately after Joshua's death, Akiba having acknowledged Bar Kokeba as Messiah despite the protests of a few prudent men. His colleague Yohanan ben Torta said, "Akiba, grass will be growing through your cheeks before the Son of David comes" (Jer. Taanith IV.7).

Though starting out with brilliant successes, the revolt ended in utter ruin. The Talmud comments briefly: "For seven years have the Gentiles manured their vineyards with the blood of Israel."

THE PERSISTENCE OF REJECTED CUSTOMS IN PALESTINE

Louis Finkelstein

It is a fundamental principle of Rabbinic Law that in any difference between the Schools of Shammai and Hillel, the opinion of the latter is always to be followed. "Both opinions are the words of the living God," says the Talmud in a characteristic paradox, "but the decision is according to the views of the School of Hillel."[1] The earlier rule that "he who desires to follow the view of Bet Shammai may do so, and he who desires to follow the view of Bet Hillel may do so," was set aside, and the very statement was prefixed with the norm: "The decision is in accordance with the views of Bet Hillel."[2] So completely was the Hillelite interpretation of the Law accepted that one famous scholar, Rab, denied that the Shammaites ever followed their own views;[3] and it was generally stated that a heavenly voice had declared in favor of the Hillelites.[4]

In spite of this academic and juristic recognition of the views of Hillelites, however, some of the practices of the Shammaites continued to be observed by large sections of the people. The Mishna itself records that R. Tarfon could not overcome his boyhood habit, developed in a Shammaite household, of lying down to read the evening *Shema,* and that he did this even when it involved considerable inconvenience.[5] The same custom was also followed by R. Eleazar ben Azariah who certainly was counted a member of the Hillelite faction.[6]

Even after the rebellion of Bar Kokeba, and the persecutions of Hadrian, when the last remnant of the Shammaite group was suppressed, there were still many who in certain details, particularly of daily ritual, followed the ways of the Shammaites, to which they had become habituated in childhood. Thus we are told that the disciples of R. Judah ben Illai declined to follow his example and wear fringes on their linen garments, because the Shammaites forbid it.[7] R. Judah the Patriarch, the compiler of our Mishna, apparently accepted the Shammaite opinion of R. Judah ben Illai's disciples;[8] and his interpretation of the Law is accepted in the later Codes.[9]

With regard to the number of strands to be inserted in each fringe, there was a further controversy between the Shammaites and the Hillelites, the former requiring four strands, the latter only three.[10]

In both passages of the Sifre where the controversy is recorded, we are expressly informed that in this instance the decision is according to the Shammaites, and this view is accepted by Tosafot,[11] and Maimonides.[12]

It is, of course, no accident that the Shammaite view was accepted particularly with regard to the law of fringes. The fringed garment is worn by a Jew from childhood, and he is naturally inclined throughout his life to observe the custom in the manner in which it was inculcated in him in his early days. No matter what the Academy might decide, people would still continue to make, for themselves and for their children, fringes after the manner used by their parents; and as a large number of the Palestinian Jews were Shammaites, the view of that group persisted in this instance.[13]

It is interesting, however, to find that the Shammaite view persisted not merely in these few instances where it was accepted as correct within a few generations after the controversies between the Schools were ended, but even in cases where the later scholars continued to reject it. Several of the differences in practice between the Babylonian Jews and the Palestinian Jews, listed in a work of geonic origin,[14] (probably about the seventh century C. E.) can be traced to the fact that the Palestinian Jews continued to follow the outlawed Shammaite rulings, which the Babylonian Jews, following the norm of the Talmud, rejected.

The first of these differences relates to the reading of the *Shema*. The geonic compilation tells us that "The Babylonians sit down when reading the *Shema;* the Palestinians, however, stand up."[15] It is clear that this disagreement has its basis in the ancient controversy between the schools of Shammai and Hillel, "The School of Shammai says that in the evening everyone must lie down to read the *Shema,* and in the morning they stand up; the School of Hillel says, 'Everyone may read the *Shema* as he chooses.' "[16]

At the beginning of the third century C. E., Samuel, doubtless reporting a custom he had seen in his youth perhaps among emigrés from Palestine, maintained that "One must read the *Shema* standing." The Yerushalmi, however, rejects the literal interpretation of this statement and comments, "This does not mean that if one is sitting one should stand up; but that if one is walking one should halt."[17] The interpretation given by the Yerushalmi is, however, forced; and it is altogether probable that Samuel meant that the *Shema* is to be recited while one is standing. The Babylonian Talmud ascribes to R. Judah, the disciple of Samuel, the view that the first three verses of the *Shema* must be recited while standing.[18] Here also Rashi insists that the meaning is not *standing up*, but *halting;* yet it is impossible to accept this interpretation. R. Johanan, who was a Palestinian, is recorded as having required the whole of the first passage (Deut. 6.4-9) to be recited while standing.

These controversies point to a difference of custom which the later scholar tried to rationalize without accepting the views of Shammaites. Actually, however, there can be little doubt that the custom of standing for the morning *Shema* is a remnant of the Shammaite practice; and that even after the Hillelites had succeeded in weaning the people away from the custom of lying down for the evening *Shema,* many of them continued to stand up for the morning *Shema*.

The predilection of the Palestinians for the Shammaite practice is even more clearly exhibited in another difference between Palestinian and Babylonian practice cited in the compilation: "The Babylonians permit a widow, whose child has died, to marry within twenty-four months after its birth; the Palestinians, however, prohibit this."[19]

The Palestinian custom was based on the rule of the Shammaites which required a woman to nurse her child for twenty-four months.[20] This view was also adopted by R. Meir who, because of it, forbade a widow to become betrothed or married until twenty-four months from the time the child was born.[21] The reason for the prohibition was that to permit a woman to marry a second time if the child died, while prohibiting her to do so while the child was alive, might lead a desperate mother to infanticide.

The Hillelites insisted that eighteen months were sufficient for the nursing of a child; their view was followed by R. Judah. Apparently the Babylonians went further than either and refused to prevent a woman from marrying if her child died. Be that as it may, the Palestinian adherence to the rule that a child should be nursed for twenty-four months proves their preservation of the Shammaite, rather than the Hillelite, interpretation of the Law.

Finally there is a paragraph in this compilation, which reads:

"The Babylonians free a man from observing the rites of mourning, if he has observed them even for one hour before a festival; the Palestinians require that he observe at least three days of mourning before the festival."[22] According to R. Eleazar b. Simeon, this was a matter of dispute between the Shammaites and the Hillelites; the Palestinian view coinciding with that of the Shammaites; the Babylonian with that of the Hillelites.[23]

Another group of opinions which, rejected by the Academy, yet survived in certain circles, appear to have been those forbidding the use of cosmetics by women during their impurity. An ancient *baraita* records that this custom had been set aside by R. Akiba; nevertheless we find it codified into law in geonic times.[24]

The Book, *Baraita d'Niddah,* in which this view occurs, evidently reflects the views of a contemporary rabbinical circle. It also reports that in one of the main controversies between the Schools of Hillel and Shammai regarding the status of women during their impurity, a heavenly Voice declared in favor of the Shammaites. Thereupon the Hillelites reversed themselves and accepted the views of the Shammaites.[25]

This story is obviously intended to offset the force of the much older legend, already mentioned, according to which a heavenly Voice declared in favor of the School of Hillel.

It is more difficult to decide whether the rule set down in this work forbidding marital relations for forty days after the birth of a son, and eighty days after the birth of a daughter, is really a survival of factional, or sectarian, views.

As is well known the Karaites forbid such relations,[26] as do also the Samaritans.[27] On the basis of these facts, and certain talmudic records, Geiger[28] advanced the theory that Sadducees accepted the prohibition; and that the Shammaites, too, adhered to it in part. This view has been opposed by Prof. Louis Ginzberg. Nevertheless, it seems clear that the prohibition was accepted in early times in certain Palestinian circles, and although the standard *halaka* rejected it, it reappears in the geonic period in the *Baraita d'Niddah.*

The persistence for centuries of these rejected rabbinical views suggests that possibly even some Sadducean views may have survived the victory of the Pharisees. This may explain the manner in which the Karaites in the seventh century C. E. were able to resurrect forgotten Sadducean doctrines and teachings. It is altogether probable that even after the overthrow of Sadducism, there were backward communities where the old Sadducean practices continued to be followed. In such places probably no fire was used on the Sabbath, even though kindled before the Sabbath;[29] and Shabuot was observed on the fiftieth day after the first day of Passover.[30] Both of these customs which the Karaites could hardly find described in Sadducean literature (of which there was probably as little available in the seventh century C.E. as today) might have survived in small communities, which Karaism absorbed.

The likelihood that this happened is increased by the fact that we find in Targum Ps. Jonathan on Deut. 22.26, another compilation of geonic times, a rule which could only have arisen in pre-Pharisaic times, namely that if a married woman is a victim of rape, she must be divorced. Rabbinic law knows no such rule; and indeed it could only have existed at a time when the intent of an act was given little consideration in meting out punishment. Its survival in Targum Ps. Jonathan is proof that some communities adhered to the primitive law in comparatively late times.

Those who wonder how traditions can survive in this underground manner, without any indication of their existence being noticed in the academic tradition, might consider the case of the Muggletonians of modern England. This sect was one of the many which arose in the middle of the seventeenth century, when all England was in a religious ferment. Its founder, Lodowick Muggleton, declared himself a prophet, with the power of damning forever all those who rose against him. In the course of his rather stormy career, he was condemned to stand in the pillory and to other indignities. Yet his sect survived; and it is said that to this day their survivors still hold a yearly meeting![31] It is altogether probable that similar stray remnants of Sadducism and of Shammaism survived the disaster which overwhelmed these groups as a whole, and here and there in Palestine some circles continued to practice the rules of their ancient factions until the seventh and eighth centuries C. E. when the rejected customs were brought to light in rabbinic and Karaite works.

THE "SONS OF LIGHT"
Theodor H. Gaster

Everyone who has read the newspapers or listened to the radio or come within earshot of a professional Bible scholar during the past ten years has heard by now of the Dead Sea Scrolls, and it is safe to say that no archeological discovery of recent times has produced a more profound or sustained public excitement. Partly, no doubt, this is due to the romantic circumstances of the discovery itself; everyone has been intrigued by the story of how an Arab boy, searching for a strayed goat in the Desert of Judah, stumbled by chance into a dark cave and found in it the oldest known manuscripts of the Bible and a collection of ancient but forgotten religious writings. Partly, too, it is due to the tantalizing mystery which surrounds the date and authorship of those writings, and to the fascination of watching scholarly sleuths cudgel their own and one another's brains in trying to solve it. Mainly, however, it may be attributed to the sensational claim (popularized especially by Edmund Wilson) that the Dead Sea Scrolls challenge or impugn the uniqueness of the Christian faith. These documents, it is alleged, attest the existence of a Jewish sect which lived at the same time and in the same general area as John the Baptist and Jesus and which not only professed many of the doctrines they taught but actually believed in a Christ-like "Teacher of Righteousness" who suffered martyrdom but subsequently "reappeared in glory" to his disciples. Small wonder that in the face of such pronouncements the general public should suddenly be manifesting a burning interest in what went on in the Desert of Judah some two thousand years ago.

In the following pages I shall try to summarize for laymen just what the Scrolls really have to say—what, in their own right, and divorced from false associations, they contribute to religion and the life of the spirit. It is necessary only to read the texts to see at once how sensation has outrun sobriety and how premature and unwarranted interpretations have been allowed to all but stifle their genuine religious message. In offering this presentation, I may perhaps be allowed to say that the more I have studied and lived with the Scrolls, the more difficult have I found it to treat them with detachment. Although I have never willfully allowed this consideration to color the statement of facts, I am conscious that in the matter of appraisal a pronounced spiritual sympathy—a process of virtual "identification"—has played its part. Indeed, what started as an objective, academic study became increasingly an act of piety toward the memory of those poor but valiant "sons of light" who gave these documents to us and who, like their greater forebear, stood in the cleft of a rock and saw the glory of God pass by.

No one yet knows for certain who wrote the Dead Sea Scrolls, when and where. Attempts to date them by radio-carbon tests, by paleography (the form of script), and by identifying purported historical allusions have alike proved inconclusive. It is now generally accepted, however—though there are still some shrill dissident voices—that whenever, wherever, and by whomsoever they may originally have been composed, they came to serve as the literature or religious repertoire of an ascetic, "protestant" and "puritan" Jewish brotherhood that lived on the western shore of the Dead Sea in the early years of the Common Era. That brotherhood (now generally identified as the Essenes) was distributed over a number of encampments, and one of its principal centers—perhaps, indeed, its "main office"—was a "monastery" situated in the forbidding gorge of Qumran, at the northern end of the area in question. The building has now been excavated, and coins found within it establish that it was occupied continuously (except for a short break due to earthquake) from about 125 B.C.E. until 68 C.E. Since the latter date coincides with that at which the Roman troops of Vespasian moved into the district on their way to suppress the First Jewish Revolt, it is a plausible conjecture that the "monastery" was abandoned at their approach and that the manuscripts of its library were then cached for safekeeping in the surrounding caves, whence they have now been miraculously retrieved.

The aims and objects of the Brotherhood, its government and constitution, its doctrines and practices, are amply described for us in two "manuals of discipline," a book of hymns, a series of commentaries on Scripture, a treatise on the final war to be waged against the forces of evil, and sundry lesser works of homiletical character.[1]

We are introduced by these documents to a group of men who, disgusted by the degeneration of religion and the corruption of the official priesthood at Jerusalem, had come to the conclusion that the only way in which Israel's traditional commitment to the Torah and Covenant could be maintained would be by establishing a select society of the faithful, duly dedicated and disciplined, and independent of such baneful influence. To this end, they betook themselves to the Desert of Judah and there organized a series of socialistic camp settlements on Scriptural lines. They believed that they constituted the true Congregation of Israel, the small remnant that had remained loyal to the Covenant and that was thereby ensuring the perpetuation of God's people, the fulfillment of its mission, and the eventual cleansing of the earth from the stain of guilt. The Covenant, they insisted, had been maintained and preserved throughout history only by a succession of such pious "remnants."

The members of the Brotherhood conceived of their adventure as a repetition in their own day and age of the experience of Israel under Moses, and entertained the hope that in return for their privations they would eventually reach a new Sinai, receive a new promulgation of the Covenant, and enter, in a more than territorial sense, into the Promised Land. There was, however, one crucial difference between them and their ancient prototypes: they were not waiting to receive the Law; they already possessed it. Their aim was simply to reassert that Law, to deliver it from the perverse and garbled interpretations that were being imposed upon it by false expositors and "men of lies." The true interpretation, they held, had in fact been transmitted by a kind of "apostolic succession" begun by the Biblical prophets and continued by a series of spiritual monitors each of whom was known as the "correct expositor" or "right guide" (*not* "Teacher of Righteousness," as it has been commonly rendered)—that is, the *orthodox* expounder of the Word. The "right guide" was apparently in every case a *priest*, his title being derived from Moses' farewell blessing upon the priestly tribe of Levi: *They have observed Thy word and kept Thy covenant. They, then, shall teach Thine ordinances to Jacob and Thy Law to Israel* (Deut. 33:9-10).

Just as Israel had been led of old by those prophets and teachers, so, it was held, a new Prophet and Teacher would arise at the end of the present era to pave the way for the Golden Age, when the scattered hosts of the faithful would be gathered in, a duly anointed high priest and a duly anointed king (called "the *messiahs* (anointed) of Aaron and Israel") installed, and "the earth filled with the knowledge of the Lord like the waters which cover the sea." The concept was derived from the words of Moses in Deuteronomy 18:15-18: *The Lord thy God will raise up unto thee a prophet from the midst of thee, from among thy brethren . . . unto him shall ye hearken . . . The Lord hath said unto me. . . . "I will raise them up a prophet from among their brethren, one like unto thee; and I will put my words in his mouth, and he shall speak unto them all that I shall command him."*

In order to emphasize the idea that theirs was but a repetition of the ancient community under Moses and that their experiences were but a fulfillment of prophecy, the Brotherhood made use of an elaborate imagery drawn from the Bible. They styled themselves the "Chosen" or "the Elect of God," in reminiscence of the election of Israel at Sinai (compare Deut. 4:37; 7:6; 14:2, etc). Their voluntary withdrawal to the desert was represented as a sojourn in "the desert of Damascus," thereby indicating that it was the fulfillment of God's word through the prophet Amos (5:25-27) that He would drive His recalcitrant people into exile *beyond Damascus*. Alternatively, echoing the words of Ezekiel (20:35), they spoke of the prevailing apostasy of Israel as "sojourn in the wilderness of the peoples." Their ancestral priests were described as "the sons of Zadok," in allusion to the foremost priestly family in the time of David (II Sam. 8:17) and to those whom the prophet Ezekiel had designated (40:46; 43:19; 44:15; 48:11) as the only legitimate priests in the restored Temple of the future.

Biblical precedents seem also to have been stressed in the actual organization of the Brotherhood. The Governing Council, we are told, had to include three priests and twelve laymen distinguished for knowledge of the Law and for holy living and it is perhaps not too fanciful to recognize in these an imitation of the priestly triumvirate of Aaron, Eleazar, and Ithamar (Num. 3:4) and of the twelve heads of the tribes associated with Moses (Num. 1:4-16; Deut. 1:13-15).

Scriptural imagery was likewise employed in speaking of the Brotherhood's opponents. The venal priests of Jerusalem who connived against their own colleagues, the successive "right guides," and allowed them without protest to be defamed and traduced, were described as "a household of Absalom," in reference to the perfidious behavior of David's son against his own father. Divisive elements within Israel itself were termed "the household of Peleg"—a clever adaptation of the Biblical name in Genesis 10:25, inspired by the fact that the Hebrew word p-l-g means "divide." The heathen forces of Belial who would be discomfited in the Day of Vengeance were defined as the "hordes of Gog," an ancient northern nation whose doom had been foretold by the prophet Ezekiel; while the Roman oppressors of the Jews were termed "the Kittians," in allusion to Balaam's prophecy (Num. 24:24; compare also Dan. 11:30) that *ships shall come from the direction of the Kittians* (originally, this was Kition in Cyprus!) *and cause tribulation.*

It would, however, be a mistake to suppose that the Brethren were inspired only by a desire to relive the past or that they betook themselves to the desert simply because they were unsettled by political turbulence or disgusted by the venality of the Jerusalemitan priests. They were swept also by other winds, and not the least of these was a strong mystical current. Adherence to the Way of God, they held, implied more than mere subscription to a legal code or a ritual discipline, or even a system of ethics and morals; it implied also the attainment, by insight, perception, and absorption, of what mystics term the "unitive state" with Him. Accordingly, they regarded themselves not only as the remnant of Israel and the replica of the pristine Mosaic community, but also as the "sons of light." The inner enlightenment which they claimed, however—the enlightenment which had led them, in fact, to embark upon their great adventure—was not attributed to any sudden spontaneous act of supernal grace. Rather was it the result of man's own voluntary exercise of that power of discernment which God had planted within every creature at the moment of its creation. All things, it was affirmed—all the phenomena of nature—had been endowed by Him with that instinctive power. It was, indeed, only by virtue of such indwelling power that sun, moon, and stars, tides, rain, and snow were able to discharge their functions in the universal scheme. In the case of man, however, God had balanced this instinct with an *evil* impulse ("the spirit of Belial") which sought ever to ensnare and enthrall him. If man vanquished that evil impulse and allowed himself to be guided only by the "spirit of God" and of God's truth, he automatically broke the trammels of his mortality. He was embraced forthwith in the communion of eternal things and with the immortal beings of the celestial realm—the holy, transfigured beings who stood forever in direct converse with God.

It was this state that the members of the Brotherhood claimed for themselves. This was the ultimate goal of their entire spiritual adventure; the aim and *raison d'être* of the Torah and of the disciplined life which it enjoined. They held that by virtue of their "enlightenment" they were members not only of the consecrated earthly fraternity but necessarily also of the Eternal Congregation. As one of their psalmists puts it, they "walked alway in uplands unbounded and knew that there is hope for what is molded of clay to hold converse with things everlasting." This is not, as all too many scholars have supposed, a mere hope for the survival of the soul in some cloudland of bliss. Rather is it the sound mystic sense that, given the right spiritual posture, given the victory over that darkness which is set before him along with the light, man may live even on earth in a dimension of eternity.

This idea too the Brethren expressed in an idiom drawn directly from the Bible. Because the prophet Daniel had spoken (11:33,35; 12:10) of the role to be played by the "enlightened" (Hebrew, *maskilim*) in the final age, they styled themselves by that name; and they termed their current tribulation "the time of trouble" or "the time of refinement," in express reference to the same prophet's declaration that *there shall be a time of trouble such as never was* and that *some of the enlightened shall stumble that they may thus be refined and purified*. Moreover, they called their enlightenment "Light-Perfection," for which the Hebrew is Or-Tôm—a play on the oracular Urim and Thummim of Scripture and more especially on that verse in the final Blessing of Moses (Deut. 33.8) which declares that *Thy Thummim and Thine Urim shall be* (ever) *with him that is loyal to Thee.*

The Brotherhood was swept also by another, no less powerful current. This was the widespread contemporary belief that the great cycle of the ages was about to complete its revolution. The belief was based on the conception (which can be traced back to remote Indian antiquity) that existence consists not in linear progressive evolution but rather in a constant cyclic repetition of primordial and archetypal events. When major upheavals occurred, it was promptly supposed that the cycle was nearing its end, that the so-called Great Year was at hand, and that cosmos was about to revert to chaos. The primal elements, restrained and controlled at the beginning of the world, would again be unleashed; all things would dissolve in an overwhelming deluge or be burned in that everlasting fire which rages in the depths of the earth. Then the cycle would begin again; a new world would be brought to birth. The picture is painted in vivid colors in one of the hymns:

> On what strength of mine own may I count
> when Corruption's snares are laid
> and the nets of Wickedness spread;
> when far and wide on the waters
> Forwardness sets her drags;
> when the shafts of corruption fly,
> with none to turn them back;
> when they are hurled amain
> with no hope of escape;
> when the hour of judgment strikes,
> when the lot of God's anger is cast
> upon the abandoned;
> when his fury is outpoured upon dissemblers;
> when the final doom of His rage
> falls on all worthless things;
> when the torrents of Death do swirl,
> and there is none escape;
> when the rivers of Belial
> burst all high banks
>
> ....
>
> rivers of fire that devour
> every foundation of clay,
> every solid bedrock;
> when the foundations of the mountains
> become a raging blaze;
> when granite rocks are turned to streams of pitch;
> when the flame burns down to the abyss,
> when the floods of Belial are loosed
> unto hell itself;
> when the depths of the sea are in turmoil
> and cast up mire in profusion;
> when the earth cries out in anguish
> for the havoc wrought in the world;
>
> ....
>
> when with a mighty roar
> God thunders forth,

and His holy welkin trembles
as His glorious truth is revealed;
when the hosts of heaven give forth their voice
and the world's foundations rock and reel;
when warfare waged by soldiers of heaven
sweeps through the universe?

For men, this theory posed the immediate problem of escape, and religion answered that problem by the postulate that "the just shall live by his faith" and that all who remained loyal to the Covenant were themselves participants in the creation of the new order. There was a sense in which, if he could not be delivered from the body of this death, man could at least be released from the trammels of this life. He could immerse himself in eternal things, divorce himself from the temporal and the mundane and, reversing the old adage, find that in the midst of death he was in fact in life.

The Brotherhood lived at a time of such "cyclic crisis." It is writ large in the non-canonical (pseudepigraphic) scriptures of the two centuries preceding the Common Era, and its fading echo may be heard in John the Baptist's cry that *the Kingdom of Heaven is at hand.* It was escape from the inexorable cycle, release not only from the guilt of sin but also from the fetters of mortality, that these men were seeking. The desert to which they repaired was not simply the Desert of Judah; it was also the mystic's Desert of Quietude—what John Tauler called "the Wilderness of Godhead, into which He leads all who are to receive the inspiration of God, now or in eternity." In that wilderness they would not merely receive a renewal of the Covenant; they would also have the vision of the Burning Bush. Removed from men, they would acquire an unobstructed view of the Divine. Thirsting in an inhospitable wild, they would drink the unfailing waters of God's grace. Shorn of earthly possessions, theirs would be the poverty of the mystics —that poverty which Evelyn Underhill has described as "complete detachment from all finite things." Burned by the scorching sun, they would see the *semplice lume* of Dante, the "infused brightness" of Saint Teresa, and by that light they would not be dazzled. They would achieve an intimacy, a communion, with the eternal, unchanging things, such as one can achieve only in a desert or on a sea. And in that experience they would reproduce and concentrate within themselves the drama of the cosmic cycle, the dissolving of the old order and the birth of the new.

In strange juxtaposition with these rarefied speculations, however, the Brotherhood also entertained a severely practical view of what was going to happen when the time for the world's renewal fell due. Even if individual men escaped the final doom, general doom there still would be, and a good deal of evil would still remain to be destroyed. The destruction would come by means of a forty years' war waged by the "sons of light," aided by the celestial hosts, against the "sons of darkness." In three campaigns they would win; in three, lose. At last, at the seventh encounter, God would triumph over Belial. This would be the Day of Vengeance. Thereafter all things would be renewed. The Era of Divine Favor (in contrast to the Era of Wrath) would be ushered in. God's light would shine sevenfold strong. He would reaffirm the Covenant with the faithful, and engrave His Law on their hearts.

The Brethren drew up an elaborate manual of operations for this war. It was cast in the form of a Roman treatise on military tactics and included explicit instructions regarding recruitment, the formations of troops, the code of signals, the inscriptions on the ensigns, and so forth. And when it describes the final battle, these are its words:

This is the day which God hath appointed for abasing and humbling the (Prince of) the Dominion of Wickedness. But He will send eternal salvation to those who have a share in His redemption through the power of Michael, the mighty ministering angel; and He will send also an eternal light to illumine with joy the children of Israel. They that have cast their lot with God shall enjoy peace and blessing. As the rule of Michael will then be exalted among the angels, so shall the dominion of Israel be exalted over all flesh. Righteousness shall flourish in heaven, and all (upon earth) that espouse God's truth shall rejoice in the knowledge of eternal things. Wherefore, sons of the Covenant, be of good courage in the trial which God visiteth upon you, until He give the sign that He hath completed His test.

Membership in the Brotherhood was open to all persons over twenty years of age. "Postulants" had to undergo a two-year probation. During the first year, they were regarded as being, so to speak, "outside affiliates" or "fellow-travelers," with no share in the communal resources and under no obligation to surrender their own private property. They did not dine at the common table. At the end of the year, however, their attitude and conduct were reviewed. If they passed the test, they qualified, as it were as "inside affiliates." They now had to deposit their possessions on trust with a special officer, but they were still excluded from any stake in the communal funds. Only if they passed a further test at the end of that second year were they deemed eligible for full membership, and even then they were admitted only by general vote and had to swear an oath of loyalty which was administered publicly to all initiants together.

No one, however, who was suffering from any unclean disease could be received into the Brotherhood, nor could anyone who contracted such a disease maintain his position within it. Similarly, no one who was lame, blind, deaf, or dumb, or afflicted with any visible bodily defect, could be elected to communal office and rank as a "dignitary."

There were various ranks of membership, and the lower had to obey the higher. These ranks involved ascending degrees of "purity"; and the precise status of each member—including even the priests— was reviewed annually at a special council, promotion or demotion being then voted in accordance with his record.

The minimum number to constitute a "chapter" or conventicle of the Brotherhood was ten, corresponding to the *minyan* of normative Jewish practice. If the ten included a priest, he was not permitted to remove himself from the other nine. Each such chapter—perhaps even each group of ten—had to appoint one of its number to serve as a full-time expositor (*doresh*) of law and doctrine, to whom recourse could be had at any hour of day or night.

Members of the Brotherhood shared all things in common. They dined, prayed together, and all were required to spend one-third of the total nights of the year in joint study and worship. They were encouraged to discuss matters of religion with one another, but were forbidden to do so, or to disclose the lore of the Brotherhood, to outsiders (styled "sons of corruption"; see Deut. 32:5; Isa. 1:4).

Children of members had to undergo a ten-year period of training in the doctrines and principles of the Brotherhood and to master a manual entitled "The Book of Study (*Hagû*)"—evidently an "official" interpretation of Biblical law, a kind of sectarian Mishnah. (Such, at least, is the provision laid dawn in a manual of discipline for the ideal congregation of the future, and we may not unreasonably suppose that it was based on current usage.)

The spiritual direction of the Brotherhood was in the hands of the priests, the sacred seed of Aaron, who were obliged to abide by a traditional interpretation of the Law laid down by the original "sons of

Zadok" and by the founding fathers. They were assisted by Levites.

There was also, however, a well-knit secular government. The chief "federal" officials were a President (or Prince) of the Entire Congregation and an Inspector-General of all Encampments. Furthermore, there was a panel of ten judges, four of whom were selected from the priests and Levites, and the remaining six from the laity. Special status was accorded also, as in ancient Israel, to "heads of families."

Each individual encampment was under the authority of a local "superintendent." His duties are thus defined in one of the manuals of discipline:

He is to enlighten the masses about the works of God, and to make them understand His wondrous powers. He is to tell them in detail the story of what happened in the past. He is to show them the same compassion as a father shows for his children. He is to bring back all of them that stray, as does a shepherd his flock. He is to loose all the bonds that constrain them, that there be none in his community who is oppressed or crushed. He is also to examine every new adherent to his community regarding his mode of life, intelligence, strength, fortitude, and wealth, and to register him in his due status, according to his stake in the portion of Truth. No member of the camp is to be permitted to introduce anyone into the community without the consent of the . . . superintendent.

Subordinate to this official were "commissioners" of work, property, charitable funds, and the like.

No one under twenty-five years of age could occupy a communal office, and no one under thirty could exercise sacerdotal authority, be reckoned as head of a family, or hold a commission in the Brotherhood's military establishment. Judges were not permitted to officiate above the age of sixty; for, says one of the manuals, "through the perfidy of Adam the potential span of human life has been reduced, and in the heat of His anger against the inhabitants of the earth, God decreed of old that their mental powers should recede before they complete their days."

The supreme authority in all lay matters was vested in a Council or Board. In this Council, we are informed, there were always to be three priests and twelve specially qualified men, "schooled to perfection in all that has been revealed of the entire Law"; but whether these constituted the total complement of members is uncertain. The twelve specially qualified men were known as "the men of perfect conduct" or "the men of holiness," and they had to undergo a two-year period of preparation. Their function was not so much juridical as spiritual: they served as moral and ethical examplars.

Their duty (we read) is to set the standard for the practice of truth, righteousness, and justice, and for the exercise of charity and humility in human relations; and to show how, by control of impulse and contrition of spirit, faithfulness may be maintained on earth; how by active performance of justice and passive submission to the trials of discipline, iniquity may be shriven; and how one can walk with all men with the quality of truth and in conduct appropriate to every occasion.

Members of the Brotherhood were subject to a rigid code of behavior. They were not allowed to swear oaths (other than the oath of allegiance), to nurse grudges, to slander their fellows, to indulge in blasphemous or lewd talk, to conceal their possessions, to appear naked, to spit at public assemblies, or to take a nap during proceedings of the Council! They were likewise restrained from "raucous, inane laughter." Breaches of this code entailed forfeiture of rations for specified periods and/or temporary exclusion from the sodality. Repeated breaches or offenses involving repudiation of basic principles were punished by irrevocable expulsion.

That there are several arresting parallels between the ideas and doctrines of the Brotherhood and those of the early Christians, and likewise between the idiom of the Scrolls and that of the New Testament, cannot be denied. Just as the Brethren called themselves "the Elect" or "the sons of light," so too did the early Christians (see John 12:36; Titus 1:1; Ephesians 5:8). Just as the Brethren claimed to be at once the "remnant" of the true Israel and participants in the Eternal Congregation, so too did the followers of Jesus (Romans 11:3-5; Ephes. 2:19). Just as the Brethren termed their spiritual monitor "the right teacher," so too was Jesus hailed as "a teacher come from God" (John 3:2). Just as the Brethren looked forward to the advent of a prophet at the end of the present era, so too Jesus was acclaimed by his followers as "that prophet that should come into the world" (John 6:14). Just as the Brethren declared that they were "preparing the highway in the desert," so John the Baptist made use of the same quotation from Isaiah (40:3) in calling the people to repentance and regeneration (John 1:23). Just as the Manual of Discipline proclaimed that if the Brethren abode by the prescribed rules, they would be "a veritable temple of God, a true holy of holies," so Paul told the Christians of Corinth that they were a "temple of God, and the spirit of God hath its house in you" (I Cor. 3:16-17). And just as the Brethren anticipated a final apocalyptic war against Belial and drew lurid pictures of a stream of fire which would burn up the wicked, so too did the author of the Book of Revelation. Indeed, the present writer has noted no less than one hundred and fifty similarities between the thought and idiom of the Scrolls and those of the New Testament Scriptures.

Similarly, there are marked affinities between the organization of the Brotherhood and that of the primitive Church. It is significant, for instance, that the term used by the Brethren to denote their total community, though itself derived from the Pentateuch, was that adopted also by the Aramaic-speaking Christians of Palestine to signify the Church; while the governing board of three priests and twelve laymen is strongly reminiscent of the three "pillars" of the Church (viz. James, Peter, and John) mentioned in the Epistle to the Galatians (2:9) and of the twelve apostles. So, too, the Hebrew word for the "overseers" or "superintendents" is the equivalent of the Christian *episkopoi* or "bishops" (in the original non-sacerdotal sense); while the rule requiring all "who perform communal service" to be at least twenty-five years old, and all "heads of families" and military officers to be at least thirty survived in the Church in the prescription of the Council of Hippo (393 C.E.) that no one was to be ordained under twenty-five, and in the Neo-Caesarean and Maronite rules that no presbyter may be under thirty.

These analogies, however, should not be pressed unduly. Insofar as ideas and expressions are concerned, just as many of them as can be paralleled from the New Testament can be paralleled equally well from the non-canonical Jewish "scriptures" that were circulating between 200 B.C.E. and 100 C.E. and from the earlier strata of the Talmud. The picture of the final conflagration, for example, is likewise painted in the so-called Third Book of the Sibylline Oracles, a basically Jewish compilation dating about 140 B.C.E. The apocalyptic war (derived ultimately from Biblical prophecy) is mentioned also in the Talmud, in the Apocalypse of Baruch and elsewhere. The doctrine of periodic world renewal, a favorite tenet of Neo-Pythagoreanism,

appears again in the pseudepigraphic Testament of Abraham and in the
Book of Jubilees; while many of the more striking images of the
Brotherhood's Book of Hymns recur in the Psalms of Solomon and in
the Odes of Solomon. Moreover, several of these ideas find place
equally in the doctrines of such sects as the Mandaeans and the Samaritans, where they may be recognized as survivals of what was anciently
common thought and folklore. Thus, the division of history into an
Era of Divine Displeasure and an Era of Divine Favor is a cardinal
dogma of the Samaritan faith; while the Mandaeans, like the Dead
Sea Brethren, style themselves "the Elect."

Similarly, in the realm of organization, there are just as many
parallels between the institutions of the Brotherhood and those of the
religious corporations of the Graeco-Roman "mystery religions" as
there are with the primitive Christian Church. The camp superintendent, for example, has his counterpart in the *koinobiarch*, and the
subordinate "overseers" in the "commissioners" (*epimeletai*) of those
groups; while there too all goods were shared in common, admission
entailed an initial oath, and there was the same emphasis upon the
"mysteries of God" and the same prohibition against disclosing the
lore of the fraternity to outsiders.

To draw from the New Testament parallels any inference of special
or unique relationship to Christianity is therefore gravely misleading.

Misleading also, and to an even greater degree, is the claim that
the Scrolls anticipate the *distinctive* tenets of the Christian faith. On
the contrary, it may now be stated definitely that on the evidence thus
far available this claim is based only on misunderstanding and misin-
terpretation and that, in point of fact, the *Dead Sea Brotherhood held
none of the fundamental theological doctrines of Christianity.*

It has been asserted, for instance, that the several references in
the Scrolls to a "right teacher" all refer to a single historical Teacher of
Righteousness, a prototype of Jesus. Anyone, however, who takes the
trouble to examine these references in the translation by me to appear
shortly will see that the term in question designates a continuing office,
not a specific individual. In some cases, it alludes to men who lived in
the past; in others, to a spiritual monitor who is to arise in the future.

It has been asserted also that a passage in the Commentary on
Habakkuk which speaks of the teacher's having been "persecuted"
but having subsequently "appeared in splendor" to the community on
the Day of Atonement foreshadows the Christian doctrine of the suffering and resurrected savior. Even, however, if the translation were

correct (which is doubtful), this would still be poles apart from the Christian belief that the crucified master was God incarnate who by his passion redeemed mankind from an inherent guilt caused by a pristine fall from grace. Of this basic tenet of Christianity there is not a shred or trace in the Dead Sea Scrolls.

There is likewise no vestige of the idea of Original Sin. On the contrary, the idea is repeatedly affirmed that every man is endowed at birth with a charisma of discernment and that any sinfulness which he manifests throughout his life is due only to his personal neglect of that gift and to his personal submission to, or entrapment by, the evil impulse (Belial).

Thus far (says the Manual of Discipline), the spirits of truth and of perversity have been struggling in the heart of man. Men have walked both in wisdom and in folly. If a man cast his portion with truth, he does righteously and hates perversity; if he cast it with perversity, he does wickedly and abominates truth. God has apportioned them in equal measure until the final age, until "He makes all things new." Howbeit, he foreknows the effect of their works in every epoch of the world, and He has allotted them to man so that man might know good and evil. But when (the time of) Inquisition (comes), He will determine the fate of every living being in accordance with which of the (two spirits he has chosen to follow).

Thus, because sin is individual and not the inherited lot of the human race, and because it is incurred only by a man's personal disposition, it can be shriven only by his own personal experience. Once he "sees the light" by the exercise of his own God-given powers, he is automatically out of darkness. In such a system of thought, since there is no concept of original, universal sin, there is obviously no place for universal, vicarious atonement. Men suffer their individual crucifixions and resurrections; there is no Calvary.

Again, there is no Communion. Certain scholars, to be sure, have claimed to find a prototype of it in the description which is given in one of the texts of a banquet attended by "the Messiah." What the document in question is really describing, however, is simply the order of precedence that is to obtain in Israel in the days of its future restoration; and in order to bring out the point that the sacred seed of Aaron is then to outrank everyone else, the writer observes that even if "the messiah of Israel"—that is, the "lay messiah" or anointed king—

should happen to be present at a communal meal, he and his retinue are not to take their seats until the priest and *his* retinue have done so, and it is to be left to the priest to pronounce the customary benediction over the food! There is no suggestion whatsoever that a Messianic banquet in the Christian sense ever formed part of the regular life of the Brotherhood, and certainly none that the bread and wine of this future meal were to be regarded as the flesh and blood of an incarnate God or that the consumption of them was to have any redemptive power. Accordingly, there is no parallel with Christian Communion. At most, what is described is some future *agape* or "love-feast."

It is, indeed, far more important to recognize the radical differences between the Dead Sea Brotherhood and Christianity than the superficial similarities. Christianity is based on the idea that salvation comes to the world by God's dying for man; the Brethren affirmed, on the contrary, that it comes by man's living for God. Christianity assumes that the Passion has to be followed by the Resurrection in order to make it completely valid. The Brethren asserted, on the contrary, that the two things are necessarily simultaneous, that suffering is itself regeneration. In their eyes, the potency of the Crucifixion (had they believed in any such doctrine) would have lain in the very fact that it evinced another scale of values in which that supreme passion became not the ultimate defeat but the ultimate triumph. The concept of a subsequent resurrection would have seemed to them a superfluous anticlimax, because it would have presumed an antecedent death; and the very thing which they claimed to have achieved by their own devotion and torment was that thereby they were living in a dimension of eternity, where life, as it were, was utterly transfigured and where death and mortality were rendered irrelevant. To them, Good Friday would have needed no Easter, and the miracle of Holy Week would have lain in the Cross and not in the Empty Tomb.

It is in the affirmation of these things that the real message of the Scrolls may be seen to reside. Viewed in this light, they are more than a mere relic of antiquity, a curious historical datum. They are witnesses to an attitude of mind and a posture of spirit which are meaningful for our own day. They represent a perennial situation—the perennial sojourn in the desert of those of us, at once restless and serene, to whom the current organs of religion seem so painfully inadequate to the intensity of our commitment. In this sense, it may indeed be said of the men of Qumran that *Ye that did cleave unto the Lord your God are alive every one of you this day.*

THE CAVE SCROLLS AND THE JEWISH SECTS
Harold L. Ginsberg

In the summer of 1947, some Bedouins of the Wilderness of Judah (the arid eastern slope of the hill country of Judah that descends to the Dead Sea) chanced upon a grotto near a ruin by the name of Khirbet Qumran, lying south from the northwest corner of the Dead Sea. The grotto contained forty or fifty large jars, of a cylindrical shape. Most of them were broken; and it was apparent that their contents had been in part removed by men, in part gnawed and scattered by rats. But from the scattered remains, and from the contents of the few comparatively intact jars, it was evident that all or most of the jars must have served as receptacles for leather scrolls—in at least one case, it later developed, for a papyrus scroll—wrapped in linen. The jars had lids.

The Bedouins, who had no idea that the writing was Hebrew, took a number of scrolls and fragments of scrolls to Bethlehem; eventually the bulk of them were acquired by the Assyrian Monastery of St. Mark in Jerusalem, and the rest by the Hebrew University. Copies and collotype photographs of all but one of the Assyrian-owned documents were pub- lished by the American School of Oriental Research under the editor- ship of Professor Millar Burrows of Yale University; the Jewish-owned ones have, unfortunately, been published only in extracts, by the late Professor E. L. Sukenik of the Hebrew University.

In 1947 Arab-Jewish tension had already made the site of the manuscript find inaccessible to Jews, and the following year all that part of Palestine was formally annexed to the Kingdom of Jordan. The cave and its environs, however, have been explored by trained scholars, especially by Father Roland de Vaux, the highly competent director of the French Dominican School of Bible and Archaeology in the Jordan sector of Jerusalem, and his assistants. Not only had additional material been recovered from the original cave that the Bedouins had ransacked, but five other caves containing manuscripts have been found in the same neighborhood (as well as several which had apparently been dwellings, not libraries). In addition, Khirbet Qumran itself, which evidently served as a communal center for the cave dwellers, has been excavated. (Important, even sensational manuscript finds have been made more recently still at two sites within a few miles of Khirbet Qumran.)

Every newspaper reader knows that the discovery at Khirbet Qumran was one of the most important finds of ancient documents ever made. We do not yet know all it can tell us of the few centuries around the beginning of the Christian Era. But the direction in which the find will increase our knowledge can already be perceived, for the evidence shows it will cast light on one of the most fascinating and perplexing problems of Jewish history—that of the three contending Jewish sects that existed around the time of the destruction of the Second Temple (70 C.E.): the Pharisees, the Sadducees, and the Essenes, their doctrines, their literature, and their character.

The struggle of the three sects, or groups of sects, eventually resulted in the triumph of the Pharisees. All modern Judaism—from the Sotmer Rebbe's to that of Lessing Rosenwald—derives from Pharisaism, in the triumph of which the facts about its rival sects were forgotten or distorted. Pharisaism itself was to suffer a similar fate in the triumph of Christianity. Just what the Sadducees (together with the related Boetheans) and the Essenes stood for has hitherto been difficult to determine; we have had only meager information and that from outsiders, and anyone who knows Judaism and Jewish life knows what fantastic things are sometimes written, even without malice, by non-Jews (or ignorant Jews). The newly found scrolls present a good deal of fresh data on one of these two heretical sects; more, they have cleared up for us the hints found in the Apocrypha and other literature suggesting the existence of a different form of Judaism from that which we know now. Let us follow the chain of historical and archaeological evidence that establishes the significance of the scrolls, beginning our detective story with the clues in the Apocrypha.

I.   THE APOCRYPHA

Before the Protestant Reformation, nearly every Christian Bible included, scattered through the Old Testament, a number of elements, ranging in size from a chapter to a whole book, which are wanting in the Hebrew Scriptures. Since then, Protestant Bibles have either relegated this group to a position between the two Testaments (as in early printings of the Authorized English Version) or omitted them altogether (as do the Revised English Versions). These writings, which Protestants describe as "apocryphal"—or the Apocrypha (plural of *apocryphon*)—and Roman Catholics call "deuterocanonical," include such familiar classics as Judith, Tobit, and the History of Susanna, the meaty Wisdom of Ben Sira (Ecclesiasticus), and the invaluable chronicle known as First Maccabees. The Hebraist can tell that all these, known to us only in Greek, were translated from the Hebrew or Aramaic (rabbinical literature actually preserves the original Hebrew of a number of verses from Ben Sira), and were obviously composed in Palestine. We can usually explain why the Rabbis denied them recognition as Holy Writ (for example, Ben Sira and First Maccabees were avowedly written centuries after that time which the Rabbis regarded as the end of the age of inspiration), but it is by no means obvious why Judaism failed to preserve these writings as edifying literature. They were not heretical; and as a matter of fact they were welcomed back into Hebrew literature in medieval (as well as modern) times in the form of actual retranslations, as well as adaptations.

But in addition to the fourteen items which used to be included as Apocrypha in the Authorized Version and are revered as "deuterocanonical" by Roman Catholics, there are a large number of books regarded as extracanonical on all sides, though early Christian writers treated them with respect. These are sometimes termed Pseudepigrapha (plural of *pseudepigraphon*), but equally often they too are simply called Apocrypha. Among them two works in particular, First Enoch and the Book of Jubilees, strike one at once as heretical. Both date events according to a calendar with an even 52 weeks, or 364 days, to the year. It is further specified that the first days of the first, fourth, seventh, and tenth months are to be special holidays—implying, no doubt, that the immediately preceding months had each an extra day, or 31 in all, as against 30 days for each of the remaining eight months. The Book of Jubilees specifically opposes the accepted Jewish calendar, on the ground that it results in the festivals being observed on the wrong days. In general, its laws are rigorous and its punishments draconic. Of interest is its polemic against the Gentiles' (Greeks') lack of shame about their bodies. (Perhaps it is not an accident that it omits from its account of Creation the Biblical statement that God created man in His own image.)

We know of another author who probably approved of the Enoch-Book of Jubilees calendar, namely, the man who wrote the Pseudepigrapha known as the Testaments of the Twelve Patriarchs (i.e., sons of Jacob). He at any rate drew upon the Book of Jubilees for biographical data on the twelve sons of Jacob. But what group ever celebrated its festivals according to that odd calendar?

II. THE GENIZAH

In Fostat, or Old Cairo, there is a synagogue which has been in existence since the ninth century. Visitors in the eighteenth and nineteenth centuries were struck by the vast amount of material in its Genizah (repository of no longer usable writings in the Hebrew script, which according to law must not be deliberately destroyed). But nothing startling was found there until 1888, when, during repairs, the inner chamber containing the really old deposits was uncovered. After that, a number of American and European travelers in Egypt with scholarly interests were able to acquire some very interesting manuscripts, partly directly from the caretakers of the synagogue and partly from dealers in antiquities. And in 1896, the late Dr. Solomon Schechter (at the time Reader in Rabbinics at Cambridge University, in England, later president of the faculty of the Jewish Theological Seminary of America in New York) went out to Cairo and acquired on behalf of the Cambridge University Library practically all of the manuscript material of the Genizah which had not yet been removed from it.

This is not the place for an appreciation of the lost works of Jewish literature and the lost chapters of Jewish history which have been recovered (and are still being recovered) from the jumbled, only half-legible leaves, strips, shreds, and scraps of manuscripts from the Cairo Genizah, now stored in libraries in Leningrad, Oxford, Cambridge, Paris, New York and elsewhere. We are only concerned here with the "Documents of Jewish Sectaries." Under this title, Schechter published fragments, from the Schechter–Taylor Collection of Genizah Manuscripts at Cambridge, of two works, one of which is known as

the "Zadokite Fragments" or the "Damascus Covenant." These fragments are composed in a kind of Hebrew which until recently was not
found in any other writing. It looks like an attempt to imitate the Bible
as closely as possible, and yet it contains a surprising number of Tannaitic—but *early* Tannaitic—terms as well as other peculiarities. The
"Damascus Covenant" was found to insist upon a more rigorous interpretation than Orthodox Judaism of the laws of ritual purity and
forbidden marriages (uncle-niece marriages and polygamy are forbidden), and of some of the dietary laws, and also to prescribe an organization into communes governed by overseers, with strict laws for
admission and expulsion. Interestingly enough, it has unmistakable
points of contact with the heretical Apocrypha referred to above. It
cites one of the Testaments of the Twelve Patriarchs by name. It refers
to the angels as "Watchers of Heaven," just like First Enoch. It employs for "evil" a special term, *mastema,* which is pecular to the Book
of Jubilees. It refers the reader, for a list of the times of Israel's "blindness" to the commandments of the Torah, to the Book of the Divisions
of Times, and evidently means First Enoch, since it is only in Chapters 89–90 of this book that we find Israel allegorically represented as
sheep that sometimes go blind and stray (corresponding to the periods
of idolatry). If we had the complete text of this remarkable screed, we
should almost certainly find some rantings against opponents for using
the wrong sort of calendar, and an emphatic insistence upon the observance of the festivals in their proper seasons—meaning on the days
on which they fell in the calendar of Enoch and the Book of
Jubilees. . . .

III. THE CAVE SCROLLS

We now come back to the scrolls that were found at Khirbet
Qumran. Many are simply copies of parts of the Hebrew Bible. By now
everybody has heard of the complete Isaiah scroll, and there are also
fragments of two other Isaiah scrolls and of most of the other books of
the Bible; and it is indeed interesting to know what the Bible copies in
use in out-of-the-way places at this early date were like. (Many of them
are full of mistakes, like the popular copies of Homer that have come to
light in recent years.) But of far greater interest are the other manuscripts in the find. These include fragments of the lost Hebrew and
Aramaic originals of the Apocrypha, fragments of the "Damascus
Covenant," and still other documents in the style and spirit of the

"Covenant." In these latter documents, by the way, we find the polemic against the celebration of the festivals on the wrong days which I surmised above must have been contained in the complete "Damascus Covenant."

Both the "Damascus Covenant" and a document very similar to it found at Khirbet Qumran, and known as the "Manual of Discipline," indicate further that the sect they represent lived in communities in which all pooled their possessions, and were governed by "overseers." The members of the sect were under strict rules of etiquette—they shared, for example, the prudishness of the Book of Jubilees about nudity. Their founder, or in any case their hero, is referred to in both these works as the "Teacher of Righteousness"; and still a third document refers to this hero's persecution by the "wicked priest" in Jerusalem. Other writings indicate that they believed in immortality.

What, then, is the age of this literature? It can be determined by internal as well as external criteria. I have not mentioned all the possible features that can serve as *internal* indications, since some would require lengthy explanation. But two obvious indications are the "wicked priest" and the "communal" societies. Jewish priests in Jerusalem ceased to exercise authority after 70 C.E. (the date of the capture of Jerusalem by Vespasian and the burning of the Second Temple); and there never have been any Jewish religious communistic societies since about the same date. As for *external* criteria: (1) All competent paleographers agree that none of the Khirbet Qumran manuscripts (which are not all of the same age) can date from later than the 1st century C.E., and some even insist that the lower limit is rather the 1st century B.C.E. (2) A carbon-14 test of the linen in which the scrolls were wrapped yielded the date 33 C.E., with a margin of error of 200 years later or earlier. (The test was carried out on the linen wrappings rather than on the writing materials, since the process of burning is involved. It is based on the observation that whereas the atomic weight of ordinary carbon is 12, a fantastically tiny but fixed proportion of all the carbon component of a living organism is present in the form of the radioactive isotope carbon-14, which begins to break down into carbon-12 at a fixed rate as soon as the organism dies. Hence the proportion of carbon-14 still present in any substance of organic origin—wood, linen, wool, etc.—is an index of its age.) (3) In some 70 separate manuscripts there is not a scrap of parchment (let alone paper!), but only leather, papyrus, and ostraca (potsherds used for writing on). (4) There are no codices (bundles of leaves, like our modern books), but only scrolls. (5) The pottery on the site is all early Roman (that is to say, of the 1st century C.E.). (6) The latest coin found on the site is of the year 68 C.E., so that the site must have been abandoned between that date and the calamity of 70 C.E. (or very soon after).

IV. THE ESSENES

I have indicated that just at this time there were two groups of sects in addition to the Pharisaic group: the Sadducees and the Essenes. We can rule the Sadducees out at once. They consisted largely of the aristocratic priests of Jerusalem, whom our documents contemn. They did not live in communes. They did not believe in immortality. And while they differed with the Pharisees regarding the date of the Feast of Weeks (Shavuot), they did not place it in the *middle* of Sivan, as the Book of Jubilees does, and they observed all the other festivals on the same days as the Pharisees.

There remain the Essenes. These did live in communes, according to both the Jew Philo and the Roman Pliny, and *were* governed by an overseer according to the former. They did believe in immortality. They were rigorists, and they were sticklers for modesty. Pliny, moreover, locates a colony of them precisely on the western shore of the Dead Sea above (that is, north of), En-gedi, at some distance back from the beach, which is insalubrious; and when we find a colony of sectarians contemporary with Pliny (he died 79 C.E.) in this very area, the burden of proof rests not upon those who assert but upon those who deny their identity with his Essenes. True, these two writers, (Philo and Pliny) state that the Essenes were recruited only from the outside, and admitted no women and begot no children, whereas the literature of our group makes provision for marriage (though it roundly condemns polygamy); and, as a matter of fact, skeletons exhumed from the Khirbet Qumran cemetery include skeletons of women. But then, both Philo and Pliny—though they had visited Judea—were writing largely from hearsay, whereas the well-known Jewish historian Josephus, who grew up in Palestine, knew that some of the Essenes did marry. The truth may be that celibacy was common among the Essenes either because their general puritanism led them to esteem it, or because there was a large excess of men over women among them, or for both reasons. The excess of males was doubtless due to the fact that outsiders were admitted to the sect, but under stringent conditions fulfillable only by a man; so that whereas the group included a large number of male neophytes in addition to the males born into it, the only females were either born into the group or had already been married to their husbands at the time they joined it.

V. THE KARAITES

But if (on the one hand) the Essene community by the Dead Sea dispersed about 70 C.E., and if no subsequent writer knows anything about the Essenes except what is to be found in Philo, Josephus, and Pliny; and if (on the other hand) the "Damascus Covenant," of which a copy was included in the library of this community, as we have seen, is a typically Essene document—then how in the world did two copies—in typically medieval hands—of this "Damascus Covenant" find their way into the Cairo Genizah whence Schechter salvaged them, as has already been mentioned? The answer is to be found in the second of Schechter's "Documents of Jewish Sectaries." Among those same manuscripts salvaged from the Genizah, Schechter found fragments of the *Sefer ham-Miṣwot* (Book of Religious Precepts) of Anan ben David, the man who founded in the 8th century the still—albeit very feebly—extant sect of the Karaites. (Some leaves of the same manuscript had already reached Leningrad—then St. Petersburg—and had been published by Abraham Harkavy.) Karaism, to be sure, is not an offshoot of Essenism. It arose after the Talmud had long been completed, and as a protest against it. Not recognizing the Oral Law, it claimed to base itself solely upon the Scriptures; hence the name Karaites—"Scripturists."

However, Father de Vaux, who has already been referred to, has called attention to the fact that Karaite and Moslem writers after 900 C.E. actually speak of an ancient sect which in the writers' own time was referred to as the "Cave Folk," and state that the reason for this designation is that "their writings were discovered in a cave." One of the Moslem writers describes some features of the "Cave Folk's" calendar—and it actually agrees with that of the Book of Jubilees. Accordingly, Professor Paul Kahle, a German Protestant now residing in England, suggested that on the occasion of the said discovery the Karaites had (by purchase?) come into possession of a number of writings from that cave, including the "Damascus Covenant."

The Karaites were interested in earlier sects and schools because the very existence of these casts doubt upon the claim of the Orthodox

Jews (whom the Karaites call Rabbanites) to possess an authentic body of oral tradition going back to Moses and therefore as old as the Written Law itself. That the Karaites made use of sectarian writings from a cave or caves is proved by testimony to which attention was recently called by Professor Saul Lieberman of the Jewish Theological Seminary in New York: a certain Rabbi Moses Taku, writing in the 13th century, accuses the Karaites of claiming to have discovered in the ground heretical writings which they have themselves fabricated and buried there. It is now evident that their claims were quite truthful. Professor Lieberman attributes to the influence of this "Cave Folk" literature some striking dietary rigorisms which the Karaites share with the "Damascus Covenant," for example, the requirement that the blood of fish be drained before they are eaten. He further suggests that the same cause may account for certain features of Karaite diction. (Thus, the epithet "Teacher of Righteousness" by which, as we have seen, the "Cave Folk" referred to the founder of their sect, is applied by Karaite writers to Elijah, the teacher of the end of the days; see Malachi 3:23-24.)

But it is evident that when all the texts from Khirbet Qumran have been published, a much larger body of "Cave Folk" literature will be available than the Karaite savants had at their disposal. A host of modern scholars will study and interpret them, and a great beam of light will be cast upon the religious and intellectual currents in Jewry at the turn of the Christian Era.

MORE LIGHT FROM JUDEAN CAVES
Harold L. Ginsberg

Both Israel and Jordan have displayed a commendable zeal in seeking, preserving, and publishing the archeological remains within their respective borders. The most sensational finds of recent years, however, have been made in the northern half of the Wilderness of Judah; actually, the decade that began in the spring of 1947 may come to be known in the history of archeological discovery in the Holy Land as the "Decade of the Wilderness of Judah." The Wilderness itself is a narrow strip of very steep, broken, and arid land running between the Dead Sea and the watershed of the hill country of Judah.

In the northern half of the Wilderness, which lies inside the Kingdom of Jordan, manuscripts dating from antiquity came to light at or near Khirbet Qumran, in 1947-52, and Wadi Murabba'at, in 1951-52. At Khirbet Mird, in 1952-53, old manuscripts were recovered in the ruins of an ancient monastery but, being medieval, they do not concern us here. Those at the other two sites were found in caves, and I shall here anticipate my conclusions to the extent of noting that the Khirbet Qumran manuscripts were abandoned in the year 68 C.E., during the First Jewish Revolt (against Rome), and the Wadi Mu-Rabba'at ones—at least the most important of them—more than sixty-five years later, in 134-5 C.E., during the Second Jewish Revolt. At Khirbet Qumran, only one manuscript cave was known from 1947 through 1951, but five more were discovered in 1952. At Wadi Murabba'at, there are two "literate" grottoes.

WADI MURABBA'AT

Wadi Murabba'at is a wild ravine extremely difficult of access. Both its two "literate" and its two "illiterate" grottoes contained abundant anepigraphic relics (remains without writing) of human occupation over a period of more than four thousand years—from the 4th millennium B.C.E. until well into the Arab period. The extreme dryness of the climate had preserved not only pottery but wooden utensils and cloth and, along with these, such perishable writing materials as papyrus and crude leather.

The period of most intensive human occupation had evidently been the Roman, which was represented by the most artifacts. These include coins of the 1st and 2nd centuries C.E. and writings in Hebrew, Aramaic, Greek and Latin; some of these mention persons, and some actual dates, of the 2nd century C.E. One very notable event of that century was the Second Jewish Revolt against Rome, which lasted from 132 to 135. Its leader's given name, Simeon, was formerly known only from coins he had minted, while his surname was not really known at all. It is indeed given as Ben Kozeba or Bar Kozeba (Son of the Disappointer), in rabbinic literature, and as Kocheba (the Star) or Bar Kocheba (Son of the Star) in the early Christian sources. But scholars have always realized that these were mere nicknames—the Christian writings preserving an earlier name from the time when the Jews had pinned great hopes on Simeon, and the rabbinic ones reflecting their disappointment. Only now do we know that his actual, official surname was Ben Kosbah. For at Wadi Murabba'at were found preserved from the time of the Second Revolt the following items: nine coins dating from that period; some Aramaic deeds dated in the "Year Three of Israel's Freedom" (134 C.E.); several fragmentary Hebrew documents dated by "the deliverance of Israel through Simeon ben Kosbah, Prince of Israel"; two letters addressed by "Simeon ben Kosbah, Prince of Israel" to one "Jeshua ben Galgola and the men of the fort"; and another letter from a different quarter addressed to the same "Jeshua ben Galgola, commander of the camp." It would seem that this Jeshua commanded a military guard which Simeon kept stationed in this desert fastness, even as the aforementioned Latin text shows that the Romans kept one stationed there subsequently—probably to keep watch over one of the roads leading to En-gedi.

The Wadi Murabba'at grottoes have further yielded some fragments of the Bible: of Genesis, Exodus, Deuteronomy, and Isaiah.

(Latest reports tell of the recovery of a defective copy of the Minor Prophets.) That they are so fragmentary is not an accident. One of the pieces of scroll has a tear which runs across three columns. The war against Ben Kosbah, as we ought now to call him, was one of the bitterest the Romans ever had to fight, and these particular grottoes in the midst of a desolate waste must have cost them heavy casualties. The pagan soldiers therefore tore the Torah scrolls and other sacred writings to shreds. Probably because of their inconspicuousness, a couple of phylacteries survived intact.

The Biblical texts found at Wadi Murabba'at (at least apart from the aforementioned unpublished scroll of the Minor Prophets) agree exactly, even to the spelling, with the Masoretic Text (our present Hebrew text), while the phylacteries contain exactly the Pentateuch sections prescribed by the Rabbis. No apocryphal texts were found and, of course, no heretical writings.

KHIRBET QUMRAN

Readers of *Commentary* (July 1953, p. 237-245 above) already know a good deal about these, the original, "cave scrolls." But abundant new data have become available in the past two years, and a certain amount of recapitulation is desirable and even unavoidable.

Whereas in our last article we were able to speak of only some forty distinct manuscripts identified with certainty and the prospect of their number being raised to seventy, we can now speak of hundreds of books dating partly from the 1st (some probably from the 2nd) century B.C.E., and partly from the 1st century C.E. The evidence for this dating—which, it is credibly rumored, has just been sensationally augmented in a manner which may soon be divulged—is at present as follows:

1. The script of the dated Wadi Murabba'at manuscripts of the year 134 C.E., which I have just mentioned, furnishes one most important piece of evidence. Next to it, even the latest scripts of Khirbet Qumran look archaic.

2. The great bulk of the inscribed material is crude leather, though there is one specimen of parchment (finely prepared skin), and also a little papyrus and three sheets of copper. There is, further, an ostracon (inscribed potsherd), which was not found in one of the caves but in a nearby spot of which more will be said below. The

important thing to remember is the negative feature that in all this vast quantity of material there is not a single piece of paper.

3. The soft materials—leather and papyrus—all constitute scrolls. Thus far there is no evidence for there having been any codices (bundles of leaves, like our modern books). And there is not, in all this mass, a single trace of vowel signs.

To be sure, some papyrus was still used in the Middle Ages, and some scrolls are used even today; e.g., our *Sifrei Torah, megillot, tefillin, mezuzot,* and—diplomas. But a library of hundreds of books comprising only scrolls, and none of paper but only of crude leather or papyrus (except for one item of parchment), is not seriously conceivable after the 3rd century C.E., if that late. And the following further observations go to show that the manuscripts were in fact stowed away in the caves as early as the 1st century C.E.

4. The manuscripts of Cave One were wrapped in linen. The age of the linen has been determined by a carbon-14 test as 33 C.E., with a margin of possible error of two centuries upward as well as downward.

5. The manuscripts of Cave One were stored in jars of a type found nowhere else except in neighboring caves (where they were used for more prosaic purposes than the storage of books) and in Level II of the nearby site of settlement known as Khirbet Qumran. Obviously, therefore, the manuscripts in question were placed in the jars and cached in the cave not later than the time when the said level of occupation of the nearby settlement was destroyed. And that date can be fixed very exactly. The latest of the many coins found in Level II is of the Year Two of the First Jewish Revolt, i.e., the year 67-68 C.E.; and we know from Josephus that Vespasian, the Roman general who was soon to be acclaimed emperor, occupied Jericho in June of the year 68. Khirbet Qumran is only eight miles south of Jericho and—unlike Wadi Murabba'at—can be reached with comparative ease; moreover, Josephus actually tells of Vespasian reaching the Dead Sea. Clearly, therefore, this was the occasion when the Romans captured and destroyed Level II of Khirbet Qumran; and it must have been in the preceding weeks or months, and in anticipation of Vespasian's coming, that the manuscripts were hidden away.

But the unusual jars are not the only objects recovered from Level II of Khirbet Qumran that bear directly upon the manuscripts in the caves of the vicinity. The settlement consisted of a single large public building of two stories. The debris of the upper story was found to include what may have been a washstand and also three tables and two inkwells, and there were benches along its walls. This was evidently the *scriptorium,* the room in which scribes sat and copied books for the community's use.

The building also had facilities for cooking and for communal meals and/or deliberations. To the east of it was a large cemetery of about eleven hundred graves, the building and the cemetery occupying between them a sort of plateau in the cliffside. A number of caves in the vicinity contained pottery but no manuscripts and evidently served as dwellings, or as storerooms for people who dwelt in tents close by. Now, it is at least a remarkable coincidence that a notable feature of Essene practice, as described in our sources, was the communal repast. The famous Roman naturalist Pliny—who accompanied Vespasian on his Judean campaign—describes the location of a colony of Essenes by the Dead Sea in terms which fit Khirbet Qumran remarkably well. The owners of the Khirbet Qumran scrolls are shown by the content of some of the scrolls to have been certainly a community of sectarians; and probably those sectarians were Essenes.

It would be too good to be true if the entire library of this community had remained intact until the recent discoveries. Khirbet Qumran is not inaccessible like Wadi Murabba'at; and although Cave One is off the beaten track, in the side of a cliff, most of its original contents were already gone when chance led a Bedouin into it in the spring of 1947. There has long been known a letter of circa 800 C.E. which mentions a discovery of Hebrew manuscripts in a cave in the vicinity of Jericho, and Karaite and Moslem writers after 900 also know of sectarian writings which were discovered in a cave. From the contents which these writers attribute to those ancient screeds it is almost certain that they belonged to the same sect as the Khirbet Qumran ones, and the cave in question may even be precisely our Cave One. But, in any case, the remains which have been salvaged from these grottoes in the last few years are epoch-making.

Here we have writings embodying the principles, regulations, liturgy, and interpretations of Scripture of a vanished Jewish sect. Here we have parts of the lost Hebrew and Aramaic originals of those remarkable works known as the Apocrypha and the Pseudepigrapha. We have even the Aramaic original of a pseudepigraphon (the Book of Lamech) whose existence was previously known only from an old book list, but of which no copy was extant in any language. And here we have the remains of an entire library of Hebrew Bible manuscripts which are centuries older than any previously known.

Of the sect's writings and doctrines, as also of its possession of some of the Apocrypha and Pseudepigrapha and their influence upon its writings and doctrines, I have spoken in my previous article. I would here merely add that we now know that the Khirbet Qumran library possessed, along with extra-canonical scriptures otherwise unknown, more than one copy each of the Book of Jubilees and First Enoch in the original Hebrew, as well as both a Hebrew and an Aramaic text of the Book of Tobit.

THE STATE AND USES OF THE BIBLE
IN GRECO-ROMAN TIMES

As is well known, the Rabbis of the Roman Age made little effort to imitate the language of the Bible in the Mishnah, Tosephta, Baraitot, and Midrashim, but employed what is called Mishnaic or Talmudic Hebrew by means of which they achieved precision, conciseness, and picturesqueness. Only in the set prayers which they prescribed—in the sections preceding and following the Shema, and especially in the Amidah—was there an obvious attempt to "talk Biblically." And even then there was no attempt to show off how many more or less apposite Biblical phrases they could think of and combine but, on the contrary, a beautiful simplicity and dignity—at least in those rabbinic prayers which ended by being adopted permanently. The sectarian Hebrew of the Khirbet Qumran manuscripts is much more "Biblical." Yet I do not think it is bias that makes me pronounce it notably inferior to the Hebrew of the Rabbis. Even the non-liturgical texts of these people read like mosaics of Biblical phrases, with a good deal of prolixity for the sake of getting in more Biblical flourishes; while their liturgies carry this tendency to monstrous extremes, with the result that the thread of thought is sometimes lost in the mass of verbiage. At the same time, the post-Biblical words with which their compositions are interspersed show that the living Hebrew of the time was actually very much like that which the Rabbis employed as a matter of course.

In other respects, however, the sectarians' use of the Bible was very similar to that of the Rabbis. Thus in two of their books, known as the "Damascus Covenant" and the "Manual of Discipline," they bolster their arguments with quotations from the Bible which they interpret midrashically; and—this was indeed a surprise—Cave One yielded a practically complete midrash on the Book of Habakkuk and fragments of midrashim on Micah and Zephaniah, while Cave Four yielded parts of one or more on Isaiah. Three different caves seem to have yielded parts of one or more "commentaries" on Psalms. Some scholars have insisted that these are not midrashim but commentaries in our sense of the word. Well, the one, or the ones, on Isaiah have not been published; but the others at any rate, are completely lacking in those things which are the very stuff of Bible commentaries in our sense of the term, and which are by no means entirely neglected even in our rabbinic midrashim: namely, grammatical, etymological, stylistic, and antiquarian notes; and any number of exegetical puzzles are not even tackled. Instead, only those verses are selected for exposition which lend themselves to a completely arbitrary interpretation as allusions to current history. Take the Book of Habakkuk, for example. It is remarkable enough according to its plain sense. A prophet here actually reproaches his God for remaining passive while the ungodly Chaldeans are having the upper hand over other, innocent nations (the prophet does not single out the wrongs done to his own Jewish people!) and then waits for and receives a reply to his reproach. ("Reproach" is the word he himself uses.) But according to the sectarian interpreter, all the prophet is concerned about is the wrong which the Teacher of Righteousness, the founder or hero of the sect, is destined to suffer half a millennium later at the hands of Hasmonean priest-princes; his reproach is directed not to God but to some human party who will be in a position to protest against the maltreatment of the Teacher of Righteousness; and the Chaldeans are none other than the Romans, whose suzerainty over Judea since 63 B.C. is represented as a punishment for the persecution of the Teacher of Righteousness and his companions.

Very similar applications of ancient oracles to their own times can be cited from the Rabbis, but by them they are meant to be understood more as *jeux d'esprit* than as insights into the actual intentions of the ancient texts. Thus, although it is true that in the Hebrew text of the oracle which announced to our mother Rebekah that "Two nations are in thy womb" the word for "nations" is spelled in such a way that it could also be read as "magnates," no Jew would be considered a heretic for doubting whether this was really meant to allude to the wealthy compiler of the Mishnah (who was of course descended from Jacob) and to the Roman emperor (supposedly descended from Esau) whose friendship the former is said to have enjoyed. On the other hand, it is well known that such "actualizations" of ancient prophecy are basic to Christianity. It is natural to surmise that this agreement between the Khirbet Qumran group and the early Christians in making every possible ancient text refer to their own times is due to the fact that both the Khirbet Qumran sect and the early Christians were persecuted and believed that they were living at "the end of the days"; the former expecting the early rise of "a Messiah from Aaron and Israel," and the latter awaiting an imminent Second Advent. For it is a fact that in an even earlier age, when Judaism was subjected to such a persecution that barring a miracle, its early disappearance seemed inevitable, it produced just such "eschatological midrashim," and these were embodied in the Bible itself.

The crisis to which I refer was the outlawing of Judaism by Antiochus Epiphanes in the years 167-64 B.C.E., and the midrashim which discovered that both this crisis and the dire end of Antiochus and the dawn of a new age had all been foretold in the ancient Scriptures are embodied in the Book of Daniel. Here (Daniel 9) we are told in so many words that the seventy years of subjection to Babylon foretold by Jeremiah were not seventy years but seventy hebdomads (weeks of years), or four hundred ninety years in all, and that they would witness many vicissitudes ending with the outlawing of the Jewish religion for half a hebdomad (three and a half years) and would be followed by the dawn of a new age. And I have shown elsewhere how a much more elaborate midrash which, among other things, turned the Assyria of Isaiah's oracles into the Syria of the 2nd century B.C.E. and the haughty king of Assyria whom Isaiah denounces into Antiochus Epiphanes, has been incorporated in Daniel 11. It is safe to say that next to Halachic midrash (see *Commentary*, September 1950, p. 283), Eschatological midrash, as exemplified by the sectarian midrashim on Habakkuk and Micah and by the even earlier midrash of Daniel 11, on Isaiah, is the oldest type of midrash there is.

These sectarians, then, were steeped in the Bible, they imitated its phraseology and meditated upon its meaning. In what form did they read it? I have already mentioned that no codices (books of leaves, like ours) were found at Khirbet Qumran, but only scrolls. It follows that these people could not possibly have possessed complete one-volume Bibles. We all know how bulky and heavy even the Pentateuch (the Torah) alone is in scroll form. But they probably did possess copies of all of the separate books in the Hebrew canon, with the possible exception of Esther. To date, fragments have been found of every book except Esther. It may well be that these sectarians did not recognize either the Book of Esther—in all probability a product of the Hasmonean Age—or the Festival of Purim, whose observance that Book enjoins. It is also far from certain that they observed Chanukah, a festival instituted by the Hasmoneans, whom they detested.

Interestingly enough, a few of the Bible scrolls are in the Old Hebrew script, which today must be familiar even to the layman from the reproductions of ancient Jewish coins on Israeli postage stamps. Even the legends on the coins of the Second Revolt minted by Simeon ben Kosbah are in the old Hebrew script. The Mishnah does not permit the use of scrolls in this script for the reading in the synagogue, but this prohibition itself reflects the existence of such scrolls among Jews of the Mishnaic period. As is well known, the Samaritans to this day use this script alone. Because of its venerable age, it was actually often regarded as more sacred than our square Hebrew letters, so that some of the sectarian documents which are otherwise executed in the square script use the Old Hebrew script for writing the name of God. Similarly, in his Greek translation of the Hebrew Bible, Aquila (a contemporary of Simeon ben Kosbah) neither translated nor even transcribed the Tetragrammaton but copied it out—in the Old Hebrew script.

The sectarians' most popular book of the Bible outside the Pentateuch was the Book of Isaiah. Khirbet Qumran has yielded one complete scroll of it, one defective one, a fragment of a third and, as we have already mentioned, parts of at least one midrash on it. In this the sectarians were by no means unique. The only books of the Bible outside the Pentateuch of which a remnant was found at Wadi Murabba'at were Isaiah and—according to latest reports—the Minor Prophets. That Daniel 11 embodies a whole midrash on Isaiah was mentioned above. Readers of the New Testament are familiar with two further instances: there is the story (Luke 4:16-22) of how Jesus went into the synagogue of Capernaum on a Sabbath, stood up to read, and was handed a scroll of Isaiah, which he opened and in which he read and interpreted a passage; and there is the other (Acts 8:26 ff.) about how the apostle Philip came upon an Ethiopian eunuch reading the prophet Isaiah and entered into a discussion with him. The reason for this popularity is not far to seek. Of the three major prophets, the Rabbis observe that Jeremiah is all calamity, Ezekiel part calamity and part consolation, and Isaiah (especially what the moderns call Second Isaiah) all consolation (Baba Batra 14b)—and, we may add, consolation in language of unforgettable beauty.

But readers will doubtless be most interested to know what light these texts shed upon higher, or literary, criticism and upon lower, or textual, criticism. Upon higher criticism, they shed no light at all. The complete Isaiah scroll, which is nearly the oldest manuscript of the lot, does not date from much before 100 B.C.E., and nobody who deserves to be taken seriously imagines that anything was added to the Book of Isaiah after that date. But for lower criticism these texts are very important. For some of them agree with our Masoretic Text in a high degree (so the first of the incomplete Isaiah scrolls) while others (notably the complete Isaiah scroll) diverge notably in spelling and grammar, and not infrequently in wording. By the way, the divergencies in spelling and grammar are nearly always in the direction of later usage—just as in the Samaritan Pentateuch and in unscholarly manuscripts of the classics.

It is of course the wording of the cave Bible scrolls that interests us in particular, and it is very interesting to find that it frequently agrees with the Septuagint, the most famous of the Greek versions, and at other points disagrees with both the Masoretic Text and the Septuagint. In one case where the Septuagint rendering reflects a different Hebrew reading from ours, that divergent Hebrew reading turns up in a Khirbet Qumran scroll and proves to be definitely superior to that of the received, or Masoretic, text. In Deuteronomy 29:1, Moses summons the Israelites for a farewell address which runs to the end of Chapter 30. This is followed by some brief instructions and dispositions. In the received text, the transition from the "ethical will" to the instructions and dispositions reads as follows (Deuteronomy 31:1-2): "Now, when Moses *had gone and spoken* (*wylk msh wydbr*) these words to all of Israel, he said to them. . . ." Obviously more correct, however, is the reading of a Khirbet Qumran scroll, which is also that which the Septuagint translator had before him: "Now, when Moses *had finished speaking* (*wykl msh ldbr*) these words to all of Israel, he said to them. . . ." For since Moses had summoned the Israelites to him, he had not gone to them.

THE MASORETIC TEXT AND ITS RIVALS IN ORTHODOX JUDAISM

But in most cases where the Khirbet Qumran Bible texts diverge from ours, the readings are inferior to ours. What I wish to stress here is merely the fact that they contain at certain points considerable divergences both from our text and among themselves. This relative fluidity of text is just what we find in ancient manuscripts of the classics, and is presupposed by the rabbinic legislation and tradition. For the rule itself that a scroll not conforming to the standard text must not be read from in the synagogue presupposes that divergent texts are in circulation for private study; and the remarkable variants reported from Rabbi Meir's copies (middle of the 2nd century C.E.) show that when he copied for private study of his own or for that of his customers he didn't bother to adhere to the standard text of the Rabbis. (On all this and more, Saul Lieberman's *Hellenism in Jewish Palestine*, Chapter One, may profitably be consulted.) It is therefore by no means unlikely that, if the Biblical remains recovered from Wadi Murabba'at were not so scanty, they would be found not to accord with the Masoretic Text so perfectly as we have noted.

There is a famous tradition in the rabbinic sources (Sifre II 356 and parallels), about how three scrolls in the Temple forecourt were compared and the reading of the majority adopted as standard wherever two scrolls agreed against one. This tradition shows that the Jewish authorities, like the Greek philologians, realized that all readings were not equally good, and set out to recover the original text by adopting the readings of a majority of superior manuscripts. The result is our Masoretic Text, which is superior to all its rivals on the whole, but certainly can be corrected by the readings of one or another of them in a number of passages. Eventually this Standard Text superseded all others even for private study, but there still survive traces of the time when it had not yet won out even in the most official religious circles. The instances of non-Masoretic Bible readings that occur in the Babylonian Talmud are listed in Rabbi Akiba Eger's *Gilyon hash-Shas* on Shabbat 55b; but the most notable one occurs in the Passover Haggadah. One of the passages in the Torah upon which the rabbinic requirement that the Haggadah be recited is based, comprises two verses which in our Standard (Masoretic) Text read as follows (Deut. 6: 20-21): "When your son asks you in time to come saying, What mean the testimonies, the statutes, and the ordinances which the Lord our God has commanded you? you shall say to your son, we were bondmen unto Pharaoh in Egypt, but the Lord took us out of Egypt with a mighty hand." The Septuagint, however, reads not "which the Lord our God has commanded *you*" but "which the Lord our God has commanded *us*," and not "out of *Egypt*" but "out of *there*," and not simply "with a mighty hand" but "with a mighty hand *and an outstretched arm*." Incredible as it may sound, our Haggadah

agrees in every one of these respects with the Septuagint. Modern
Occidental Haggadahs, to be sure, have corrected the son's question
into "commanded *you*" so as to make it agree with the Masoretic Text,
but early and Oriental Haggadahs still have the Septuagint reading
("commanded us") even here, and all Haggadahs have retained the
Septuagint wording of the father's reply. In these two verses, therefore, the Rabbis obviously had before them the same Hebrew text as
was used by the Septuagint translator.

In the daily liturgy, on the other hand, they have followed, at least
at one point, a reading which disagrees with those both of the Masoretic Text and of the Septuagint, but agrees with that of the (complete)
Isaiah cave scroll. The Amidah with which we are all familiar includes
the sentence "And may our eyes behold how Thou returnest unto Zion
in mercy." It is true that the old Palestinian Amidah lacked this sentence. But the Rabbis who introduced it—whether Palestinian or
Babylonian—must have been inspired by a non-Masoretic text of that
grand book of consolation, Isaiah. (As was noted above, the Rabbis
did try to "talk Biblically" in the prayers which they composed, and
Isaiah was everybody's favorite comforter.) To be sure, the main
clause, "And may our eyes behold," was inspired by the Masoretic
Text of Isaiah 33:17a, "Thine eyes shall behold a king in his beauty,"
and not by the divergent reading which is common to the Septuagint
and the Cave Scroll. But as for the rest of the sentence in the Amidah,
that can only derive from the Cave Scroll text of Isaiah 52:8b. For
the Masoretic Text has here merely "Yea, eye to eye they shall see how
the Lord returns unto Zion," without the addition of "in mercy." The
Septuagint, on the other hand, has the "mercy" without the "returning,"
since it substitutes "takes pity on" for "returns unto." Only in the
Cave Scroll do we find precisely what is presupposed by the wording
of the Amidah: "Yea, eye to eye they shall see how the Lord *returns*
unto Zion *in mercy*." To which we may add: Amen.

LAW

We have already discussed in the general introduction the attitude of the Rabbis to law. Faced with an entrenched law, they yet had to face the challenge of a changing world. They found their solution in interpretation, which enabled them to make changes which were yet no changes and received so-to-say retroactive authority from Sinai. This approach was made possible by their belief in the verbal inspiration of Scripture, for there flowed from this the theory that no word or even letter could be superfluous and hence the precise mode of expression, and the precise words used lent themselves to interpretation and the production of "new" laws. The Jews never developed the belief that the Bible was stylistically perfect, unlike the Moslems who claimed just such perfection for their holy book. In fact, it was stylistic or grammatical imperfections (e.g. repetition, anomalous spellings) which were the most favored pegs on which to hang a new interpretation. The rules for making interpretations became codified and fixed in later times. The relationship between laws that have no apparent Scriptural basis and those which are derived from Scripture is discussed by J. Z. Lauterbach in a long article to which the interested reader is referred.[1] Finkelstein discusses the social consequences of the Rabbinic approach to law. Daube deals with the formalized rules which enabled this interpretation to take place within specified guidelines. Zeitlin gives us an overview of Tannaitic jurisprudence, and discusses other mechanisms that were available for legal development. Blidstein discusses some aspects of crime and punishment, in particular the still unsettled issue of the desirability of retaining capital punishment. Cohen's article enables us to see how the rabbinic mind worked in a specific area of civil law, and illustrates how Jewish law was fully developed to cover all areas of life.

LIFE AND THE LAW
Louis Finkelstein

To many people today the adjustment of Jewish law to life implies simply the shortening of the prayers and the creation of a less complicated religious ritual. This is a grotesquely simple-minded conception of the history and sweep of Jewish law. Historically, Jewish law, even more than Roman law or Common law, has covered the whole of human relations, or as near the whole as any law can reach. A true measure of rabbinic adjustment of law to life is to be found in the difference between the small pocket Pentateuch and the massive tomes of the Talmud. For example, the two hundred folios of *Kiddushin* and *Ketubot* into which the Babylonian Talmud expands the six or seven verses of biblical marriage law are filled, not with additional severities, but with judicial decisions tempering the rigor of abstract law to the weakness of mortal man.

Unless, like the Pauline Christians, we abolish the law and completely reject its authority, we can adapt it to the needs of a growingly complex civilization only by reinterpreting and enlarging it. Half a century ago the historian of rabbinic tradition, I. H. Weiss, recognized (though the full significance of his discovery escaped him) that the sages most active in developing talmudic law were precisely those who were most keenly aware of the social needs of their times: Hillel, R. Joshua ben Hananya, R. Akiba, and their disciples. So too the Supreme Court of the United States, seeking guidance in the small written Constitution for the government of the continually expanding Republic, has amplified and broadened the original instrument far more than have the twenty-one actual amendments. So, again, have British judges drawn out of the meager traditions of the twelfth and thirteenth centuries that system of the Common law which is at once the dismay of the student and the delight of the scholar.

It is the purpose of this paper to show how the Jewish sages proceeded to interpret and expand their written law so as to keep it flexible and pertinent to the problems of changing life.

I. EXTRA-LEGAL INSTITUTIONS

The most important adjustment of Jewish law to life was the creation of the synagogue. Biblical law provides for only one sanctuary—the Solomonic temple at Jerusalem. Sacrifices outside of Jerusalem were forbidden. But there was no such prohibition against prayer. And if prayer was permitted in private, why not in public? Whether we suppose that the synagogue originated among the deported Judeans of the Babylonian exile, who sought in it a substitute for the destroyed temple; or among the post-exilic villagers, for whom it took the place of the earlier *bamot*, the provincial altars; or, as I am inclined to think, during the long reign of Manasseh when the prophetic following, driven from the polluted temple, sought a new avenue of approach to God—no matter when the synagogue originated, it arose as an extra-legal institution. If nothing in the law prohibited its organization, neither was there any authorization for it. No recognized authority ever sanctioned it; no one even realized that in creating the new institution the biblical law against public worship outside of Jerusalem had been circumvented and practically nullified! Thus the greatest revolution in the history of Jewish ceremonial—the substitution of prayer for sacrifice, of an institution for an edifice, of a democratic sanctuary for a hierarchic temple—was accomplished without removing an iota from the law.

Of importance not only for Israel but for the Western world was the creation of that other extra-legal institution of pre-talmudic Judaism: the prophetic canon. The prophets are mentioned in the Torah, i.e. the Pentateuch, and their authority in their own time is recognized. But there is no suggestion whatever that their words were to be collected or handed down to later ages as authoritative. The Hasidean or Maccabean scholars, who some time in the second century B.C.E. gathered together the fragments of prophetic writing, acted on no warrant but their own. The time needed decisive action if the books of Isaiah and Jeremiah and the rest were to be saved from the oblivion which had overtaken the *Midrash* of Iddo the Prophet and the even older *Sefer Hayashar* and the *Sefer Milhamot Hashem*. The sages rose to the demands of the occasion.

The creators of these two institutions, the synagogue and the prophetic canon, were as unaware of their contribution to history as were the Pilgrim Fathers of theirs. Let us now consider some later extra-legal innovations whose authors seem to have understood fully the implications of their words and deeds, and yet proceeded, perhaps in the teeth of determined opposition.

An interesting talmudic record tells us how, in the third century C.E., Abba Areka, appearing before the patriarch Rabbi Judah I for permission to return to Babylonia, was granted authority to decide questions of ritual and civil law, yet was arbitrarily forbidden to pass upon the ceremonial fitness of first-born animals. The later Babylonian authorities (the *amoraim*) who looked back to Abba Areka, known to them as Rab, as the greatest scholar of their land, could not conceal their surprise at this reservation. It seemed all the more remarkable because Abba Areka's less learned cousin, Rabbah bar Hanah, had received complete unreserved ordination. Nor could they ascribe Abba Areka's limited authority to his youth and inexperience, for another tradition told them that he had spent eighteen months with a shepherd studying the diseases of domestic animals in order to prepare himself for expertness in the very field which was now closed to him. While the explanation offered by the Talmud—Rabbi Judah's fear that Rab might establish precedents misleading to others less expert—cannot be accepted, it points to the truth of the situation. Rabbi Judah doubtless apprehended exactly what came to pass in time: that his young promising pupil would establish in Babylonia an academy rivaling that of Palestine, perhaps even wresting the hegemony from it. Unable to prevent Rab's return to Babylonia, perhaps even desirous of spreading the Torah through him, he was yet determined to save the prestige of the Palestinian academy, and thought he might do so by limiting Rab's authorization.

But life is stronger than men, with their ingenious verbal distinctions. When Rab arrived in Babylonia he found Rabbi Judah's fetters no more consequential than did Samson the ropes of the Philistines. Establishing his academy on the banks of the Euphrates, Rab proceeded to teach and graduate disciples. If he could not grant them the traditional *semikah* (ordination) with the title *Rabbi* ("my master"), for that title could not be conferred outside of Palestine, he invented a new degree, that of *Rab* ("master"), and declared that its holders might act as teachers of the people and as judges in matters of everyday occurrence. As questions of ritual and civil law could not possibly be sent to Palestine for decision, the Babylonian Jews needed to receive answers from their local authorities. On the other hand, questions of criminal law involving fines and stripes, being unusual, were to be outside the province of these new *amoraim*.

Continually harassed by the persecutions of Christian Rome and Byzantium, the Palestine schools weakened. At the same time these new Babylonian academies rose in influence. By the time of the *geonim* (i.e. after the sixth century C.E.) they were the accepted centers of Jewish authority for the whole world; even Palestine, while at times challenging their prerogatives, generally obeyed their decisions.

An extra-legal institution still more important, because it helped Israel pass through a more dangerous crisis, was the west-European *kehillah* ("community"). The organized communities of talmudic and pre-talmudic times had enjoyed but scant authority over their members. They were authorized to sell public buildings, and to fix weights and measures; but it was the scholar who was arbiter in all matters affecting Jewish law and ceremonial. Yet when the Jewries of Western Europe emerge out of the dark ages into the dawn of the tenth and eleventh centuries we find them provided with a definite community organization wherein the scholar was merely the spokesman of the popular will. It was now the *kehillah* that acted as arbiter between rival litigants: it regulated business dealings, it issued ordinances, it excommunicated the recalcitrant and the obdurate, and in general performed for its limited territory all the functions of the ancient Sanhedrin.

Thus, in issuing their decrees, scholars like Rabbenu Gershom (960-1040) derived their authority not from their learning, as had Hillel (*ca.* 20 B.C.E.) and Simeon ben Shatah (ca. 75 B.C.E.), but from their recognition by the communities.

For example, the ordinances against plural marriage and compulsory divorce, which we usually ascribe to Rabbenu Gershom, were known to his contemporaries as "Ordinances of the Communities." The same title was applied to the remarkable "constitution" established by Rabbenu Gershom and his colleagues for the Federation of the Rhine communities. Men like Rabbenu Tam (1100-1171) and his brother R. Samuel ben Meir (*ca.* 1085-1174) tried in vain to limit the power of the "community" and to restore the scholar to full and undivided authority. The democratic communities refused to yield their prerogatives; and only gradually, under the influence of men like R. Meir ben Baruch of Rothenburg (1215-1293), were they induced to recognize a legal jurisdiction in the scholar.

Similar examples of extra-legal institutions, and their value in adjusting law to life, might be cited from other parts of Jewish law, as indeed from almost any system of living jurisprudence. The English system of equity came into being first as an extra-legal supplement to the Common law. The American party system, without warrant or even mention in the Constitution, has destroyed the whole constitutional theory of presidential elections.

II. RADICAL INTERPRETATIONS

Extra-legal institutions by themselves, however, are not adequate to provide the full measure of necessary adjustment of law to life. A new house can scarcely be built every time a leak appears in the roof of the old one. Frequently the difficulty is not serious enough to warrant a new institution: what is needed is an "interpretation" of the law which will remain loyal to its spirit, even though it does some violence to the letter.

In a sense every application of law to life involves interpretation, for no formula in words can cover the intricate facts of human life. Hence the judge very frequently injects his personality into the application of a law. The legislator must pass over infinite variations of daily problems if he is to provide us with a code less than encyclopedic. The judge or teacher, on the other hand, must answer each specific question as it arises. If he can find no guidance in the letter of the law he must seek it in its spirit. He must interpret the will of the lawgiver as displayed in the code as a whole. In so doing, he is influenced necessarily by his own inclinations and understanding.

From time to time a situation arises demanding more than mere additional details beyond the scope of a written code. A social cataclysm occurs: the people are driven into exile; the laws of peace are challenged by the conditions of war; the inherited agricultural traditions are found unsuitable for a growingly commercial society. The judge's task now is to decide whether the accepted interpretation of the law, frequently whether the law itself, was intended to apply under these altered circumstances. He is no longer an expounder of the law, he becomes a quasi-legislator, practically offering amendments to the law. Jewish civilization, often called static, was remarkably rich in such violent changes. The Babylonian exile, the restoration, the Maccabean rebellion, the destruction of the Maccabean state, the rise of the Herodians, the fall of the Temple, the destruction of Judea, the removal of the Jew from the soil into the town, the transfer of the center of Jewish spiritual life first to Babylonia and then to Western Europe—all these were crises that required fundamental reinterpretations of the law.

The earliest recorded interpretation of this type is that of the Hasmonean court which permitted war in self-defense on the Sabbath. It was this court (beth din)—not Jesus—that first established the principle that the Sabbath is made for man, not man for the Sabbath. The earlier conception of the Sabbath had forbidden fighting even to save one's life. Jerusalem was taken without resistance on the Sabbath day by Ptolemy I. At the beginning of the Maccabean revolt a number of Hasideans permitted themselves to be slain in cold blood when attacked by the Syrian soldiers: "they answered them not, neither cast they a stone at them, nor stopped up the secret places, saying, 'Let us die all in our innocency.' " (I Macc. 2, 36.) But Mattathias and his friends, constituting themselves an emergency Sanhedrin, "took counsel on that day saying, Whosoever shall come against us to battle on the Sabbath day, let us fight against him, and we shall in no wise all die, as our brethren died in the secret places." To this decision, doubtless, we must trace back the famous talmudic principle that "the Sabbath law may be set aside in order to save human life."

Significantly, the new authority for making such radical decisions, at variance with accepted traditions, was first exercised by what we may call a "War Sanhedrin." While the Hasmonean decision to permit war in self-defense on the Sabbath may seem only obvious common sense to us, in its day much courage and self-confidence were required to issue it. The following generation accepted it as orthodox teaching. But many of the contemporary Hasideans must have been shocked by its heterodoxy.

No less extraordinary was the Hasmonean legal reinterpretation which gave women equal status with men. In early pastoral and agricultural Palestine, there could be no independent woman. As long as a woman remained unmarried she was a member of her father's family and entirely under his control; when she married, she passed into the possession of her husband. To flee from either of them was to face destitution and starvation, or degradation. To obtain employment in another family, except as slave or concubine, was impossible. A widow who had children remained on her husband's estate; a childless widow was either taken back by her father or inherited, together with the rest of her husband's property, by his nearest male relative.

The development of Jerusalem as a great urban center brought about a veritable revolution in the relation between the sexes. In the metropolitan market-place a woman could earn her living without dependence upon the landed estates of either father or husband. Whether married or not, she could "make fine linen and sell it, and deliver girdles to the merchant." Yet the current interpretation of the law still held her bound under the rules established by an earlier civilization. She could not retain her wages or earnings; they had to be given to her nearest male relative, her father or her husband, who in turn supported her. She could not choose her husband; that was done by her father. The father received and kept the marriage payment made by the bridegroom; thus the right to choose the bridegroom was an economic asset. If a woman suffered injury, the person responsible made restitution not to her but to her husband or father. She could not even take a binding vow; her husband or father, hearing of it, could annul it.

The Hasmonean sages were without authority to reject this old interpretation of the law. But they could define it. They maintained that the word *na'arah* (maiden) in the sense used in Scripture applied only to girls *under twelve years of age*. All others were quite free. This interpretation, which is basic to all talmudic law, is actually referred to in such works as the *Testaments of the Twelve Patriarchs* and the *Book of Jubilees* composed early in Hasmonean times.

Another remarkable interpretation of the law, possibly under the influence of the Roman legal system, established for the first time a system of wills and testaments in Judaism. Biblical law, as ordinarily interpreted, does not permit any interference with the usual rules of inheritance. Even the right of primogeniture, giving the first-born a double share in his father's property, cannot be transferred to another child. In primitive times this regulation represented an important reform; it was a necessary limitation of despotic paternal authority. The father could not do what he pleased with his estates; the right of his children to inherit them was inalienable.

However, such a rule was necessary only when property consisted of landed estates. In a commercial and artisan community a man would frequently wish to leave mementoes of himself to friends and relatives besides his immediate heirs. This would not deprive his children of their means of livelihood; and yet, under the law, such a legacy could not be made. Though the father could of course request his sons to make gifts to his friends, such a request was not binding.

To meet the situation a new principle was evolved. While a person on his deathbed could not interfere with the law through the execution of a testament, he could make gifts to whomever he pleased, and it was ruled that such gifts required no legal formalities of the usual kind. There need be no documents, no symbolic handing over of the property; not even the presence of the recipients was required. All that was needed was the oral statement of the sick person, attested by two witnesses who had heard it. "The statement of a sick person is as binding as though the property had actually been handed over." There was only one difference between the effect of a gift made in sickness and that made in health. If the sickness passed and the person became well, the gift was void. It had obviously been made in anticipation of death, and was valid only in that event.

The most interesting rule of all was that fixing the status of Gentiles within the Jewish state. The Scriptures offered no guidance to the Maccabean governors as to treatment of their heathen subjects. Were they to be forcibly converted, or permitted to continue in their idolatry? Were they to be subject to their own law or to the Jewish law? Might they pursue their own customs in whole or in part? Were they to be tried for civil and criminal offenses by the regular courts?

The liberal Pharisaic Sanhedrin answered these difficult questions by an interpretation which imposed on the "sons of Noah" (that is, the Gentiles) seven commandments only: to observe the civil law, to refrain from murder, unchastity, robbery, blasphemy, cruelty to animals, and idolatry. No attempt was made to compel their observance of the Jewish Sabbath or festivals. We cannot doubt that this decision—so definitely opposed to King Hyrcan's policy as exhibited, for instance, in his fateful treatment of the Idumeans—was in part responsible for the break between its Pharisaic authors and the growingly imperialistic Hasmonean dynasty.

Further adjustment of the law was temporarily suspended by the withdrawal of the Pharisees from the Sanhedrin after their quarrel with Hyrcan. We hear of no innovations by the Sadducean Sanhedrin till the rise of Simeon ben Shatah in the reign of Queen Salome (70-64 B.C.E.).

The most important innovation enacted under Simeon's guidance was the *ketubah,* the Jewish marriage contract. In primitive times husbands had purchased their wives, giving as their price a dower called *mohar.* This custom was a natural appendage to plural marriage under which the status of wife is not essentially different from that of slave: she had definite work assigned to her on the farm or in the house, and is thus an economic asset to the family. The demand for these wife-slaves inevitably gave them a market value. This was true in ancient Palestine as it still is true among the Moslems, and for that matter among the Yemenite Jews who continue to this very day to practise plural marriage.

But plural marriage, profitable on the farm, was an institution quite unsuited to artisan and commercial life, in which each man earns his livelihood by personal craft or cunning. The tendency toward monogamy, reflected as early as Malachi, Job, and Proverbs, destroyed the old institution of *mohar* and marriage by purchase. The maiden whose conservative father demanded a price for her "became old without marriage"; prospective husbands could find others, whose fathers were more liberal. Popular custom met the situation by whittling down the *mohar* to a mere nominal sum, given as *kiddushin*; and even in less advanced circles, the father would use the *mohar* to furnish his daughter's home.

Simeon ben Shatah thought the time ripe to introduce some uniform practice. He offered a new interpretation, suggested to him perhaps by his enforced exile in Egypt, where we now know a similar institution had been established for centuries. He maintained that the husband, instead of giving his wife's father the *mohar,* might merely obligate himself to pay an equivalent sum to the wife out of his estate whenever the marriage might terminate. This arrangement not only did away with the hardships of providing the women with husbands; it had the advantage of giving them some safeguard against arbitrary divorce, or complete destitution in the event of the husband's death.

Of the same interpretive form was Hillel's activity (*ca.* 20 B.C.E. —*ca.* 20 C.E.) in adjusting the law to life. His famous *takkanah* of "Prosbol," often cited as a typical rabbinical amendment to the biblical law, was frankly intended to adjust the law of the sabbatical year to the new commercial status of Jerusalem. According to this *takkanah,* the biblical law providing that no debts might be collected after the sabbatical, *i.e.* the seventh year, was not to apply if the creditor appeared before a duly authorized court and declared that he gave over to the court the debt due to him from such and such a person, and that "thereafter I may collect it whenever I desire to do so." But was this not an annulment of the biblical law? Raba maintains that it was, and that it was based on the right of the Sanhedrin to confiscate property. But if this interpretation of Hillel's action be accepted, how can we explain the form which he gave it? Why did he not simply declare the biblical law inoperative? Why did the creditor have to transfer his debt to the court? Those who adhere to the talmudic interpretation of Hillel's decree are forced to the assumption that there were in fact two amendments to the biblical law, the first permitting a creditor to collect a debt if he transferred it to the court, and the second, that of Hillel, making the transfer a mere matter of form.

It seems to me that this supposes needless complications in what must have been a relatively simple matter. Hillel, finding that the law of the annulment of debts in the sabbatical year interfered with the growing credit system of the community, offered a new judicial interpretation of it. He maintained that only individuals, and not the courts, are prohibited from collecting a debt after the sabbatical year. In order then to meet the law, a creditor had but to assign the debt due him to the court. Since debts as personal obligations are not transferable according to Jewish law, Hillel further explained that a "Prosbol" could be executed only if the debtor had landed property. The possession of land made the debt a *jus in rem*, a right against the property, and therefore transferable to the court.

The effect of this interpretation was the same as would have been that of an amendment, but it was made within the framework of the law rather than outside it.

Hillel's other great *takkanah* was even more clearly interpretive rather than legislative. The biblical law provided that a house sold in a walled city could be redeemed at the original price during a whole year. To prevent redemption, buyers would often hide on the last day, or the last days, of the year of sale. Hillel provided that if the purchaser were not available the redemption money might be left for him at a special office in the Temple. This arrangement offered a remedy at least for the inhabitants of Jerusalem, the main "walled city" of ancient Palestine.

Neither of these interpretations marks a very radical change in the law. In fact, as I. H. Weiss observes, Hillel's usual opponent, Shammai, does not appear to have objected to them. They were accepted by all as ingenious interpretations making the law suitable to the needs of the time.

A far more serious interpretive change was that made by the conservative Shammai (*ca.* 10 B.C.E.). Since the days of the Hasmoneans, as we have noted, it had been orthodox tradition that soldiers might fight in self-defense on the Sabbath. But they were still forbidden to take the offensive on the Sabbath. So that when Pompey besieged Jerusalem he used the Sabbath day (according to Josephus) to strengthen his outworks and prepare for better attack on the city. Since he did not actually threaten lives of the soldiers they could not interfere with his tactics. Departing from tradition, Shammai offered a new interpretation of the law, permitting all war on the Sabbath: "And thou shalt make war upon it till it be reduced (Deut. 20:20)—that means even on the Sabbath," he said.

Still more bold, radical and interesting is the famous interpretation of R. Simeon ben Gamaliel (*ca.* 60 C.E.) in the matter of pigeon-profiteering. The biblical law provides that after childbirth a woman must bring to the Temple as sacrifice a lamb and a pigeon or, if she cannot afford that, two pigeons. Apparently most women, living at a distance from the national shrine, would visit it not after each childbirth but only after many years, when they would bring sacrifices for all the children they had borne. Naturally, too, they would all gather to the Temple on the Passover, the most popular of the annual pilgrimages. The demand for pigeons then led to such unscrupulous profiteering that R. Simeon ben Gamaliel determined to put an end to it. As President of the Sanhedrin he announced without even consulting his colleagues, so far as we know, that no matter how many children a woman had borne one pair of pigeons satisfied all her obligations to the Temple. There occurred at once what we might call a "crash" on the pigeon exchange, and, reports the Mishnah, a pair of pigeons, selling in the morning at a golden dinar (about six dollars) could be bought that evening for half of a silver dinar (about twelve cents).

It was in this spirit that R. Johanan ben Zakkai, after the destruction of the Temple in the year 70 C.E., transferred to his academy at Jabne most of the prerogatives that had formerly been considered limited to Jerusalem. The Talmud has preserved a graphic picture of the debate that ensued when R. Johanan insisted that the *shofar* be sounded at Jabne on Rosh Hashanah even when it occurred on the Sabbath, just as had been the custom at the Temple. His opponents said to him, "Let us argue the matter first." R. Johanan, realizing the urgency of the issue and impatient with the obstructionists, replied, "First let us sound the *shofar* as part of the service; we shall then have time to argue the law." So the *shofar* was sounded. And when the nationalist opponents of transferring Jerusalem's prerogatives to Jabne came to R. Johanan to argue the matter he calmly said, "The *shofar* has already been sounded in Jabne, and one cannot argue a law after a precedent has been established"! And, indeed, that was no time for academic debate; the whole future of rabbinic Judaism depended on the universal recognition of Jabne as the rightful successor to Jerusalem.

Hundreds of radical interpretations of the law have been offered since the day of R. Johanan ben Zakkai down to our time. They are to be found among the *amoraim,* among the *geonim,* among the French *tosafists,* and among modern orthodox rabbis.

One interpretation among many of very modern interest may be cited. It applied the rabbinic principle of *hazakah* (seizin or prescription), which recognized the unchallenged possession of a farm or a house for three years as *prima facie* evidence of ownership. The rule was extended in early times to easements, rights of way, and similar less concrete property rights. Finally it was made to cover the conduct of business or work which might interfere with neighbors. They cannot complain, the law says, of the noise made by the anvil of the smith or the mill of the flour merchant if he is established in business.

By a curious extension this old rule was made to include the right to hold one's job, especially a communal office. A person who had held a position for three years could not be removed except by due trial and by the submission of evidence proving that he had forfeited his trust. Otherwise, he had *hazakah,* a prescriptive right to maintain it for life. Sometimes it was even held that the right was inherited, and could be disposed of by his wife and children.

III.   ACTUAL LEGISLATION

The history of Jewish law offers no example of actual legislation by the Sanhedrin before the year 66 C.E. The earlier innovations were all made through extra-legal institutions or radical interpretations such as we have discussed. While Rabban Gamaliel I—he who is so highly praised for his liberalism by the author of Acts—was responsible for several reforms in judicial procedure, none of them was legislative. He substituted, for the traditional oath taken by a widow collecting her dower, a less grave vow; he forbade a husband, who had appointed an agent to divorce his wife, to withdraw the power of attorney except in the presence of the agent; he ordered people having both Hebrew and Greek names to mention both in legal documents they drew up.

A similar judicial ordinance was established by the Shammaitic judges. If a slave of two masters had been freed by one of them, he was held by the School of Hillel to be obligated to "serve his remaining master and himself on alternate days." The Shammaitic judges protested that such a decision left the half-slave with no recognized social status. "You have provided for the master," they said, "but you have not provided for the slave. He cannot marry a free woman, for he is still half slave; he cannot live with a slave, for he is already half free." Their policy was therefore to allow the slave to buy his full freedom from the remaining master with a note of indebtedness for half his value. This decision was afterward adopted also by the Hillelite judges.

It was the War Sanhedrin, meeting in the year 66 C.E. at the outbreak of the revolt against Rome, that for the first time claimed the authority to establish new ordinances, frankly without basis in biblical law. Their resolutions were formulated in Eighteen Decrees, directed primarily against the heathen population of Palestine. Among these decrees were prohibitions against buying from Gentiles wine, bread, cheese or oil, and against selling them land or animals to till the land. In other words, this Sanhedrin, preparing for war, declared a religious boycott against the Romans and their allies. There was bitter opposition to this radical departure from traditional procedure, this new usurpation of power by the war-mad zealots. In vain did the pacifist Hillelites denounce the whole proceeding; the fateful laws were passed over their protest.

In spite of the precedent thus established, no other legislative acts were passed by the Sanhedrin for more than sixty years, till after the war of Bar Kokba. In their attempt to reconstruct Jewish life after the ill-starred venture, the sages found mere reinterpretation of the law insufficient: once more they had recourse to the usurped authority of legislation. The havoc wrought in second-century Judaism by the crushing defeat of Bar Kokba, and the subsequent persecutions of Hadrian, are nowhere more clearly reflected than in the ordinances adopted as a result of them. For the first time in their recorded history the Jews faced the problem of loosening family ties. In the impoverishment and desolation of the country, men and women lost their mental balance. In their desperation—seeing tens of thousands of dead unburied; watching their children being sold into slavery and prostitution; deprived of their ancestral lands and all means of livelihood; in perpetual danger of arrest and punishment for observance of Jewish law —fathers abandoned their minor children; children refused to support their parents; wives sold their personal property away from their husbands' right to inherit it; and men were quite willing to rob their families by giving all they had to the poor. The so-called *Takkanot Usha,* directed against these practices, were like the Eighteen Decrees, not founded on bibilical law; they were announced as frank innovations.

The later *tannaim*, the *amoraim*, the *geonim*, the west-European rabbis, all took it upon themselves to add new legislative ordinances of this type. The very biblical commandment against adding to the Torah was interpreted out of its original significance in order to make room for the preservation of the law itself. The new rabbinic attitude toward the law was summed up by R. Johanan when he said: "Better that one commandment be torn out of the Torah, than the whole Torah be forgotten."

RABBINIC METHODS OF INTERPRETATION
David Daube

The way in which the Rabbis built up the colossal system of
Talmudic law by means of an exegesis of the relatively few provisions
contained in the Bible is still a mystery. To outsiders, the whole development appears arbitrary, a mass of sophistic and involved deductions governed by no coherent first principles and serving no valid
communal needs. Orthodox Jews affirm that the methods used by the
Rabbis and the results reached by them are of Sinaitic origin: God
revealed them all to Moses during the forty days Moses stayed with
him, and Moses, though not writing them down, transmitted them to
Joshua, Joshua to the elders and so on. This dogma goes back to the
Talmud itself and, as we shall see, it made good sense in that period;
but, as proposed today, it amounts to an admission that the evolution
cannot be justified on rational grounds. Some liberal Jewish scholars,
on the other hand, have tried to show that the Rabbis were guided by
pure logic,[1] but that is hardly more convincing. No real attempt, however, has so far been made to understand the growth of Talmudic law
against its historical background, and to investigate the relationship
with other Hellenistic systems of law, such as the Greek ones or the
Roman. The reasons for this failure are not far to seek. Apart from the
usual difficulties where several fields of study are concerned, the modern exponents of Greek and Roman law are often quite unaware of
some of the mainsprings of their systems, namely, the conventions
among the ancient jurists as to types of arguments admissible or in-

admisible, the relative weight of arguments and the like. But it is precisely in this province of 'legal science' that may be found the really important points of contact between the Talmud and other Hellenistic creations.

The thesis here to be submitted is that the Rabbinic methods of interpretation derive from Hellenistic rhetoric.[2] Hellenistic rhetoric is at the bottom both of the fundamental ideas, presuppositions from which the Rabbis proceeded and of the major details of application, the manner in which these ideas were translated into practice. This is not to detract from the value of the work of the Rabbis. On the contrary, it is important to note that, when the Hellenistic methods were first adopted about 100 to 25 B.C., the 'classical,' Tannaitic era of Rabbinic law was just opening. That is to say, the borrowing took place in the best period of Talmudic jurisprudence, when the Rabbis were masters, not slaves, of the new influences. The methods taken over were thoroughly Hebraized in spirit as well as form, adapted to the native material, worked out so as to assist the natural progress of Jewish law. It is the kind of thing which *mutatis mutandis,* happened at Rome in the same epoch. Later on, from A.D. 200, in 'post-classical,' Amoraic law, the development was in several respects more autonomous, less open to foreign inspiration, yet at the same time there was a distinct lack of vitality and originality, the most prominent tendency now being ever greater specialization. However, in its beginnings, the Rabbinic system of hermeneutics is a product of the Hellenistic civilization then dominating the entire Mediterranean world.

Let us begin by recalling a few matters concerning date and geography. It is to Hillel, the great Pharisee who flourished about 30 B.C., that we owe the oldest rules in accordance with which Scripture is to be *nidhrasheth,* 'interpreted.' He himself says that he learned them from his teachers Shemaiah and Abtalion,[3] and, indeed, they are the first Rabbis to be called *darshanim,* 'interpreters of Scripture.'[4] The Talmud represents them as proselytes. The historicity of this feature has been doubted; but it is agreed that, if they were not natives of Alexandria, they studied and taught there long enough to go on using Egyptian measures even after settling in Palestine.[5] So there is a *prima facie* case for a direct connection between Hillel's seven norms of interpretation and Alexandria, a centre of Hellenistic scholarship.

The historical situation in which Hillel found himself may next be considered. For centuries before him, Scripture had been subjected to the most scrupulous philological analysis, each word and sentence being inspected with a view to establishing its exact sense and grammatical status.[6] But treated in this conservative manner, the Bible yielded comparatively little law; and it is not surprising that a large body of law, religious and secular, grew up in addition to that contained in Scripture. This non-Scriptural law consisted of various elements. Some of it indeed was still almost Scriptural: the meaning of an obscure verse would be fixed, a very inconvenient precept would be credited with a somewhat more desirable meaning, the claims of flagrantly inconsistent ordinances would be settled. But a great part was avowedly novel, extensions of Biblical provisions designed to deal with fresh cases or also, in the words ascribed to the men of the Great Synagogue, 'to make a fence around the Torah.'[7] In either case, what was the ground of recognition of this vast body of non-Scriptural law? It was the authority of the people promulgating it. The correctness of a decision was guaranteed by the character and learning of him who delivered it. Significantly the *dibhere sopherim,* the 'sayings of the ancient scribes,' are never supported by any arguments. The wise man simply knows the true import of a Biblical commandment or the proper supplement to add.

The non-Scriptural law was aptly termed 'the tradition received from, or handed down by, the fathers,' $\pi\alpha\tau\acute{\epsilon}\rho\omega\nu$ $\delta\iota\alpha\delta\circ\chi\acute{\eta}$ or $\pi\alpha\rho\acute{\alpha}\delta\circ\sigma\iota\varsigma$ $\tau\hat{\omega}\nu$ $\pi\alpha\tau\acute{\epsilon}\rho\omega\nu$ *qabbalath ha'abhoth, masoreth ha'abhoth.*[8] From Akiba's statement, about A.D. 120, that 'tradition is a fence around the Torah,' we may gather that the extensions for the purpose of ensuring strictest observance of the Biblical law were regarded as the chief component of the non-Biblical,[9] and it may be remarked, in passing, that this adage is surely indebted—however indirectly— to Plato's praise of 'ancestral customs which, if well established, form a cover around the written laws for their full protection.'[10] The trouble was that important groups refused to consider the tradition binding, above all, the Sadducees (but also the Samaritans). For them, the text of the Bible was of God, but nothing beyond it. The Pharisaic 'fence' they rejected and even ridiculed. When the Pharisees insisted on purification of the golden candlestick in the Temple in case it had contracted some uncleanness, the Sadducees commented: 'Look how they purify the light of the moon!'[11]

Josephus has an interesting remark: the Sadducees, he says, hold it a virtue to dispute against their own teachers.[12] Evidently, they had taken over from the Hellenistic schools of philosophy the ideal of working out any problem by unfettered argument and counter-argument. Their encounter with Jesus in the New Testament provides support; they attempt to reduce to absurdity the belief in a resurrection of the body, and the point they make might well figure in a philosophical dialogue of the time.[13] It is worth noting that very similar arguments—also in the form of 'teasers'—are attributed by the Talmud to the citizens of Alexandria[14] and (which comes to the same thing) to Queen Cleopatra.[15]

There were, then, these diametrically opposed views: the Pharisaic, according to which the authority of the fathers must be unconditionally accepted, and the Sadducean, according to which the text alone was binding, while any question not answered by it might be approached quite freely, in a philosophical fashion. In this situation, Hillel[16] declared that Scripture itself included the tradition of the fathers; and that it did so—here he took a leaf out of the other party's book—precisely if read as, on the most up-to-date teaching of the philosophical schools, a code of laws ought to be read. There existed, he claimed, a series of rational norms of exegesis making possible a sober clarification and extension of legal provisions. If they were applied to Scripture, the opinions expressed by the fathers would be vindicated, would turn out to be logical, not arbitrary; and in fact, he contended, some measure of traditional, Rabbinic authority would always remain indispensable—not everybody was in a position to judge the merits of a doctrine approved by the experts.[17] While this part of his program was addressed to the Sadducees, he pointed out to his own group that his hermeneutics, if they vindicated the tradition of the fathers, must themselves enjoy a degree of sanctity and be put to further use: the tradition of the fathers (he urged) had evidently been evolved along these lines all the time. His first public debate before the Pharisaic officers—on the question whether the paschal lamb might be slaughtered even if Passover fell on a Sabbath—culminated in the demonstration that what he concluded from the Bible by means of his system of interpretation coincided with the traditional ruling. It was then that the Pharisees made him their leader and accepted his innovation.[18] Let us just note that the very setting of this historic debate was that of the 'disputatio fori.'[19]

Hillel, by introducing this system into Talmudic jurisprudence, accomplished two things. He not only created the basis for a development of the law at the same time orderly and unlimited,[20] but also led the way towards a bridging of the gulf between Pharisees and Sadducees. On the one hand, he upheld the authority of tradition. Actually, in a sense, he increased it: as, for him, the traditional decisions were all logical, necessary inferences from the Bible, they were equal in rank to the latter. He went as far as to speak of two Toroth, a written one and an oral one[21]—an idea governing all subsequent thought. On the other hand, his modern, scientific technique and, above all, the very conception of the oral Torah as deriving from, and thus essentially inherent in, the text implied a profound appreciation of the Sadducean standpoint and must have brought over a good many who embraced it. Clearly, his work in this field was not the least of his achievements in the service of unity and peace.

We may now examine the main ideas underlying Hillel's program.

First, the fundamental antithesis he tried to overcome was that between law resting on the respect for a great man, on the authority of tradition, and law resting on rational, intelligible considerations. This antithesis is common in the rhetorical literature of the time. His contemporary Cicero distinguishes between arguments from the nature of the case and arguments from external evidence, that is to say, from authority. An example of the latter type would be the decision: 'Since Scaveola said so and so, this must be taken as the law.'[22] In 137 B.C., Cicero reports, P. Crassus, after first 'taking refuge in authorities,' had to admit that Galba's 'disputation' founded on arguments from analogy and equity led to a more plausible result.[23]

Secondly, Hillel claimed that any gaps in Scriptural law might be filled in with the help of certain modes of reasoning—a good, rhetorical theory. Cicero has much to say about 'ratiocination,' by which 'from that which is written there is derived a further point not written,'[24] while Auctor ad Herennium defines 'ratiocination' as the method to be applied where 'the judge has to deal with a case not falling under a statute of its own, yet covered by other statutes in view of a certain analogy.'[25]

Thirdly, the result of such interpretation was to be of the same status as the text itself, was to be treated as if directly enjoined by the original lawgiver. This view also can be paralleled. Of a certain institution, Gaius tells us that it is called 'statutory' because 'though there is no express provision about it in the statute (the XII Tables), yet it has been accepted through interpretation as if it had been introduced by the statute.'[26] Another time he even omits the 'as if,' representing as laid down by the XII Tables a rule in reality deduced from that code by its interpreters.[27] As is well known, the term *ius civile* was occasionally employed for the body of law evolved by interpretation.[28] This reflects a stage where the law evolved by interpretation was so different from, and so much fuller than, the statute law to which it attached that it had practically buried the latter and usurped its place.

Fourthly, Hillel's assumption of 'a written Torah and an oral Torah' is highly reminiscent of the pair   νόμοι ἔγγραφοι   and νόμοι ἄγραφοι or *ius scriptum* and *ius non scriptum* (*or per manus traditum*). It is superfluous to adduce references, but it may be worth noting that the terms νόμοι ἄγραφοι and *ius non scriptum* do not always signify the natural law common to all men. They frequently signify the traditional, customary law of a particular community as opposed to its statute law.[29] Plato, in the same section where he describes the customs of the fathers as a protective covering around the written laws, says expressly that 'what people call customs of the fathers are nothing else than the sum of unwritten laws.'[30] They are even used of the law created by the interpreters of statutes.[31] Since, on the other hand, Hillel's 'oral Torah' was still of a wide range, embracing ethics as well as law in the narrow sense, his dependence on Hellenistic philosophy seems beyond doubt.

Fifthly, there is an idea which at first sight looks the exclusive property of the Rabbis, for whom the Bible had been composed under divine inspiration: the lawgiver foresaw the interpretation of his statutes, deliberately confined himself to a minimum, relying on the rest being inferable by a proper exegesis. (It is this idea which gradually led to the doctrine that the oral Law no less than the written is of Sinaitic origin: God, by word of mouth, revealed to Moses both the methods by which fresh precepts might be derived from Scripture and all precepts that would ever be in fact derived.) But even this is a stock argument of the orators. Cicero observes that the application of a statute to a case not mentioned in it may be justified by pleading that the lawgiver omitted the case 'because, having written about another, allied one, he thought nobody could have any doubt about this one,' or that 'in many laws many points are omitted which, however, no one would consider as really omitted, since they can be deduced from other points that are put down.'[32] Auctor ad Herennium advises him who wishes to go beyond the letter of a law to 'extol the appropriateness[33] and brevity of the author's style, since he put down only as much as was necessary, but deemed it unnecessary to put down what could be understood without being put down;' only by going beyond the letter are we giving effect to 'the will of the author.'[34] When Sabinus extended a mode of assessment prescribed in the first chapter of the *lex Aquilia* to the third where it was not prescribed, he maintained that 'the lawgiver thought it sufficient to have used the relevant word in the first chapter.'[35] The Romans inherited the idea from the Greeks. Lysias, for instance, as-

serts that the law-giver who declared punishable the use of certain offensive words meant to include all equivalent ones.[36] If one wonders
how Greeks and Romans could talk in this 'religious' way, it should be
remembered that there had been periods when their ancient legislations
also enjoyed a semi-divine standing, much as the Bible did among the
Jews.

Sixthly, it is the task of a lawgiver to lay down basic principles
only, from which any detailed rules may be inferred. Just so, Cicero,
in the imaginary role of a legislator, announces that 'the statutes will
be set forth by me, not in a complete form—that would be endless—
but in the form of generalized questions and their decisions'; and according to Suetonius, Caesar planned to replace the embarrassing mass
of statutes by 'a few books, containing what was best and necessary.'[37]

Seventhly, it is the task of a lawgiver, if he wants to regulate a
series of allied cases, to choose the most frequent and leave the others
to be inferred on the ground of analogy.[38] Just so, Cicero argues that
the edict directed against violence with the help of men 'brought together' covers the case where men had assembled uninvited and were
then made to participate in some violence; the edict is framed in this
way because 'normally, where numbers are needed, men are brought
together,' but 'though the word may be different, the substance is not,
and the same law will apply to all cases where it is clear that the
same principle of equity is at stake.'[39] In opening that half of his *Digest*
where he discusses *leges* and *senatusconsulta*, Julian explains that neither
'can be formulated so as to comprise all cases that may occur at any
time, but it is sufficient that the most frequent happenings should be
regulated.'[40]

Hillel's jurisprudence, then, i. e. his theory of the relation between
statute law, tradition and interpretation, was entirely in line with the
prevalent Hellenistic ideas on the matter. The same is true of the
details of execution, of the methods he proposed to give practical effect
to his theory. The famous seven norms of hermeneutics he proclaimed,
the seven norms in accordance with which Scripture was to be interpreted, hitherto looked upon as the most typical product of Rabbinism,
all of them betray the influence of the rhetorical teaching of his age.

The first of these norms is the inference *a fortiori*, or *a minori ad
maius*—in Hebrew *qal wahomer*, 'the light and the weighty.' Ex. 20.25
gives permission to build the altar of stone, brick or anything else.[41]
By means of a *qal wahomer*, it is concluded that, since the material may
be chosen in the case of this most important object of the Temple, it

may *a fortiori* be chosen for the other, less important objects. The second, third and fourth norms in Hillel's plan are various kinds of inferences from analogy. For example, just as the daily sacrifice, which Scripture says should be brought 'at its appointed time,' is due even on a Sabbath, so the Passover lamb, which Scripture also demands 'at its appointed time,' must be slaughtered even if Passover falls on a Sabbath.[42] Rhetorical parallels abound. 'What applies to the *maius*,' says Cicero, 'must apply also to the *minus*, and *vice versa*. Again, what applies to one thing must apply to that which is equal.'[43] To discover the meaning of a problematic phrase, its 'normal force,' the 'usage of language' and the 'analogies and examples of those who have used it thus' will have to be considered;[44] and the definition should not 'clash with the usage in the writings of others, certainly not with that in other writings by the same author.'[45]

It might perhaps be objected that it is so natural to argue *a fortiori* or from analogy that the parallels cannot prove any borrowing on Hillel's part. Postponing this problem for a moment, we would draw attention to the arrangement of his norms: first *a fortiori*, then analogy. One could imagine the reverse order. But it is interesting that, right from Aristotle,[46] wherever in rhetorical literature the methods of interpretation are set forth in a tabulated form, this is the order we find. We have already quoted Cicero: 'What applies to the *maius* must apply to the *minus*, and *vice versa*; what applies to one thing must apply to that which is equal.'[47] Auctor ad Herennium declares that the first thing to be asked when filling the gaps of the law by 'ratiocination' is 'whether anything comparable has been laid down concerning greater, smaller or equal matters.'[48] There is a standard sequence, and it is observed in Hillel's list.

Still deferring the question of the naturalness of his first four norms, let us proceed to the fifth, which is more complicated, the rule of 'the general and the specific,' *kelal upherat*. It says that if the range of a statute is indicated both by a wider and a narrower term, it is the one put second that counts; that is to say, if the narrower term comes second, it restricts the wider one, while if the wider one comes last, it includes and adds to the narrower one. Lev. 1.2 ordains that 'ye shall bring your offering of the beasts, of the oxen and sheep'; the general term 'beasts' is restricted by the following more specific 'oxen and sheep'—so wild animals are excluded.[49] By way of contrast, Ex. 22.9 (10) fixes the liability of a man charged by another with the custody of 'an ass, an ox, a sheep or any beast'; here the specific terms 'ass, ox, sheep' are covered and added to by the following more general 'any beast'—so the regulation extends to wild animals as well.[50]

The latter half of the norm, about the order specific—general, is fully given by Celsus (who was particularly interested in hermeneutics): 'It is not unusual,' he tells us, 'for a statute first to enumerate a few cases specially and then to add a comprehensive term by which to embrace any special cases.' [51] The rule underlies certain older decisions, for instance, one by Q. Mucius. A will provided that 'X shall be my heir if he ascends the Capitol; X shall be my heir,' and Mucius held that 'the second clause should prevail, since it is fuller than the first.'[52] However, the other part of this norm of interpretation, i. e. that concerning the order general—specific, also seems to have been familiar to the earlier classical Roman jurists. A man, in conveying land, gave an assurance that 'it was first class (free from servitudes) and he had not allowed its legal position to deteriorate (had not allowed any servitudes to be imposed).' Proculus held that only the second, narrower clause was binding: 'though the first clause alone, without the addition of the second, would mean the complete absence of any servitudes, yet I believe the second clause releases him sufficiently to limit his responsibility to such servitudes as were imposed through himself.'[53] The specific term, the *perat,* which comes second, restricts the general one, the *kelal,* which comes first.

To turn now to the question we have put off: can it be argued that the first four norms of Hillel are so natural that the rhetorical parallels constitute no evidence of a genetic connection? For one thing, the argument is greatly weakened by the existence of parallels to the fifth norm, of 'the general and the specific,' which is rather subtle (not to mention the Hellenistic colouring of Hillel's doctrine of the role of interpretation as a whole). But even the first four are not so very simple. If we take as illustration the inference *a fortiori*—to be sure, any layman might reason thus: 'Here is a teetotaller who does not touch cider; he will certainly refuse whisky.' Three points, however, must not be overlooked. First, the deduction will not always be made in this direct, almost technical manner; more often than not there will be some twist somewhere. Secondly, the ordinary person will rarely perceive the exact nature of his deduction. There is a considerable difference between merely using various modes of deduction and being aware of using just these modes, defining, distinguishing and tabulating them. Thirdly, the recommendation of a series of such modes of deduction as an instrument —or indeed, as the only satisfactory instrument—with which to build up a complete legal or theological system manifestly involves a further step. Medieval Icelandic law is of a high standard; if the norms of exegesis here discussed were so natural, we should expect to find them there, but there is no trace of them. Actually, it is by no means clear to what extent our modern lawyers are consciously applying a coherent system of hermeneutics.

A comparison between the Old Testament and the New is instructive. Both contain inferences *a fortiori*; the Old Testament cases were already collected by the Rabbis of the Talmud (occasionally, indeed, their eyes were too sharp). But there is a difference. The old Testament cases are popular, the New Testament ones technical. A good Old Testament instance is the reply of Joseph's brothers when accused of the theft of his cup: 'The money which we found in our sacks' mouths we brought again unto thee—how then should we steal silver or gold?'[54] Apart from a slight irregularity in the structure of the argument—an action, 'we brought again,' in the premise, an omission, 'we did not steal,' in the conclusion[55]—it is relevant to note that the statement occurs in the course of a dispute concerning facts, namely, the guilt or innocence of Joseph's brothers. It is a far cry from here to the methodical elaboration of law and theology by means of the norm *a minori ad maius*. This stage, however, is reached by the time of the New Testament. According to Matthew, Jesus, asked about healing on the Sabbath, answered: 'What man shall have one sheep, and if it fall into a pit on the sabbath, will not lift it out? How much better then is a man than a sheep! Wherefore it is lawful to do well on the sabbath.'[56] According to Luke, he argued: 'Doth not each man on the sabbath loose his ox for watering? And ought not this woman, being a daughter of Abraham, whom Satan hath bound these eighteen years, be loosed?'[57] These are academic, 'Halakhic' applications of Hillel's first rule of exegesis. No less significant an example may be met with in Paul's theological discourse: 'While we were yet sinners, Christ died for us; much more then, being now justified by his blood, we shall be saved from wrath through him.'[58] The technique is exactly the same as that of the Roman jurists, whose 'ratiocination' respecting the *lex Aelia Sentia* is recorded by Gaius. The statute laid down that the property of certain *dediticii* should on death be treated like that of citizen freedmen. The jurists, however, decided that the *dediticii* were not thereby given the citizen freedmen's power of making a will: seeing that even Junian Latins, superior in status to *dediticii*, were incapable of making a will, it could not have been the lawgiver's intention to grant this facility to 'men of the very lowest rank.'[59]

The point is that Hillel's system—and not only the first four norms[60]

—is 'natural' in the sense of 'grown out of intelligent observation, consistent and useful.' (So, presumably, is the theory of relativity). But, like the theory of relativity it is not 'natural'—not even the first four norms—in the sense of 'obvious, readily hit upon by any student of these matters.' It is the naturalness of the rhetorical categories and methods in the former sense, their soundness as doctrine and in practice, which accounts for their adoption, in one form or another, in so many parts of the Hellenistic world. Recently, it has been shown that Philo was acquainted with them, and the conclusion has been drawn that he was influenced by Palestinian Rabbinism. But it is far more likely that he came across them in the course of his general studies at Alexandria. We have before us a science the beginnings of which may be traced back to Plato, Aristotle and their contemporaries. It recurs in Cicero, Hillel and Philo—with enormous differences in detail, yet *au fond* the same. Cicero did not sit at the feet of Hillel, nor Hillel at the feet of Cicero; and there was no need for Philo to go to Palestinian sources for this kind of teaching. As we saw, there are indeed signs that Hillel's ideas were partly imported from Egypt. The true explanation lies in the common Hellenistic background. Philosophical instruction was very similar in outline whether given at Rome, Jerusalem or Alexandria.

It is not necessary to dwell on the remaining norms of Hillel, beyond noting a clear parallel to the seventh, the rule that an ambiguity in the law may be settled by adducing the context, *dabhar hallamedh me'inyano*. The commandment 'Thou shalt not steal' is interpreted as referring to theft of a person, not of property, since it appears together with other capital crimes against a person, namely, murder and adultery.[61] Cicero writes: 'It ought to be shewn that the ambiguous passage becomes intelligible from what precedes and comes after it.'[62] It may well have been this norm of interpretation which Celsus had in mind when he declared, in discussing *leges dotis*, that 'it was not in accordance with the science of the civil law to judge or give an opinion on the basis of a mere fragment of a *lex*, without inspecting the whole.'[63]

A few remarks may be added about terminology. We have already pointed out that, just as the Romans succeeded in latinizing the rhetorical notions they used, so the 'classical,' Tannaitic Rabbis succeeded in Hebraizing them. There was no slavish, literal rendering. In fact, it is fascinating to watch the transformation the Hellenistic concepts underwent as they were freely adapted to the Jewish milieu. To take a small example, we mentioned above the introduction by Hillel of the antithesis 'a written Torah and an oral Torah,' an antithesis owing much to that of νόμοι ἔγγραφοι and ἄγραφοι or *ius scriptum* and *non scriptum* or *per manus traditum*. Yet look at the Hebrew term for 'oral Torah:' *torah shebbe'al pe*, 'Torah by mouth.' The words *'al pe*, 'by mouth,' frequently signify 'by heart,' 'from memory,' and this meaning is certainly relevant. But for the Rabbis of the Talmud, a good many other ideas were evoked by the phrase. We need only consider passages like the following: 'According to the mouth of the Lord they rested, and according to the mouth of the Lord they journeyed; they kept the charge of the Lord according to the mouth of the Lord in the hand of Moses';[64] again, 'The Torah of thy mouth is better unto me than thousands of gold and silver; give me understanding that I may learn thy commandments';[65] or again, 'This book of the Torah shall not depart out of thy mouth, but thou shalt meditate therein day and night, that thou mayest observe to do according to all that is written therein.'[66] The latter verse in particular must have been in Hillel's mind when he coined the antithesis in question (or in the mind of whoever coined it about that time). It advocates the constant study, interpretation, of Scripture,[67] for the sake of being able scrupulously to fulfil all precepts. When we remember the function of 'a fence' around Scriptural law assigned to the tradition of the fathers in the age of Hillel, and when we consider that the verse quoted enjoins constant interpretation by saying that 'the Torah shall not depart out of thy mouth' and describes as the object the keeping of all 'that is written therein,' we can hardly doubt that here is a main root of Hillel's contrast between the 'written Torah' and the 'Torah by mouth.' The Hellenistic scheme has been completely Judaized.

Nevertheless there are instances of the Greek or Latin terms being still noticeable in the Hebrew. In some cases, this is almost inevitable. Rules concerning deduction from analogy will naturally operate with concepts like ὅμοιον in Greek—as when Aristotle explains this method as 'the comparison of like with like, when both of them come under the same genus but one is more familiar than the other'[68]—*simile* or *par* in Latin—as when Cicero says that 'the doubtful matter to be deduced must appear similar to one as to which there is certainty'[69] or that 'like is compared to like'[70]—*shawe* in Hebrew.[71] Again, rules concerning general and specific laws could scarcely avoid expressions like καθόλου — κατὰ μέρος (καθ' ἕκαστον), γενικόν (περιέχειν , περιλαμβάνειν)— ἴδιον , *generale* (*complecti*)—*speciale* (*singula*), *kelal—perat*. However, on occasion, the Rabbis employ words less obviously suitable, when it is worth searching for the possible Greek or

Latin model. The sixth of Hillel's norms is called *keyotse' bo bemaqom 'aher*, literally, 'as what is going out with it in another passage of Scripture.' The verse 'When Moses held up his hand Israel prevailed'[72] is taken as meaning that Israel prevailed when directing their thoughts on high; 'as what is going out with it thou shouldest say, Make a serpent and set it upon a standard and every one that seeth it shall live[73] also means that they were healed when directing their thoughts on high.'[74] The phrase *yotse' bo* (in Aramaic *naphiq be*), 'going out with it,' in this sense of 'corresponding to,' is rare. Its use in the norm under discussion may well be due to συμβαίνω, which signifies not only 'to correspond to,' but also 'to follow from reasoning.'[75]

Another case seems to be the familiar *(shen)ne'emar*, '(as) it is said.'[76] Like '(as) it is written,' it exclusively introduces quotations from Scripture—never an oral tradition. It is tempting to explain this by the influence of ῥητόν which, in rhetorical works, though literally 'what is said,' has the technical sense of 'the written document to be subjected to interpretation.'[77] The Roman orators translated it by *scriptum*.[78] The Rabbis, in addition to *kathubh* (Aramaic *kethibh*), 'it is written,' evolved a term more faithfully rendering the Greek: *ne'emar*, 'it is said.'

In conclusion, attention may be drawn to four points that should be borne in mind when these matters are pursued in greater detail.

First, the influence of Hellenistic philosophy was not confined to the period of Hillel. It had started before; and it went on afterwards, in an increasing degree, for a long time. The systems of interpretation advocated by Ishmael and Akiba some 150 years later can be understood only against the background of the rhetorical teaching of the time. Josiah, a disciple of Ishmael, about the middle of the second century A.C., favoured the method *seres*: a verse at first sight illogical may be made logical by re-arranging its parts. In Num. 9.6 ff., we are told that certain men brought a problem 'before Moses and before Aaron' and that Moses transmitted it to God, thus obtaining the correct solution. Josiah explains[79] that the passage cited must be re-arranged: the men evidently came first before Aaron, who did not know, and then before Moses, who approached God. The name of the method is curious, the literal meaning of *seres* being 'to castrate.' It becomes intelligible, however, when we remember that τέμνειν also signifies 'to castrate,' 'to divide logically,' 'to distinguish,' τομή 'castration,' 'logical division,' 'distinction,' 'precision of expression,' 'caesura.' Even ideas which *prima facie* one would incline to put down as peculiarly Rabbinic may turn out to have been, if not borrowed from rhetoric, at least supported, helped on, by it. The oral Torah, in the eyes of the Rabbis, is the particular glory of Israel; the gentiles cannot grasp the secret, mysterious way Scripture is interpreted.[80] Cicero, as an argument in favour of 'interpretation,' i.e. of following the spirit rather than the letter of a statute, refers to the lawgiver's decree that judges must be of a certain rank and age, capable not only, as anybody would be, of reciting a statute, but also of discovering its intention: 'if the author of a statute, committed his work to simple men and primitive judges, he would diligently put down every detail, but since he knows how well qualified the judges will be, he does not add what he deems to be obvious.'[81] It is the same thing in a Roman dress.[82]

Secondly, the influence of Hellenistic philosophy was not confined to the domain of interpretation. Such fundamental matters as the distinction between *mishpatim*, rational, natural laws, 'commandments which, were they not laid down, would have to be laid down,' and *huqqoth*, inexplicable laws, 'commandments which the evil impulse and the heathens refute,'[83] are not of purely Jewish origin; and even the teaching that 'you have no right to criticize the *huqqoth*'[84] was probably a commonplace before Plato. He has a profound discussion as to how far it is proper 'to be wiser than the laws'[85]—this sounds like a reference to an earlier slogan—, and Aristotle advises us, if our case is favoured by a statute which, though still technically in force, is clearly obsolete, to argue 'that there is no advantage in being wiser than the physician, for an error of the latter is less harmful than the habit of disobeying the authority; and to try to be wiser than the laws is precisely what is forbidden in the best of them.'[86] Students of Roman law are familiar with the statements by Julian, 'It is impossible to give reasons for everything that our forefathers laid down,'[87] and by Neratius, 'Wherefore it is not correct to inquire into the reasons of what they laid down, otherwise much that is secure would be undermined.'[88]

Thirdly, if the Roman and Greek sources can help us to elucidate the Jewish side, the converse is also true. To some extent, this may have become clear already. But to take a fresh exampde, about 200 B.C., Aelius Paetus wrote a "tripertita,' where 'the law of the XII Tables was given first, then the interpretation was joined to it and finally the *legis actio* was appended.'[89] Scholars are still divided as to whether there were three large parts—first the complete XII Tables, next all results of interpretation and then a list of all *legis actiones*—or whether each provision of the XII Tables (or each group of provisions) was accompanied by its interpretation and *legis actio*. Comparison of the Rabbinic material should settle the controversy in favour of the latter alternative. Aelius Paetus wrote a Midrash. The old, expositional (as distinct from the homiletical) Midrash takes the form of a running commentary on Scripture.[90] It is significant, however, that there is nothing on the Jewish side to correspond to the *legis actio*. So even here, no sooner have we noted a parallel than we are struck by the profound difference between the two legal systems.

This brings us to the fourth and last point. The next task, of course, is to conduct a thorough inquiry into the debt of Talmudic jurisprudence to Hellenistic rhetoric. The present study is only a first beginning, intended to open the subject and to show that some debt there is, but to do no more. We have merely touched the fringe. Yet it is greatly to be hoped that, once this immediate task has been carried out, with all that belongs to it (it will, for example, be necessary to answer such subsidiary questions as whether the influence was greater or smaller at different times and on different schools, and through what channels it was chiefly exercised), the second, subtler one will not be forgotten: a working out of the differences between Greek and Roman rhetoric and Talmudic rhetoric, of the factors that determined the Rabbinic selection of certain notions and rejection of others, of the changes that the Hellenistic concepts suffered—singly and as a system—in the course of being transferred to an alien soil.

THE HALAKA

Solomon Zeitlin

Demosthenes, in defining law, said that its purpose was to deter any man from doing what is wrong and punish transgressors to make the rest better men.[1] Law is the foundation of society.[2] Since primitive times, when man saw the need of being united, laws came into existence to safeguard the individual as well as society. It is said that the people are worthy of their leaders. Certain it is that the people have the laws that they deserve, of which they are the creators. They may introduce laws which enslave themselves or laws which promote their progress.

The halaka reflects the way of life of the Jewish people. It was the creation of the genius of the Jews of the Second Commonwealth. It was progressive and plastic. The sages strove to bring the halaka into consonance with life.

THE WRITTEN AND UNWRITTEN LAWS

Jewish laws are considered divine, delivered by God to the children of Israel; some, like the Ten Commandments, revealed by God Himself,[3] others through Moses. They were all embodied in the Code called the Law of Moses,[3a] or the Law,[3b] commonly known to us as the Pentateuch. Violations of these laws are called sins. Some transgressors are to be punished either by death or corporal punishment, while others must bring a sacrifice to God in order to obtain atonement.

Most of the laws in the Pentateuch concern the relation between man and God. Every transgression was considered a crime against God.

Not only was the worship of foreign gods considered such but even the profanation of the sabbath, incest and adultery. Among the civil laws in the Pentateuch mention is made of a judge, God himself sometimes acting as a judge. For example—in the Book of Exodus we read, "What if the servant shall plainly say, 'I love my master, my wife and my children; I will not go out free'; then his master shall bring him unto Elohim (God)";[4] the Septuagint rendering *Elohim* the Court of God.[5] The rabbis, on the other hand, interpreted this word to mean judges.

The Law of Moses was canonized by Ezra (the High Priest) after the Restoration. By this I mean that the Pentateuch became the constitution of the Jewish people. While the Law of Moses is referred to in the prophetic books it was not accepted as the constitution by the Jewish people.[5a] In the Northern Kingdom (in the State of Israel) the principal tenet of the Pentateuch, that there is only one God and no other is to be worshipped, was not adhered to by the kings of Israel who all worshipped foreign gods. Even in the Southern Kingdom (in the State of Judaea) many kings were equally guilty. Solomon himself, according to the Book of Kings, followed foreign gods,[6] while the kings Ahaz and Manasseh brought foreign altars into the Temple for worship. If the heads of the nation acted thus it is evident that the Pentateuch was not the constitution of the people. No individual could be punished for transgressing the precept of the Pentateuch when the basis of the Book, that there is only one God, was not accepted by the kings. After the Restoration the Jewish community of course did not permit the worship of idols. Monotheism, the belief in one God, was the guiding principle of the new community—the Torah became the law of the land.

There is no doubt that parallel with the laws of the Pentateuch were many not embodied therein. They were the outcome of customs, unwritten laws—halakot. Philo, in explaining why Moses added the Book of Genesis to the Torah, which deals only with the history of the Patriarchs, said that the Patriarchs actually followed all the laws which were unwritten but were later given by God to Moses. According to Philo the written law is the product of the unwritten law—"One might properly say that the enacted laws are nothing else than memorials of life of the ancients, preserving to the later generations their actual words and deeds."[7] The view that the Patriarchs had observed all the laws of the Torah is also expressed in the Mishna.[8] This was the opinion of orthodox Jewry of the Second Commonwealth. Others had the view that the laws were enacted and written on tablets at the time of the Patriarchs and were held in heaven until God gave the Tables of the Law to Moses on Mount Sinai. This is told in the so-called Book of Jubilees which I believe was originally called תורת משה the Law of Moses, and was written in opposition to the Pentateuch.[9]

The writings of the prophets as well as the Hagiographa contain references to laws not mentioned in the Pentateuch. In the Book of Haggai it is stated that God told the Prophet to examine the priests on the laws of sanctity and impurity. "Thus said the Lord of Hosts. Ask now the priests Torah (Law) saying, 'If one bear hallowed flesh in the skirt of his garment, and with his skirt do touch bread or pottage, or wine, or oil, or any food, shall it become holy?' And the priests answered and said 'No.' Then said Haggai, "If one that is unclean by a dead body touch any of these, shall it be unclean?' And the priests answered and said, 'It shall be unclean.' "[10] These two halakot about which the Prophet Haggai questioned the priests are not found in the Pentateuch, but apparently the Prophet thought that they should be familiar with the laws of sanctification and defilement. In the first question the priests were asked whether a person carrying holy flesh קדש with him, could thus transfer his sanctity to other subjects. The second question was whether a person who had become unclean by contact with a dead body could transfer impurity to others.[11]

We learn from the Book of Jeremiah that when the Prophet bought a field from Hanamel he wrote a deed in the presence of witnesses who affixed their signatures.[12] In the Pentateuch there is no requirement of a deed and witnesses in the transfer of personal property. In the Book of Tobit it is related that when Raguel gave his daughter as a wife to Tobit "he wrote an instrument of cohabitation."[13] The author continues "He gave her to wife according to the decree of the Law of Moses."[14] From the Pentateuch we know that a father had full rights over his daughter, even the right to sell her.[15] If a girl was seduced the seducer had to pay a penalty for this act but the money was paid to her father, not to her.[16] The Pentateuch does not say that if the father gives his daughter away in marriage he must write a deed. The deed which Raguel wrote was most likely one of transfer of his rights over his daughter, Sarah, to Tobit, her future husband. According to the Book of Nehemiah the Jews were prohibited from carrying any burden on the sabbath or buying and selling,[17] while in the Pentateuch the Jews are forbidden to work on the sabbath; the nature of the work is not defined. From Nehemiah, however, we learn that the transaction of any business on the sabbath formed part of such forbidden work.

In the Book of Ruth it is stated that Boaz told his kinsman that he would have to marry Ruth when he purchased the field of Naomi "to raise up the name of the dead upon his inheritance." "Now this was the custom," we are informed, "in former time in Israel concerning redeeming and concerning exchanging, to confirm all things. A man drew off his shoe and gave it to his neighbor; and this was the attestation in Israel."[18] When Boaz acquired the field the author says, "he drew off his shoe." Among the sages there was a discussion as to who removed the shoe and who gave it, whether the kinsman gave his shoe to Boaz, i.e. as a sign of transfer of the property, or whether Boaz gave the shoe as a sign of purchase of the property.[19] It is clear, however, that it was the custom in ancient Israel in the transfer of immovable property to resort to a symbol of transfer either by the one who transferred the property or by the new owner. There is no mention whatsoever in the Pentateuch of this law or custom.

When Naboth, the Jezreelite, according to I Kings, refused to give or to sell his vineyard to King Ahab, his wife Jezebel proclaimed a fast and had two men testify falsely that Naboth had cursed God and the king. For this he was put to death and thus King Ahab acquired the vineyard.[20] God then said to Elijah, "Go to Ahab, the King of Israel, and tell him, Thus saith the Lord, 'Hast thou murdered and also inherited?' "[21] It is evident that God was opposed to Ahab's acquiring possession of the vineyard of Naboth who was put to death on false testimony by a scheme of Jezebel. If, however, Naboth had cursed God and the king, Ahab, the King of Israel, would have become the legitimate heir of the vineyard. Such a law of forfeiture is not found in the Pentateuch. But in the tannaitic literature we learn that when a man committed a crime against the state and was executed his property was not inherited by his children but was forfeited to the state.[22]

From the Book II Kings we may infer that a law existed in Israel in regard to the status of the debtor to the creditor. It is told that, a certain woman of the wives of the sons of the prophets cried to Elisha saying: "Thy servant, my husband, is dead; and thou knowest that thy servant did fear the Lord; and the creditor is come to take unto him my two children to be his bondsmen."[23] From the complaint of the widow we may deduce that in ancient times if a debtor did not pay his debts the creditor had the right to take him into servitude and if he died and the debt was unpaid to take his children into bondage. The principle of *obligatio*, that the debtor was bound to the creditor who had the right to sell him and even his children into slavery or to imprison him, if he did not pay his debt to the obligator is evident from a story in the Gospel according to Matthew.[23a] The law that if a debtor did not pay his debt the creditor had a right not only over his person but also over his children is not in the Laws of Moses.

The principle of *hiyub, obligatio in person,* that the obligator had the right in person and not in property, goes back to the Pentateuch. According to the Torah if a man had stolen property he had to return it to the owner and pay him a fine. If it was an ox his penalty was double, but if he no longer had the ox in his possession that is, if he had slaughtered or sold it, he had to pay a fine five times its value. If the thief did not have the money to pay to the owner for the value of the stolen property he was sold into slavery. From this we can readily see that the *hiyub, obligatio,* to pay for the stolen property, lay in person. According to tannaitic law the thief could be sold only when he was unable to pay the principal of the value but not if he could not pay the fine.[23b] Since *furtum* (theft) was considered *delicta privata,*[23c] the fine which the thief was supposed to pay (for that matter any fine) according to tannaitic law as well as according to the Roman law, could not be collected by the heirs until after *litis contestatio* had taken place.

The few laws which we have just recorded are based purely on customs. They were most likely put into effect by public opinion, because of the antiquity of their practice. After the Restoration they were enforced by the authorities.

The decree which the Persian king gave to Ezra included the authority to appoint judges and to punish those who would not follow דתא ד' אלהיך the law of God and the law of the king. "Let judgment be executed" it read "upon those with diligence whether it be unto death or to banishment or to confiscation of goods or to imprisonment."[24] Thus Ezra received authority to exercise full jurisdiction over those Jews who did not obey all the laws, whether they were the laws of the Torah or unwritten laws. The latter became known in rabbinic literature as halakot. The word halaka means custom, law; it is derived from הלך walk. Similarly the Greek word νόμος law had the original connotation of custom, usage.[25] Hence the laws embodied in the Torah were the written laws, תורה שבכתב and called דברי תורה while those not included in the Pentateuch, which sprang from the customs of the people, and although sanctioned by the authorities, were called halakot תורה שבעל פה , unwritten laws, or דברי סופרים *jus non scriptum,* ἄγραφοι νόμοι.[26]

At the time of the Restoration many laws not found in the Pentateuch prevailed among the Jews, but many beliefs and doctrines not mentioned there were in vogue. Some of these were established through the influence of the prophets.

One of the main contentions between the Judeans and the Samaritans was that the former wanted Jerusalem to be the site of the new Temple. The Samaritans objected because the city was not mentioned in the Pentateuch. The importance of Jerusalem above all other cities of Judea arose through history and the prophetic teachings. The family of David reigned there for centuries and the Temple of God was there.

Although the new community was established as a Theocracy and the High Priest became the vicar of God, who had authority over the entire Jewish community, not only spiritual but also temporal, not all the Jews favored such a government. Many looked forward to the day when the Davidic dynasty would be reestablished,[26a] since God through his prophets had promised David that his dynasty would last forever.

From the tannaitic literature, as well as from Josephus, we learn that the Sadducees rejected the unwritten laws while the Pharisees accepted them. Josephus, in his book, *Jewish Antiquities,* writes as follows, "The Pharisees had passed on to the people certain regulations received from their forefathers but not recorded in the Laws of Moses, for which reason they are rejected by the Sadducean group, who hold that only those laws should be considered valid which were written down and those which had been handed down by the forefathers need not be observed."[27] However, we must assume that the Sadducees could not reject all the laws which were not the Laws of Moses. No state, large or small, could function without customs, unwritten laws.[28] Cicero has well remarked that the law had its origin ages before any written law existed or any state had been established.[29] The Sadducees could not reject many laws in vogue after the Restoration which were in force either by public opinion or by the vicar, the High Priest. Many of these customs had become part of the written law and to this Josephus apparently refers, "Only those laws should be considered valid which were written down." The Sadducees particularly opposed the ideas and beliefs of the Pharisees regarding the Davidic family.

We must assume that the account of Josephus is based on a source later than the Restoration, when the Pharisees and the Sadducees were two distinct political and religious groups. At this time the Pharisees had developed an array of laws which they held were based not only on tradition but also on the Pentateuch and which were derived by her-

meneutic rules. The Sadducees opposed these views. The Pharisees, on
the other hand, maintained that the halakot as well as the Torah were
revealed by God. According to the Talmud, "In the days of mourning
for Moses thousands of halakot were forgotten."[30] The same thought
was expressed by a Palestinian Amora of the third century C.E. when
he said, "Many halakot were transmitted to Moses on Mt. Sinai and all
of them are embodied in the Mishna."[31]

The conception that the unwritten law was really a gift of God was
entertained by the Greeks as well as the Romans. Demosthenes said
that law though made by wise men was the gift of the gods.[32] Cicero
also said that law came into existence through the divine mind, "The
true and the primal law," he wrote, "applied to command and prohibition is the right reason of supreme Jupiter."[33] Elsewhere he wrote,
"that law which the gods have given to the human race has been justly
praised; for it is the reason and mind of a wise lawgiver applied to
command and prohibition."[34]

At times the sages considered the halakot the laws enacted by the
Soferim more important than the laws of the Pentateuch,[35] and even
favored them above the Torah.[36] A similar opinion of the greater importance of unwritten laws was held by the Greek philosophers. Aristotle said that customary laws are more sovereign than the written
laws.[37] There is a statement in the Talmud in the name of Rabbi Ishmael that in three instances the halaka superseded the Torah. These
were cases where the blood of a beast or a fowl which was slaughtered
was to be covered only with dust, could according to the halaka be
covered with anything at all; where, according to the Pentateuch, a
Nazir was forbidden to cut his hair with a razor, was not allowed to
cut his hair with any instrument at all; and finally where though, according to the Pentateuch, a decree of divorce had to be written in a
book to be valid, it could be written on anything, on pottery, book or
leaves, according to the halaka.[38]

The Jews, in order to enforce the unwritten laws, maintained that
these like the written laws were revealed by God. When the unwritten
laws were codified they became written laws and hermeneutic rules
were applied to them to infer new halakot.[38a] While common law—
unwritten law—may be enforced by authorities new laws cannot be inferred from them. Hermeneutic rules may be applied to written laws but
not to customs, unwritten laws.

The sages of the Talmud who said that many halakot were revealed
to Moses on Mount Sinai held that these were incorporated in the Mish-

na.[39] The word Mishna is derived from the word שנה to study. The term Mishna has also the connotation of "second" and I think that these halakot, which were assembled in one collection and made into a code were purposely called Mishna to signify that it was the Second Code to the Laws of Moses.

The halakot codified in the Mishna ceased to be unwritten laws; they were now considered *written laws*. The statement in the Talmud that it is permissible to put into writing the Laws of Moses but not the halakot,[40] I venture to say that this refers to the halakot before the codification of the Mishna or to such halakot which were not included in the Mishna. They remained the unwritten law.[41]

One may question, if the Mishna is a code, why are differences of opinion found there in connection with the halakot. A code is a set of laws recorded without any dissension—like the Torah, and the codes of the Roman law like the *Institute of Gaius* for example. We must take into consideration however the fact that Judaism at the time of the codification of the Mishna was a nomocracy, i. e. a government under the rule of the law. The Mishna, being a code, records different opinions but rules are laid down as to which laws are to be observed. Where there is both a majority opinion and a minority opinion the majority opinion must be followed. At times when Rabbi, who was the real architect of the Mishna, thought that the law as interpreted by a particular sage should be followed, he recorded such a view or opinion in the Mishna, either as anonymous or in the name of the sages,[42] i.e. he made it the majority opinion. Rabbi set down numerous opinions in the Mishna, even those which he did not accept as halaka. The reason for this was that if sometime in the future some halakot suggestions should arise the rabbis should be able to support their decisions on those opinions recorded in the Mishna.[43] Hence the Mishna, even though a code, cannot be compared to the Torah. The Torah was revealed by God to Moses and had to be administrated by the High Priest, the vicar of God. The code of the Roman law certainly cannot be compared to it. Its authority came either from kings, senate or magistrates. The sages of the Second Commonwealth did not derive their authority from kings, senate or magistrates but from their profound knowledge of the Law and their ability to interpret it. Some of the sages were called דרשנים interpreters.[44]

The halakot in the Mishna are arranged according to the subject matter and generally make no reference to the Pentateuch. The halakot in the *Mekilta Sifra* and *Sifre*, however, are arranged according to the pentateuchal passages and are interpreted by biblical verses. This type of legal interpretation is also found throughout the Talmud.

THE HALAKA AND MIDRASH

The question confronting modern scholars has been what form of law came first, that form of law given in the Mishna or that form of law recorded in the *Mekilta Sifra* and *Sifre*? It has been the consensus of opinion among scholars that the teaching of the law as recorded in the *Mekilta Sifra* and *Sifre*, which they call *Midrash Halaka*, is older than that in the Mishna.[45] Likewise it has been generally assumed that the teaching of the halaka in the Mishna form took place after the period of the *Soferim*.[46] There is a wide difference of opinion as to when the period of the *Soferim* ended. According to some Simon I was the Just and he was the last of the *Soferim*. Hence this period ended about 300-270 B.C.E.[47] According to others Simon II was the Just, and he was the last of the *Soferim*[48]; hence, according to this view the end of the period of *Soferim* came circa 210-190 B.C.E. Those who held that the teaching of the Midrash form is older than the Mishna find support for their theory in the literature of the Gaonim.[49]

The theory that the teaching of the Midrash form is older than the Mishna is historically untrue. 1—The Gaonic statement in advancing this view is not sufficient proof. The Gaonim lived centuries after the compilation of the Mishna and therefore the statement is questionable. On the contrary we may deduce from the tannaitic literature that the Mishna form was older and hence the Gaonic statement is refuted. To establish what form of teaching is the older we must go to tannaitic literature, the product of the builders of the Mishna and the Midrash halaka. Only the literature of the Tannaim and the early Amoraim can be conclusive in this matter.

Again the theory that the period of the *Soferim* lasted until Simon I (300-270 B.C.E.) or Simon II (210-190 B.C.E.) is refuted by many passages in tannaitic literature, according to which the period of the *Soferim* continued down to the time of the destruction of the Second Temple. In the Mishna Yad. 3 it is stated that, "the Holy Scriptures defile the hands,"[50] was decreed by the *Soferim*. This law was decreed about the year 65 C.E. a few years before the destruction of the Temple. Again in the Tosefta Tebul Yom 2, it is stated that Rabbi Joshua said, "This is new which the *Soferim* innovated."[51] Rabbi Joshua's statement refers to the decree which was introduced a few years before the destruction of the Temple, hence it is quite evident that the theory that the *Soferim* ceased to exist before the time of the Maccabees is erroneous and must be disregarded.

The contention that the name *Soferim* designates a group who occupied themselves with the Book and taught the Book alone is refuted by the Mishna Yad. 3 and by the Tosefta Tebul Yom 2. The halaka quoted in this tannaitic literature is not derived from the Book. We may disregard the theory that, "This name (*Soferim*) has been applied to the earliest teachers of the Halakah, because they imparted all their teachings in connection with the Book of the Law either as an exposition of it or as a commentary on it, that is to say in the form of the Midrash."[52] The halakot just quoted came not from the "earliest teachers" but from the teachers of the period shortly before the destruction of the Second Temple. They are independent halakot. Again it is not true that the name *Soferim* was applied only to the early teachers while that of the Tannaim was applied to the later teachers who began to teach the abstract halakot.

The scholars who have dealt with the problem of halakot have not only failed to see that the term *Soferim*, as applied to the sages, was used down to the destruction of the Second Temple but they have not shown a true comprehension of the philosophy of Jewish history during the Second Commonwealth. Most of these scholars were theologians —academicians. They were accustomed to analyze written words and thus they applied the same method to the study of the halakot during the Second Commonwealth. They ignored the fact that the Jews of that period were a living nation, the creators of the laws. It is well known that every people, besides having statutory laws, have also common laws, customs, which had originated among the people. In the same way the Jews at the time of the Restoration, when the Pentateuch was canonized, had many halakot outside of the Pentateuch which were as old or even older.

That the halakot preceded the Midrash form is manifest from two events in the life of Hillel. According to the Palestinian Talmud there were three reasons for Hillel's coming to Palestine.[53] He found three contradictory verses in the Pentateuch:

1. With regard to leprosy one verse reads טהור הוא "he is clean," which means that a person is considered clean when his leprosy is cured. In another verse, however it is stated וטהרו הכהן "the priest shall pronounce him clean," which means that although a man is cured from leprosy he is not considered clean unless pronounced so

by the priest. Hillel interpreted these two verses and said that both
conditions were necessary. The one stating that the man must be first
cured and that the other that he must be pronounced cured by the
priest.[54]

2. In one verse it is written that the Paschal Lamb must be brought
from the flock and the herd while another passage reads that the
Paschal Lamb must be brought from the sheep and the goats. Hillel interpreted this to mean that the Paschal Lamb is to be taken from the
flock while the sacrifice called *hagiga* is to come from the herds.[55]

3. In one verse it is stated that unleavened bread is to be eaten for
six days but another verse says seven days. Hillel interpreted and reconciled these two verses by referring the seven days to the old harvest
and the six days to the new harvest.[56] The Jews were not allowed to eat
of the new harvest until the sixteenth day of Nisan, i. e. the second day
of the Festival of Unleavened Bread. Thus the unleavened bread from
the new harvest is to be eaten only six days.

The Talmud continues דרש והסכים ועלה וקיבל הלכה .

Hillel interpreted and reconciled[57] these passages after he arrived in
the Land of Israel when he discovered that his interpretations were
halakot, i. e. the Jews had been practicing as he had interpreted. Since
these three laws were not applicable in Babylonia, for there was no
law of leprosy there, nor was there sacrifice of the Paschal Lamb, nor
was there any law regarding the new harvest,[58] Hillel interpreted the
verses referring to them in accordance with the halaka in vogue in
Palestine. Thus it is evident that the halaka supersedes the Midrash.

The other event in Hillel's life from which we may deduce that the
halaka preceded the Midrash was in connection with the slaughter of
the Paschal Lamb on the sabbath. In both Talmuds it is related that
once, when the eve of Passover (14th of Nisan) fell on sabbath, the
B'nei Bathera did not know whether the Paschal Lamb might be slaughtered on the sabbath. They were advised, there is a man named Hillel, a
disciple of Shemaiah and Abatalion, who possibly knows; let us ask
him. "They sent for him and asked him whether the Paschal Lamb
could be slaughtered on the sabbath." He replied that it could and
proved it by hermeneutic rules; by קל וחומר   *a minori ad majus,* by
גזירה שוה analogy of words, by היקש   analogy of subjects. The B'nei
Bathera however, did not accept his ruling, but when he said that he
had this tradition from Shemaiah and Abatalion they accepted it. Hillel
was then appointed Nasi over the Bet Din.[59] The Talmud adds that
the B'nei Bathera did not know whether it was permissible to carry the

knives for the slaughter of the Paschal Lamb on the sabbath. When they asked Hillel he answered that he had a tradition of "the halaka but that he had forgotten it." However, said he, "leave it to Israel, if they are not prophets they are sons of prophets."[60] The Jews who brought lambs for the sacrifice stuck knives in the wool of the lambs.[61] It is evident from this story that although the B'nei Bathera did not know that the Paschal Lamb could be slaughtered on the sabbath, and although Hillel to sanction this had to resort to hermeneutic rules, the farmers knew this and when preparing to bring the Paschal Lamb for slaughter on the sabbath they stuck knives in the wool of the lambs. Thus it is clear that this halaka, i. e. the custom of slaughtering the Paschal Lamb on the sabbath, was in vogue long before the time of Hillel. The reason why the B'nei Bathera did not know of this is that they were new in the Bet Din, having come from outside of Eretz Israel. Hillel sought to make this halaka—unwritten law—a statutory law by interpreting the Torah.

It has been suggested that from a particular passage in the Talmud it is evident that the Midrash form was older than the Mishna form.[62] The passage referred to contains a story in which R. Johanan speaks to Simon b. Lakish about a statement by R. Eleazar b. Pedat, and remarks: "I see that the son of Pedat interprets in the way as Moses did from God."[63] Thus the opinion is expressed that to study or teach in the Midrash form as it is given in the *Mekilta Sifra* and *Sifre* is as old as Moses. This interpretation however is erroneous. R. Eleazar b. Pedat had a reputation for quoting the opinions of others and not giving original opinions. Simon b. Lakish particularly criticized him for this.[64] Once R. Eleazar b. Pedat expressed an opinion which R. Johanan thought original and told Simon b. Lakish how much he admired the originality of Ben Pedat who, like Moses, interpreted the law as received from God without any intermediary. To this Simon b. Lakish replied that even here Ben Pedat was not original for he took the opinion from the Sifra.[65] Hence there is no basis whatsoever for the contention that the Midrash form is older than the Mishna form.

SOURCES OF TANNAITIC LAW

The sources of the law may be divided into the following categories: The Law of Moses—the written law; halakot—customs, unwritten laws; g'zera—decree; *takkana*; סיג fence around the law.

The Laws of Moses were the basic laws of the Jews. However they underwent great modification by interpretation and fiction. The sages declared that some of them were applicable to the time of Moses only and were not for posterity.[66]

Halakot which were codified in the Mishna, even those which before the codification through interpretation of the Pentateuch were accepted by the Bet Din, became statutory laws and were used as a basis for new laws. This method of development of law is called *Midrash Torah* and *Midrash Halaka*.

G'zera is a decree—independent legislation by an authority. During the Second Commonwealth many laws were decreed by the authority of the Bet Din or by the head of this institution. A decree was promulgated for a particular reason. When the reason for it disappeared the decree automatically became void. This may be illustrated by an example from tannaitic literature. It is stated that Jose b. Joezer and Jose b. Johanan decreed that the land of the pagans was in a state of levitical uncleanliness.[67] This decree was issued during the time of the Maccabean struggle for freedom. It was promulgated to prevent the Jews from migrating to foreign countries and it was also directed against Onias's temple. With the decree declaring the land of the pagans in a state of levitical uncleanliness, the rivalry between the temple in Egypt and the temple in Jerusalem was destroyed.[68] When both the menace of emigration and the rivalry of the temple of Onias were thus removed the *g'zera* automatically disappeared. When a new cause arose and the sages thought that, for the benefit of the Jews and Eretz Israel, the land of the pagans should again be declared in a state of levitical uncleanliness they decreed another such *g'zera*.

From this point of view a perplexing talmudic passage becomes clear. The question was asked, if Jose b. Joezer and Jose b. Johanan declared the land of the pagans to be in a state of levitical uncleanliness why is it said that the schools of Shammai and Hillel had such a decree promulgated?[69] Furthermore, the Talmud says that, according to tradition, the "rabbis of the eighty years" (i. e. the rabbis who lived eighty years before the destruction of the Temple) had promulgated such a decree.[70] The answer given in the Talmud is that although Jose b. Joezer and Jose b. Johanan decreed the land of the pagans to be in a state of levitical uncleanliness the people did not accept their decree; but that when the later rabbis issued such a decree it was accepted by the people.[71] According to our opinion the reason why this decree was repeated three times is not that it was not accepted by the people but that when the reason for the decree vanished, *ipso facto,* the decree became null and void. When the reason arose again the later sages reissued the decree.

Another source of law was *takkana*. *Takkana* is an amendment of early law, either pentateuchal or halaka, introduced by the sages generally for the purpose of harmonizing religion and life. They did not hesitate to amend a pentateuchal law if such was life's demand. Hence *takkana* has a lenient tendency. In introducing a *takkana* the sages sought support for it in the Bible. The *takkanot* recorded in tannaitic literature either appeared under the name of an individual authority, like the *takkana* of *Ketuba*, ascribed to Simon b. Shetah, or the *takkana* of *Prosbol*, ascribed to Hillel, while other *takkanot* were ascribed to Ezra and Solomon. As I have pointed out elsewhere the *takkanot* ascribed to Ezra and Solomon were not introduced by them but were the results of the evolution of the halakot developed during the time of the Tannaim. Some of the *takkanot* were of ancient origin while others came into being shortly before the destruction of the Second Temple and even after that period.[72]

The introduction of takkanot was either by the method of *interpretio* or *fictio* and sometimes by both. To illustrate I shall give an instance of one *takkana*. The Talmud ascribes the *takkana* of Erub to Solomon.[73] In the Book of Exodus we read,[74] "Ye shall sit each of you in his place, let no man go out of his place on the seventh day." Literally the meaning is that the ancient Hebrews had no right to leave their "place" on the sabbath day. The Septuagint however renders the words, "his place" his house.[75] This would mean that the Hebrews had no right to go out of their houses on the sabbath day. They were allowed to walk only four cubits from their homes.[76] Later the words "his place" were interpreted to mean his city. Accordingly they were permitted to walk not only four cubits but two thousand cubits.[77] But if a Jew was forcibly taken into another city on the sabbath day, i. e. kidnapped by pagans, he could walk only four cubits on the sabbath because that city was not his abode.[78] Similarly if a Jew traveled to Jerusalem on the sabbath day to give testimony on the birth of the new moon, in which case the prohibition to travel was suspended, he had no right to walk around in Jerusalem on the sabbath; he had to stay in one place. Actually there was a court in Jerusalem called Beth-Yazek where the witnesses who arrived on the sabbath to give testimony on the birth of the new moon assembled. Rabban Gamaliel the Elder, amended the law so that such witnesses were to be considered inhabitants of Jerusalem, (i. e. it was their abode), and have the right to walk two thousand cubits in any direction on the sabbath.[79] The law was further amended so that a Jew had the right to walk throughout the city on the sabbath and two thousand cubits beyond.

The sages introduced *takkanot* to amend the pentateuchal laws as well as the halaka. From the Talmud we learn that if Rosh Hashana fell on the sabbath the sounding of the *shofar* was suspended. In the Temple however the blowing of the *shofar* took precedence over the sabbath, a custom which was in vogue during the Second Commonwealth. After the destruction of the Temple, Rabban Johanan b. Zakkai introduced a *takkana* that in the city of Jabne, where the Bet Din was sitting, the blowing of the *shofar* should take precedence over the sabbath.[80] By this *takkana* Rabban Johanan b. Zakkai sought to demonstrate that the Bet Din took the place of the Temple.

The sages not only amended ritual laws but also laws in relation to the family and civil laws. In the early period of Jewish history, i. e. in the time of the Pentateuch, a woman was considered the property of her father and, later, of her husband. The father had the right to sell her and give her in marriage; the groom had to pay a certain sum of money, called *mohar,* to the father of the girl.[81] A *takkana* was introduced by Simon b. Shetah to amend this ancient halaka. Instead of the groom paying the father money for taking his daughter in marriage he had to write a writ, *ketuba,* in which he pledged all his property as security for two hundred *zuzim* in the case of his death or divorce. The purpose of this *takkana* was to raise the social and economic life of the woman. She was protected economically in case of divorce or the death of her husband and she was no longer the property of her father but possessed rights in herself.[82]

The *takkana* of *Prosbol,* introduced by Hillel, was a modification of a pentateuchal law necessitated by the economic life of the Jews during the period of the Second Commonwealth.[83]

A *g'zera* is a decree of the authorities absolutely independent of the Torah and for a certain period and may be local. A *takkana,* on the other hand, is universal and applicable to all classes like halaka.[83a] It must be supported by a biblical verse.[83b]

Another source of law was *Minhag*—usage. Some of the *minhagim* were local, confined to a particular city[84] or to a particular group, like the usage among shippers,[85] or among members of a caravan.[86] The difference between *minhag* and halaka is that although the origin of halaka is custom, most customs became laws and were so interpreted in the academies.[87] On the other hand *minhag* never became a part of law but was only a custom of a particular group or locality; hence the members of the group or locality had to follow the custom. A *minhag* was never interpreted in the academies.[88] It was pointed out above that there was an opinion that halaka even supersedes the Torah.[89] Similarly it was the opinion of the Amoraim that a *minhag* sometimes nullifies a halaka.[90]

In the study of tannaitic jurisprudence סיג must be taken into consideration. The term סיג means "a fence around the law." In order to prevent the possibility of transgressing the law the sages introduced what is known as "a fence around the law." Although the term סיג in connection with halaka is found in but a few places in the tannaitic literature, the principle involved shaped many of the tannaitic halakot. It is worth noting that the school of Hillel, which was generally lenient in the interpretation and application of the law, resorted to this principle. According to the halaka, fowl and cheese must not be eaten at the same time. There is no law, however, which prohibits them from being placed on the same table. According to the school of Shammai fowl and cheese may be so placed but may not be eaten simultaneously.[91] However, according to the liberal school, the Hillelites, fowl and cheese were not allowed to be placed on the same table,[92] for the reason that one might be tempted to eat both, which was forbidden. Therefore, as a preventive measure, they introduced a fence around the law, not to place fowl and cheese on the same table.

The principle of "a fence around the law" was not used as frequently in the tannaitic literature as *takkana* and *g'zera*. It came to be used as an important principle in the shaping of the halaka after the Jews had lost their independence, when it became necessary for them to make a fence around the law.[92a]

INTERPRETATION AND LEGAL FICTION

From time to time the Tannaim, in order to carry out the current needs of the people, adapted the laws to the changing conditions of society. They sometimes interpreted the biblical verses so as to bring the pentateuchal law into consonance with life. We give an example of such an interpretation. According to the Pentateuch if water was put upon the seed the latter became susceptible to levitical uncleanliness.[93] The word זרע may have the meaning, "seed attached to the ground and seed which is plucked from the ground." During the period of the Second Commonwealth the Jews of Palestine were dependent on the grain imported from Egypt, then the granary of the world. It is well known that the fields of Egypt were irrigated with water from the Nile, thus water was poured on the seed. Hence, according to the Pentateuch, the seed was susceptible to levitical uncleanliness. In order to make it possible for the Jews of Palestine, who were concerned about the laws of levitical uncleanliness, to import the grain from Egypt, the sages interpreted the word זרע to mean seed detached from the ground."[94] Thus the law of levitical uncleanliness did not affect the grain imported from Egypt since it was watered while still attached to the ground. This *takkana* was introduced by the sages in order to facilitate the economic life of the Jews.

Legal fiction is a process whereby a possible state of things was assumed as actually existing.[95] It was applied throughout the entire tannaitic law. I shall cite two examples. The pentateuchal words, "he shall sit in his place," were, as we have already remarked previously, explained to mean sitting, i. e. a Jew had the right to walk throughout the city on the sabbath and two thousand cubits beyond. Then a new law was introduced that if a Jew deposited food in a place located at a distance of two thousand cubits from the city he had the right to walk that distance from the place of depository on the sabbath. This law was promulgated on the assumption that the place where the Jew had deposited food for the sabbath became his abode. This law, known as *Erubin* is a legal fiction—an assumption that the place where a person deposited food on the eve of sabbath could have been made his abode. Thus the Tannaim considered it a fact that it was his abode, and hence he could walk two thousand cubits beyond it.

The idea of legal fiction was introduced by the Tannaim not only into ritual law but into civil law as well. According to the Pentateuch every seventh year was called the sabbatical year, in which, "Every creditor shall release that which he has lent unto his neighbor; he shall not exact it of his neighbor and of his brother because God's release had been proclaimed."[96] Thus, according to the Pentateuch, if a man made a loan and was not paid before the sabbatical year he could not claim it or sue for it. According to the Mishna, if a debtor gave the creditor security for the loan even if the security was not equal to the value of the loan he was not entitled to a release of his unpaid debt because of the sabbatical year.[97] The assumption was that when the creditor received the security from the debtor the loan was repaid, being actually in exchange for the debt, even though the security was not equal in value to the loan.

Although legal fiction was often applied by the Tannaim no term for it is found in tannaitic literature. Some students are of the opinion that the word הערמה was the term used by the Tannaim for legal fiction. They point out the tannaitic passage where it is stated that, according to Rabbi Joshua if a dam and its young fall into a pit on a holiday one may pull out the dam in order to slaughter it and then change one's mind about which animal to slaughter, and also pull out the young in order to slaughter it.[98]

According to the halaka, the Jews were allowed to work on a holiday only for the need of their sustenance. Hence, if an animal fell into a pit they had the right to lift her out of the pit for slaughter. However it was not permitted that a dam and its young be slaughtered on the same day. Hence, in order to release both of them from the pit, a Jew may mentally designate the dam for slaughter and then he may change his mind and decide to slaughter its young instead; thus he acquires the right to lift the young out of the pit. Now that both are out of the pit he may slaughter either one. We have here not a legal fiction but a loophole in the law. Because of the ambiguity of the law an astute person may find the loophole and get around the law.[99] Legal fiction is a branch of law and had great influence in molding the halaka, while הערמה is only a loophole to get around the law, and it was a question among the authorities whether a person had the right to take advantage of the ambiguity of the law for his own benefit.[100]

THE SCHOOLS OF SHAMMAI AND HILLEL

Jurisprudence of the time of the Second Temple may be divided into two branches, one dealing with the laws from the time of the Restoration to the time when Simon the Hasmonean was elected High Priest and Ethnarch, when the theocracy was abolished and was succeeded by a commonwealth; and the other relating to the second period from the establishment of the Commonwealth to the suppression of the revolt of Bar Kokba, when the sages assembled in Galilee, in the city Usha. Up to the time of Simon, the High Priest had full power over the Jews, both spiritually and temporally, appointing judges and sanctioning and interpreting the laws. After the establishment of the Commonwealth a supreme court—Bet Din—was instituted, most likely by the Great Synagogue which elected Simon as the High Priest and Ethnarch. At the head of the Bet Din were two men, one had the title *Nasi,* and the other *Ab Bet Din.*

These two, *Nasi* and *Ab Bet Din,* were the representatives of two schools of thought in Jewish law. The first three presidents were of the conservative and the first three *Ab Bet Din* were of the liberal school. The last two presidents were of the liberal and the last two *Ab Bet Din* were of the conservative school.[101] After the death of Hillel and Shammai the office of *Ab Bet Din* was abolished. Gamaliel, the grandson of Hillel, had the title Rabban since he was the sole head of the *Bet Din.*

While the schools named after their great masters, Hillel and Shammai, represented liberalism and conservatism respectively, they had their beginning with the "first pair" Jose ben Joezer and Jose ben Johanan. A parallel instance of the origin of similar schools of thought is found in Roman jurisprudence. It is known that in the time of August Caesar there came into being two schools of strongly contrasting characters and tendencies. The actual founders of these two schools were two jurists, Ateius Capito and Antistius Labeo; the former was a strong supporter of imperial despotism and of conservative tendencies, while the latter, who was of an independent spirit, upheld republicanism and was more inclined to break with established institutions if such were life's demands. The schools, however, were named after later jurists, their disciples. The followers of Capito were usually called Sabinians, after his pupil Masurius Sabinus; those of Labeo were called Proculians, after Julius Proculius, a pupil not of Labeo, himself, but of his disciple, Nerva, the grandfather of the Emperor Nerva. For several generations, from the days of Augustus to the days of Antonines, every jurist enrolled himself under one flag or the other and was known as a Sabinian or Proculian. Similarly the schools of Shammai and Hillel were most likely older than their teachers, and many halakot of these two schools had been formulated before the time of Shammai and Hillel.

Some of the sages were not at all in sympathy with the change from High Priest to *Bet Din,* i. e. from theocracy to nomocracy. This feeling is reflected in two passages in the Talmud. One reads: "All the schools (teachers) which arose in Israel from the days of Moses until the days of Jose ben Joezer studied the Torah as Moses did, but afterwards they did not study the Torah as Moses did."[102] The other passage reads: "All the schools (teachers) which arose in Israel from the days of Moses until the days of Jose ben Joezer were without reproach but afterwards they were of reproach."[103] Before the establishment of the *Bet Din* there were no halakic controversies, the High Priest was the sole authority. He decided the law as Moses did. With the establishment of the *Bet*

Din there arose halakic controversies. The first controversies recorded were between Jose ben Joezer, who was the first *Nasi,* and Jose ben Johanan, who was the first *Ab Bet Din.*[104]

After the establishment of the *Bet Din* Jewish law was revolutionized. Although the Pentateuch was the basis of Jewish law and was the constitution of the people, the sages, in order to bring the halaka into consonance with life, interpreted and amended the pentateuchal laws. While the laws of the Pentateuch still had a system of tribal justice, the tannaitic laws, however, represent the justice of a great civilization and had far-reaching influence on other civilizations. We refer to that upon the canon law of the Church in spite of the fact that in the early days of Christianity the leaders of the Church were opposed to what they called tradition and the laws of the scribes.

TANNAITIC JURISPRUDENCE

Furtum (theft) was regarded in the Pentateuch as among *delicta privata,* that is matters in which the state had no right to interfere. The *actio furti* could only be brought by the victim, not by the state. Even the penalty, a fine paid by the offender, had to be turned over to the injured person and not to the state as in modern laws. Moreover the injured person could forgive the transgressor and refuse to accept any fine. If he acted so the state had no authority to interfere, since the transgressor was not considered a criminal in the eyes of the state. According to tannaitic law, however, the transgressor, besides paying a fine to the victim, was punished by the court.[105] Theft became a crime against society.

Not only theft but maiming or bodily mutilation had been considered a private wrong. The injured person had the right to fix the punishment for the offender, and if the former suffered the loss of an eye or a tooth he was allowed to gouge out an eye, extract a tooth of the offender. That was the law of the Pentateuch, "An eye for an eye, a tooth for a tooth."[106] However the victim could absolve entirely the man who caused the injury. *Talio* was only the extreme satisfaction which an injured person could demand, the state had no right to interfere. The state could not punish the offender since he was not held guilty of a crime against society. A similar conception was held in ancient Rome. *Si membrum rupsit, ni cum eo pacit talio esto,* (the Twelve Tables) that is, if the injured man did not get any satisfaction he might apply to *talio.*[107]

Even homicide in the Pentateuch was not considered *delicta publica,* a crime against society, but against the family of the victim; hence the kin of the family had to avenge the murder. The authorities had to decide whether a person was killed by accident or deliberately.[108] The execution was carried out by "the avenger of the blood." According to the Pentateuch the slayer could flee to a city of refuge and if he could prove that the dead man had been killed by accident and was not his enemy, he had to remain in the city of refuge until the death of the high priest[109] (the head of the community). There he was to be protected from the "avenger of the blood." However, if it was proved that the accused had killed the man deliberately, the authorities had to deliver him to the "avenger of the blood" who was supposed to kill him. In all primitive society the kin of the victim had the right to take ransom from the murderer and could make private arrangements with him. Such arrangement was called *compositio.* According to the Pentateuch the "avenger of the blood" had no right to take ransom from the murderer but had to kill him.[110] With the establishment of the *Bet Din,* homicide became a *delicta publica,* a crime against the state; the institution of the "avenger of the blood" was abolished and the accused was brought before a constituted court. Lynching which was practiced in primitive society became a crime against the state since no individual had the right to administer justice.

In the Pentateuch only a person's act is recognized. The idea of intention is not found there. An act takes place when a voluntary movement of the body is made, while an accident or an event occurs where there is no such voluntary movement. If a man jumps from a bridge it is an act because it is accompanied by volition. If he falls or is pushed from a bridge it is an accident or an event because there is no volition. Similarly if the hand of a person is forcibly guided into writing a signature, this is not considered an act since will is absent. Intention, however, refers only to a future act—the consequence of the first act; in other words to the ultimate purpose—to the end and not to the means. If a person throws a missile in order to break some object or to injure some one, the breaking and the injuring are the consequences of the first act of throwing. The first act resulted from the will of throwing and that was the means to the end of injuring. Intention refers only to the end—to the consequence of the first act and not to the means. The idea of intention as a legal principle was introduced by the school of Hillel and had a revolutionary effect on Jewish jurisprudence.[111]

Tannaitic jurisprudence was progressive, always with a view to the advancement of society. Its legal principles were founded on equity and morals, and revolutionary modifications of the Pentateuch are evident in all its branches. The progressiveness of tannaitic jurisprudence is exemplified in all the halakot. The pentateuchal laws dealing with inheritance indicate that while man is mortal, property is permanent. If a person dies his estate is inherited by his sons; where there are no sons it passes to his daughters and where there are no daughters it goes to the nearest kin.[112] It must always remain in the family or tribe. If a man sells his real property it must be redeemed and returned to him; if it is not redeemed then it is returned to him in the year of the Jubilee, except if he sells his house in a "walled city" and has not redeemed it within a year, in which case the house remains in the hands of the purchaser,[113] apparently as a punishment for not redeeming it. The idea of testament is not found in the Pentateuch for the simple reason that property cannot be transferred to a stranger. But according to the tannaitic law a man may write a testament[114] so that after his death part of his property may go to a stranger. This law completely reversed the pentateuchal conception of inheritance, wherein a man was considered mortal and property permanent. According to tannaitic jurisprudence man is immortal but the title to property is limitable by time. A man may give away his property by will even ten years after his death and the authorities must carry out his provision.[115]

The conception of partnership, that more than one person may have rights and title to the same property, and the idea of agency, that a person may transfer his rights to another man to act for him, is not recognized in the Pentateuch. The view that a person may acquire property by possession and also that he has the right to relinquish privileges and liabilities connected with a property is not found. Neither does the Pentateuch speak of *res nullis*. The entire conception of *jus in rem* and *jus in personam* was highly developed in tannaitic jurisprudence.

THE HALAKA AS A MODE OF LIFE

Tannaitic law actually shaped and molded the lives of the Jews. The Greeks made law a philosophy, the Romans made it a science, the Jews made law their religion. Judaism, from the time when it became a nomocracy, became a religion of laws based on equity and

high moral principles. As a matter of fact the word that has the connotation of religion is *dat*—law. In the tannaitic literature the phrase
המיר את דתו   means "he changed his religion."[116] The author of III
Maccabees says that Dositheus, who was by birth a Jew and later
gave up his religion, used the words "he changed his law."[117] In biblical
times the expression used was changed his god.[118] In the tannaitic period, when Judaism became a universal religion and the God of Israel
was considered the God of the entire universe, no person could change
his God since there was only one God. Thus, to say of a person that
he left the Jewish people, the term used was "he changed his law." The
term *dat* was used by the Jews in the same manner as *religio* by the
Romans.[119]

It has been shown above that the Tannaim always bore in mind
that the law was made for man and not man for the law. One sage
expressed it well in saying that sabbath is for the man and not man for
the sabbath;[120] the halaka was not to be a burden upon the Jews. It
has also been shown that although they deviated from the Pentateuch
they always enacted laws in its spirit. They never abrogated the biblical
law but interpreted it. Some people believe that the pentateuchal and
tannaitic laws are not adjusted to our present civilization and would
like to have them abrogated, while others do not recognize the fact
that some laws, particularly decrees, are obsolete and are not observed
today. Both groups are mistaken. Jewish law cannot be abrogated nor
can the chain of Jewish tradition be broken. If one seeks to abrogate
the Jewish law one will ultimately be lost to the Jewish fold, as happened
with the Karaites. Some laws, however, must be interpreted, but this
must be done in the spirit of Judaism and by authorities in Rabbinical
law—תלמידי חכמים   .

Let us hope that the Third Commonwealth, the Republic of Israel,
will follow the spirit of the sages of the Second Commonwealth by en-
acting laws in consonance with life. This must be done in the true
spirit of universal Judaism. We should take a lesson from the history
of the Second Commonwealth. Let us hope that the Synagogue will not
be involved in political struggles. There must be a Religious Court
(Sanhedrin) separated from the political Sanhedrin.

CAPITAL PUNISHMENT — THE CLASSIC JEWISH DISCUSSION

Gerald J. Blidstein

I

"KILL" and "MURDER" are words whose integrity is carefully guarded. "Kill" designates any taking of human life, while "murder" is reserved for unauthorized homicide, usually of a malicious nature. This fine distinction has become a vital one, serving in both legal and ethical Jewish thought.

Contemporary Jewish translators of the Bible have unanimously read the Sixth Commandment as a ban upon what we call murder: Old JPS gives, "Thou shalt not murder"; New JPS, "You shall not murder"; Buber-Rosenzweig, "*Morde nicht.*" The Children of Israel were thus commanded at Sinai to desist from unauthorized killing, but they were not commanded regarding homicide of, say, a judicial or military nature.[1] The ideological conclusions to be drawn from this fact would tend to confirm Judaism as a realistic, hard-headed system, committed to a law of justice rather than a chaos of love. An obvious line is being drawn between a faith that reads, "You shall not murder," and one that naively and unrealistically demands, "You shall not kill."

This Jewish translation is also insisted upon by the twelfth-century exegete, R. Samuel b. Meir (Rashbam), who states in his notes to *Exodus* 20:13: "*Rezichah* means 'unjustifiable killing' wherever it is used . . . but *harigah* and *mitah* can be used for both unjustifiable (killing) . . . and justifiable . . . ."[2] These definitions were denied,

313

however, by Isaac Abarbanel, who finds in the Sixth Commandment a
ban on killing *per se,* and in the word *rezichah* the equivalent of homicide. To illustrate such usage, he cites *Numbers* 35:27.[3] Actually,
Numbers 35:30 makes the point even more dramatically:

‎27. ומצא אותו גואל הדם מחוץ לגבול עיר מקלטו ורצח ⁴ גואל הדם את הרוצח אין
‎לו דם.

‎30. כל מכה־נפש לפי עדים ירצח ⁵ את הרוצח ועד אחד לא יענה בנפש למות.

Both verses certainly describe legal killings. In one, the blood-
avenger takes advantage of the murder's abandonment of the city of
refuge to kill him. In the other, the murderer is killed after his guilt is
established by witnesses.

Consider our three translations of these verses:

*But if the manslayer shall at any time go beyond the border of his
city of refugee, whither he fleeth; and the avenger of blood find him
without the border of his city of refuge, and the avenger of blood
slay* (ve-razach) *the manslayer, there shall be no blood-guiltiness
for him . . .*

* * *

Whoso killeth any person, the murderer shall be slain (yirzach et
ha-rozeach) *at the mouth of witnesses.*

(Old JPS)

In the first passage, *razach* is consistently rendered "slay." In the second,
the *rozeach* is branded a murderer, yet rather than being "murdered"
himself (as a consistent translation of *yirzach* would require) he is
"slain." Obviously, in English one cannot translate a judicial ("at the
mouth of witnesses") killing, "murder"—but the Hebrew text does not
allow any such latitude.

The New JPS (of which I give the crucial phrases) goes the old
version one better.

. . . and the blood-avenger kills the manslayer . . .

*   *   *

*If anyone kills a person, the manslayer may be executed only on
the evidence of witnesses; . . .*

We have three persons in our drama, all described by some form of the root *r-z-h* and all, surprisingly, with different English names: the *man-slayer*, the *killing* blood-avenger, and the *executioner*. Translation, then, reflects contemporary values; slayer, killer, and executioner are named with little regard for their Hebrew root but with much concern for the role (condemned or approved) each plays in our society.

Our third version, Buber-Rosenzweig, has the merit of consistency (of a rather didactic nature, one suspects):

. . . und der Bluteinloser mordet den Morder ab . . .

* * *

nach dem Mund von Zeugen soll man[6] *den Morder abmorden*[7] . .

Both Old and New JPS, by their discriminations, refuse to admit that the Bible makes no verbal distinction between a murderer and the approved surrogate of either family or society. Only Buber-Rosenzweig pursue an offending consistency with the vengeance of *had gadya*: *r-z-h* is uniformly rendered "murder." But since, on the one hand, "murder" is to be defined by contemporary usage, and, on the other, the killing of the murderer is either commanded or regulated by Divine law, it can only be called killing. The conclusion will then have to be that *r-z-h* must be rendered "kill" in all instances of its use.

One is, therefore, taken aback by the ingenious obscuring of Biblical thought in our contemporary translations, by the costuming of Biblical statement in diplomatic prose. There are, of course, instances where a translator must interpret an obscure text, but, on the other hand, a translator must always resist the impulse to manipulate the clear yet disconcerting phrase or sentence. This is especially so where preconceived moral judgments threaten to be imposed upon dissenting texts. Otherwise, the original statement becomes at best the victim of oversight; it is subdued by habit.

II

What of Rabbinic usage? Does it make a hard and fast verbal distinction similar to that made between murder and kill? How does it deal with *razach*?

Exodus 21:14 states that a murderer is to be brought to justice even from the altar, which implies, if necessary, delaying the sacrificial service. The *Mekhilta* (ed. Horowitz-Rabin, p. 263) wishes to argue from this that executions could take place even on the Sabbath; it uses the term *rezichah*. One might object that the *rezichah* here spoken of is the case of murder committed by the accused,[8] rather than the execution administered by the court. The ensuing discussion in the *Mekhilta* (p. 264, 1:1-4) specifically includes within the scope of the argument, however, all modes of execution, and hence all to be executed, not merely murderers. Still, the critical reader could justifiably bisect the two passages.[9]

The parallel passage in the Jerusalem Talmud (*Sanhedrin* 4:6; 22b) places the matter beyond all doubt:

> Resh Lakish says: "Let them try him, convict him, and execute him on the Sabbath. For if the service, which overrides the Sabbath, is overridden by an execution (*rezichath-mitzvah*), . . . certainly the Sabbath, which is overridden by the service, should be overridden by execution (*rezichath-mitvah*)."

The term *rezichath-mitzvah* could hardly refer to an act of murder: it must, then, denote an execution. *Mitzvah* is perhaps used in its usual sense of "commanded," as opposed to "permitted";[10] it may even emphasize that the only valid motive for the act is the fulfillment of the Divine command (see the discussion of R. Isaac b. Abdimi, *Yebamot* 39b). Whatever the correct explanation, one thing is clear: the Biblical meaning of *razach*—"to kill"—was perpetuated in Talmudic times.

A passage (seemingly from our *Mekhilta*) in the *She' iltot* (*Vayechi*, No. 34) is equally illuminating:

> The burial of a *met mitzvah* [neglected corpse] does not override the Sabbath, as it is stated: [*And if a man be put to death*] . . . thou shalt surely bury him the same day (Deut. 21:23), on the day on which you execute him (*rozcho*), do you bury him . . .

—and since no executions *(rezichot)* took place on the Sabbath, neither were such burials permitted. This passage is of the same fabric as the one previously discussed; in both *rezichah* hardly
Rezichah is used similarly in the *Midrash Hagadol*:[11]

> Most severe is the spilling of blood, which finds its atonement only in *rezichah*, as it is stated (*Num.* 35:33): . . . *and no expiation can be made for the land for the blood that is shed therein, but by the blood of him that shed it.*

This verse refers, of course, to the execution of the murderer. (A similar use of the term occurs in a medieval *midrash*.)[12] The citation of *Numbers* 35:33 is indeed relevant in our context. For the Bible pointedly indicates here the reciprocity[13] demanded by the execution of the killer—a reciprocity in harmony with the fact that Biblical language does not discriminate between executions and other killings.

The word is similarly understood by the *Zohar*. Noting the dual system of cantillation and pronunciation provided for the Ten Commandments, it comments that without the caesura thus created in v. 13 ". . . it would be illegal to kill anyone in the world, though he had violated the law of the Torah. . . ."[14] The verbal (as distinguished from the substantial) point implied here is that *razach* is best understood as "killing," rather than as "murder." So too Maimonides: "Anyone who kills a human being violates *lo tirzach* (*Hilchot Rozeach* 1:1)." And in the *Sefer Ha-mizvoth* (negative command 289):[15] "We are commanded not to kill one another, as it is stated, *lo tirzach*." The dialectic of Halachah can, of course, comprehend both a ban on killing and the duty to execute—much as it comprehends a ban on physical violence and a command to administer stripes.[16] Other resolutions of this problem could be suggested. But whatever the final nature of the dialectic, one thing is clear: Maimonides, both in the *Sefer Ha-Mizvoth* and in his *Code,* applies the Sixth Commandment to killing in general.[17]

We have thus seen that Biblical usage does not limit *rezichah* to murder, rather extending it to describe all killing, even to that which is Biblically ordained. We have also seen that subsequent Jewish usage never totally abandoned the Biblical insight that no word for the spilling of human blood could bear a less prohibitive denotation than any other.

The conclusion to be drawn from this usage is as concerned with the moral vision of the Hebrew language as it is with the proper rendering of the Sixth Commandment. For in the creation of certain words and their meanings and the non-creation of others a basic and irretrievable moral step is taken. Some speak of the genius of the language. This is imprecise, for language itself is but the manifestation of a more significant and responsible entity.

Western thought distinguishes, at a basic and indelible level—at the level of the word—between homicide and murder. Jewish usage does not make this distinction. The verbal integrity of the spilling of human blood is never violated; homicide is not splintered into the justifiable and the criminal. Obviously, I do not speak here of Biblical law, which knows of authorized killings of war, self-defense, and execution. I speak of language, of the stuff in which law is articulated, from which it is nourished, and with which it (or any healthy human activity) is ultimately harmonized.

III

Is there a drive within Judaism that reflects the verbal scheme outlined above? Do we have here a linguistic quirk or rather the organic expression of a deeply rooted attitude? Let us examine the debate carried on in the study halls of Talmudic Palestine over the propriety and wisdom of capital punishment.

The famous clash of R. Akiba and R. Tarfon with R. Simeon ben Gamaliel is provocative and ambiguous:

> R. Tarfon and R. Akiba say: "Were we in the Sanhedrin [during that period when it possessed capital jurisdiction], no man would ever have been killed." R. Simeon ben Gamaliel says: "They, too, would multiply spillers of blood in Israel."[18]

It is clear that R. Tarfon and R. Akiba could not have expected mere sentiment to make the application of capital punishment impossible. They needed a device that would legally bind the Sanhedrin to their point of view; as the Talmud explains, such a device was to be found in an intense and meticulous questioning of witnesses (e.g., "Did the murderer kill a man about to die anyhow?" "Perhaps the murderer's dagger pierced the body at the very spot of the mortal weakness?"), a questioning designed to find the witness wanting. Yet while their strategy is clear enough, the motive of R. Akiba and R. Tarfon is not discussed. Why this radical and total disclaimer of a recognized judicial procedure?

Three possibilities suggest themselves. First, the very device sketched above may embody the germ of their opposition. R. Akiba and R. Tarfon feared human weakness, the inability of man ever to know an event in its accurate facticity. No witness can ever testify with an absolute knowledge, as their examination was designed to show. Execution then becomes no more than a judicial gamble—and the dice are always loaded when a man's life is the stake. The Sanhedrin, they held, must never arrogantly assume a certainty it cannot truly possess.

Yet this approach, though reasonable, is not totally satisfactory. In the Talmud the device of close interrogation answers the question, "What would they have done (to prevent execution)?" It is not adduced to explain the source of R. Akiba's and R. Tarfon's opposition to capital punishment. Furthermore, and most crucially, R. Simeon ben Gamaliel's retort("They,too, would multiply spillers of blood in Israel")is a *non sequitur*. For once the possible innocence of the man in the dock is admitted, one cannot have his head merely to insure public safety.

A second approach would be that R. Akiba and R. Tarfon agreed that human observation of events could be accurate enough to establish the guilt of an individual but that a society that practiced capital punishment was bound to err, that this license would, by the very frailty of human judgment, be abused, leading to the execution of an innocent. Yet, once again, R. Gamaliel's reply is not to the point: can society purchase health at the price of innocent lives?

Perhaps, then, the opposition to capital punishment is rooted elsewhere; perhaps its source is not a fear of killing the innocent but a reluctance to kill the guilty. This reluctance to take the life of even a criminal could be translated into an effective legal restraint by the type of questioning outlined above—an interrogation on the unknowable. R. Gamaliel's retort is now very much to the point: "You would not kill the guilty," he says, "because of your disdain to take the life of man; but you will in reality cause many more deaths than the one you now seek to avoid."

It were well to emphasize at this point the fact that this approach to capital cases was not a "mere theoretical" one.[19] True, both R. Tarfon and R. Akiba lived at a time when the Sanhedrin did not sit on such cases; hence their teachings had no immediate application. Yet they also lived at a time of intense political and military activity designed to regain for the Jews full autonomy, including, of course, the re-establishment of the Sanhedrin. The precise role played by R. Akiba in this struggle may be a matter of debate; but the existence of this struggle is a fact against which all utterances of the time must be measured. Hence, the teaching of these Tannaim cannot be relegated to the limbo of pure theory. It were also well to emphasize that R. Akiba hardly sanctifies human life beyond all other values. Did he not deliver up his own life for the love of God and His Torah? Naturally, he retained his objectivity in the construction of the Halachic scheme: while many sages understood the "death" decreed for the non-*Kohen* who performed the Temple service (*Num.* 18.7) as "heavenly (*biydei shamayim*)," R. Akiba maintained that capital punishment was intended.[20] Indeed, Jewish law abolished capital punishment in fact not by denying its conceptual moral validity but rather by allowing it *only* this conceptual validity.

This teaching of R. Akiba would be an accurate reflection of the categories of the Hebrew language. For when a language does not verbally distinguish between authorized and unauthorized killing, it implies one possibility of its people's morality. The point in time at which this morality becomes explicit, the moment at which linguistic insight crystallizes into legal fact, is irrelevant. We must see R. Akiba, then, as the final expositor of a muted tradition. Significantly, R. Akiba is identified as using the term *rezichah* for execution (*Mekhilta Ki Tissah*, p. 304, 1:13). Other teachings of this Tanna and his school fit into this same pattern. Thus, "R. Akiba says: 'Whoever spills blood destroys the image (of God).' "[21] This is the metaphysical fact of the matter, a fact unchanged by the motives behind the slaying. R. Meir (a student of R. Akiba) points out that the sight of an executed criminal hanging from a tree (Deut. 21:22-3) provokes the thought that the King (God, as it were) himself is hung.[22]

IV

It has long been a truism that Jewish law is so weighted as to make execution a virtual impossibility. Again, such an attitude was not "merely theoretical": the young R. Yochanan ben Zakkai attempted the actual disqualification of murder-witnesses by questioning them concerning the stems of the figs growing on the tree underneath which the crime was committed (*Sanhedrin* 41 a). Such questioning (the Talmud [81 b] tells us) had as its sole end the possible evasion of the death penalty; it could not prove the innocence of the accused or free him. Similarly, Samuel regards the stringent requirements for proper *hatra'ah* (warning) of the murderer as relevant only to his execution but not to his imprisonment. These devices, then, were hurdles placed between the criminal and his execution.[23]

Yet R. Tarfon and R. Akiba go farther—if not in fact, then at least in formulation. Disdaining legal propriety, they bluntly do away with all pretense and announce their goal, a goal which legal ingenuity would then have to achieve. R. Jochanan had attempted the same result (see Rashi, 41 a, *s.v. ke-hakiroth*)[24] but had not, to our knowledge, publicly acknowledged his aim. (R. Akiba similarly "teaches" a teleological orientation in *Shabbat* 64b.)

As we have seen, R. Tarfon and R. Akiba met with opposition. R. Gamaliel was probably not alone in protesting this virtual abolition of the death penalty. His is merely the clearest voice. As we note some other expressions of opposition, we shall also see more fully the basis of the debate.

In *Midrash Tannaim* (p. 115) we find the following comment to *Deuteronomy* 19:13:

Do not pity him—this is an admonition not mercifully to spare the killer; we should not say, "The one has already been killed— of what use is the killing of the other?" Thus the execution will be neglected. Rather, he must be killed. Abba Hanon says in the name of R. Eliezer: "Wherever the Torah specifies an (apparently)[25] unjust punishment, it is written, *Do not pity*."

Here we find R. Eliezer (an older contemporary of R. Tarfon) emphasizing the duty to execute; the passage as a whole rebukes those who would eliminate the death penalty as useless.

The corresponding comment in the *Sifre* (*Deut.* 18:7) is, despite its terseness, most instructive:

> Perhaps you will say, "Since the one has been killed, why should we incur the guilt of spilling the other's blood (*la-hov be-damo*)?"[26] Therefore the Torah says, *Do not pity him.*

Both passages deal with a man whose guilt is established beyond doubt. Nevertheless, there are those who protest his execution. In the *Midrash Tannaim* the uselessness of such execution is cited; the objecting voice in the *Sifre* would take the argument one step further— if such execution is useless, it is *eo ipso* criminal, a "guilty spilling of blood." This is not merely circumstantial opposition to the death penalty; it cuts at the very root of the institution.[27] The guilt of the court, it contends, would be similar to that of the murderer: both would have spilled blood.

Yet the *Sifre* and *Midrash Tannaim* reject the suggestion that the death penalty is useless and immoral. Rather, it is both useful and moral; it functions as a deterrent (as R. Gamaliel points out), and its morality is established by the fact that it is an ordinance of the Torah. To paraphrase, "The Judge of all the world has done justly"; is man to be more just than his Lord? In a similar vein, the Talmud tells that God rebukes him who mourns overmuch: "Do you love the departed more than I" (*Mo'ed Katan* 27b)? The correct response to such situations is not to be forged in human freedom. Man must abide not only by the pattern devised by God; he must also accept the evaluation and judgment implied by the set pattern.

This response is a natural one in a religious community; one expects to find it hurled as a general accusation at all departures from the popularly accepted norm. Furthermore, the accusation that man is arrogantly assuming Divine prerogative can, by slurring over man's dynamic responsibility of interpreting and implementing the Divine imperative, simplify the issue to a question of antinomianism.

One senses in the following Aggadah, too, an admonition to man to forego all reliance upon his own erratic judgment, especially in areas where he claims to be motivated by his moral or ethical sensibility:

> *Be not righteous overmuch* (*Eccles.* 7:16)—do not be more righteous than your Creator. This refers to Saul . . . who debated with his Creator and said, "God said, 'Go and smite Amalek.' If the men are guilty, the women and children are yet innocent; the oxen and donkeys are innocent too." A voice answered from heaven, "Be not more righteous than your Creator." . . .
>
> Resh Lakish said: "Whoever pities where he should be cruel will ultimately be cruel where he should pity. Whence do we learn that Saul was cruel instead of merciful? As it is stated: *And Nob, the city of the priests, smote he with the sword, both men and women, children and sucklings, and oxen and asses and sheep, with the edge of the sword* (1 *Sam.* 22:19). Is Nob less than the seed of Amalek?"[28]

The problem with which the Aggadah grapples is clearly a crucial one—can man's moral insight, an insight implanted by God and further educated by Him, ever become self-reliant? Can man ever be master in his own house? In fact, any slackening of the rigor of the law is censured; again we hear that the universal terminus of such a course is moral bankruptcy. However generous the motive, the perversion of justice is evil, its motivation misguided. The Rabbis feared that true love of humanity could only be undermined by indiscriminate recourse to "mercy," which, as R. Gamaliel pointed out, would deny to an innocent society the concern shown the criminal.

But thus stated, the problem is a simplistic, indeed meaningless, contrast in black and white—just as the situation selected by the Aggadist offers only the two opposed options of adherence to the command of God or total revolt against it. The Aggadah illustrates an instance where the answer had to be "No," for an absolutely unconditioned ethos is imposible. And so the Aggadist points out the incontrovertible: man never advances far beyond brutality; he is never educated out of cruelty. The tower, says Pascal, rises on an abyss.

Rabbi Jose b. Bon said: "They do not well who turn God's *middoth* (attributes) into mercy, and also those who translate: 'My people Israel, just as I am merciful in heaven, so be you merciful on earth—*be it cow or ewe, you shall not kill it and its young both in one day (Lev. 22:28).*' "[29] The ban against killing both mother and young on the same day was apparently a favorite text of those who would sweep away law and enshrine mercy. R. Jose was contending with a spiritual temper that has always had its adherents and which read Leviticus 22:28 as a charge and a program. That the text was so used we see from the following:

> Bar Kappara said: "Doeg is called the Edomite because he forbade Saul to shed the blood (*dam*) of Agag. For Doeg said: 'It is written in the Torah, *Ye shall not kill it and its young both on the same day*; yet you are about to kill young and old, children and women in one day.' "[30]

Doeg (and those he represents) argues that the manifestation of God's mercies in certain rules should become the standard of all conduct. The Rabbis reject this as a superficial understanding of mercy.

V

Yet such statements always remained only one pole of the tension we have been examining; the act of mercy towards those held undeserving of it was practised and praised, for it was motivated by *imitatio Dei.* Thus we read[31] of R. Joshua b. Levi:

> In the neighborhood of R. Joshua b. Levi there lived a Sadducee (*min*) who used to trouble him greatly with (his interpretations of) texts. One day the Rabbi . . . thought . . . "I shall curse him." When the moment (propitious for cursing) arrived, R. Joshua was dozing. (On awakening) he said: "I see from this that my intention was improper. For it is written, *And His mercies are over all His works,* and it is further written, *Neither is it good for the righteous to punish.*"

A Scripture-quoting heretic may not be a menace of the first rank. Yet R. Joshua's motive for abandoning the matter remains of interest. He does not withdraw because of the insignificance of the episode, nor because the heretic did not objectively deserve his curse. Rather, he takes his sleep as a sign that justice is to be subdued by mercy. For does not

God extend His mercy even where He should visit justice upon the world? The righteous, then, must also stay their hand.

The Aggadah would praise even those reluctant to exact their due from the murderer: "The priests forgave (Saul, for his role in the slaughter at Nob), but the Gibeonites did not forgive him, and therefore God rejected them."[32] We have, then, come full circle: for some, the murder of the priests of Nob limns the irresponsibility and bankruptcy of Saul's earlier desire to save the Amalekite innocents, while for others it proves the opportunity for a merciful act of forgiveness to the guilty. We see, thus, that both legal and Aggadic discussions give witness to two tendencies, one that regards the enforcing of retribution as most just and hence most merciful, and another, which finds mercy too divinely dynamic a quality to be forever defined and controlled by the demand for retribution.

Both approaches, curiously enough, contend in the Midrashic interpretation of *Deuteronomy* 13:18: *And there shall cleave nought of the devoted thing to thy hand, that the Lord may turn from the fierceness of His anger, and show thee mercy, and have compassion upon thee, and multiply thee, as He hath sworn unto thy father*:

> *Show thee* (literally, "give" Thee): to your people is the quality of mercifulness given, and not to others, as we, read, *And the Gibeonites were not of the children of Israel.*

> *Have compassion upon thee*: the punishing of the wicked is an act of mercy to the world.[33]

AN ESSAY ON POSSESSION IN JEWISH LAW
Boaz Cohen

The general word for property is נכסים . The Tannaim distinguished as we are accustomed to do in modern legal systems, between real and personal property. The former was designated by the circumlocution נכסים שיש להם אחריות while the latter was denoted by the phrase נכסים שאין להם אחריות.[1] Again they differentiated between goods which had an owner נכסים המיוחדים (T. B. K. 1.1) and ownerless property נכסי הפקר.[2] It is important to recall that the term הפקר embraces both res nullius, such as wild animals in the state of freedom, actually belonging to no one, and res derelictae, i. e. property which was abandoned with the intention of relinquishing ownership.

Possession is disengaged from ownership by the use of divergent terms. Thus an ancient halakah reads רשות ההדיוט בחזקה [3] i. e., a private individual acquires ownership over property he purchases by taking possession of it. The word designating ownership is רשות akin to the late Biblical רשיון . The primitive significance of the Aramaic word רשי , is to have power.[4] In Arabic רסא means to be firm. In Aramaic the term אחסין which is employed in the sense of possession is derived from חסן meaning strong. In Latin "dominus" designates ownership, while in Russian "wladets," to possess, can be traced to "vlast," signifying power. Besides a number of passages in Tannaitic sources where רשות[5] is used to connote ownership,[6] there are others where רשות signifies possession. Thus in T. Maaser Sheni 1.5, we read אין מחללין על המעות שאינן ברשותו . One may not exchange produce of Maaser Sheni with money which is not in one's possession. This meaning might have insinuated itself into the word because originally the criterion for distinguishing possession from ownership was not clearly established. Thus Joseph Duquesne[7] has pointed out that a similar confusion in terminology is found among the Roman lawyers. Professor Ginzberg suggested to me that we might have before us two words רְשׁוּ and רְשׁוּת. In Assyrian rašu signifies to seize, to take, to possess, and it may well be that the Hebrew רשות meaning possession, is derived from the same root as the cognate word in Assyrian.

However the technical term for possession in Tannaitic jurisprudence is חזקה. Thus in the ancient Mishnah previously cited רשות ההדיוט בחזקה,[8] we are informed that chattels are acquired by the purchaser when he takes possession of them. In later Tannaitic parlance the expressions משיכה (traditio), מסירה and הגבהה are commonly employed. In the Digest[9] too, we read that dominiumque rerum ex naturale possessione coepisse, i. e. ownership began with actual possession. Not only moveable objects but real estate and slaves were acquired by חזקה.[10] In regard to finding a lost object, the law states that if one noticed an object upon the road, and fell upon it, while another came and took hold of it, the latter acquired it זה שהחזיק בה זכה בה.[11] Anyone who appropriated the estate of a proselyte after his death, which was regarded as a res nullius, became its owner.[12] If an executor obligated himself to take charge of the estate of orphans he must fulfil his fiduciary relations once he has taken possession of their property. אפיטרופסין .... משהחזיקו לנכסי יתומין אין יכולין לחזור בהן.[13] Finally, חזקה is used to denote usucapion, i. e. uninterrupted possession of land for three years upon which one has a valid claim.[14] En passant we wish to call attention to certain characteristic peculiarities in the use of the juridical terms זכה and קנה. As a general rule it may be stated that קנה[15] is used to denote purchase, and is employed also in connection with marriage which is formally an act of purchase.[16] Hence we read in the Mishnah I:1, a woman is acquired in three ways (האשה נקנית).[17] Similarly we find in Ned. X:6 מה אם אשה שקנה הוא לעצמו.[18]

When property is acquired in any other way, the term זכה is generally employed, e. g. by barter, when commodities are given and taken without the intervention of money. We read in M. Kid. I:6, if one exchanges an object for another, as soon as one party has taken possession of the one object (זכה) the other party is obliged to give him the other in exchange.[19] It is used also in reference to finding a lost object,[20] dividing an inheritance,[21] seizing a res derelicta,[22] or receiving a gift,[23] and in cases of doubtful purchases.[24] There are, of course some exceptions, thus a Tannaitic statement reads: ... האומר נתתי שדה פלוני לפלוני ר'מאיר אומר קנה.[25] Maimonides in the chapter זכייה ומתנה of his code employs זכה merely to denote the acquisition of derelict property. So much for terminology.

Although the Tannaim were not given to formulating legal principles, the latter are undoubtedly presupposed in their juristic writings. Thus they do not define the constituent elements of possession. Yet we may infer what their doctrine was, from their statutes concerning property which was abandoned, lost, or taken by superior force. Possession involved the physical control over an object, whereas ownership continues even after the loss of possession, for it is the legal right to possess an object which is not forfeited as long as the owner means to keep it as his own or as the Roman jurists put it, he has the animus rem sibi habendi.[26] Consequently when one purposely abandons his property with the intention of losing ownership, it becomes a res derelicta. Loss of ownership of an object is brought about by being deprived of possession as well as by a cessation of the will to hold it as one's own. Similarly, the Digest[27] informs us. "Just as no possession can be acquired except by a physical and mental act, so none is lost unless where both acts are reversed."

In contradistinction to the res derelicta which becomes the property of the first one who seizes it, there are instances where one is constrained to renounce one's possessions and no one is permitted to claim them. According to Scripture, no leaven may be seen or found in the house of an Israelite during the Passover festival. The rabbis accordingly ordained on the basis of Deut. 16.4 that it is mandatory on the eve of the festival to renounce ownership of the leaven in one's possession[28] (בטל מלבך).

According to Jewish law, it is not permitted to carry on the Sabbath from the house to a courtyard without making an Erub. If several brothers live in different houses that open into one courtyard, each is required to make an Erub. If one had forgotten to do so, he may renounce by means of a legal fiction his right to the premises (מבטל רשותו) and will thus enjoy the same privileges as the others.[29]

The views of the Tannaim concerning possession are also reflected in their discussions of the law touching objects from which one may not derive any benefit (אסורי הנאה). Thus if a man affiances a woman with any such objects his action has no effect.[30] Should a person steal such objects he would not be obliged to make restitution.[31] If a Jew notices an idolatrous object on the ground and wishes to acquire it, he should request a Gentile to deface it somewhat, and then he may take possession of it.[32] The rabbis held that the right of property carried with it the privilege of disposing of it; only when such right was entirely extinguished was true ownership lost. Hence they considered the action of a non-priest who betrothed a woman with Terumah, as valid, inasmuch as he had the right to dispose of it, although he could not eat it.[33]

In the case where property is lost or stolen, the law is more complicated for, in this instance, one parts with the object involuntarily. The law concerning lost objects may be briefly summarized as follows: First, if the property that was lost had no marks of identification and the owner was unknown, then the finder acquired title to it, because it is assumed that the original owner had abandoned it מפני שהבעלים מתיאשין מהן [34] or, as it is put in another source, lost property is to be returned only when it has a claimant יש לו תובעין.[35] Secondly, if one loses his property through an act of God and fails to make an effort to recover it, one may assume that he has relinquished the property. Thus we read,[36] if a river overflowed its banks and carried away one's trees, stones, or beams into the field of a neighbor, it belongs to the latter if the original owner abandoned it; on the other hand, if he made attempts to rescue his property, or was not present at the time of the accident, the original owner retains title.

Thirdly, we find the law of salvage, which in modern systems plays an important role in maritime law. It has reference to property which was lost through an act of God or force majeure, and an outsider steps in to save it. The rabbis deal with five such instances; namely: where one rescues an object from a river, invading troops, robbers, wild animals, or a conflagration. In case of the first three, if it is known that the original owner abandoned it, then it belongs to the salvager, in the last two instances, it is generally supposed that the original owner had abandoned it, and title forthwith passes to the rescuer.[37] A similar view is preserved in the Digest where we read "A thing rescued from the sea does not become the property of the rescuer until the owner has begun to regard it as abandoned."[38]

One of the peculiarities of Tannaitic jurisprudence which vexed sorely the minds of the Amoraim was the law of possession as applied to larceny and robbery. They noticed both the contradictory rules on the subject in the Mishnah and Baraitot, and perceived the anomaly of giving title to a thief for stolen goods, or as they put it דבאיסורא

אתאי לידיה [39]. The difficulties inherent in the law can only be resolved if we realize that the legislation on this point was modified during the Mishnaic period, due to the political and social conditions of the time. There can be no doubt that the older halakah would not confer ownership of a stolen thing upon a thief. As Jenks says "No system of law will recognize a title acquired by theft, for theft is a breach of the law, and for the law to recognize an interest acquired by defying its clearest mandates, would be to stultify itself plainly."[40] This attitude is certainly reflected in the ancient halakah which disallowed the offering of a stolen sacrifice קרבנו ולא הגזול.[41] Similarly in regard to the celebration of the Feast of Tabernacles, the Mishnah proscribes the use of a stolen lulab as well as the other three species of plants,[42] while according to R. Eliezer it is also forbidden to sit in a stolen Sukkah.[43] Furthermore, if one robbed land he may not bring first fruits from it, for Scripture says ראשית בכורי אדמתך.[44] While these instances are from the domain of the ritual, there can be no doubt that the same rule applied to civil cases.

This notion of the inviolability of property was subjected to a rude shock after the Roman subjugation of Palestine in 70 C.E. Surely many took advantage of the confusion of the times and the prevailing chaos, to seize property of others with the connivance of the Roman government. This species of robber was termed אנס . The rabbis for the sake of law and order, and in the interest of the public good, were compelled to recognize de facto possession as true ownership.

Consequently we read in Mishnah Kilaim VII:6 מאימתי הוא נקרא (של) אנס משישקע.[45] When does the robber acquire title to the field, when the name of the original owner is no longer associated with it. If a man robbed a field, and planted it, the fruits are subject to the Law of Orlah.[46] If he set aside Terumah, or Maaser, or dedicated stolen objects to the sanctuary, his action is valid.[47] If he stole skins and intended to use them, they became susceptible to Levitical impurity.[48]

The view presupposed in the cases just cited, is that the thief acquires title to objects after it is known that the goods were abandoned, or in some instances, it is merely presumed that they were relinquished. We find however, that unlawful possession is sometimes transformed into ownership in other legal systems. "Why the law should ascribe possession to wrong-doers," says Pollock, "may be difficult to explain completely. It is one thing to recognize the fact that physical control of things of value is often wrongfully acquired, another thing to attach definite legal incidents, nay right which ultimately may ripen into indisputable ownership, to such facts when entertained."[49]

RELIGIOUS IDEAS

It has been said that Judaism is a religion without dogmas, and it is true that belief in dogmas has never been the *test* of the adherent in the way it was in other religions. "Good deeds" whether ethical or ritual have been not only the road to Divine favor, but the assurance of obtaining it. "Eat thy bread with joy, and drink thy wine with a merry heart; for God hath already accepted thy works." It is of course on this crucial point that Judaism parts company with Christianity, which may see good deeds as a *symptom* of grace but not a means to attaining it.

Despite the stress on works, Judaism has been a fruitful supplier of religious and ethical ideas. Some of the notions of Talmudic Judaism may seem strange to us, e.g. the idea that the Patriarchs created a fund of Divine goodwill on which their ancestors can draw in time of need, or that the righteous may be punished in this world in order to expiate any minor sin, and so leave him open to a perfect reward in a future existence. Yet many have had a lasting impact on Western civilization, and only some of them can be alluded to here.

First we must mention the notion of the "special relationship between God and Israel." The God of the Talmud is far from being a tribal god; he is the universal creator of all men and all things. Yet he has elected Israel, and placed upon Israel special responsibilities and privileges symbolic of the mutual and eternal love between them. This idea undoubtedly played a part in the survival of the Jews in highly adverse circumstances; the Israelite though chastened never felt unloved. None could remove the inner strength that came of this conviction.

Next comes the notion of revelation. God's will has been made known once for all in a theophany, witnessed by multitudes and of unquestionable veracity. All the mechanisms and results of Rabbinic homiletic and legal activity derive their authority and peculiar flavor from this eruption of the Divine into history. And history itself is not cyclic, but progressive, albeit in unequal leaps; it began at one point and is proceeding to another, the Messianic age, when all the horrors of the world will be laid to rest and all puzzles will be solved. This process is inexorable, yet it may be speeded or impeded by man's individual actions. These doctrines gave a purposefulness to life as seen through Talmudic eyes which many a modern mind may envy.

Germane to all this is the doctrine of free will. Probably no religion has ever held so tenaciously to this notion as has Judaism, undeterred by the difficulties of reconciling this belief with the belief in an omnipotent and omniscient God. The rabbis, many of whom lived in the home of astrology, Babylonia, had a suspicion that planetary influences might have their effects on the gentiles, but Abraham, in becoming an uncompromising monotheist had put those influences to an end for himself and his descendants. A man could be what he chose to be, morally, spiritually, perhaps even academically. The modern psychologist or sociologist may have good reason to differ with this; they too however would probably agree with the notion of the importance that such a doctrine must have on the individual, even if only as part of the environment which determines his behavior. The Talmudist lived in the glow of freely choosing to follow the behests of a loving, living God and he achieved independence and security at once.

Many texts illustrative of the notions outlined above will be found in C. G. Montefiore and H. Loewe's *Rabbinic Anthology* (republished in New York, 1960); part of the function of this reader is to enable the student to read such materials without being puzzled or put off by the garb in which they are clad. The ethical ideals of the Talmud and Midrash on such areas as goodness, justice, honesty, charity and hospitality are also well illustrated by selections to be found there; and these ideals are further illuminated by the essays which follow in this section.

THE RELIGIOUS IDEAS OF TALMUDIC JUDAISM

Julius Guttmann

Jewish Hellenism was a transitory phenomenon in the development of Judaism. The dominant form of Jewish religion since the last centuries of antiquity—and the one that served as the foundation for the development of Judaism in the Middle Ages and modern times—was Talmudic Judaism, which developed in Palestine and Babylonia. Until the end of the first century of the Common Era, the most diverse religious tendencies flourished in Palestine, and many of the apocryphal books show the extent to which the Jews of Palestine were influenced by the religious syncretism of late antiquity. However, after the destruction of the Second Temple by Titus (70 C.E.), all the religious currents that had competed with Pharisaic Talmudic Judaism quickly disappeared, and the latter achieved a unified form. The significance of the Talmud for coming generations resides mainly in religious law, which does not concern us here. The ritual, ceremonial, and legal provisions of the Talmud gave Jewish religious life its fixed and distinct form, which maintained itself until the end of the eighteenth century. The basic religious ideas of Judaism, on the other hand, were never given a similarly definitive form by the Talmud. The Talmud never attempts to formulate religious truths in fixed dogmatic expressions. The borderline between those binding doctrine and individual opinion is extremely fluid, and there is far greater variety between different generations and individuals than in the realm of religious law. The most diverse religious ideas were current between the last centuries B.C.E., when the development of the Talmud began to take place, and its final redaction at the end of the fifth century. Many of the foreign doctrines which had penetrated into Judaism during the syncretistic period reappeared in Talmudic literature. Many of them, however, like those fantastic eschatological descriptions which we have already seen in the apocryphal literature, should be considered simply as the free play of imaginative fancy or the product of popular faith, rather than as doctrine in the precise sense. It is possible, after all, to detect a common and permanent pattern of basic ideas which proved of the greatest importance for subsequent developments.

The faith of Talmudic Judaism rests completely on biblical foundations. Central to it are the simple and sublime ideas of the Bible concerning a transcendent God, the Torah as the embodiment of his moral demands, the moral nature of the relationship between God and man, the wisdom and justice of divine providence, the election of Israel, and the promise of the coming kingdom of God. No theoretical reflection diminishes the living reality of God. Even speculations concerning hypostases and other mediating agencies could not affect His immediate presence to the world or remove Him to an unapproachable distance. God acts as much in the present as he did in the past. It is true that prophecy and the miraculous events of biblical times belong to the past, and that the salvation announced by the prophets belongs to the future —the "end of days." This distinction between the present, on the one hand, and the mighty revelations of God in the past and future, on the other, is a necessary corollary of the historical character of the Jewish concept of revelation, and the expectation of a future (historical) salvation. Similar causes operated in Christianity and in Islam and led to similar distinctions between the present and the time of revelation— that is, the past. But even if the present was devoid of historic revelation, men still felt the immediate presence of God in their lives. Every individual Jew knew himself under the same divine providence which had governed the lives of his ancestors, and through some chosen pious persons, even miracles would be wrought—though these could not, of course, be compared to those wrought by the prophets.[1] In order to express the consciousness of the presence of God, the religious imagination did not stop even before the most daring anthropomorphisms. In order to emphasize the value of the study of Torah, the Talmudic rabbis describe God himself as studying the Torah. The faith that the sufferings of Israel could not destroy the intimate bond between God and his people was expressed by saying that God not only lamented over the sorrows that he had brought upon Israel, but actually shared their exile.[2]

But the Talmudists clearly recognized the nature of the anthropomorphisms of their own religious fantasy, as well as those of the Bible. They pointed out how God revealed himself according to the varying historical situations, and how the prophetic utterances were influenced by the individual personality of each prophet; in fact, they even suggested that every Jew standing at Sinai saw God in a slightly different fashion.[3] These notions were never systematically developed; no attempts were made to distinguish between anthropomorphic forms of expression and the actual content of the idea of God, but their intention is quite clear. The idea of the personal and moral nature of God remains beyond all criticism, and provides the basic common core of the different concrete images.

The passionate violence of the religious ethos of the prophets had given place, in Talmudic times, to a quieter, more restrained, and in a way even sober piety, bound to history and tradition. However, the activist character of Jewish religion was preserved. Religious life was still centered on the divine "commands," in which God addressed himself to the human will, and showed the way of communion between man and God. Human destiny is conceived in different ways. Piety is not so much the mere observance of the divine commandments as the imitation of a divine model. The biblical commandment to be holy even as the Lord God is holy, and the injunction to walk in the ways of God, are interpreted as demands to imitate the divine qualities of love and mercy.[4] Love of God and faithful trust in Him are considered the foundation of the right observance of the commandments. The spirit of rabbinic religion is thus elevated above mere submission or obedience of the will. Its religious activity is rooted in the inner certainty of community with God, yet its piety remains one of precept and duty. Consequently, much stress is laid on moral freedom: man's actions are his own, even in relation to the divine omnipotence. The Torah is the embodiment of the divine will, and the observance of its commandments is the task given to Israel by God. The universality of the divine commandment is established by the notion of an original, pre-Israelite revelation, addressed to all nations and containing the foundations of morals.[5]

However, the perfect divine revelation is the Torah given to Israel. As a divinely revealed law, all its parts—ritual as well as moral—are of equal validity, and equally constitute the religious duty of Israel. The idea of equal and unassailable validity—from a formal point of view—of all parts of the Torah follows as a logical consequence from the biblical notion of a divine legislation; at the same time the rabbis—

from the material point of view—distinguished between central and marginal laws, between means and ends. The Talmud frequently interprets ceremonial and cultic items of the biblical legislation as means toward the ultimate moral ends of the divine law, subordinating the former to the latter in spite of their common divine origin.[6] Psychologically of course, it is only to be expected that sometimes one, and sometimes the other of these two facets comes to the fore; at times the observance of the commandments is permeated by ethical attitudes; at other times, the distinction between ethics and ritual becomes blurred.

The messianic promises of the prophets were the mainstay of the Jewish community. We need not concern ourselves here with the transformation of the relatively simple expectations of the prophets into the more complicated notions of the later eschatologies developing in the last centuries of the pre-Christian era, or with the differences between the more national and the more universalistic versions of the messianic ideal, or with the changing ideas about the imminence or distance of the messianic coming. All these, though of considerable consequence for later times, are largely irrelevant to our present theme. Throughout all these variations on the messianic theme, the historical character of the prophetic hope for the future is preserved intact. An expectation of an entirely different sort is found in the ideas of the resurrection of the dead and the immortality of the soul. In a way, the resurrection of the dead still links up with the expectations of an historical fulfillment. It will take place at the end of time, and the resurrected will take part in the miraculous events of that age. The individual hope for an eternal life was thus combined with the idea that past generations too, would share in the promise of the kingdom of God. The personal longing for eternal life is satisfied within the framework of collective historical eschatology.

These two elements are completely separated by the belief in the immortality of the soul. Frequently, the idea of immortality is overshadowed by that of resurrection. The Talmud, like the apocryphal literature, knows of a kind of intermediate state of the soul between death and resurrection; true retribution will be dispensed only after the resurrection of the body.[7] But along with it, we also find the faith in a retribution coming immediately after death, and in a life of blessedness for the soul in the beyond.[8] According to the latter view, the individual hope for the future has no connection whatsoever with history. "The world to come," the place of reward and punishment beyond, is distinct from the future "kingdom of God" even in its most eschatological form. "The world to come" does not succeed "this world" in time, but exists from eternity as a reality outside and above time, to which the soul ascends. This view faces a double opposition—on the one hand between the present reality of history and the future kingdom of God, and on the other, between life on earth and life beyond. The two orientations do not necessarily exclude each other. The original Jewish eschatology with its historical and collective hopes did not lose its power or intensity because of the belief in individual immortality, and the latter, as we have seen, could combine with the idea of the resurrection of the dead. Nevertheless religious interpretation of the world had taken a new and decisive turn which provided starting points for the most diverse developments of Jewish thought in latter periods.

The belief in another world, above and beyond time, led to a new evaluation of the present world. It was not enough that this world should find its perfection and fulfillment in a world to come, and that the wrongs of this earthly life should be made good there, but the ultimate end of man was shifted to the world to come. Our life in this world came to be conceived as a mere preparation, whether in terms of the resurrection of the dead or of the immortality of the soul. According to a well-known Talmudic saying, this world is like a vestibule in which man should prepare himself for entering the banquet hall of the world to come.[9] The blessedness of the world to come is understood as consisting of the pious enjoying the radiance of the presence of God.[10]

Nevertheless, this rabbinic view is very different from the dualistic contempt for the world of the senses exhibited, for example, by Philo, under Platonic influence. The Talmud emphatically repeats the biblical affirmation of this world and interprets the words of Genesis, "and God saw everything that He had made and behold it was very good," as referring to *both* worlds.[11] The good things of this world, including sensual pleasures, may be enjoyed simply and naturally; only in rare instances do we find any ascetic tendencies. Even more important is the fact that asceticism plays no role in the understanding of ethics. Although the moral act was understood as a preparation for the future world, it lacked the negative connotation of separation from the world of the senses. Its meaning was rather wholly positive: to serve God in this world, to fulfill His will, and to build a social order in accordance with his will. The religious value of moral action is maintained even in the face of eschatological communion with God, since fulfilling the will of God in this world is no less communion with God than the state of blessedness in the hereafter. The same Talmudic teacher who described this world as only a vestibule to the coming world, also said that although one hour of blessedness in the world to come was worth more than all the life of this world, yet one hour of repentance and good deeds in this world was worth more than all of the life of the world to come.

What has been said regarding the rabbinic view of the world applies as well to the idea of man. The Bible had ascribed a divine origin to the human spirit, but now we find an explicit dualism. The body and the soul are seen in sharp contrast. Because of his soul, which is destined for eternal life, man belongs to the superior world of the spirit; in his body, he belongs to the earth. Thanks to his soul, he resembles the angels; thanks to his body, a beast. Following the Stoics and Philo, the relationship of the soul to the body is compared to that of God to the world.[12] The idea of the pre-existence of the soul is also known to the Talmud.[13] Man's higher powers, such as his reason and moral consciousness, are attributed to the soul; his lower passions are assigned to the body. The corollary of man's intermediate position between the higher and lower worlds is that by observing the divine commandments, he can rise to the rank of the angels, but by transgressing them he descends to the level of the beasts.[14]

But this dualism is far from identifying evil with man's sensual nature. The body is not the ground of evil, and consequently man's moral task does not consist in his separation from the body. The warfare between good and evil is fought out *within* man's soul; it is there that good and evil impulses face each other.[15] They represent two directions of the human will, and man must choose between them. As the source of temptation, sensuality occasionally is identified with the "evil impulse," but in itself it is ethically indifferent and has its legitimate sphere of existence. In spite of the Talmudic praise of the virtue of frugality as practiced by the pious, sensuality—provided it is kept under control—is considered unobjectionable, and the body is regarded as an essential part of man's God-given nature. Even the evil impulse is a necessary part of human nature, and the Talmud voices the remarkable demand to love God with both of our impulses—the good and the evil.[16] Here again the end of ethics is seen not as separation from the world of the senses, but rather serving God within that world, with all available human powers. The body and the senses should be subordinate and subservient to the soul; they are not, of themselves, enemies of its heavenly destiny. Nonetheless, the whole complex of ideas described so far—the belief in a spiritual world above the world of the senses, the eternal destiny of the soul, and the dualistic conception of man, could easily be turned in the direction of an ascetic contemplative religion; it did, in fact, provide the opening through which the Neoplatonic type of spirituality entered Judaism in the Middle Ages.

Along with these speculative developments, there emerged another, more formal, though no less significant phenomenon: the growth of theoretical reflection on the contents of religion. Inquiry into fundamental religious questions is no longer an expression of the religious consciousness itself, seeking an answer to its doubt and anxieties (as in the later prophets, or in the Book of Job), but acquires an independent value. The basic religious ideas of the Bible, as well as the commandments of the Law, become objects of theoretical reflection. Particularly in regard to ethical questions, a high degree of abstraction was reached. Of particular interest is the attempt to reduce the entire content of the biblical commandments to one principle. The Talmud, like the gospels, seeks to determine the "major principle" of the Torah. One Talmudic master finds it in the commandment, "But thou shalt love thy neighbor as thyself" (Leviticus 19:18); another finds it in the sentence, "This is the book of the generations of Adam. In the day that God created man, in the likeness of God made He him" (Genesis 5:1). Similarly, a well-known legend has Hillel, the greatest of the Talmudic sages, declare that the rule, "That which is hateful unto thee, do not do unto thy neighbor," was the "entire Torah," and everything else was only a commentary on it.[17] By declaring love of one's neighbor to be the supreme ethical virtue, the Talmud does not make any material addition to the teaching of the Torah; the novelty lies in the theoretical formulations which describe the commandment of love as the greatest and most inclusive commandment of the Torah, or assert the whole Law to be merely a commentary on this superior ethical rule, to which both ethical and ritual laws are thus made subordinate. Elsewhere a comment on Leviticus 18:4, "Ye shall do my judgments and keep mine ordinances," emphasizes the difference between ethical and ritual commandments. These "judgments," which include the ethical commandments of the Torah, are defined as those laws that "ought to have been written" even if Scripture had not stated them.

The incomprehensibility of the ritual commandments is expressed in the saying that they were open to the objections of the "evil impulse and the nations of the world."[18] The idea of the intrinsic self-evidence of the ethical commandments which God gave to man is essentially a biblical heritage; it is merely the theoretical formulation that is new. The self-evidence of the moral law, implied by the Bible, is emphasized in obvious imitation of the Greek notion of an "unwritten law" in the pointed formulation that moral laws are laws that "ought to have been written down." True, according to the Talmud, the biblical laws which lack this intrinsic evidence possess the same unconditioned validity as the self-evident "judgments of the Lord." The Talmudic doctrine that the whole biblical law, by virtue of its divine origin, is equally and unconditionally authoritative—although material distinctions can be drawn between ethical and ceremonial precepts—appears here in its utmost clarity.

The doctrine of retribution is strongly emphasized and elaborated in considerable detail; yet the Talmud demands the disinterested observance of the divine commandments. It is not demand in itself, but the theoretical precision with which it is formulated, that is of immediate relevance to our theme. In the saying to which we have already referred—"Better is one hour of repentance and good deeds in this world than the entire life of the world to come, and better is one hour of blessedness in the world to come than all of the life of this world"—the religious pathos employs conceptual language. Elsewhere the same demand is stated in sober theoretical language.

In connection with the commandment to love God, the Talmud discusses the difference between those who serve God out of love, and those who serve him out of fear. The question is raised in the form of a casuistical problem, whether an observance of the Law because of a desire of reward or fear of retribution has any value at all. The decision is that observance of the Law, even for ulterior motives, was not devoid of value, for through it men could rise to a disinterested observance.[19] To this ideal of the observance of the commandments is added the study of the Law. The latter was not only a divine commandment in itself but also gave full scope to the desire for education. Discussing the primacy of "theory" (learning), over "practice" (the observance of the commandments), the Talmud solves the dilemma on one occasion by declaring that the study of the Law was equivalent to the observance of all the commandments, and on another by concluding that not theory but deeds were what mattered. Elsewhere a kind of compromise is reached: the dilemma is decided in favor of study, but the reason given is that "study leads to practice."[20]

Some of these ethical questions also led to theological discussions of dogmatic problems. Belief in the freedom of the human will, which in the Bible is an immediate religious certainty, becomes a doctrinal proposition in the Talmud. Talmudic predilection for pointed formulations produces the paradox: "Everything is in the hands of Heaven, with the exception of the fear of Heaven."[21] The difficulty of reconciling man's freedom with God's omniscience was fully realized, but was not resolved. Instead, the rabbis held fast to both horns of the dilemma: "Everything is foreseen, yet permission is given; the world is judged with mercy, yet the verdict is according to one's deeds."[22] The second half of this sentence refers to a question which greatly preoccupied the Talmudic sages. Once we realize that even the righteous are not free of sin, and that there is no wicked man who has not done some good, what is the line of division between the righteous and the wicked? The answer, though somewhat primitive, states that man is to be considered good or evil according to the preponderance of his good or evil deeds.[23] The biblical question "Why do the righteous suffer and the evil men prosper?" is treated in many and varied ways, and though faith in a future life dulled the point of this question to some extent, it did not solve it in principle. The meaning of human suffering remained a riddle. The Talmud stresses the purgative quality of suffering, and in some of its reflections on this subject it touches the most profound reaches of the religious consciousness.[24] But in addition to such levels of insight we also find a mechanical explanation: the sufferings of the righteous in this world are punishment for those sins they have committed, and the prosperity of the wicked represents a reward for the good deeds that they have done; ultimate retribution for both is left to the world to come.[25]

The rabbinic manner of thinking is seen in the form in which it is expressed. The terse and pithy formulations we have cited suggest its capacity for conceptual thinking. This appears at its best in those sentences and maxims in which the Talmudic masters enunciate with extraordinary concision fundamental religious and ethical doctrines. The art of coining such maxims was apparently cultivated in the schools of the Talmudic sages. One tractate of the Mishna—known as the Sayings of the Fathers—consists of a collection of sentences by some of the greatest Talmudic masters (some of which have already been quoted). Comparing these maxims with the proverbs or sayings in the biblical wisdom literature, one is immediately struck by the vast difference between them in regard to their subject matter, and perhaps even more, to their form of thought.

The Talmudic epigram is built on the pointed abstraction; its charm resides in its striking felicity and terseness of form. The epigram just quoted, concerning the relationship between divine providence and human freedom, may be taken as a complete theology in one sentence; in its power of compression it is not alone among rabbinic sayings. Even where the specific form of the epigram is not intended, rabbinic thought almost instinctively expresses itself in this way. The saying that certain precepts would have to be written down if they had not *already* been written down in the Torah, and the statement that everything is in the hand of God except the fear of God, are not less pungent than the maxims proper. A more precise formal analysis, which until now has never been attempted, would probably reveal, in addition to the characteristics described above, a whole series of typical forms of thought recurring again and again in rabbinic discussion of religious fundamentals.

These hints must suffice for our present purpose. They also enable us to recognize the limitations within which this type of thought moves. Its form of expression shows that the systematic treatment of religious problems is not intended; it is satisfied with an individual maxim or comment on a Scriptural verse and at the utmost proceeds from there to the discussion of a particular question. This lack of system is characteristic of Talmudic discussions of theology. Problems are taken up one by one; there is never an attempt to combine isolated conclusions in a coherent framework. As our examples have shown, there are insights into the most basic problems of religion, with full awareness of their fundamental significance; but fundamentals are discussed in the same way as details, and no attempt is made to follow them systematically to their conclusions. The Talmud is content with the abstract statement that the love of one's neighbor was the supreme principle of the Torah, but it never attempts to trace the different moral laws to this supreme principle or to demonstrate concretely (apart from a few occasional examples) the moral purpose of the ceremonial law. The demand of a completely disinterested worship of God does not in itself contradict the doctrine of retribution which occupies so important a place in Talmudic ethics; but the problems posed by the juxtaposition of these two ideas are never properly discussed.

All the most important ideas in connection with the problem of theodicy can be found in the Talmud; yet it is impossible to construct from them a systematic doctrine. This is especially true of the metaphysical aspects of theology. The Talmud repeatedly emphasizes that the anthropomorphic expressions of the Bible are only metaphors, but it never enquires into the criteria for delimiting metaphorical from literal utterances. We may therefore speak of a definite and consistent over-all religious viewpoint of the Talmud, but no correspondingly consistent and unified theoretical comprehension of the central questions of religion. What the Talmud has produced is not theology, but scattered theological reflections. This accounts for the sometimes strange coexistence of ideas; next to insights of the utmost profundity there are other pages which show a primitive thought wrestling laboriously with its problems. Lack of theoretical maturity is often found in conjunction with sharp and pointed conceptual formulations.

The difference between the righteous and the wicked man consists, as we have seen, in the preponderance of good over evil deeds. This atomistic conception of man characterizes not so much the moral view of the Talmud as the adequacy of its conceptual tools, which can measure the good or evil in man only according to the number of individual acts. Equally naive is the answer which tries to solve the profound question of theory versus practice by pronouncing in favor of the superiority of learning because it leads to practice. Rabbinic thought is struggling to master the content of religion, but seems still unable to grasp it in its wholeness and unity.

After what has been said, it is hardly necessary to point out that rabbinic Judaism was little affected by the scientific philosophy of the Greeks. Only the most popular forms of these Greek doctrines, in which they were spread among the masses, whether orally or in writing, seem to be echoed in the Talmud. Much in Talmudic ethics is reminiscent of Stoic popular philosophy. Both teach that everything that man possesses is borrowed from God, and therefore man should not complain if God demands the return of that which is properly His. Both consider the soul as a stranger in this world, praise the virtue of moderation as the true riches, and advise man to live every day as if it were his last.[26] Some of the rabbinic maxims which ask man to do his duty without thought of reward bear a strong formal resemblance to Stoic sayings. The dependence on Stoic models may be doubtful in the case of individual parallels. Stoic influence as such is beyond doubt. The comparison of the soul to God derives from Stoic metaphysics; the soul fills and vitalizes the body as God fills the world, and like God, it sees but cannot be seen.[27] The Talmud incorporates Platonic as well as Stoic ideas, which, divorced from their systematic context, were part and parcel of general Greek culture. The Talmud not only knows of the pre-existence of the soul, but also says that before birth the soul knew the entire Torah, forgetting it only at the moment of birth. Here the Torah takes the place of the Platonic Idea, as also in the saying that God looked at the Torah and from this model created the world. The invisibility of God is exemplified by the Platonic parable of the human eye which cannot bear to look even at the brightness of the sun.[28] The Talmud uses such ideas in order to rebut the arguments of Gentile opponents and Jewish skeptics. The admonition, "Know what to answer to an Epicurean," (the Epicurean is, for the rabbis, the typical free-thinker)[29] proves that the knowledge of foreign ideas was promoted by apologetic considerations. However, since the attacks emanated from popular philosophy rather than from strictly scientific circles, popular Greek wisdom could suffice for their rebuttal.

Gnostic speculation exerted a profounder influence than philosophy on the Talmudic rabbis. Particularly in the first and the beginning of the second century, Gnosticism fascinated many of the leading teachers. Later the suspicions against this trend, which had been present from the very beginning, gained the upper hand, and the Mishnah pronounced an anathema on it: "Whosoever speculated on these four things, it were better for him if he had not come into the world—what is above? what is beneath? what was beforetime? and what will be hereafter?"[30] This hostility to Gnosticism, or at least to its more extreme forms, did not destroy it but definitely broke its power. From its very beginning Gnosticism was considered an esoteric doctrine that could be propagated only in the narrow circle of the elect. Naturally, Judaism had no room for its dualistic and antinomian doctrines.

In its teaching that the creation of the world and the biblical legislation were not the work of the supreme good God but rather of a hostile demiurge, Gnosticism meant to hit and destroy its hated enemy, Judaism. The Gnostic doctrine of the "two powers" consequently became the worst heresy in Jewish eyes.[31] Accordingly, Jewish Gnosticism was unable to accept the pessimistic Gnostic doctrine of matter as an essentially evil principle completely independent of God. After discarding these elements, Jewish thought nevertheless preserved a number of characteristic and decisive Gnostic traits. The two main subjects of Jewish esotericism—the "work of creation" (maaseh bereshit) and "the work of the chariot" described by Ezekiel (maaseh merkabah)[32] correspond to the central themes of Gnosticism. The world of the chariot—that is, the throne of glory and the angels surrounding it —corresponds to the highest spiritual sphere, the pleroma of the Gnostics. It is the terminus of the soul's mystical journey, the ascension to heaven, which is portrayed in similar terms by Jewish as well as non-Jewish Gnosticism.[33]

The doctrine of creation presents speculation concerning the origin of the world in the form of mystical interpretation of the biblical text. Gnostic ideas are adapted to the biblical notion of creation, but in such a way that the act of creation becomes merely the starting point of a highly mythological cosmogonic process. In the spirit of Gnostic metaphysics of light, God wraps himself in the radiance of a light that fills the world.[34] When God created the world, the latter sought to expand to infinity, until God set limits to its expansion.[35] In connection with the biblical idea of the upper and lower waters, Jewish Gnostics speculate on water as the primal matter of the world, and declare in thoroughly mythological fashion: "Three creations preceded the world: water, spirit, and fire; water conceived and gave birth to darkness, fire conceived and gave birth to light, the air conceived and gave birth to wisdom."[36] The continuation of these Gnostic doctrines can be found in post-Talmudic Jewish mysticism, but for the religious development in Judaism as a whole, they merely represent a sideline. Both in the Talmudic and post-Talmudic eras, they were cultivated only in small circles. Even if at times their influence was relatively great, they never determined the general religious scene.

Nothing so well indicates the limits of theological reflection in the Talmud as the absence of any dogmatic formulation of the substance of Jewish teaching. Attacks from the outside on certain doctrines, like the resurrection of the dead, are refuted, or those who deny them are excluded from the fellowship of Israel.[37] The Talmud nowhere systematically attempts to fix the contents of the Jewish faith; hence the impossibility of establishing with any precision the boundary between a generally valid doctrine and a teacher's individual opinion. This proved of far-reaching consequence for the later development of Judaism.[38] The flexible form in which the faith of Judaism was cast allowed the religious thought of later generations a great deal of freedom. Medieval Jewish philosophy was able to reinterpret traditional religious beliefs with a freedom that was denied to Christian scholasticism. Attempts were made in the Middle Ages to limit this freedom by formulating articles of faith, but since Jewish spiritual authorities could demand general recognition of their rulings only insofar as they acted as interpreters of the Talmud, such efforts could at best have limited success. Nevertheless, the freedom with regard to the tradition of faith had certain boundaries set to it from the beginning. The basic principles of the Jewish faith needed no dogmatic systematization in order to be clearly determined. The belief in the divine origin of the Bible as well as of the complementary oral tradition authoritatively bound the individual both in matters of belief and religious law.

Religious truth had been given once and for all in the Bible and the oral tradition, and it was the absolute norm for faith. All freedom was merely a freedom to interpret this truth, which by its very nature was valid for everybody. Also with regard to the material contents of faith, this freedom was bound to certain fixed principles. Thus the Jewish belief in revelation entailed a whole series of religious assumptions, sharing the authority of revelation and consequently not requiring explicit dogmatic emphasis in order to assert their authority over the faithful. The ideas of providence, retribution, and miracles were firmly established as elements of the Jewish faith through their connection with belief in revelation. Their factual truth was beyond doubt; only in regard to their precise understanding was there freedom for philosophical interpretation. Other religious ideas, though they lacked this close formal relationship to the notion of revelation, attained such prominence in liturgy and public worship that their authority was unquestioned. The whole complex of religious convictions that had grown up in the Talmudic period served as an incontestable, valid norm of faith for future Jewish generations and for their philosophies. Both facts—the existence of a norm of faith and the absence of a systematic formulation of dogma—are of equal importance for subsequent developments: both the freedom and constraint of medieval Jewish philosophy derive from them.

THE RELIGION OF THE JEWS AT THE TIME OF JESUS

Louis Ginzberg

A FAMOUS DOCTOR of the Synagogue, living in the third century remarked, "Israel went into exile only after it became divided into twenty-four sects." The pragmatism of the Rabbi is open to serious objection, although modern historians uphold his view that the downfall of the Jewish state was the direct consequence of the internal disunion. That a united Israel would have withstood the power of Rome a little longer than the state torn by dissensions and factions is very likely, but the doom of Jewish independence was sealed at the moment Rome entered upon its policy of aggression in the East. However there can be no doubt that about the time of the downfall of the Jewish state, that is, the time of the rise of Christianity, Israel was divided into many sects.

You are, of course, all acquainted with the three main sects the Pharisees, Sadducees, and Essenes, concerning whom we have a good deal of contemporary information, though unfortunately not as adequate as some may believe it. But what do we know about the numerous currents and sub-currents in the wide stream of religious life of the Jews of that period? Take, for instance, the Pharisees; only quite recently scholars have learned to differentiate between the apocalyptic and legalistic wings of Pharisaism, and let me add that even the so-called legalistic Pharisaism was not uniform. In the histories of the Jews we are told that about a generation before the time of Jesus, there lived the two great doctors of the Synagogue, Hillel and Shammai, the

founders of the schools later known as the houses of Hillel and Shammai. This statement is, however, far from being quite accurate. A
critical study of the old rabbinic sources reveals the very interesting
fact that Pharisaism at its very appearance in history, about 170 b.c.,
represented two distinct currents, the conservative and the progressive.
Thus Hillel and Shammai far from being the founders of schools, were
rather the last representatives of the two wings of Pharisaism. Now I
have no intention of discussing the doctrinal differences between the
numerous schools, still less those between the different sects. These
introductory remarks will give you, however, some notion of the difficulty that lies before us. Our subject is the religion of the Jews in the
time of Jesus. But of what Jews? Of the Pharisees, the Sadducees,
or the Essenes? And if the Pharisees,—of what branch of Pharisees,
the apocalyptic or legalistic, and if the latter,—of what shade, the
progressive or conservative? And again, what are the sources which
we may draw upon for an unbiased and fair representation of the religion of the Jews at the time of Jesus? Roughly speaking, there are
three distinct groups of literary sources to be considered: (1) The
literature of the Alexandrian Jews, of which the works of Philo are
the most important, (2) the Palestinian Pseudepigrapha, and (3) the
vast resources of the so-called rabbinic literature. Now, permit me to
describe briefly the point of view from which I shall attempt to approach
the subject.

All creative activities of nature consist in producing new forms of
existence—new beings and new functions—by means of new combina-
tions of the given elements and the elemental individual. Christianity
saw the light in Palestine and the given elements from which it was
created must be looked for in the religious thoughts of Palestinian
Jewry and not in the Alexandrian Hellenism of the Diaspora Jew.
Even granted that Hellenism was not without influence upon Palestinian Judaism—and this influence is to my mind of a very problematic nature,—we must not forget that the Jew always had a genius
for assimilating foreign matter by impressing upon it his own individuality. Hence it is Judaized Hellenism that might have had its share
in the mental makeup of the Palestinian Jew, and not Hellenism, pure
and simple. The Hellenism of the Diaspora Jew may have been of
great importance for the development of Christianity of the second
century, but it can be disregarded in the study of the rise of Christianity.

The attractiveness of the novel is responsible for the exaggerated
claims put up by some scholars for the apocalyptic Pseudepigrapha as

the main source for the religious life of the Jew. The most important works of this branch of literature came to light in comparatively recent times, and scholars are human enough to be dazzled by a sudden light. There is, however, no fear in my mind that we shall have to wait too long for a sober judgment upon the real value of the apocalyptic literature, and that this will be that the apocalyptic Judaism or apocalyptic Pharisaism was neither the Judaism of the time of Jesus nor the religious atmosphere in which the latter and his disciples breathed.

Of apocalyptic Pseudepigrapha, it may well be said that the new therein is not Jewish, and the Jewish is not new. Only those who misunderstood Pharisaism, pure and simple, could see in the universalistic and Messianic ideas of apocalyptic Judaism something new and hostile to the former. The true understanding of the religion of the Jews at the time of the rise of Christianity can, therefore, be gained from the Pharisaic sources which express the religious consciousness of the bulk of the nation or Catholic Israel. Taken at bottom the nation was for the most part Pharisaically minded; in other words, the Pharisees were only the more important and religiously inclined men of the Jewish people who gave the most decided expression to the prevailing belief and strove to establish and enforce it by a definite system of teaching and interpretation of the sacred books.

Our attempts must be, however, to derive the religious thought of the Jew from the spirit of the literature as a whole rather than from single formal doctrine. Of our subject it is eminently true that the details of a written tradition are intelligible only through the whole. Every member of a living organism depends for its health and function upon the whole more than the whole depends upon its separate organs. So the true bearing of single features of Pharisaic literature can be learned only from their relation to the whole.

Pharisaism, or to use the more comprehensive term Rabbinism, is inseparable from Biblical Judaism, yet not entirely identical therewith. Without drawing a sharp distinction between religion and theology, it would be good to remember that the Rabbis were as little theologians as the prophets philosophers. As the latter did not reason out but experienced the truths to which they gave utterance, so the theology of the former is not based upon cold speculation but upon warm feeling. The most characteristic feature of the rabbinical system of theology is its lack of system. With God as a reality, revelation as a fact, the Torah as a rule of life, and the hope of redemption as a most vivid expectation, one was free to draw his own conclusions from these axioms and postulates in regard to what he believed.

A story is told about Hillel, the great doctor of the Synagogue, who flourished about a generation before Jesus, that a heathen approached him with the request to give him the contents of the Torah—the main tenets of Judaism—while standing on one foot. Hillel replied, "What is hateful to thee, do not unto thy fellowman. This is the entire Torah. Go and study the rest, which is merely commentary." Paul, the pupil of Hillel's grandson, Gamaliel, repeated almost literally this idea when he said, "For all the law is fulfilled in one word even in this,—thou shalt love thy neighbor as thyself."

With all due reverence to such great men as Hillel and Paul, I am rather distrustful of all attempts at constructing an acrobatic religion. One cannot go on forever standing on one foot. I prefer, therefore, to quote to you the following legend, occurring in rabbinic literature in many versions, that will give you a more complete and vivid picture of the religion of the Pharisaic Jew than any learned definition. The legend reads: "When God resolved upon the creation of the world, He took counsel with the Torah—that is Divine Wisdom. She was skeptical about the value of an earthly world on account of the sinfulness of man who would be sure to disregard her precepts. But God dispelled her doubts. He told her that Repentance had been created long before and sinners would have the opportunity to mend their ways. Besides good work would be invested with atoning power, and Paradise and Hell were created to dispense reward and punishment. Finally, the Messiah was appointed to bring salvation which would put an end to all sinfulness."

Divested of its fantastic garb, this legend contains a fair summary of the tenets of the religion of the Pharisaic Jew. God is the creator of the world and in His goodness and wisdom, created man. It is the duty of man to obey Him. He has made known the will of God by the revelation of the Torah; God rewards those who fulfill His commands and punishes those who disobey. But even the vilest sinner can repent, and if he does, he will be forgiven. Wickedness will however disappear from among men when the Messiah will arrive and the Kingdom of God be established on earth.

It would take a dozen lectures to discuss in detail these religious ideas in which Jewish legend saw the essence of Judaism. I will limit myself to discuss their bearing on a favorite thesis of a famous theologian of our day, concerning the gospel. Prof. Adolph Harnack grouped the teachings of Jesus under three heads; they are, firstly, the Kingdom of God and its coming; secondly, God, the father, and the infinite value of the human soul; thirdly, the higher righteousness and the commandment of love. I have, of course, no intention of discussing the thesis of Prof. Harnack, but whether we accept it or not, there can be no doubt that these teachings ascribed by him as the message of Jesus do represent fundamental religious ideas. It may, therefore, be profitable in a sketch of the religion of the Jews in the time of Jesus, to ascertain what the Kingdom of God, the Fatherhood of God, and the Commandment of Love meant to the Jew of that time.

Any student of the New Testament, of course, knows that the expression "Kingdom of God" belongs to the religious language of the Jew; in Matthew's "Kingdom of Heaven" we still have the exact rendering of the Hebrew מלכות שמים (Malkut Šamâyîm). A feeling of reverence led the Jews at a very early date to avoid as far as possible, all mention of the name of God, and Heaven is one of the usual substitutes for it. Hence, expressions like "Kingdom of Heaven," "Sake of Heaven," "Fear of Heaven," and many like them are very frequently met with in rabbinic literature. As the term "Kingdom of Heaven" is less expressive of an accomplished fact than of an undefined and undefinable idea, the only safe way to ascertain its actual meaning is to let the Rabbis speak their own language. What is the section of the Torah where there is to be found the receiving of the Kingdom of Heaven to the exclusion of the worship of idols? ask the Rabbis. The answer given is, "This is the Shema the section containing the words: Hear—Shema—O Israel, the Lord is our God, He is One, and thou shalt love the Lord, thy God, with all thine heart, with all thy soul, and with all thy might." The implicit acceptance of God's unity as well as unconditional surrender of mind and heart to His holy will which the love of God expressed in the "Shema" implies, this is what is understood by the receiving of the Kingdom of God.

Commenting upon Ps. 81.10 "There shall be no strange God in thee," the Rabbis remarked, "By this is meant, the strange God in the very heart of man, his evil inclination." The acceptance of the Kingdom of Heaven meant, therefore, the denial of one's selfishness which is polytheism in disguise, the worship of God combined with the devotion to one's desires and passions. When Rabbi Akiba, who died the death of a martyr, was in the hands of his torturers, he, in the words of the Talmud, joyfully received upon himself the yoke of the kingdom of Heaven, that is, he recited the "Shema." When asked why he did so, he answered, "All my life I have recited the words: 'And thou shalt love the Lord, thy God, with all thine heart, with all thy soul, and with all thy might,' and have longed for the hour when I could fulfill it. I loved Him with all my heart, I loved Him with all my fortunes, now I have the opportunity to love Him with all my soul, giving my life for His sake. Therefore, I repeat these words in joyfulness." And thus he died. The idea of the Kingdom of Heaven was accordingly for the Pharisees, neither eschatological nor political but that of the rule of God in the heart of the individual.

To conclude our discussion on this point, I would add the following remarks on the relation of the Messianic idea to that of the Kingdom of Heaven. As in the case of all ideas, the occasion for the rise of the Messianic idea is to be looked for in the particular circumstances of the historical factors which determine the genuine originality of a historical idea. The material starting point for the Messianic idea is, of course, to be looked for in the particular circumstances of the national and political life of the Jewish nation. Israel in suffering and agony clung to the hope of seeing a scion of the glorious house of David as its annointed king—Messiah—restore its old glories. But soon the view changes. The Messiah does not merely mean king; he becomes the symbolic figure of human suffering, from whom alone, genuine hope can issue and who alone can bear within himself the genuine warranty for the restoration and regeneration of the human race.

The truth of the saying: "there is only a hair's-breadth between the sublime and the ridiculous" is best illustrated by the fate that befell the Messianic idea, that noble product of the religious genius of the Jew. Disregarding the phantasmagoria of the apocalyptic Pseudepigrapha and the fancies of popular imagination—it is time to distinguish more clearly between folklore and theology—I shall quote to you the following prayer, very likely composed about the beginning of the second century and still recited in the Synagogue, which to my mind represents the Messianic hopes of the Pharisees at the time of the rise of Christianity. The prayer known as the "Kingdom Prayer" reads, "Our God, and God of our fathers, reign Thou in Thy glory over the whole universe, and be exalted above the earth in Thine honor and shine forth in the splendor and excellence of Thy might upon all the inhabitants of the world, that whatsoever has been made may know that Thou hast made it and whatsoever has been created may understand that Thine hand created it, and whatsoever has breath in his nostrils may say the Lord God of Israel is King and his dominion ruleth over all. O, purify our hearts to serve Thee in truth, for Thou art God in truth."

Here we find expressed not only the universal aspect of the Kingdom of God but also the conception of religion freed from the idea which represents it as serving only the interest of a world beyond and not, primarily and above all things, of the world we live in. Not that the thought of the world beyond was in any way to be curtailed; on the contrary, the Rabbis often speak of the reward awaiting the righteous after their death as consisting not in material pleasure but in feeding on divine glory. Nevertheless, the development of the religious thought of the Jew shows the marked tendency to fix the center of gravity of religion not in the thought of a world beyond but rather to fasten and establish it in the actual life of man on earth. In this respect the scribes and Rabbis were the true successors to the prophets. For the latter, morality was the most essential feature of religion and there is an ethically weak point in even the purest and loftiest ideas concerning the bliss of future life. All these ideas take into account only the individual but in morality, society occupies the chief consideration; ethics is, if not entirely, at all events preeminently social. Accordingly, the highest ideal of the Pharisees was the Kingdom of God in this world and not in the other world. The position of Rabbinism with regard to mundane morality and supermundane bliss is best expressed in the following saying of a famous Rabbi. After remarking that this world is the vestibule where man prepares for the hall, the world to come, he adds, "Better is one hour of returning to God and good works in this world than all the life of the world to come; yet better is one hour of bliss in the world to come than all the life of this world." No happiness of this life can be compared to heavenly bliss, but the highest that man can achieve is living a religious life in this world.

The realization of morality presupposes, as we have remarked, the existence of society and this meant for antiquity, national society. Even Plato, in his "Outline of an Ideal State," has the Greeks arrayed against the Barbarians, the non-Greeks, in constant warfare. The Messianic ideal, as preached by the prophets and taught by the Rabbis, is against particularism but not against nationality. It is quite erroneous to assert that the prophets hated the State as such and desired its destruction because they regarded its very existence as essentially inconsistent with that spiritual life which was their aim. What the prophets combated was the materialistic view of the national life as they combated the materialistic view of the life of the individual; they were strongly nationalistic but of a spiritual kind. The Messianic hopes of the Pharisees were as we have seen universalistic, yet at the same time, national. The two ideas, the Kingdom of Heaven over which God reigns and the Kingdom of Israel in which the Messiah, the son of David, holds the sceptre, became thus almost identical. This identification gave substance and reality to the idea of the Kingdom of God without diminishing its spiritual value. The combination of the national idea in its spiritualized form with the universal is well expressed in another Kingdom prayer composed at the same time as that mentioned before. It reads:

"Now, therefore, O God, impose Thine awe upon all Thy works that they may fear Thee and that they may all form a single band to do Thy will with a perfect heart. Give then glory, O Lord, unto Thy people, joy to Thy land, gladness to Thy city, a flourishing horn unto David, Thy servant, and a clear shining light unto the Son of Jesse, Thy Messiah. Then shall the just be glad and all wickedness shall be wholly consumed like smoke when Thou makest the dominion of arrogance to pass away from the earth. And Thou, O Lord, shalt reign, Thou alone over all Thy works on Mount Zion, the dwelling place of Thy glory and in Jerusalem, Thy holy city."

We come now to the second head under which Prof. Harnack grouped the teaching of Jesus,—the Fatherhood of God and the infinite value of the human soul. The term "Father in Heaven" is certainly one of the greatest watchwords of spiritual religion and it is now generally admitted that it was not new at the time of Jesus but a part of the common stock of religious ideas and a natural element in the Jewish religion at that time. I shall not discuss the meaning which Jesus put into this common term of his people, but will limit myself to quote a few sayings of the Rabbis in which it occurs, that we may be able to ascertain the meaning they gave to it. Rabbi Eliezer ben Hyrkanos, a younger contemporary of the apostles, dwelling on the moral degeneration of his age, explaimed, "In whom, then, shall we find help if not in our Father who is in heaven!" His pupil and later colleague, the famous Rabbi Akiba, remarked: "Blessed are ye, O Israelites! Before whom do you purify yourself from your sins and who is it that purifies you? Your Father in Heaven." These and many similar sayings show how baseless a fiction the view is that the Pharisee thought of God only, or even mainly, as distant and inaccessible or as a taskmaster whose service was hard. The very apostrophe of many Pharisaic prayers, "Our Father" or "Our merciful Father" exhibit the steady faith of those who knew that they are safe in God and certain of being heard by Him.

The words of Rabbi Akiba quoted contain not only the declaration of belief in direct access to God himself through prayer and repentance, but also the repudiation of any mediator. Every man, says he Talmud, has a patron—a friend at court. If there comes trouble upon him, he does not go directly to the patron but goes and stands at the door and goes to a servant or to a member of the household who tells the patron, "so and so" is standing at the door of thy yard. Perhaps the patron has him admitted, perhaps he leaves him alone. But the Holy One, Blessed be He, is not so. If trouble comes on a man—notice the text speaks of a man generally and not of a Jew in particular—God says, "Let him pray not to Michael and not to Gabriel but to Me and I will answer him at once" and this is that which is written, "Everyone that calleth on the name of the Lord shall be delivered." The methodological error in overestimating the value of the Apocalyptic literature as a source for the main current of the religious life of the Jew at the time of the rise of Christianity is fraught with serious consequences for the proper understanding of the problem. In a history of the Jewish religion based upon the study of rabbinic sources, angelology and demonology would hardly play any important part at all—certainly not that part which is ascribed to them by those who see in apocalyptic Judaism the religion of Israel in the time of Jesus. The Pharisaic Jew, as we have seen, did not pray to the angels to intercede in his behalf to God that he may be saved from the evil caused by demons, but sought help from God "like a child from his father"—to use the words of a leading Pharisee about 80 B.C.,—that he may be sustained in his struggle against the evil in himself. In approaching God, the Pharisaic Jew knew that the divine rule goes as far as life itself—life down even to its smallest manifestation in the order of nature, or in the words of the Rabbis, "one does not hurt his small toe without it being decreed by Heaven," or to use a phrase more familiar to you, "A bird perishes not without the will of Heaven."

The man who can come to the Ruler of Heaven and Earth like a child to his father is thereby raised above nature and has a value higher than heaven and earth. The Rabbis often speak of the righteous who by their noble deeds associate themselves with God in the work of creation. The thought underlying the figurative language of the Rabbis is that the universe with its endless array of life forms and its unchanging definite laws of necessity reaches perfection only in the presence of the soul of man who, endowed with free will, rises above nature by his God-fearing actions and thus becomes an associate of God in the work of creation.

Man as the quasi-associate of God is mostly spoken of by the Rabbis in reference to his moral deeds. For instance, they say, "He who suffers himself to be insulted without taking offence, thereby associates himself with God in the work of creation." This leads us to the conception of morality of Pharisaism and its relation to the third head under which the whole of the Gospel is embraced, according to Harnack: "The higher righteousness and the commandment of love." The following remarks of the Rabbis will indicate to you their view on morality and ethics.

I had occasion in the course of this lecture to refer to the saying of Hillel that the commandment of love is the essence of the Torah. More characteristic of the Pharisaic conception of morality is the theory of the Rabbis with regard to the use of the Tetragrammaton, that the name expressive of God's being, the "I am," stands for love and mercy. In modern phraseology the thought expressed by the Rabbis is: the moral law based on love does not exist by virtue of a divine act or an authoritative fiat; it flows from the essence of God's being, from His absolute and infinitive moral nature. The divine Being knowable to men only in its attribute of love combined with the endeavor to emulate Him in man's finite way constitutes at once the rule and the reason of morality. In the words of the Rabbis, "Because I am merciful, thou shalt be merciful," the reason underlying the moral can and should be the same for man as for God. If God can have no reason for morality but the nature of the moral, so there shall be no reason for man. The principle of morality is accordingly autonomous, but its archetype is God's. And now let me add one sentence as to the universal character of ethics as taught by the Rabbis. A great leader among them remarked as follows: "The most comprehensive principle of the Torah is expressed in the words: in the day that God created man in the likeness of God made He him!" In these words of Scripture, the Rabbis found expression not only of the unity of mankind as an ethical idea but also the reason thereof—the likeness of man to God.

No description of the religion of the Jews in the time of Jesus could be adequate which would leave out of account one of its main features, its being a Torah-religion. You will have noticed that I have used all through my lecture the term "Torah" and not "Law." It must first be stated that the term "Law" or its Greek equivalent

"Nomos" is a very misleading rendering of the word "Torah." "To the Jew," Professor Schechter aptly remarked, 'Torah' means a teaching or instruction of any kind. It may be either a general principle or a specific injunction, whether it be found in the Pentateuch or any other parts of the Scripture or even outside of the Canon." "Torah" to the Jew is the sum total of the contents of revelation without special reference to any particular element in it. Eternal truths about God's love and justice, laws and commandments leading the individual as well as society to a noble life, symbolic observances, worship and discipline, diverse of character as they otherwise might be, are of equally binding power as they all were revealed by the same God. The Jew must embody in his practical life the teachings of Moses and the prophets, concerning God and man. It is not enough to know; the Jew is required to do and to be.

The most distinctive aspect of a Torah-religion is obedience to the will of God. In the Torah, as in nature, the two revelations—God is the ultimate cause in the Torah, as in nature,—no part may be denied, even though the reason and the connection may not be comprehended; as in nature, so in the Torah, the traces of divine Wisdom must ever be sought for. His ordinances must be accepted in their entirety as undeniable phenomena. They are laws for us, even if we do not comprehend their reason and purpose. They are like the phenomena of nature which we recognize as facts, though their cause and relation to each other are not always understood by us. And as we endeavor to interpret the working of nature by observing carefully its phenomena and their relation to one another, so will we be able to comprehend the spirit of the Torah by a diligent study of its individual laws and doctrines, teachings and commandments.

Therein lies the great contribution of Pharisaism to the development of Judaism. The Sadducee taught the immobility of the Torah, the Pharisee its immutability which is not stereotyped oneness but impossibility of deviating from its own course. To understand its course, the knowledge of the entire Torah, law as prophecy, commandments as doctrines, was an absolute necessity. It was this conception of the Torah that saved it from becoming a sacred relic, a revered mummy without spirit and life.

As true virtuosi of religion, the Rabbis knew that in religion the irrational elements must not be entirely eliminated, if it should not degenerate into a shallow rationalism. But they also knew that religion, if not saturated with rational elements must necessarily sink to the level of an anti-cultural mysticism, hostile alike to true religion and to progress. The Torah with its numerous commandments and laws of practice and love, of righteousness and holiness, but also with an elaborate system of ritual and service offered them a harmonious blending of the rational with the irrational elements of religion. Their guide for life was: It is good that thou shouldst take hold of the one, yea, also from the other withdraw not thy hand. Obey the will of God as expressed in His revealed Torah, try to penetrate into the spirit of the word of God, but whether you are able to discern the reason of a divine commandment or not, thy first duty is to fulfil it, and its fulfillment will be unto thee a source of inspiration and joy.

Conformity with the will of God and communion with God are the two outstanding features of a spiritual religion. The Pentateuch and the Psalms, the *Halakah* and the *Haggadah* are not contrasts but necessary complements to one another. Of course, no one will deny that a Torah-religion, that is one that lays great stress upon the conformity to the will of God, might become for some a set of rules and forms without inwardness and spirituality. But no less deniable is the fact that a religion which overemphasized the communion with God might degenerate into antinomianism. The one as the other has frequently happened and is happening daily. To characterize, however, rabbinic Judaism as legalism is as justified as to identify Christianity with antinomianism. The Rabbis, who after all ought not to be entirely ignored in judging or rather in sentencing Judaism, are at least as severe in their censure of legalism as the church fathers in their denunciation of antinomianism.

The precepts of the Lord are according to the words of the Psalmist, not only right, but also "rejoicing the heart." It may therefore not be out of place to correct another prevailing error with regard to rabbinic Judaism. We hear quite often of the yoke of the law under which burden the Pharisees groaned, but little is said of the joy they experienced at the fulfillment of the divine commandments, שמחה של מצוה is the expression used by the Rabbis. The daily prayer of the Jew, in a part composed very likely in pre-Christian times, we read as follows: "With everlasting love Thou hast loved the House of Israel, Thy people." Can there still be any doubt that those who lived and died for the Torah considered it as a blessing, the affluence of God's mercy and love?

With respect to the work of art which we term religion, says a modern philosopher, idealization is as necessary as elsewhere, the primary condition for each of its adherents, but no less so for the foreign student. In my attempt to sketch before you the religion of the Jews at the time of Jesus, I was guided by this thought, that without idealization even the historical ascertainment of facts would be impossible, at least insofar as such an attempt is aimed at presenting one collective spiritual view of its matter. Of course, I have not lost sight of the absolute necessity of an exact study of the available sources. For without this latter, it would not be possible for the process of idealization itself to come into operation; a mere subject phantom would ensue. I am thoroughly convinced that statistics may become as dangerous to theology as theology is to statistics. We will never do justice to the religion of a group by following the method of statistics, and attempt to ascertain the "average" because there is not such a thing as the average in religion. As each man's emotions, needs, and longings must differ, so must each man's religion differ. Each man lives his religion in his own way. To gain insight into the life of a foreign religion, we must never forget that where there is no sympathy there is no understanding. Your being here today to listen to the exposition of Judaism by a Jew shows that you possess the only means of comprehending and interpreting a foreign religion, which is the mental readiness for sympathy. I hope that your sympathy will find its reward.

SOME RABBINIC IDEAS ON PRAYER
Israel Abrahams

It is, one must admit, not easy to speak of a Rabbinic conception of prayer at all. Rabbinic theology is a syncretism, not a system. To the earliest Pharisees the Bible as a whole, to the later Rabbis the Bible literature as a whole, were the sources of inspiration. Hence they adopted and adapted ideas of many ages and many types of mind, and in consequence you may find in Rabbinic Judaism traces of primitive thought side by side with the most developed thought. Especially is this true of prayer. A conspectus of Rabbinic passages on prayer would cover the whole range of evolution, from the spells of a rain-producing magician to the soul-communion of an inspired mystic. A slip in uttering the formulae of prayer was an evil sign.[1] The Rabbis, again, believed on the one hand in the efficacy of the prolonged prayers of the righteous in general, and on the other hand they, like a certain school of modern Evangelicals, sometimes confided in the possession by gifted individuals of a special faculty for influencing the powers above. Such individuals were mighty men of prayer, able to force their will on a reluctant providence; they would argue, importune, persuade. It has always remained an element in the Jewish theory of prayer that man can affect God; what man does, what he thinks, what he prays, influence the divine action. It is not merely that God cares for a man, is concerned with and for man. God's purpose is affected, his intention changed by prayer. These phases of belief are, however, never altogether absent from prayer, even in its most spiritualized varieties. They are noticeable in the Psalms, and, when one remembers the influence of the Psalter, one need not wonder to find these phases of belief in the extant liturgies of all creeds. Perhaps we may put it that in the Pharisaic theology there was a fuller belief in special providences than is now thought tenable; but after reading some of the papers in a recent Christian volume entitled "In Answer to Prayer"[2] one must hesitate before making this assertion to the detriment of Pharisaism. The Rabbis somewhat mitigated the crudity of the belief in special providences by holding that all miracles were preordained, and were inherent in the act of creation. But the order of nature is a modern theory: you will look for it in vain whether in Rabbinic or early Christian books. Now so soon as you believe in special providences, you are liable to seek them by special petitions, and prayer may degenerate into importunity. Onias the circle-drawer would not leave his circumscribed standing-place until the rain fell, and he told people in advance to place under cover all perishable things, so sure was he that God must send the rain for which he prayed.[3] Hanina ben Dosa could always tell from his fluency or hesitancy when he prayed for sick men whether the patients would live or die. And though such cited cases are rare in the Talmud, and are perhaps Essenic rather than Pharisaic, still it was generally believed that specific prayer for a specific end might hit the mark.

It *might* hit the mark, but it was not certain to do so. Therein lies the whole saving difference. If Rabbinism is firm in its assertion that prayer *may* be answered, it is firmer still in its denial that prayer *must* be answered. The presumptuous anticipations of Onias the circle-drawer were rebuked by some Rabbis. Prayer was efficacious, but its whole efficacy was lost if reliance was placed upon its efficacy. As the Prayer Book version of Psalm xxvii. 16 runs: "O tarry thou the Lord's leisure; be strong and he shall comfort thine heart: and put thy trust in him." But the wicked man is in a hurry. Like Tom Tulliver in *The Mill on the Floss,* his faith cannot survive the failure of divine answer to a petition that he may know his Latin verbs in school next morning. The recovered Hebrew original of Sirach gives us the fine text: "Be not impatient in prayer."[4] The Rabbis put it that the wicked denies God if he happen to pray in vain; the righteous man receives affliction as the mead of virtue yet never questions the justice of God. Solomon's Prayer on dedicating the Temple is thus summarized in the Midrash: When, O Lord, a Hebrew prays to thee, grant what seems *good to thee*; when a heathen prays, grant what seems *good to him*.[5] The meaning of this fine Rabbinic saying is: the heathen entirely rests his belief in God on an immediate, specific answer to his prayers, and Solomon entreats God to give the heathen such specific answer in order to retain his allegiance. The true believer is, on the contrary, free from such reliance on the objective validity of his supplication; to him *that* is good which God pleases to ordain.

At this place a word must be interposed on a category of what the Rabbis call Vain or Fruitless prayer (*tephillath shav*). "Though a sharpened sword is held at a man's throat, he shall not withhold himself from mercy,"[6] that is: Prayer and penitence may avail even at the eleventh hour. But not at the twelfth. I do not assert that the Rabbis disbelieved in the possibility of salvation after death. But they held that it was in this life futile to pray *ex post facto*. Thus: "He who supplicates God concerning what has already come to pass utters a vain prayer."[7] If you are going to look at an honours list, you waste your time in praying that your name may be found there or found in a particular position. As the Rabbis otherwise put it, You must not *rely* on miracles. Thus certain prayers are excluded by the Rabbis from the very possibility of answer. To this category belong also such prayers as one which Raba overheard and blamed. He once heard a man praying that he might win the love of a certain maiden. Raba bade him cease his prayer, urging: "If she be destined for thee, nothing can part you; if thou art not destined to get her, thou deniest providence in praying for her."[8] For marriages are made in Heaven, and are beyond praying for.

Even more to the point is the Rabbinic denunciation of what they term *Iyyun Tephillah*. The word *Iyyun* means thought, calculation. Sometimes it is used with regard to prayer in a good sense, to connote careful devotion as opposed to mechanical utterance of prescribed formulae. But there is another word for that, viz. *kavvanah*, which may be rendered devotion, than which no more necessary quality can be conceived of in the Rabbinic theory of prayer. But *Iyyun Tephillah* is very often used in a bad sense. Calculation in prayer is the expectation of an answer to prayer as a due claim, and the Rabbis protest with much vehemence against such *expectation* of a divine response to prayer of any kind whatsoever. "He who prays long and relies on an answer ends in disappointment." Again: "To three sins man is daily liable—thoughts of evil, reliance on prayer, and slander."[9] Thus the expectation of an answer to prayer is an insidious intruder, difficult to avoid, and branded as sin. Perhaps the point can be best illustrated from another side. Not only do the righteous expect no answer to prayer, but they are reluctant to supplicate God for personal benefits. "The Holy One," we are told, "yearns for the prayers of the righteous." God's throne was not established until his children sang songs to him; for there can be no king without subjects. And as God wishes for man's praise, so he longs for man's petitions. But the righteous cannot easily be brought to make petitions. This is the Talmudic explanation of the barrenness of the Patriarchs' wives; God withheld children to compel the reluctant saints to proffer petitions for them. And so also, from a somewhat different point of view, with the whole people of Israel. Why did God bring Israel into the extremity of danger at the Red Sea before effecting a deliverance? Because God longed to hear Israel's prayer. Said R. Joshua b. Levi: To what is the matter like? It is like a king who was once travelling on the way, and a daughter of kings cried to him, "I pray thee, deliver me out of the hand of these robbers." The king obeyed and rescued her. After a while he wished to make her his wife; he longed to hear her sweet accents again, but she was silent. What did the king do? He hired the same robbers again to set upon the princess, to cause her to cry out, that he might hear her voice once more. So soon as the robbers came upon her, she began to cry to the king. And he, hastening to her side, said "This is what I yearned for, to hear thy voice."—Thus was it with Israel. When they were in Egypt, enslaved, they began to cry out, and hang their eyes on God, as it is written: And it came to pass . . . that the children of Israel sighed because of their bondage . . . and they cried. Then the Scripture immediately follows: And God looked upon the children of Israel. He began to take them forth from Egypt, with a strong hand and an outstretched arm. And God wished to hear their voice a second time, but they were unwilling. What did God do? He incited Pharaoh to pursue them, as it is said: And he drew Pharaoh near. Immediately the children of Israel cried unto the Lord. In that hour God said: For this I have been seeking, to hear your voice, as it is written in the Song of Songs (which Rabbinic exegesis interpreted as an allegory of the love of God and Israel) "My dove in the clefts of the rock, let me hear thy voice; thy voice, the same voice which I first heard in Egypt."[10]

There is a hint here of another note, but we can hear it elsewhere more unmistakably. "Honour the physician before thou hast need of him," says Ecclesiasticus. This passage is used in the Talmud to criticize the common practice of praying only under the pressure of necessity. "The Holy One said: Just as it is my office to cause the rain and the dew to fall, and make the plants to grow to sustain man, so art thou bounden to pray before me, and to praise me in accordance with my works; thou shalt not say, I am in prosperity, wherefore shall I pray; but when misfortune befalls me than will I come and supplicate. Before misfortune comes, anticipate and pray."[11] It will be seen that such passages as this carry us far beyond the conception of prayer as petition. It is an attitude of mind, a constant element of the religious life, independent of the exigencies of specific needs or desires. And that, one may say, on a review of the whole evidence, is the predominant thought in the Rabbinic theory of prayer.

From one side this is illustrated by the importance attached to public worship. This importance partly arose from the regularity of that worship. It was not a casual impulse, but a recurrent feature of the daily round. But there lay much more than this in the Rabbinic glorification of public prayer. The prayer of a community may be selfish as against the welfare of other communities, but the selfishness is less demoralizing than when an individual prays for what may entail injury to another individual. Even selfishness of the first kind, that is, communal selfishness in prayer, is castigated in some famous Rabbinic passages. "The Angels," it is said, "wished to sing praises to God while the Egyptians were drowning in the sea, and God rebuked them, saying, Shall I listen to your hymns when my children are perishing before my eyes?"[12] This was no mere pious expression, for the Passover liturgy of the synagogue has been permanently affected by this Rabbinic idea. On the Jewish festivals the noble series of Psalms of Praise (Hallel)—Psalms cxiii to cxviii—are a regular feature of the synagogue service. But on the seventh day of Passover—the traditional anniversary of the drowning of the Egyptians in the Red sea— these psalms are curtailed, on the basis of the Talmudic utterance just cited. Thus did the Pharisees, and the religion derived from them, honour the text: "When thy enemy falls do not rejoice."

There are, no doubt, imprecatory passages in the Psalter, and some (by no means all) of these have found their way into the service of synagogue and church. But, except in times of bitter persecution (as in the Puritan struggle against tyranny in England, or during the Crusades), these imprecatory petitions have not been interpreted personally. Still, Jew and Christian could do without them. There is enough in the Psalter without these.

An interesting incident bearing on the same point is related by Josephus. Aretas, the Nabatean king, was besieging Jerusalem about 67 B.C. with a combined force of Arabians and Jews. "Now there was a man whose name was Onias, a righteous man, and beloved of God, who in a certain drought, had prayed to God to put an end to the intense heat, and whose prayer God had heard and had sent rain. This man had hid himself, because he saw that this civil war would last a long while. However, they brought him to the Jewish camp, and desired that as by his prayers he had once put an end to the drought, so he would in like manner utter imprecations on Aristobulus and those of his faction. And when, on his refusing and making excuses, he was still compelled to speak by the multitude, he stood up in the midst of them, and said: 'O God, King of the whole world, since those that stand now with me are thy people, and those that are besieged are also thy priests, I beseech thee that thou wilt hearken neither to the prayers of those against these, nor bring to effect what these pray against those.' " Such impartiality was not pleasing to the lower minds and violent partisans who claimed God as exclusively on their side, as is the wont of the mean and the partisan in all ages. When the "wicked among the Jews who stood around him" found that he, whom they had brought to curse, refused the amiable rôle assigned to him they speedily made an end of Onias.[13] But the underlying idea of Onias's prayer meets us elsewhere. A human judge, we are reminded, hears only one side at a time; God hears the whole world at once. The Shechinah, or divine presence, rests on ten when praying together—ten forming a quorum for public worship. It is possible that some irresistible power was attributed to the prayers of a congregation, and one catches suspicious echoes in Rabbinic literature of this unworthy belief, but it is nowhere explicitly enunciated. The idea rather seems that the individual petition counts less in such prayers, and the individual's own peculiar claims are merged in and reinforced by the mass. "All are equal when they pray before God, women and slaves, sage and simpleton, poor and rich." "When one prays with the congregation it is like a number of rich men who are making a crown for the king, and a poor man comes and inserts his mite. Shall the king think less of the crown because of this poor man's contribution? So when a wicked man joins in prayer with the righteous, shall God reject this joint prayer because of him?" Congregational prayer thus levels up, and makes irrelevant any distinction between righteous and unrighteous. Or take this saying, "When various congregations pray, the angel appointed over prayer gathers their supplications together and sets them as a garland on the brow of the Most High."[14] That, at all events, part of the Rabbinic predilection for public prayer was due to this greater unselfishness, is seen by the frequency with which men are urged to pray for one another. "A prayer uttered in behalf of another is answered first"; "He who loses a chance of praying for another is termed sinner"; "Elimelech and his sons were punished for their failure to pray for their generation."[15] They left Judea, it will be remembered, for Moab, and thus subtracted their prayers from those that ascended on behalf of the famine-stricken congregation. Perhaps this point best comes out in a Rabbinic prayer which at first sight may seem queer enough. "Let not the prayer of wayfarers find entrance, O Lord, before thee."[16] For wayfarers would selfishly ask for fine weather when the general good of the land needed rain. Selfishness can no further go, nor can one conceive a subtler rebuke of selfishness than this.

Now, all the Pharisaic ritual laws which so trouble the spirit of German theologians refer to this public prayer. That this ritualism had its serious dangers is clear enough. The inevitable result of a fixed liturgy is rigidity. The fixation of times and seasons and formulae for prayer does tend to reduce the prayer to a mere habit. But what can be done at any time and in any manner is apt to be done at no time and in no manner. The Rabbis thus attached great importance to habits. "Fix a period for thy study of Scripture"[17] is a well-known Rabbinic maxim. The study of Scripture was, of course, an act of worship, it was higher than prayer. Raba declaimed against men who "put aside everlasting life (the Scriptures) and concern themselves with temporal life" (prayers for maintenance). To know the will of God was more important than to seek to turn God's will in man's favour. Therefore, "Fix a period for thy study of Scripture." Dangerous fixity of a good custom, we exclaim. But is it not curious how inclined we are to detect this danger only in our more ideal habits? We read our morning newspapers as a matter of habit, yet we do not fear to become thereby only mechanically interested in the news of the world. But in the case of prayer the difficulty is supremely urgent. If prayer is to mean anything it must retain its spontaneity. And therefore the Rabbis did their utmost to counteract the inherent weakness of a settled liturgy. Hebrew was the preferable but not the necessary language of prayer; men might pray in any tongue. And though the study of the Law was to be a fixed thing, prayer was not to be a fixed thing. The Rabbis formulated this in a general principle: "Make not thy prayer a fixed thing but a supplication for mercy."[18] Fix the study of God's word by which his will was made manifest, but do not make a fixed thing of prayer, for prayer is at once the human attempt to realize God's will and the human confession of inability to realize that will,—prayer is at highest a cry for mercy. What is the objectionable fixed thing in a prayer? One Rabbi answers: "If a man's prayer is a burden"; another answers: "If the man does not pray as one seeking mercy"; a third answers "If the man fails to introduce personal variations into the fixed forms." Ostentation was particularly discouraged. Again and again worshippers are cautioned not to pray too loudly. "He who shouts in prayer belongs to those who are of little faith."[19] A devotional heart, a humble attitude, are prescribed. The Pharisee, boasting in his prayer that he is not as other men, is not typical, for Pharisaism conceives all men equally destitute of saving virtue. Confession of sin, not profession of superior sinlessness, was the Pharisaic accompaniment of prayer. Eyes to earth, heart to heaven—is the Rabbi's suggestion for a prayerful posture.

These prescriptions could not completely succeed. But at this early period one must remember that public worship was of short duration. The length to which Jewish services have now grown was a slow evolution, and until the first decades of the fourteenth century the actual ritual of public worship was to a large extent in a very fluid condition. In the time of Jesus, you will recall the freedom with which any one could read and expound the Scriptures in the synagogue of Galilee. It is even possible that Jesus was able to select his own reading from Isaiah. And as to prayers, the same comparative freedom existed. When we talk, then, of a fixed liturgy in the time of Jesus, we must not think of anything like the current synagogue liturgies or the Anglican Book of Common Prayer. Nothing is more remarkable than the extraordinary number of original individual prayers in the Talmud, and the faculty and process of ready improvisation for public as well as private worship has continued with copious flow to our own times in the synagogue, though the stream of such inspiration was more generous in the spacious times which preceded the age of printing. The latter invention did more than Pharisaism to give rigidity to Judaism. It is not possible to give by quotations any true impression of the vast mass of new prayers which entered the publicity of the synagogue liturgy or the privacy of the Jewish home during the first fourteen centuries of the Christian era.

Then again, the Rabbis, though they sometimes emphasize the value of lengthy prayer, often declaim against it. The subject was not always approached from the same point of view, and it was admitted that there is a time to prolong and a time to shorten prayer. The Emperor Antoninus asked R. Judah the Prince: "May one pray at all

times?" "No!" said the Rabbi, "it is treating God with levity." The
Emperor was not convinced. So the Rabbi got up early next morning,
went to the Emperor, and greeted him with the salutation, "My Lord!"
An hour later he returned, and exclaimed, "O Imperator!" After another hour the Rabbi accosted him for the third time, with "Peace be to
thee, O King!" Antoninus could no longer endure it. He angrily retorted
to the Rabbi: "You are making mock of my royalty." "So!" said the
Rabbi, "Thou, a king of flesh and blood, find these repeated greetings
disrespectful; shall then man trouble the King of Kings at all times?" [20]

But the parable of Rabbi and Emperor is dangerous teaching if it
mean more than this: Man must not importune God. Against this may
be set another Rabbinic parable.[21] A man visits his friend and the
friend greets him cordially, placing him on the couch beside him. He
comes again, and is given a chair; again and receives a stool. He comes
a fourth time and the friend says, "The stool is too far off, I cannot
fetch it for you." But God is not so; for whenever Israel knocks at the
door of God's house the Holy One rejoices, as it is written: For what
great nation is there that hath a God so nigh unto them as the Lord
our God is, *whenever* we call? The Rabbis, like ourselves, would have
been shocked at the supposition that God is at any time inaccessible to
the broken-hearted and contrite. "The gate of tears is never shut," said
a Rabbi.[22]

Much of what precedes touches only the surface of the subject;
we must now try in the few minutes that remain to penetrate a little
deeper. The essential relevancy of prayer depends on the nature of
God and his relation to man. If God is the absolute, if he is the unchangeable, then prayer must be identical with submission and praise.
The worshipper registers his sense of the divine power and as a corre-
lative his own weakness; he adds the corollary that the all-powerful is
likewise the all-good. Praise has therefore always formed a large item
in the liturgies of the religions which had their source in Judaism. In
the Psalter, in the Prayers of Nehemiah and Daniel, on which so
many subsequent prayers were modeled, praise is introductory to
petition. The oldest of old Psalmic refrains is the *Hodu*: O give thanks
unto the Lord for he is good; for his loving-kindness endureth for ever.

Rabbinic Judaism took a very strong line on this subject.[23] It attributed to Adam the authorship of Ps. xcii: It is a good thing to give
thanks to the Lord and to sing praises to thy name, O Most High; and
it declared that when all sacrifices cease in the Messianic age, for as
men will no longer sin they will offer no more sin-offerings; when all

propitiatory and penitential prayers are discontinued, for men will in that period of grace have nothing to repent of or ask pardon for,— when all other sacrifices and prayers cease, the thank-offering and the service of praise will remain eternally. Thus from Adam to the Messiah, in the Rabbinic conception, man's duty and delight is to utter the praises of God. First praise, then supplicate, is the recurrent Rabbinic maxim for writers of prayers. Praise God for sorrow as well as for happiness. What is an affliction of Love, asks the Talmud? It answers: Such affliction as does not deprive the sufferer of the power to pray.[24] So long as prayer is possible, God's hand, though heavy on the unhappy, rests on the unhappy not in anger but in love. The countless benedictions prescribed in the Talmud for every conceivable and inconceivable act of life are all praises. There may have been in this some notion of gratitude for favours to come; but this notion, however degrading as between man and his fellow, is not a low conception as between man and his God—even if, while testifying thanks, the worshipper implies a hope. Or again, there may be in this rubric of praise an element of propitiation—you mollify an irresponsible autocrat by the incense of flattery. But such an idea cannot be said to have consciously invaded the mind of Judaism. The *mind* of Judaism came largely into the domain of prayer, for the study of the Law was not only in itself an act of worship, but the school was often the place of prayer. And the intellect, whether directed to universal history or to personal experience, perceived recurrent ground for praise and thanksgiving. But prayer is not only or chiefly a matter of the mind; it is a matter of the heart.

Now, while the mind appreciates that the only prayer should be praise, the heart is not satisfied by eulogizing God. Through the whole history of human life runs the cry for mercy. As men suffer irrespective of creed, so do they all appeal to God's mercy; to quote the late S. Singer, "pain is undenominational and so is pity." And here we come face to face with a peculiar Rabbinic dualism—the Mercy and the Justice of God. A few citations will be better than a long exposition of this dualism. The righteous are they that strengthen God; they help him to be merciful. Why are the prayers of the righteous symbolized as a spade? Just as the spade turns the grain from place to place, so the prayers of the righteous turn the divine attributes from the attribute of wrath to the attribute of mercy.[25] And God himself prays to himself in the same strain. At the Creation God made himself a tent in Jerusalem, and therein he prayed. And he said: May it be my will that my children do my will, so that I destroy not my house of prayer. But when Israel's sins made the Holy One destroy the house, then God prayed: May it be my will that my children repent, so that I may rebuild my house. Rabbi Ishmael relates how he once (as a priest) entered the innermost sanctuary to offer incense, and saw there God who asked a blessing, and Rabbi Ishmael said: May it be thy will that thy mercy subdue thy wrath, and God nodded in assent.[26] Weber, with German wrongheadedness, sees in such passages merely the notion of a supreme despot who may or may not permit mercy to temper justice. But though some of these passages are crude, and even childishly naïve, they represent a phase of the attempt to bring God into relation with man, an attempt which is at once the supreme aim and the despair of every religion. And the climax is reached when the Rabbis tell us that God teaches man the very formulae of prayer; he bids Moses to pray to him, and tells him to say: O God, turn the bitter into sweet.[27] "From thee I fly to thee," wrote Solomon ibn Gabirol in his *Kether Malchuth,* the most inspired Hebrew hymn after the Psalter.

The just God judges, but his tender mercies are over all his works. It is this belief in the all-pervading mercy of God that makes Jesus' words, "Thy will, not mine," the supreme utterance of the Jewish consciousness on the subject of prayer. These words express more than resignation: they express also a confidence that God's will is man's ultimate good. Prayer thus becomes something more than petition, something beyond praise; it becomes a harmony between the human and the divine. It is the divine in man going out to meet the divine in God; it is the upward rise of the soul to its heavenly fount. A praying man is in the divine presence.[28] Prayer, in the language of a Jewish mystic, is as flame to coal: it unites the upper and the lower worlds.[29] Prayer, said a Rabbi, is heart-service;[30] it lays the heart of man on the altar of God. No man prays acceptably unless he makes his heart flesh.[31] Thou shalt love the Lord thy God with all thy heart: thus is Israel warned that in the hour of prayer he must not have a divided heart, part for God, and part for worldly aspirations.[32] It is the fear of God that gives virtue to prayer. One self-inflicted heart's pang is more saving than many stripes.[33] Prayer turns aside doom, but it is prayer associated with charity and penitence.[34] Note, in passing, how the old magical force of prayer has been transfigured in such a saying—one of the most popular in the Jewish liturgy. God wants the heart, is another famous utterance. Prayer purifies.[35] God is the Fountain of Israel. As the water cleanses the unclean, so the Holy One cleanses Israel. Which goeth to which? The fountain to the defiled or the defiled to the fountain? The defiled goeth to the fountain, descends, and bathes. Thus is it with prayer. But the fountain is near. If thou canst not go to the house of prayer, pray on thy couch: if thou art unable to frame words, let thy heart meditate in silence.[36] And finally, Rabbi Eliezer said: Thus shall a man pray: "Do thy will, O God, in heaven above, and bestow tranquillity of spirit on those who fear thee below, and what is good in thine own sight do. Blessed art thou, O Lord, thou that hearest prayer."[37]

But there is neither time nor need to add more quotations. In his fine book *The Psalms in Human Life,* Mr. R. E. Prothero says: "The Psalms, then, are a mirror in which each man sees the motions of his own soul. They express in exquisite words the kinship which every thoughful human heart craves to find with a supreme, unchanging, loving God, who will be to him a protector, guardian, and friend. They utter the ordinary experiences, the familiar thoughts of men; but they give to these a width of range, an intensity, a depth, and an elevation which transcend the capacity of the most gifted. They translate into speech the spiritual passion of the loftiest genius; they also utter, with the beauty born of truth and simplicity, and exact agreement between the feeling and the expression, the inarticulate and humble longings of the unlettered peasant. So is it that, in every country, the language of the Psalms has become part of the daily life of nations, passing into their proverbs, mingling with their conversation, and used at every critical stage of existence."

Mr. Prothero traces out, by well-chosen and eloquently described historical instances, how these Psalms, with their deep consciousness of sin, their fine note of humility in the hour of victory, "Not unto us, O Lord, not unto us," their contrite yet assured aspiration after a renewed communion with God,—how these Psalms have become the breviary and viaticum of humanity. And lo! though the book is entitled The Psalms in *Human* Life, Mr. Prothero practically ignores their power and influence in Jewish life. All the world is marshalled to testify to the undying value of the Psalms: only the Jews, who wrote the Psalms, are omitted.

It was necessary for me to make this comment, in sadness rather than with indignation. For, too many, in estimating the Jewish conception of prayer, forget that the Psalms were not only Jewish in origin, but the most constantly prized, the most dearly beloved of all the sacred literature of Judaism.[38] Priests and Levites sang Psalms at the daily sacrifices, and when the Temple fell, Psalms took the place of sacrifices.

The Psalms have been to the Jews a well-spring of consolation, a support in tribulation, a reassurance under sin. And the Jewish theory of prayer is—the Psalter. Rabbinism re-interpreted and re-enforced the Psalter, but abated nothing and surrendered nothing of it. Rabbinism saw in the Psalter, in Heine's words, "sunrise and sunset, birth and death, promise and fulfilment—the whole drama of humanity." And the synagogue absorbed the Psalter into its inmost soul. In the eleventh century, Ibn Gabirol wrote the following Invocation to Prayer, which appears in many modern Jewish liturgies, and is uttered by countless myriads of Jewish worshippers daily in the early morning:

> At the dawn I seek thee,
>   Refuge, Rock sublime;
> Set my prayer before thee in the morning,
>   And my prayer at eventime.
> I before thy greatness
>   Stand and am afraid:
> All my secret thoughts thine eye beholdeth
>   Deep within my bosom laid.
> And withal what is it
>   Heart and tongue can do?
> What is this my strength, and what is even
>   This the spirit in me too?
> But indeed man's singing
>   May seem good to thee;
> So I praise thee, singing, while there dwelleth
>   Yet the breath of God in me.

This rendering is by Mrs. Salaman,[39] and it beautifully and exactly reproduces the Hebrew. "Mechanism," "Pharisaism," and all such phrases are intolerably inappropriate when applied to a Rabbinic theory of prayer which finds its frequent expression in such meditations as this.

THE RABBINICAL CONCEPTION OF HOLINESS

Solomon Schechter

The conception of holiness in the Rabbinic literature is rather complicated, being a composite of various aspects not easily definable, and at times seemingly even contradictory. But diverging as the ideals of holiness may be in their application to practical life, they all originate in Israel's consciousness of its intimate relation to God, which is, as I have endeavoured to show in many places in this Review, the central idea of Rabbinic theology.[1] In fact, in its broad features, holiness is but another word for *Imitatio Dei,* a duty dependent upon Israel's close contact with God. "Ye shall be holy, for I the Lord am holy" (Lev. xix. 2). These words are explained by the ancient Rabbinic sage Abba Saul to mean "Israel is the *familia* (suite or bodyguard) of the King (God), whence it is incumbent on them to imitate the King."[2] The same thought is expressed in different words by another Rabbi, who thus paraphrases the verse from Leviticus which has just been cited: "Ye shall be holy, and why? because I am holy, for I have attached you unto me, as it is said, 'For as the girdle cleaves to the loins of a man, so I have caused to cleave unto me the whole house of Israel' " (Jer. xiii. 11).[3] Another Rabbi remarked, "God said to Israel, Even before I created the world you were sanctified unto me; be ye therefore holy as I am holy"; and he proceeds to say, "The matter is to be compared to a king who sanctified (by wedlock) a woman unto him, and said to her: Since thou art my wife, what is my glory is thy glory, be therefore holy

373

even as I am holy."[4] In other words, Israel having the same relation to God as the *familia* to the king, or as the wife to the husband, or as children to the father,[5] it follows that they should take him as their model, imitating him in holiness.

Before proceeding to some analysis of this *Imitatio Dei* or holiness, as suggested by the Rabbinic literature, it must be remarked that the Hebrew term *Kedushah* does not quite cover our term "holiness," the mystical and higher aspect of it being better represented by the Hebrew term *Chasiduth* (saintliness), for which Kedushah is only one of the preparatory virtues;[6] though the two ideas are so naturally allied that they are not always separated in Rabbinical texts. I shall, nevertheless, in the following pages classify my remarks under the two headings of *Kedushah* and *Chasiduth*. The former moves more within the limits of the Law, though occasionally overleaping it, whilst the latter, aspiring to a superior kind of holiness, not only supplements the Law but also proves a certain corrective to it.

As we have seen, holiness, according to Abba Saul, is identical with Imitation of God. The nature of this Imitation is defined by him thus: "*I and He,* that is like unto him (God). As he is merciful and gracious, so be thou (man) merciful and gracious."[7] The scriptural phrases "walking in the ways of God" (Deut. xi. 22), and "being called by the name of God" (Joel iii; 5) are again explained to mean; "As God is called merciful and gracious, so be thou merciful and gracious; as God is called righteous, so be thou righteous; as God is called holy, so be thou holy[8]." "The profession of the holy one, blessed be he, is charity and loving-kindness, and Abraham, who will command his children and his household after him 'that they shall keep the way of the Lord' (Gen. xviii. 19), is told by God: 'Thou hast chosen my profession; wherefore thou shalt also become like unto me, an ancient of days.' " [9] The Imitation receives practical shape in the following passage: "The members of the house of Israel are in duty bound to deal with one another mercifully, to do charity (*Mizwah*), and to practise kindness. For the holy one, blessed be he, has only created this world with loving-kindness and mercy, and it rests with us to learn from the ways of God." Thus said R. Chama b. Chanina, " . . . Walk in the attributes of God (or rather, make his attributes the rule for thy conduct). As he clothes the naked (Gen. iii. 21), so do thou clothe the naked; as he nurses the sick (Gen. xviii. 1), so do thou nurse the sick; as he comforts the mourners (Gen. xxv. 11), so do thou comfort the mourners; as he buries the dead (Deut. xxxiv. 5), so do thou bury the dead."[10] Again, when R. Judah

b. Ilai interrupted his lectures in order to join the bridal procession, he used to address his disciples with the words: "My children! rise and show your respect to the bride (by joining the procession), for so we find that the holy one, blessed be he, acted as best man to Eve."[11] The Imitation is further extended to mere good manners, in which God is also taken as a model. As, for instance, when we are told by the Rabbis: "Let man learn proper behaviour from the Omnipresent, who, though knowing the absence of righteous men from Sodom and Gomorrah, did not interrupt Abraham in his intercession for these cities, but waited until he finished his pleading, and even took leave before parting from him."[12]

It is to be remarked that this God-likeness is confined to his manifestations of mercy and righteousness, the Rabbis rarely desiring the Jew to take God as a model in his attributes of severity and rigid justice, though the Bible could have furnished them with many instances of this latter kind. Interesting in this connection is the way in which the commandment of the Imitation was codified by some of the later authorities: "The holy one, blessed be he, ordained that man should cleave to his ways, as it is written, 'Thou shalt fear the Lord thy God, him shalt thou serve, and to him shalt thou cleave' (Deut. x. 19). But how can man cleave to the *Shechinah*? Is it not written, 'For the Lord thy God is a consuming fire, a jealous God'? (Deut. iv. 24). But cleave to his ways: as God nurses the sick, so do thou nurse the sick, and so forth."[13] The feature of jealousy is thus quite ignored, whilst the attributes of mercy and graciousness become man's law. The prophet Elijah, who said, "I have been very jealous for the Lord God of hosts" (I Kings xix. 10), and even repeated his denunciation of Israel (ibid. ver. 14), was, according to the Rabbis, rebuked by God, who answered him, "Thou art always jealous," and was removed from his prophetic office, Elisha being appointed prophet in his room.[14]

The second or negative aspect of holiness is implied by the Hebrew word *Kedushah*, the original meaning of which seems to be "separation" and "withdrawal."[15] So the Rabbis paraphrase the verse, "Sanctify yourselves, therefore, and be holy, for I am holy" (Lev. xi. 44), with the words, "As I am separated, so be ye separated."[16] By the separatedness of God is not meant any metaphysical remoteness, but merely aloofness and withdrawal from things impure and defiling as incompatible with God's holiness, whence Israel should also be removed from everything impure and defiling.

Foremost among the things impure, which range very widely, are:

idolatry, adultery, and shedding of blood. To these three cardinal sins the term *Tumah* (defilement) is especially applied.[17] The defiling nature of the second (including all sexual immorality) is particularly dwelt upon in the Rabbinic literature. Thus the Rabbis interpret the verse, "And ye shall be unto me a kingdom of priests and a holy nation" (Exod. xix. 6), with the words, "Be unto me a kingdom of priests, separated from the nations of the world and their abominations."[18] This passage must be taken in connection with another, in which, with allusion to the scriptural words, "And ye shall be holy unto me . . . and I have severed you from other people that you should be mine" (Lev. xx. 26), the Rabbis point to the sexual immorality which divides the heathen world from Israel.[19] In fact, all such incontinence was called *Tumah* (impurity), indulgence in which disqualifies (or cuts man off) from God; God says, "What joy can I have in him?"[20] but he who surrounds himself with a fence against anything unchaste is called holy,[21] and he "who shutteth his eyes from seeing evil (in the sense of immorality) is worthy of receiving the very presence of the *Shechinah*."[22]

The notion of impurity is further extended to all things stigmatized in the Levitical legislation as unclean, particularly to the forbidden foods "which make the soul abominable." The observance of these laws the Rabbis seem to consider as a special privilege of Israel, marking the great distinction between them and the "descendants of Noah,"[23] whilst in the transgression of them they saw the open door leading to idolatry; in a word, to a deeper degree of impurity.[24]

The soul is also made abominable—and hence impure—according to the Rabbis, by doing anything which is calculated to provoke disgust, as for instance, by eating from unclean plates or taking one's food with filthy hands.[25] In fact, to do anything which might have a sickening effect upon others is ranked among the hidden sins which "God shall bring into judgment";[26] but he who is careful to refrain from things filthy and repulsive brings upon himself a particular holiness purifying his soul for the sake of the holy one; as it is said. "Ye shall sanctify yourselves."[27]

Lastly, we have to record here that view which extends the notion of impurity to every transgression of Biblical law. Every transgression has the effect of stupefying the heart,[28] whilst the observance of the laws in the Torah is productive of an additional holiness.[29] According to this view, all the commandments, negative and affirmative, have to be considered as so many lessons in discipline, which if only as an education in obedience, result in establishing that communion between man and God which is the crowning reward of holiness. Thus the Rabbis say, with allusion to the verse "That ye may remember and do all my commandments and be holy unto your God" (Num. xv. 40), "Heart and eyes are the two middlemen of sin to the body, leading him astray. The matter is to be compared to a man drowning in water, to whom the shipmaster threw out a cord, saying unto him, Hold fast to this cord, for if thou permit it to escape thee there is no life for thee. Likewise the holy one, blessed be he, said to Israel, 'As long as you cling to my laws, you cleave unto the Lord your God (which means life) . . . Be holy, for as long as you fulfil my commandments ye are sanctified, but if you neglect them you will become profaned.' "[30]

Thus far holiness still moves within the limits of the Law, the obedience to which sanctifies man, and the rebellion against which defiles. There is, however, another superior kind of holiness which rises above the Law, and which, as already indicated in the opening remarks of this essay, should be more correctly termed *Chasiduth* (saintliness). The characteristic of the Chasid, as it is somewhere pointed out, is that he does not wait for a distinct commandment. He endeavours to be pleasant to his Maker, and like a good son studies his father's will, inferring from the explicit wishes of the father the direction in which he is likely to give him joy.[31] Hence the tendency of the Chasid to devote himself with more zeal and self-sacrifice to one law or group of laws than to others, just according to the particular bent of his mind, and his individual conception of the will of his father. Thus Rab Judah perceives the "things of *Chasiduth*" in paying particular attention to the tractates *Nezikin* (Damages, including the laws regarding the returning of lost goods, prohibition of usury, etc.), and in avoiding anything which might result in doing injury to a fellow man. Raba again defines *Chasiduth* as carrying out the prescriptions in the tractate of Aboth; a tractate, be it observed, in which the ritual element is quite absent, as it is limited to the moral sayings and spiritual counsels given by the ancient Jewish authorities. Another (anonymous) author thinks that *Chasiduth* consists in closely observing the laws prescribed in the (liturgical) tractate *Berachoth* (Benedictions), prayer and thanksgiving having been probably the particular passion of this Rabbi.[32]

The principle of *Chasiduth* is perhaps best summarized by the Talmudic formula: "Sanctify thyself even in that which is permitted to thee." [33] R. Eleazar, of Worms, who takes this saying as the motto to one of his chapters on the *Regulations of Chasiduth*, comments

upon it: "Sanctify thyself and thy thoughts, reflect upon the Unity
(of God, and think of) whom thou art serving, who (it is that) observes thee, who it is that knows thy deeds, and who (it is) to whom
thou wilt return . . . Hence be (in ritual questions) stringent with
thyself and lenient towards others . . . The Torah in certain cases
made concessions to the weakness of the flesh (hence the law cannot
always be taken as the supreme standard of conduct). Take no oath
even for the truth . . . Keep thee from every wicked thing (Deut.
xxiii. 11), which means, among others, not to think even of things
impure, etc. etc."[34] Impure thinking was, in the Rabbinic view, the
antecedent to impure doing, and the ideal saint was as pure of heart
as of hand, acting no impurity and thinking none.

Very expressive is Nachmanides, whose comments on the injunction of separatedness—"As I am separated so be ye separated"—are
to the following effect:

"According to my opinion, by the Talmudical term פרישות,
separatedness, is not meant the abstaining from *Arayoth* (sexual intercourse forbidden in the Bible), but something which gives to those
who practise it the name of Perushim. The matter (is thus): The
Torah has forbidden *Arayoth* as well as certain kinds of food, but
allowed intercourse between man and his wife as well as the eating
of meat and the drinking of wine. But even within these limits can
the man of (impure) appetites be drenched in lusts, become a
drunkard and a glutton, as well as use impure language, since there
is no (distinct) prohibition against these things in the Torah. A man
could thus be the worst libertine with the very licence of the Torah.
Therefore the scripture, after giving in detail the things forbidden
absolutely, concluded with a general law (of holiness), to show that
we must also abstain from things superfluous. As for instance, that
even permitted sexual intercourse should be submitted to restrictions
(of holiness), preserving it against degenerating into mere animal
lust; that the drinking of wine should be reduced to a minimum, the
Nazir being called holy because he abstains from drink, and that one
should guard one's mouth and tongue against being defiled by glut-
tony and vile language. Man should indeed endeavour to reach a
similar degree of holiness to R. Chiya, who never uttered an idle word
in his life . . . The scripture warns us to be clean, pure, and separated
from the crowd of men who taint themselves by luxuries and
ugliness."[35]

It will be observed that this correction of the Law is not considered by Nachmanides as a new revelation: according to him it is implied by the general scriptural rule of holiness, which, of course, considering the undefinable nature of holiness can be extended to any length. Nor were the Rabbis conscious of any innovation in or addition to the Torah when they promulgated the principle of sanctifying oneself by refraining even from things permitted; a principle which can be and was applied both to matters ritual as well as to morals and conduct.[36] As it would seem they simply looked upon it as a mere "fence" preventing man from breaking through the limits drawn by the Torah itself. Very instructive in this respect is the conversation which the Talmud puts in the mouth of King David and his friend Hushai the Archite. When David was fleeing before his rebellious son Absalom, he is reported to have been asked by Hushai, "Why hast thou married a captured woman?" For it is supposed by the Rabbis that Absalom's mother Maacah (2 Sam. iii. 3) was a woman taken captive in the war. Hushai thus accounts for the misfortune which has befallen David by this unhappy marriage. But David answers him, "Has not the merciful allowed such a marriage?" (Deut. xxi. 10–13), whereupon Hushai rejoins: "Why didst thou not study the order of the scripture in that place?" In other words the fact that the regulations regarding the woman taken captive in war are closely followed by the law concerning the stubborn and rebellious son (Deut. xxi. 18–21), indicates that the Torah, though not absolutely forbidding it, did not wholly approve of such a marriage, but foretold that its offspring was likely to prove a source of misery to his parents.[37] The correction of the Law, for neglecting which David is so terribly punished, is thus effected, not by something antagonistic to or outside of it, but by its own proper interpretation and expansion. As another instance of this kind I quote the following, which, rendered in the old Rabbinic style, would run thus: "We have heard that it is written, 'Thou shalt not kill' (Exod. xx. 13). We should then think that the prohibition is confined to actual murder. But there are also other kinds of shedding blood, as, for instance, to put a man to shame in public, which causes his blood to leave his face. Hence to cause this feeling is as bad as murder, whence he who is guilty of it loses his share in the world to come.'[38] Again, we have heard that it is written, 'Thou shalt not commit adultery' (Exod. xx. 14). But the phrase in Job (xxiv. 15), 'The *eye* also of the adulterer waiteth for twilight,' teaches us that an unchaste look is also to be considered as adultery; and the verse, 'And that ye seek not after your own heart and your own eyes, after which ye used to go a whoring' (Num. xv. 39), teaches that an unchaste look or even an unchaste thought are also to be regarded as adultery."[39]

The crowning reward of *Kedushah*, or rather *Chasiduth*, is, as already indicated, communion with the Holy Spirit, "Chasiduth leading to the Holy Spirit," or, as it is expressed in another place, "Holiness means nothing else than prophecy."[40] This superior holiness, which implies absolute purity both in action and thought, and utter withdrawal from things earthly, begins, as a later mystic rightly points out, with a human effort on the part of man to reach it, and finishes with a gift from heaven bestowed upon man by an act of grace.[41] The Talmud expresses the same thought when we read, "If man sanctifies himself a little, they (in heaven) sanctify him much, if man sanctifies himself below (on earth), they bestow upon him (more) holiness from above."[42] "Everything is in need of help (from heaven.[43] Even the Torah, which is called pure and holy, has only this sanctifying effect, when man has divested himself from every thought of pride, when he has purified himself from any consideration of gold and silver, when he is indeed quite pure from sin."[44] Only Torah with holiness can bring about communion with God. Thus runs a prayer, or rather prophecy, by an ancient Rabbi: "Learn with all thy heart and all thy soul to know my ways, and to watch the gates of my Torah. Preserve my Torah in thy heart, and may my fear be present before thy eyes. Guard thy mouth against all sin, and make thyself holy against all sin and injustice, and I will be with thee."[45] Hence the prayer which so often occurs in the Jewish liturgy, "Sanctify ourselves by thy commandments,"—for any thought of pride or any worldly consideration is liable to undo the sanctifying effect of the performance of any divine law.

DIVINE RETRIBUTION IN RABBINIC LITERATURE

Solomon Schechter

"Blessed be he who knows." These are the words with which
Nachmanides, in his classical treatise on Retribution ("Shaar Hag-
gemul"), dismisses a certain theory of the Geonim with regard to
this question; after which he proceeds to expound another theory,
which seems to him more satisfactory. This mode of treatment implies that, unsatisfactory as the one or other theory may appear to
us, it would be presumptuous to reject either entirely, there being
only one who knows the exact truth about the great mystery. But we
may indicate our doubt about one doctrine by putting another by its
side, which we may not affirm to be more absolutely true, but more
probable. This seems to have been the attitude, too, of the compilers
of the ancient Rabbinical literature, in which the most conflicting
views about this grave subject were embodied. Nor did the synagogue
in general feel called upon to decide between these views. There is
indeed no want of theodicies, for almost every important expounder
of Job, as well as every Jewish philosopher of note, has one with its
own system of retribution. Thus Judaism has no fixed doctrine on the
subject. It refused a hearing to no theory, for fear that it should contain some germ of truth, but on the same ground it accepted none to
the exclusion of the others.

These theories may, perhaps, be conveniently reduced to the two
following main doctrines that are in direct opposition to each other,
whilst all other views about the subject will be treated as the more
or less logical results of the one or other doctrine.

1. There is no death without (preceding) sin, nor affliction without (preceding) transgression (*Sabbath*, 55*a*). This view is cited in the name of R. Ammi, who quoted in corroboration verses from Ez. xviii. 20, and Ps. lxxxix. 33. Though this Rabbi flourished towards the end of the third century, there is hardly any doubt that his view was held by the authorities of a much earlier date. For it can only be under the sway of such a notion of Retribution that the Tannaim, or doctors of the Mishnah, were so anxious to assign some great crime as the antecedent to every serious calamity by which mankind was visited. The following illustrations of my meaning will suffice:— "Pestilence comes into the world for capital crimes mentioned in the Torah, which are not brought before the earthly Tribunal. . . . Noisome beasts come into the world for vain swearing and for profanation of the Name (of God). Captivity comes upon the world for strange worship and incest, and for shedding of blood and for (not) giving release to the land."[1] As an example of the misfortune befalling the individual I will merely allude to a passage in *Arachin*, 16*a*, according to which leprosy is to be regarded as the penalty for immorality, slander, perjury and similar sins.

If we were now to complement R. Ammi's view by adding that there is no happiness without some preceding merit—and there is no serious objection to making this addition—then it would resolve itself into the theory of measure for measure, which forms a very common standard of reward and punishment in Jewish literature. Here are a few instances:—"Because the Egyptians wanted to destroy Israel by water (Exod. i. 22), they were themselves destroyed by the waters of the Red Sea, as it is said, Therefore I will *measure* their former work into their bosom (Is. lxv. 7)." Whilst, on the other hand, we read, "Because Abraham showed himself hospitable towards strangers, providing them with water (Gen. xviii. 4), God gave to his children a country blessed with plenty of water (Deut. viii. 1)." Sometimes this form of retribution goes so far as to define a special punishment to that part of the body which mostly contributed to the committing of the sin. Thus we read, "Samson rebelled against God by his eyes, as it is said, Get her (the Philistine woman) for me, for she pleases *my eyes* (Jud. xvi. 21); therefore, his *eyes* were put out by the Philistines (*ibid.* xviii. 9)"; whilst Absalom, whose sinful pride began by his *hair* (2 Sam. xiv. 25) met his fate by his *hair* (ibid. xviii. 9).[2] Nachum of Gamza himself explained his blindness and the maimed condition of his arms and legs as the consequence of a specific offence in having neglected his duty of succouring a poor man.

Addressing the dead body of the suppliant who perished while Nachum was delaying his help, he said, "Let my eyes (which had no pity for your pitiful gaze) become blind; may my hands and legs (that did not hasten to help thine) become maimed, and finally my whole body be covered with boils" (*Taanith,* 21*a*). "This was the hand that wrote it," said Cranmer at the stake; "therefore it shall suffer first punishment."

It is worth noticing that this retribution does not always consist in a material reward, but, as Ben Azai expressed it in the Mishnah (*Aboth,* iv. 5): "The reward of a command is a command, and the reward of a transgression is a transgression." So again: "Because Abraham showed himself so magnanimous in his treatment of the King of Sodom, and said, I will not take from thee a thread; therefore, his children enjoyed the privilege of having the command of Zizith, consisting in putting a thread or fringe in the border of their garments" (*Chulin,* 88*b*). In another passage we read, "He who is anxious to do acts of charity will be rewarded by having the means enabling him to do so" (*Baba Bathra,* 9*b*). In more general terms the same thought is expressed when the Rabbis explained the words, Ye shall sanctify yourselves, and ye shall be holy (Lev. xi. 44) to the effect that if man takes the initiative in holiness, even though in a small way, Heaven will help him to reach it to a much higher degree (*Yoma,* 39*a*).

Notwithstanding these passages, to which many more might be added, it cannot be denied that there are in the Rabbinical literature many passages holding out promises of *material* reward to the righteous as well as threatening the wicked with *material* punishment. Nor is there any need of denying it. Simple-minded men—and such the majority of the Rabbis were—will never be persuaded into looking with indifference on pain and pleasure; they will be far from thinking that poverty, loss of children, and sickness are no evil, and that a rich harvest, hope of posterity, and good health, are not desirable things. It *does* lie in our nature to consider the former as curses and the latter as blessings; "and if this be wrong there is no one to be made responsible for it but the Creator of nature." Accordingly the question must arise, How can a just and omnipotent God allow it to happen that men should suffer innocently? The most natural suggestion toward solving the difficulty would be that we are not innocent. Hence R. Ammi's assertion that affliction and death are both the outcome of sin and transgression; or, as R. Chanina ben Dossa expressed it, "It is not the wild beast but sin which kills" (*Berachoth,* 33*a*).

We may thus perceive in this theory an attempt "to justify the ways of God to man." Unfortunately it does not correspond with the real facts. The cry wrung from the prophets against the peace enjoyed by the wicked, and the pains inflicted on the righteous, which finds its echo in so many Psalms, and reaches its climax in the Book of Job, was by no means silenced in the times of the Rabbis. If long experience could be of any use, it only served to deepen perplexity. For all this suffering of the people of God, and the prosperity of their wicked persecutors, which perplexed the prophets and their immediate followers, were repeated during the death-struggle for independence against Rome, and were not lessened by the establishment of Christianity as the dominant religion. The only comfort which time brought them was, perhaps, that the long continuance of misfortune made them less sensible to suffering than their ancestors were. Indeed, a Rabbi of the first century said that his generation had by continuous experience of misery become as insensible to pain as the dead body is towards a prick of a needle (*Sabbath* 13*b*). The anaesthetic effect of long suffering may, indeed, help one to endure pain with more patience, but it cannot serve as an apology for the deed of the inflictors of the pain. The question, then, how to reconcile hard reality with the justice of God, remained as difficult as ever.

The most important passage in Rabbinical literature relating to the solution of this problem is the following (*Berachoth, 7a*):—With reference to Exod. xxxiii. 13, R. Jochanan said, in the name of R. José, that, among other things, Moses also asked God to explain to him the method of his Providence; a request that was granted to him. He asked God, Why are there righteous people who are prosperous, and righteous who are suffering; wicked who are prosperous, and wicked who suffer? The answer given to him was according to the one view that the prosperity of the wicked and the suffering of the righteous are a result of the conduct of their ancestors, the former being the descendants of righteous parents and enjoy their merits, whilst the latter, coming from a bad stock, suffer for the sins of those to whom they owe their existence. This view was suggested by the Scriptural words, "Keeping mercy for thousands (of generations). . . . visiting the iniquity of the fathers upon the children" (*ibid.* xxxiv. 7), which were regarded as the answer to Moses' question in the preceding chapter of Exodus. Prevalent, however, as this view may have been in ancient times, the Rabbis never allowed it to pass without some qualification. It is true that they had no objection to the former part of this doctrine, and they speak very frequently of the

"Merits of the Fathers" (זכות אבות) for which the remotest posterity is rewarded; for this could be explained on the ground of the boundless goodness of God, which cannot be limited to the short space of a lifetime. But there was no possibility of overcoming the moral objection against punishing people for sins they have not committed.

It will suffice to mention here that with reference to Joshua vii. 24, 25, the Rabbis asked the question, If he (Achan) sinned, what justification could there be for putting his sons and daughters to death? And by the force of this argument they interpreted the words of the Scriptures to mean that the children of the criminal were only compelled to be present at the execution of their father.

Such passages, therefore, as would imply that children have to suffer for the sins of their parents are explained by the Rabbis to refer to such cases where the children perpetuate the crimes of their fathers.[3] The view of R. José, which I have already quoted, had, therefore, to be dropped, and another version in the name of the same Rabbi is accepted. According to this theory the sufferer is a person either entirely wicked (רשע גמור) or not perfectly righteous (צדיק שאינו גמור), whilst the prosperous man is a person either perfectly righteous (צדיק גמור) or not entirely wicked (רשע שאינו גמור).

It is hardly necessary to say that there is still something wanting to supplement this view, for the given classification would place the not entirely wicked on the same level with the perfectly righteous, and on a much higher level than the imperfectly righteous, who are undoubtedly far superior. The following passage may be regarded as supplying this missing something:—"The wicked who have done some good work are as amply rewarded for it in *this* world as if they were men who have fulfilled the whole of the Torah, so that they may be punished for their sins in the next world (without interruption); whilst the righteous who have committed some sin have to suffer for it (in this world) as if they were men who burned the Law, so that they may enjoy their reward in the world to come (without interruption)."[4] Thus the real retribution takes place in the next world, the fleeting existence on earth not being the fit time either to compensate righteousness or to punish sin. But as, on the one hand, God never allows "that the merit of any creature should be cut short," whilst, on the other hand, he deals very severely with the righteous, punishing them for the slightest transgression; since, too, this reward and punishment are only of short duration, they must take place in this short terrestrial existence. There is thus established a sort of divine economy, lest the harmony of the next world should be disturbed.

Yet another objection to the doctrine under discussion remains to be noticed. It is that it justifies God by accusing man, declaring every sufferer as more or less of a sinner. But such a notion, if carried to its last consequences, must result in tempting us to withhold our sympathies from him. And, indeed, it would seem that there were some non-Jewish philosophers who argued in this way. Thus a certain Roman official is reported to have said to R. Akiba, "How can you be so eager in helping the poor? Suppose only a king, who, in his wrath against his slave, were to set him in the gaol, and give orders to withhold from him food and drink; if, then, one dared to act to the contrary, would not the king be angry with him?"[5] There is some appearance of logic in this notion put into the mouth of a heathen. The Rabbis, however, were inconsistent people, and responded to the appeal which suffering makes to every human heart without asking too many questions. Without entering here into the topic of charity in the Rabbinic literature, which would form a very interesting chapter, I shall only allude now to the following incident, which would show that the Rabbis did not abandon even those afflicted with leprosy, which, according to their own notion, given above, followed only as a punishment for the worst crimes. One Friday, we are told, when the day was about to darken, the Chassid Abba Tachnah was returning home, bearing on his shoulders the baggage that contained all his fortune; he saw a leprous man lying on the road, who addressed him; "Rabbi, do with me a deed of charity and take me into the town." The Rabbi now thought, "If I leave my baggage, where shall I find the means of obtaining subsistence for myself and my family? But if I forsake this leprous man I shall commit a mortal sin." In the end, he made the good inclination predominant over the evil one, and first carried the sufferer to the town (*Kohelet Rabba,* ix.7). The only practical conclusion that the Rabbis drew from such theories as identify suffering with sin were for the sufferer himself, who otherwise might be inclined to blame Providence, or even to blaspheme,[6] but would now look upon his affliction as a memento from heaven that there is something wrong in his moral state. Thus we read in *Berachoth* (5a): "If a man sees that affliction comes upon him, he ought to inquire into his action, as it is said, Let us search and try our ways, and turn again to the Lord (Lam. iii. 40)." This means to say that the sufferer will find that he has been guilty of some offence. As an illustration of this statement we may perhaps consider the story about R. Huna, occurring in the same tractate (p. 7b). Of this Rabbi it is said that he once experienced heavy pecuniary losses, whereupon his friends came to his house and said to him, "Let the master but examine his conduct a little closer." On this R. Huna answered, "Do you suspect me of having committed some misdeed?" His friends rejoined, "And do you think that God would pass judgment without justice?" R. Huna then followed their hint, and found that he did not treat his tenant farmer as generously as he ought. He offered redress, and all turned out well in the end. Something similar is to be found in the story of the martyrdom of R. Simon ben Gamaliel and R. Ishmael ben Elisha. Of these Rabbis we are told that on their way to be executed the one said to the other, "My heart leaves me, for I am not aware of a sin deserving such a death"; on which the other answered, "It might have happened that in your function as judge you sometimes—for your own convenience—were slow in administering justice."[7]

But even if the personal actions of the righteous were blameless, there might still be sufficient ground for his being afflicted and miserable. This may be found in his relations to his kind and surroundings, or, to use the term now more popular, by reason of human solidarity. Now, after the above remarks on the objections entertained by the Rabbis against a man's being punished for the sins of others, it is hardly necessary to say that their idea of solidarity has little in common with the crude notions of it current in very ancient times. Still, it can hardly be be doubted that the relation of the individual to the community was more keenly felt by the Rabbis than by the leaders in any other society, modern or ancient. According to the *Mechilta* (63a) it would, indeed, seem that to them the individual was not simply a member of the Jewish commonwealth, or a co-religionist, but a limb of the great and single body "Israel," and that as such he communicated both for good and evil the sensations of the one part to the whole. In *Leviticus Rabba* (ch. 4), where a parallel is to be found to this idea, the responsibility of the individual towards the community is further illustrated by R. Simon ben Yochai, in the following way: "It is," we read there, "to be compared to people sitting on board a ship, one of the passengers of which took an awl and began to bore holes in the bottom of the vessel. Asked to desist from his dangerous occupation, he answered, 'Why, I am only making holes on my own seat,' forgetting that when the water came in it would sink the whole ship." Thus the sin of a single man might endanger the whole of humanity. It was in conformity with the view of his father that R. Eliezer, the son of R. Simon (ben Yochai) said, "The world is judged after the merits or demerits of the majority, so that a single individual by his good or bad actions can decide the fate of his fellow-creatures, as it may happen that he is just the one who constitutes this majority."[8] Nor does this responsibility cease with the man's own actions. According to the Rabbis man is responsible even for the conduct of others—and as such liable to punishment—if he is indifferent to the wrong that is being perpetrated about him, whilst an energetic protest from his side could have prevented it. And the greater the man the greater is his responsibility. He may suffer for the sins of his family which is first reached by his influence; he may suffer for the sins of the whole community if he could hope to find a willing ear among them, and he may even suffer for the sins of the whole world if his influence extend so far, and he forbear from exerting it for good.[9] Thus the possibility is given that the righteous man may suffer with justice, though he himself has never committed any transgression.

As a much higher aspect of this solidarity—and as may have already suggested itself to the reader from the passage cited above from the *Mechilta*—we may regard the suffering of the righteous as an atonement for the sins of their contemporaries. "When there will be neither Tabernacle nor the Holy Temple," Moses is said to have asked God, "what will become of Israel?" Whereupon God answers, "I will take from among them the righteous man whom I shall consider as pledged for them, and will forgive all their sins"; the death of the perfect man, or even his suffering being looked upon as an expiation for the shortcoming of his generation.[10]

It is hardly necessary to remind the reader of the affinity of this idea with that of sacrifices in general, as in both cases it is the innocent being which has to suffer for the sins of another creature. But there is one vital point which makes all the difference. It is that in our case the suffering is not enforced, but is a voluntary act on the part of the sacrifice, and is even desired by him. Without entering here on the often-discussed theme of the suffering of the Messiah, I need only mention the words of R. Ishmael who, on a very slight provocation, exclaimed, "I am the atonement for the Jews," which means that he took upon him all their sins to suffer for them.[11] This desire seems to have its origin in nothing else but a deep sympathy and compassion with Israel. To suffer *for,* or, at least, *with* Israel was, according to the Rabbis, already the ideal of Moses: He is said, indeed, to have broken the Two Tables with the purpose of committing some sin, so that he would have either to be condemned together with Israel (for the sin of the golden calf), or to be pardoned together with them.[12] And this conduct was not only expected from the leaders of Israel, but almost from every Jew. Thus we read in *Taanith* (11*a*), "When Israel is in a state of affliction (as, for instance, famine) one must not say, I will rather live by myself, and eat and drink, and peace be unto thee, my soul. To those who do so the words of the Scriptures are to be applied: And in that day did the Lord God of Hosts call to weeping and to mourning, . . . and behold joy and gladness. . . . Surely this iniquity shall not be purged out from you till ye die (Is. xxii. 12-14)." Another passage is to the effect that when a man shows himself indifferent to the suffering of the community there come the two angels (who accompany every Jew) put their hands on his head, and say, "This man who has separated himself shall be excluded from their consolations." (*Taanith, ibid.*)

We might now characterize this sort of suffering as the chastisement of love (of the righteous) to mankind, or rather to Israel. But we must not confuse it with the chastisement of love (יסורין של אהבה) often mentioned in the Talmud, though this idea also seems calculated to account for the suffering of the righteous. Here the love is not on the side of the sufferer, but proceeds from him who inflicts this suffering. "Him," says R. Huna, "in whom God delights he crushes with suffering." As a proof of this theory the verse from Is. liii. 10 is given, which words are interpreted to mean: Him whom the Lord delights in he puts to grief. Another passage, by the same authority, is to the effect that where there is no sufficient cause for punishment (the man being entirely free from sin), we have to regard his suffering as a chastisement of love, for it is said: "Whom the Lord loveth he correcteth" (Proverbs iii. 11).[13] To what purpose he corrects him may, perhaps, be seen from the following passage: "R. Eleazar ben Jacob says: If a man is visited by affliction he has to be thankful to God for it: for suffering draws man to, and reconciles him with God, as it said: For whom God loveth he correcteth."[14]

It is in conformity with such a high conception that affliction, far from being dreaded, becomes almost a desirable end, and we hear many Rabbis exclaim, "Beloved is suffering," for by it fatherly love is shown to man by God; by it man obtains purification and atonement, by it Israel came in possession of the best gifts, such as the Torah, the Holy Land, and eternal life.[15] And so also the sufferer, far from being considered as a man with a suspected past, becomes an object of veneration, on whom the glory of God rests, and he brings salvation to the world if he bears his affliction with joyful submission to the will of God.[16] Continuous prosperity is by no means to be longed after, for, as R. Ishmael taught, "He who passed forty days without meeting adversity has already received his (share of the) world (to come) in this life."[17] Nay, the standing rule is that the really righteous suffer, whilst the wicked are supposed to be in a prosperous state. Thus, R. Jannai said, "We (average people) enjoy neither the prosperity of the wicked nor the afflictions of the righteous,"[18] whilst his contemporary, Rab, declared that he who experiences no affliction and persecution does not belong to them (the Jews).[19]

2. The second main view on Retribution is that recorded in the Tractate *Sabbath* (56b) as in direct opposition to that of R. Ammi. It is that there is suffering as well as death without sin and transgression. We may now just as well infer that there is prosperity and happiness without preceding merits. And this is, indeed, the view held by R. Meir. For in contradiction to the view cited above, R. Meir declares that the request of Moses to have explained to him the mysterious ways of Providence was *not* granted, and the answer he received was, "And I will shew mercy on whom I will shew mercy" (Exod. xxxiii. 19), which means to say, even though he to whom the mercy is shown be unworthy of it. The old question arises how such a procedure is to be reconciled with the justice and omnipotence of God. The commentaries try to evade the difficulty by suggesting some of the views given above, as that the real reward and punishment are only in the world to come, or that the affliction of the righteous is only chastisement of love, and so on. From the passages we are about to quote, however, one gains the impression that some Rabbis rather thought that this great problem will indeed not bear discussion or solution at all. Thus we read in a Baraitha: "The angels said to God, Why have you punished Adam with death? He answered, On account of his having transgressed my commandment (with regard to the eating of the tree of knowledge). But why had Moses and Aaron to die? The reply given to them is in the words, Eccl. ix.2: 'All things come alike to all, there is one event to the righteous and the wicked, to the good and clean and unclean' " (*Sabbath*, 55b). In Tractate *Menachoth, 29b,* we again find a passage in which we are told how, "when Moses ascended to heaven, God showed him also the great men of futurity. R. Akiba was sitting and interpreting the law in a most wonderful way. Moses said to God: Thou hast shown me his worth, show me also his reward: on which he is bidden to look back. There he perceives him dying the most cruel of deaths, and his flesh being sold by weight. Moses now asks: Is this the reward of such a life? whereupon God answers him: Be silent; this I have determined."

It is impossible not to think of the beautiful lines of the German poet:—

> Warum schleppt sich blutend, elend,
> Unter Kreuzlast der Gerechte,
> Während glücklich als ein Sieger
> Trabt auf hohem Ross der Schlechte?
>
> Also fragen wir beständig,
> Bis man uns mit einer Handvoll
> Erde endlich stopft die Mäuler—
> Aber ist das eine Antwort?

Still, when examined a little closer, one might perhaps suggest that these passages not only contain a rebuke to man's importunity in wanting to intrude into the secrets of God, but also hint at the possibility that even God's omnipotence is submitted to a certain law—though designed by his own holy will—which he could not alter without detriment to the whole creation. Indeed, in one of the mystical accounts of the martyrdom of R. Akiba and other great Rabbis, God is represented as asking the sufferers to accept his hard decree without protest, unless they wish him to destroy the whole world. In *Taanith* (25a) again we read of a certain renowned Rabbi, who lived in great poverty, that once in a dream he asked the divine Shechinah how long he would have still to endure this bitter privation. The answer given to him was: "My son, will it please you that I destroy the world for your sake?" It is only in this light that we shall be able to understand such passages in the Rabbinic literature as that God almost suffers himself when he has to inflict punishment either on the individual or whole communities. Thus God is represented as mourning for seven days (as in the case when one loses a child) before he brought the Deluge on the world (*Gen. Rabbah,* c. 27); he bemoans the fall of Israel and the destruction of the Temple (see *Pessikta* 136b), and the Shechinah laments even when the criminal suffers his just punishment (*Mishnah Sanhedrin,* vi. 5). And it is not by rebelling against these laws that he tries to redeem his suffering. He himself has recourse to prayer, and says: "May it be my will that my mercy conquer my wrath, that my love over-rule my strict justice, so that I may treat my children with love" (see *Berachoth,* 7a). If now man is equal to God, he has nevertheless, or rather on that account, to submit to the law of God without any outlook for reward or punishment; or, as Antigonos expressed it, "Be not as slaves that minister to the Lord with a view to receive recompence."[20] Certainly it would be hazardous to maintain that Antigonos' saying was a consequence of this doctrine; but, at any rate, we see a clear tendency to keep the thought of reward (in spite of the prominent part it holds in the Bible) out of view. Still more clearly it is seen when, with reference to Ps. cxii., "Blessed is the man . . . that delighteth greatly in his commandments," R. Joshua ben Levi remarks that the meaning is that the man desires only to do his commandments, but he does not want the rewards connected with them.[21] This is the more remarkable, as the whole content of this chapter is nothing else than a long series of promises of various rewards, so that the explanation of R. Joshua ben Levi is in almost direct contradiction to the simple meaning of the words. On the other hand, also, every complaint about suffering must cease. Not only is affliction no direct chastisement by God in the way of revenge, for, as R. Eleazar teaches: "With the moment of Revelation (that is to say, since moral conduct became law) neither bliss nor adversity came from God, but the bliss comes by itself to those who act rightly, and conversely" (*Deut. Rabba,* c. 42); but even when it would seem to us that we suffer innocently, we have no right to murmur, as God himself is also suffering, and, as the Talmud expresses it, "It is enough for the slave to be in the position of his master" (*Berachoth,* 58*b*).

This thought of the compassion—in its strictest sense of suffering-with—of God with his creatures becomes a new motive for avoiding sin. "Woe to the wicked," exclaims a Rabbi, "who by their bad actions turn the mercy of God into strict justice." And the later mystics explain distinctly that the great crime of sin consists in causing pain, so to speak, to the Shechinah. One of them compared it with the slave who abuses the goodness of his master so far as to buy for his money arms to wound him.[22] But, on the other hand, it becomes, rather inconsistently, also a new source of comfort; for, in the end, God will have to redeem himself from this suffering, which cannot be accomplished so long as Israel is still under punishment.[23] Most interesting is the noble prayer by a Rabbi of a very late mystical school: "O God, speedily bring about the redemption. I am not in the least thinking of what I may gain by it. I am willing to be condemned to all tortures in hell, if only the Shechinah will cease to suffer."[24]

If we were now to ask for the attitude of the Synagogue towards these two main views, we would have to answer that—as already hinted at the opening of this paper—it never decided for the one or the other. R. David מרטיקא dared even to write a whole book in defence of Adam (זכות אדם) proving that he committed no sin in eating the fruits of the tree of knowledge against the literal sense of the Scriptures, which were also taken by the Rabbis literally.[25] By this he destroyed the prospects of many a theodicy, but it is not known to us that he was severely rebuked for it. It has been said by a great writer that the best theology is that which is not consistent, and this advantage the theology of the Synagogue possesses to its utmost extent. It accepted with R. Ammi, the stern principle of divine retribution, insofar as it makes man feel the responsibility of his actions, and makes suffering a discipline. But it never allowed this principle to be carried so far as to deny the sufferer our sympathy, and by a series of conscious and unconscious modifications, he passed from the state of a sinner into the zenith of the saint and the perfectly righteous man. But, on the other hand, the Synagogue also gave entrance to the very opposite view which, abandoning every attempt to account for suffering, bids man do his duty without any hope of reward, even as God also does his. Hence the remarkable phenomenon in the works of later Jewish moralists that whilst they never weary of the most detailed accounts of the punishments awaiting the sinner, and the rewards in store for the righteous, they warn us most emphatically that our actions must not be guided by these unworthy considerations, and that our only motive should be the love of God and submission to his holy will.[26]

Nor must it be thought that the views of the Rabbis are so widely divergent from those enunciated in the Bible. The germ of almost all the later ideas is already to be found in the Scriptures. It only needed the progress of time to bring into prominence those features which proved at a later period most acceptable. Indeed, it would seem that there is also a sort of domestication of religious ideas. On their first association with man there is a certain rude violence about them which, when left to the management of untutored minds would certainly do great harm. But, let only this association last for centuries, during which these ideas have to be subdued by practical use, and they will, in due time, lose their former roughness, will become theologically workable, and turn out the greatest blessing to inconsistent humanity.

HONOR IN RABBINIC LAW AND ETHICS

Chaim W. Reines

Honor, a sentiment which exerts a strong influence in all human societies, involves certain moral and legal problems of considerable practical import. From the ethical standpoint, it is necessary to define the place of the sense of honor in the moral life of man. Legally, we must determine the law's attitude toward the various offences against honor.

First, what does the concept of honor involve? Most of the thinkers who treat the subject give the concept an explanation that is purely sociological; honor is the expression of the individual's position in society.[1] However, honor's social, as well as its ethical meaning, can be explained only on the basis of the idea of the dignity of man.[2] A similar conception of honor is found in the work of a noted jurist (K. Binding, *Die Ehre und ihre Verletzung*). Man is a self-conscious personality, endowed with reason and the power of self-determination (animals, as well as the mentally deficient, lacking these faculties, lack a sense of honor as well). Consequently, the human personality as a subject for ends and an end in itself, possesses an inherent dignity and commands the respect of others.[3] Human society is based on mutual respect of individuals for each other. Since a human being can develop his spiritual capacities only in society, he must secure the "acceptance" of his fellow men, who evaluate him according to his skills, (moral) virtues, and merits (in terms of society). The concept of honor, therefore, signifies the dignity of the person, and the esteem in which the individual is held in society.

Every society possesses certain rules for social contact (manners and customs), aimed to protect the dignity of the individual. The sense of honor is intimately bound up with the self-consciousness of the individual. An offense against a fellow human being's honor, therefore, constitutes an affront to his self-consciousness, and usually provokes a strong emotional and affective outburst.[4] Further, it is an offense against the dignity of man and the respect due all human beings in society; it may also damage an individual's reputation and social position. These considerations clarify the relevance of the concept of honor to ethics and the law. Ethics are generally based on the notion of the dignity of the person; it demands consideration for the interests and feelings of fellow human beings. Consequently, it should also stress consideration for a person's honor. Hence it was that Maimonides[5] pointed out that the commandment to "love thy neighbor as thyself" implies that one should regard one's neighbor's property and honor as highly as one does one's own. The concept of rights denotes the individual's legitimate sphere of interests; honor, on the other hand, signifies the individual's inner worth, the esteem in which he is held by his fellows. There is, therefore, a close logical connection between the concept of honor, which signifies the dignity of the individual as a "person," and the latter's civil status and rights.[6] Consequently, since the law is concerned with the protection of rights, its scope includes the protection of honor.[7] However, since the law is in the main interested in the minimum demands of security for the individual and society, and omits the more subtle cases of personal offense, its concern with the protection of honor is a limited one (this fact has been frequently deplored in recent times). Gradually, however, the law has extended the range of cases of this kind for which a fine may be imposed. This point will be made clear in this paper with regard to rabbinic law.

Views and attitudes concerning honor are, however, influenced by certain sociological factors; sometimes, honor's importance is stressed extravagantly. The aristocratic "code of honor" demands that the individual should at all costs defend his honor, killing the offender or sacrificing his own life in the process.[8] According to a view long current among European nations, and one which still prevails in certain circles, honor is man's highest good. It should be placed above all other (moral) considerations, and prized even above life itself.[9] Regarded as an expression of courage and of a heroic attitude to life, actually this view is based on extreme vanity and egocentricity, on the perversion of the true (ethical) meaning of the concept of honor. In reaction to this extreme position, a contrary position developed which attached little or even no importance to the concept of honor.[10] This view is equally repugnant, since it overlooks honor's ethical significance. A correct and balanced view of the sense of honor would be based on its ethical and social relevance, and would, at the same time, repudiate its egotistical manifestations. As noted, honor has a double aspect: it signifies both the individual's *inner* worth and the esteem in which society holds him. Now, a man cannot in any way be damaged inwardly by an insult; he can, however, impair his own inner worth by (immoral) actions. To be sure, social esteem is no indifferent matter. Everyone is eager, even obliged, to guard his honor in society. However, it must be left to the discretion and tact of the person concerned to decide, in individual cases, how much weight to attach to considerations of honor; and sometimes it is imperative that one disregard offenses against one's honor for the sake of a higher moral cause.

Judaism proclaimed the idea of the dignity of man. Consequently, Jewish ethics placed the utmost stress on consideration for the honor of a fellow human being.[11] Rabbinic ethics lay particular emphasis on this point. The rabbis said: "When you insult a fellow human being, know that you are insulting one created in the image of God."[12] Another rabbinic statement expresses the same idea: Slapping a fellow Jew in the face is equivalent to slapping the face of the *Shekhinah,* the Divine Presence.[13] These statements were apparently intended to convince people that they ought to take a more serious view of offenses against honor —acts usually committed thoughtlessly. Hence, the deduction that an act of this nature constitutes a graver moral sin than others (e.g., adultery, punishable by death according to Jewish law), and that the offender in this regard loses his share in the Hereafter.[14] The rabbis also enacted various laws, aimed to protect the public honor of all classes of people (especially the poor).[15] It was further ruled that the "dignity of God's creatures" (*kvod-ha-briyoth*) is so important that a religious law may be disregarded in order to maintain that dignity.[16] In addition, the rabbis showed remarkable insight into the individual's psychological need to be honored according to his worth. This insight is expressed in the story about Honi "the circle-drawer."[17] When, according to legend, Honi awoke from his long sleep and went to the Beth Hamidrash, he was not recognized by the scholars, nor given due honor. Honi took this affront so to heart that he died. The Talmud comments that this story illustrates the accuracy of the popular proverb: "Give me companionship, or give me death."

Society without the proper esteem of one's fellows offers no satisfaction. The rabbis apparently had their own inner circle of scholars in mind. Although they urged students not to undertake scholarly study with an eye to honorific rewards, they were, nevertheless, careful to add that scholarship would be crowned with respectful recognition.[18] A Talmudic legend expresses the insight that an insult is not only a grave moral sin but—by evoking retaliation on the part of the offended individual—it may even cause considerable harm to the community as a whole. The legend associates the destruction of the Second Temple with just such a calamitous incident. The story[19] goes that a man in Jerusalem planned a banquet, to which he told his servant to invite a friend of his called Kamza. Instead, the servant invited another man named Bar Kamza, an enemy of his master. When the host recognized Bar Kamza among the guests, he ordered him to leave the house. Deeply insulted, Bar Kamza pleaded that he be spared that humiliation, going so far as to offer to cover the costs of the banquet. But his offer was rejected, and Bar Kamza was forced to leave. Enraged by the silence and apparent acquiescence of the rabbis present, he denounced the Jewish leaders to the Roman emperor as plotting a revolt; the emperor came to Jerusalem with his troops and destroyed the Temple.[20] Rabbi Elazar commented: "Come and see how far-reaching is the effect of insult, because of which the Lord helped Bar Kamza destroy His Temple."

As noted, the insulted individual feels a stronger impulse to retaliate than any other aggrieved person. Recognizing this psychological fact, a medieval rabbinic authority ruled that the insulted individual, who replies in kind, cannot be held responsible, since not everyone has the necessary self-control to keep calm under insults.[21] However, Jewish ethics, which generally frowns on revenge, urges the victim of an insult not to retaliate. This thought is expressed in a source[22] which declares: "They that are shamed, and do not shame others, that hear their disgrace and do not retort, that act out of love, and rejoice in chastisement—it is of them that the Writ says: 'But they that love Him are as the sun when it goeth forth in its might.' "[23] The attitude of those, who do not reply to insults in kind, is here considered extremely virtuous, because it requires a large measure of self-control. The same counsel—to keep silent when insulted—is also given in the Biblical wisdom literature: "He that despiseth his neighbor lacketh understanding; but a man of discernment holdeth his peace."[24] The stoic philosopher Epictetus, also, observed that the hurt derives really not from the insulter, but from the injured party's own thoughts. He counsels the victim therefore, to master his mind so as to gain time to think things over and retain his self-control.[25] It is interesting to quote the view of Maimonides on this subject. In several of his letters to his favorite pupil, that reveal a glimpse of his personality, Maimonides urges his disciple to disregard the insults flung at him by his opponents. As for himself, Maimonides observes, his sense of dignity saves him from replying to fools according to their folly. He who wishes to fulfill man's real destiny—reason— ought to pay no heed to such follies."[26] And, in his Code, Maimonides declares that insults from the ignorant or spiritually inferior ought to be ignored; one ought not even take the trouble to reprove the culprit though one is obliged to do so in the case of other sins. Rather, one ought to forgive the culprit straight away. However Maimonides was an exception in taking this position, one which reflects only his own philosophical attitude, prompted, no doubt, by his opinion of the low spiritual level of the "masses." Far from accepting insults with equanimity, whatever their source, the rabbis were quite sensitive on this point.[28]

Rabbinic ethics demand that the offender repeatedly beg forgiveness, as in the case of any act of injustice committed against one's fellow man.[29] It was stressed that the sin could not be exculpated by the payment of indemnities alone; the culprit had to obtain the victim's forgiveness. On the other hand, a victim who refused to grant forgiveness for an offence against his ego, was considered cruel.[30] An exception was made in the case of slander, which it was said, could not be forgiven.[31] This opinion is apparently based on the reasoning that the rabbis consider slander, which destroys an individual's reputation, as one of the most heinous of sins. Rabbinic law imposes definite monetary fines on the various kinds of physical assault which are disrespectful of the person—such as slapping the face, spitting, pulling the ear, plucking the hair, etc. A substantial fine was also imposed for other acts, which put a person to shame by forcing him to violate the accepted customs of decency, such as uncovering a woman's head in a public place.[32] The rule was formulated that the amount of the fine is proportionate to the status of the offender (the higher the status of the offended, and the lower the status of the offender, the larger the fine). This rule is based on the insight that society honors each individual according to his status, and that the dishonor inflicted by the offensive act differs accordingly. Since, however, the rich enjoyed high social prestige, while the poor were held in low esteem, it follows that the rich should be awarded a greater indemnity than the poor.[33]

Another opinion, apparently finding this rule to be impractical—

since it varies the amount of the indemnity according to each individual case—holds that all persons who have some means should receive the same indemnity, on the fiction that they were all men of good family who had lost their fortune. The implication is that the middle class and the very rich should be awarded equal indemnities. However, the poor should be awarded lesser amounts.[34] This distinction is the recognition of the sharp class division that developed in Jewish society; the law had to take into account the actual fact that the poor were not esteemed as much as the rich. (In all other instances, Jewish law recognizes no class divisions.) However, Rabbi Akiba, who enunciated the maxim of the dignity of man formed in the image of God, and of Israel as the recipient of the Torah,[35] holds that the poor, too, should be awarded equal indemnities with the rich, as the descendants of Abraham, Isaac, and Jacob.[36] The latter formula, indicating the common spiritual heritage of the Jewish people, endows all Jews with a nobility that persists, despite any accidental class distinction. Talmudic law imposes a fine for offenses against honor only in the event the offense is *active*; but not for purely verbal offenses,[37] though the slander may, sometimes, seriously damage the reputation of the individual (and indirectly cause material damage, as well). As a general rule, Biblical-Talmudic law imposes punishment only for actions, not for words.[38] However, in some cases, punishment is imposed for slander, as well. Thus, the Mishnah points out[39] that the fine of one hundred silver coins which, according to Biblical law[40] is imposed on a newly-wed husband, who falsely accuses his wife of adultery, is imposed only for the slander. The rabbis further derived, from this case, that the punishment imposed for slander is even more severe than that imposed for a physical act of abomination, the fine levied on the slanderous husband being twice as high as the fine for rape.[41] In cases where a solitary witness appeared in court to testify that he had seen an individual perform an immoral act, some rabbis used to sentence the witness to flagellation. Since the testimony of one witness is not sufficient, according to Jewish law, the surmise was that the witness had testified solely with the malicious intent of damaging another man's reputation.[42]

One source declares that he who calls his fellow "slave" should be placed under ban; he who calls him "bastard" should be sentenced to flagellation; he, who calls him "wicked" (*rasha*), may have his very life threatened by the maligned.[43] The first two epithets constitute a grave threat to the maligned individual's place in the community, since a person stigmatized as slave or bastard may not intermarry with other members of the community. Consequently, the court imposes various punishments for the use of these epithets in order to prevent the spreading of malicious rumors about legitimacy.

The epithet "wicked" (*rasha*), meaning that the individual so labeled is a man of bad character, who does not meet his obligations toward his fellow men, may damage the social position of the individual concerned; a person with a reputation of this kind is neither respected nor trusted, and people refuse to do business with him.[44] However, according to our text, the court does not intervene; it is the offended person, himself, who theratens the offender's "very life." The commentators explain that the latter phrase means that the maligned may deprive the maligner of his sources of livelihood (by unfair competition).[45] However, Rashi objected to this interpretation, on the ground that it cannot be assumed that the sages would allow such an act of revenge. Rashi interprets "very life" to mean that the offended will quarrel with the offender and make threats against him.[46] This interpretation is partly correct, since the phrase is a general expression of the offended individual's violent reaction, and should not be taken literally. But the phrase does imply that in the absence of any action on the part of the court, the offended individual may be prompted to take the law into his own hands, rebuking the offender to prevent future assaults on his honor. However, in the post-Talmudic period, the Geonim ordered that in all cases of verbal insult, the court should impose a ban on the offender until he should agree to conciliate the offended individual, either by words or (when the latter was unwilling to accept verbal reconciliation) by the payment of a monetary fine.[47] Speaking in more general terms, Maimonides[48] declares that the court, acting according to its lights, has to take appropriate measures in each case of this kind. There was, however, no uniform usage in this matter, every community having its own regulations. Generally, the prevailing practice was for the offender to be sentenced to either flagellation or a monetary fine;[49] but, at the same time, the court explained to the offended individual that it was unbecoming for a Jew to derive material gain from such a case, and that the money ought to be donated for some worthy cause, such as the support of poor scholars.[50] In addition to this fine, the offender was induced to declare publicly during the synagogue service that he had sinned against the Lord and the person he had maligned by his slander. Thus, the offender received his due punishment and was sufficiently humiliated; at the same time, the offended individual was prevented from taking undue advantage and from seeking further revenge, and a reconciliation was achieved.

The foregoing review proves that the rabbis were concerned with defending the honor of all classes of society, including the *am haaretz* (ignorant). However, special stress was naturally laid on the honor of the learned (*talmid chacham*). The latter were the teachers and spiritual leaders of the nation; they, also, acted frequently in the capacity of local judges and leaders, and it was essential that the people show them due respect. Consequently, it was said that he who insults a *talmid chacham* or even another man in the presence of a *talmid chacham,* is to be considered an *apikores* (one who behaves insolently toward the word of the Lord)—since the *talmid chacham* represents the moral teaching and authority of the Torah, insulting him is equivalent to insulting the Lord himself.[51] However, at the same time, it was recognized that the honor bestowed on a scholar is actually not intended for the Torah as an abstract entity, but for the individual who excels in learning (and in moral virtue). So it was ruled that a scholar may, at his will, disregard (or allow others to disregard) his honor, and to perform actions unseemly in a person of his dignity (such as serving his guests at a banquet, an action attributed to the Patriarch Rabbi Gamaliel).[52]

The most famous rabbis did, indeed, act on this principle, sometimes humbling themselves, and even enduring grave insults for the sake of a higher cause, such as preserving peaceful relations between husband and wife.[53] On the other hand, it was said that a scholar should not leave unavenged an offense against his honor, since such an act damages the prestige of the Torah.[54] Maimonides explains, however, that this rule is valid only in situations where a scholar is insulted publicly; on all other occasions, he should be forgiving.[55] In the same connection, Rabbi Meir of Rothenburg wrote to a colleague that scholars are not to pay much heed to insults to their person—rather they should emulate the patience shown by the master prophet (Moses). But scholars should be all the more zealous to avenge insults shown to other people.[56]

According to Talmudic law, he who insults a scholar may be placed under ban, either by the insulted person or by the courts.[57] This measure was so freely applied in the Middle Ages that some rabbis voiced their opposition to it.[58] There was another ruling to the effect that an insulted scholar should be awarded (by the offender) a full fine (*boshto meshalem*) according to his dignity and not the minimum fine fixed for the insults suffered by the unscholarly.[59] It was also applied in Spain and elsewhere during the Middle Ages.[60] However, some scholars declined to take advantage of it.[61] On the other hand,—there were vigorous complaints in later centuries that some officiating rabbis were taking advantage of the law to extort money from the wealthy members of their communities. As a consequence of these protests, the imposition of special fines for insults to a scholar was abolished.[62] However, a Sephardic rabbi, Samuel Alkalai, strongly defended the scholars in this matter.[63] He admitted that the vain scholar, who sought to dominate others and derive undue advantages from his scholarly position, was certainly not entitled to extort fines for slights.[64] However, the presence of isolated cases of this nature could not, in Alkalai's opinion, serve as a ground for depriving other honest scholars of the rights the Talmud grants them to protect their honor.

Our survey has shown that the rabbis had a deep understanding of the ethical, social, and legal aspects of the concept of honor. Their regulations, in this matter, were intended to meet both the demands of justice (the punishment of the offender) and of morality (forgiveness and reconciliation). These regulations were also flexible enough to meet the varied needs of the times. In addition, the stress laid on the protection of the honor of scholars, and the laws enacted to this end—though there were some abuses in their application, and they were in large part abolished in later centuries—helped to maintain the respect for learning characteristic of the Jewish people throughout the ages. In this, as in other respects, the Jewish past may serve as a shining example for our own times, when consideration for the dignity of man, and respect for learning, have sunk so low.

IN PRAISE OF THE TALMUD

Jacob Neusner

The Talmud records not only laws, but the process by which laws are uncovered. By describing that process, it posits, and proposes to resolve, the tension between ordinary life and logic. The argument develops its themes through inquiry into fundamental principles and the application of those fundamental principles to ordinary affairs. These principles themselves are then subjected to analysis and a search for still more basic and ultimately unifying conceptions. The conceptions prove to be highly relative and abstract. So even the placing of a napkin at a meal is turned into a discipline for living, a discipline which requires that logic and order everywhere prevail, and demands that concerns for a vast world of unseen, principled relationships come to bear. Humble and thoughtless action is elevated and made worthy of thought, shown to bear heavy consequences.

The Talmud is a fundamentally non-historical document. The argument, though unfolding by generations of rabbis, does not center upon the authority and biography of the ancients, but about their timeless, impersonal reasons for ruling as they do. The participants in the argument sometimes are named, but the most interesting constructions are given anonymously: "What is the reason of the House of Shammai?" "Do not the House of Shammai and the House of Hillel agree with R. Yosi and R. Meir, respectively?" Elegant analytical structures are not assigned to specific authorities, because to the Talmud the time and place, name and occupation of the authority behind an inquiry are of no great interest. Logic and criticism are not bound to specific historical or biographical circumstances. Therefore the principles of orderly, disciplined life are not reduced to the personalities or situations of the men who laid down or discovered those principles.

Talmudic thinking stands over against historical, including psychological, interpretation because of its preference for finding abstraction and order in concrete, timeless problems of daily life. What counts is reason, ubiquitous, predominant, penetrating. The object of reason is twofold: the criticism of the given by the criterion of fundamental principles of order; and the demonstration of the presence, within commonplace matters, of transcendent considerations. Casuistical controversy over trivialities does not always link up to a transcendent concern; but always is meant to. For the ultimate issue is how to discover the order of the well-ordered existence and well-correlated relationships; and the prevalent attitude is perfect seriousness (not specious solemnity) about man's intention and his actions.

The presupposition of the Talmudic approach to life is that order is better than chaos, reflection than whim, decision than accident, ratiocination and rationality than witlessness and force. The only admissible force is the power of fine logic, ever refined against the gross matter of daily living. The sole purpose is so to construct the discipline of everyday life and so to pattern the relationships among men that all things are intelligible, well regulated, and trustworthy. The Talmud stands for the perfect intellectualization of life, the subjection of life to rational study; nothing is so trivial as to be unrelated to some deeper principle.

The Talmud's conception of man is this: man thinks, therefore both he and what he does are worth taking seriously. Man will respond to reason and subject himself to discipline founded upon criticism. His response will consist in utter self-consciousness about all he does, thinks, and says. To be sure, man is dual, composed of the impulse to do evil as much as the impulse to do good. As the famous saying about not interrupting one's study even to admire nature makes clear, man cannot afford even for one instant to break off from consciousness, to open himself to the utterly natural, lest he lose touch with revealed order and revealed law, the luminous disciplines of the numinous.

Nor is the ultimate issue of man solely ethical. To be sure, one must do the good, but Torah encompasses more than ethical behavior. The good is more than the moral; it is also the well-regulated conduct of matters to which morality is *not* important. The whole man, private and public, is to be disciplined. Etiquette is blended with theology, furthermore with something one might call metaphysics, and finally with social law—relationships with sages, on the one side, and idolaters, on the other. No limits are set to the methods of exploring reason and searching for order. Social order with its concommitant ethical concern is no more important than the psychic order of the individual, with its full articulation in the ritual life. All reality comes under the examination of the critical intellect.

The Talmud's single-minded pursuit of unifying truths constitutes its primary discipline. But the discipline does not derive from the perception of unifying order in the natural world. It comes, rather, from the lessons imparted by the supernatural, in the Torah. The sages perceived the Torah not as a mélange of sources and laws of different origins, but as a single, unitary document, a corpus of laws reflective of an underlying, ordered will. The Torah revealed the way things should be, just as the rabbis' formulation and presentation of their laws tell how things should be, whether or not that is how they actually are done. The order derives from the plan and will of the Creator of the world, the foundation of all reality. The Torah was interpreted by the Talmudic rabbis to be the architect's design for reality: God looked into the Torah and created the world, just as an architect follows his design in raising a building. A single, whole Torah—in two forms, oral and written, to be sure—underlay the one, seamless reality of the world. The search for the unities hidden by the pluralities of the trivial world, the supposition that some one thing was revealed by many things—these represent in intellectual form the theological and metaphysical conception of a single, unique God, creator of heaven and earth, revealer of one complete Torah, revelation, guarantor of the unity and ultimate meaning of all the human actions and events that constitute history. The Talmud therefore links the private deeds of man to a larger pattern, provides a great general "meaning" for small, particular, trivial doings.

Behind this conception of the unifying role of reason and the integrating force of criticism lies the conviction that God supplies the model for man's mind, therefore man, through reasoning in the Torah's laws, may penetrate into God's intent and plan. The rabbis of the Talmud believed they studied Torah as God did in heaven; their schools were conducted like the academy on high; they performed rituals just as God performed rituals, wearing fringes as did He, putting on phylacteries just as God put on phylacteries. In studying Torah, they besought the heavenly paradigm revealed by God "in his image" and handed down from Moses and the prophets to their own teachers. If the rabbis of the Talmud studied and realized the Divine teaching of Moses, whom they called "our rabbi," it was because the order they

would impose upon earthly affairs would replicate on earth the order
they perceived from heaven. Today these beliefs may be seen as projections of Talmudic beliefs onto heaven. But the Talmudic sages believed
they themselves were projections of heavenly "values" onto earth. And
what they saw projected from heaven to earth was, as I have said, the
order and rational construction of reality.

To the Talmudic way of thinking, man is liberated, not imprisoned,
by reason, which opens the way to true creativity, the work of finding,
or imposing, form and order upon chaos. The wherewithal of creativity
is triviality, and what is to be done with triviality is to uncover, within
or beyond the simple things of chaos, the order, the structure, the co-
herence of the whole. What is concrete therefore is subordinate to what
is abstract. It is the construction of the larger reality that reveals the
traits of that reality. And to the Talmudic rabbi, the most interesting
aspect of reality is the human and the societal: the village, the home,
the individual. Talmudic Judaism, because of its stress on what and
how one eats and drinks, has been called a religion of pots and pans.
And so it is, if not that alone, for its raw materials are the irreducible
atoms of concrete life. But these come at the beginning; they stand
prior to what will become of them, are superficial by contrast to what
lies beneath them.

What is to be done with these atoms, these smallest building blocks
of reality? They are to be subjected to control, the man to self-control.
All impulses are to be carefully regulated in accord with the Divine plan
for reality; all are good when so ordered, evil when not. The robust
sexuality of the Talmudic laws of marital relations testifies to the rabbis'
seriousness and matter-of-factness about what today is highly charged
material.

So the regulation of the impulse was the opposite of its suppression;
it was its liberation. But what was done had to be done rightly. The
nuptial bed was the right circumstance. To be sure, appropriate social
and legal regulations brought the couple to their bed; but (in theory at
least) if an unmarried man, legally permitted to marry his beloved, engaged in sexual relations with an unmarried woman, the couple thereby
consummated a legitimate union and were regarded as fully and legally
married in all respects. It is assumed that a man does not enter sexual
relations lightly or licentiously; it is taken for granted that people intend to do the right thing. Again, the time had to be right. The Torah

prohibited sexual relations during a woman's menstrual cycle. Then not during that cycle relations are to be encouraged. The circumstances then had to be discussed: Is it all right in not completely private conditions? The ultra-pious would drive away even flies and mosquitoes. So the course of law rolls on, regulating what is natural and enhancing it through good order, bringing to consciousness what is beneath the surface, through the therapy of public analysis and reasoned inquiry legitimizing what might be repressed.

Certainly, the Talmudic way of thinking appeals to, and itself approves, the cultured over the uncultured, those capable of self-conscious criticism over those too dull to think. "An ignorant man cannot be pious." Fear of sin without wisdom is worthless. The sages encouraged the articulate over the inarticulate: "The shy person cannot learn." For the give-and-take of argument, one cannot hang back out of feigned or real bashfulness. Reason makes men equals and reveals their inequalities. Reason is not a quirk of personality, but a trait of mind, therefore must be shamelessly and courageously spelled out. The ideal is for intellectuals, devoted to words and the expression, or reduction, of reality to the abstractions constituted by words.

The Talmud contains few simple, declarative sentences. The primary mode of expression is those joining-parts of language which link thought to thought, or set thought against thought: "but," "however," "do you reason so," "what is for the presupposition?" What is Talmudic about the Talmud is expressed in the Aramaic mortar, not in the Hebrew stones. The near-grunts of the uneducated, "I want this, I do that," "That is my opinion"—these are virtually absent in the Talmud's extended discourse. The argument is expressed in terse, apocopated phrases, moving almost too rapidly for the ordinary ear to grasp.

What is Talmudic, too, is perpetual skepticism, expressed in response to every declarative sentence or affirmative statement. Once one states that matters are so, it is inevitable that he will find as a response: Why do you think so? Perhaps things are the opposite of what you say? How can you say so when a contrary principle may be adduced? Articulation, forthrightness, subtle reasoning but lucid expression, dialectic and skepticism—these are the traits of intellectuals, not of untrained and undeveloped minds, nor of neat scholars, capable only to serve as curators of the past, but not as critics of the present.

Above all, Talmudic thinking rejects gullibility and credulity. It is, indeed, peculiarly modern in its systematic skepticism, its testing of each proposition, not to destroy but to refine what people suppose to be so. The Talmud's first question is not *"Who* says so," but, "Why?" "What is the reason of the House of Shammai?" In the Talmudic approach to thought, faith is restricted to ultimate matters, to the fundamental principles of reality beyond which one may not penetrate. Akabya warned to try to find out what is whence one comes and whither one is going. The answers will yield humility. But humility in the face of ultimate questions is not confused with servility before the assertions, the truth-claims, of putative authorities, ancient or modern, who are no more than mortal.

Since the harvest of learning is humility, however, the more one seeks to find out, the greater will be one's virtue. And the way to deeper perception lies in skepticism about shallow assertion. One must place as small a stake as possible in the acceptance of specific allegations. The fewer vested convictions, the greater the chances for wide-ranging inquiry. But while modern skepticism may yield—at least in the eye of its critics—corrosive and negative results, Talmudic skepticism produces measured, restrained, and limited insight. The difference must be in the open-endedness of the Talmudic inquiry. Nothing is ever left as a final answer, a completed solution. The fruit of insight is inquiry; the result of inquiry is insight, in endless progression. The only road closed is the road back, to the unarticulated, the unconscious, and the unself-conscious. For once consciousness is achieved, a reason spelled out, one cannot again pretend there is no reason, and nothing has been articulated. For the Talmud the alternatives are not faith against nihilism, but reflection against dumb reflex, consciousness against animal-instinct. Man, in God's image, has the capacity to reflect and to criticize. All an animal can do is act and respond.

That is why energy, the will to act, has to be channelled and controlled by law. Deed without deliberation is not taken seriously. Examination of deeds takes priority over mere repetition of what works or feels good. For this purpose, genius is insufficient, cleverness irrelevant. What is preferred is systematic and orderly consideration, step by step, of the principles by which one acts. The human problem in the Talmudic conception is not finding the motive force to do, but discovering the restraint to regulate that protean, elemental force. In the quest for restraint and self-control, the primal energies will insure one is not bored or lacking in purpose. For the Talmudic mode of thought perceives a perpetual tension between energy and activity, on the one side, and reflection on the other. To act without thought comes naturally, is contrary, therefore to the fact of revealed discipline. The drama of the private life consists in the struggle between will and intellect, action and reflection. If the Talmud is on the side of the latter, it is because the former require no allies. The outcome will be determined, ultimately, by force of character and intellect, these together. And the moot issue is not how to repress, but how to reshape, the primal energy.

Yet it is an error to focus so one-sidedly upon the Talmudic mind and so to ignore the other formative force in culture, the community. The Talmud, for its part, fully recognizes the social force, the pressures to conform and to follow established custom and habit. That is why so much attention centers upon people's doing things together. The Talmudic rabbis exhibit keen awareness that restraint is societal before it is personal. Community takes priority over individuality and gives the private person nearly the whole of the structure of symbols and values that render living meaningful. "Give me fellowship, or give me death," said one of them. The more important parts of the Talmud, furthermore, deal with civil regulations: What to do if a cow gores another cow? How to divide a disputed prayer-shawl? How to litigate a contested will, in which the material results affect the disposition of a palm-tree or a tiny bit of land?

The Talmudic rabbis are well aware that society forms the individual. If one seeks to create a disciplined individual, whose life is regulated by revealed law, one must give priority to the regulation of the society which forms the ground of individual existence. And to regulate society, one must concentrate upon the conflicts among men, the conflicting claims to unimportant things which, all together, will add up to justice and make possible dignity and autonomy. It is through law that one will revise habit, establish good customary behavior. It is through a lawful society that one will create an environment naturally productive of restraint and rational behavior. If, therefore, it is correct to claim that what is Talmudic about the Talmud is the application of reason and criticism to concrete and practical matters, then the Talmud is at its core an instrument for the regulation of society in the most humble and workaday sense of the words.

To be sure, to regulate society one must have access to the institutions that exercise and confer legitimate power, and the Talmudic rabbis knew the importance of various sorts of power. They understood, first of all, the intrinsic power of law itself, which rendered unnecessary constant, *ad hoc* intervention of puissant authority into routine affairs. Once law has established how things should be done, the enforcement of the law becomes necessary only in exceptional circumstances. In normal ones the law itself ensures its own enforcement, for most men most of the time are law-abiding. The Talmudic rabbis actively sought access to the instrumentalities of Jewish autonomous government made available by the authorities of Roman Palestine and Iranian Babylonia. If the imperial regimes were content to have the Jews regulate their own affairs and fundamentally disinterested in meddling in ritual and community regulations, the rabbis were eager to take over the institutions authorized to regulate the people's lives. They worked their way into these institutions, formed by the Patriarch of Palestine and the Exilarch of Babylonia, and made themselves the chief agents for the day-to-day government of the local communities. So far as the state stood behind the Jewish community's officials, the rabbis enjoyed the benefit of state-power and therefore mastered the intricacies of politics.

The Talmudic rabbis, moreover, exercised a kind of "moral authority," sufficient to make people do what the rabbis wanted without the intervention of this-worldly authorities. That moral authority was based upon multiform foundations. First, the rabbi was understood to have mastery of the Divine revelation and unique access to part of it, the Oral Torah handed down from Sinai. So his rule was according to heavenly principles. Second, the rabbi was seen as himself paradigmatic of the Torah's image of man. Therefore what he did was revelatory. Common folk who proposed to obey the will of Heaven as the rabbis explained it would not have to be coerced to do what the rabbis said. They might just as well imitate the rabbi, confident that he did what he did in order to imitate Moses "our rabbi" and God, Moses's rabbi. The Talmud is full of stories of what individuals said and did on specific occasions. In some instances the abstract law is conveyed by such stories. In most others, the point of the story is to show, by relating the rabbi's deed, what the law is, how one should conduct himself. These are not "political" stories, yet they have a pronouncedly political result, for the story influences behavior no less than a court-decree shapes action.

Finally, among the rabbis were some believed able to exercise miraculous and even supernatural powers. A modern anthropologist having spent a few years in Talmudic circles to study the social role of the rabbi might well call his consequent book, "The Lawyer-Magicians of Babylonia." But the exercise of supernatural power, the ability to appeal to the fantasies of ordinary folk—fantasies the rabbis themselves certainly shared—these too constituted a kind of "moral authority." Intellectual achievement produced theurgical power. The righteous were believed to have the creative power of God: "If a righteous man desires it, he can create a world." And why should the rabbi not have such power, given his knowledge of the Torah, which contained the plan and pattern for God's own creation of this world? Learning reshaped a man into the likeness of God and therefore endowed him with God's powers of creation. In a secular sense, belief in the supernatural consequences of the natural power of mastery of Torah-traditions and reasoning about them produced a practical power considerably more efficient than political instrumentalities in moving people to do the right thing. The charisma represented by brilliance in reasoning and argument was effective outside of the circle of intellectuals, just as it is today, but with better reason then. The luminous thus became numinous.

One can hardly refer to politics without alluding, as well, to the rabbis' reconstruction of the family, the relationship of father to son. Here Talmudic rabbis discerned a tension, and resolved it in their own favor. They understood the primacy of the father in the formation of the personality of the child and the shape of the family. At the same time they claimed they, as masters of Torah, should shape personality and provide the model for the family. They admitted that the father brought the child into this world. But, they quickly added, the teacher brings him into the next world, therefore is entitled to the honor owing from the child to the father. The teacher is better than the father, above the father, just as God is the ultimate father of the child and giver of his life. If, therefore, a son sees the ass of his father struggling under his load and at the same time he sees the ass of his teacher about to stumble, he helps the ass of his teacher, then that of his father, for the one has brought him into this world, the other, to eternity. Just as the rabbi placed his rule over that of the state and the state's functionaries, the Patriarch and Exilarch, so he sought to take precedence over the primary component of the community, the family, by laying claim to the position of the father.

In larger terms, the effort to replace the father by the rabbi symbolized a struggle equivalent to the effort to replace the concrete, this-worldly natural government of ordinary officials by the abstract, non-natural or supernatural authority of the rabbi, qualified by learning of the Torah and capacity to reason about it. The Roman authority and his agent, the patriarch in Jewry ruled through force or the threat of force. The rabbi effected his will through moral authority, through the capacity to persuade and to demonstrate through affective example what the law required. Both political and familial life thus was to be rendered something other than what seemed natural or normal. Everyone could understand the authority of the gendarme, the priority of the father. But to superimpose the rabbi both in politics and in the family represented a redefinition of the ordinary sense of politics and the plain, accepted meaning of the family. It made both into something more abstract, subject to a higher level of interpretation, than an ordinary person might readily perceive. Political life to the rabbi was not merely a matter of the here and now, nor was the family what it seemed. Both were to be remodeled in the image of Heaven, according to the pattern of the Torah. That is to say, they were to be restructured according to the underlying principles of reality laid down by the Divine plan as undercovered by rational inquiry. Society was to be made to conform to the heavenly definition of the good community; the family was to be revised according to the supernatural conception of who the father really was: God and his surrogate, the rabbi—the man most closely conforming to His image.

The Talmudic stress upon criticism, therefore, produced a new freedom of construction, the freedom to reinterpret reality and to reconstruct its artifacts upon the basis of well-analyzed, thoroughly criticized principles revealed through the practical reason of the sages. Once one is free to stand apart from what is customary and habitual, to restrain energies and regulate them, he attains the higher freedom to revise the given, to reinterpret established perceptions of reality and the institutions which give them affect. This constitutes, to begin with, the process of the mind's focusing upon unseen relationships and the formation of imposed, non-material considerations.

One recalls in this connection the extensive ritual-purity laws, which play so considerable a role in the rabbis' regulation of eating and other fundamental things, for instance, sexual relations. These laws seem to have comprised and created a wholly abstract set of relationships, a kind of non-Euclidean geometry of the levitical realm. Yet those high abstractions are brought down to earth to determine in what order one washes his hands and picks up a cup of wine. So what is wholly relative and entirely a matter of theory, not attached to concrete things, transforms trivialities. It affects, indeed generates, the way one does them. It transforms them into issues of some consequence, by relating them to the higher meanings (to be sure, without much rational, let alone material substance) associated with the pure and the impure. The purity-laws stand at the pinnacle of Talmudic abstraction and ratiocination.

One may supply a social explanation for the intellectuality and abstraction of the Talmudic rabbis' approach to reality. They themselves stood apart from the larger Jewish society, much as the Jews stood apart from the majority. Their intent was to reshape and improve society. But they were different from other men because of their learning and intellect. They lived in this world, but in another too, one in which, for example, the unseen realities and unfelt relationships of purity and impurity were taken so seriously as to determine behavior in the world of material realities and perceived, concrete relationships. They stood apart not because they alone believed in God, for everyone did, or because they alone revered the Torah, for they were not alone, but because they alone conceived it possible for man to elevate himself heavenward through Torah, rationally apprehended. They participated in the history of this world, but were aware of the precariousness and imperfection of this world when perceived and measured by the standard of the next. Their capacity to criticize therefore derived from their situation of detachment. They knew that what is now is not necessarily whatever was or what must always be. Able to stand apart because of the perspective of distance attained through rational criticism of the practical life, they realized men have choices they themselves may not perceive. There have been and are now other ways of conducting life and living with men, of building society and creating culture, than those the ordinary people supposed were normative. Able to criticize from the perspective of a transcendent perception of the principles of being, they could evaluate what others took for granted, could see the given as something to be elevated and transcended.

In a word, the Talmud is a document of the moral intellect. It takes for granted that man's primary capacity is to think; he therefore is to be taken with utmost seriousness. The Talmud endures as a monument to intellectualism focused upon the application of practical rationality to society. It pays tribute, on every page, to the human potential to think morally, yet without lachrymose sentimentality, to reflect about fundamentals and basic principles, but for concrete purposes and with ordinary society in mind. The good, well-regulated society will nurture disciplined, strong character. The mighty man—"one who overcomes his impulses"—will stand as a pillar of the good society. This is what I understand as the result of the intellectual activity of the moral intellect. Reason, criticism, restraint, and rational exchange of ideas— these are not data for the history of Talmudic literature alone. The Talmud itself testifies to their necessary consequences for the personality and for society alike.

What is contemporary man to make of the Talmudic approach to life? How is he to appropriate the Talmud's moral intellectualism for contemporary sensibility?

Perhaps you think I have claimed too much for the Talmudic mode of thought, but I fear I have claimed too little. For what the Talmud accomplished, in the formation of a specific civilization—that of the Jewish people—was to lay the foundations for a society capable of rational, supple response to an irrational situation. The Jews lived as aliens, so they created a homeland wherever they found themselves. They effectively and humanely governed themselves without the normal instruments of government, lacking much of a bureaucracy, having no consequential power at all. They created not one culture but multiple cultures, all of them quintessentially "Jewish," out of the materials of many languages, many societies, many sorts of natural environments, many histories, and many cultured traditions. The Talmud's construction of a world of ideas and principles, corresponding to, but transcendent of reality, is a paradigm for the Jews' capacity to reinterpret reality and reconstruct culture in age succeeding age, their non-material power fully, rigorously, and robustly to live the life of the mind. Beyond the Jews' capacity for fantasy—after all, not unique to them—was their power to reflect, reconsider, stand back from reality and revise its interpretation. This, it now is clear, is the end-result of a society which trained its young in the Talmud and rewarded its mature and old men alike for lifelong devotion to its study.

It was the rationality and intellectuality of the Jews' culture which led them to a way of living with one another, not in perfect harmony—they were flesh and blood—but in mighty restraint and mutual respect. The inner life of the Jewish community was so organized that the people might conflict with one another, yet not through the total free expression of the impulse toward mutual annihilation. Renunciation of brute power, affirmation of the force of ideas and reason—these represented the Jews' discovery. They cannot claim to have uncovered these principles, but they rightly can claim meaningfully to have effected them in the formation of their community-life and the reestablishment of their protean culture. Reason applied to practical affairs through the acute inquiry of Talmudic argument—this I think accounts for the Jews' capacity for so many centuries to accommodate themselves to a situation of worldly powerlessness. For they knew ideas could be powerful; criticism could constitute a great force in society. In the end, the sword, once sheathed, could change nothing, but an idea, once unleashed, could so persist as to move men to move the world.

The Talmud lays the foundation for the rational, therefore the moral culture. I refer to Philip Rieff (*The Triumph of the Therapeutic. Uses of Faith after Freud* [N. Y., 1966: Harper], p. 232) who speaks of the functions of culture: "(1) to organize the moral demands men make upon themselves into a system of symbols that make men inelligible and trustworthy to each other, thus rendering also the world intelligible and trustworthy; (2) to organize the expressive remissions by which men release themselves, in some degree, from the strain of conforming to the controlling symbolic, internalized variant readings of culture that constitute individual character." Clearly, the Talmud exhibits the capacity to organize "the moral demands" of men into a system of orderly, integrated symbols. These take the form of actions to be taken, others to be rejected. The degree of order and integration depends upon the rabbis' success in locating the fundamental principles which draw together and show the interrelationships among discreet actions.

But what is the form of the "expressive remissions"? How does the Talmud make room for individual character? The answer lies in the Talmud's stress on the reasons for its rules. Once the reason is made known, one makes room for contrary reason, for reason to reject or revise the established position. Not only does the individual have the place to differ, but he also has the power through criticism to move the entire community to appropriate what to begin with expressed his private judgment, his individuality. This I think is not only to the advantage of the individual, but also fundamentally therapeutic for the community as a whole.

For contemporary man the Talmud must stand as a formidable source of criticism, for by it the correlated values, "follow your own impulse," and "do your own thing," are rejected. The Talmud gives contrary advice. "Tame your impulse," regulate, restrain, control energies through the self-imposition of the restraining rule of law. At the same time, the Talmud demands that one *not* do "his own thing" alone, but persuade others to make what is his own into what is to be shared by all. The Talmud therefore subjects the individual to restraints on pure individuality, while opening for individuality the possibility of moral suasion of the community at large. "Unrestrained" and "individualism" therefore are set over against "regulated" and "rationality," for it is rationality which overcomes the isolation of the individual, connecting one mind to another through the mediating way of reason. Through the imposition of rational, freely adopted rules, one restrains those destructive elements of the personality which potentially are damaging for both the individual and the community.

To be sure, the supernatural world-view of the Talmud cannot claim a serious hearing among Jews who stand at a distance from the traditional world of faith, let alone among gentiles. But even for these the Talmud serves a good purpose nonetheless, for it contains within its pages a detailed demonstration of how practical reason may be applied to humble affairs. As a whole document within the multiform, historical civilization of the Jewish people, it testifies to the concrete possibilities of rational and critical approaches to human affairs. This it does not only in generalities, but, as I have stressed, in strikingly trivial details. The course of the Talmudic argument shows it is possible commitedly, involvedly, to argue about changing hypotheses, to take seriously culturally neutral matters, and to find important principles in ordinary affairs. The Talmudic rabbi takes a clinical attitude toward his own ideas, and certainly toward those of his fellows. They are there for analysis, not for either gullible acceptance or utter rejection. The purpose of the analysis, moreover, is not final commitment to some one conclusion, but a provisional decision, laying the way open to further inquiry.

The open-ended character of the Talmudic argument bears considerable contemporary pertinence. Since one expects no final solutions, man is prepared for a succession of intermediate, provisional ones. He learns, therefore, the discipline of commitment within open-mindedness, the capacity to hold conviction loosely, to refrain from imposing on the other person the task of verifying, by assenting to, one's own deeply held convictions. It is the undogmatic quality of Talmudic discourse which contemporary men might well learn to emulate. They will do so when their commitment is to method, rather than to its results, and when the method, or mode, of thought recovers the form prefigured in the Talmud: skepticism, criticism, above all, easy and free movement.

The tradition of Talmudic learning prepared the Jews for the modern situation and even in pre-modern times carried within itself the qualities we now associate with modernity. So far as modernity requires man to take this world seriously, the Talmud met the requirements of modernity. So far as modernity is characterized by cosmopolitanism and the relativity of values, the Talmud, which could be both studied and realized in many countries and various cultures, prepared the Jews for the modern situation. By its stress on the unfolding possibilities of reason and by its relentless testing of all propositions against the measure of skeptical reason, the Talmud prepared the Jews to recognize the relativity of successive truth-claims, the probability that each would in its turn have to give way to the next.

The Talmud thus taught its disciples to deny the need they must have felt, the need to judge all values, all assertions, all theories by their own, particular, self-authenticating system of thought while affirming the Torah and the final truth of all contained therein. The Talmud prepared its students to see as merely transitory and useful artifacts and ideas the world understood to be absolute and perfected. The Talmud disciplined its devotees to preserve a thoroughly doubting attitude toward the perfections of the hour. It imparted both the view that reality—the immutable truth of others—was something to be criticized, and the humility likewise to perceive one's own.

The Talmud nurtured abiding skepticism about what people offered as salvation, as final solutions to the problems of "the human condition." The Talmudist did not expect final solutions, was trained to ask simple, therefore devastating questions about their finality, and so readied the Jews for the modern situation of provisional truths and hypotheses subject to testing and revision. True, the Talmud did come to decisions. But these were in matters or detail. No one ever resolved any of the really interesting questions of logic and reasoning. The Talmudic rabbi remained open to the good insights that might come, denying at the same time the finality of what was already present. This gave him the freedom to criticize the Mishnah, the *Gemara,* Rashi, and whatever was to come thereafter. The Talmudist could deny the present achievements of the mind because he hoped for ultimately better ones.

The Jew, disciplined in the Talmud's mode of thought, could accommodate himself to the modern world's relativization of values precisely because he had already seen the vision of greater perfection than what was originally present. The Talmud produced an activist tradition of men interested in daily affairs and in their proper regulation, a tradition which told men they were partners in the task of perfecting the world under the dominion of God. If the world was perceived to be insufficient and incomplete, it was man's task to help complete it. If men saw values as in a measure relative to the situation of specific men and groups, and understood reason to be something provisional and transitory, the Talmud taught the Jews their duty was to criticize and purify their ideas by skeptical criteria at once most ancient and still not wholly realized.

Finally, the Talmud taught the Jews not to be terrified by the necessity to face, and to choose among, a plurality of uncertain alternatives. The Talmud testified that men must choose, if tentatively and for a time only, among competing interpretations, so that the law might in fact be applied, and the ordinary man might know what to do. So the Talmud forced choices, in a tentative and austere spirit, among the many truths available to reasonable men. It insisted one cannot be paralyzed before contrary claims and equally persuasive reasons. The House of Shammai and the House of Hillel both laid claim to sound law and excellent reasoning; neither party could be shown inferior to the other in critical acumen. But a choice had to be made. If Heaven had to resolve the formidable problem of choice, it set a good example and did not have to intervene again.

The Talmud taught that men must end up doing some one thing when faced with conflicting choices. Values may be relative, but men must choose some ideal by which to guide their lives. Men could not endure in indecision. They had to decide to be more than nothing in particular, for their capacity for rational thought is insufficient without an equivalent ability to make and carry out rational decisions. The best proof of the duty to make reasonable decisions among unreasonable alternatives was the Jews themselves, who, because of their international character and their memories of many lands and empires, saw the world in all its complex diversity, but also chose to form the most vivid and intense of all groups, to sustain what is, after all, one of the most particular of all literary traditions, the Talmud itself. Yet they did so in full knowledge that their group was not co-extensive with society, and that their Talmudic tradition did not contain everything worth knowing about the right way of living life.

So the Talmud imparted the lesson that while man faces a relativity of values, he must choose life in some specific place, among some particular group of people. And the values that shape those lives are not relative to the conditions in which they are lived. When all values are seen to be relative and all reasons may be criticized with equally good reasons, that is when men most need the fellowship produced by access to a common, deeply held and widely shared, discipline of thinking. The conclusions will vary; the mode of thought and argumentation must then be constant and enduring.

Having emphasized the priority of making difficult choices, we come to the final, peculiarly modern, trait of the Talmudic mind, its pragmatism. What shall we say of a tradition of thought which laid greatest emphasis upon deed, upon a pattern of actions and a way of living, but that it is pragmatic? What shall we say of a perspective upon the world that focused on practical reason, but that it is worldly? What shall we conclude of a religious language which called honesty or charity a *kiddush hashem,* a sanctification of God's name, but that it is deeply secular? A legal system whose deepest concerns were for the detailed articulation of the this-worldly meaning of love for one's fellow man here and now is one which long ago brought the Jews into the pragmatic, this-worldly framework of modernity.

That is why the Talmud not only relates to the contemporary world, but may stand in judgment of it. And it surely will judge a world willing to reduce man to part of himself, to his impulses and energies, than to validate the unrestrained expression of those energies as the ultimate, legitimate adumbration of what is individual about the person, as though he had no mind, no strength of rational thought. It will condemn a world of enthusiasts who make an improvement and call it redemption, come up with a good idea and, without the test of skeptical analysis, pronounce salvation. The Talmud shows a better way; it demonstrates that men have the capacity to assess the unredemption of the world, to perceive the tentativeness of current solutions to enduring problems, and at the same time to hope and work for salvation. It is this unfulfilled yet very vivid evaluation of the world, the power to take the world so seriously as to ask searching questions about its certainties, which, I think, explains the Jew's capacity to love so much, and yet to doubt; to hold the world very near and close, with open arms. The Jew has been taught by the Talmud to engage realistically in the world's tasks, to do so with a whole heart, yet without the need, or even the power, to regard completion of those tasks as the threshold of a final fulfillment of history.

Because of its dialectic, the Talmud teaches men to take seriously the wide range of worldly problems without expecting that in solving them—provisionally, let alone finally—he might save the world. If the Jew has found the modern situation congenial and congruent to his perception of humanity, it is because the Talmud, writ large across the traditional culture of the Jewish people, uniquely prepared him for the conditions of modernity, readied him not only to participate in those conditions, but deeply and unstintingly to criticize them, and, finally, in full rationality to reform them.

GLOSSARY[1]

Ab—the month of the Hebrew calendar in which the Temple was destroyed.

abodah—worship, especially the sacrificial cult.

Aboth, Pirke Aboth—a tractate of the *Mishna* containing sayings of the sages.

agada, aggada—the non-legal portions of the rabbinic writings e.g. legends, folklore, homiletics. Opp. of *halacha*.

am ha-aretz—peasant, ignoramus.

Amidah—a prayer consisting of eighteen (later nineteen) benedictions recited at prescribed times.

Amora (plur. *Amoraim*)—a religious authority of the *Gemara*.

Apikores—an unbeliever, heretic.

Ashkenazic—relating to Jews of German and Polish origin.

Baraita—a tannaitic statement not included in the *Mishna* but still authoritative.

Beth Din—court of law.

bet ha-kneset, beth hakeneseth—synagogue.

chasiduth—saintliness.

derash, drash—the deeper meaning of a scriptural verse derived by *midrash*.

---

[1]No attempt has been made to harmonize the many different transliteration methods used by the various writers.

421

derek erez, derech eretz—the way things should be done; decent conduct.

din—judgment, law.

erub, eruv—a procedure permitting the carrying of items within a certain area or the preparation of food on days when these activities would normally be forbidden.

Gemara—the later stratum in the *Talmud* which expands and clarifies the *Mishna*.

geonim—post-talmudic religious authorities.

gezerah—decree of the authorities.

haber, chaver—associate; member of a group devoted to acts of special piety.

haggadah—(1) the home ritual for the eve of Passover (2) same as *agada*.

hagigah—(1) the festal offering; (2) name of a tractate of the *Mishna*.

ha-Kadosh Baruch Hu—a rabbinic name of God.

halacha, halaka,—(1) rule of law (2) legal portions of the rabbinic writings.

hallah, challah—a priestly due on grain.

imitatio Dei—imitating the attributes of God.

kaddish—the doxology. A prayer in praise of God marking the end of a section of the service.

kabbalah—(1) tradition (2) mystic lore.

kasher—ritually fit.

kavanah, kawwanah—intent, proper direction of mind while performing a religious act.

kedushah—holiness.

kehillah—Jewish community.

kiddush—a ceremonial proclaiming the sanctity of the Sabbath.

ketubah, kethubah—marriage contract.

kiddush ha-shem—a signal act of religious devotion.

kohen (plur. *kohanim*)—priest.

lishmah—for its own sake, without ulterior motive.

maaser—the priestly tithe.

ma'arib, maariv—the evening service, also called *'arbith*.

makom—a rabbinic name of God.

massechta, massichta—a tractate of the Talmud.

Megillah—(1) scroll (2) scroll containing the Book of Esther (3) name of a tractate of the *Mishna*.

mezuzah—a small box attached to the doorpost of a Jewish house containing quotations from the Pentateuch.

midrash—rabbinic exegesis of scripture (2) a collection embodying such exegesis.

Minha, Mincha—the afternoon prayer.

minhag—local usage, custom.

minim—heretics, sectarians.

Mishna, Mishnah—(1) a thesaurus of oral law compiled in the 3rd century C.E. (2) a sub-section of this thesaurus.

mitzvah, mizwah, (plural *mitzvot*)—commandment; virtuous deed.

Musaf—additional prayer or sacrifice prescribed for feast days.

nasi—prince, patriarch, leader of the Jewish community.

olam ha-ba—the world to come.

olam ha-zeh—this world, as opposed to the world to come.

parnasim—community leaders.

perushim—Pharisees.

peshat, pshat—the plain meaning of a scriptural verse.

prosbul—a legal device enabling transactions to be effective beyond the sabbatical year.

Purim—the Feast of Lots, commemorating the deliverance of the Jews of Persia.

Rashi-R. Solomon ben Isaac—famous commentator on Bible and Talmud.

resh galuta—exilarch: the head of Babylonian Jewry.

seder—(1) one of the six major divisions of the Mishna (2) the home service for the eve of Passover.

sefer Torah—scroll of the pentateuch.

semikah, semikha, semichah—ordination.

Sephardic—relating to Jews of Spanish, Portuguese and Mediteranean origin.

shavuot—Feast of Weeks.

Shechinah, Shekhina, Shekina—the Divine Presence.

shema—passages from the Pentateuch, to be recited night and morning.

Shemone Esreh—same as *Amidah.*

Sheol—the grave, the underworld.

shofar—the ram's horn, blown on certain religious occasions.

sopherim—scribes; early rabbinic authorities.

takkana—amendment to a law.

tallith—fringed garment (Num. 15.38).

talmid chacham—talmudic scholar.

Talmud—the *Mishna* and *Gemara* combined.

tamid—the perpetual offering, formerly sacrificed daily in the Temple.

Tanna (plur. *Tannaim*)—(1) a religious Authority of the Mishna (2) a professional memorizer of rabbinic traditions.

Targum—Aramaic translation of the Bible.

Tefillah—(1) prayer (2) same as Amidah.

tefillin, tephillin—phylacteries.

terumah—heave offering.

tetragrammaton—the four letter name of God.

Torah min ha-shamayim—Divine Law.

tosafist—a writer of *tosafot*.

tosafot—medieval glosses on the Talmud.

Tosephta, Tosifta—a thesaurus of oral law similar in character to the *Mishna*.

tumah—impurity.

tsaddik, tzadik—(1) righteous man (2) a Hasidic rabbi.

tzedakah, zedakah—almsgiving, charity.

tzitzith—fringes prescribed to be worn on the garments (Num. 15.38).

yetzer ha-ra—the evil inclination in man.

yetzer ha-tov (*tob*)—the good inclination in man.

yom tov, jom tob—festival; religious holiday on which work is prohibited.

zugoth—"pairs"; pairs of rabbinic authorities (see Aboth chap. 1.)

A NOTE on the LANGUAGE of the TALMUD

The language of the Mishna is Hebrew, but it is distinctly different from the language of the Bible. The differences are explained partly by the constant change that takes place in all languages; partly by the effect of other languages known to the Jews, especially Aramaic and Greek; and partly because the language of the Mishna may in any case be descended from a dialect of Hebrew not identical with Biblical Hebrew even in Biblical times.

Mishnaic Hebrew possesses many words unknown in the Bible, including many technical words. The syntax is much closer to that of European languages. Many grammatical forms are different. Certain typical constructions of Biblical Hebrew are absent to the extent that the reading of one line is enough to tell whether the Hebrew is Biblical or Mishnaic. Mishnaic Hebrew is the underlying idiom of writers as diverse as the medieval sage Moses Maimonides and the Nobel Prize winner S. Y. Agnon; modern Hebrew draws on both the Biblical and Mishnaic language, and the skilled writer can add nuances to his work by leaning on one or the other, giving effects which defy translation. Hitherto unknown documents in Mishnaic Hebrew have been discovered by Hebrew University expeditions to highly inaccessible caves in the Judean desert.

The language of the Gemara is Aramaic, often quoting earlier statements in Mishnaic and Biblical Hebrew. Aramaic is a language closely related to Hebrew, but quite distinct from it; the languages were no more mutually intelligible than are English and German. Aramaic once occupied the position in the Middle East now filled by Arabic; it is still spoken by a few people in Iraq and elsewhere. It exists in several dialects, and several different scripts have been used to write it down, including the Hebrew alphabet and other related ones. The two old Bible translations into this language known as *Peshitta* (in a dialect called *Syriac*) and Targum are of importance to Bible scholars.

The Aramaic of the Gemara is rich in technical terms used in the talmudic dialectic, mostly brief but often requiring clumsy translations into other languages.

The Midrashim are written in both Mishnaic Hebrew and in Aramaic, the dialect of the latter depending on the provenience of the particular Midrash.

All these works are customarily written without vowel points and without punctuation. This fact must have greatly influenced the manner in which they have traditionally been studied. The absence of vowel points is not as serious as it may seem, since once the language is mastered, the vowel points are not normally necessary. But the absence of punctuation has made "skimming" practically impossible, unless the text had been previously thoroughly studied on a previous occasion. Hence the habit has been fostered in the traditional Talmudical academies of spending hours, even days, over a single page. The manner in which the modern reads a novel, a newspaper, or even a textbook was discouraged by the pages of unvowelled, unpunctuated text.

The standard dictionary of both the Hebrew and Aramaic parts of Talmud and Midrash is M. Jastrow, *A Dictionary of the Targumim the Talmud Babli and Yerushalmi and the Midrashic Literature* (reprinted in New York, 1950). Additional works are listed in Hermann L. Strack, *Introduction to the Talmud and Midrash* (reprinted in Cleveland and New York, 1959).

NOTES

NOTES TO THE INTRODUCTION (Pg. 1-2)

1. A. J. Arberry, *The Seven Odes* (New York, 1957), p. 20.
2. J. Vansina, *Oral Tradition* (Chicago, 1965), p. 34.

OPEN THOU MINE EYES (Pg. 55-61)

1. See H.A. Wolfson, *The Philosophy of the Church Fathers,* Vol. 1, Cambridge 1956, p. 24.
2. Abot 5.25
3. Leo Baeck, *Judaism and Christianity,* 1958, p. 167.
4. *The Midrash on Psalms,* 92.3.
5. Ibid.
6. Gen. Rabbah 12.6.
7. Gen. Rabbah 17.6.
8. Robert Burton, *Anatomy of Melancholy,* Pr. III sec. 2, mem 2, subs. 2.
9. Midrash on Psalms 9.1.
10. Abot de R. Nathan A 16, Baba Mesi'a, 58b and Abot 3.15.
11. Abot 2.15.

RABBINIC EXEGESIS (Pg. 62-64)

1. Cf. *Nishmath, Malchuyoth, Zichronoth,* and *Shofaroth.*
2. Cf. also S. R. Edelman, *Sefer Hamesiloth* and *Hatirosch,* as well as Z. W. Einhorn, Commentary to *Midrash Rabbah.*
3. I Samuel 15.1; see note of R. Samuel Strashun ad locum.
4. See Mandelkern's Concordance.
5. In Jer. 18.19 the expression *ushema lekol* has no reference to obedience but to listening to rantings and tumults.
6. Genesis *Rabbah* 20:8.
7. God is the Artist who fashions life in the mother's womb.
8. See *Baba Kamma* 65a, 85b.
9. *Ibid.* 22.14.
10. For other views, see Heineman, *Darkhe ha-Agada,* Jerusalem, 1940. Chap. I.

THE ECONOMIC CONDITION OF JUDEA AFTER THE DESTRUCTION OF THE SECOND TEMPLE (Pg. 73-106)

1. It remained in this condition for two years, and only after the Roman conquest of Galilee some refugees began to rebuild it (III, 9, 2), but the Romans destroyed it utterly a second time (III, 9, 3). They placed there a garrison of foot and horsemen who plundered the neighborhood of Joppé and destroyed the neighbouring villages and townlets (II, 9, 4) and turned the whole district into a real desert. Lydda must also have been rebuilt by the Jewish general appointed after Cestius's defeat by the revolutionists for Thamna including Lydda, Joppé, and Emmaus (II, 20, 4).
2. See Reland; Kohut, *Flavius Josephus,* 660, note 487, suggests Gazara, Gezer.
3. In *Vita,* 75, Josephus reports how he, after the conquest of Jerusalem, delivered from among the captives several men, his brother and fifty friends, and from among the great mass of women and children kept as captives in the Temple about 190 whom he had recognized as belonging to his friends and companions; he freed them without ransom. In Thekoa he saw many captives crucified, among them three of his friends who at his request were taken down, but only one survived.
4. Baraitha in *Joma,* 59a: two high priests survived the first Temple; one said that in the service on the Day of Atonement he had sprinkled the blood of the sin-offering on the four corners of the altar while standing in the same place, the other

said that he had walked around the altar for the purpose of sprinkling the blood, and both gave their reasons. In the *Mishnah Joma*, V, 5, R. Eliezer holds the view of the first high priest, the same in *Baraitha Joma*, 59 a, *jer.*, V, 442 d, 62. The parallel account, *jer.*, V, 42 d, 66, reads: two priests fled in the wars, one said that he had stood, the other that he had walked while atoning. This shows, what is otherwise clear, that high priests of the second Temple are meant, as Ishmael, son of Fiabi, the best known high priest in the Talmud, who survived the destruction and was later in Kyrene (*Wars*, VI, 2, 2; in *Sotah*, IX, 15: since Ishmael b. Fiabi died, the glory of the priesthood ceased); he could have given the information quoted.

5. Jelamdenu in *RÉJ*, 1887, XIV, 93, *Joma*, 21 b, 39 a, *'Eduj.*, II, 1-3, *Pesah.*, I, 6, *Shekal.*, VI, 1.

6. *Ta'an.*, 13 a, *jer. Beṣah*, II, 61 b, 51, and parallels.

7. *Tos. Hallah*, I, 10; when he was to be executed, he said to the Roman executioner: 'I am a priest, the son of a high priest,' *ARN*, XXXVIII, 57 b, the parallels make him himself a high priest. As Samuel the Young, who died before R. Gamaliel II (*Semah.*, VIII), prophesied before his death the end of R. Ishmael (*Tos. Sotah*, XIII, 4, *jer.*, IX, 24 b, 38; *Synh.*, ii a; *Semah.*, VIII; Bacher, *Tannaiten*; I; 234, 3) R. Ishmael's death seems to have been brought about by the political unrest in the year 117.

8. A Simeon b. Jehosadak, a priest, died in Lydda (*Semah.*, IV, 11); when his brother came from Galilee to engage in his burial and defile himself, Simeon was already buried, and the rabbis—in *Conforte R. Tarfon*—would not allow him to defile himself (Brüll, *Jahrbücher*, I, 38). As R. Tarfon's name is doubtful, most scholars take Simeon b. Jehosadak to be identical with R. Johanan's teacher in the first half of the third century (Bacher, *PA*, I, 119).

9. *Tos. Joma*, I, 12, *jer.*, II, 39 d, 15, b. 23 a.

10. R. Jehudah in *Bekhor.*, 45 b, *Tos.*, V, 7, reports how R. Tarfon said to a man with twelve fingers on his hands and twelve toes on his feet and inquiring whether he was fit (to be a priest): May, like you, many be (high) priests in Israel; according to R. José he said to the man: Few shall be, like you, Mamzers and Nathins in Israel. This man was a priest.

11. *Joma*, 38 a, b, *jer.* III, 41 a, 63; *Tos.*, II, 7.

12. The priests continued to guard their purity of stock against the intrusion of tainted or doubtful families. R. Johanan's decrees could have been issued before the year 70; but nothing is otherwise known of similar decrees of his at that time, and, from the subject-matter, it is almost certain that the ruling mentioned belongs to the period of his activity in Jamnia. And there is evidence for the same attitude of the priests even later. Rabba b. bar-Hanna (*Kiddush.*, 78 b) and R. Assi in R. Johanan's name (*jer. Bikk.*, I, 64 a, 27) remark that since the destruction of the Temple the priests have guarded their dignity by not marrying a woman both whose parents were proselytes. Other peculiarites of priests proving their number in Baraitha Bekhor., 30 b. reported by R. José b. Halaftha: since the destruction of the Temple priests have guarded their dignity by not entrusting their levitically pure food to a non-priest. In *Tos, 'Eduj.*, I, 9. it is stated that priests followed R. Ishrael's view on a point of law discussed in *'Eduj.*, II, 6. In *Tos. Ahil.*, XVI, 13, *Mikw.*, VI, 2, *Pesah.*, 9 a, *jer.* 1, 27c, 39, R. Jehudah and R. Simeon b. Gamaliel report incidents in Rimmon with several priests.

13. *Gittin*, V, 2; *'Eduj.*, VII, 9; *Jebam.*, XIV, 2, *Hull.*, 55 b. In *Tos. Arakh.*, I, 15, R. Haninah b. Antigonossays that he know certain when who had blown the flute in front of the altar in Jerusalem, and that they were Levites. Either he lived before the destruction of the Temple and survived it, or those Levites lived long after the year 70 and R. Haninah met them when they were old. Now he quotes a statement of R. Eleazar Hisma (*Tos. Temur.*, IV, 10) who was a disciple of R. Gamaliel II (*Sifrê Deut.*, 16; *Horaj.*, 10 a, b) and discussed a question with R. Meir, R. Jehudah, and R. José (*'Arakh.*, II, 4) after the year 136, so that there appears to be no foundation for Weiss's view (II, 121) that R. Haninah lived before the year 70. On the other hand, as he died in the times of R. Jehudah and R. José

(*Bekhor.*, 30 b), he could have been born before the destruction of the Temple, and if he died very old, could have been, as a young priest (*Bekhor.*, 30 b), observed the things reported by him from the Temple; see also Hyman, *Toldoth*, 480 a. In *Jebam.*, XVI, 7, R. Eliezer and R. Joshua tell R. Akiba how once several Levites went to So'ar, the town of date palm-trees; on the way one of them was taken ill and brought to the nearest inn. On their way back they learnt from the female innkeeper that their companion had died and she had buried him, and on her evidence the rabbis allowed the widow to re-marry. This seems to have happened in the times of the rabbis mentioned, so that the Levites as their contemporaries would also have survived the destruction of Jerusalem.

14. Aptowitzer in *MGWJ*, LII, 1908, 744 ff.

15. *Jebam.*, VIII, 4; see Brüll, *Einleitung*, I, 30.

16. *Jer. Hag.*, II, 77 c.

17. *'Erub.*, 27 a, bottom; *Tos. Ma'as. sheni*, I, 14. His father came only on pilgrimage to Jerusalem, as no man of the capital was allowed to redeem the tithe; but *Tos.* has, 'was selling,' so that the man lived in Jerusalem (see Schwarz, *Tosifta*, I, 174 a). We find that the Galilean R. Josê, after the year 136, met Abba Eleazar, who told him how he had sacrificed in Jerusalem (*Hag.*, 16 b), and that R. Josê could have received information about the Temple and Jerusalem from his father Halaftha, who had seen even R. Gamaliel I on the Temple mount (*Tos. Sabb.*, XIII, 2, and parallels). Those and other scholars who lived in Galilee are not discussed here.

18. *Midrash Threni*, I, 16, *jer. Kethub.*, V, 30 b, c, *Gitt.*, 56 a; Bacher, *Tannaiten*, I, 47, 6.

19. *Sifrê Deut.*, 305; *Kethub.*, 66 b; *Mekhiltha* on Exod. xix. 1, 61 a.

20. *Jer. Kiddush.*, IV, 65 c, 59; in *b. Jebam.*, 79 b, top, Rabbi is mentioned instead, evidently the name Eleazar having fallen out.

21. See, for instance, Munk, *Palestine*, 604 b; Besant-Palmer, *Jerusalem*, 52, and others.

22. See Herzog-Hauck, *RE*, VIII, 687 ff.

23. See the pilgrimages of people of Asia to Jamnia in *Tos. Hull.*, III, 10; *Parah*, VI, 4; *Mikw.*, IV, 6.

24. *Ma'as. sh.*, II, 7; it naturally seems more probable to refer it to the time of the Temple, but then R. Gamaliel II lived in Jerusalem and had there no occasion for redeeming that tithe. And when R. Joshua and R. Gamaliel knew R. Akiba, it was long after the year 70; for all attempts to place Akiba's time of study before that year seem futile.

25. R. Eleazar b. 'Azarjah is in *Sabb.*, 54 b, *Besah*, 23 a, said to have given thousands of calves as tithe. This, however, had to be offered as peaceoffering, and was, according to *Bekhor.*, 43 a, not to be given after the destruction of the Temple; see *Tosafoth* to all the passages. On the other hand, the *Mishnah Bekhor.*, IX, 1, states that it had to be given, but not what should be done with the tithe from cattle.

26. *Genes, r.*, 32, 10, *Cant. r.*, 4, 14, *Deut. r.*, III, 6, 7, 14.

27. See Lewy in *haMaggid*, 1870, 149 b, top.

28. Krauss in I. Lewy's *Festschrift*, 21 ff.

29. Cf. R. Jehudah's report in *'Erub.*, IV, 4, and *jer.*, IV, 22 a, with *Baraitha b. Erub.*, 45 a: R. Tarfon entered on a Sabbath morning the school and taught all day.

30. *Jer. Besah*, III, 62 a, 55; see my *'Am ha'ares*, p. 302, 5.

31. *Mekhiltha*, 53 b; *R. Simeon*, p. 82; *Bekhor.*, 5 b; *REJ*, 1910, LX, 107 ff.

32. *Nazir*, 52 a; the parallels in *Tos. 'Ahil.*, IV, 2, *jer. Berakh.*, I, 3 a, 19, do not give the name.

33. *Sabb.*, 29 b; *Tos.*, II, 5; cf. *Tos. 'Erub.*, IX, 2.

34. *Tos. Jadaj.*, II, 16. In *Tos. 'Ahil.*, XVIII, 18, about the year 200 Rabbi, R. Ishmael b. R. Josê and R. Eliezer haKappar stayed for the Sabbath in the food-shop of Pazzi in Lydia, and R. Pinhas b. Jair, who lived in Lydda, sat in front of them discussing with them halachic questions.

35. *B. mes.*, IV, 3; they are mentioned also in *Tos. Pesah.*, X, 10, but see b. 116 a. e.g. *jer. Shebi.*, IX, 38 d, 69; s' e Klein in *RÉJ*, LX, 1910, 106.

36. *Kiddush.*, 66 b; *jer. Terum.*, VIII, 45 b, 36; *Tos. Mikw.*, I, 17.

37. *Tos. Hag.*, II, 13; in *Rosh haShan.*, 29 b, on the day of a New Year which fell on the Sabbath, all the towns had assembled in Jamnia around R. Johanan b. Zakkai. The Munich MS. and other authorities in Rabbinowicz, however, have only, 'and all had assembled.' In *Rosh haShan.*, I, 6, it is reported: once over forty pairs of witnesses who had observed the appearance of the new moon, passed on their way to the beth-din in Jamnia through Lydda, where R. Akiba stopped them from proceeding; R. Gamaliel blamed him for it. In the parallel *Baraitha*, 22 a, top, *jer.*, I, 57 b, 70, R. Jehudah says that R. Akiba would not have committed such a mistake, but that it was Shazpar, the head of Gadar, who did it and who was for it deposed by R. Gamaliel. The incident shows how many men in the neighbourhood of Lydda were ready to go and give such evidence.

38. *Rosh haShan.*, 31 b; it is again mentioned in *Tos. 'Ahil.*, IV, 2, *jer. Berakh.*, I, 3 a, 18, *Nazir*, 52 a: R. Jehudah said: boxes containing human bones were brought from Kefar-Tabi to a synagogue in Lydda.

39. *Synh.*, 32 b, and *Pesaḥ-Haggadah*; in *Tos. Sabb.*, III, 3, b. 40 a, R. Jehudah reports that R. Akiba and R. Eleazar b. 'Azarjah bathed in a bath in benê-Berak; see also *Synh.*, 96 b, and Rabbinowicz. R. Akiba taught also in Lydda, *Semah.*, II, 4, *Nazir*, 52 a.

40. *Hag.*, 3 a, *jer.*, I, 75 d, 59; *Tos. Sotah*, VII, 0; *Synh.*, 32 b. He once went to R. Johanan b. Zakkai to berû-Hajil, and the inhabitants of the villages brought them

41. *Kil'aj.*, VI, 4. As R. Joshua visited him there (*Tos.*, IV, 7), it cannot have been far from Peki'in; and as R. Ishmael attended discussions in Jamnia (*Jadaj.*, IV, 3) with other teachers, and on the death of his sons was visited by R. Tarfon, R. Josè the Galilean, R. Eleazar b 'Azarjah, and R. Akiba (*Moëd k.*, 28 b), he cannot have lived far from Lydda and Jamnia; see Brüll, *Jahrbücher*, I, 41. According to R. Josè (*Kethub.*, V, 8), he lived near Edom, and Neubauer, *Géographie*, 117; *PEF*, Mem., 3, 348 ff.; Buhl, *Geographie*, 163, identify on that Kefar-'Aziz with Hirbet 'Aziz not far south of Jutta, but it seems improbable on the evidence adduced. Edom need not mean ancient Idumaea, but the part of Judaea that in Roman times was called Idumaea. In that district beth-Gubrin had Jewish inhabitants, for Jehudah b. Jacob of beth-Gubrin gave evidence with Jacob b. Jiṣhak of beth-Gufnin concerning Caesarea in *Tos.' Ahil.*, XVIII, 16. Rabbi declared beth-Gubrin free from priestly dues, *jer. Dammai*, II, 2, c, 55; *JQR*, XIII, 683.

42. *Midr. Tannaim*, ed. Hoffmann, 175, אמהוס with *h* instead of the usual alef, e.g. *jer.* Shebi. ix. 38d, 69; see Klein in REJ, LX, 1910, 106.

43. *Hull.*, 91 b; *Kerith.*, III 7, 8, here spelled עימאוס ; Nehemiah עמסחי is also probably of Emmaus, Grätz in *MGWJ*, II, 1853, 112. Against the identity of the two tells the essential difference of their rules of interpretation, R. Johanan reporting כלל ופרט of Nehunjah in *Shebu.*, 26 a, whereas Nehemiah applied רבוי ומעוט ; *jer. Berakh.*, IX, 14b, 68, and *Pesah.*, 22 b. Klein thinks that the discussion between R. Nehunjah and R. Joshua took place in Emmaus, but the report does not suggest it.

44. G. A. Smith, *Histor. Geography*, 209 ff.

45. *Kohel. r.*, 7, 7; *Sabb.*, 147 b; *ARN*, XIV, 30 a; 2 *ARN*, XXIX, 30 a; it is not Ḥamtha near Tiberias, but in Judaea, Bacher, *Tann.*, 1, 76, 3; by removing from the second version the word Jerusalem all contradictions disappear.

46. *Jebam.*, XII, 6; but the Mishnah in *jerus. Jebam.* reads Kefar-'Ibdas, the Cambridge Mishnah Kefar-'Akkô.

47. In *Beṣah*, 21 a; *Tos.*, II, 6; *Mekhiltha R. Simeon*, 17, it is reported: When on one holy day Simeon of Thimnah had not come to the school, R. Jehudah b. Baba asked him the next morning for the reason. Now from *Tos Berakh.*, IV, 18, we learn that Simeon belonged to R. Tarfon's school in Lydda, and from *Tos. Synh.*, XII, 3, b. 17 b; *B. kam.*, 90 b; Bacher, *Tann.*, I, 444 ff., we see that he had discussions with R. Akiba, as R. Jehudah b. Baba with R. Akiba and R. Jehudah b. Bethera, so that Simeon belonged to the school of Jamnia or Lydda.

48. See Guérin, *Judée*, 1, 202.

49. *Tos. 'Ahil.*, XVI, 13; *Mikw.*, VI, 2; *Pesah.*, 9 a, *jer.*, I, 28 a, 39. fruit (*Tos. Ma'as.*, II, 1; *jer.*, II, 49 d, 24). R. Johanan lived in that place (*Synh.*, 32 b), but it has not been identified yet, nor is there anything to suggest even the

district where it was. If the incident refers to a time after the year 70, berûr-Hajil must be sought in Judaea in a part inhabited by Jews.

50. Zech. xiv. 10; *Tos. Sotah*, XI, 14; S. Klein, *Beiträge z. Geographie*, 94, 3, thinks of Rimmon in Joshua xix. 13, but the two teachers report, as in many other instances, Judaean experiences. R. Simeon b. Johai in the lifetime of his teacher R. Akiba stayed for the Sabbath in Kefar-beth-Fagi (*Tos. Me'ilah*, I, 5, b. 7 a), where he met another disciple of R. Akiba. As it was on his way from Judaea to Galilee, the position is difficult to define.

51. Pliny, *H. N.*, V, 15; Galerius, vol. XIV, p. 25, Kühn; cf. Hölscher, *Palaestina in d. pers. u. hellen. Zeit*, 49. In *Midr. Cant.*, ed. Grünhut, to i. 14, it is said that 'En-gedi was beautiful, and wine was made there in levitical purity for libations in the Temple; and R. Josef the Babylonian from a Baraitha states in *Sabb.*, 26 a, that balsam was gathered in from 'En-gedi to Ramatha. The vineyards there bore four times a year fruit (*Agad. Cant.* on i. 14).

52. *'Eduj.*, VII, 5, reads Hadar, but the Cambridge and Naples *Mishnah* and other texts quoted by Rabbinowicz have Hadid, the place mentioned in Ezra ii. 33; Neh. vii. 37, xi. 35; 1 Chron. viii. 12, as Adida in 1 Macc. xii. 38, xiii. 13; in the Bible passages together with Lydda and 'Onô, as they were neighbours, similarly in *'Arakh.*, IX, 6, b. 32 a, Hadid and 'Onô in Judaea as fortified since ancient times. In *Kethub.*, 111 b, bottom, R. Jacob b. Dosithai says that he walked from Lydda to 'Onô to his ankles in fig honey.

53. *Gitt.*, VI, 7. In *Tos Synh.*, II, 13, b. 11 b, *jer.*, I, 18 d, 76, he testifies that the intercalation of a year may take place only in Judaea, exceptionally also in Galilee. It is obvious that that evidence was taken when owing to the Hadrianic persecutions the religious life of the Jewish community had to be guided from Galilee. Therefore the words 'before R. Gamaliel' in *Tos.* are a mistake. In *Sifrê zutta* on Num. xv. 4 in *Jalkut*, Num. 746, *Horovitz*, 92, a R. Papias of 'Onô is mentioned; whether he is identical with R. Papias, a colleague of R. Akiba, is uncertain. About the year 200 R. Simai and R. Sadok went to Lydda to intercalate the year and, when staying for the Sabbath in 'Onô, gave a decision on religious law (*Hull.*, 56 b). R. 'Aibo of the fourth century says (*Cant. r.*, 2, 2;*Lev. r.*, 23, 5; *Threni r.*, 1, 17): God ordered Jacob's enemies to surround him, so Halamish surrounds Naweh, Castra Haifa, Susitha Tiberias, Jericho No'aran, and Lydda 'Onô. As 'Onô is mentioned as an old fortress, we would suggest 'Ono to Lydda, but Lydda rose in importance and may have superseded 'Onô even as fortress or merely as city (*JQR*, XIII, 733). In *jer. Gitt.*, IV, 46 a, 36, R. 'Ammi ruled that if a slave escaped from abroad and reached 'Oni, he must not be surrendered to his master (for the place is in Palestine), if to 'Antris, he may be surrendered (for it is not in Palestine), if to 'Aparkoris, it is doubtful. 'Antaris cannot be Antarados, as Krauss, *Lehnwörter*, II, 72, suggests, for the place must be on the border of Palestine. Where is 'Oni? Is it identical with 'Onô, and are the other two places in Philistia? Another place is mentioned in *jer. Synh.*, I, 18 c, 71: 'we still find that the year was solemnly initiated in Ba'alath (in Judaea). This was at times reckoned to Judah, sometimes to Dan. But do we not find that the year was initiated in Balath? Here the houses stood in Judah, the fields lay in Dan.' In the two places mentioned the ceremony of initiating the new year was performed after the authoritative beth-din had long been transferred to Galilee. We learn that there were Jews in those places in the fourth century, though it may confidently be assumed that the same applied to earlier times, as Ba'alath was last in the line Lydda—Modeim —Ba'alath (see, however, Neubauer, 99 ff.). The same may apply to 'Ekron, of which Eusebius says that it was east of Jamnia between this and Azotus and a great Jewish village.

54. It is again mentioned in *jer. Dammai*, II, 22 c, 47: the law of Dammai applies to Samaritans in Pondaka of 'Ammuda and of Tibatha to Kefar-Saba; see Schürer, II, 156 ff. Antipatris seems to have been raised at some time or other in character as town, for *Threni r.*, 1, 5; ed. *Buber*, 33 a, says: You find that before the destruction of Jerusalem no city was in their sight of value, but after the destruction Caesarea became a metropolis, Antipatris a central town, and Neapolis a colony.

As the latter became a colony only under Philip Arabs, the statement was made at the earliest in the year 250; yet Antipatris may have been distinguished at a much earlier time.

55. *Tos. Niddah*, VIII, 7; in the parallel *Baraitha Niddah*, 61 a, the informant is Abba Saul, and the scholar who suggested a new method of examining the rock was R. Joshua.

56. Eusebius, p. 220; Schürer, *Geschichte*, I, 218, 28.

57. *Jer. B. kam.*, III, 3 d, 37; Bacher, *Tann.*, II, 371, 3.

58. In *Nedar*, 81 a, a statement of Isi b. Jehudah is identical with that of Jehudah of Ḥuṣa (see Ratner on *Shebi'ith*, VIII, 38 b, 10, p. 77); see also *Kiddush.*, 58 b, top, and Derenbourg, *Essai*, 483.

59. *Tos. Kelim*, I, IV, 4, variants in *MGWJ*, 1901, XLV, 22.

60. *Tos. Terum.*, III, 18; from the same place wine was in Temple times taken for sacrifices, *Menaḥ.*, VIII. 6. Neubauer, 84, suggests Sukneh near Joppé, but the statement that Kefar-Signa was in the valley is too vague for definition.

61. In *Tos. Hull.*, III, 23, b. 62 a, the opponents of R. Eliezer refer to the fact that the people of Kefar-Thamartha in Judaea ate a certain fowl as permitted, because it had a crop, a sign of purity. They were Jews; but it is not clear whether this refers to our period after the year 70.

62. *Jer. Ta'an.*, IV, 69 a, 23; *Threni r.*, 2, 2. In *Seder 'Olam, XXX*, it says: From Vespasian's war to that of Quietus were 52 years; see Ratner, p. 73 b, note 78; Schürer, *Geschichte*, I, 696, note.

63. In the parallel in *B. kam.*, 83a R. Simeon b. Gamaliel says that in his father's house (school) were a thousand children, 500 learned Torah, and 500 Greek science, and of all only he and his cousin in Asia remained. Betthar is not mentioned, but apparently Jamnia is meant.

64. *Semaḥ.*, VIII: מכאן ועד שנים עשר חדש פסקו בולאות שנאמר חרדו שאננות רמזה בוטחות, שאננות אלו בולאות שביהודה, בוטחות אלו קרקסיאות, לא היה בו לשון בוטחות אלא טרכסין. Two groups of places are referred to: one בולאות, the other קרקסיאות, for which 80, 1, reads חרדו שאננות אלו טרקסיאות. The verb פסק without complementary verb can hardly refer to persons, but only to inanimate things, best to cities that felt too secure, open places as opposed to fortified towns that offered safety, as already N. Brüll in his *Jahrbücher*, I, 41, 89, explained them. As כרקום means a fortress in *T. Jebam.* XIV, 8: fortress of Betthar, קרקסיאות, is most probably a corruption of that word. As to the meaning of בולאות a Baraitha cited by R. Josef in *Gitt.*, 37 a, top, reads: I shall break the pride of your might (Lev.xxvi. 19), these are the בולאות in Judaea (not to be identified with the interpretation of the same verse in *Sifra*, 111 d, §2: These are the nobles who are the pride of Israel, as Pappos b. Jehudah and Lulianus, Alexandri and his companions, for the characteristic word is not there, see Bacher, *Tann.*, I, 52, 6). And in *Jer. Nedar.*, III, 38 a, 13, *Pesiktha r.*, XXII, 112 b ff., R. Samuel b. Naḥman says: Twenty-four בוליות were in the Darom and all were destroyed owing to a useless, though true oath. Here it is evident from the word חרבו that buildings or towns are meant. R. Ḥaninah, the vice high-priest, says in *'Abôth R. Nathan*, XX, 36 b: The sons of my mother were angry with me (Cant. i. 6), referring to בולאות in Judaea, who shook off the yoke of God and set over them a human king. Here either leading men of the country are referred to or the elders in I Sam. viii. 4 who committed that mistake; as R. Ḥaninah hardly knew bar-Kochba, and as far as we know, in the year 116 no king of Judaea was elected, the reference is still obscure. If he meant towns with proper constitutions, he may have referred to the revolution in the years 66–70, though we only know of Menaḥem as a kind of king (Geiger in *ZS*, VIII, 39, and Schlatter, *Zur Topographie*, 121 ff.).

65. His wealth and his position are described in *ARN*, XVII, 33 a, VI, 16 a, b; 2 *ARN*, XIII, 16 a; *Kethub.*, 66 b, bottom.

66. *Sifré Deut.*, 305, 130 a; *Kethub.*, 66 b; *ARN*, XVII, 33 a; Bacher, *Tannaiten*, I, 42. R. Eleazar b. Sadok met her in Akko in adject poverty, *Tos. Kethub.*, V, 10; *jer.*, V, 30 b, 76 ff., b. 67 a.

67. Josephus in *Wars*, VI, 5, 2, reports that the treasure houses of the Temple were burnt, in which an enormous sum of money ,a mass of garments and other precious things, in short, the whole wealth of the Jews was kept, as the wealthy had brought there all their effects.

68. The same in *jer. Gitt.*, V, 47 b, 11: the enemy decreed persecutions first against Judaea, subdued its people, took their fields and sold them to others.

69. In 2 *ARN*, XXXI, 34 a, a sentence introduced by הוא היה אומר attributed to R. Joḥanan b. Zakkai, reads: Force the children (students) away from haughtiness and separate them from בעלי בתים for these keep people away from the words of the Torah. The wealthy landowners are referred to who not only had no interest in learning, but also dissuaded others from joining the schools. They are identical with the עמי הארץ, to whom R. Dosa b. Harkinas refers in *'Abóth* III, 10: Sleep in the morning and wine in midday and sitting in the houses of assembly of the 'Amme ha'ares remove man from the world. The comfort described here points to a class of wealthy men. It may be pointed out here that the sentence quoted is in *ARN*, XXI, 37 b explained to refer to those who sit at the corners in the market and divert one from the Torah. The contemporary of R. Johanan b., Zakkai, Neḥunjah b. Hakanah, in his prayer in *Baraitha Berakh.*, 28 b, said: I thank Thee God that Thou hast given my lot with those who sit in the school and not with those who sit at the corners; for we both rise early, I for the words of the Torah, they for vain things; I toil and they toil, I receive a reward, they do not; I run to eternal life, they run to hell (in *jer. Berakh.*, IV, 7 d, 39, instead of the corners, theatres and circuses). R. Akiba termed himself an 'Am ha'ares in *Pesaḥ.*, 49 b, and in *ARN*, XI, 37 b he said in his later years when a scholar: I thank Thee my God that Thou hast given my lot with those who sit in the school and not with those who sit at the corners in the market. This shows the identity of the latter men with the 'Am ha'ares.

70. He lived in Jamnia, *Tos. Kelim.*, 3, II, 4; *Sabb.*, VII, 18; *Mikw.*, VI, 3; *jer. Meg.*, I, 71 c, 11; *Genes. r.*, 70, 5; *Kohel. r.*, 7, 8; *Num. r.*, 8 end; *Pesik. r.*, XXIII, 117 a.

71. *Sifra*, 106 c, § 9. When R. Gamaliel died, Akylas burnt more than seventy manehs of money in his honour, *'Abod. z.*, 11 a; *Tos. Sabb.*, VII, 18; *Semaḥ.*, VIII; this shows his wealth. R. Tarfon in Lydda once after the harvest plucked figs from another man's tree, *Nedar.*, 62 a; when the owner of the field found him doing this, he seized him and put him in a sack to drown him. When R. Tarfon sighed and said: Woe to Tarfon, for he will be killed, the man left him and ran away. R. Haninah b. Gamaliel reports that R. Tarfon through all his life could never forgive himself that he had derived this benefit from his position as scholar. The parallel in *jer. Shebi.*, IV, 35 b, 17, reports the incident to have occurred in the sabbatical year, so that the owner of the field was a Jew. As the field-guards who struck R. Tarfon knew when hearing the name who R. Tarfon was, they seem Jews.

72. *Jer. Berakh.*, II, 5 d, 5, and *Ratner*, p. 62; in the parallel *B. kam.*, 81 b, the same is told of Jehudah b. Nekosa who was met by Rabbi and R. Hijja in Sepphoris about the year 200.

73. Reference is made to a מציק in Rimmon in *Tos. 'Ahil.*, XVI, 13; *Mikw.*, VI, 2 (see p. 11, 1), who seems to have been a Jew in the service of the Romans, and who, by their assistance, acquired property (*JQR*, XVI, 153). In *Derekh 'ereṣ*, VI, Gaster, מעשיות, 103, a Simeon b. Antipatris received many wayfarers and provided food, drink, and lodging, but striped all visitors who swore by the Torah that they would not eat, but in the end ate. R. Joḥanan b. Zakkai and the teachers, hearing of this, sent R. Joshua b. Ḥananjah to rebuke Simeon. As his place had a bath, it was a town, perhaps Antipatris, as a part of his name.

74. *Lev. r.*, 34, 16; *Pesik. r.*, XXV, 126 b; in *Kallah* the incident is reported differently: R. Tarfon was wealthy, but not liberal. Once R. Akiba suggested to him to buy one or two places (?fields), and R. Tarfon handed to him 4,000 gold denars which R. Akiba distributed among the poor. After that, R. Tarfon gave him more money for distribution. Interesting is his definition of a wealthy man in *Baraitha Sabb.*, 25 b: He who has a hundred vineyards, a hundred fields and a hundred slaves

to work them. It shows his standard of wealth and, if the figures are to be taken strictly, also the relation between a unit of field and the number of slaves required for it.

75. *Sifrê Num.*, 116; *Pesaḥ.*, 72 b; *Sifrê zutta Num.*, 18, 7, *Horowitz*, 112.

76. *Tos. Kethub.*, V, 1; *jer. Jebam.*, IV, 6 b, 59. In *jer. Kethub.*, V, 29 d, 46, R. Tarfon says that all the food due to a betrothed woman after twelve months should be given to her in the form of priestly due, for such is found everywhere. The parallels do not contain the last sentence; it would imply that there were fields in Jewish possession everywhere.

77. In a *Baraitha Berakh.*, 35 b, R. Jehudah reports: Earlier generations were different from the present one: those brought in (from the fields) their produce by the way of טרקסימין in order to make the produce liable to tithe; the present generation bring in their produce by the way of courts and enclosures in order to free it from tithe. In the parallel in *jer. Ma'as.*, III, 50 c, 8, R. Jehudah says to Rabbi and R. Josê b. R. Jehudah: See, R. Akiba bought three kinds of produce for one Perutah in order to give tithe of each.

77a. *Tos. Dammai*, V, 22; *jer.*, V, 24 d, 69; *b. Menah.*, 31

78. A case concerning his cow is specially discussed in *Sabb.*, V, 4; *Besaḥ*, II, 8, because he allowed her, against the opinion of the rabbis, to go out on the Sabbath with a strap between her horns. In *jer. Sabb.*, V, 7 c, 28, the rabbis asked R. Eleazar either to leave the school or to stop his cow being let out in that way; see *Ratner* and *Sabb.*, 54 b, bottom. It is evident that the controversy occurred when R. Eleazar was not yet the president of the school in Jamnia.

79. The garden had two entrances, one in a levitically pure, the other in an unclean place (reported by R. 'Abba in *jer. Ma'as. sheni*, V, 56 b, 71; *b. Jebam.*, 86 b). R. Akiba objected to a priest's taking a tithe which in his opinion was due to Levites only, and he persuaded the owner of the garden to keep the pure entrance shut and, if R. Eleazar should send a disciple for the tithe, to tell him that tithe must be called for by its claimant. R. Eleazar soon found out the author of this trouble, and recognizing his mistake, returned all the tithe which he had ever received.

80. R. Josê in *Terum.*, IV, 13, reports that a case came before R. Akiba of fifty bundles of vegetables having been accidentally mixed with a bundle, half of which was priestly due. This landowner observed also the rabbinic extension of the duty of tithing to vegetables. A landowning priest was R. Ishmael in Kefar-'Aziz (*Kil'aj.*, VI, 4) who planted vines, figs, and sycamores in his garden, so that he must have otherwise provided for his maintenance (see p. 83, n. 41). Another priest was Zechariah b. haKassab, who, with his wife, had escaped from Jerusalem when the Romans took possession of it (*Kethub.*, II, 9, above, p. 77). He assigned to his wife a separate house in his court (*Baraitha Kethub.*, 27, b, bottom; *Tos.*, III, 2; *Semah.*, II), and she lived there. There seems hardly any interval between his escape from Jerusalem and his settling on his property. Where he lived is not stated, but as R. Joshua quotes in *Sotah*, V, 1, to R. Akiba a statement of R. Zechariah, the latter seems to have lived in Jamnia. This is confirmed by his giving evidence with R. Josê the priest ('*Eduj.*, VIII, 2). As R. Eleazar b. R. Josê, who lived in the Darom, probably Lydda, reported some of his statements, one in *Tos. B. bath.*, VII, 10 (in *b.* 111 a, R. Josê b. R. Jehudah and R. Eleazar b. R. Josê, cf. *jer.*, VIII, 16 a, 17), and another in *Tos Meg.*, I, 6, it is just as possible that he lived in Lydda.

81. *ARN*, VI, 15 b; 2 *ARN*, XIII, 15 b; *Genes. r.*, 42, 1; *Pirkê R. Eliezer*, I.

82. *Synh.*, 68 a; *Berakh*, 16 b; *jer.*, II, 5 b, 66; *Semah.*, I, 10.

83. In a Baraitha in *Sabb.*, 127 b, a man of Upper Galilee served for three years with a farmer in the Darom. At the conclusion of his service on the eve of the Day of Atonement, he asked for his wages in order to return home and to provide for his wife and his children. The master replied that he had neither money, nor produce, nor field, nor cattle, saddles, or cushions, which the servant asked in succession. He took his luggage and, greatly disappointed, went home. After the feast of Tabernacles the master took the servant's wages, a load of three asses of food, drink, and sweet things, and took all this to his former servant. In the conversation it turned out that the servant had thought his master had expended all his money on cheap articles for business, his cattle had been hired by somebody, his field leased, his produce had

not been tithed yet, and all his other possessions consecrated to God. The master then explained that, in order to force his son Hyrkanos to study Torah, he had prohibited himself by a vow the use of all his property, but now his vow was annulled by his colleagues in the Darom. This scholar, living in the Darom, father of a Hyrkanos, and having relations with Upper Galilee, is evidently R. Eliezer b. Hyrkanos, as She'iltoth, *Exodus*, § 40, in the same report expressly state, and give as the name of the servant Akiba b. Josef. Though the source of this is unknown to me, the Baraitha itself, with its references to property of all kinds in Lydda, deserves special attention.

84. A female slave of his was once baking loaves of priestly due, and another time she was stopping jugs of wine of such due (*Niddah*, 6 b). RSBM and *Tosafoth* refer this to R. Gamaliel I, though as a rule he is called Gamaliel the Old; in *jer. Niddah*, II, 49 d, 36, the wine was for libations in the Temple.

85. *Dammai*, III, 1. The Jew was not trustworthy in matters of tithes and priestly dues. Such landowners were termed 'Am ha'ares, as we find R. Sadok asking R. Joshua whether a distinction was made between Haber and 'A ha'ares as to blemishes of a firstborn animal (*Bekhor.*, 36 a); and also in a discussion between Shammaiites and Hillelites, here R. Eliezer and R. Joshua, about levitical purity (*Hag.*, 22 a, b; *'Eduj.*, I, 14).

86. *Nedar.*, 50 a, b; *ARN*, VI, 15 a, b; 2 *ARN*, XII, 15 b, describe his furniture of gold and a jewel of his wife.

87. *Jer. Pe'ah*, I, 15 b, 39; a Baraitha in *Kethub.*, 50 a, merely reports: A man wanted to give away more than a fifth of his property, but his colleague would not allow it; some say that it was R. Jesheb'ab and R. Akiba.

88. To this may be added the legend in Hegesippus (Eusebius, *Hist. Eccl.*, III, 20) in which the relatives of Jesus were questioned by Domitian as to their financial position, and they answered: 'We both possess only 900 denars, of which a half belongs to each, and even this we possess not in cash, but in land consisting of 39 plethras.'

89. Another instance of lending money on fields is found in R. Akiba's advice to his disciple R. Simeon b. Johai in *Pesah.*, 112 b, top: If you want to do a good deed and at the same time profit by it, lend money to your fellow on a field to enjoy its income as instalment, and the borrower has also a profit from your money.

90. R. Jehudah in *Tos. Sabb.*, III, 4, reports that Boethos had a bucket of water prepared on Friday to have it poured over him on the Sabbath.

91. A man bought something from one of two men, but did not know from which, and both claimed the price; R. Tarfon advised him to put the purchase-money between both and go away. R. Akiba said there was no other solution but to pay both. *B. kam.*, 103 b.

92. Baraitha *'Ab. zar.*, 13 a; *Tos.*, I, 8, speaks of slaves, male and female, of houses, fields, and vineyards, purchased and brought before the office of non-Jews; similarly *Tos. 'Ab. zar.*, VI, 2; Baraitha *Gitt.*, 44 a; *Tos. B. bathra*, VIII, 2; *Sifrê Num.*, 117. As the office is already mentioned by R. Akiba in Baraitha *Gitt.*, 11 a; *Tos.*, I, 4 (see my *'Am ha'ares*, 244, 37), those passages could not very well be referred to Galilee after the year 135.

93. *Midrash Esther*, VI begin. on 2, 5, and *Midr. Psalms*, 106, 3, see Buber, and Bacher, *Tannaiten*, I, 188, 4. As R. Eleazar of Modeim is asked to give his opinion, the discussion took place in R. Tarfon's time; in *Kethub.*, 50 a, the interpretation is quoted in the name of R. Samuel b. Nahman. In *Midr. Proverbs*, 6, 20, R. Meir asks Elisha b. 'Abuja, his teacher, whether there is a remedy for an adulteress, and Elisha cites a statement of ben-'Azzai, his colleague, who recommended as a remedy for such a woman the bringing up of an orphan in her house and teaching him Torah and observance.

94. In spite of his poverty he received a wayfarer whom he provided with food and drink, and, as he had no room for him, he took him to the roof of his house (*Derekh 'eres*, V, end). About midnight the stranger stole all things which he found on the roof, and not knowing that his host had removed the steps, tried to descend and broke his collar-bone.

95. A worse case was that of Nahum of Gimzô (*Ta'an.*, 21 a) who, deprived of the use of his limbs, arms, eyes, and visited by leprosy, lived in a house in very bad

repairs. For his terrible condition he accounted to his disciples as follows: When once on my way to my father-in-law with three asses laden with food, drink, and sweet things, I met a poor man who asked for my help; while I unloaded my ass, the man died and I cursed my limbs and my body.

96. Of R. Gamaliel's household it is said in *Sabb.*, 113 a, bottom, *Tos.*, XII, 16, that they did not fold their garments on the Sabbath, because they had another set to change; it seems to imply that ordinary people had only one set.

97. R. Akiba terms poverty an ornament of Israel (*Lev. r.*, 35, 6), but says that even the poor are nobles (*B. kam.*, VIII, 6); he himself walked, when he was a scholar, bare-footed even in Rome, and was jeered at by an eunuch (*Koh. r.*, 10, 7), and enjoined on his son Joshua among other things not to withhold shoes from his feet (*Pesah.*, 112 a; Bacher, *Tannaiten*, I, 270, 2). It is not evident whether he did so owing to poverty. R. Tarfon wore shoes, *Tos, Neg.*, VIII, 2; *Sifra*, 70 c; *jer. Sotah*, II, 18 a, 7.

98. *Kethub.*, 8 b; *Tos. Nid.*, IX, 17; *jer. Berakh.*, III, 6 a, 34; *Semah.*, XIV, end.

99. R. Eliezer in *Cant. r.*, introduction, § 9, said: Nobody ever was before me in the house of learning or left by me there; once I rose early and already met the manure- and straw-labourers, they were early workers; should not we be at our work as early as they? Bacher, *Tannaiten*, I, 101, 3. The rabbis worked all day long in their respective occupations, and in the evening they attended the school, even on Friday and holy day night, *Tos. Sabb.*, V, 13; *Sifrê Num.*, 116; *Pesah.*, 72 b. R. Tarfon, *Pesah.*, 109 a R. Akiba, *Tos. Besah*, II, 16 R. Jehudah b. Baba and R. Simeon of Timnah. On some occasions also ordinary people were present in greater numbers, *Berakh.*, 27 b; *jer.*, IV, 7 d, 5, 6, if העם means such, and not the usual audience of scholars.

100. We find rabbis riding on asses, as R. Johanan b. Zakkai in *Kethub.*, 66 b; *Sifrê Deut.*, 305; *Hag.*, 14 b, and parallels; R. Gamaliel riding from Akko to Ekdippa in '*Erub.*, 64 b., *Tos. Pesah.*, 1, 28; *jer. 'Abod. zar.*, 1, 40 a, 65. An ass of R. Gamaliel was loaded for too many hours with honey and died, *Sabb.*, 154 b. R. Gamaliel gave a Libyan ass as bribe to a philosopher and judge who pretended to be incorruptible, *Sabb.*, 116 b. When finding that he will have to pay for the consequences of a wrong judgment, R. Tarfon said: Thy ass is gone, Tarfon, *Synh.*, 33 a. Doves in Lydda are mentioned in *Tos. Tohar.*, IX, 14; a dove-cote in Lydda in *Tos. Berakh.*, IV, 16; *Mekhiltha*, 31 b.

101. *B. kam.*, 80 a, top, and my *'Am ha'areṣ*, 191 ff.

102. *Revue des Études Juives*, 1907, LIII, 14 ff.

103. In a Baraitha in *Sabb.*, 53 b, R. Jehudah reports that the family of Antiochia had goats with large breasts and had to tie bags on them to prevent their wounding them. Perhaps that family lived in Lydda or Jamnia.

104. In *Kiddush.*, 82 a, Abba Gorja says that no one should train his son to be an ass- or camel-driver, nor a coachman or a boatman, herdsman or grocer, because their occupation implies dishonesty. He seems to make no distinction between herds and flocks; but from the several references to shepherds as robbers it is probable that he referred in the first instance to shepherds.

105. See also the report in the tractate of *Kalleh*, ed. Coronel, 19 a: Once R. Akiba sat as his table under an olive-tree owing to religious persecutions, and said: Those who rear small cattle and cut down good trees, and children's teachers who do not do their work properly, will see no sign of blessing (see also *Pesah.*, 50 b). The persuasive tone of the statement suggests that some people were acting against the prohibition.

106. Judaean wine never turned sour in the times of the Temple, but it did so in R. Jehudah's days, *jer. Dammai*, I, 21 d, 8; *Tos.*, I, 2; *b. Pesah.*, 42 b. R. Eliezer never suffered any loss by his wine turning sour, or by his flax being smitten, or his oil smelling badly, or his honey fermenting, *Synh.*, 101 a.

107. *Tos. Ta'an.*, II, 5; *jer.*, II, 66 a, 44; *b. Rosh haShan.*, 18 b.

108. R. Jehudah speaks of a year of drought when men in places left their Lulabs to their sons as inheritance (*Tos. Suk.*, II, 9); perhaps it was the same year when on his sea voyage with R. Joshua, R. Eleazar b. 'Azarjah, and R. Akiba, only R. Gamaliel had a Lulab which he had bought for a thousand zuzs (*Suk.*, 41 b). There

seem to have been unsatisfactory years not due to drought; for R. Joshua accounts by special sins for the lack of blessing in produce and for man's toil not being rewarded by sufficient food (*ARN*, XXXVIII, 57 a). R. Eliezer's or R. Ishmael's remark that when the Jews do not fulfil God's will they are compelled to keep four years of rest instead of the one prescribed (*Mekhil.*, 23, p. 100 b), also suggests sad times.

109. The parallel in *jer. Pe'ah*, VII, 20 a, 70, by R. Hijja b. 'Abba, does not mention Judaea. The price of land is nowhere stated, except in the legend of Hegesippus about Jesus' relatives (p. 91, n. 88), where they state their property to be 900 denarii in the shape of 39 plethra of land. Though the historical value of the report is very doubtful, it may have been made up on real conditions in Palestine of the time of Hegesippus, when 1 plethra of land was worth 23-3/39 denarii.

110. Rabbi once came to benê-Berak and saw lying there a cluster as big as a calf of three years; *Midrash Tannaim*, ed. Hoffmann, 173 ff.

111. R. Gamaliel bought corn from a Jew who seemed unreliable as to giving tithes, and fed his labourers with it, *Dammai*, III, 1.

112. The rabbis urged the Jews to teach their children a craft; R. Gamaliel describes it as giving security, *Tos. Kiddush.*, I, 11, and R. Ishmael in *jer. Pe'ah*, I, 15 c, top, explains 'choose life' in Deut. xxx. 19 to refer to a craft. Judaea had places engaged in the wool industry, not only women working in their household (*B. kam.*, X, 9), but, as R. Hosha'jah in the first half of the third century reports (*Tanhuma*, נשׂא , 8, see Buber, § 14, note 70), there were villages in the Darom engaged in dyeing purple, and there most men had dyed hands. See for the fourth century 'Totius urbis descriptio' (Müller, *Geographi Graeci minores*, II, 513; Schürer, *Geschichte*, II, 56, 173), which mentions Lydda, Neapolis, Caesarea, Sarepta 'purpuram praestant'.

113. Also R. Ishmael said in *B. bath.*, 60 b, bottom; *Tos. Sotah*, XV, 10, that we ought to abstain from everything, but it could not be carried out by the people. R. Joshua himself had at first to be comforted by his teacher R. Johanan b. Zakkai in *ARN*, IV, 11 a; 2 *ARN*, VIII, 11 b.

114. Of feasting at circumcisions and weddings we read in the Baraitha *Synh.*, 32 b; *jer. Kethub.*, I, 25 c, 32; *Tos. Sabb.*, VII, 9, and elsewhere, p. 96.

115. *Tos. Synh.*, XII, 10; in an anonymous Baraitha in *Synh.*, 101 a, Joshua b. Hananjah denounces the same; in *ARN* XXXVI, 54 b, it is ascribed to R. Johanan b. Nuri.

116. *Tos. Sotah*, end; *B. bath.*, 60 b; Bacher, *Tannaiten*, I, 159, 3. Other things of luxury ceased to be used, as white glass. Though in the report in Baraitha *Sotah*, 48 b: Since the destruction of the first Temple the use of Pranda silk, of white glass and iron chariots ceased, according to some also the jelly of wine from Senir that resembled fig-cakes, this is connected with the destruction of the first Temple (cf. *jer. Sukkah*, IV, 54 d, 13), it is evident from Baraitha *Moëd kat.*, 27 a, bottom; *jer. Dammai*, IV, 24 a, 66; *Tos. Niddah*, IX, 17, that the second Temple was meant. For first wealthy people went to comfort mourners with wine in bottles of white glass, the poor in such of coloured glass, and as the poor were hereby put to shame, it was instituted that everybody should use coloured glass. This institution and the others reported there belong to a very late period of the second Temple.

117. *'Erub.*, 41 a; *Ta'em.*, 13 a; *jer. Beṣah*, II, 61 b, 51.

118. Weiss, II, 73 ff.; Bacher, *Tannaiten*, I, 89.

119. *Tos. Jebam.*, VIII, end; b. 63 b; *Genes. r.*, 34, 14; *Sotah*, 4 b.

120 A very interesting question addressed to R. Eleazar b. R. Sadok by his disciples indicates an otherwise unknown, but very instructive fact; Why does everybody want to mary a proselyte, but not a freed maid-servant (*Horaj.*, 13 a)? We known only of few proselytes in Judaea in our period, and cannot account for the statement. Is it perhaps the Galilean R. Eleazar b. Sadok?

121. *Jer. Jebam.*, IV, 6 b, 37; *Semah.*, VII; *Moëd kat.*, 23 a.

122. R. Akiba bought for his wife a golden ornament representing Jerusalem, *Sabb.*, 59 a, b *jer.*, VI, 7 d, 65. When R. Gamaliel's wife envied her for it, her husband referred her to the great share which A. Akiba's wife had in his greatness.

123. *Kiddush.*, 31 b; *jer.*, IV, 61 b, 18; *Nidd.*, 48 b; *Tos.*, VI, 8.

124. *Tos. Kethub.*, IV, 7; *Niddah*, 48 b; VIII, 3; *Kethub.*, 10 b; *Jadaj.*, III, 1; *Hag.*, 20 a.

125. *Joma*, 66 b; in *jer. Sotah*, III, 19 a, 5, the woman is a matrona, a non-Jewess.

126. Little is known about the relations between rabbis and women of the people. R. Joshua once stayed with a woman who cooked his food (*'Erub.*, 53 b). When R. Ishmael died, the women of Israel bewailed him (*Nedar.* L, IX, 10 ff.; *Baraitha*, 66 b).

127. *Sotah*, III, 4; the translation of the word by separation from intercourse seems to me to follow from the context; see also *jer. Nedar.*, XI, 42 c, 65.

128. Baraitha R. Meir in *Gitt.*, 90 a; *Tos. Sotah*, V, 9.

129. R. Akiba in *ARN*, XXVI, 41 b, in 2 *ARN*, XXXV, 41 a, Josê the Babylonian accounts for the death of young scholars; the frequency of the sad occurrence demanded an explanation. R. Akiba visited one of his disciples who was ill and visited by nobody (*Nedar.*, 40 a, 41 a).

130. *Baraitha Jebam.*, 122 b; *Tos.* XIV, 9, 10; *jer.*, XVI, 15 d, 38.

131. *Baraitha Jebam.*, 25 b; *Tos.*, IV, 5; *jer.*, II, 4b, 2.

132. *Tos. Jebam.*, XIV, 5; *jer.*, XVI, 15 d, 14; b. 121 a. R. Akiba in *Semah.*, IV, 34; *Derekh'eres z.*, VIII, relates how in his earlier days he once found a murdered man and carried the body 6,000 cubits till he reached a place of burial, and buried him. When he reported his act to the rabbis, they (R. Eliezer and R. Joshua) told him that he ought to have buried the man where he found him.

133. Simeon of Timnah tells R. Jehudah b. Baba how the night before a troop of non-Jews came to his town and wanted to spoil the whole place; by slaughtering a young cow for them, they got rid of them in peace, *Besah*, 21 a; *Tos.*, II, 6. Rashi explains the Hebrew word as a great band of raiders who search everything; see the dictionaries.

134. Punishments inflicted by the Romans on Jews also suggest violent acts in Judaea. A Jew in prison freed without witnesses the childless widow of his brother from marrying him (*Jebam.*, XII, 4 and 105 b, bottom), and R. Akiba declared it valid. Originally the rabbis said: when one goes away in a collarium and asks that a bill of divorce should be written for his wife, it should be written and delivered; later they added: a man who goes on a sea journey or with a caravan. R. Simeon Shezuri added: a man who is dangerously ill, *Gitt.*, VI, 5. Now this disciple of R. Tarfon knew already the first additions to the original rule, so that this must have belonged at the latest to the time of his teacher. Executions, see in *Semah.*, II, 11, 13. Galilean Jews suspected of murder came to R. Tarfon and asked for shelter, but he refused, *Nidd.*, 61 a, bottom.

135. R. 'Aibo's statement about hostile fortresses in Palestine, p. 84, note 53 ff., must not be adduced, for he lived in the fourth century.

136. Here *Rashi* and *Tosafoth* read R. Gamaliel instead of R. Johanan.

137. See Grätz in *MGWJ*, 1885, XXXIV, 17 ff.; Bacher, *Tannaiten*, I, 36; *Krauss, Lehnwörter*, II, 106. *Midrash haGadol Deut.*, 33; *Midrasch Tannaim*, 215, read in the *Sifrê* passage: Agrippas hegemon asked R. Johanan b. Zakkai.

138. 'Instead of me from the stores' cannot be correct, as the continuation clearly shows; cf. the Baraitha in *'Ab. zar.*, 71 a: A Jew must not ask a non-Jew to enter for him into the stores; see Rashi.

139. From an economic point of view *Tos. Damm.*, I, 11, is very instructive: He who buys produce from a ship in Joppé or in Caesarea must give tithe. R. Jehudah said: The produce on the shore (?) of Jishub and of Antipatris and in the market of Patros was at first declared not certainly tithed, because it generally came from the King mountains; but now our rabbis said . . . Jishub was a Samaritan place (Neubauer, *Chronique Samaritaine*, 19), further south was Antipatris, so that the unknown Patros was further south. We learn that Judaea and the places in the central range north of Judaea exported produce via Joppê and to the three places.

140. The occasional visit of stratiotai in the school of Jamnia in the days of R. Gamaliel who came to learn the law of the Jews, *Sifrê Deut.*, 344, 143 b; *jer. B. kam.*, IV, 4 b, 29; b. 38 a, proves nothing for a garrison in the town.

141. In an Aramaic story in *Ta'am.*, 21 a, the Jews sent through Nahum of Gimzo

a box of precious stones as a gift to the emperor; the Roman governor is meant. R. Joshi'a, R. Ishmael's disciple, in *ARN*, XXXVIII, 57 a, says that owing to neglect in giving priestly dues and tithes the skies withhold dew and rain, and the people is handed over to the government. This is taken from life, and refers to Roman confiscations of property.

142. The presence of soldiers constituted a danger for Jewish women, as the case before R. Haninah in *jer. Nedar.*, XI, 42 d, 58, shows: When once soldiers came into a city, the wife of a priest came to the beth-din and complained that a soldier had embraced and assulted her; but the rabbis permitted her to continue to eat of her husband's priestly due. Also the *Mishnah Nedar.*, XI, 12, reflects such a danger. First the rabbis said: In three cases a woman must be divorced and receive her marriage settlement: when she says to her husband, I am defiled for you, God is between us, and I am removed from the Jews. Later the rabbis altered that rule in order that a woman should not commit adultery because she wants to marry somebody else. It seems that violation of women and persuading them to leave Judaism reflects Roman times.

143. *She'iltoth*, בראשית read R. Meir, which is merely a misreading of the form *Midrash haGadol* to Exod. xxi also has R. Tarfon, and for agoras ארכיות.

144. Otherwise the Jews had their own jurisdiction in civil cases and the right to impose fines, as the judgments of R. Akiba show (p. 77 ff.), and also the statement of Rabh in *Synh.*, 13 b, 14 a, that if R. Jehudah b. Baba during the Hadrianic persecutions had not ordained five disciples, the law about fines had been forgotten in Israel. There were no courts for capital punishment, in spite of Origen's remark to the contrary; for R. Akiba and R. Tarfon say in *Makk.*, I, 10, if they had been on a Synedrion, nobody would have ever been executed. The past tense clearly shows that in their times no such court was in existence. Scholars frequently point out that the rabbis applied the ban to force recalcitrant parties to obey their judgments. But as evidence not one single occurrence could be adduced; for all cases reported concern rabbis who either persisted in their individual teachings and had to be banned, or such as had disobeyed the orders of R. Jehudah haNassi.

145. In Jellinek's *bath-haMidrasch*, I, 1; *Esther r.*, introduction, §9, 'Abba Gorjon, in the name of R. Gamaliel, says: Since untrue judges increased, false witnesses increased; since delatores (informers) increased, the robbing of people's money (confiscations) increased, . . . since the beloved children provoked their father in heaven, he raised over them a wicked king to punish them. This statement, obviously picturing the times of R. Gamaliel, reveals sad conditions in Judaea under Roman rule, especially the evil of informers. Perhaps R. Eleazar b. 'Azarjah's sentence against the evil tongue in *Makk.*, 23 a, refers to the same: He who speaks evil language and he who receives evil language and he who gives false testimony, deserve to be thrown before dogs. See Bacher, *Tannaiten*, I, 91, 1.

146. Not merely in Caesarea where R. Eliezer was once tried on the bêma by a hegemon as judge, *Kohel. r.*, 1, 8, 3; '*Abod. z.*, 16 b; *Tos. Hull.*, II, 24, and R. Akiba by Tineius Rufus, Bacher, *Tannaiten*, I, 287, and *Midr. Prov.*, 9, 2. R. Eliezer's statement made in connexion with his trial in '*Ab. zar.*, 17 a, on Prov. v. 8 b: Draw not near to the entrance of her house, to the government, also warns against relations with the Romans. But the two parallels quoted do not contain that word.

147. *B. bathra*, 10 b; *Pesik.*, 12 b; Bacher, *Tannaiten*, I, 34, 4. Of Roman charity in Palestine about the year 300 speaks R. Jishak in *Pesik.*, 95 b: The governors go out to the villages, plunder the farmers, return to their town and say: Call the poor together, for we want to give them charity. In *Midrash haGadol* on Deut. vii. 26, quoted by Dr. Schechter in his '*Agadath Canticum*, p. 71, the kindness of the nations in Prov. xiv. 34 is referred to the Romans building public and other baths for the poor and rich, but leaving there a place for worshipping idols and for immoral women. But there is beside a doubtful reference of R. Gamaliel none mentioning such institutions in Judaea before the year 135.

148. See also *Tos. Sotah*, XIV, 10: Since the number of those increased who accepted charity from non-Jews, non-Jews began to increase and Jews to decrease, and the latter have in the world no pleasure. If this statment could be dated, it would be an instructive parallel to the above passage.

149. *Mekhil.* on 15, 2; *Mekhil. R. Simeon,* 60; Bacher, *Tannaiten,* I, 285, 4.

150. In *'Agadath Canticum,* 1,6, a similar but anonymous passage occurs: You would not guard the Temple as required, now they guard the great fortress. Schechter, p. 58, thinks it a corruption of the *Mekhiltha* passage, but there is hardly a trace of it here. If שוקלין were from שומרין the sentence would be clearer: They have to pay taxes to Caesarea or Rome.

151. *Geschichte der röm. Kaiserzeit,* I, 881.

152. Galenus, vol. XIV, p. 25, ed. Kühn; Marquardt, *Röm. Staatsverwaltung,* II², 258.

153. Galenus, XIV, 7; Pliny, *Nat. Hist.,* 12, 111, 113, 123. In whose hands 'Engedi had been before the war is not evident. Though it was one of the eleven toparchies (*Wars,* III, 3, 5), but not mentioned as such by Pliny (V, 14, 70), and though Eusebius, *Onom.,* 254, terms it a very great Jewish place, its plantations may have been already before the year 70 in Roman hands. During the revolution the sicari of Masada attacked it (*Wars,* IV, 7, 2) in the night of Passover, scattered the population and drove it from the town, and women and children about 700 were killed. All the villages around Massada were laid waste and the whole district made desolate. It is difficult to see why the sicarii should have killed Jewish women and children, as they could have taken the victuals which they wanted from the women. It seems, 'En-gedi was either in favour of peace or partly inhabited by Romans.

154. Cp. Hölscher, *Judäa in pers. u. hell. Zeit,* 49.

155. The version of R. Nehunja b. Hakanah's sentence in 2 *ARN,* XXXII, 34 b: From him who takes upon him the yoke of the Torah, the yoke of the government and of business is removed, and upon him who shakes off the yoke of the Torah, the yoke of the government and of business is imposed, suggests that scholars were exempted from taxes, regular or irregular. See Krakauer in *MGWJ,* 1874, XXIII, 60 ff.; *RÉJ,* 1912, LXIV, 60, which, however, refer to the edicts of the emperors of the courth century, as perhaps *ARN;* 'Aboth, III, 8, does not contain the 'yoke of the government'.

156. Marquardt, *Staatsverwaltung,* II², 222.

157. C. Wessek, *Student z. Palaeogr, u. Papyruskunde,* 1901, 9.

158. Schürer, *Geschichte,* III⁴, 46 ff.

159. Krauss in *Berlinger-Hoffman's Magazin,* XIX, 110, without sufficient evidence applies the words to military fortifications.

160. Marquardt, 1. c., 232.

161. The wording is doubtful; see Schechter, 12, who quotes a version במאות altars.

162. *Tosafoth Zebah.,* 91 b, quoting from memory attribute the first anonymous sentence to R. Akiba, but his name is even in the second part doubtful; see Rabbinowicz and R. Isaiah Trani the elder in *JQR,* IV, 93 ff.

163. Schlatter, *Tage Trajans,* 68, states that the Roman legion brought its cult with it, and refers to the stone still standing in the Nebi Daud gate in Jerusalem set by the legio III Cyrenaica in 116 for the welfare and victory of Trajan and the Roman people to Jupiter Optimus Maximus Sarapis.

164. In *Midrasch Tannaim,* 58; 2 *ARN,* XXXI, 33 b ff., R. Johanan b. Zakkai says: Be not hasty in pulling down the altars of heathens that thou shouldst not have to rebuild them with thy hand; pull not down any of bricks that they should not ask thee to rebuild them of stone; nor of stone that they should not ask thee to rebuild them of wood. This shows that there were in Judaea heathen altars which some Jews were eager to pull down; but it is possible and even probable to refer such statements to the time before the War. Cf. also the parallel in *Meg.,* 31 b; *Tos. 'Ab. z.,* I, 19; Bacher, *Tannaiten,* II, 425, 3.

165. *'Abod. z.,* 55 a; Bacher, *Tannaiten,* I, 294.

166. R. Eliezer referred to a man in Askalon who honoured his father greatly. *Kidd.,* 31 a; *jer. Pe'ah,* I, 15 c, 18; *Pesik. r.,* XXIV, 123 b.

167. *Jer. Sotah,* III, 19 a, 7; in the parallel *Joma,* 66 b, only a woman is mentioned.

168. *Sabb.,* I, 9; *Baraitha,* 19 a; *Tos.* I, 22.

169. *Mekhil.,* 12, 48. p. 18 a; *Jebam.,* 46 a; *Gerim,* II, 4.

THE STRUGGLE BETWEEN SECULAR AND RELIGIOUS FORCES
FOR LEADERSHIP (Pg. 107-118)

1. Comp. Hag. 1.14; 2.4 וחזק יהושע ... ועתה חזק זרבבל.

2. Comp. Zech. 6.12–13. ....ועשית עטרות ושמת בראש יהושע בן יהוצדק הכהן הגדול
...והוא יבנה.

3. Ezra 4.6–22. A letter was sent by the enemies of the Jews to the King of Persia informing him that the Jews were contemplating the establishment of an independent state. ...מגדה בלו והלך לא ינתנון...חלק בעבר נהרא לא איתי לך... על מלכין מתנשאה.
ומלכין תקיפין הוו על ירושלם... ומדה בלו והלך מתיהב להון.

4. During the period of the First Temple there was friction between the Priests and Prophets and the kings.

5. Ezra 7.21–26. ....ואנת עזרא כחכמת אלהך די בידך מני שפטין ודינין די להון דאנין לכל עמא
וכל די לא להוא עבד דתא די אלהך ודתא די מלכא... הן למות הן לשרשו הן לענש נכסין
ולאסורין.

6. S. Zeitlin, *History of the Second Jewish Commonwealth*, pp. 18–26.

7. I. Macc. 14.41-47.

8. S. Zeitlin, ibid., pp. 39–40.

9. Ben Sira 38.31–34.

10. Ibid. 45.17; comp. also Deut. 33.10.

11. See S. Zeitlin, ibid., pp. 39–40.

12. Idem, ibid.

13. Jose ben Joeser was a priest; see Hag. 2.3, יוסי בן יעזר היה חסיד שבכהונה.

14. Shemaiah and Abtalyon were no longer priests. Comp. Yoma 71b, ייתון בני עממין
ולא ייתי בר אהרון ...לשלם. See S. Zeitlin, *JQR*, VII (1916–17), 512, n. 21.

15. See idem, *The Jews: Race, Nation or Religion?* p. 38.

16. See Yer. Tan. 68a, אמר ר' לוי מגילת יוחסין מצאו בירושלים וכתוב בה הלל מן דדוד.
Comp. also Sanh. 5, לא יסור... ומחוקק מבין רגליו אלו בני בניו של הלל שמלמדין תורה.
Also Ket. 62b and Sanh. 12, ועמוסי יריכי נחשון. See Israel Levi, *REJ*, 1895.

17. Comp. Josephus, B.J.2.

18. Tos. Men. 13.21, אוי לי מבית ביתוס...אוי לי מבית ישמעאל בן פיאבי, שהם כהנים
גדולים ובניהם גזברין וחתניהן אמרכלין.

19. Vita, 190; B.J., 2.563; 4.159.

20. See Mak. 24, וכבר היה ר' גמליאל ורבי אלעזר בן עזריה ור' יהושע ור' עקיבא מהלכין
דלמא ר' אליעזר ורבי יהושע ורבן גמליאל, Yer. Sanh. 25d. בדרך ושמעו קול המונה של רומי
מעשה שהיו רבותינו ברומי ר' אליעזר, Mid. Rab. Deut. 2, ורבי יהושע ורבן גמליאל סלקון
לרומי ור' יהושע ורבן גמליאל, וגזרו סנקליטין של מלך לומר מכאן ועד שלשים יום לא יהיה בכל
העולם יהודי.

21. Comp. Tosefta, Para, 4.7, שאלו תלמידיו את רבן יוחנן בן זכאי פרה במה נעשית אמר
להם בבגדי זהב אמרו למדתנו בבגדי לבן אמר להם יפה אמרתם מעשה שעשו ידי...ויש אומרים
שאלו תלמידיו את רבן, Comp. Sifre, ed. Friedmann, 123, הלל הזקן שאלו לא שלא היה יודע
יוחנן בן זכאי באיזו כלים פרה נעשית....ויש אומרים הלל הזקן היה אלא שלא יכול לומר מה
ששרתו ידי.

22. Git. 56b, בעי מינאי מידי דאתן לך אמר ליה תן לי יבנה וחכמיה ושושילתא דרבן גמליאל.

23. According to the Talmud Rabban Jochanan ben Zakkai prophesied that Vespasian would be Emperor; according to Josephus he foretold that Vespasian would be crowned as Emperor, B.J., 3, 399–407. Comp. also Suetonius, *Vesp. 14; Tacitus, Hist.* 5.

24. Tos. Ber. 2.6. See also n. 20 above. רבן גמליאל ובית דינו ביבנה היו עסוקין בצרכי צבור.
Comp. also Ber. 27b דאי אית ליה לפלוחי לבי קיסר אף הוא אזיל ופלח.
Josephus in *Contra Apionem* II, 22, which was written after the destruction of the Temple, still pictured the Jewish state as controlled by the priests:

"And where shall we find a better or more righteous constitution than ours, while this makes us esteem God to be the governor of the universe, and permits the priests in general to be the administrators of the principal affairs, and withal intrusts the government over the other priests to the chief high-priest himself? These men had the main care of the law and of the other parts of the people's conduct committed to them: for they were the priests who were ordained to be the inspectors of all, and the judges in doubtful cases, and the punishers of those that were condemned to suffer punishment."

25. Ber. 27*b*, עד כמה נצעריה וניזל בראש השנה אשתקד צעריה... תא ונעבריה. See R. H. 25a, Yer. Ber. 7d, אמרו לו על מי לא עברה דעתך תמיד הלכו ומינו את רבי אלעזר בן עזריה בישיבה.

26. Ber. 27*b*, והוא עשירי לעזרא.

27. Although the Temple was destroyed the Jews continued to live in Jerusalem. Many Jews even continued to sacrifice the paschal lamb. See at length S. Zeitlin, *Horeb*, 1938, טומאת נכרים בזמן הבית השני.

28. See Yer. Ber. 7d, מינו אותו אב בית דין. The expression מינו אותו can mean only his appointment to the position of *Ab Bet Din*.

29. Sanh. 11b, מעשה ברבן גמליאל שהיה יושב על גב מעלה בהר הבית... ושלש אגרות... וכתוב לאחנא בני גלוותא... ושפרא מילתא באנפיי ובאנפיי חביריי ואוספת על שתא דא יומין תלתין.

30. Sanh. ibid., דילמא בתר דעברוה. The Gamaliel here referred to is the second, who lived after the destruction of the Temple. This can be deduced from the contents, where it is said: דילמא בתר דעברוה. Further proof is offered by the Palestinian Talmud where it is stated that Rabbi Joshua participated with Rabban Gamaliel in sending these epistles, which shows conclusively that it could only be the second Gamaliel. שהיה ר׳ יהושע בן חנניה תמן, Ma'as. Sh. 56c.

31. 'Eduy. 7.7, מעשה ברבן גמליאל שהלך ליטול רשות מטפסר בסוריא ושהא לבא ועברו את השנה על תנאי לכשירצה רבן גמליאל. See also Sanh. 11a.

32. See S. Zeitlin, *JQR*, XXVII, 393.

32a. Only זקנים could participate in the session of the Sanhedrin when intercalation of the year was under discussion. Comp. Yer. Sanh. 18c. חברים מהו ליכנס לעיבור השנה נישמעניה מן הדא מעשה ברבן גמליאל שאמר יקרוני שבעה זקנים לעלייה ונכנסו שמונה אמר מי הוא שנכנס שלא ברשות ואפילו כן לא עיברוה, Comp. S. Zeitlin, *Horeb*, 1939, הפרושים.

33. Hor. 13b.

34. Sanh. 11, Tosefta, ibid. מהודעין... ושפרת מילתא באנפי ואוסיפת על שתא דא תלתין יומין.

35. Yer. Sanh. 19a, אמרו בית דין שמינה שלא לדעת הנשיא אין מינויו מינוי, ונשיא שמינה שלא לדעת בית דין מינויו מינוי, חזרו והתקינו שלא יהו בית דין ממנין אלא מדעת הנשיא, ושלא הנשיא ממנה אלא מדעת ב״ד.

35a. Comp. Yoma 78a, שאלו את ר׳ אלעזר זקן ויושב בישיבה צריך ליטול רשות... דבר זה הניחו להם לבי נשיאה כדי להתגדר בו צריך ליטול רשות.

36. Ibid., תמן קריי למנוייה סמיכתא. אמר רבי בא בראשונה כל אחד ואחד ממנה את תלמידיו כגון רבן יוחנן בן זכאי מינה את רבי ליעזר ורבי יהושע ורבי יהושע את רבי עקיבא. Rab Ba used the term מנוי which was prevalent only in his own time.

37. Yer. Ned. 42b. All authorization given by scholars was with the consent of the Patriarch. See notes 35 and 35a, Sanh, 14, Yer., ibid. It was also called נטילת רשות. See Sanh. 5, לשקול רשותא.

38. Yer. Bik. 65d, ר׳ יצחק בר נחמן הוה בעזה ומנוניה, ר׳ זמינא הוה בצור ומנוניה ע״מ לחזור יהודה בן טיטס הוה ברומי ומנוניה. Comp. also *Leges Novellae ad Theodosianum*, XVI, ed. Th. Mommsen, 1905, Lib. XVI.

39. Yer. Ned. 42b; see also ibid. Bik. 65d, חיא בר אבא אתא לגביה, ר׳ לעזר אמר ליה פייס לר׳ יודן נשייא... הרי ששלחני לכם אדם גדול... עד שינע אצלנו. See also Sanh. 5b.

40. Ibid., ר׳ זעירא וחד מן רבנן הוון יתיבין עבר חד מן אילין דמתמני בכסף See Sanh. 7b,
דבי נשיאה אוקמי דיינא דלא הוה גמיר.

41. Sanh.5a, לשקול רשותא.

42. Comp. Yer. Yeb,13a, ... בני סימוניא אתין לגבי רבי אמרין ליה בעא תתן לן חד בר נש;
also ibid., Pea 21. ר׳ יוסי עאל לכפרה בעא מוקמה לן פרנסינ׳ולא קבלין עליהון ר׳ חני כד
הוה מקים פרנסין.

43. Git. 60a., ת׳׳ח הממונים פרנסים.

44. *The Works of the Emperor Julian* (*The Loeb Classical Library*) III, 178, τὸν ἀδελφὸν
Ἰουλον, τὸν αἰδεσιμώτατον πατριάρχην.

45. Yer. Ter. 46b; Midr. Rab. Gen. 78.

46. Theodosius, op. cit. XVI, 8, 29, p. 895.

47. Sanh. 5a, לא יסור...ומחוקק מבין רגליו אלו בני בניו של הלל שמלמדים תורה ברבים.
See Hor. 11b.

48. See S. Zeitlin, *The History of the Second Jewish Commonwealth*, pp. 6–18.

49. Idem, ibid., pp. 11–12.

50. Sanh. 5a, לא יסור שבט מיהודה אלו ראשי גליות.

51. The Jews in the Diaspora depended for the order of the holidays upon the
calendar as fixed by the Sanhedrin in Palestine.

52. Dr. Kaminka in the *JQR*, XXX, 107, maintains that Hillel was not a Babylonian
but an Alexandrian. His hypothesis is based on a misunderstanding of a talmudic text.
In the passage in the Talmud which reads כשהיו בני אלכסנדריא מקדשין נשים ... אמר
...להם הלל הזקן הביאו לי כתובת אמכם the phrase בני אלכסנדריא does not mean, as
Kaminka translated it, "happened in Alexandria, " but rather refers to the people of
Alexandria who were in Palestine. (See S. Zeitlin, *The Jews: Race, Nation or Religion*? p.
14, n. 22; comp. also Yer. Meg. 73d, מעשה בר׳ אלעזר בן צדוק שלקח בית הכנסת של
אלכסנדרים ועשה בה כל צרכיו.)
As to the talmudic usage "Hillel of Babylonia," Kaminka tries to dispose of this by
saying that the Talmud sometimes called Alexandrians Babylonians, and refers to Men.
100. However, the passage reads as follows ...אמר רבה בר חי...והבבלים אוכלים אותו כשהוא
חנה אמר ר׳ יוחנן לא בבליים הם אלא אלכסנדרים הם ומתוך ששונאים את בבליים קורין אותם
על שם בבליים, which means that Palestinians did not like the Babylonians because
of their lack of culture and therefore anyone who acted boorishly was called in reproach
a Babylonian. Comp. also Rashi, ad. loc.

53. Ḥul. 48a, מעשה ועלו עליה בני עסיא ג׳ רגלים ליבנה לרגל שלישי התירוה להם.

54. Yer. Ned. 40a. חנינא בן אחי ר׳ יהושע עיבר בחוץ לארץ שלח ליה רבי תלת אגרין...גדיים
...שהנחת נעשו תישים....אם אין את מקבל עליך צא לך למדבר האטד ותהא שוחט ונחונין זורק.
Comp. also ibid., Sanh. 19a.

55. Sanh. 5a.

56. Ibid., אמר רב האי מאן דבעי למידן דינא ואי טעה מיבעי למיפטריה לישקל רשותא מבי
ריש גלותא.

57. Ibid. 17b, דיינא גולה קרנא.

58. B.B. 89, דבי נשיאה [ריש גלותא]אוקמי אגרדמין בין למדות בין לשערים א׳׳ל שמואל לקרנא.
Comp. Yer. ibid. 15b, רב מנייה ריש גלותא אנגרמוס והוה מחי על מכילתא ולא על שיעוריא,
עאל רב קרנא.

59. Sanh. 5a, רבה בר רב הונא כד הוה מינצי בהדי דבי ריש גלותא אמר לאו מינייכו נקיטנא
רשותא, נקיטנא רשותא מאבא מרי ואבא מרי מרב מרב ורב מרבי חייא ורבי חייא מרבי.

60. Git. 59a, שאני הונא בר נתן דמיכף הוה כייף ליה לרב אשי.

61. Ber. 64a; Hor. 14a.

62. Yer. Sanh. 19a, ‫תמן קריי למנייה סמיכותא‬. See also I. A. Herzog, *Sinai*, 1939, ‫הערות‬
‫היסטוריות בהלכות סנהדרין‬.

63. Only a few names of the Exilarchs are recorded in the Talmud, which indicates that the Amoraim tried to ignore them. All important documents to be considered valid had to be recorded in the courts of the academies. See Git. 36b.
‫לא כתבינן פרוסבול אלא אי בבי דינא דסורא אי בבי דינא דנהרדעא‬.

BACKGROUND—THE WORLD WITHOUT (Pg. 119)

1. R. Travers Herford, *The Pharisees* (New York, 1924), G. F. Moore, *Judaism in the First Centuries of the Christian Era* (Cambridge, Mass., 1927-30.)

THE TALMUD IN HISTORY (Pg. 120-123)

1. *Novellae Constitutiones,* 146.
2. The view of Justinian's rescript given in the text is the one usually adopted. It is by no means the only possible explanation, for it is possible that what Justinian prohibited was the use of the traditional Aramaic translation.
3. S. R. Hirsch, *A Book of Essays, London,* 1905, p. 14.
4. *A Book of Essays,* p. 141.

THE BURNING OF THE TALMUD ... (Pg. 127)

1. Properly, *Sire* Leon: the respectful title given a rabbi in medieval French.

GRAECO—ROMAN VIEW OF JEWS ... (Pg. 142-148)

1. Cited in Augustine, *De Civ. Dei,* VI, 10.
2. *Syrian Wars,* ch. 50.
3. Epit. Bk. 68, 22.
4. Ep. Bk. 69, 12 and 13.
5. Bk. 37, ch. 17.
6. *Hist. Aug. Hadrian* ch. 5 and 14.
7. *Petr. Poems,* 24.
8. *Persius Sat.* V, 176.
9. *Juv. Sat.* XIV, 96.
10. *Plut. Moralia, Superstit.* 8.
11. *Dio Cass. Ep. Bk.* 65, 7.
12. *Apoll. Vit.* V, 27.
13. Ib. V, 33.
14. *Instit. Or.* III, 7.21.
15. *Med.* II, 9, 19.
16. *Med.* IV, 7.6.
17. Pliny *Epist.* X, 96.
18. *Hist. Aug. Severus,* ch. 22.

A UNITARIAN MINISTER'S VIEW ... (Pg. 152)

1. Sabb. 13b.

THE IDEA OF TORAH IN JUDAISM (Pg. 172)

1. Idolatry and immorality.

THE PHARISEES IN THE LIGHT OF MODERN SCHOLARSHIP
(Pg. 178-191)

1. George Foot Moore, *Judaism,* I, 16.
2. Leo Baeck, *The Pharisees,* p. 14.
3. *Happerushim we-anshe kneseth haggedolah* (New York, 1960).
4. *Jesus and the Pharisees* (Chicago, 1928), p. 178.

PHARISEES, ESSENES AND GNOSTICS (Pg. 193-197)

1. See Ralph Marcus, "The Pharisees in the Light of Modern Scholarship," above, pp. 178–192.

2. J. M. Baumgarten, "Sacrifice and Worship among the Jewish Sectarians of the Dead Sea (Qumran) Scrolls," *Harvard Theological Review*, XLVI (1953), 141–57, argues (p. 157) that "both the Essenes and the Dead Sea Sectarians honor the temple and the priesthood as holy institutions, although they ceased to offer sacrififices." In spite of Josephus' statement it seems unlikely that the Essenes actually sacrificed animals in their own communities. It seems even more unlikely that the unorthodox calendar of Jubilees and the Manual of Discipline was carried out in practice—otherwise these covenanters would have been stigmatized as heretics.

3. "Some Observations on the Attitude of the Synagogue toward the Apocalyptic Eschatological Writings," *JBL*, XLI (1922), 115–36.

4. See, e. g. Gershom Scholem, *Major Trends in Jewish Mysticism* (Jerusalem, 1941), p. 355; Morris Goldstein *Jesus in the Jewish Tradition* (New York, 1950) chapters 1 and 2. I have a private communication from Louis Ginzberg dated September 24, 1943, in which he writes *inter alia* "I may state with certainty that only in a very few places does *Minim* refer to Judeo-Christians, while in most cases it describes Gnostic Jews."

5. "The problem of the Minim Reconsidered," *G. A. Kohut Memorial Volume.* (New York, 1935), pp. 359–60.

6. Essenism is characterized as "an early form of Jewish gnosis" by W. Bauer, art. *Essener* in PWRE, Suppl. IV (1924) SP. 386–430. On the proto-Gnostic and early Gnostic elements in Jewish apocalyptic, see Kershom Scholem, *op. cit.,* lectures 1 and 2. On the Gnostic elements in the Qumran scrolls see Isaiah Sonne, "A Hymn against Heretics in the Newly Discovered Scrolls and Its Gnostic Background," *Hebrew Union College Annual*, XXXIII, Part 1 (1950–51), 225–313.

7. So, most recently, A. Dupont-Sommer, *Nouveaux apercus sur les manuscrits de la Mer Morte* (Paris, 1953), ch. VII.

THE PERSISTENCE OF REJECTED CUSTOMS ... (Pg. 216-220)

1. 'Erubin 13b.
2. Hullin 44b; Tosefta Yebamot 1.13, p. 242; Tosefta 'Eduyyot 2.3, p. 457.
3. Yebamot 14a.
4. Yer. Berakot 1.7, 3b B. 'Erubin 13b.
5. Mishna Berakot 1.2.
6. Tosefta Berakot 1.4, p. 1; Yer. ibid. 1.6, 3b; Babli ibid. 11a; Sifre Deut. 34.
7. Sabbath, 25b.
8. Menahot 40a.
9. Maimonides, *Yad, Zizit* 3.6.
10. Menahot 41b; Sifre Numbers 115; Sifre Deut. 234.
11. Bekorot 39b.
12. *Yad, Zizit* 1.6.
13. In a few instances, scholars of the second century consciously accepted Shammaite views. So R. Meir, apparently, B. Ketubot 60b, Tosefta Niddah 2.2, p. 642; B. Niddah 65b; and R. Jose ben Halafta in Yer. Terumot 3.4, 42a; Tosefta ibid. 3.12, p. 29, which reads R. Judah instead of R. Jose; and Tosefta Kelim, B.B., 1.12, p. 591.
14. *Hillufe Minhagim,* ed Mordecai Margulies, Jerusalem, 1938; another edition by B. M. Lewin is also appearing in *Sinai.*
15. Ed. Margulies, p. 75.
16. Mishna Berakot 1.6.
17. Yer. Berako. 2.1, 4a.
18. Berakot 13b.
19. Ed. Margulies, loc. cit.
20. Ketubot 60b.
21. Ibid.

22. Ed. Margulies, p. 76.

23. Tosefta Moʻed Katan 2.9, p. 230; so also R. Gamaliel in *Masseket Semahot* 7.2, ed. Higger, p. 137.

24. *Baraita d'Niddah* 1.3, published in Horowitz, *Tosefta 'Atikata*, Frankfurt, 1890, IV, p. 5; and 3.1, p. 21.

25. Ibid., 3.1, p. 21.

26. See B. Revel, *The Karaite Halakah and its Relation to Sadducean, Samaritan, and Philonian Halakah*, Philadelphia, 1913, p. 42.

27. See Leopold Wreschner, *Samaritanische Traditionen*, Berlin, 1888, p. 38.

28. *Kebuzzat Maʻamarim*, second edition, Warsaw, 1910, pp. 55 ff., and 90 f.; *Jued. Zeitschrift*, I, p. 51; II, p. 27; *Nachgelassene Schriften*, III, p. 316; Hebrew section, pp. 138 ff. and 163 ff. For Prof. Ginzberg's views, see his notes on *Kebuzzat Maʻamarim*, second edition, pp. 385 and 392–93.

29. The view that the Sadducees prohibited the use of fire on the Sabbath was set forth by A. Geiger, *Nachgelassene Schriften*, III, 287 ff.

30. Cf., however, Ginzberg, *Kitbe Ha-Geonim*, New York, 1929, p. 478.

31. See C. E. Whiting, *Studies in English Puritanism from the Restoration to the Revolution, 1660–1688*, London, 1931, p. 258.

THE "SONS OF LIGHT" (Pg. 223)

1. One of the manuals of discipline, styled conventionally "the Zadokite Document," was already known from a 12th-century copy found, some sixty years ago, by the late Solomon's Schechter in the famous Cairo Genizah, but its relation to the Dead Sea Brotherhood became apparent only when the Qumran scrolls were brought to light and when fragments of a far more ancient copy were actually retrieved from one of the caves. The hymns are known conventionally as "the Psalms of Thanksgiving" because many of them begin, "I thank Thee, O Lord." The commentaries thus far published cover the first two chapters of the book of Habakkuk, sundry verses of Micah, Nahum, and Zephaniah, and Psalm 37. There is also a paraphrase of Moses' farewell address to Israel in the Book of Deuteronomy. The text of the treatise on the war has been brilliantly edited by General Yigael Yadin, who has shown that the organization of the army and the plan of battle which it describes are patterned on Roman models. The work would seem, indeed, to be a kind of religious "skit" on Roman military manuals.

LAW (Pg. 223)

1. "Midrash and Mishna" in Rabbinic Essays (Cincinnati, 1951) pp. 163–256.

RABBINIC METHODS OF INTERPRETATION (Pg. 275-289)

1. Adolf Schwarz's works are the outstanding example of this sort.

2. See some provisional observations by the present writer in Law Quarterly Review 1936, 265 f., Journal of Roman Studies 1948, 115 ff., Cambridge Law Journal, 1949, 215.

3. Palestinian Pes. 33a, Babylonian Pes. 66a.

4. Bab. Pes. 70b, a passage all the more reliable as it is a Sadducee who describes them as such, and probably in a sneering tone: 'It is curious that these wonderful interpreters of Scripture did not realize. . . .'

5. Graetz, *Geschichte der Juden*, 5th ed. by Brann, vol. 3, pt. 2, 711 ff.

6. Bab. Kid. 30a says that *sopher*, 'scribe,' originally meant 'one who counts': the ancient scribes counted all the letters in the Bible. Whatever the original meaning of the word, there is no reason to doubt the information concerning the activity of the early scholars. We can go further. Most, if not all, of the early *gezeroth shawoth* (inferences from analogy, in accordance with the second of Hillel's norms of interpretation) are based on expressions which occur only in the two passages concerned and nowhere else in the Bible (Schwarz, *Die Hermeneutische Analogie*, 61 ff.) Thus the Mekhiltha tells us that from the use of *ʼasher loʼ ʼorasa* in Ex. 22. 15 (16) and Deut. 22.28 it follows that the penalty is 50 shekels

for seduction (Exodus) just as for rape (Deuteronomy). The phrase *'asher lo' 'orasa* occurs only in these two verses. It is safe to conclude that there existed, before Hillel, collections of ἅπαξ λεγόμενα, δὶς λεγόμενα etc. The norm of *gezera shawa* would have been impracticable without them. How far even this old, narrowly grammatical and lexicographical analysis and statistics may have been influenced by Greek ideas we need not here decide. In Rome, Varro, about 100 B.C., wrote monographs about synonyms, about the formation of words, about rare words in Plautus. He followed Greek models.

7. Mishnah Ab. 1.1.

8. Josephus, Ant. 13.10.6, Targum on Job 15.18. A synonym is παράδοσις τῶν πρεσβυτέρων, occurring in Matthew 15.2, Mark 7.3, 5; it would correspond to *masoreth hazzeqenim* (cp. *dibhere hazzeqenim*, e.g. in Pal. Berakhoth 3b).

9. Mishnah Ab. 3.14. Certainly, for Akiba, *masoreth* had come to signify, more specifically, 'the tradition concerning the exact state of the sacred text' (see Bacher, *Älteste Terminologie*, 108, *Tradition und Tradenten*, 3). But for one thing, it must not be forgotten that this particular branch was of such importance for him precisely because—in opposition to Ishmael—he used technicalities like the presence or absence of the optional accusative sign for deriving fresh law; hence 'the tradition concerning the state of the text' so to speak swallowed up the tradition of the fathers in general, it more or less represented the entire oral Law. For another thing, the adage 'tradition is a fence around the Torah' is doubtless older than Akiba, dating from a time when *masoreth* had its original, wider sense. The point of Abhoth 3.14 is the putting together of this maxim with 'tithes are a fence around riches' etc.

10. Laws 7.793B (πάτρια νόμιμα ἃ καλῶς ἐθισθέντα πάσῃ σωτηρίᾳ περικαλύψαντα ἔχει τοὺς τότε γραφέντας νόμους).

11. Tosephtha Hag. 3.35, Pal. Hag. 79d. The Samaritans, as they disallowed any 'interpretation,' and yet found it impossible to go on sticking to the text in its literal form, were driven to the only alternative—emendation; see the present writer's discussion in *Zeitschrift für die Alttestamentliche Wissenschaft* 1932, 152. The Rabbis saw through this: cp. e.g. Bab. Sota 33b.

12. Ant. 18.1.4.

13. Matthew 22.23 ff., Mark 12.18 ff., Luke 20.27ff.

14. Bab. Nid. 69b ff.: 'Does Lot's wife, a pillar of salt, convey uncleanness? (Strictly, she is a corpse.) Does the child raised from the dead by Elisha convey uncleanness? When the dead are raised, will they need sprinkling on the third and seventh days, having been in contact with a corpse? The Talmud terms these scoffing questions *dibhere boruth*, 'sayings of a vulgar nature.'

15. Bab. Sanh. 90b. The Queen admits that the dead will rise but wonders whether they will be naked or dressed? Bacher, *Agada der Tannaiten*, vol. 2, 68 (followed by Strack and Billerbeck, *Kommentar zum Neuen Testament*, vol. 1, 897), thinks that 'Cleopatra' must be emended because she was not contemporary with Meir, A. D. 150, to whom she is represented as talking. But Talmudic legend was never afraid of anachronisms, and whoever wanted to indicate that Meir's opponents were Alexandrians, i. e. addicts to Greek philosophy, might find Cleopatra particularly suitable in view of the rather improper flavour of the question. A most unsavoury story is told about her in Bab. Nid. 30b.

giving," because many of them begin, "I thank Thee, O Lord." The commentaries thus far published cover the first two chapters of the Book of Habakkuk, sundry verses of Micah, Nahum, and Zephaniah, and Psalm 37. There is also a paraphrase of Moses' farewell address to Israel in the Book of Deuteronomy. The text of the treatise on the war has been brilliantly edited by General Yigael Yadin, who has shown that the organization of the army and the plan of battle which it describes are patterned on Roman models. The work would seem, indeed, to be a kind of religious "skit" on Roman military manuals.

16. The Talmud is fully aware of the dicisive role played by him; he is compared to Ezra in Bab. Suk. 20a, Sota 48b. The four legends in Bab. Shab. 30b f. are

designed to illustrate (*inter alia*) four cardinal teachings of his: (1) every question deserves a well-reasoned answer, (2) tradition must inevitably command some authority, (3) by applying the norms of interpretation, the entire Law might be inferred from a single, ethical principle, and (4) the tradition of the fathers contains nothing but what follows from Scripture on proper exegesis. Ad (1): Somebody asks Hillel questions like 'Why have the Babylonians such round heads?,' to which he replies 'A weighty queslion—because they have no skillful midwives.' Ad (2): A gentile undertakes to become a convert if he need submit only to the written Law. The severe Shammai rejects him, Hillel accepts him. The first day, he teaches him the Hebrew alphabet; the second, he reverses the order of the letters. The proselyte protests, whereupon Hillel tells him that if he trusts him as to the alphabet, he might do so as to the oral Torah. Ad (3): A gentile undertakes to become a convert if he can be taught the entire Torah while standing on one foot. Shammai rejects him, Hillel accepts him. He teaches him 'What is hateful to you, do not to your fellowman:' all the rest, he says, is interpretation. Ad (4): A gentile undertakes to become a convert if he will be made High Priest. Shammai rejects him, Hillel accepts him. In the course of his instruction, Num. 1.51 is reached: 'And the stranger that cometh nigh shall be put to death.' Hillel explains that even King David is a 'stranger' for this purpose, whereupon his pupil, by a *qal wahomer,* an inference *a minori ad maius,* deduces the utter unfitness of a proselyte. He then returns to Shammai to ask him why he dogmatized instead of drawing his attention to Num. 1.51: once he (the convert) knew that verse, and the method of *qal wahomer,* he himself (the convert) agreed with the traditional attitude, he himself shuddered at his original request.

17. See the legends numbered (2) and (4) in the preceding footnote. According to Pal. Pes. 33a, Hillel went from Babylonia to Palestine in order to get it confirmed that the results of his interpretation agreed with tradition. Jesus' reply to the question about resurrection (see above, p. 277) is twofold: he not only propounds a theological argument—there might be a rejoinder to that—but also quotes a verse from Scripture to be taken as alluding to a quickening of the dead.

18. Pal. Pes. 33a, Bab. Pes. 66a.

19. That ancient Roman 'interpretation' assumed the form of a public debate is stated in D. 1.2.2.5. A vivid illustration may be found in Cicero, De Or. 1.56.240; see below, p. 246 n. 24.

20. The possibilities of the new method were clearly seen from the outset, as emerges from legend (3), above, p. 278 n. 16; all Law might at a pinch be deduced from one principle.

21. Bab. Shab. 31a. Shammai also used these terms: in this respect, there was no disagreement between him and Hillel. The equality of the oral Torah is strikingly brought out by the fact that the principle from which, in Hillel's view, the entire Law might be deduced, 'What is hateful . . .' (see legend (3), above, p. 278 n. 16), belongs, not to Scripture, but to traditional ethics.

22. Top. 2.8, 4.24 ('quae autem adsumuntur extrinsecus, ea maxime ex auctoritate ducuntur, ut si respondeas: quoniam P. Scaevola dixerit, id tibi ius videri'). Cp. Aristotle, Rhet. 2.23.12, Quintilian 5.11.36.

23. De Or. 1.56.240 ('Galba autem multas similitudines afferre multaque pro aequitate contra ius dicere; atque illum ad auctores confugisse, ac tamen concessisse Galbae disputationem sibi probabilem videri'). Of course, it was also possible to 'dispute,' 'interpret a statute,' so as to reach results in conflict with equity; D. 50.16.177, 50.17.65.

24. De Inv. 1.13.17 ('ex eo quod scriptum est aliud quod non scriptum est inveniri'); cp. 2.50.148 ff.

25. 1.13.23 ('cum res sine propria lege venit in iudicium, quae tamen ab aliis legibus similitudine quadam occupatur'); cp. Aristotle, Rhet. 2.23.1 ff., Quintilian 7.8.3 ff.

26. 1.165 ('quae tutela legitima vocatur, non quia nominatim ea lege de hac tutela cavetur, sed quia proinde accepta est per interpretationem atque si verbis legis introducta esset'); cp. 3.218. The term *iura condere* may have originated as describ-

ing the activity of the ancient interpreters: see G. 4.30.

27. 2.42: 'fundi vero et aedium biennio, et ita lege XII tabularum cautum est. The XII Tables, as Gaius doubtless knew, mentioned only *fundus*, the interpreters, reasoning from analogy, added *aedes;* Cicero, Top. 4.23, Pro Caec. 19.54.

28. D. 1.2.2.5, 12.

29. Aristotle, Rhet. 1.13.2 *(λέγω δὲ νόμον ἴδιον μὲν τὸν ἑκάστοις ὡρισμένον πρὸς αὐτούς, καὶ τοῦτον τὸν μὲν ἄγραφον τὸν δὲ γεγραμμένον κοινὸν δὲ τὸν κατὰ φύσιν)*, also D. 1.1.6.1, 1.3.32 *pr.*, I. 1.2.3.9. That *ius scriptum as* understood in the *Digest* is not quite the same as statute law in the modern sense need hardly be mentioned. The term *per manus traditum* is, of course, always confined to the custom of a certain people; cp. Livy 5.51.4, D. 29.7.10.

30. Laws 7.793A *(οὓς πατρίους νόμους ἐπονομάζουσιν οὐκ ἄλλα ἐστὶν ἢ τὰ τοιαῦτα (ἄγραφα νόμιμα) ξύμπαντα*. In the Statesman, *ἀγράμματα* or *ἄγραφα* is regularly paired off with *πάτρια*; e.g.295A, 298D f.

31. Cicero, De Inv. 1.13.17, 2.50.148, *Quintilian* 7.8.3, D. 1.2.2.5, 12; see above, p. 278 n. 19, p. 279 nn. 24, 25, 28.

32. De Inv. 2. 50.150 f. ('idcirco de hac re nihil esse scriptum quod, cum de illa esset scriptum, de has is qui scribebat dubitaturum neminem arbitratus sit . . . multis in legibus multa praeterita esse quae idcirco praeterita nemo arbitreur quod ex ceteris de quibus scriptum sit intellegi possint'); cp. 2.47.39 f., 2.50.152; De Leg. 2.7.18.

33. Cp. *commodissime* in Cicero, De Inv. 2.50.152, cited in the preceding footnote.

34. 2.10.14 ('laudabimus scriptoris commoditatem atque brevitatem, quod tantum scripserit quod necesse fuerit, illud quod sine scripto intellegi potuerit non necessario scribendum putaverit . . . contra eum qui scriptum recitet et scriptoris voluntatem non interpretetur'); cp. 2.12.18.

35. G. 3.218: 'nam legislatorem contentum fuisse quod prima parte eo verbo usus esset.' Note the close similarity in expression to Auct. ad Her. 2.10.14, 2.12.18, cited in the preceding footnote. I. 4.3.15 says: 'nam plebem Romanam, quae hanc legem tulit, contentam fuisse'. Possibly, Tribonian no longer understood the doctrine of interpretation underlying Sabinus' remark and believed that the omission in the third chapter was to be explained by the character of the *lex Aquilia* as a plebiscite, the *plebs* being a careless and lazy law-giver.

36. Contra Theomn. I 8 *(περὶ ἑνὸς εἰπὼν περὶ πάντων ἐδήλωσεν);* cp. also (despite important differences) Aristotle, Rhet. 1.13.13, 17, in turn dependent on Plato, Statesman 294A f.

37. Cicero, De Leg. 2.7.18, referred to above, p. 249 n. 33 ('leges a me edentur non perfectae—nam esset infinitum—sed ipsae summae rerum atque sententiae'); cp. 2.19.47 ff., Aristotle, Rhet. 1.13.12 ff., Nic. E. 5.10.4 ff., Plato, Statesman 294A f. Suetonius, Div. Jul. 44.2 ('optima quaeque et necessaria in paucissimos conferre libros'); cp. the use of *necessarius* in Auct. ad Her 2.10.14, quoted above, p. 280 n. 34.

38. It is not certain that this idea goes back to Hillel's time, but it cannot be much later: see Mishnah Edhuyoth 1.12, where the School of Shammai accounts for a traditional ruling, which they desire to extend, by saying that it speaks about 'what happens normally,' i. e. gives only the principal example. By Ishmael's age, the idea was fully established.

39. Pro Caec. 21.59 ('quia plerumque, ubi multitudine opus est, homines cogi solent, ideo de coactis compositum interdictum est; quod etiamsi verbo differre videbitur, re tamen erit unum, et omnibus in causis idem valebit in quibus perspicitur una atque eadem causa aequitatis').

40. D. 1.3.10; see Lenel, *Palingenesia*, vol. 1, 464 ('neque leges neque senatus-consulta ita scribi possunt ut omnes casus qui quandoque inciderint comprehendantur, sed sufficit ea quae plerumque accidunt contineri').

41. At least that was what the Rabbis took to be the force of 'if' in 'And if thou wilt make me an altar of stones:' Mekhiltha *ad loc.* For the present purpose, it is immaterial whether or not this view is tenable.

42. Pal. Pes. 33a, Bab. Pes. 66a, Num 28.2, 9.2. The writer refrains from being more explicit about Hillel's second, third and fourth norms because their original nature and history has not so far been appreciated, but it would lead too far afield here to go into them. For a certain aspect of the second, *gezera shawa,* see above, p. 277 n. 6.

43. Top. 4.23: 'quod in re maiore valet valeat in minore, item contra; item quod in re pari valet valeat in hac quae par est.' As an illustration of the latter argument he adduces the extension of the XII Tables' rule concerning usucapion of *fundus;* see above, p. 279 n. 27.

44. Part. Or. 36.123, 126 ('communis verbi vis,' 'consuetudo sermonis,' 'similia exemplaque eorum qui ita locuti sunt').

45. Part. Or. 37.132 ('discrepare cum ceteris scriptis vel aliorum vel maxime eiusdem').

46. Rhet. 2.23.4 f.

47. Top. 4.23; see above, p. 282 n. 43. Cp. 18.68, De Or. 2.40.172, De Inv. 1.28.41, 2.17.55; also Quintilian 5.10.86 ff. There are one or two exceptions to the rule, but they can shewn to be secondary.

48. 2.13.18 ('in causa ratiocinali primum quaeretur ecquid de rebus maioribus aut minoribus aut similibus similiter scriptum aut iudicatum sit').

49. Siphra *ad loc.*

50. Mekhiltha *ad loc.*

51. D. 9.2.27.16: 'non esse novum ut lex specialiter quibusdam enumeratis generale subiciat verbum quo specialia complectatur.' Celsus is discussing the *lex Aquilia,* which, as we saw above, p. 249, Sabinus also treated on approved rhetorical lines. In non-legal prose, the summing up of a detailed exposé was, of course, a recognized stylistic device. Cicero, in De Inv. 2.5.18, uses almost the same words as Celsus: 'denique, ut omnia generatim amplectamur. . . .'

52. D. 28.5.68, from Pomponius on Mucius, but doubtless going back to the latter ('si ita scriptum fuerit "Tithasus si in Capitolium ascenderit heres esto, Tithasus heres esto," secunda scriptura potior erit; plenior est enim quam prior').

53. D. 50.16.126: 'si, cum fundum tibi ' manicipio ' darem, legem ita dixi "uti optimus maximusque esset" et adieci "ius fundi deterius factum non esse per dominum praestabitur," amplius eo praestabitur nihil; etiamsi prior pars "ut optimus maximusque sit" liberum esse significat eoque, si posterior pars adiecta non esset, liberum praestare deberem, tamen inferiore parte satis me liberatum puto ne quid aliud praestare debeam quam "ius fundi pr dominum deterius factum non esse." ' For ' mancipio ' , see Lenel, *Palingenesia,* vol. 2, 164. The present writer has changed the current punctuation of the text, which takes no account of the doctrine of interpretation behind it. It is unfamiliarity with this doctrine which explains the large scale excisions and emendations proposed by some modern scholars.

54. Gen. 44.8.

55. A perfectly straight inference *a fortiori* would run either 'we did not retain the money found, still less did we steal' or 'we brought again the money found, still more did we refrain from stealing.'

56. Matthew 12.10 ff.

57. Luke 13.14 ff. It is interesting that the mode of reasoning is the same as in Matthew 12.10 ff., a *gal wahomer,* though the substance of the argument is not a little different. The argument of Luke 14.3 ff., on the other hand, is very close to Matthew 12.10 ff. in substance, but there is no longer an obvious *gal wahomer.* If we did not know Matthew 12.10 ff. and Luke 13.14 ff., we should probably see in Luke 14.5 a reasoning from analogy: as one may help a beast, so one may a man.

58. Romans 5.8 f.; much more = πολλῷ μᾶλλον, *multo magis.* John 13.14 is curious. According to the prevalent reading, Jesus, as Lord and Master, sets an example, ὑπόδειγμα, to be imitated by his disciples; this idea recurs in many passages of the New Testament. But D θ insert πόσῳ μᾶλλον before καὶ ὑμεῖς ὀφείλετε, thus turning the argument into a technical qal wahomer: if the Master performs this servile duty, *a fortiori* the disciples must do it.

59. 3.75: 'pessimae condicionis hominibus.' Note the ascription of the result to the will of the lawgiver; cp. above, pp. 280 ff. The term *incredible* is technical and rhetorical hermeneutics: *verisimile* or *credible* designates what may be presumed, in view of all circumstances or on ratiocination to be the import of an arrangement or law, *incredible* what cannot be regarded as such. See e.g. Cicero, De Inv. 2.40.117, D. 12.4.6 *pr.*, 15 I.9.4, 15.I.57.2, 18.1.39.1, 19.1.13.22, 20.1.6, 20.4.13, 28.6.31.5, 30.1.47 *pr.*, 34.2.8, 34.5.24, 35.1.36, 48.19.41; 50.16.142, 50.17.114. Later the exclusion of dediticii was based not on an inference a minori ad maius, but on an entirely different argumenti: Ulp 20.14.

60. The fifth, 'the general and the specific,' is applied, more or less consciously, in innumerable cases in modern law. The *Travelers' Guide* handed to those spending a holiday abroad, forbids you 'to cash cheques on your sterling account, to borrow currency or to enter into any other agreement to obtain foreign currency'—clearly a provision which 'specialiter quibusdam enumeratis generale subiciat verbum quo specialia complectatur.'

61. Mekhiltha *ad loc.*, Bab Sanh, 86a.

62. De Inv. 2.40.117 ('ex superiore et ex inferiore scriptura docendum id quod quaeratur fieri perspicuum').

63. D. 1.3.24; Lenel, *Palingenesia*, vol. 1, 141 ('incivile est nisi tota lege perspecta una aliqua particula eius proposita iudicare vel respondere'). On Celsus, see above, p. 285.

64. Num. 9.23; cp. Josh. 22.9, Ex. 17.1, 38.21, Num. 3.51, Ezra 1.1, II Chron. 36.22.

65. Ps. 119.72 f.

66. Josh. 1.8.

67. Exactly what the original author meant by this does not here matter. The Rabbis understood the verse as referring to the kind of study they practised. It is note worthy that the verb *hagah*, 'to meditate,' is actually used as denoting 'to deduce a further law from an existing one' in Pal. Meg. 72b.

68. Rhet. 1.2.19 *(ὅμοιον πρὸς ὅμοιον, ὅταν ἄμφω μὲν ᾖ ὑπὸ τὸ αὐτὸ γένος, γνωριμώτερον δὲ θάτερον τοῦ θατέρου).*

69. De Inv. 2.50.150 ('ut id de quo quaeritur rei de qua constat simile esse videatur').

70. Top. 10.43 ('par pari comparatur').

71. Occurring in the second of Hillel's norms and several other Tannaitic rules of interpretation.

72. Ex. 17.11.

73. Num. 21.8.

74. Mishna R.H. 3.8.

75. See Plato, Gorg. 479C *(συλλογίζομαι τὰ συμβαίνοντα ἐκ τοῦ λόγου)*, Phaedo 74A *(κατὰ πάντα ταῦτα συμβαίνει τὴν ἀβνάμνησιν εἶναι ἀφ᾽ὁμοίων)*, Aristotle, Nic. E. 7.12.1 *(οὐ συμβαίνει διὰ ταῦτα)*, Demosthenes, Contra Aristog. I 792A *(ἐκ γὰρ ὧν νῦν ὅδ᾽ἀξιοῖ ταῦτα συμβαίνει)* — the conclusion drawn is involved but, if the rhetorical scheme underlying it is recognized, makes perfect sense). Other terms deserving consideration in this connection are *διεξέρχομαι περί τινος*, 'to expound' (e.g. Plato, Laws 9.857 E) and even the Latin *(per)venire* (e.g. Cicero, De Inv. 2.50.148 f., 152—see above p. 279 n. 24).

76. It does not figure in Hillel's norms, but that it goes back to his epoch may be seen from *ἐρρέθη* in Matthew 5.21, 31, Romans 9.12; cp. *εἴρηκεν* in Hebrews 4.3, *ῥηθὲν* in Matthew 1.22, 2.17, 23, 4.14, 8.17, 12.17, 13.35, 22.31, 24.15, and *εἰρημένον* in Luke 2.24, Acts 2.16, 13.40, Romans 4.18.

77. The fact that later scholiasts emphasize that the spoken word also may form a *ῥητόν* only confirms the original limitation. See also the next footnote.

78. They soon noticed that *scriptum* in this technical sense might consist in a purely verbal utterance; see e.g. Quintilian 7.5.6 Cp. the preceding footnote.

79. Siphre *ad loc.*
80. Tanhuma Wayyera par. 6 on Gen. 18.17.
81. De Inv. 2.47.139 ('demonstrabit illum scriptorem, si scripta sua stultis hominibus et barbaris judicibus committeret, omnia summa diligentia perscripturum fuisse; nunc vero, quod intellegeret quales viri res judicaturi essent, ideirco cum quate perspicua videret esse non adscripsisse').
82. Needless to say, an advocate using Cicero's argument would at the same time flatter the judges. Even this element was hardly unwelcome to the Rabbis: the people would be more willing to shoulder the burden of the oral Law if that gave them a feeling of superiority.
83. Siphra on Lev. 18.4, Bab. Yoma 67b.
84. *Ib.*
85. Statesman 299C (οὐδὲν γὰρ δεῖ τῶν νόμων εἶναι σοφώτερον).
86. Rhet. 1.15.12 (οὐ λυσιτελεῖ παρασοφίζεσθαι τὸν ἰατρὸν, οὐ γὰρ τοσοῦτο βλάπτει ἡ ἁμαρτία τοῦ ἰατροῦ ὅσον τὸ ἐθίζεσθι ἀπειθεῖν τῷ ἄρχοντι καὶ ὅτι τό τῶν νόμων σοφώτερον ζητεῖν εἶναι τοῦτ᾽ ἐστὶν ὅ ἐν τοῖς ἐπαινουμένοις νόμοις ἀπαγορεύεται. The argument is strongly influenced by Plato. Even the comparison with the physician occurs in Statesman 294 ff.
87. D: 1.3.20 ('non omnium quae a maioribus constituta sunt ratio reddi potest').
88. D. 1.3.21 ('et ideo rationes eorum quae constituuntur inquiri non oportet, alioquin multa ex his quae certa sunt subvertuntur').
89. D. 1.2.2.38 ('lege XII tabularum praeposita iungitur interpretatio, deinde subtexitur legis actio'). The same threefold division comes earlier on in the same fragment, in the first half of 1.2.2.12 (that the part up to 'continent' goes back to an older source than the rest is suggested by the fact that the second half begins by 'aut plebiscitum' instead of 'aut est plebiscitum'), and it recurs in 1.3.13.
90. True, the Midrash was not written down till long after the period of the 'tripertita.' But in its oral form, it certainly dates from the 1st century B.C. (The recent discovery of a homiletical Midrash on Habakkuk 1 f., possibly written down in the 1st century B.C., is significant in this connection: the first steps towards a Halakhic Midrash can hardly be later.) Moreover, the Targum, the free rendering of Scripture into the vernacular for use in liturgy, is as old as Aelius, and the rule was that each verse of Scripture was at once to be followed by its paraphrase.

THE HALAKA (Pg. 290-312)

1. ὧν ἕνεκα πάντες τίθενται οἱ νόμοι τοῦ τε μηδένα μηδὲν ὅ μὴ δίκαιόν ἐστι ποιεῖν καὶ τοῦ τοὺς παραβαίνοντας ταῦτα κολαζομένους βελτίους τοὺς ἄλλους ποιεῖν...Against Aristogeiton, 1.17.
2. Next after the gods, the laws preserve the State. Demosthenes, *ibid.* ἐπειδὴ τοίνυν οἱ νόμοι μετὰ τοὺς θεοὺς ὁμολογοῦνται σῷζειν τὴν πόλιν. Est enim ius, quo devincta est hominum societas, et quod lex . . . Cicero, Laws 1.15.
3. See Ex. 20; Shab. 88; comp. also Mak. 24a אנכי ולא יהיה לך מפי הגבורה שמענום.
3a. תורת משה.
3b. ספר התורה.
4. Ex. 21, והגישו אדניו אל האלהים: עד אלהים יבא דבר שניהם אשר ירשיען אלהים.
5. τὸ κριτήριον τοῦ θεοῦ.
5a. Comp. also II Chron. 15. וימים רבים לישראל ללא אלהי אמת וללא כהן מורה וללא תורה.
6. ויהי לעת זקנת שלמה נשיו הטו את לבבו אחרי אלהים אחרים...אז יבנה שלמה במה לכמוש שקץ מואב.
7. ὁπότε καὶ ἀγράφῳ τῇ νομοθεσίᾳ πρίν τι τὴν ἀρχὴν ἀναγραφῆναι τῶν ἐν μέρει ῥᾳδίως καὶ εὐπετῶς ἐχρήσαντο οἱ πρῶτοι ὣς δεόντως ἄν τινα φναι τοὺς τεθέντας νόμους μηδὲν ἀλλ᾽ ἤ ὑπομνήματα εἶναι βίου τῶν παλαιῶν ἀρχαιολογοῦντας ἔργα καὶ λόγους οἷς ἐχρήσαντο.

לשלשה דברים הללו והסכים להלכה ועלה לא״י לדרוש כן, וקבל הלכה, בני א״י קבלו ממנו
גם כן להלכה שכך קיבל ג״כ מפי שמעיה ואבטליון. The commentators did not understand
this talmudic passage and hence misinterpreted it.

58. Comp. M. Kid. 1. כל מצוה שהיא תלויה בארץ אינה נוהגת אלא בארץ ... ר׳ אליעזר
מתניתא דר׳ אליעזר .Yer. ibid, החדש אסור מן התורה בכל מקום M. Orla; אומר אף החדש
דתנינן תמן...ר״א אף החדש.

59. זו הלכה נעלמה מבני (מזקני) בתירה פעם אחת חל י״ד להיות שבת ולא היו יודעין אם פסח
דוחה את השבת אם לאו אמרו יש כאן בבלי אחד והלל שמו ששמש את שמעיה ואבטליון...התחיל
דורש להן מהיקש, ומקל וחומר, ומגזירה שוה...לא קיבלו ממנו עד שאמר להן יבוא עלי כך
שמעתי מפי שמעיה ואבטליון...עמדו ומינו אותו נשיא עליהן Pes. 66a, Yer. ibid. 6.

60. Ibid.

61. מי שפסחו טלה תוחבו בצמרו...ראה מעשה ונזכר הלכה.

62. Lauterbach, op. cit., p. 32.

63. ראיתי לבן פדת שיושב ודורש כמשה מפי הגבורה, Yeb. 72b.

64. Comp. Mak. 5b, א״ל ר׳ אלעזר אם היא הוחזקה כל ישראל מי הוחזקו זמנין הוו יתבי...
קמי דר׳ יוחנן אתא כי האי מעשה לקמייהו אמר ריש לקיש הוחזקה זו א״ל ר׳ יוחנן אם הוחזקה
זו כל ישראל מי הוחזקו הדר חזיא לר׳ אלעזר בישות אמר ליה שמעת מילי מבר נפחא ולא
אמרת לי משמיה.

65. See Yeb. 82b, אמר ליה ריש לקיש דידיה היא מתניתין היא היכא תנא ליה, בתורת כהנים...

66. Comp. Tosefta Pes. 8, פסח מצרים מקום אכילה שם לינה ופסח דורות אוכלין במקום
אחד ולנים במקום אחד. See also S. Zeitlin, The Liturgy of the First Night of Passover,
JQR, April 1948.

67. דתני יוסי בן יועזר איש צרידא ויוסי בן יוחנן איש ירושלים גזרו טומאה על ארץ העמים,
Shab. 14b.

68. See S. Zeitlin, The History of the Second Jewish Commonwealth, Prolegomena, pp.
26–9; comp. also L. Ginzberg, מקומה של ההלכה בחכמת ישראל, ירושלים תרצ״א.

69. See Yer. Shab. 1, ולא כן א״ר זעירא בר אבונא בשם רב ירמיה יוסי בן יעזר...גזרו טומאה...

70. See Shab. 15a, והא רבנן דשמונים שנה גזור.

71. see אלא מעיקרא גזור ולא קיבלו מיניהו ואתו רבנן דשמונים שנה וגזרו וקיבלו מיניהו
ואתו רבנן דשמונים שנה....לשרוף אינהו גזור אתו Tosefot ibid.

72. See S. Zeitlin, Takkanot Ezra, JQR, viii.

73. Shab. 14b, בשעה שתיקן עירובין ונטילת ידים.

74. 16.29, שבו איש תחתיו אל יצא איש ממקומו ביום השביעי.

75. καθίσεσθε ἔκαστος εἰς τοὺς οἴκους ὑμῶν.

76. Comp. Er. 51; Yer. ibid., שבו איש תחתיו אלו ארבע אמות; see also M. ibid. 4,...
ר׳ יהושע ור׳ עקיבא אומר אין לי אלא ד׳ אמות.

77. See ibid., נאמר כאן מקום ונאמר להלן ושמתי לך מקום מה מקום שנאמר להלן אלפים...
ואנשי עיר קטנה אין להן .comp. also Tosefta ibid אמה אף מקום שנאמר כאן אלפים אמה
אלא אלפים אמה בלבד.

78. M. Er. 4, מי שהוציאוהו גוים או רוח רעה אין לו אלא ארבע אמות.

79. See R. H. 23a חצר גדולה היתה בירושלים ובית יעזק היתה נקראת ולשם כל העדים
מתכנסין...לא היוזזין משם כל היום התקין רבן גמליאל הזקן שיהו מהלכין אלפים אמה לכל
מי שיצא Comp. also M. Er. 4 רוח...הרי הם כאנשי העיר ויש להם אלפים אמה לכל רוח
ברשות...יש לו אלפים אמה.

80. יום טוב של ראש השנה שחל להיות בשבת במקדש היו תוקעין אבל לא במדינה כשחרב בית
המקדש התקין ר׳ יוחנן בן זכאי שיהו תוקעין בכל מקום שיש בו ב״ד אמר ר׳ אלעזר לא התקין ר׳
יוחנן בן זכאי אלא ביבנה בלבד M. R. H. 4.

81. Ex. 22.16. see S. Zeitlin, The Origin of the Ketubah, JQR, 1933, L. Epstein,
The Jewish Marriage Contract.

82. S. Zeitlin, ibid.

83. Idem, JQR, 1947.

83a. The Greeks likewise held that law must be universal. Οἱ δὲ νόμοι κοινὸν καὶ τεταγμένον ταὐτὸ πᾶσιν, Demosthenes, *op. cit.*

83b. Hul. 106; מכאן סמכו לפרוזבל שהוא מן, מכאן סמכו חכמים לנטילת ידים מן התורה Ket. 10a, מכאן סמכו חכמים לכתובת אשה מן התורה; Yer. Sheb. 10; התורה

84. מנהג העיר, מנהג המדינה.

85. מנהג הספנין.

86. מנהג הולכי שיירא.

87. Tan. 26b, מאן דאמר הלכה כר׳ מאיר דרשינן לה בפירקא.

88. מאן דאמר מנהג מידרש לא דרשינן.

89. See above, p. 296.

90. See Yer. B. M. 7.1, אמר ר׳ הושעיה זאת אומרת המנהג מבטל את ההלכה.

91. Hul. 104b, העוף עולה עם הגבינה על השלחן ואינו נאכל דברי ב״ש ובית הלל אומרים לא עולה ולא נאכל.

92. Comp. also Eduy. 1, שמאי אומר כל הנשים דיין שעתן והלל אומר מפקידה לפקידה; השוחט חיה ועוף ביום טוב בית שמאי אומרים יחפור בדקר ויכסה ובית הלל אומרים Beza 1, לא ישחוט אלא א״כ היה לו עפר מוכן מבעוד יום. Comp. S. Zeitlin, "Les Principes des Controverses Halachiques entre les écoles de Schammai et de Hillel." *REJ.* 1932.

92a. In the Talmud there are some halakot which are defined as הלכה למשה מסיני. These are few and are not of a major importance in the development of halaka.

93. Lev. 11.38. וכי יתן מים על זרע.

94. Sifra, 11, כשאתה אומר מחוברים טהורים ותלושים טמאים טמאת מקצת וטהרת מקצת. See S. Zeitlin, Takkanot Ezra, *JQR*, VIII.

95. On legal fifiction see *The Institutes* by R. Sohm; T. E. Holland, *The Elements of Jurisprudence.*

96. Deut. 15.1–3.

97. Tos. Sheb. 8.5, המלוה את חברו על המשכון אף על פי שההחוב מרובה על המשכון אינו משמט. See also B. M. 82, לבעל חוב שקונה משכון . . .

98. Beza, 37, אותו ואת בנו שנפלו לבור ר׳ אליעזר אומר מעלה את הראשון על מנת לשחטו ושוחטו והשני עושה לו פרנסה במקומו כדי שלא ימות ר׳ יהושע אומר מעלה את הראשון על מנת לשחטו ואינו שוחטו וחוזר ומערים ומעלה השני רצה זה שוחט רצה זה שוחט.

99. See Pes. 9a, מערים אדם על תבואתו ומכניסה במוץ שלה כדי שתהא בהמתו אוכלת ופטורה מן המעשר.

100. See M. K. 12b, תנאי היא דתניא אין מערימין בכך ר׳ יוסי בר יהודה אומר מערימין.

101. Tosefta Hag. מימיהם לא נחלקו אלא על הסמיכה, חמשה זוגות הן שלשה מזוגות הראשונים שאמרו שלא לסמוך היו נשיאים ושנים אבות בית דין, שנים מזוגות האחרונים שאמרו לסמוך היונשיאים ושנים אבות בית דין דברי ר׳ מאיר וחכמים אומרים שמעון בן שטח היה נשיא ויהודה בן טבאי אב בית דין; comp. also Yer. *ibid.* 2. See S. Zeitlin, The Semikah Controversy between the Zugoth, *JQR*, VII, *idem.* חורב תרצ״ז, ט, הפרושים; L. Ginzberg, *op. cit.*

102. Tem. 15b, כל אשכולות שעמדו להן לישראל מימות משה עד ימות (שמת) יוסי בן יעזר היו, לומדין תורה כמשה רבינו מכאן ואילך לא היו לומדין תורה כמשה רבינו. The reading עד ימות יוסי was suggested by Graetz, *Monatsschrift*, 1869.

103. כל אשכולות שעמדו לישראל מימות משה עד ימות(שמת) יוסי בן יעזר לא היו בהם שום *ibid.* דופי מכאן ואילך היה בהם שום דופי,

104. See Yer. H. 2, בראשונה לא היתה מחלוקת בישראל אלא על הסמיכה בלבד.

105. B. M. 91a, לוקה ומשלם.

106. עין תחת עין שן תחת שן כאשר יתן מום באדם כן ינתן בו.

107. Compare also Josephus, *Ant.* 4.8.35. "He that maimeth any one, let him undergo the like himself and be deprived of the same member of which he deprived the other, unless he that is maimed will accept money instead of it; for the law makes the sufferer the judge of the value of what he hath suffered and permits him

to estimate it, unless he will be more severe." On the attitude of the Pharisees and of Jesus toward the law of *talio*, see S. Zeitlin, *Who Crucified Jesus*, pp. 114-121.

108. See Numb. 35.24. ‏ושפטו העדה בין המכה ובין גאל הדם...והצילו העדה את הרצח‏ ‏ולא ימות ביד גאל הדם עד עמדו לפני העדה‏ ,Josh. 20.9; ‏מיד גאל הדם‏

109. ‏וישב בה עד מות הכהן הגדול‏, *ibid*. It is worthwhile noting that Demosthenes relates that in Greece manslaughter was punished by exile. ἐὰν τίς ἐπ'ἀκουσίῳ φόνῳ πεφευγώς, μήπω τῷ ἐκβαλόντων αὐτὸν ᾑρημένον αἰτίαν ἔχῃ ἑτέρου φόνου ἑκουσίου. (*Against Aristocrates*, 77).

110. Numb. 35. ‏גאל הדם ימית את הרוצח...ולא תקחו כפר לנפש רצח‏.

111. See S. Zeitlin, Studies in Tannaitic Jurisprudence, *Journal of Jewish Lore and Philosophy*, Vol. 1; idem. Asmakta or Intention, *JQR*, V.XIX.

112. Numb. 27. ‏איש כי ימות ובין לו והעברתם את נחלתו לבתו...ונתתם נחלתו לשארו‏ ‏הקרוב אליו ממשפחתו‏.

113. Lev. 25, ‏בשנת היובל הזאת תשבו איש אל אחזתו...ואיש כי ימכר בית מושב עיר חומה‏ ‏והיתה גאלתו עד תום שנת ממכרו...ואם לא יגאל עד מלאת לו שנה תמימה וקם הבית אשר בעיר‏ ‏אשר (לא) לו חמה לצמיתות לקנה אותו‏.

114. See B. B. chs. 8–9.

115. See H. S. Maine, *Ancient Law*, Ch. VI. The early history of testamentary succession.

116. See Suk., 56b, ‏שהמירה דתה‏; Pes. 96a ‏המרת הדת‏.

117. τοῦτον δὲ διαγαγὼν Δωσίθεος ὁ Δριμύλου λεγόμενος τὸ γένος Ἰουδαῖος ὕστερον δὲ μεταβαλὼν τὰ νόμιμα καὶ τῶν πατρίων δογμάτων ἀπηλλοτριωμένος. (1.3) Comp. also Josephus, *Jewish War*, VII; II Mac. 6.24.

Charles (*The Apocrypha*, ad. loc.) translated the words μεταβαλὼν τὰ νόμιμα "abandoned the observance of the law." He did not recognize that these Greek words μεταβαλὼν τὰ νόμιμα were actually a rendering of the Hebrew ‏המיר את דתו‏ "he changed his religion."

118. Jer. 2.11. ‏ההימיר גוי אלהים‏.

119. Modern etymologists are of the opinion that the word *religio* is derived from the root *ligo* — to tie, bind together. Cicero (*De Natura Deorum* 11.28,72) derives the word *religio* from *relegere*, to relate.

Dr. M. Kaplan in his recent book, *The Future of the American Jew*, 1948, made the following assertion, "In fact, there is really no word for religion in the entire Biblical and Rabbinical literature. Even in the medieval philosophical literature there is no exact equivalent for the concept *religion*. The Hebrew word *dat*, which occurs frequently in Jewish theological writings of the Middle Ages, is wrongly translated by the word religion; it really means law." Dr. Kaplan is apparently unaware of the fact that the word *dat* was used in tannaitic literature in the sense of religion and overlooks the fact that in the Hellenistic literature the term *dat*, νόμος was used in the sense of changing one's religion.

Those who believe that Judaism is a civilization are either unaware of or ignore Jewish history. Judaism is a religion — a nomocracy. In the Bible the term for worship of God, religion, was ‏אמונה‏ *fides*. Likewise in the New Testament, as well as in the writings of the Church Fathers, the word religion does not occur. The word πίστεως, *fides*, faith, belief in Jesus, is used. Only the Fathers who wrote in Latin used the word *religio*. In the Hellenistic literature the term for worship, religion, was εὐσέβεια or θρησκεία, ὁσιότης. Thus Kaplan's assertion "there is really no word for religion in the entire Biblical and Rabbinical literature," is erroneous.

120. Yoma 86b ‏היא מסורה בידכם ולא אתם מסורים בידה‏.

CAPITAL PUNISHMENT . . . (Pg. 313-324)

1. The Leeser translation (first published in 1855) does read, "Thou shalt not kill." Among the lexicographers, Gesenius' *Handwortebuch* . . . *über Das Alte Testament* (17th ed.) translates *r-z-h* "*tödten, morden*" (earlier editions give only *tödten*). Ben-Yehudah allows that the word can mean either murder or kill but stipulates that it means murder in the Decalogue. Brown, *et al. (Lexicon of the O. T.)* takes the word to mean either "kill deliberately" or "murder."

2. R. Joseph Behor-Shor (12 cen.) adds to the explication of R. Samuel, "This is what is called 'murder' in the language of the land." See also n. 17 in D. Rosen's edition of *Rashbam;* both R. Samuel and R. Joseph were in polemic contact with Christians. R. Samuel further discusses *Deut.* 4:42 in the light of his distinction, but his remarks should not be applied to *Num.* 35:27. 30.

3. Warsaw, 1886, II, 38c. The editions of Abarbanel I was able to consult all cite a non-existent verse. With the emendation of two letters, however, we have *Num.* 35:27.

4. The Talmudic discussion (*Makkoth* 12a) as to whether the blood-avenger's act of vengeance is required or optional in this context revolves around the conditionality of the sentence, not around the approval or disapproval expressed in *ve-razach*. The Torah itself, while allowing the slaying of the unintentional homicide before he reaches the City of Refuge or upon his leaving it (in this last case, one Tanna makes his slaying a *mitzvah;* see *Makkoth* 12a), and exonerating the blood-avenger ("there shall be no blood-guiltiness for him"), sees the accidental homicide as pitiably caught in the situation and in some way undeserving of the death he faces: ". . . he shall flee to one of the cities and live. Lest the avenger of death pursue the manslayer . . . and kill him, whereas he is not deserving of death (so in Old JPS; New JPS gives, 'he was not guilty of a capital crime'; the crucial *mishpat* may also carry the connotation here of a normative judgment of some sort, rather than implying innocence—see *Ex.* 21:9) . . . then shalt thou add three cities beside these three, that innocent blood be not shed" (*Deut.* 19:5, 6, 9, 10). The Torah paradoxically recognizes the legal right to kill a man in some sense undeserving of death, a right based upon the demands of "blood" and "earth." It was, perhaps, the unconditionally of this last statement ("innocent blood"), taken with a literal understanding of the introductory *vav* of v. 10, that led the Talmud (*Mo'ed Katan* 5a) to understand this verse as an admonition to the courts generally to maintain the safety of the roads.

5. The subject of *yirzach* is unclear and unexpressed (see n. 6). In pseudo-Jonathan either the blood-avenger or the court can function as subject. Y. Kaufmann (*Toledot*, II, p. 560; see also *I. C. C. ad loc.*) contends that the Torah knows of execution only at the hands of the blood-avenger supervised by the court. Apparently, then, the subject of *yirzach* would be the blood-avenger. The Talmud (*Sanhedrin* 45b) states that should no familial blood-avenger exist the court must appoint one. R. Nissim (*ad loc.*) takes this to mean that the court-appointed avenger functions both as prosecutor and as executioner; hence, every execution of a homicide could be seen, ideally, as the final working out of the process of blood-vengeance (see *Deut.* 19:12, *Ex.* 21:20 and *Mekhilta ad loc.*), and the subject of *yirzach* is in truth the avenger. Nahmanides, however (in his additional *'aseh* 13 to Maimonides' *Sefer Ha-Mitzvoth*), carefully avoids this approach, making both natural and appointed blood-avengers responsible only for the apprehension but not for the execution of the homicide where a court is capable of taking care of the latter. This places the execution of the murderer in a totally different judicial light.

6. In the use of the impersonal *soll man* Buber-Rosenzweig perhaps followed Luther's *soll man tödten*. In any case, it avoids assigning a subject to *yirzach*.

7. This consistent translation preserves the power and intent of the original, in which the murderer is paid back in fitting verbal coin (as Rabbi M. Bernstein of Yeshiva pointed out to me)—a stylistic *middah k'neged middah*. Indeed, a *baraitha*

quoted in the Jerusalem Talmud (*Sanhedrin* 7:3; 24b; *Mekhilta d'RSBI*, p. 169, 1. 19) would deduce from these words that murderer should suffer the same death that he inflicted, were it not for verses to the contrary. (A vocalized fragment published by Prof. L. Ginzberg in *Yerushalmi Fragments from the Genizah*, p. 258, 1. 14, takes *y-r-z-h* as a *nif'al* form.) Such, in fact, was the demand of the *Book of Jubilees*, 4:31-33.

8. See *Mekhilta d'RSBI*, p. 171, 1. 23. *Tosafot, Sanhedrin* 35b, *c. v. she-ne'emar* argue from the Biblical case. See, however, J. Levy, *Wortebuch über die Talmudim*, IV, 465.

9. Thus, *Mekhilta Vayakhel*, p. 347, 1:1 ff. On the literary relationship of these sources, see Prof. A. Weiss, *Le-Heker Ha-Talmud*, pp. 425-9. R. Ishmael (*Mekhilta Ki Tissah*, p. 340, 1. 10) uses the expression, "*shefichuth damim* [spilling of blood], which pollutes the land and drives away the *shekhina* [after *Num.* 35:34]," to describe killing in self-defense. Though such killing is permitted and its legal status thus transmuted (see Rashi, *Yomah* 85a, *s.v. u-shefichuth*), there is a descriptive and Halachic level on which it remains "shedding of blood," with its usual adverse connotations. Interestingly enough, the Midrash takes note of the bloodshed in approved wars and condones it. Abraham, distraught over his role in the war of the kings ("perhaps I have violated the command of God, 'He who sheds blood . . .' ") is reassured: "Fear not Abram, I shall reward you greatly, for you have rooted out the thorns, as it is stated, 'And the people shall be . . . as thorns cut down . . .' " (*Tanhuma*, ed. Buber I, p. 76; contrast the rebuke delivered to a self-justifying Jewish informer: "Let the owner of the vineyard [God] root out his thorns himself [B. M. 83b]). David is similarly reassured: ". . . When David heard that the blood on his hands prevented him from building the Temple [*I Chron.* 22:8] he feared he was unfit to build the Temple. R. Judah b. Illai said, "God said to him, 'Do not fear—by your life, all the blood you shed is as [permitted as] the blood of the gazelle and of the hart' . . ." (*Midrash T'hillim*, 62).

10. Maimonides (who uses the phrase *s'refath mitzvah* in his *Sefer Ha-Mitzvoth*, ed. R. Chayyim Heller, *shoresh* 14, p. 30a) apparently understands it in this sense. A parallel construction would be *milhemeth mitzvah* (*Sotah* 8:7). Note also the expression in *Midrash Shir Ha-Shirim* 4:10—". . . for they [the Sanhedrin] order [*mezavin*] stoning, strangulation, etc."

The precise relation of the words attributed to Resh Lakish with our *Mekhilta* is obscure. Certainly, the term *mitzvah* may be a later, explanatory addition—but then it may not. Such an addition would, however, be meaningless if *rezichah* here meant murder. In the passage under discussion we have, then, either another version of our *Mekhilta* or an early Amoraic explanation of it.

11. *Midrash Hagadol, Exodus*, ed. Prof. M. Margulies, p. 428.

12. Quoted by Prof. S. Lieberman, *Hilchoth Ha-Yerushalmi La-Rambam*, p. 21, n. 24.

13. Maimonides, *Guide*, III, chap. 41; see also *Hovel U-Mazzik*, 1:3.

14. Vilna, 1894, II, 93b. See also *Meshekh Hokhma*, 70d.

15. *Sefer Ha-Mitzvoth*, ed. R. Chayyim Heller, p. 172, and see the editor's comments on p. 13. The peculiar placing of this command in the judicial section remains of interest.

16. See Rashi to *Deut.* 25:3; *Kethuboth* 33a (top), 32a; Rashi to *Yoma* 85a, *s.v. u-shefichuth*.

17. Maimonides' words in the *Code* bear a striking resemblance to the statement in *Midrash Tannaim* (*Deut.* 5:17), p. 23: "*lo tirzach*—this is a ban on killing." But this segment of *M. T.* was collated from the *Midrash Ha-Gadol*, which is known to have incorporated Maimonidean material. Note also the unusual proof-text given in *M. T.*

18. *Makkoth* 7a.

19. See G. F. Moore, *Judaism*, II, pp. 186-8; Prof. L. Ginzberg, *On Jewish Law and Lore*, p. 6.

20. *Sanhedrin* 81b, 84a.

21. *Tosefta Yebamoth,* 8:4. This same teaching is found in anonymous form as comment to "You shall not kill" (*Mekhilta Yithro,* p. 233).

22. See A. J. Heschel,*Torah Min Ha-Shamayyim,* pp. 220-3. This last teaching of R. Meir is, of course, of a different order; it lives with the paradox of execution as a metaphysically destructive *desideratum.* Removal of the hung man at nightfall merely ends this tension.

23. *Hatra'ah* is apparently understood in this formal sense by the sages in their disagreement with R. Jose b. Yehudah, *Sanhedrin* 8. Compare Maimonides, *Code, Hilchoth Eduth* 12:1.

In practice the Rabbinic authorities found the abolition of capital punishment inherent in Jewish law impossible to maintain (see S. Assaf, *Ha-Onshin Ahar Hatimath Ha-Talmud*). The large majority of medieval decisors balanced this abolition of capital and corporal punishment by citing the discretionary power granted, indeed imposed upon, the court to suspend all normal procedures and requirements should the general well-being of the community demand such action. Though some limited the scope of these powers (which are rooted in the *baraitha* cited in *Sanhedrin* 46a) in various ways, the majority read it as a *carte blanche* for effective government at all times and in all places (see *Tur* and *Bet Yossef, H. M.,* sec. 2, 425).

Yet if medieval practice is clear, Talmudic practice itself remains ambiguous. J. Mann's presentation of the evidence (*Ha-Zofe Le-Hochmath Yisrael,* X (1926), pp. 202 ff.), though debatable at points (e.g., his rejection of Origen's testimony concerning the activities of the Palestinian Patriarch in the third century, and his interpretation of certain Talmudic practices), does lead one to conclude that the Babylonian Amoraim did not practice capital punishment. I would simply add to his discussion of *Sanhedrin* 27a-b that, while the court did in that case wish to inflict a punishment unknown to standard Jewish law, the witnesses were subject to Mishnaic requirements, and were ultimately disqualified by them. This practice would support the view of R. Jose (Jerusalem Talmud, *Hagigah* 2:2; 78a) that a court may only waive the requirement of *hatra-ah,* but may never act without competent witnesses (as the *P'nei Moshe* interprets the passage; here too we have a discrimination based on the obviously Pentateuchal requirement of witnesses and the formal nature of *hatra'ah* discussed above). One also wonders whether the disagreement over King Solomon's right to try cases with neither warning nor witnesses (*Rosh Ha-Shanah* 21b denies him this right, while R. Yochanan [*Yalkut* to *Psalms,* 72] and other Palestinian Amoraim [*Midrash Shir Hashirim,* 1:10] grant it to him) is an Aggadic reflection of a contemorary problem. These last sources, in any case, present problems of internal analysis.

Even the medieval practice could be guided by Talmudic law. Thus we find R. Abraham b. Isaac of Narbonne (12th cen.) refusing—on various grounds of Talmudic law—to execute a murderer, though he does impose corporal punishment and financial liability upon the homicide (responsum published by S. Assaf, *Sifran Shel Rishonim,* pp. 42-4). Generally speaking, medieval practice also remained true to the theoretical structure of these discretionary powers, which stipulated that punishment be carried out for its salutary social effect rather than as a mode of dispensing justice to the body and soul of the criminal; see the responsum cited above, p. 43 (bottom) and that of R. Meir of Lublin (16 cen.) in the 1st or 2nd edition of his responsa (no. 138). This responsum was deleted in subsequent editions.

24. R. Yochanan's intentions in this matter are not yet clear. See Prof. A. Weiss, *Seder Ha-Diyyum,* p. 207, p. 5. As *bedikoth* ("examinations") such questions could only serve to disqualify witnesses who contradicted each other in their answers, not witnesses ignorant of such information.

25. *Sic.* Rabbi David Hoffman.

26. The expression *la-hov* indicates a fear of actual guilt.

27. I am taking the view dismissed by the *Sifre* as representative of an existent tendency rather than as a rhetorical strawman, as we apparently find in *The Midrash on Psalms* (trans. Braude; to *Ps.* 56), I, p. 497. Yet even in this anonymous *midrash* the question presupposes a real problem; compare note 11 above.

28. *Koheleth Rabbati* 7:33. This same *midrash* appears (in perhaps a more

original form) with significant variations in *Yoma* 22b (and in R. Hananel) and *Midrash Zutah, Koheleth* (ed. Buber), p. 138. The words here attributed to Resh Lakish are also found, with a slightly different twist to them, in the mouth of R. Joshua b. Levi (he and Resh Lakish share a nearly identical abbreviation of names) in *Yalkut* to *I Samuel*, sec. 121 (see also *Midrash Shmuel*, ed. Buber, p. 100, n. 8).

29. Jerusalem Talmud, *Berachoth*, 5:3; 9c.

30. *Midrash on Psalms* (to *Ps.* 52), I, p. 479; see II, p. 474, n. 11. See also, *I Corinthians*, 9:8–10.

31. *Berachoth*, 7a.

32. *Shmoth Rabbah*, 30:12 (end). For the authors of the *midrash*, of course, Saul was not legally liable—there is no agency in criminal acts. In *Yebamoth* 79a the Gibeonites are criticized for not forgiving Saul, but no mention is made of the priests' contrasted behavior. Elsewhere (*Vayyikrah Rabbah*, 26:7) the ineradicability of Saul's murder of the priests is stressed, but here the king is arraigned before the heavenly court.

33. *Midrash Tannaim*, p. 69.

POSSESSION IN JEWISH LAW (Pg. 325-329)

1. These two terms are interchangeable with קרקע and מטלטלין.

2. Cf. also the phrase שאין להם בעלים Pes. 118b.

3. Kid. 1:6.

4. Lewy, *Worterbuch* IV, 473b asserts that in Syriac רשי means to seize, but I could not find any indication for this statement in the Syriac dictionaries.

5. In the Mishnah, ownership is also expressed by the preposition שלו *e. g.* אין אדם מקדיש דבר שאינו שלו, Arakin VII: 5 and T. Peah, III, 13. מקדש דבר שאינו שלו Kil. VII: 5, and אין אדם מקדיש דבר שאינו שלו

6. cf. BB. VIII:7 and Pes. 6b, and T.B.M. VIII:23.

7. Distinction de la possession et la detention en droit romain, Paris 1898, p. 5.

8. This passage is explained in T. Kid. I: 9 as follows: אבל ההדיוט לא קנה עד שעה שהחזיק.

9. 41, 2, 1, English translation by Zulueta, Oxford 1922, p. 47.

10. Kid. 1:3, B.B. IV:9.

11. B.M. I.3.

12. T. Peah II:10.

13. T. B. B. VIII:12.

14. B.B. III:1.

15. For the term לקיחה, cf. T. B. M. IX: 9.

16. Cf. Westermarck, History of Human Marriage, Vol. II, 5th Edition, New York 1922, pp. 354 ff.

17. For the sake of parallelism, the Mishnah says היבמה נקנית בביאה; cf. however Yeb. IV: 7 הכונס את יבמתו זוכה בנכסים של אחיו.

18. It is rather unusual that in Ket. VIII: 1 the text reads: הואיל וזכה באשה לא יזכה בנכסים. Perhaps here too זכה is used on account of the second phrase.

19. כל הנעשה דמים באחר כיון שזכה זה נתחייב זה בחליפיו T. Kid. I:9 paraphrases the words כל הנעשה דמים באחר by the phrase החליף עמו. The words כל הנעשה דמים באחר mean "any object which he evaluated for the purpose of exchange," cf. the statement in B.M. V:9 זוכן היה הלל אומר לא תלוה אשה ככר לחברתה עד שתעשנו דמים see also Pes. VII: 3, and Temurah V: 5. Possibly in Kid. I: 6 זכה is employed because it is in opposition to נתחייב.

20. B.M. I:3, 4.

21. B. B. IV: 9. Inherited property before it is divided is termed תפיסת הבית; Bek. IX. 3. For this phrase, cf. Jer. 40.10 and Kid. 26a.

22. T. Maaser Rishon III:11, cf. also M. B.K. III:3.

23. T. B.B. VIII:11, IX:13.
24. B.M. VIII:4, T. VIII:23.
25. Git. 40b, cf. T. B.B. IX:13.
26. Savigny, *Treatise on Possession,* London 1848, pp. 266–272; Sohm, *Institutes of Roman Law,* 3rd. Ed., pp. 330–331; Dernburg, *System des Romischen Recht,* Berlin 1911, pp. 292–293; Hollander, *Ueber den Animus im Recht des Besitzes der Romer,* Halle 1903.
27. 41.2.8. English translation of Zulueta, p. 56.
28. Sifre. Deut. 131 note cf. also M. Pes. III:7, and baraita in Pes. 7a and statement of Rab in Pes. 6b. Rashi's view in Pes. 4b that the law is derived from Ex. 12.15 which implies השבתה בלב goes back to Mekilta di R. Shimon (ed. Hoffmann, p. 15). According to R. Tam (some authorities read R. Isaac) renouncing one's leaven means declaring it free property (*Tosafot* Pes. 4b s.v. מדאורייתא). Nahmanides who took R. Tam's view too literally raised objections to it on eight grounds (*Novellae* to Pesahim). Meiri, without mentioning Nahmanides by name tried to refute every one of his arguments; see *Magen Abot,* ed. Last, p. 73–78, cf. *Rabiah,* ed. Aptowitzer, Vol. II, p. 25, and *Semag,* Positive Command, no. 39, ed. Kopys, p. 17b.
29. Erubin VI:7.
30. Kid. II:9 enumerates nine instances.
31. T.B.K. VII: 11 cf. Schwarz *ad loc.* p. 70 and Mek. to Exod. 22.3.
32. T. Ab. Zarah V (VI): 3 ישראל שמצא עבודה זרה עד שלא באת לרשותו אומר לגוי ומבטלה of the incident of R. Joshua b. Levi and Bar Kappara in Babli 43a. One does not acquire a lost object before one gains physical control over it (B.M. 2a). The theory underlying this passage of the Tosefta is that one cannot acquire an object which one cannot own. For a similar conception in Roman Law see Cuq, *Manuel des institutions juridiques des Romains,* Paris 1917, p. 313.
33. Kid. II:10 and T. Peah II:13.
34. T. B.M. II:2, Babli 22a.
35. B.M. II.5.
36. T. B.K. X:24 and parallel passages.
37. M. B.K. X:2, T. B.M. II:2, Yer. B.K. X:2.
38. 41, 1, 58 translation of Zulueta, p. 43.
39. B.K. 66a.
40. *Law and Politics in the Middle Ages,* N.Y. 1898, p. 189.
41. B.K. 66b.
42. Sukkah III:1, 2, 3 and 5.
43. Sukkah 27b, Yer. III:1.
44. Bik. I.2.
45. I have inserted the word של which is not in the text, for it is unintelligible without it.
46. Orlah I:2.
47. T. Terumah I:6.
48. Kelim XXVI:7, Sifra 76b, T. Kelim B.B. IV:11.
49. *Essay on Possession in the Common Law,* Oxford, 1883, p. 3.

THE RELIGIOUS IDEAS OF JUDAISM (Pg. 334-346)

1. Cf. *Talmud Yerushalmi,* ed. Krotoschin, Berakhot 13 a, b; *Midrash Tehillim,* edited by Buber, p. 314. Further material in R. Travers Herford, *The Pharisees,* and G. F. Moore, *Judaism in the First Centuries,* etc., I, 439 ff. On the subject of God's hearkening to prayer and present-day miracles, cf. Büchler, *Some Types of Jewish Palestinian Piety,* pp. 196–264.
2. Babylonian Talmud: Abodah Zarah 3b; *Sifre Numbers,* par. 84; Berakhot 9b.
3. *Mekilta to Exodus,* 15:3; Hagigah 13b.; *Pesikta,* ed. Buber, p. 109b, 110a.
4. *Sifra to Leviticus,* 19:1; *Sifre Deuteronomy,* 49; cf. *Mekilta to Exodus,* 15:2.

5. Sanhedrin 56a, b.

6. In general, the commandments were given to man only in order to purify his character. In detail, many ceremonial and cultic regulations were given ethical interpretations.

7. Shabbat 152b; Hagigah 12b; Sanhedrin 91a, b.

8. *Sifre Deuteronomy*, 307; Berakhot 28b; Shabbat 153a; Berakhot 17a.

9. Pirke Abot 4:16.

10. Berakhot 17a.

11. *Bereshit Rabbah*, 9:3.

12. *Sifre Deuteronomy*, 309, edited by Friedmann, p. 132a; *Bereshit Rabbah*, 8:11. Berakhot 10a.

13. Hagigah 12b; Niddah 30b.

14. *Sifre Deuteronomy, loc. cit.*

15. Berakhot 61a.

16. *Sifre Deuteronomy*, 32; cf. *Bereshit Rabbah*, 9:7.

17. *Sifra to Leviticus*, 19:18; Shabbat 31a.

18. Sifra to Leviticus 18:4.

19. *Sifre Deuteronomy*, 32, p. 73a; Pesahim 50b.

20. Mishnah Peah, 1:1; Abot 1:17; Kiddushin 40b.

21. Berahot 33b.

22. Abot 3:15.

23. Kiddushin 39b; Rosh Hashanah 17a.

24. Berahot 5ab; Sanhedrin 101a, etc.

25. Kiddushin 39b; *Bereshit Rabbah*, 33:1.

26. Cf. Bergmann, "Die stoische Philosophie und die jüdische Frömmigkeit," *Judaica, Festschrift zu Hermann Cohens 70. Geburtstag*, pp. 145–166.

27. Berakhot 10a; cf. Seneca, *Epistolae Morales*, 65:24.

28. Niddah 30b (cf. Plato, *Phaedo*, 76D, and *Responsa of the Geonim*, X, 621A); *Bereshit Rabbah*, 1:1 (cf. *Timaeus*, 29a); Hullin 59b (*Responsa*, VIII, 514 ff). According to Freudenthal (*Hellenist. Studien*, I, 69) and other scholars, the ideas of Plato were transmitted to the rabbis through the media of Jewish-Helenistic writings, and especially through Philo, where these doctrines are also found. But despite all the exegetical parallels between Philo and Talmudic literature, it is very questionable if he was known to the Talmudic rabbis. Their knowledge of philosophic ideas, which, in general, was quite limited, was probably drawn from wandering Greek philosophic preachers or through personal contact with Hellenistic Jews, who were also probably mediators of Alexandrian exegesis. Neumark (*History of Jewish Philosophy*, German edition, II, 89–91) claims that Platonic ideas had a decisive influence upon Talmudic Judaism, but very few of his arguments can withstand close scrutiny.

29. Abot 2:3.

30. Mishnah Hagigah 2:1.

31. Berakhot 33b; Hagigah 15a; *Sifre Deuteronomy*, 329.

32. Mishnah Hagigah, *loc. cit.*

33. Hagigah 14b; cf. Grätz, *Gnostizismus und Judentum*, p. 56 ff.; Bousset, "Die Himmelsreise der Seele," *Archiv für Religionswissenschaft*, IV, 145 ff.

34. *Bereshit Rabbah*, 3:4; *Tanhuma*, edited by Buber, on Exodus 37:1. Cf. Freudenthal, *Die dem Flavius Josephus*, p. 71, who brings a parallel from Philo, *De fuga*, 110; Aptowitzer, MGWJ, LXXII, 363 ff; Ginzberg, *The Legends of the Jews*, V, 8, 9. For detailed treatment of the light metaphysics of ancient mysticism, *vide* Baeumkers, *Witelo*, pp. 361 ff.

35. Hagigah 12a; cf. Grätz, *op. cit.*, p. 39; Joël, *Blicke in die Religionsgeschichte*, I, 147. With reference to the preceding it is worth while to consult Joël, *op. cit.*, pp. 114–170.

36. *Exodus Rabbah*, 15:22; cf. Freudenthal, *op. cit.*, p. 71. This saying is undoubtedly ancient, despite its recent context.

37. Mishna Sanhedrin 10(11).

38. Cf. my essay: "Die Normierung des Glaubeninhalts in Judentum," MGWJ, LXXI, 241–255.

SOME RABBINIC IDEAS ON PRAYER (Pg. 360-372)

1. Mishnah, *Berachoth*, V end (Talmud B. *Berachoth*, 54 b). The passage concerning Hanina b. Dosa cited later on occurs at this same reference.

2. London, Isbister, 1904.

3. Mishnah, *Taanith*, III.8. Cf. note 10 below. Onias and Hanina are both held to have been Essenes. Prayer for rain must only be uttered near the rain-season (ibid., 1, 2). Does this imply a belief in the order of nature? Such a prayer had to be sincere; on Tabernacles men did not pray for rain till the end of the festival, when the duty of dwelling in the tabernacle was over, so that "men might pray for rain with a perfect heart."

4. Sirach (Hebrew) vii.10.

5. Buber's *Tanchuma*, Genesis p. 134 (Toledoth, 14).

6. T.B. *Berachoth*, 10 a (foot).

7. Mishnah, *Berachoth*, IX; T. B, *Berachoth*, 60a, has many sayings on תפלת שוא.

8. T. B. *Moed Katon*, 18 b.

9. See on עיון תפלה, T. B. *Berachoth*, 32 b, 55 a; *Baba Bathra*, 164 b. He who prays thinking he deserves answer receives none. *Rosh Hashanah*, 18 a. On the other hand: "Whoever performs the will of heaven and directs his heart devoutly to his prayer receives an answer." *Exod. Rabba*, § 21; cf. *Berachoth*, 6 b (foot). The distinction may be said to be in this. Devout prayer is answered, *but* the expectation of an answer is not to enter into the thought of the utterer of the prayer. And the failure of an answer must not disconcert the worshipper. As he does not start by relying on an answer, he is not overwhelmed by receiving none. "What is good in thine own sight do" (see note 40 below). This was the final attitude. Of course God does what he thinks good; prayer makes man perceive that what God thinks good is good.

10. *Exodus Rabba*, ch. xxi.

11. Ibid., ch. xxiii. *Tanchuma*, § מקץ (near end).

12. T.B. *Yebamoth*, 64 a. On public worship see *Berachoth*, 8 a. Prayer for the wicked (that they may repent and be saved) is enjoined. T.B. *Berachoth*, 10 a. For the passage about the Egyptians see T.B. *Megillah*, 10 b; *Sota*, 36 a.

13. Josephus, *Antiquities*, xiv. 2. § 1. Schürer's treatment of the episode (I, 293, 294) is worth noting. He includes it as one of the "Episodes highly characteristic of the contemporary Jewish pietism (*Frömmigkeit*)." His final comment is: "But the people was so little in sympathy with this brotherly spirit of Onias that they at once stoned him." But Josephus says that the stoning was done by οἱ πονηροὶ τῶν 'Ιουδαίων, "the wicked of the Jews, "and has pointedly stated previously that the noblest of the Jews had left the country for Egypt *(οἱ δοκιμώτατοι τῶν 'Ιουδαίων ἐκλιπόντες τὴν χώραν εἰς Αἴγυπτον ἔφυγον)*. This Onias becomes a popular hero in the later Jewish tradition, and it was "highly characteristic" of the Jewish *Frömmigkeit* that it held precisely the brotherly view of Onias in the positive as his was in the negative form. "A human being cannot hear two people appealing to him at once; but the Holy One, even though *all creatures on earth* come and cry before him, hears their cries, as it is written, O thou that hearest prayer, unto thee shall all flesh come" (*Mechilta*, Shira, § 8; ed. Friedmann, 41 b).

14. *Exodus Rabba*, xxi; *Echa Rabba*, 9v.,

15. *Baba Kama*, 92a; *Baba Bathra*, 90a-91b; *Berachoth*, 10b.

16. *T.Jer. Yoma*, v.Hal. 2. (Cf. Buber, *Tanchuma*, Lev. p. 5 for parallel.)

17. Mishnah, *Aboth*, i. 15. In the *Jewish Encyclopaedia* X. p. 166 b, Dr. J. D. Eisenstein writes: "The higher class, that is the scholars, would not be disturbed in their studies, which they considered of superior importance to prayers. R. Judah recited his prayers only once in thirty days (*Rosh Hashana*, 35a). R. Jeremiah,

studying under R. Ze'era, was anxious to leave his study when the time for prayer arrived; and Ze'era quoted: He that turneth away his ear from hearing the Law, even his prayer shall be abomination (Prov. xxviii.9; T.B. *Sabbath,* 10a)." The reference here is to the set times and forms of prayer. Individuals prayed spontaneously at all times. R. 'Akiba, we are expressly told, prayed briefly in public, but lengthily in private.

18. *Aboth,* II, 13; *Berachoth,* IV, 4 (cf. Talmud *Berachoth,* 28b) "At first," writes Prof. L. Blau, "there were no written prayers; a scribe of the end of the first century says: The writers of benedictions are as those that burn the Torah. A man who was caught copying some at Sidon threw a bundle of his copies into a wash-tub (*Sabbath,* 115b): In no case was written matter used during public worship. Prayerbooks appear about the seventh century" (*Jewish Encyclopedia,* art Liturgy, Vol. VIII, p. 138b).

19. *T.B. Berachoth,* 24b, 29a. For the next citation see *Yebamoth,* 105b.

20. *Tanchumay* מקץ . The passage, taken from Miss Wolfenstein's story, is quoted from *A Renegade and other Tales* (Philadelphia: the Jewish Publication Society of America, 1905; p. 200). R. Jochanan thought that men might pray all day, but others limited the lawful times of prayer to three (Berachoth, 21a, 31a).

21. Midrash on Ps. iv.

22. T.B. Berachoth, 32b.

23. Leviticus Rabba, 9: T.B. Berachoth, 6 and 31b, and 32a.

24. T.B. Berachoth, 5a.

25. *Tanchuma,* מקץ (end); T. B. *Succah,* 14 a.

26. Midrash, *Yalkut,* on Ps. lxxvi. 3; T.B. *Berachoth,* 7a.

27. *Exodus Rabba,* 43.

28. T.B. *Sanhedrin,* 32a; *Yoma,* 53b.

29. *Zohar,* ויקהל, 213 b. See *Jewish Encyclopedia* (J. W. Eisenstein), Vol. X, p. 169 b, for further citations.

30. *Sifri,* ed. Friedmann, p. ס (on Deut. xi. 13); T. B. *Taanith,* 2 a.

31. T.B. Sota, 5a.

32. *Tanchuma,* on Deut. vi. 5.

33. *T.B. Berachoth,* 7a.

34. *Jer. Sanhedrin,* X, 28c; *Numbers Rabba,* 12.

35. *Exodus Rabba,* xxii; *Mechilta* (בשלח), § 6.

36. Yalkut, on Ps. iv.

37. *T. B. Berachoth,* 29 b (towards end).

38. An inspiring and pathetic chapter could be written on the use of the Psalms in Jewish life. *The Authorized Daily Prayer Book,* ed. S. Singer, contains about half the Psalter. The whole of the Psalms are read in daily instalments in many synagogues. But besides this liturgical use, there are many historical records of the application of the Psalms in times of stress under danger and martyrdom, of gratitude under salvation, of acceptance of God's will and inspiration to courageous endeavour—which prove the fertile influence of the Psalter on Jewish life in all ages. Here is one famous instance. In the tenth century, the captain of a corsair vessel had captured Moses b. Hanoch and his fair wife. The pirate became enamoured of his beautiful captive. One day she asked her husband in Hebrew if those drowned in the sea rose again at the Resurrection. He answered her with the Psalmic text: "The Lord said, I will bring again from Bashan, I will bring again from the depths of the sea" (Ps. lxviii. 22). Fortified with this hope, and resolved to save her honour, she threw herself in the sea.

39. In *Songs of Exile* (Macmillan) and *Service of the Synagogue* (Routledge). In Hebrew the prayer is included in Baer's classical edition of the daily Liturgy, and in many other editions.

THE RABBINICAL CONCEPTION OF HOLINESS (Pg. 373-380)

1. See JEWISH QUARTERLY REVIEW, vols. VII and VIII.

2. Sifra. 86 c. Cp. Bacher, Agada der Tannaiten, II, 367, and Lewy, Uehr einige Fragmente aus der Mischna des Abba Saul, p. 28.

3. *Tanchuma*, קדושים, § 5. Cp. also *Pesikta*, ed. Buber, 16 a.

4. *Tanchuma*, ibid, 2.

5. See Lev. Rabbah, xxiv. 4.

6. See *T. B. Abodah Zarah*, 20 b, and ר״ס to the passages. All the parables, however (given by Bacher in his *Agada der Tannaiten*, II, p. 796, note 5. p. 460, to which *Midrash Mishle*, XV, is also to be added), have חסידות close to רוה״ק.

7. *Mechilta*, 37 a, and *T. B. Sabbath*, 133 a, and parallels. The interpretation of Abba Saul is based on the word ואנוהו in Exod. xv. 2, which he divides into אני והו, meaning "I (man) and he (God)."

8. *Sifra*, 85 a. It seems that the Rabbis read in Joel יְקְרָא.

9. See Gen. Rabbah, lviii, 9.

10. *T. B. Sotah*, 14 a. The beginning of the passage is taken from the שאילתות פ׳ בראשית. According to the Agadic explanations Abraham was in an invalid state when God appeared to him in the plains of Mamre. The blessing, again spoken of in Gen. xxv. 11, which took place after the death of Abraham, was meant as a message of condolence.

11. See *Aboth d. R. Nathan*, c. iv. The words "And he brought unto the man" (Gen. ii. 23) are understood by the Rabbis that God took particular care to represent Eve to Adam in the adorned state of a bride.

12. See דרך ארץ רבה, c. v. I supplemented the passage with the parallel in *Aboth d. R. Nathan*, c. xxxvii.

13. ספר יראים, § 3.

14. See תדא״ז, c. viii, and *Yalkut Shimoni*, II, § 217. Cp. also *Rabbah* to Canticles i. 6. *Agadath Shir Hashirim*, p. 45.

15. See Robertson Smith's *Religion of the Semites* p. 140 about the uncertainty of the original meaning of the word.

16. *Sifra*, 57b.

17. See *Moreh Nebuchim* III, 47. Maimonides' explanation was undoubtedly suggested to him by *Sifre* 81a (to Lev. xvi. 16).

18. *Mechilta*, 63 a. A few lines before, there is given another explanation to the words וגוי קדוש, which was taken by the great master of the Agada, Lector Friedmann, to contain a protest against proselytizing. The text, however, seems to be corrupt, and reads in the *Midrash Haggadol* יכול מלכים ובעלי מלחמה ת״ל כהנים או כהנים יכול בטלנים כענין שנ׳ ובני דוד כהנים היו ת״ל וגוי קדוש.

19. *Sifra*, 93b.

20. *Sifra*, 86d.

21. *Lev. Rabbah*, xxiv. 6.

22. See *Lev. Rabbah*, xxiii, end.

23. See *Exod. Rabbah*: xxx, 9 about the end.

24. This seems to me to be the meaning of the words in דרך ארץ זוטא, III, תחלת טומאות לע״ז פתח. See *Sifra*, 57 b, ואם טמאים אתב בהם סופכם ליטמא בם, and comp. the פרוש הראב״ד. The other explanation given there suggests our passage to be a parallel to that quoted in the preceding note from the דא״ז. Perhaps we should read in the *Sifra*, סופכם ליטמא בע״ז.

25. See *T. B. Makkoth*, 16 b, and Maimonides, הלכות מאכלות אסורות, § xvii, the last five הלכות.

26. See *T.B. Chagigah,* 5a, the explanation of *Rab* to Eccles. xii.14.

27. Maimonides, ibid. Cp. T.B. *Berachoth,* 53b, the last lines of the page.

28. See *T. B. Yoma,* 39 a, תני דבי ר׳ ישמעאל עבירה, &c. By עבירה in this passage is meant the transgression of any law.

29. See *Mechilta,* 98 a, and *Sifra,* 35 a and 91 d, קדושת כל המצות. The *Midrash Haggadol* also seems to read in *Sifra* (to Lev. xi. 44) והתקדשתם זו קדושת מצות; a reading which is confirmed by Maimonides when he says (*Moreh Nebuchim,* iii. 33 and 47), אמנם אמרו יתעלה והתקדשתם... לשון ספרא זו קדושת מצות.

30. *Numbers Rabbah,* xvii. 6.

31. See מסילת ישרים.

3|2. See *Baba Kama,* 30 a, text and commentaries, especially the ר״ן to their corresponding place in the רב אלפס. For the ten things of the *Chasiduth* which Rab is said to have observed (mixture of the ceremonial and the moral) see *Yuchasin,* ed. Filipowski, p. 180.

33. *T.B. Jebamoth,* 20a.

34. Introduction to the רוקח.

35. Commentary to the Pentateuch, Lev. XIX. 2.

36. See רוקח, ibid., where he deducts from it both certain stringent rules regarding forbidden food, as well as others teaching morality.

37. See *T. B.* Sanhedrin, 107 a.

38. See *T. B. Baba Mezia,* 59a.

39. See *Lev. Rabbah,* xxiii. Cp. *Pesikta Rabbathi,* 124 b, text and notes. See also *Midrash Haggadol* ד״א לא תנאף שלא ינאף... ולא בעין ולא בלב... ומנין שהעין והלב מזנין דכת׳ ולא תתורו אחרי לבבכם ואחרי עיניכם. Cp. also New Testament, Matt. v. 21 and 27. I suspect that the expression in the N. T., "Ye have heard," had originally something to do with the Talmudic formula שומע אני or ת״ל..., לא שמענו..., or ,ל״ת..., במשמע אלא...ת״ל... (see *Mechilta,* 81 b, 82 b, and 84 a)

40. ואת הקדוש והקריב אין קדושה אלא נבואה שנ׳ אין קדוש כה׳. *Midrash* in MS.

41. ענין הקדושה... תחלתו השתדלות וסופו מתנה ch. xxvi מסילת ישרים.

42. *T.B. Yoma,* 39a.

43. Midrash to Ps. XX. Cp. Tanchuma, קדושים, § 9.

44. Midrash MS. in פ׳ יתרו.

45. T. B. Berachot, 17a. See also ר״ס to the passage.

DIVINE RETRIBUTION IN RABBINIC LITERATURE (Pg. 382-393)

1. *Aboth* (ed. C. Taylor), v. 12-15. See also *Sabbath,* 32 *seq.,* and *Mechilta* (ed. Friedman), 95*b*.

2. See *Mechilta,* 259*a,* 32*b.* Gen. Rabbah, ch. 48, and *Tossephta Sotah,* IV. 7 and parallels.

3. See *Mechilta,* 68*b* and parallels. *Sifra,* 112*b. Pessikta* of R. Kahana, 167*b.* Cp. *Sanhedrin,* 44*a.*

4. *Aboth* de R. Nathan, 40*a,* 59 *b,* and 61*b. Pessikta* of R. Kahana, 73*a,* and parallels.

5. *Baba Bathra,* 10*a.* See Bacher, *Hagada der Tannaiten,* I., 295.

6. See *Aboth* de R. Nathan, 65*b* and notes.

7. See *Mechilta,* 57*b,* and parallels.

8. See *Kedushin,* 40*b.*

9. See *Sabbath,* 54*a.*

10. See *Exodus Rabbah,* c. 35 and parallels.

11. See *Negaim,* ii. 1, and compare *Aruch, s.*iv.

12. *Exod. Rabbah,* c. 46.

13. See *Berachoth,* 5*a.*

14. Tanchuma, כי תצא § 2.

15. See *Sifré*, 73*b*, and parallels.
16. See *Taanith*, 8*b*.
17. See Arachin, 16*b*.
18. *Aboth*, iv. 15.
19. See *Chagigah*, 5*a*.
20. *Aboth*, i., 3., p. 27, ed. Taylor. See also note 8.
21. *Abodah Zarah*, 19*a*. See also *Sifré*, 79*b*.
22. See ראשית חכמה I, 9.
23. See *Exod. R.*, 30, and parallels.
24. See רמתים צופים 33 *b*.
25. See *Sabbath*, 55 *b* and *Sifra*, 27 *a*.
26. See for instance, מנורת המאור (Amsterdam, 1720), p. 4, *seq.*, and 94 *seq.*, and much more in the ראשית חכמה, in the two chapters שער היראה ושער האהבה, where also the views of other authors are given.

HONOR IN RABBINIC LAW AND ETHICS (Pg. 394-402)

1. Eugene Terraillon, *L'Honneur.*
2. Hermann Cohen, *Ethik des Reinen Willens*, 2, 464: "*Das Wesen des Menschen ist sein Ehre.*"
3. Cf. I.Kant, *Metaphysik der Sitten* (edit. Vorlander), 322.
4. The rabbis (*Baba Mezia* 58b) emphasized this fact by pointing out that when a person is put to shame, the blood runs to his face. They say, therefore, that shaming a fellow-man is equivalent to shedding blood.
5. *Deoth*, VI, 3, based on *Aboth* II, 12.
6. The connection between honor and rights is also obvious from the fact that the slave, who lacks legal status, according to one opinion (*Baba Kama* 87a), is not entitled to indemnities for the shame suffered during an assault.
7. Cf. Mommsen, *Roemisches Strafrecht*, 788; Buckland, *Main Institutions of Roman Private Law*, 337. Roman law uses the technical term "*injuria*" for a complaint that an individual's honor has been offended. (cf. Thering, *Aufsaetze* III, 251). The rabbis use the term *onaah* in regard to a (verbal) injury (*Baba Mezia* 58b). The Hebrew term has a meaning similar to that of the Latin one ("injury", "oppression" "infringement of rights").
8. The law's failure to provide adequate punishment for an offense against honor is in no way an explanation for the custom of dueling (as has been often assumed). Rather, duelling was the result of the view that the individual should personally avenge his offended honor (cf. H. Reiner, *Die Ehre*, 62ff. 67).
9. Cf. Jacob Burckhardt, *Die Kultur der Renaissance in Italien*, 406ff. The same view is expressed by Norfolk is Shakespeare's Richard II.
10. This view, expressed by Falstaff in Shakespeare's drama *Henry IV*, was particularly stressed by Schopenhauer (*Werke*, V., 403f). Schopenhauer's disparagement of honor may be understood as part of his general rejection of the idea of the dignity of man (cf. *Ibid*. p. 409. However, a similar view was also expressed in antiquity by the Stoic philosophers, who, stressing the self-sufficiency and *inner* dignity of the individual, deprecated external honor. (Epictetus, *Handbook of Morals*, pp. 23, 24).
11. Cf. Psalms 15:3; Proverbs 11:12, 17:5.
12. Genesis Rabbah XXIV.
13. *Sanhedrin 58b*. It is instructive to contrast this rabbinic statement with Schopenhauer's comment (*op.cit.*, 208) that a slap is a slight physical affront, unworthy of attention.
14. *Baba Mezia* 58b; 59a.
15. Cf. C. W. Reines, *Torah Umusar*, 193f. Maimonides (Sanhedrin XXIV, 10) stressed this point with regard to the criminal—viz., that although punishment necessarily involves degrading the offender and shaming him publicly, he ought not be dishonored beyond the necessity of law.

16. *Berakhoth* 19a.
17. *Taanith* 23a.
18. *Nedarim* 62a.
19. *Gitt'n* 55b, 56a.
20. *Gittin* 57a.
21. Responsa of Rabbi Isaac Bar Sheshet, No. 216.
22. *Yoma* 23a.
23. *Judges* 5:31.
24. Proverbs 11:12.
25. Epictetus, *Manual of Morals,* 20.
26. *Iggeroth Harambam,* edit. M. Z. Baneth, pp. 56, 61, 90.
27. *Deoth* VI, 9. *Talmud Torah* VII, 1.
28. As is apparent from various incidents reported in the Talmud (cf. *Baba Kama* 117a; *Baba Mezia* 84a; *Ketuboth* 69a).
29. *Yoma* 87a.
30. *Baba Kama* 92a.
31. Yerushalmi *Baba Kamma* VIII, 10.
32. Mishnah *Baba Kama* VIII, 4.
33. Roman law also imposes different fines for offenses, according to the class allegiance of the offended (Buckland. *Main Institutions of the Roman Law,* 337). The same was also true among the Babylonians and other ancient peoples.
34. *Baba Kama* 86a. This opinion is accepted by the medieval authorities (cf. Rabbi Asher to *Baba Kama,* chapter VIII, 7; Maimonides *Chovel Umazik* III, 1a; and see the comment of R. Judah Rosanes *ad loci*).
35. *Aboth* III, 14.
36. *Baba Kama* 92b.
37. *Baba Kama* 91a.
38. Maimonides (*Moreh Nevuchim* III, 41) explains this rule on the ground that verbal offenses are very common. Spinoza (Ethics III, propos. II) also observes that people are least able to control their tongues. The death punishment that the Bible prescribes for indignities committed against one's parents is meted out only where the culprit is guilty of striking his parents, not for verbal insults (cf. Maimonides, *Mamrim* V, 16). Maimonides adds, however, that the court must impose flagellation (*makoth marduth*) for this offense).
39. *Arachin* 15a.
40. Deuteronomy 22:19.
41. *Arachin* ibid.
42. *Yerushalmi Pesachim* III b.
43. *Kid ushin* 28a.
44. Cf. *Tosaphoth* of R. Isaac the Elder *ad loci.*
45. Rashi, *Kiddushin ad loci;* Aruch sub *Chaj.*
46. Rashi, *Baba Mezia* 71a.
47. Responsa of R. Meir Rottenburg edit. Bloch, par. 293.
48. *Chovel Umazik* III, 5. *Sanhedrin* XXVI, 5.
49. Mordecai to *Baba Kama* chap. VIII, par. 81.
50. R. Solomon Luria, *Yam shel Shlomo, Baba Kama* VIII, 49.
51. *Sanhedrin* 99b; cf. Responsa of R. Samuel Alkalai *Mishptai Shmuel,* par. 119.
52. *Kiddushin* 32a.
53. *Nedarim* 66b; *Yerushalmi Sotah I,* 4.
54. *Yoma* 23a.
55. *Talmud Torah* VII, 1. Cf. *Aboth* VI, 1.
56. *Tshuvoth Psakin Uminhagim,* edit. Cahana p. 69.
57. *Kiddushin* 79a.
58. Responsa of Israel Bruna, 189.
59. Yerushalmi *Baba Kama* VIII, 6; *Ketuboth* VIII, 4.
60. Maimonides, *Chovel Umazik* V, 6; Responsa of Rabbi Asher XV, 10. Responsa of Rabbi Isaac Bar Sheshet, par. 27.

468

61. Maimonides, *ibid*.
62. Responsa of Rabbi Joseph Cologne, par. 161.
63. Responsa *Mishptai Shmuel,* par. 119.
64. Cf also response of Rabbi Asher XII, 10.